THE BOURGEOIS VIRTUES

DEIRDRE N. McCLOSKEY

The Bourgeois Virtues

ETHICS FOR AN AGE OF COMMERCE

THE UNIVERSITY OF CHICAGO PRESS ॐ CHICAGO AND LONDON

DEIRDRE N. MCCLOSKEY is distinguished professor of economics, history, English, and communication at the University of Illinois at Chicago. Among her many books are *Crossing: A Memoir* (University of Chicago Press, 1999), and *If You're So Smart: The Narrative of Economic Expertise* (University of Chicago Press, 1990).

The University of Chicago Press, Chicago 60637
The University of Chicago Press, Ltd., London
© 2006 by The University of Chicago
All rights reserved. Published 2006
Printed in the United States of America
15 14 13 12 11 10 09 08 07 06   2 3 4 5
ISBN: 0-226-55663-8 (cloth)

Library of Congress Cataloging-in-Publication Data

McCloskey, Deirdre N.
    The bourgeois virtues : ethics for an age of commerce / Deirdre N. McCloskey.
        p. cm.
    Includes bibliographical references and index.
    ISBN 0-226-55663-8 (cloth : alk. paper)
        1. Capitalism—Moral and ethical aspects. 2. Commerce—Moral and ethical aspects.
3. Social ethics—History. 4. Business ethics—History. 5. Virtues—History. 6. Economic
history. I. Title: Ethics for an age of commerce. II. Title.
    HB501.M5534 2006
    174—dc22

                                                            2005029657

To my mother,

Helen Stueland McCloskey

CONTENTS

While on an airplane reading John Casey's *Pagan Virtue: An Essay in Ethics* (1990), then recently published, it struck me suddenly that *bourgeois* virtue needed a similar treatment. Maybe it was the thinness of the air. I took out my primitive laptop and hammered away. The flight attendant asked me to quiet down. Out of the hammered notes came an essay, "Bourgeois Virtue" (1994), in the *American Scholar*.

Age fifty or so, my second education began. As Peter Dougherty put it in a book with a theme similar to mine, a few economists now understand the blessed Adam Smith's "lesser known, yet surpassingly powerful, civic, social, and cultural legacy, lodged in the phrase 'moral sentiments.' "[1] We few—lagging many decades behind sociologists and social psychologists and literary folk—have finally noticed the ethical soil in which an economy grows. We came to the understanding through economic history (my own case) or game theory, through experimental economics or economic policy, through confrontations with personal faiths, political and religious. A theory of moral sentiments beyond utilitarianism requires stepping outside of economics. You can see it better there.

As you will soon realize, though, even an economist with some historical and rhetorical and philosophical interests is badly educated for moralizing the bourgeois life. I discovered that the story of the demoralization of our economic theories, and the hope for their remoralization, was about much more than the internal history of economics or of economists or even of the economy. To tell the Adam-Smithian story of bourgeois virtues required schooling in ethics, theology, classics, poetry, sociology, social psychology, literary history, art history, intellectual history, philosophy, and twenty other fields in which I am embarrassingly far from expert.

The present book tells what the "virtues" are and how they flourish—or wither—in a commercial society. The next, *Bourgeois Towns: How a Capitalist Ethic Grew in the Dutch and English Lands, 1600–1800*, will tell how in the seventeenth and eighteenth centuries the virtues fared theoretically and practically in northwestern Europe, and with what consequences for the nineteenth century, material and spiritual. *The Treason of the Clerisy: How Capitalism Was Demoralized in the Age of Romance* will tell of the sad turn after 1848 against the bourgeoisie by the artists and intellectuals of Europe and its offshoots. It too had consequences, among them August 1914 and October 1917. And *Defending the Defensible: The Case for an Ethical Capitalism* will tell how bourgeois values have on balance helped rather than hurt the poor and the culture and the environment. The four books propose a fresh start in our attitudes—or at any rate the clerisy's attitudes—toward how we earn a living. Let's chat about it, at http:\\www.press.chicago.edu, under "Electronic projects."

A wise historian said, "Study problems, not periods." All right: the present book asks, "How are the virtues relevant, if they are, to a bourgeois life?" The second asks, "How did Europe and its offshoots become probourgeois yet antivirtuous, 1600–1800?" The third, "How did the Europeans become antibourgeois, though still antivirtuous, after 1848?" And the fourth, "How can we regain a virtuous respect for who we are, bourgeois and capitalist and commercial nowadays, all?"

To put it another way, using the vocabulary that we Americans have heard so much during recent elections, the project is to explain the red states to the blue. *Ad bellum purificandum*, as Kenneth Burke once put it, to make our differences less lethal. Or it is to explain the Midwest and South to the East and West, the Flyover States to the Coasties. The conservatives to the progressives. Or, in an older vocabulary, to explain America to Europe. Or older yet, Rome to Greece.

ACKNOWLEDGMENTS

Joseph Epstein, the editor of the *American Scholar* in 1994, was helpful and encouraging. My colleagues in the Project on Rhetoric of Inquiry (Poroi) at the University of Iowa gave me encouragement and instruction over many years. In March of 1996 John and Christine Blundell and the Institute for Economic Affairs in London, where I delivered an early version of the case to MPs and academics, were kind, as was the University of California, Berkeley, Seminar in Economic History in April 1996. Dutch, Italian, Portuguese, Turkish, Greek, Iranian, and other students at Erasmus University of Rotterdam in various courses on bourgeois virtues during 1996 and then again during annual two-month visits there 2002 to the present have pushed me forward. So have students in courses touching on the matter at the University of Illinois at Chicago since 1999, as did students at Iowa during the 1990s—such as my graduate students in the Sunday Seminar and my undergraduates in a business ethics course taught twice, first with Colin Bell. Students and colleagues at the annual seminar in southern France of EDAMBA (the European Doctoral Association in Management and Business Administration) heard the ideas at length, as later did two springtime sessions in Barcelona lovingly scripted by Eduard Bonet at the Escola Superior d'Administració i Direcció d'Empreses. Teaching a graduate English course with Ralph Cintron and Walter Benn Michaels at UIC in 2004 was eye-opening, too.

For their generous interest I thank in rough chronological order audiences at the Institute for Advanced Study at Princeton, the University of Groningen, the dean's seminar on ethics at the Tippie College of Business at the University of Iowa, the Technical University of Delft, the Free University of Brussels, the University of Gothenburg, the University of Amsterdam, the Humanities Institute and the Social and Political Theory and Economics Program of the Research School of Social Sciences at Australian National University, the Institute for Historical Research (Senate House, London), the University of Western Michigan, Indiana University, the Free University of Amsterdam, Bowling Green State University, Ohio State University, University of Cincinnati, Middlebury College, MIT, the universities of Regina, Edmonton, Calgary, and Lethbridge (these organized by Morris Altman), Jönköping Business School, the New School University, Santa Clara University, the University of Puget Sound, Texas Christian University, George Mason University (on at least three occasions: Don Lavoie and then David Levy were behind these), Georgia Tech, Poroi at the University of Iowa again, Grinnell College, the University of Colorado, the University of Zurich, the University of Århus, the Judge Institute at the University of Cambridge, the University of New South Wales, again the Research School of Social Sciences at Australian National University, Capital University, Ball State University, New Mexico State University, the University of Texas at El Paso, Washington University of St. Louis, the economic history seminar at the University of Michigan, the Art and Cultural Studies seminar at Erasmus University, and the Columbia Seminar in Economic History.

My participation in the Lilly Endowment's multiyear research project "Property, Possession, and the Theology of Culture," directed by William Schweiker, began my education in theology and biblical studies, just as I was becoming on other grounds religious. I have long been a participant in Liberty Fund conferences on human freedom, on subjects ranging from Greek tragedy to Frank Knight, and they have been a big part of my adult education on these matters, especially in political philosophy. I acknowledge here, too, the educational contribution of the Teaching Company lectures, which have accompanied my treadmill walking for some years.

I thank the journal *In Character* for permission to use chapter 42, "God's Deal," originally published there, and the *Anglican Theological Review* for permission to use chapter 14, "Humility and Truth." Chapter 29, "Ethical Realism," appeared in part in Uskali Mäki, ed., *Fact and Fiction in Economics: Models, Realism, and Social Construction* (Cambridge: Cambridge University Press, 2002). And scattered bits in *Reason*.

Stanley Lebergott was encouraging at an early stage. At a later stage I incurred a debt to readers of the preliminary manuscript: Paul Oslington,

Anthony Waterman, Stephen Ziliak. They set me straight on matters of theology and arrangement. My acquisitions editor and friend at the University of Chicago Press, Douglas Mitchell, showed again the imagination and good faith that has made him an institution in the business. Writing for the Press, Dick Lanham was his usual warm yet sharply discerning self. Tyler Cowen displayed his astounding breadth, and kept me from making many mistakes. The final editor at Chicago, Carol Saller, caught many other mistakes and disciplined my prose. My brother John McCloskey of Lafayette, Indiana, the best writer among the scribbling McCloskeys, edited the book with loving care, rewriting whole passages and suggesting scores of new ideas. From all these I have stolen freely. My mother didn't raise a fool.

My presidential addresses at the Economic History Association meeting in New Brunswick in 1997 and the Eastern Economic Association meeting in Washington in 2004 and the Tawney Lecture to the British Economic History Association meeting in Durham in 2003 were good occasions for airing my thoughts. I gave talks on the matter to various meetings of the Eastern Economic Association and the American Economic Association, and, in October 2003, to the Spiritual Capital Planning Meeting sponsored by the Templeton Foundation and to an economics session at the Society for the Scientific Study of Religion. It was a pleasure to bring these notions to a nonacademic audience in Colorado at the 56th Annual Conference on World Affairs at Boulder in April 2002. I thank president Elizabeth Hoffman for initiating that visit. In May 2004 Arjo Klamer of Erasmus University (with the Vereniging Trustfonds), the Studium Generale, and Altuğ Yalçintaş of the Erasmus Institute for Philosophy and Economics sponsored a symposium on Dutch Identity: Virtues and Vices of Bourgeois Society, at which I and others spoke.

I thank the Laura C. Harris Fund at Denison University, in particular Robin Bartlett, David Anderson, Marilyn Tromp, and Sandy Spence, for a very productive two-month stay there in Women's Studies in the spring of 2003. Robin and David, both eminent academics, did me the honor of being "students" in the undergraduate course I gave on a crude form of my manuscript, and I participated with David in a discussion group on theology as well. I thank the University of Illinois at Chicago, especially Stanley Fish, for a visiting research professorship in the fall of 1999; and the University of California at Riverside's Center for Ideas and Society, especially Emory Elliott, Stephen Cullenberg, Richard Sutch, Susan Carter, Joe Childers, Ken Barkin, Jim Parr, Trude Cohen, and Laura Lara, for a fellowship and for deep intellectual and personal engagement at a crux in the spring of 2000. The Earhart Foundation has supported my strange vision of an ethical capitalism early and late, financing students at Iowa during the early 1990s and my research in the Netherlands at the end.

You see that I have gotten a great deal of help over a long period of time. The extent of the help shows how hard it was for an economist and calculator to get the point. It is still another measure of the gap in our culture between the Sacred and the Profane.

And I thank four unusual people who have sustained me for decades in this and all my work: Arjo Klamer of Erasmus University of Rotterdam, John Nelson of the University of Iowa, Stephen Ziliak of Roosevelt University, and above all my mother, an aristocratic poet of bourgeois origin, Helen McCloskey—reading voraciously, taking new residences yearly, publishing in her eighties amazing poetry. I have dedicated the book to her. She and the others have done me the favor, all these years, of disagreeing with me about the bourgeois virtues.

Apology

A BRIEF FOR THE BOURGEOIS VIRTUES

I. Exordium: The Good Bourgeois

I bring good news about our bourgeois lives. You will find here, in the vocabulary of Christianity, from the Greek for the defendant's side in a trial, an "apology" for capitalism in its American form.

I do not mean "I'm sorry." The book is an *apologia* in the theological sense of giving reasons, with room for doubt, directed to nonbelievers. It is directed toward you who are suspicious of the phrase "bourgeois virtues," pretty sure that it is a contradiction in terms. And the book is directed, with less optimism about changing your minds, toward you who think the phrase is worse: a lie.

"Bourgeois virtues" is neither. The claim here is that modern capitalism does not need to be offset to be good. Capitalism can on the contrary be virtuous. In a fallen world the bourgeois life is not perfect. But it's better than any available alternative. American capitalism needs to be inspirited, moralized, completed. Two and a half cheers for the Midwestern bourgeoisie.

Of course, like an aristocracy or a priesthood or a peasantry or a proletariat or an intelligentsia, a middle class is capable of evil, even in a God-blessed America. The American bourgeoisie organized official and unofficial apartheids. It conspired against unions. It supported the excesses of nationalism. It delighted in red baiting and queer bashing. It claimed credit for a religious faith that had no apparent influence on its behavior. The country club is not an ethical graduate school. Nowhere does being bourgeois ensure ethical behavior. During the Second World War, Krupp, Bosch, Hoechst, Bayer, Deutsche Bank, Daimler Benz, Dresdner Bank, and

Volkswagen, all of them, used slave labor, with impunity. The bourgeois bankers of Switzerland stored gold for the Nazis. Many a businessman is an ethical shell or worse. Even the virtues of the bourgeoisie, Lord knows, do not lead straight to heaven.

But the assaults on the alleged vices of the bourgeoisie and capitalism after 1848 made an impossible Best into the enemy of an actual Good. They led in the twentieth century to some versions of hell. In the twenty-first century, please—dear Lord, please—let us avoid another visit to hell.

I don't much care how "capitalism" is defined, so long as it is not defined a priori to mean vice incarnate. The prejudging definition was favored by Rousseau—though he did not literally use the word "capitalism," still to be coined—and by Proudhon, Marx, Bakunin, Kropotkin, Luxembourg, Veblen, Goldman, Polanyi, Sartre. Less obviously the same definition was used by their opponents Bentham, Ricardo, Rand, Friedman, Becker. All of them, left and right, defined commercial society at the outset to be bad by any standard higher than successful greed.

Such a definition makes pointless an inquiry into the good and bad of modern commercial society. I think this is what economists like Douglass North, looking recently into the history of institutions, have been seeing: that there's something going on from 1500 to the present beyond maximum utility on a narrow definition. That is what the middle ground of social thinking in the past three centuries, with which I associate myself, has believed: Montesquieu, Smith, Tocqueville, Keynes, Aron, Hirschman. If modern capitalism is defined to be the same thing as Greed—"the restless never-ending process of profit-making alone . . . , this boundless greed after riches," as Marx put it in chapter 1 of *Capital,* drawing on an anticommercial theme originating in Aristotle—then that settles it, before looking at the evidence.

There's no evidence, actually, that greed or miserliness or self-interest was new in the sixteenth or the nineteenth or any other century. *Auri sacra fames,* "for gold the infamous hunger," is from *The Aeneid,* book 3, line 57, not from Benjamin Franklin or *Advertising Age.* The propensity to truck and barter is human nature. Commerce is not some evil product of recent manufacture. Commercial behavior is one of the world's oldest professions. We have documentation of it from the earliest cuneiform writing, in clay business letters from Kish or Ashur offering compliments to your lovely wife and making a deal for copper from Anatolia or lapis lazuli from

Afghanistan. Bad and good behavior in buying low and selling high can be found anywhere, anytime.

You can see that I am wishy-washy and empirical, not pure and rationalist, about "capitalism." As Kwame Anthony Appiah said about a similar messiness in the word "liberalism," it seems wise to use a "loose and baggy sense."[1] We can't do with philosophical definition a job that needs to be done with factual inquiry. Better stay baggy. Suppose we knew at the outset the real essence of capitalism. Then we would already have answered by philosophical magic the chief question of the social sciences—why is the world today so very different from that of our ancestors? And we would have answered too the chief question of the humanities—is our human life good, evil, or indifferent? I think we're unlikely to make progress in answering either question if we insist at the outset that "capitalism" just *means* modern greed.

To put the matter positively, we have been and can be virtuous and commercial, liberal and capitalist, democratic and rich, all these. As John Mueller said in a book in 1999 anticipating my theme, *Capitalism, Democracy, and Ralph's Pretty Good Grocery*, "Democracy and capitalism, it seems, are similar in that they can often work pretty well even if people generally do not appreciate their workings very well."[2]

One of the ways capitalism works "pretty well," Mueller and I and a few other loony procapitalists such as Michael Novak and James Q. Wilson and Hernando De Soto and the late Robert Nozick claim, is to nourish the virtues. Mueller argues for the one direction of causation: "Virtue is, on balance and all other things being equal, essentially smart business under capitalism: nice guys, in fact, tend to finish first."[3] Max Weber had a century earlier written to the same effect: "Along with clarity of vision and ability to act, it is only by virtue [note the word] of very definite and highly developed ethical qualities that it has been possible for [an entrepreneur of this new type] to command the indispensable confidence of his customers and workmen."[4]

Yes. Countries where stealing rather than dealing rules become poor and then remain so. The historical anthropologist Alan Macfarlane explains the "riddle of the modern world" in such terms. What was odd about northwestern Europe in the eighteenth century, he says, is that it escaped from "predatory tendencies" common to every "agrarian civilization" since the beginning. Because of a change in the technology of war, northwestern

Europe escaped for a time external predation from the Steppe, "but equally important, [it escaped] internal predation . . . of priests, lords, kings, and even over-powerful merchant guilds."[5]

It doesn't matter what kind of predation/stealing it is—socialist stealing such as in Cuba, or private/governmental stealing such as in Haiti, or bureaucratic stealing such as in the Egypt of today or of ancient times, or for that matter stealing at the point of a sword in France during the Hundred Years' War or stealing at the point of a cross in Germany during the Thirty Years' War or stealing at the point of a pen by CEOs in America during the 1990s. By doing evil we do badly. And we do well by doing good.

But I go further. Capitalism, I claim, nourishes lives of virtue in the non-self-interested sense, too. The more common claim is that virtues support the market. Yes, I agree. Other economists have started to admit so. It's been hard, because it goes against our professional impulse to reduce everything, simply everything, to prudence without other virtues.

I say that the market supports the virtues.[6] As the economist Alfred Marshall put it in 1890, "Man's character has been molded by his every-day work, and the material resources which he thereby procures, more than by any other influence unless it be that of his religious ideals; and the two great forming agencies of the world's history have been the religious and the economic."[7] The two are connected. If one is persuaded a priori to find the economy wholly corrupting—"the restless never-ending process of profit-making alone"—then of course no virtues or religious influences can come of it. But such an opinion doesn't fit our experience.

A little farmers' market opens before 6:00 a.m. on a summer Saturday at Polk and Dearborn in Chicago. As a woman walking her dog passes the earliest dealer setting up his stall, the woman and the dealer exchange pleasantries about the early bird and the worm. The two people here are enacting a script of citizenly courtesies and of encouragement for prudence and enterprise and good relations between seller and buyer. Some hours later the woman feels impelled to buy $1.50 worth of tomatoes from him. But that's not the point. The market was an occasion for virtue, an expression of solidarity across gender, social class, ethnicity.

In other words, markets and the bourgeois life are not always bad for the human spirit. In certain ways, and on balance—and here I take up themes articulated by eighteenth-century theorists of capitalism, and in the late twentieth century by Wendy McElroy, Daniel Klein, Paul Heyne, Peter Hill,

Jennifer Roback Morse, and Tyler Cowen—they have been good. We have sometimes become good by doing well.

Are such propositions true? "What is truth?" asked jesting Pilate. Stay, I beg you, for an answer, the apology. In the early 1990s, a month before the presentation of a crude version of the answer to the Institute for Advanced Study at Princeton, the secretary of the School of Social Science telephoned me in far Iowa and asked me for the title. I replied, "Bourgeois Virtue." She paused—startled it seemed, and then . . . *laughed*. My purpose is to examine her laughter, with sympathy but with attention, to find where it is justified and especially where it is not.

Flocks of literate people East and West, left and right, would think her laughter very well justified. They are my implied readers, people who think that capitalism is probably rotten, and who believe that a claim to bourgeois "virtues," of all things, is laughable.

Such a laughing sophisticate would not be a Pakistani British shop owner, say, or a Norwegian American electrical contractor. Such people have actually lived the bourgeois virtues, and some of the bourgeois vices, too. They would find an apology, or even an *apologia*, lacking in point. "What's to apologize for? What's to defend in our lives? We came to Bradford in Yorkshire or to St. Joseph in Michigan and made good livings, honestly."

My implied readers are instead the theoreticians and the followers of theoreticians, what Coleridge and I call the "clerisy," opinion makers and opinion takers, all the reading town, the readers of the *New York Times* or *Le Monde*, listeners to Charlie Rose, book readers, or at any rate book-review readers. My people. Like me.

Many of them—the people I am mainly anxious to chat with here—take it as given, undiscussably obvious, that "bourgeois virtues" is an oxymoron on the level of "military intelligence" or "academic administration." "Many persons educated in the humanities (with their aristocratic traditions)," writes Michael Novak of the problem, "and the social sciences (with their quantitative, collectivist traditions) are uncritically anticapitalists. They think of business as vulgar, philistine, and morally suspect."[8] They have stopped listening to the other side. If a channel click accidentally gives a glimpse, they wax indignant, and hurry away.

If politically speaking they are on the Hampstead Village/Santa Monica left wing, the members of the clerisy believe that capitalism and profit are evil, that the American soul has been corrupted by markets and materialism, and that the enrichment of the West depends on stealing from the third world or the poor or the third-world poor. "We—the middle classes, I mean, not just the rich—have neglected you," confessed the economic historian and settlement-house pioneer Arnold Toynbee in 1883 to an audience of workingmen. "But I think we are changing. If you will only believe it and trust us, I think that many of us would spend our lives in your service. . . . You have to forgive us, for we have wronged you; we have sinned against you grievously."[9]

If by contrast the doubters are on the City of London/Wall Street right, they believe that capitalism and profit are good for business but have nothing to do with ethics, that the poor should shut up and settle for what they get, and that we certainly don't need a preacherly ethic of sin and service for a commercial society. They think Jesus got it all wrong in the Sermon on the Mount. They reply as the English businessman did when Friedrich Engels, also a businessman, harangued him one day on the horrors of an industrial slum: "And yet there is a great deal of money made here. Good morning, sir."

And if they are in the middle, bobos in paradise, nowadays the south-of-the-Thames clerisy, the Montgomery County suburbanites, the Tokyo commuters, they believe moderate versions of both sides. Anyway they agree with the harder folk to the left or right about the laughably nonethical character of capitalism. As Mort Sahl put it, "Liberals feel unworthy of their possessions. Conservatives feel they deserve everything they've stolen."

Thus from the left, André Comte-Sponville, a teacher of philosophy at the Sorbonne who doesn't really claim to know much about economics, feels confident in declaring without argument that "Western prosperity depends, directly or indirectly, on third world poverty, which the West in some cases merely takes advantage of and in others actually causes."[10] This is mistaken, though I myself would not claim, understand, that every Western policy is ethical. Even a defender of capitalism thinks that protection for Western agriculture against third-world farmers, for example, is decidedly unethical.

Or from the center-left, James Boyd White, a teacher of law and literature at the University of Michigan from whom I have been learning for decades, declares that "economic 'growth,' that is to say, the expansion of the exchange system by the conversion of what is outside it into its terms . . . is a kind of steam shovel chewing away at the natural and social world."[11] This too is mistaken—not that I think everything marketed, understand, is good. College term papers and Asian children are for sale, and shouldn't be. I told you I was wishy-washy.

Or from the conservative right, John Gray, a political philosopher at the London School of Economics who doesn't really claim to know much about empirical sociology, yet from whom I have also learned a good deal, feels confident in declaring that recent neoliberal theory "failed to anticipate that among the unintended consequences of its policy of freeing up markets was a fracturing of communities, and a depletion of ethos and trust within institutions, which muted or thwarted the economic renewal which free markets were supposed to generate."[12] Mistaken again—not that all consequences of markets are desirable.

Or from another version of the right, the libertarian version, any one of my fellow Chicago School economists who don't really claim to know much about philosophy or the Middle Ages—Friedman, Becker, Barro, step forward—would protest, "Philosophy? What scientist needs that? *Ethics?* Bosh. I'm a positive scientist, not a preacher. Capitalism is efficient, which is all I preach. Who needs faith? Put your faith in Prudence Only." Mistaken yet again—not that all philosophy is useful.

I suggest gently to such people, my good friends of the clerisy left, center, and right who believe bourgeois life must be unethical, that they might possibly be making a mistake when they attribute amorality to markets. I am attempting here a *Summa contra gentiles*, a treatise on the virtues of capitalism directed at people who believe it has very few. The book and its sequels will try to disestablish their pessimism, which since about 1848 has been the high orthodoxy of the West. "I do not welcome the fact that most people I know and respect disagree with me," said Robert Nozick in 1974, making as a philosopher a point similar to mine.[13] But it is our duty nonetheless to give it the old college try.

Note well that some parts of the orthodoxy are shared by left and right and center. Each politics has its own special topics of dismay or celebration concerning capitalism. But they use topics in common, too. The left believes capitalism is a matter of Prudence understood as ruthless self-interest, and therefore is an ethical catastrophe. The right also believes that capitalism is a matter of Prudence understood as ruthless self-interest—but it believes on the contrary that capitalism therefore is a practical triumph. I claim in what follows that neither left nor right, neither the Department of English nor the country club—nor the center, eyeless in Starbucks, uneasily ruminating on morsels taken from both sides—is seeing bourgeois life whole.

Capitalism is not a matter of Prudence Only. It has not followed Prudence Only over its short history as the ruling ideology of our economies. Prudence Only is not how it actually works. Property is not theft—yet neither is property everything there is. Ruthless self-interest is not the life of capitalists—yet neither is every capitalist ethical. Bourgeois life has not in practice, I claim, excluded the other virtues. In fact, it often has nourished them.

II. Narratio: How Ethics Fell

A Western framework for the analysis of ethics was built in classical and Christian times, paralleled in Confucianism and other ethical traditions. It combined four "pagan" virtues, above all aristocratic Courage, with three so-called Christian virtues, above all peasant/proletarian Love.

The ethical framework, most gloriously developed by St. Thomas Aquinas in the middle of the thirteenth century, assigned a place of honor among the seven virtues to Prudence—that is, to know-how, competence, a thrifty self-interest, "rationality" on a broad definition. Prudence is the storied prime virtue of a bourgeoisie. But from the time of Machiavelli and Hobbes to the time of Bentham and Thomas Gradgrind, the system of four pagan plus three Christian virtues was gradually pushed out of balance, at any rate theoretically, by the rising dominance of Prudence. Among non-Romantics such as Bentham the virtue of Prudence by the nineteenth century came to be regarded theoretically as the master virtue, with lessened theoretical esteem for, say, love or courage. The Romantics such as Carlyle therefore seized on the other end of the stick, elevating fancy over calculation, theoretically.

And yet in eighteenth-century Europe certain theorists such as Montesquieu and Voltaire and Hume and Smith had articulated a balanced ethical system for a society of commerce, veritable "bourgeois virtues," fanciful and calculative together. Japan embarked independently on an eerie parallel of this European venture, starting from a different theory of the good.[14]

In the late eighteenth and early nineteenth centuries the European venture, tragically, was spoiled. It was spoiled as I said by a reaction among

Romantics in favor of unbalanced love and courage, by an apotheosis among Benthamites of prudence only and among Kantians of reason as justice and temperance only. The vision of a balanced ethical system was further spoiled by an enthusiastic belief in antimarket versions of faith and hope among the new evangelicals, religious and secular. John Stuart Mill contained in his life most of these early nineteenth-century strains of thought (except the important one of evangelical Christianity), embodying many of the shifting faiths of his age. A lot changed in the mind of Europe from the Lisbon Earthquake to the June Days, from 1755 to 1848.

Nonetheless until those June Days most artists and intellectuals, the new clerisy, accepted capitalism, well before much of its material fruit was evident. J. S. Mill in the first edition of his *Principles of Political Economy* in 1848 and Daniel Defoe and Thomas Paine and Thomas Macaulay and Victor Hugo and Alessandro Manzoni had associated free markets with liberalism and with the new freedoms of 1689, 1776, 1789, and 1830. By 1848, materially and politically speaking, capitalism had in practice triumphed, at least in Europe and its offshoots. It was beginning—just beginning—to uplift the wretched of the earth. Macaulay wrote in 1830:

> If we were to prophesy that in the year 1930 a population of fifty millions, better fed, clad, and lodged than the English of our time, will cover these islands; that Sussex and Huntingdonshire will be wealthier than the wealthiest parts of the West Riding of Yorkshire now are, . . . that machines constructed on principles yet undiscovered will be in every house . . . many people would think us insane. . . . If any person had told the Parliament which met in perplexity and terror after the crash in 1720 that in 1830 the wealth of England would surpass all their wildest dreams, . . . that London would be twice as large and twice as populous, and that nevertheless the rate of mortality would have diminished to one half of what it was then, . . . that stage coaches would run from London to York in twenty-four hours, that men would be in the habit of sailing without wind, and would be beginning to ride without horses, our ancestors would have given as much credit to the prediction as they gave to *Gulliver's Travels*. Yet the prediction would have been true.[15]

Yet after 1848, or a little before, the European clerisy formed up into antibourgeois gaggles of bohemians and turned to complaining about the bourgeois virtues that had nourished them. Marx at the dawn observed that a "small section of the ruling class cuts itself adrift, and joins the revolutionary class," as, for example, Engels and especially he himself had.[16] It was not such a small section. What César Graña described as the "modern literary irritability" about bourgeois life, evident in Stendhal, Poe, Baudelaire, Flaubert, and late Dickens, became after the failed revolutions of 1848 a political creed.[17] The sons of bourgeois fathers became enchanted in the 1840s and 1850s by the revival of secularized faith called nationalism and of secularized hope called socialism.

In the late nineteenth and early twentieth centuries they brought European high civilization and then its rulers along with them, and afterward the whole world: thus Mill (in his later years), Marx, Engels, Mazzini, Carlyle, Morris, Ruskin, Chernyshevsky, Renan, Zola, Kropotkin, Bellamy, Tolstoy, Shaw, Hobson, Lenin. Thus the "International" (1871/1888), from the French original: "Arise ye prisoners of starvation, / Arise ye wretched of the earth. / For justice thunders condemnation: / A better world's in birth."[18] Or on its nationalist side in 1841—the poem was in fact an appeal for German unity at a time when nationalism was liberal, not an appeal for the German conquest of Europe—"Deutschland, Deutschland über alles, / Über alles in der Welt."

In its hopeful faith the clerisy—Emerson in 1858 spoke of "the artist, the scholar, and in general the clerisy"—sometimes evoked a nostalgia for the aristocratic virtues of a Europe before the economists and calculators took charge.[19] Sometimes it imagined a peasant-cum-proletarian future, a Nowhere of postbourgeois virtues. Sometimes both. Baudelaire in 1857 quoted with approval Poe's sour observation in 1849, "The world is infested now with a new sect of philosophers. . . . They are the *Believers in everything Old*. . . . Their High Priest in the East is Charles Fourier, in the West Horace Greeley."[20]

As George Bernard Shaw noted in 1912, "The first half of the 19th century"

> despised and pitied the Middle Ages as barbarous, cruel, superstitious, and ignorant. . . . The second half saw no hope for mankind except in the recovery of the faith, the art, the humanity of the Middle Ages. . . . For that was how men felt, and how some of them spoke, in the early days of the Great Conversion, which produced, first, such books as the *Latter Day Pamphlets* of Carlyle, Dickens' *Hard Times*, and the tracts and sociological novels of the Christian Socialists, and later on the Socialist movement which has now spread all over the world.[21]

For such antibourgeois nostalgias the twentieth century paid the butcher's bill. Everywhere except in the United States the payoff from capitalism to the ordinary man came too late to stop the rise of socialist parties.

Everywhere the ruling class found it could use patriotism to stay in charge, and anyway believed most ardently in its own racism, nationalism, imperialism, and clericalism. The result was a clash of isms in the European Civil War, 1914–1989, and its spawn overseas. Capitalism was nearly overwhelmed by nationalism and socialism and national socialism, Kaiser Billy to the Baathists.

Yet during the late twentieth century capitalism and its bourgeois virtues resumed their triumphs. Countries which appeared hopelessly poor in 1950, such as Japan and South Korea and Thailand, became under capitalist and bourgeois auspices well-to-do. Countries which in 1950 were relatively rich but still had large portions of their populations ill-housed, ill-clad, ill-nourished, such as Britain and Italy and the United States, became richer in housing and clothing and food. Latin American and Caribbean incomes per head doubled in thirty years.

The worldwide enrichment made possible a cultural and ethical enrichment, too. The breaking of constraints in the 1960s that so irritates neoconservatives was not the beginning of cultural rot, as the neocons declare. In rich countries it was the fulfillment of a promise, a spread of freedoms won by rich white European men a century before. It promised equality now for women, blacks, browns, gays, handicapped people, colonial people, ethnic minorities, the poor—in short, for a growing share of the people left out of politics under the previous dispensation. In poor countries it was the beginning of the end for patriarchy and village tyranny. The neocons seem often to want order at any cost in freedom, rather than freedom achieved in an orderly manner. I say: Hurrah for late twentieth-century enrichment and democratization. Hurrah for birth control and the civil rights movement. Arise ye wretched of the earth.

True, the 1960s worldwide saw itself as antibourgeois, even socialist, and this intemperance of freedom had costs—small costs in the broken windows of the Hoover Institution and large costs in the broken economies of sub-Saharan Africa. It would have been better if every social movement of the 1960s had adhered to nonviolence and self-discipline and mutual respect, and had therefore joined the bourgeois project down in the marketplace. But in the late twentieth century even sophisticated capitalists came to recommend a devotion to Prudence Only, Wall Street's "greed is good." Bourgeois theorists, in other words, overstressed the virtue of prudence.

The theoretical impulse to collapse everything into prudence is as old as Mo-zi in China in the fifth century BC, or the Epicurean school of the Greeks and Romans, or Machiavelli, or Hobbes, or Bernard Mandeville in his *Fable of the Bees* (1714). In 1725 Bishop Butler complained about "the strange affection of many people of explaining away all particular affections and representing the whole of life as nothing but one continued exercise of self-love."[22] "It is the great fallacy of Dr. Mandeville's book," wrote Adam Smith in 1759, "to represent every passion as wholly vicious which is so in any degree and any direction."[23] Bourgeois life, I repeat, and as Butler and Smith said, does not in fact exclude the other virtues. Look around at your bourgeois friends. At your sweet self, at your colleagues in the office, at the clerks in the shops giving the lady what she wants.

The left side of the clerisy has never wavered in its 150-year-old campaign against the system that has made its arts and sciences possible. Most educated people in our time, though enriched by bourgeois virtues in themselves and in others, imagine the virtue of their lives as heroic courage or saintly love uncontaminated by bourgeois concerns. They pose as rejecting bourgeois ethics.

Even so wise a man as the Israeli writer Amos Oz allows himself this sort of blast, at the "ancient Jewish diseases." "One of them," he wrote, "perhaps the most repulsive, is the petit-bourgeois sickness which makes 'upright Israelis' force their offspring to take piano lessons and learn French and make good marriages and settle down in a quality flat in a quality job and bring up quality children, clever but devoted to their family."[24]

Appalling. Making them learn French! Forced piano lessons! Respectability looks boring to the Romantic, and if he is comfortable enough to be bored he is repelled. He looks for an *exciting* life.

Capitalism has triumphed in our time, which I claim is a good thing, though boring. The coming of bourgeois society to northwestern Europe was good. So was the theorizing of bourgeois virtues in Holland and Scotland and France. So were the early successes of bourgeois society in England and Belgium and the United States. So was the enlargement of the clerisy. So was the global triumph of capitalism from 1848 to 1914 and again from 1945 to the present in its spread to the second world and to more and more of the third. It has allowed the escape from deadly poverty by hundreds of millions in the late twentieth century, the defeat of Fascism and then of Communism, the revolts against the tyrants from Marcos to the House of

Saud, the liberal hegemony of the early twenty-first century. All of these, I say, are good things.

One can think of the calamities of the twentieth century as caused by the sins of capitalism. The left does. Capital was born, wrote Marx, "dripping from head to foot, from every pore, with blood and dirt."[25] I think on the contrary that most of the calamities were a consequence of the *attacks* on capitalism.

Either way, the twentieth century and especially its first half were without question very sad. Indeed, the ethical history leading up to and through the twentieth century could be viewed as more than sad—it could be viewed as "tragic," in the strict, literary, ancient Greek sense. Perhaps there was lurking in the hubris of each triumph a tragic flaw leading ineluctably to a reversal of fortune, which we are just now realizing.

Maybe, that is, a tragic pessimism worthy of Sophocles is justified. Maybe, as the economist/sociologist Max Weber predicted in 1905, the very rationalization he detected in modern capitalism will lock it in an iron cage, stifling the creativity of the bourgeoisie. Maybe, as the economist/historian Joseph Schumpeter believed in the darkest days of the last century, it is not possible to sustain capitalism and democracy, together, in the long run. "The very success [of capitalism]," Schumpeter wrote, "undermines the social institutions which protect it."[26] Maybe.

But I want to persuade you that Schumpeter in 1942, with Weber in 1905, Daniel Bell in 1976, and Francis Fukuyama in 1999 positing likewise a cultural contradiction in capitalism, were wisely, eloquently mistaken. Capitalism has retained its creativity; and yet it has not abandoned ethics. I think a worse "tragedy," in the sense of "an exceptionally bad turn, avoidable if we had been less proud," would be to accept the pessimistic view and abandon the daily task of moralizing capitalism.

The cynic, exploiting our first doubts, is always in fashion. His less cool and more vocal cousin, Jeremiah, exploiting our later regrets, is fashionable, too. Yet fashionable and seductive though they are, they are not always correct. Since 1800 in truth they have often been mistaken. As both would say, to be sure, the hypocrites flourish, everywhere, and our former days were glorious indeed. Yet bourgeois creativity has enriched the world. The sky has not in fact fallen. The situation, though always serious, is not always hopeless.

A democratic but cultured and creative capitalism *is* possible, and to our good. It needs to be worked on. You come, too.

III. Probatio A: Modern Capitalism Makes Us Richer

The first generations of professional historians, chiefly Catholic intellectuals and German nationalists allied with Romantic litterateurs, had claimed that all things French and English and Enlightened and Revolutionary are dirty. They argued that people in olden times were innocent and good, and that a market-absent purity is to be found in the medieval history of *Das Volk*. Since 1900, though, historians have found reason to doubt their German *Doktorvaters*. They have found markets and maximizing in the thirteenth as much as in the twentieth century.

Most of what we are taught in school about the economy of traditional Europe turns out to be wrong, because it is inspired by the earlier, anticapitalist tale. Max Weber in 1905, beginning the revision, declared that greed is "not in the least identical with capitalism, and still less with its spirit." "It should be taught in the kindergarten of cultural history that this naïve idea of capitalism must be given up once and for all." The lust for gold "has been common to all sorts and conditions of men at all times and in all countries of the earth."[27]

I mean by "capitalism" merely private property and free labor without central planning, regulated by the rule of law and by an ethical consensus. Above all *modern* capitalism encourages innovation. Joel Mokyr has emphasized the institutions of modern Europe that prevented the sins of envy or of anger or injustice from killing innovation.[28]

None of the features of such a "capitalism," however, were entirely unknown, or even very rare before 1800 or 1600 or 1453, in Aleppo or Timbuktu or Tlatelolco. Encouragement to innovation is certainly not unique to modern capitalism, or to modern Europe. Otherwise we would not have woven clothing and tossed pottery—though nowadays the encouragement to innovation is very great, bordering on lunacy. Long-distance trade carried Mayan obsidian to Oklahoma and Baltic amber to Egypt. Large-scale enterprise and sophisticated financial markets, too, can be found in Ming China and fourth-century Athens. One could get rich in ancient Rome without inspiring retaliation by the state. Official governmental sympathy to profit making is less common outside of bourgeois Europe, but it is not unheard of in Phoenicia and Bombay.

"Capitalism existed," declared Weber, "in China, India, Babylon, in the classic world, and in the Middle Ages."[29] The historical anthropologist Jack

Goody writes that merchants "developed an independent secular culture . . . in Hangzhou or Ahmadabad, in Osaka or in London, where they were very roughly on the same level of complexity and achievement" still in the nineteenth century.[30] I am going to use the word "capitalism" here to mean, usually, *modern, European-style* capitalism. But I will bear in mind that its elements are not all modern and not all Western.

When Schumpeter wrote his *Capitalism, Socialism, and Democracy* most people were persuaded that every Western institution from capitalism to democracy was failing, that the clerisy of 1848 had got it right. A couple of years later Jean-Paul Sartre in similar terms announced "on the whole, the failure of the democratic point of view."[31]

Considering the apocalyptic battles raging then, a retribution on the twentieth-century for the intellectual sins of its grandparents, such opinions were not unreasonable. Most thinking people in 1942 and 1944 and for a long time afterward believed them to be true. Christopher Lasch wrote *The Culture of Narcissism* in 1979, at another moment of pessimism in the West, after Vietnam but before the British coal miners' last strike, after President Carter's "malaise" talk but before the democratization of the Philippines, Korea, and Taiwan, before the collapse of the Soviet empire, before the liberalization of Latin American governments, before the prowl of Asian and Celtic tigers. He believed then that "Bourgeois society seems everywhere to have used up its store of constructive ideas. . . . The political crisis of capitalism reflects a general crisis of western culture. . . . Liberalism, the political theory of the ascendant bourgeoisie, long ago lost the capacity to explain events."[32]

Viewed over a longer period, however, the most amazing political fact since, say, 1800, as Tocqueville noted as early as 1835, is the spreading idea of equality in freedom, that theory of the ascendant bourgeoisie. Cynics and Jeremiahs to the contrary, it spreads yet. According to Freedom House, the percentage of "free" countries rose from 29 percent in 1973 to 46 percent in 2003, containing 44 percent of the world's population.[33] Think of Ukraine and South Korea. The world continues to draw on a lost, failed, used-up liberalism. Liberal democracy keeps on explaining events.

And the first of the two most amazing *economic* facts about the modern world keeps on explaining events as well: the world's population increased from 1800 to 2000 by a factor of about *six*.[34] The nineteenth and twentieth centuries have witnessed the fastest growth of human population since the drought-pushed, language-enabled march of a little group of *Homo sapiens sapiens* out of the African homeland around 50,000 BC.[35] Think of it: six times more souls.

The second, and still more amazing, fact uncovered by the economic historians in the past fifty years is that despite the rise in population since 1800 the goods and services consumed by the average person has not fallen. The forecasters of doom from Thomas Malthus to Paul Ehrlich have been mistaken.

"We cannot absolutely prove, wrote Macaulay in 1830, "that those are in error who tell us that society has reached a turning point, that we have seen our best days. But so said all who came before us, and with just as much apparent reason." Amazingly, the optimistic, Whiggish Macaulay was exactly right. The amount of goods and services produced and consumed by the average person on the planet has *risen* since 1800 by a factor of about eight and a half. I say "about." If the factor were four or five, or ten or twelve, the conclusion would be the same: liberal capitalism has succeeded. And like liberal democracy, its success continues. In these latter days the fact should delight and amaze us.

Never had such a thing happened. Count it in your head: *eight and a half* times more actual food and clothing and housing and education and travel and books for the average human being—even though there were six times more of them. Of course not every sort of person on the planet got exactly 8.5000000 times more. Averages are averages. But the figure's rough magnitude, I repeat, is not in doubt, and the success of capitalism has left no class of people on the planet entirely behind. Even unhappy Africa's income per head has in real terms—that is, allowing for mere monetary inflation of prices, as do all these figures—more than tripled since the early nineteenth century, despite an alarming collapse in some parts after the 1970s.

In places like Hong Kong or Taiwan or France or the United States that have had the luck or the skill to let the bourgeois virtues flourish, national income per head has risen by a factor of as much as, for example, nineteen.[36] Goodness. Nineteen. Understand, that's not a mere 100 percent or 200 percent more to eat and read and wear than two centuries ago. It is eighteen hundred percent more.

"Ah, but at the cost of a worse quality of life." Briefly for now, no. Consider that you may be mistaken. The quality of life you personally lead, dear reader, is better than the lives of your thirty-two great-great-great-great

grandparents. I'll speak for myself. An Irish peasant woman digging prat-
ties in her lazybed in 1805 or a Norwegian farmer of thirty acres of rocky
soil in Dimmelsvik in 1800 or the American daughter of poor English
people in 1795 Massachusetts had brutish and short lives. Many of them
could not read. Their horizons were narrow. Their lives were toilsome and
bitter.

Ask them. They said so. Martha Ballard of Hallowell, Maine, among the
literate half of adult women in the United States then (she was the great
aunt of Clara Barton, the founder the Red Cross), kept from 1785 until her
death in 1812 a diary as wife and midwife on the hardscrabble inner frontier.[37] Some of the 10,000 entries:

> I attended funeral of [name of child obscure], who deceased 19th instant, being
> 4 years and 1 day old.... Captain Lamb's wife, [and] Solon Cook's and Ebeneezer
> Davis, Jr.'s wives, died in child bed; infants deceased also. . . . A storm of snow;
> cold for March. . . . I had two falls; one on my way there, the other on my return.
> . . . I traveled some roads in the snow where it was almost as high as my waist. . . .
> I was at home this day . . . making soap and knitting. . . . Was called at a little past
> 12 in [the] morning by Mr. Edson, to go to his wife being in travail. . . . The river
> [was] dangerous but [I] arrived safe through Divine protection. . . . I could not
> sleep for fleas. I found 80 fleas on my clothes after I came home. . . . Cleared some
> of the manure from under the out house. . . . Iced-over [rain] barrel.[38]

Martha Ballard lived a typical precapitalist life. Is any of this, dear reader,
typical of your life in a modern bourgeois society?

"Ah, but the environment was better." Briefly for now, no. Consider that
you may be mistaken. Air quality during the past fifty years has improved in
some respects in every rich city in the world. Let us then be rich. Remember smoky crofters' cabins. Remember being tied in Japan by law and cost to
one locale. Remember American outhouses and iced-over rain barrels and
cold and wet and dirt. Remember in Denmark ten people living in one
room, the cows and chickens in the other room. Remember in Nebraska sod
houses and isolation. Remember a very reasonable terror in the face of
nature, wolves roaming in packs during the seventeenth century even in the
highly urbanized Low Countries. Remember horse manure in New York
and soft coal in London. This is what we have escaped, thanks to that used-
up liberal capitalism.

For 150 years water has been getting better in countries that can afford to
indulge such an interest. In 2004 the World Health Organization and

UNICEF announced that half the world's population now had clean water piped into the home, and 83 percent were within half an hour's walk of a clean water source. If that sounds awful, then you don't grasp how bad it once was, and how important water-borne disease has been in human history. From 1990 to 2002 Angola, the Central African Republic, Chad, Malawi, and Tanzania, some of the poorest countries in the modern world, have increased access to clean water by 50 percent.[39] Remember why a third of the grain crop went into water-preserving beer in the European Middle Ages. Remember cholera in Chicago in 1852 and 1854 and 1873, typhoid in 1881 and 1891.

You will say that social, humanitarian, and cosmopolitan forces have achieved the improvement. Your opinion deserves sympathetic scrutiny. But for now consider that you might be mistaken, that enrichment rather than regulation is the main cause of our better human environment. Consider, too, that the social, humanitarian, and cosmopolitan forces you admire, supporting the United Nations and the relief of disasters, were themselves a result of liberal capitalism.

Consider.

IV.   Probatio B: And Lets Us Live Longer

Clean water, inoculation, better food, and penicillin purchased with the higher income raised the expectation of life at birth in the world from roughly 26 years in 1820 to 66 years in 2000—with variation, but no place left behind: from 39 to 77 in the United States, for example; from 23 to 52 (before AIDS) in Africa; up in Russia, then down during its halfhearted move to capitalism, now up again.[40]

Goodness: 26 years to 66 years. Linger a while on those numbers, if you like that sort of thing. They imply that over the past two centuries the adult years over age 16 have increased in expectation for the average newborn from the 10 years from 16 to 26 to the 50 years from 16 to 66. The expectation of adult life in other words has grown by a factor of 5. Not 5 years or 5 percent, but 5 times.

This would be the relevant statistic for someone, say a father, gazing on his son and heir and speculating about what length of adult life he could be expected to have. An economist would claim that a father would think this way when deciding at the birth how much to invest in him. With 50 adult years in prospect the father might well plan for a thorough education, in which the son would learn to read and to figure, to recite his paternoster and to grind lenses. But with only 10 adult years in prospect, why bother?

From the child's own point of view the more relevant statistic maybe is the historical rise in expectation of life at, say, age 16 itself, on setting out into the adult world. At that age it is the grown child's turn—or so the economist claims in her prudence-loving way—to form a plan of investment in education or migration.

Because the fall in early child mortality is such an important matter in the history of the past two centuries, looked at this way the change in years of expectation of later adult life is smaller. In 1800 life expectancy at age 16 was perhaps age 40; it is now perhaps age 70. It is at either date only a little above the expectation *at birth* because, to repeat, it is child and especially infant mortality that has fallen furthest. By age 16 much of the chance of death per year the young man was to face until he was quite old had already occurred. Anyway, in 1800 a young person could expect to live another twenty-four years. But in 2000 he could expect to live another 54 years.[41] Adult years from the perspective of age 16, then, increased by a factor of about 2, not 5.

Such a person experiencing, depending on the point of view one adopts, a factor of increase of 2 or 5 times more years, was to become equipped by the end on average with that 8.5 times more goods and services. The combination of longer and richer lives is historically unique. It is one reason that liberalism has spread. There are by now many more adults living long enough lives sufficiently free from desperation to have some political interests. The theory that desperation leads to *good* revolution is of course mistaken, or else our freedoms would have emerged from the serfs of Russia or the peasants of China, not from the bourgeoisie of northwestern Europe, as they in fact did. Material wealth can yield political or artistic wealth. It doesn't have to; but it can. And it often has. What emerged from Russia and China, remember, were the antibourgeois nightmares of Stalin and Mao.

Montesquieu long ago noted that in a state of nature people are not bold but timid, crushed by necessity. Observe that 64-year-old men vote at many times the rate of 22-year-old men. Imagine then a political society without the triple revolutions of freer and longer and richer lives. A churning mass of impoverished juveniles makes for easy tyranny. Such a political society is not difficult to imagine, because it still exists in some parts of the world, such as Sudan or Myanmar. In 1800 it existed almost everywhere.

Gather together the figures on the quantity and quality of life since 1800. In "adult years of goods-supplied life" the resulting factor of increase since great-great-great-great grandma's day is therefore 17 (= 2 times 8.5) or 42.5 (= 5 times 8.5), depending on one's point of view. Note that larger figure: forty two and a half times. Listen to that phrase "adult years of goods-supplied life." The number is reasonably solid and pretty much knowable and exhibits a growth of 17 or 42.5 times since liberal capitalism began its work.

You can go one better. The longer, richer average now applies to those 6 billion rather than to the former 1 billion people.[42] So multiply each by a factor of six to get the increase in "*world* adult materially supplied years." These nurture the flowers of world culture, low and high, politics and music. Beethoven, for example, in a world sized about 1.0 in such terms was among the first highbrow musicians to support himself by selling his compositions to the public rather than to a noble patron. A market of bourgeois minipatrons was just emerging.[43] Haydn had shown what could be done for musical art on the frontier of capitalism, moving in 1791 from the livery of Prince Miklós Esterházy of Hungary to popular acclaim and commercial success as a bourgeois composer in London.

In the two centuries since the young Beethoven's time the market for music has increased if you look at it from the point of view of the 16-year-old setting out on adult life by a factor of 2 times 8.5 times 6—a factor of 102 in total. That's not 102 *percent*, class. That's a *factor* of 102, which is to say about *9,000* percent. Do you see? *One hundred* times, or *9,000* percent, more music, painting, literature, philosophy, cuisine, cocktails, medicine, sports.

Or one better again. From the proud parent's point of view the market increased 5 times 8.5 times 6—or by a factor of 255. That's 255 times more music, painting, and the rest, good and bad, glorious and corrupting. Good Lord. As a couple of acute observers, Marx and Engels, put it when all this was getting under way, "What earlier century had even a presentiment that such productive forces slumbered in the lap of social labor?"

"Modern economic growth," as the economists boringly call the fact of real income per person growing at a "mere" 1.5 percent per year for two hundred years, to achieve that rise by a factor of nineteen in the countries which most enthusiastically embraced capitalism, is certainly the largest change in the human condition since the ninth millennium BC. It ranks with the first domestications of plants and animals and the building of the first towns.

Possibly modern economic growth is as large and important an event in human history as the sudden perfection of language, in Africa around 50,000 BC. In scarce two hundred years our bourgeois capitalism has domesticated the world and made it, Chicago to Shanghai, into a single, throbbing city.

Some people have lagged, though not most people in countries that have allowed capitalism to flourish. The laggards have been the countries experimenting with socialism or fascism or mere violent cronyism—Cuba, North Korea, Zimbabwe. They have suffered mainly by their own bad politics, not through some internal contradiction of capitalism or through imperialist aggression. Prices in dollar-accepting department stores in Havana in the period 1993 to 2004, when Fidel Castro permitted the domestic use of American dollars, were much the same as they were in Miami. This would not have been so if the bizarre American refusal to trade had been the actual cause of Cuban poverty. If Cuba's trade in general were actually being cut off from the world by the American action, the Cuban price system would not look like the rest of the world's. But in fact Cuba trades freely with every country *except* the United States, and so has almost all the benefit it would get from direct trade with the perfidious Yanquis.

Castro has nationalized all large businesses, closed vegetable markets, refused to allow small businesses or independent professionals to set up shop, and in 2004 he reversed his previous dispensation and outlawed dollar transactions. *That* is why Cuban real income per head has fallen by a third since 1959—while it has doubled everywhere around Cuba, except Haiti (see "violent cronyism").

By adopting the bourgeois virtues the Cubans, Haitians, North Koreans, Congolese, Sudanese, Myanmarians, and Zimbabweans can be enriched and liberated, as billions already have been. Witness the Peoples' Republic of China, which has already begun to follow Taiwan and Korea in transitioning from a very poor, socialistic autocracy into a much more rich, capitalistic autocracy. One day China may take the next step to democracy, as Taiwan and Korea did. By the 1990s India had joined the modern economic world, freed at last from the "license Raj" that had ruled since 1947. John Mueller and Amartya Sen both point out that capitalism and democracy do not have to go together.[44] All the more reason to make a thankful offering to Ganesha for a democratic and now frankly capitalist and increasingly rich Republic of India.

V.   Probatio C: And Improves Our Ethics

But.

If we had gained a better material world, two cars in the garage and Chicago-style, deep-dish, stuffed-spinach pizza on the table, but had thereby lost our souls, I personally would have no enthusiasm for the achievement. I urge you to adopt the same attitude. A good name is rather to be chosen than great riches. For what is a man profited, if he shall gain the whole world, and lose his own soul?

I do not want to rest the case for capitalism, as some of my fellow economists feel professionally obligated to do, on the material achievement alone. My apology attests to the bourgeois *virtues*. I want you to come to believe with me that they have been the causes *and consequences* of modern economic growth and of modern political freedom.

True, any well-wisher of humankind will count the relief of poverty over large parts of the world as desirable, at least if she could be sure that no excess corruption of souls was involved. No good person delights in the misery of others. Even many people skeptical of a Washington consensus of neoliberal capitalism agree that globalization has been desirable materially. It has, as one of the skeptics, Joseph Stiglitz, wrote in 2002, "helped hundreds of millions of people attain higher standards of living, beyond what they, or most economists, thought imaginable but a short while ago."

He means bringing the 1.3 billion people—70 percent of them women— now living on a dollar a day to two dollars, and then to four, and then to eight, not merely the further enrichment of the West, which neither he nor I regard as especially important. "The capitalist achievement," wrote Joseph Schumpeter in 1942, "does not typically consist in providing more silk stockings for queens." That can be achieved merely by redirecting aristocratic plundering to silk factories. The achievement consists "in bringing [silk stockings] within the reach of factory girls in return for steadily diminishing amounts of effort."[45]

To halt such a good thing, as some of the Seattle-style opponents think they wish, would be according to Stiglitz "a tragedy for all of us, and especially for the billions who might otherwise have benefited."[46] The economist Charles Calomiris, who supports globalization on egalitarian grounds, as I do, argues that "if well-intentioned protestors could be convinced that reversing globalization would harm the world's poorest residents (as it surely would) some (perhaps many) of the protestors would change their minds."[47] One would hope so.

But fattening up the people, or providing them with inexpensive silk stockings, I will try to persuade you, is not the only virtue of our bourgeois life. The triple revolutions of the past two centuries in politics, population, and prosperity are connected. They have had a cause and a consequence, I claim, in ethically *better* people. I said "better." Capitalism has not corrupted our souls. It has improved them.

I realize that such optimism is not widely credited. It makes the clerisy uneasy to be told that they are better people for having the scope of a modern and bourgeois life. They quite understandably want to honor their poor ancestors in the Italy of old or their poor cousins in India now, and feel impelled to claim with anguish as they sip their caramel macchiato grande that their prosperity comes at a terrible ethical cost.

On the political left it has been commonplace for the past century and a half to charge that modern, industrial people, whether fat or lean, are alienated, rootless, angst-ridden, superficial, materialistic; and that it is precisely participation in markets which has made them so. Gradually, I have noted, the right and the middle have come to accept the charge. Some sociologists, both progressive and conservative, embrace it, lamenting the decline of organic solidarity. By the early twenty-first century some on the right have schooled themselves to reply to the charge with a sneering cynicism, "Yeah, sure. Markets have no morals. So what? Greed *is* good. Bring on the pizza."

The truth I claim is closer to the opposite. In his recent book on the intellectual history of modern capitalism Jerry Muller notes that "the market was most frequently attacked by those who viewed its intrinsic purposelessness as leading to an intrinsic purposelessness in human life as such, and who sought radical alternatives on the left and right."[48] That is indeed what the left and right believed, and still believe. They believe in the *cultural* critique of capitalism, a critique which once justified the Arts and Crafts movement and socialist realism on the left and the architecture and poetry of fascism on the right, and justifies now sneering at red states by blue.

I say that the cultural critique is mistaken. Production and consumption, to be sure, are "intrinsically purposeless." Mere eating is not a "purpose" in the sense that people mean the word as a commendation. But this is true of any production and consumption, in any economy imaginable, in a medieval or pastoral utopia as much as in actually existing socialism or capitalism.

Humans make their consumption meaningful, as in the meal you share with a friend or the picture frame in which you put the snapshot of your beloved. It is not obvious that consuming in Midtown Manhattan is less purposeful than consuming in an anticapitalist North Korea or in an antibourgeois hippie commune. Isn't it *more* purposeful, speaking of the transcendent? The grim single-mindedness of getting and spending in a collectivist village is not obviously superior to the numberless levels, varieties, and capacities of Paris or Chicago. Vulgar devotion to consumption alone is more characteristic of pre- and anticapitalist than of late-capitalist societies.

I claim that actually existing capitalism, not the collectivisms of the left or of the right, has reached beyond mere consumption, producing the best art and the best people. People have purposes. A capitalist economy gives them scope to try them out. Go to an American Kennel Club show, or an antique show, or a square-dancing convention, or to a gathering of the many millions of American birdwatchers, and you'll find people of no social pretensions passionately engaged. Yes, some people watch more than four hours of TV a day. Yes, some people engage in corrupting purchases. But they are no worse than their ancestors, and on average better.

Their ancestors, like yours and mine, were wretchedly poor, engaged with getting a bare sufficiency. It does not have to be that old way. In 1807 Coleridge quoted an economist of the time, Patrick Colquhoun, asserting that "poverty is . . . a most necessary . . . ingredient in society, without which nations . . . would not exist in a state of civilization. . . . Without poverty there would be no labor, and without labor no riches, no refinement." This was a standard argument against the relief of poverty, joining eight other ancient arguments against doing something about poverty—the eight are a recent count by the philosopher Samuel Fleischacker.[49]

Coleridge sharply disagreed with Colquhoun's pessimism. A man is poor, he wrote, "whose bare wants cannot be supplied without such unceasing bodily labor from the hour of waking to that of sleeping, as precludes all improvement of mind—and makes the intellectual faculties to the majority of mankind as useless as pictures to the blind."[50] Can such waste be necessary for a high civilization? Coleridge didn't think so.

In 1807 the debate was still unsettled. Is a class of exploited people necessary for high civilization, as Colquhoun, or Nietzsche, claimed? Or is the disappearance of such a class as a result of material progress exactly how we get a mass *high* civilization, as Coleridge, or Adam Smith, claimed?

The results are now in. Modern economic growth has led to more, not less, refinement, for hundreds of millions who would otherwise have been poor and ignorant—as were, for example, most of your ancestors and mine. Here are you and I, learnedly discussing the merits and demerits of capitalism. Which of your or my ancestors in 1800 would have had the leisure or education of a Colquhoun or a Coleridge to do that? As the economic historian Robert Fogel noted in 2004, "Today ordinary people have time to enjoy those amenities of life that only the rich could afford in abundance a century ago. These amenities broaden the mind, enrich the soul, and relieve the monotony of much earnwork [Fogel's term for paid employment]. . . . Today people are increasingly concerned with the meaning of their lives."[51] He points out that in 1880 the average American spent 80 percent of her income on food, housing, and clothing. Now she spends less than a third. That's a rise from a residual 20 percent of a very low income spendable on "improvements of mind" to about 70 percent of a much larger income. All right: a lot of it is spent on rap music rather than Mozart, alas; and on silly toys rather than economics courses, unfortunately. But also on book clubs and birdwatching.

Some noble savages have been ripped or enticed from admirable cultures by capitalism. But some ignoble savages, too, have learned a better life free of tribal patriarchy and family violence. You yourself probably have, for example, by comparison with your ancestors of, to put it conservatively, some dozens of generations ago. The cultural relativist claims that one cannot tell whether it is better to be a Tahitian as idealized by Paul Gauguin or a realtor of Zenith as satirized by Sinclair Lewis. I say that idealizations or satires aside, a soul choosing from behind a prenatal veil would opt for bourgeois life now over Tahitian agriculture in 1896. Their mothers and fathers surely would, for their children. Billions have voted this way with their feet.

And whether or not one honors such personal choice, hypothetical or actual, if you adopt an Aristotelian criterion, then most people after capitalism are more fulfilled as humans. They have more lives available. The anthropologist Grant McCracken has written of the "plenitude" that the modern world has brought. He half-seriously instances fifteen ways of being a teenager in North America in 1990: rocker, surfer-skater, b-girls, Goths, punk, hippies, student government, jocks, and on and on. By now the options are even wider. "In the 1950s," he notes, there were only two categories. "You could be mainstream or James Dean. That was it."[52] I was there in the 1950s, and agree—though in places like California, richer and fresher than Ontario or Massachusetts in the 1950s, the options were richer, too. The plenitude has come from free people sifting through the cornucopia, making themselves in their music and their clothing.

As the economic historian Eric Jones put it, "There is a tendency to lament the loss of earlier values and practices, however inappropriate they may be for modern circumstances"—think of French village life in Lorraine in 1431 or headhunting Ilongot in the Philippines in 1968—"without allowing for the greater wealth of opportunities and novelties that is continually being created."[53] Mario Vargas Llosa does not believe that globalization has impoverished the world culturally. On the contrary, Vargas Llosa writes,

> globalization extends radically to all citizens of this planet the possibility to construct their individual cultural identities through voluntary action, according to their preferences and intimate motivations. Now, citizens are not always obligated, as in the past and in many places in the present, to respect an identity that traps them in a concentration camp from which there is no escape—the identity that is imposed on them through the language, nation, church, and customs of the place where they were born.[54]

Participation in capitalist markets and bourgeois virtues has civilized the world. It has "civilized" the world in more than one of the word's root senses, that is, making it "citified," from the mere increase in a rich population. It has too, I claim, as many eighteenth-century European writers also claimed, made it courteous, that is, "civil." "The terrestrial paradise," said Voltaire, "is Paris."

Richer and more urban people, contrary to what the magazines of opinion sometimes suggest, are *less* materialistic, *less* violent, *less* superficial than poor and rural people. Because people in capitalist countries already possess the material, they are less attached to their possessions than people in poor countries. And because they have more to lose from a society of violence, they resist it.

You can choose to disbelieve if you wish some of the things said to go along with the capitalist revolution of the past two centuries, such as the emerging global village, the rise in literacy, the progress of science, the new rule of law, the fall of tyrannies, the growth of majority government, the opening of closed lives, the liberation of women and children, the spread of free institutions, the enrichment of world culture. But if only a few of these alleged consequences were justified, then capitalism itself would be justified. And not by bread alone.[55]

The late Robert Nozick wrote that "what is desired is an organization of society optimal for people who are far less than ideal, optimal also for much better people, and which is such that living under such an organization itself tends to make people better and more ideal."[56] Nozick and I say it's capitalism. We say that socialism works only for an impossibly ideal Socialist Man, or a Christian saint, and that socialism tends to make people worse, not better.

The ethical betterment is not achieved, I repeat, at the cost of the remaining poor people. That is a fact to be established. I do not expect you to agree with everything I am saying. If you do, you are not the antibourgeois, anticapitalist, or antiethical reader I am trying to persuade. I need to persuade you that capitalism and bourgeois virtues have been greater forces eliminating poverty than any labor union or welfare program or central plan. We have the eight-hour day mainly because we got rich, and therefore we won't tolerate eleven-hour days—unless we are yuppie attorneys in New York fresh from Yale Law School making well over $100,000 a year in exchange for a seventy-seven-hour work week. Some poor people now work long hours and can't make it. No one should deny that. But it was worse in 1900, and worse yet in 1800. Better working conditions have prevailed not because of union negotiations or governmental regulations, but because capitalism has worked.

I need to persuade you also that, contrary to Colquhoun, poverty is not a most necessary ingredient in society. I need to show you empirically, for example, and will try in volume 4, what most economists know: that if the allegedly exploitative trade of the first world with the third were halted tomorrow the first world would suffer a mere hiccup in its rate of growth. I need to show you empirically that if presently poor people in rich countries all became engineers and professors, the presently rich people would be better off, not worse off, though with fewer poor people to bus the tables and mind the children.

We will not have the heaven-on-earth of perfect equality, ever, and I lament this fact. But equality over the long term—despite an unhappy reversal in the trend in the United States in the 1980s—has been increased by capitalism, and in absolute terms the poor even in the 1980s and after got better and better off.

In asserting capitalism's innocence of causing poverty, understand, I am not simply disrespecting the poor, or elevating material abundance to trumps, or recommending a cold heart. I have emphasized that all our ancestors were poor, that everyone descends overwhelmingly from poor people, even from slaves, since almost all societies before the eighteenth century had lesser or smaller numbers of slaves and all such societies were by your standards and mine astoundingly poor. Try to imagine living on one dollar a day, with the prices of food and clothing and housing as they now are. Imagine, if you wish, an economy with very many such people, and so having commercial provision for mats to sleep hundreds abreast on the streets of Calcutta and for rice-by-the-bowl with pebbles and clay mixed in. It's still no picnic. Ninety-nine percent of our great-great-great-great grandparents lived on a dollar a day, and more than a billion people I said do still.

I am not disdaining the once and present poor. I am merely repeating what the poor themselves say—that "I been poor and I been rich," in Sophie Tucker's words, "and, honey, rich is best," for stomachs, for brains, for souls. No one in a *favella* behind the Copacabana thinks her life is made more admirable in a spiritual sense by living in a cardboard box. Only saints and intellectuals can believe such a paradox for longer than it takes the sun to go down over Corcovado. The poor person wants the fruits of capitalism, first the material fruits and then the spiritual fruits. The poor are not better than you and me. They're just poorer. We bourgeois do not make them better off by being ashamed of being rich, since it's not our fault that they are poor, and there is therefore no original sin in our being rich. We should instead work to make them rich, too, by spreading the used-up liberal capitalism.

The richer, more urban, more bourgeois people, one person averaged with another, I claim, have larger, not smaller, spiritual lives than their impoverished ancestors of the pastoral. They have more, not fewer, real friends than their great-great-great-great grandparents in "closed-corporate" villages. They have broader, not narrower, choices of identity than the one imposed on them by the country, custom, language, and religion of their birth. They have deeper, not shallower, contacts with the transcendent of art or science or God, and sometimes even of nature, than the superstitious peasants and haunted hunters-gatherers from whom we all descend.

They are better humans—because they in their billions have acquired the scope to become so and because market societies encourage art and science and religion to flourish and because anyway a life in careers and deal making and companies and marketplaces is not the worst life for a full human being. As the economist and philosopher Amartya Sen puts it, "The freedom to exchange words, or goods, or gifts does not need defensive justification in terms of their favorable but distant effects; they are part of the way human beings in society live.... We have good reasons to buy and sell, to exchange, and to seek lives that can flourish on the basis of transactions."[57] He instances the liberation of women worldwide through access to markets.[58]

You need to be careful here. Not all market behavior is good for the soul, and I am not claiming it is. If you listen to Ted Fishman on NPR describing the horrible behavior of his erstwhile colleagues in the options pit at the Chicago Mercantile Exchange you are liable to think, "Ah hah! Thus capitalism and the *betterment* of human beings!"[59] And that's right. Fishman says that his mentor at the exchange told him to go after every dollar as though his life depended on it. Not good. Spirit-corrupting.

But the bad things in a capitalist world are not all testimony to the badness of capitalism. Much of human good and evil arises from our fallen natures, and has nothing to do with the circumstances in which we are put. Or to be more exact, it "has to do" with the circumstances, but only in the sense that capitalist circumstances evoke a certain kind of greedy behavior in Ted, while socialist circumstances would evoke in him . . . *another* kind of greedy behavior. Ted, like you and me, is fallen. This is a crucial point. We must not tolerate bad behavior, anywhere. But we must in our moralizing not mistake human failing for specifically capitalist failing. To attribute every badness to the system is like blaming everything on the weather. It's not smart or useful.

The Capitalist Man in his worst moments is greedy. And so are you and I. And so, I note, is Socialist Man, in more than his worst moments. If capitalism is to be blamed for systemic evils, then it also is to be given credit for systemic goods, compared not with an imaginary ideal but with actually existing alternatives. The economist Michael Kalecki moved from his good academic position in England back to Poland to help with the imposition of communism there. After some years he was asked about whether Poland had succeeded in abolishing capitalism. "Yes," he replied. "All we have to do now is to abolish feudalism."[60]

Capitalism has not corrupted the spirit. On the contrary, had capitalism not enriched the world by a cent nonetheless its bourgeois, antifeudal virtues would have made us better people than in the world we have lost. As a system it has been good for us.

Jonathan Sacks, the chief rabbi of Britain and the British Commonwealth, sometimes repeats the usual claim of religious leaders, unsubstantiated, that "the dominance of the market [has] had a corrosive effect on the social landscape" and that "the institutions of civil society . . . have become seriously eroded in consumption-driven cultures." He is mistaken. It is a mistake for one thing to think of bourgeois life as "consumption-driven," if one means that spend, spend, spend is necessary for its survival. An aristocrat or a peasant will spend, spend, spend when he can, yet his life consists of more. So too the bourgeois. Since capitalism took command, the social landscape has been enriched, not eroded, as many modern sociologists have discovered—at any rate those who have looked into the matter rather than accept nineteenth-century German romanticism and twentieth-century Catholic nostalgia.[61]

But Rabbi Sacks gets it right when he tells us "It is the market—the least overtly spiritual of contexts—that delivers a profoundly spiritual message." What message? "It is through exchange that difference becomes a blessing, not a curse." This from a man who has given some thought to the costs and benefits of difference. Sacks understands that "the free market is the best means we have yet discovered for alleviating poverty," yes, but also for "creating a human environment of independence, dignity and creativity."[62]

Capitalists ended slavery and emancipated women and founded universities and rebuilt churches, none of these for material profit and none by damaging the rest of the world. Bourgeois virtues led us from terrified hunter bands and violent agricultural villages to peaceful suburbs and lively cities. Enlightened people such as Voltaire, Montesquieu, Adam Smith, and Mary Wollstonecraft believed that work and trade enriched people in more than material things. They believed that a capitalism not yet named broke down privileges that had kept men poor and women and children dependent. And for the soul they believed that labor and trade were on the whole good, not dishonorable. Work is "rough toil that dignifies the mind," wrote Wollstonecraft, as against "the indolent calm that stupefies the good sort of women it sucks in."[63] Commerce, the French said, was a sweetener: *le doux commerce*. Commerce may have lowered the spirit of the proud noble, Voltaire noted with little regret, having suffered literal beatings at his behest, but it sweetened and elevated the rude peasant.

Ulysses is an old man in Tennyson's poem of 1833, about to take ship for one last, heroic adventure. He describes his unheroic, even bourgeois, son Telemachus left to govern Ithaca, "by slow prudence to make mild / A rugged people, and thro' soft degrees / Subdue them to the useful and the good." *Boring*. So inferior to Ulysses' knightly irresponsibility. Unlike their Romantic successors, the writers of the Enlightenment did not yearn for knighthood and sainthood and peasant solidarity reimagined. "Gothic" in 1733 was a term of contempt, meaning "of the Goths and Vandals," then descriptive of the Middle Ages, again "chiefly with reprobation." Only in the nineteenth century did it become a commendation from the Believers in Everything Old like Tennyson and William Morris and John Ruskin. The tradition of the pastoral from Theocritus to Wendell Berry romanticizes rural poverty, viewed from a couch in town.

The bourgeois life rejects the romance of the old and the rural. A good thing, too. Toward the end of the first liberal hour, Tocqueville, who was neither a pastoral poet nor a Romantic, remarked, "The principle of self-interest rightly understood produces no great acts of self-sacrifice, but it suggests daily small acts of self-denial. . . . If [it] were to sway the whole world, extraordinary virtues would doubtless be more rare; but I think that gross depravity would then also be less common."[64] *Doux commerce* makes for Temperance. And also for part of Justice. The philosopher Lester Hunt recently imagined that "if the rules and practices of commercial transactions were plucked out of the world and gift-exchange were carried on without them, . . . self-respect would lack some of the support it is granted in [our actual, capitalist world]."[65] Hunt seems to consider his mental experiment to be improbable. It is not. It is a description of the ethical world of the West before the triumph of the bourgeoisie. Richard II and Harry Bolingbroke followed no rules and practices of commercial transactions. Self-respect in their world, and on Shakespeare's stage, lacked any support but rank and violence.

Since 1848 the critic of capitalism has made three counterclaims, all of them I am sorry to say mistaken. As a practical project, the critic says, capitalism works poorly, immiserizing us or subjecting us to chronic collapse.[66] Such a claim, I shall try gradually to persuade you, is mistaken. And capitalism, the critic also says, generates inequality.[67] A class of poor people, at home or abroad, is supposed to be necessary for bourgeois prosperity. That, too, is mistaken. And to come to the present point, capitalism, he says, has debased values, making people greedy, vulgar, alienated, and depraved.[68] Mistaken again. The play-by-play man would remark that our anticapitalist critic, coming up to bat late in the ball game, is "oh for three."

The theologian William Schweiker expresses the criticisms succinctly: "The modern age in the West . . . brought great rewards. . . . Yet it has led, ironically, to the demeaning and the profaning of human existence and all of life through wars, ecological endangerment, and cultural banality."[69] With great respect for the person and the generous sentiment, I would reply: no. The reaction to the project, not the project itself, brought the wars. The absence of property rights brought the ecological endangerment. And human culture has always been banal, mostly. What survives into museums and history books is normally the nonbanal, giving us an exalted notion of the past, an anxiety of influence.

The claim on the left, in short, is that regardless of the individual capitalist's virtue or vice the *system* of capitalism leads to evil. The claim is mistaken.

We need to defend a defensible capitalism. We citizens of the bourgeois towns need to rethink our love and courage. We need to nourish the commercial versions of temperance, justice, and prudence that were admired during the eighteenth century by some in the commercial societies of northwestern Europe, and by at least the merchants themselves in Japan.[70] And we need to find a safe home for our faith and hope. For failures in just these regards, see the Muslim, and especially the Arab, and especially the Saudi Arabian world, 1967 to the present. And see, for an earlier case, the Christian, and especially the Western European, and especially the German- and English-speaking world 1517 to 1689.

If we can do all this ethical reinvestment, we can avoid repeating the slaughters and lesser sadnesses of the twentieth century.

VI.   Refutatio: Anticapitalism Is Bad for Us

The danger is not from the natural environment, as so many physical and biological scientists believe. Modern economic growth has made the "resources" that everyone except economists thinks of as especially scarce— oil, fresh water, chromium—into an unimportant share of national income.

An item's share of national income is a rigorously justifiable measure of its economic importance. The biggest one by far is labor, laborers now rich in self-owned human capital, the "ultimate resource," as the economist

Julian Simon called it. Physical capital in factories and machines and houses is a much smaller share, though still big. But rental income from resource-bearing land of all sorts in the United States in 2002 was a mere 1.7 percent of national income. Take a little if you wish from corporate profits (9.4 percent) or business-owners' income (9.1 percent), as perhaps including by mistakes in accounting a bit of resource land rent, too, and you will have difficulty getting up to 3 percent of national income.

Or so at least modern economists believe.[71] The modern followers of Henry George, dismissed by most other economists, object to the claim that rents of all sorts have become trivial. They point out that urban land rents to location, location, location have risen, and new forms of land-like rent such as the very large rental value of the electronic spectrum are big shares of national capital.

That may be, but even the Georgists agree with their colleagues that in the usual meaning "natural *resource*" rents—rents on oil, coal, iron ore, and agricultural land—have fallen dramatically since *Progress and Poverty* was first published. If national income were measured to include the value of nonmarketed services such as homemakers' time and the like, as it properly should, the share would be even smaller.

You can see in other ways, too, that natural resources, vital though they sound to the noneconomic mind, can't be all that important nowadays. The unimportance of oil and diamonds and land are why Russia or, worse, the Congo and Bolivia, with all those "natural resources," are still poor, while Japan or, better, Singapore and Hong Kong, with practically none, are rich. In fact, in the modern world "resources" are commonly an impoverishing "Dutch disease" rather than a way to wealth. See oil-rich Nigeria—and the numerous other cases of an inverse relationship between wealth in natural resources and human capital. The human capital makes one truly wealthy in the modern world.[72] Saudi Arabia has squandered its oil wealth on Rolls Royces and London department stores instead of educating its people, for example, its women, in preparation for the time when the oil runs out.

Truly wealthy countries now are not like the United States in 1879 (the year of George's *Progress and Poverty*), employing 48 percent of the labor force in agriculture, or like the United Kingdom in 1817 (the year of David Ricardo's *The Principles of Political Economy and Taxation*), getting 15 percent of all its income from land rents.[73]

The claim on the left is that "the first person who, having enclosed a plot of land, took it into his head to say *this is mine* and found people simple enough to believe him, was the true founder of political society. What crimes . . . would the human race have been spared had someone pulled up the stakes . . . and cried out to his fellow men: 'Do not listen to this imposter. You are lost if you forget that the fruits of the earth belong to all!' "[74] In 1755 it was not unreasonable of Rousseau to focus on landownership. But to focus on the original appropriation is a mistake in a progressing economy. The philosopher David Schmidtz explains the economics against Rousseau: "Philosophers . . . tend to speak as if people who arrive first . . . are much luckier than those who come later. . . . Consider the Jamestown colony of 1607. Exactly what was it, we should ask, that made their situation so much better than ours? They never had to worry about being overcharged for car repair. . . . They never had to agonize over the choice of long-distance phone companies. Are these the things that make us wish we had gotten there first?"[75]

Today in places like Europe and the United States the share of income earned from all the original and indestructible powers of the soil is, I say, below 3 percent.[76] Even in overheated, supercooled, and gas-guzzling America we earn only about 4 percent of our national income from crude oil, reckoned at the well head or the point of importation. And only part of the 4 percent is an income to the land involved. Much of it is the income of roughnecks and drill bits and oil tankers, not the oil land itself. Therefore the oil geopolitics which so fascinates deep thinkers—besides being socially cruel and politically shortsighted and militarily impractical—is economically silly.

The real danger comes from assaults on the *human* capital that made land scarcity irrelevant in the first place. We can pollute Lake Erie. In fact, we did. During the 1960s every environmentalist declared with angry assurance that Erie was biologically dead forever, kaput, finite, over. And yet in the 1990s we can bring it back for fishing and swimming, and did, *if* we have our wits about us.

If we have our wits about us we can in the next fifty years use up the oil in the Middle East and yet replace it in automobiles and heating with hydrogen. We can drain the Oglala aquifer in the next twenty years, and yet one day replenish it—mad thought—from desalinized seawater piped to Nebraska using that cheap and clean hydrogen fuel, if we have our wits about us. The modern world is different from a zero-sum world, which Malthus theorized just as it was disappearing forever. We can keep on innovating, keep up the factor of 8.5 or 19. If we have our wits about us.[77]

Responding to the real danger threatening our future, I argue, requires attention to human freedom. It is human freedom which has given us the wits to prosper. This again is not obvious, but volume 2 will try to show that it is true.

A bright future for human freedom therefore requires curbing our present lords. These are not the corporations, which after all control only our consumption of hamburgers and athletic shoes, and, in view of their competition, "control" even those feebly, McDonald's against Burger King or Nike against New Balance. Observe that the terrible corporate trusts of earlier times, such as the great and imposing United States Steel, the horrific Amalgamated Copper Company, the appalling American Telephone and Telegraph Company, the gouging Erie and New York Central railway pools, are one with Nineveh and Tyre.

A farmer-captured Department of Agriculture, though, and a corrupt United States Congress live on and on and on. At the end of 2004 the growers of taste-free little machine-harvested tomatoes in Florida were able to block the exportation from the state of ugly but delicious handpicked varieties by using the governmental system of "marketing orders" first promulgated as a New Deal measure in 1937. When American steel producers get tariffs or when sugar beet growers get import quotas it is not because of their market power but because of their political power, their access to an all-powerful state.

The ongoing danger to freedom, in other words, is from the powers of the modern state. Its powers have been justified, ironically, by the alleged need to protect us from the monopoly of United States Steel, say, or from the low price of world sugar, or from terrorists provoked by the same government's adventures in oil geopolitics.

It has long been so. Adam Smith warned in 1776 against imperial adventures and against the monopolizing spirit of merchants and manufacturers. "The interest of the dealers . . . in any particular branch of trade or manufactures is always in some respects different from, and even opposite to, that of the public."[78] What's good for General Motors is not, in general, good for the generality.

But in Smith's analysis the bourgeoisie would have little power against competition if they did not have a powerful state to corrupt. "To found a great empire [or to restrict domestic competition] for the sole purpose of raising up a people of customers. . . . is . . . a project altogether unfit for a nation of shopkeepers, but extremely fit for a nation whose government is *influenced* by shopkeepers."[79] The more comprehensive and effective is the state, the greater is the incentive for interests and parties to seize control of it, there being in that case more to gain.

Smith would have found highly amusing the notion that the government itself, such as George III's United Kingdom, could be a "countervailing power" to corporate interests or a "referee" between labor and capital or a "regulator" of professions or a "planner" of technological change. He himself in his old age, by the way, held a sinecure collecting the customs revenues he railed against in *The Wealth of Nations*. Thus the corrupting power of the state, even against its severest critic.

It is surprising how quickly some have forgotten what even naïve people outside it discovered after the fall of Communism. An all-encompassing state, regardless of an official ideology of equality, yielded, in the words of the Bulgarian-French critic Tzvetan Todorov, "a reign of unrestrained personal interests . . . [which] corrupted political institutions, . . . ravaged the environment, the economy, and human souls."[80] And so too it might be said, as Adam Smith did say, about unrestrained personal interest misusing the powers of capitalism, corrupting political institutions.

The historian William McNeill is one of many recent scholars to make the point that "gunpowder empires" after 1400 or so in Japan, China, India, the Middle East, Russia, and in seagoing form in Spain and Portugal, could control their merchants and then their speech. By contrast, Spain and Portugal at home faced competition from other cannon-owning governments, and depended, as every Western European government did, and still does, on loans and taxes from the bourgeoisie.

Adam Smith noted that uncivilized, that is, un-city-rich, kings had to have literal gold stocks to finance foreign adventures.[81] Modern governments have instead the bourgeoisie. That is why Philip II of Spain, though rich in New World gold, was desperate to keep the merchants of the Netherlands under his taxing power. That is why the Puritan merchants of London could defy Charles I of England.

The "macroparasites," as McNeill dubs those who run states for their own profit, the predatory priests, kings, lords, and guilds of Macfarlane's version, could not regain their grip in Europe for a long while, a grip loosened in the Middle Ages. "The tendency to form vast homogeneous empire," writes Macfarlane, "the dream of Charles V, Louis XIV, Napoleon, or Hitler, was never realized."[82] In China anciently and in the Ottoman lands after 1453 and in Japan after 1603 it was. In Europe the land-war struggle between the Hapsburgs and the Bourbons, and then the sea-war struggle between France and first the Dutch Republic and then Britain, had no decisive imperial winners until the nationalisms of the nineteenth century. Until then therefore the long spine of little states in Europe from Northern Italy to Holland, what Geoffrey Parker called the "Lotharingian axis" after Charlemagne's grandson Lothar, stayed independent of big national states, though a cockpit of European warfare.

Because European kingdoms and duchies and city-states competed with each other, McNeill argues, "European rulers and state officials [even] in the nineteenth century did not begin to sop up all of the new forms of wealth," as elsewhere and earlier such governments had been so skillful at doing.[83] Macfarlane quotes the historical sociologist Ernest Gellner on the "thug states": "in a multi-state system, it was possible to throttle Civil Society in some places, but not in all of them."[84]

Even big states in Europe have until recently been incompetent at taxing and repressing their subjects. Charles V and Philip II sent marauding armies into the Low Countries for eighty years but in the end got only half a loaf. The much-maligned tsarist state was unable in the nineteenth century to run even a secret service with ruthlessness.[85] Stalin, after all, was sent to Siberia *twice*. One wishes the police had in his case done a better job.

In the twentieth century, though, as a result of the Great War, Western governments got more skilled at violence. They reasserted an encompassing control over people's wealth and minds that had been routine in the ancient examples of, say, Egypt, Assyria, Sparta, Ch'in dynasty China, Rome.[86] We are at present in a race between on the one hand ever freer markets and on the other hand ever worse tax systems, drug regulations, attorneys general, electronic eavesdropping, regulatory populism, and state-sponsored violence.

We must keep our bourgeois wits about us. If we let our wits become enchained, we cannot then whine about the loss in body and soul. If people allow themselves to be treated like serfs rather than merchants they become serfs rather than merchants. Witness Russian history, except for the hopeful episodes 1801–1812, 1905–1914, and 1989–2003.

Modern economic growth and modern ethical improvement I would claim—the claim is controversial, and needs to be proven—are a consequence of personal freedom in places like Amsterdam in 1568, London in 1689, Philadelphia in 1776. Such commercial places viewed freedom as relief from an oppressive government that would restrict if it could thought and expression, shut down the newspapers, monopolize the early modern equivalents of TV stations.

Men and women of commerce came to believe in a Lockean right of self-ownership, on the analogy with other ownership. The Swiss-French political philosopher of early nineteenth-century liberalism, Benjamin Constant, called it "modern" freedom. "Ancient" freedom was rather the *collective* autonomy of the community, and the right of individuals to participate in its politics. The ancients "admitted as compatible with this collective freedom the complete subjection of the individual to the authority of the community. . . . Among the Spartans, Therpandrus could not add a string to his lyre without causing offense to the ephors. . . . The individual was . . . subservient to the supremacy of the social body [even] in Athens."[87]

Why, for example, did Japan, which in the mid-eighteenth century was in so many other ways ready for economic growth, wait another hundred years to embark on it, only after humiliations by Western powers? Because, I would claim—this is not a controversial claim—the shogunate restricted access to foreign thought and expression, closing Japan to most foreign contact. The turmoil of ideas in the West was forbidden under the Tokugawa shogunate. The initial impetus was fear of Christianization. By a law of 1635 any Japanese who came back from abroad was executed, which permanently stranded many thousands of Japanese in places all over Southeast Asia.[88] Foreign trade therefore was a mere 1 or 2 percent of national income, which made internal control easy. The shogunate exercised a monopoly of gunpowder and anyway a dominance over the numerous lesser *daimyo*—something like half of the income of the lesser lords was wasted in compulsory attendance at the court at Edo. For 264 years the government faced little competition, and after the suppression of the Shimabara revolt in 1638 and before the disintegration of Tokugawa power in the 1860s in the face of Western challenge, no competition at all. The closing of the country was meant to achieve exactly this, by cutting off competitors for power within Japan from potential allies abroad, for example, Christian Europeans.

European governments on occasion also devised laws restricting, say, the clothing of various of their social classes. But the Japanese government could actually enforce such laws, and did with rigor. European governments like that of Russia or Spain *wanted* to be as effective in controlling their populations as the Tokugawa, but they were not. The shogunate intervened in technical progress repeatedly. It banned ship construction above coasting size—following in this the Central Kingdom across the Sea of Japan—and banned, of all things, wheeled vehicles. As late as the 1850s you will find no carts in prints of Japanese city scenes. The rickshaw is a Meiji invention. Most bridges were pulled down by the authorities, to force the travelers afoot to pass through the numerous barriers at which passports were inspected.[89]

The Japanese state's busybodyness from 1603 to 1868 would surprise even a Frenchman. In the autumn of 1794, for example, the Tokugawa bureaucracy saw it as urgent to ban the use of mica in the background of prints, a luxurious technique suddenly popular. Compare Therpandrus adding a string to his lyre. The printmaker Toshusai Sharaku shifted immediately to yellow ground and smaller portraits. The 6 percent of the population who were samurai, much more numerous than Western European nobilities, functioned after 1603 as a bureaucracy enforcing such laws. A samurai, the only person allowed to have swords, could preemptorily behead anyone he felt was insufficiently respectful. The Japanese social anthropologist Chie Nakane put it mildly: under the Tokugawa, "administrative control was thorough and far-reaching."[90]

Such intrusions, to be sure, were little different in spirit from those of the Inquisition, or as I say of French mercantilism then and now. In France during the term of the laws 1686–1759 prohibiting the importation or making of printed calicoes—this to protect wool and linen manufacturers—Eli Heckscher reports that the measures "cost the lives of some 16,000 people, partly through executions and partly through armed affrays, without reckoning the unknown but certainly much larger number . . . sent to the galleys. . . . On one occasion in Valence, 77 were sentenced to be hanged, 58 were to be broken on the wheel, 631 were sent to the galleys."[91] But Europeans could at least flee to Switzerland or England or America. The calicoes, and the later idea of machine-made cotton, continued to leak through the frontiers. In

Europe the frontiers were close by, the countries small. "Even this vigorous action," writes Heckscher, "did not help to attain the desired end. Printed calicoes spread more and more widely among all classes, . . . in France and everywhere else."[92] Japan under the Tokugawa was a prison, locked down by the shogunate—though a peaceful and self-satisfied prison for much of the time. The Japanese case, and the Chinese, too, shows that peace alone does not suffice for an industrial revolution. Maybe freedom does.

In parts of Europe, beginning in the Netherlands, the censors and ayatollahs lost their power, if gradually. By 1600 the Dutch had taken over from the Venetians the role of the unrestricted publishers of Europe, publishing the books of heretics like John Locke in English and Pierre Bayle in French. The free press grew in Western Europe, while it continued to be repressed in China and Japan. In the late eighteenth century a Chinese lexicographer who violated the imperial dictum that the written characters for "Confucius" and for the Ch'ing emperors themselves were never to be seen in full was executed and five of his male offspring sold into slavery. A Japanese writer with the temerity to issue a pamphlet in 1834 recommending the opening of the country was arrested and forced to commit suicide.[93] When in that same year Louis Philippe enacted laws against cartoons making fun of his pear-like visage and the corruptions of his regime, the French purchased their cartoons instead abroad, continuing to make merry of Louis Philippe, and at length toppled his throne.

So it was that in Europe the competing states, as McNeill and many others such as Alan Macfarlane and Eric Jones and Jean Baechler have stressed, made for a certain intellectual and therefore economic freedom. "The expansion of capitalism," wrote Baechler in 1971, "owes its origins and raison d'être to political anarchy."[94] "The plurality of small states in Europe," Macfarlane argues, "autonomous but linked by a common history, religion, and elite language, almost incessantly at war and when not at war, in fierce cultural and social competition, was the ideal context for rapid productive and ideological evolution."[95] "In purely dialectical fashion," writes Joel Mokyr in 2002, echoing Schumpeter's logic, "technological progress creates [vested interests] that eventually destroy it. . . . For a set of fragmented and open economies . . . this result does not hold."[96] Think of the Renaissance, the Reformation, the glories of a Dutch Republic beset on every side.

In the way that American cities and states compete for corporate headquarters—economists call it the Tiebout effect—the Spanish crown in the

1490s competed with France, Portugal, England, and the Dukedom of Medina Celi for the services of Cristoforo Colombo, admittedly in a competition less than fierce. John Cabot, the English explorer for Henry VII of England, was Giovanni Caboti of Genoa and Venice. He had hawked his project for the Northwest Passage around Europe. Henry Hudson did two voyages for the English Muscovy Company, but his third for the Dutch East India Company, and his fourth and last, after being arrested for going over to the Dutch, for another English company. As McNeill observes, "The European state system was crucial in preventing the takeover of mercantile wealth by bureaucratic authority in the way Chinese, Mughal, and Ottoman officials were able to do as a matter of course."[97] I would add Tokugawa Japanese officials to the list, and would worry nowadays about European Community and American federal officials, too.

In China and the Ottoman Empire invention was secret and monopolized and under suspicion. The sultan was as likely to throw an inventor off a cliff as to reward him for his trouble. In 1603 Japanese technology was equal to that of Western Europe, and in some matters—musket making, for example, and carpentry—it may have been superior. Geoffrey Parker argues that the reason the Far Eastern powers were not victims in the sixteenth and seventeenth centuries of Europe's "military revolution"—cannon-proof fortifications and volley firing of muskets, for example—is that they had already had the revolution—in Japan's case decades and in China's centuries before.[98] But by 1800, despite a trickle of "Dutch learning" into the country, Japan was a century behind. Around 1600 Western mathematics embarked on two centuries of improvement in the solution of actual physical problems, at the same time that Japanese mathematics became as ornamental as Western mathematics became after 1800.

As Mokyr argues in *The Gifts of Athena* (2002), "to create a world in which 'useful' knowledge was indeed *used* with an aggressiveness and a single-mindedness that no other society had experienced before was the unique Western way." The way led through an "Industrial Enlightenment."[99] The more general Enlightenment, by means of free speech and uncensored publication about the things of this world, "unlocked the doors of prosperity and threw them wide open." Mokyr quotes Hume in 1742 arguing that "the emulation [of neighbors] . . . is an obvious source of improvement. But what I would chiefly insist on is the stop which such limited [but competing] territories give both to power and authority."[100] Competition often breeds freedom, and always change. Free minds invent.

The same European competition worked of course in politics, too. Luther could play off the elector Frederick of Saxony against Pope Leo X. The allies of the deposed Stuarts could find refuge in France; the allies of the deposed Bourbons could find refuge in England. In much of Europe city air made one free, so long as cities remained free of the center, which in Germany, for example, was true well into the nineteenth century.

For centuries republics like Venice or Switzerland or the Netherlands irritated their monarchical neighbors by giving refuge to almost anyone. José Martí wandered in exile from imperial Cuba to the republics of Guatemala, Venezuela, and, 1881–1895, New York, until he invented the Cuban nation. Most governments in Europe except Britain had a price on the head of Giuseppe Mazzini. So Britain was the place in which after 1837 he lived and was lionized and from which he invented the Italian nation. Prince Kropotkin was during 1883–1886 jailed even in republican France, but found refuge in Britain to write encyclopedia articles about his pacific brand of anarchism. Lenin, whose theories were not pacific, was transported like a human time bomb from neutral and tolerant Switzerland through the front lines of the Central Powers to the Finland Station. Not all of these competitions had good results. But they were better for speech and for dealing, and so for innovation and for economic growth, than a one-voiced empire.

The serfdom in rich countries now is governmental, not private—in olden days it was governmental *and* private, since an aristocracy regards its office as its property. To be perfectly candid—you will have detected my politics anyway, and it would be churlish not to state it forthrightly—I advocate laissez-faire, and dream of literally one-third to one-fifth of the government we now have. My friend Milton Friedman is fond of remarking that we should be thankful we do not get as much government as we pay for. My friend Robert Higgs views the government, as I do, as a voracious leviathan. Funnily enough, leviathan has long been financed in the United States by withholding taxes invented as a war measure by . . . a young Milton Friedman.[101]

I doubt you will in the end be persuaded by Milton or Bob or me to let government revert to pre–Great War levels. In 1910 the American local, state, and federal governments spent altogether a mere 7 percent of the goods and services produced, as against 20 percent in recent decades; they handed out 7 percent of the incomes received, as against 36 percent in the early 2000s, including, that is, social security and other transfer payments.[102] The rise in other rich countries, such as the UK, or Sweden, has been larger, to around 50–60 percent at the end. And as Higgs has often observed, these measures do not capture the growing role of government in compelling or forbidding this or that behavior, preventing wheeled vehicles or executing people for importing calicoes.

I know, I know. You think that most of that government expenditure goes for "programs," as the politicians put it, that benefit you, and especially the poor. So we all wish. If it were so, if modern government were in fact effective in giving a hand up to the deserving poor, if most of its expenditure were on behalf of such people, I would be very much more happy with it. But as it stands in the United States the typical government program is more like road building than Head Start. It benefits politically well-connected construction unions and the owners of paving firms, not little kids from the inner city.

I agree with my favorite Marxist economist, Nancy Folbre, that education should be financed from the center, that maternity care and early child care should be expanded and be state financed, that inheritance taxes should be steep, that corporate welfare should be eliminated, that military expenditures should be cut to a tiny fraction of their present levels, that a modest minimum income should be given to every American, that tax laws should "encourage both men and women to combine paid work with family and community work."[103] We agree in short that France, minus its own thicket of corporate and union and farmer welfare and its large military expenditures, has some good ideas. I would nonetheless have to note with Robert Nozick that the taxes to pay for the ideas, good or bad, are a kind of slavery. But I would be a more cheerful slave if my masters, as under the Folbre-McCloskey plan, were actually the poor.

We followers of Adam Smith are egalitarians. Gertrude Himmelfarb has noted that Smith's *The Wealth of Nations* "was genuinely revolutionary in its view of poverty and its attitude towards the poor."[104] Samuel Fleischacker has shown this in detail.[105] We antistatist egalitarians want the poor to prosper. But we have proposals to achieve that desirable result which for two hundred years, contrary to the proposals of our socialist friends, have actually worked.

The tempting shortcut of taxing the rich has not worked, for two reasons. First, I repeat, taxation is taking, and as the philosopher Edward Feser puts it, "Respecting another's self-ownership . . . [reflects] one's recognition that that other person does not exist for *you*. . . . The socialist or liberal egalitarian . . . rather than the Nozickian libertarian . . . is . . . more plausibly accused of 'selfishness.' "[106] No left egalitarian has explained how such takings square with Kant's second formulation of the categorical imperative: "So act as to use humanity, both in your own person and in the person of every other, always at the same time as an end, never simply as a means."[107] Taxing Peter to pay Paul is using Peter for Paul. It is corrupting. Modern governments have been encouraged to think that any abuse of Peter is just fine, that Peter is a slave available for any duty that the ruler has in mind. A little like nonmodern governments.

And, second, the existing governmental programs to help the poor are too small to do their alleged job, for the excellent reason that the relatively rich arrange this to be so. Think for a minute about the statistics in the distributive-justice argument. If the one-third and more of national income that the American government collects *actually* went to the poor, would there be any American poor? Of course not.

Imagine that as much as a quarter of the one-third went to the poor—below the fraction I suppose people have in mind when defending governments of the twentieth century as "helping the poor." That's $\frac{1}{3} \times \frac{1}{4} = \frac{1}{12}$ of gross domestic product, earmarked in such a hypothetical world for transfers to the poor. That would be about $1,000 billion.

According to the official definitions of numbers living in poverty, 34 million Americans do, over 10 percent of the population. The poverty figure, though it has fallen dramatically since Presidents Kennedy and Johnson drew sharp attention to it in the 1960s, appalls me as much as it appalls you. It is important to realize that some of the poor are in fact temporarily so. The optimistic news is that according to a tracking study of 50,000 Americans collected by researchers at the University of Michigan and reported in a 1999 book by W. Michael Cox and Richard Alm, only 5 percent of those who started in the bottom 20 percent in 1975 were still there in 1992.[108] Peter Gottschalk and Sheldon Danziger take a much less optimistic view of the statistics, noting that the "mobility" of a bourgeois teenager working part-time is not what we want to measure. They find much less mobility measured more relevantly, 1968–1991. Yet even by their reckoning some 60 percent who started in the bottom fifth got out of it.[109] That figure is similar to the rate at which Britons and Americans in the third quarter of the twentieth century moved out of unskilled occupations.[110]

Whatever the dimensions of the problem, government doesn't seem to be the solution. If it were, then each poor person would be getting, according to the one-fourth of one-third hypothesis, goods and services from the government equal to $1,000 billion divided by 34 million. That's about $30,000 for every man, woman, and child in poverty. Thirty thousand is still below the average gross domestic product per capita, which is about $40,000. Yet no one would call a family with two adults and two children getting goods and services in the amount of $120,000 a year "poor." With such an income, obviously, the poor would not be poor. But they *are* poor, namely, poor in those appalling 34 millions of souls. So it must not be true that the government's taxes go mainly, or even much at all, to the poor.

You can reason the other way, too, asking what low fraction of government programs would constitute transfers to the poor under the (true) condition that the existing poor are nonetheless left in poverty. Even if poor people earned nothing in the market, the implied fraction is very low indeed—not a quarter or an eighth but more like one-sixteenth of what government collects and disburses. One sixteenth. Is *that* the figure you have in mind when on tax day you comfort yourself that "after all, my tax dollar is going to help the poor?" Fifteen-sixteenths of the dollar is not.

Something else must be motivating government to collect and disburse the large share of national income that it does in the modern world. I don't suppose I will succeed in persuading you that in the United States the country club rules, and that therefore the government programs benefit mainly the rich, or at best the middle class—certainly not the poor. Or that you, dear reader, are part of the rich, or at best the middle class. Or that important beneficiaries of government programs ranging from the Department of State down to local public schools are not the poor but the well-to-do government employees themselves—such as me, an upper-middle-class employee of the State of Illinois. It's the Golden Rule: those who have the gold, rule. "The social confederacy . . . provides a powerful protection for the immense possessions of the rich," noted Rousseau at the dawn of serious concern in France for the poor. "Are not the privileges and exemptions reserved for them alone?"[111]

Rousseau believed that privileges and exemptions granted by the general will, that is, majority voting, would solve the problem of government by and for the rich. Not likely. Economists speak of a "median voter theorem," namely, that the benefits to the swing voters in a democracy get overrepresented, because the swing voters decide who wins. In a 49-51 institution the half of 1 percent in the middle will decide who wins. In a 40-60 institution the 10 percent in the middle will. Anyway, the middle, the median, runs the show. And the median person in the United States, who is very well off by historical and international standards, earning $40,000 per capita a year, is not enthusiastic about helping the poor of the world or the poor of the United States. The politicians therefore give what they can extract in taxes to *her*, not to the poor. The median voter decides who wins and, not surprisingly, *she* is the winner.

The news from the median voter theorem is nothing like all bad. Democracy is a good thing, and a great improvement over the *non*–median voter theorem, under which a tiny elite of aristocrats or property owners or samurai wins, every time. Sen has argued persuasively, for example, that democratic rule prevents moral horrors such as famines. "No famine has ever taken place in the history of the world," he observes, "in a functioning democracy."[112] He notes that the largest famine in history, in China after the socialist experiment of the Great Leap Forward, 1958–1961 (I remember well, by the way, the enthusiasm we American lefties of 1958–1961 had for this noble experiment) took place in a socialist autocracy, "whereas India has not had a famine [of any sort] since independence" and democratic rule.[113]

But in rich countries like the United States or France the subsidies to the median voter are in effect subsidies to pretty high-income people, unless offset by an ideology of egalitarianism and by accounting above the average. A good example is public higher education. The average taxpayer in California has a lower income than the typical coed at the University of California, reckoning her income either by that of her family of origin or by that of her college-enabled future. This was even more true around 1960 than it is now, and it is still strikingly true in Europe. It is worse in, say, Africa. "Zambia," writes Robert Guest, "spends 135 times more public money on each university student than on each primary school pupil despite the fact that university students typically come from affluent families."[114] I regard public higher education as one of the great projects of modern civilization, and I told you that I am employed at the University of Illinois at Chicago. But we are speaking here not of its existence, but of the peculiar way in which it is financed, especially in states or times of very low tuitions, as in the western U.S. states, such as California in 1960. State financing of higher education under the no-pay scheme takes from the relatively poor taxpayer and gives to the relatively rich college student. The relatively rich, after all, as Guest notes, send more of their kids to college. Those who have the gold, rule. In logic it need not have this regressive effect. If tuitions were raised for the rich—for example, the median voter in a rich country or the predatory class in a poor country—and "scholarships" (that is, price breaks) given to the poor, it would not. But in the political world we actually have it works in the regressive way. No one who understands the median voter theorem, or governmental predation, should be surprised.

I don't suppose you are open to persuasion that in consequence of the way politics actually works the American farm program, say, benefits not poor farmers but big farmers with access to senators in farm states—thus sugar quotas and cotton price supports. Or that restrictions on the practice of medicine and limitations on the power of prescription impoverish and sicken poor patients. Or that shop laws and planning permission in Britain and Holland raise the rental incomes of rich High Street or Hoogstraat landlords at the expense of mothers holding badly paying jobs.

All right. We can agree to disagree. But I beg you for your own sweet good not to flee unthinkingly to the other extreme, which regards every problem as an occasion for more state coercion and more corporate welfare and more governmental transfers to the median voter or to the country club buying her vote. We ride the back of a tiger when we give the Vladimir Vladimirovich Putins of our world more power. We damage the poor to boot. I beg you to consider that there might be such a thing as bourgeois virtues, the modern freedoms, and that letting people alone to make deals in a law-respecting society with low taxes helps them *and their poor neighbors* to flourish, materially and ethically, as Western Europe did 1600 to the present, increasingly bourgeois. "It seems safe to say," writes Joseph Ellis celebrating in 2000 the founding brothers of the American republic, "that some form of representative government based on the principle of popular sovereignty and some form of market economy fueled by the energies of individual citizens have become the commonly accepted ingredients for national success."[115] Yes, it seems safe to say.

In *The Origins of Virtue* (1996), Matt Ridley "glimpses . . . a better way, . . . a society built upon voluntary exchange of goods, information, fortune and power between free individuals in small enough communities for trust to be built. I believe such a society could be more equitable, as well as more prosperous, than one built on bureaucratic statism."[116] So do I, and admire with Ridley the bourgeois towns. A society of free individuals in small enough communities for trust to build was in fact Prince Kropotkin's pacific brand of anarchism, though he thought of capitalism as state-sponsored monopolies and therefore believed that he opposed it. Ridley and I both think that an unsubsidized capitalism works, and that state socialism, or a subsidized and regulated capitalism, does not. Ridley instances as a sad example his own city of Newcastle-upon-Tyne: "In two centuries it has been transformed from a hive of local enterprise and pride . . . into the satrapy of an all-powerful state. . . . In two centuries the great traditions of trust, mutuality and reciprocity on which such cities were based have been all but destroyed—by governments."[117]

Our communitarian friends, to the contrary, say that public goods are not provided in capitalist societies, and that therefore we should steadily expand the power of the state. The communitarians, unfortunately, are mistaken. I *do* wish the way forward were expanding the power of philosopher kings and queens over our lives. That would be convenient for us all, and consistent with the self-interest of corporations and NGOs and, as a bit of a philosopher herself, Deirdre McCloskey. But unhappily it isn't so.

Philip Selznick concedes at the end of his eloquent book advocating a Deweyan communitarianism, *The Moral Commonwealth*, that "The 'bourgeois virtues' of thrift and fair dealing are real enough. But those virtues do not insure that collective goods will be protected or achieved."[118] I say that thrift and fair dealing are only the beginning—that civic solidarity, inventive courage, and the human connections of the marketplace *are* bourgeois virtues. If the assertion is that bourgeois virtues do not ever, or even usually, choose the collective goods we need, it is factually mistaken, as Ridley's Newcastle of 1800 and a hundred other examples could show. The private provision of lighthouses on Britain's coasts in the nineteenth century is a famous one, "famous" at any rate among economists.[119]

We have a choice between a collective good springing from bourgeois virtues or a collective good ordered up by the government. Neither is perfect, but perfect worlds are not on offer. I would say that most public/collective goods are best provided by free exchange and bourgeois citizenship within a minimal state . . . all right: by a *much* smaller state than the one we at present have.

Economists would admit that the bourgeois virtues do not "insure" that public goods are provided, "insuring" like a proof on a blackboard. That little word "insure," by the way, has caused much mischief in the last hundred years. It embodies a lawyerly view that the only way to "insure" such-and-such a social result is to make still another law, instead of depending on self-organizing systems like markets and morals, or for that matter common-law decisions of courts. The economists point out, in any case, that many public goods get provided as spillovers from self-interested action, as when a private police force in a building discourages crime even out on the street, or when a billboard on the highway advertising a restaurant serves as a vivid pointer to the downtown, or when educated people raise the tone of public discourse, when they do.

And "collective action to sustain the infrastructure of civil society . . . heavily dependent on governmental protection and support" does not *insure* that *good* public goods get provided.[120] It *insures* merely that the Putins get more power over our lives. After all, Selznick's main point, and mine, and Ridley's, and Adam Smith's, is that without virtue the machinery of neither the market nor the government works for our good. That is why we preach. Let us therefore turn to preaching the civic and bourgeois virtues.

I am puzzled when my friends on the right preach freedom for the owner of an assault weapon loaded with dum-dum shells hung on a rack in his Hummer, but then preach, too, intrusions by the government into that same man's sexual practices or his taste in recreational drugs or the care of his brain-damaged wife. But I am also puzzled when my friends on the left preach still more power for a government that has in its time shot Kentucky strikers and electrocuted Italian anarchists and jailed Muslim radicals without trial.

Selznick and other capitalism-skeptics do not sufficiently acknowledge that market societies like seventeenth-century Holland provided voluntarily for universities and churches and opera houses, and invented the social safety net. As Sen points out, "The contribution of economic growth has to be judged not merely by the increase in private incomes, but also by the expansion of social services (including, in many cases, social safety nets) that economic growth may make possible."[121] The Catholic church's charity, the model for the clerisy's theory of a social gospel, had until then gone mainly to keep abbots supplied with the better wines.

Nor do the capitalism-skeptics acknowledge what is statistically true, as I have said, that the "public goods" so uncritically praised by the center left consist in good measure of welfare for the rich and warfare for the poor. In the early 2000s in America, for example, corporate welfare alone cost annually about $87 billion. You can think of it as a transfer of a little under 1 percent of national income from you and me to the owners of corporations, ignoring deadweight and rent-seeking losses.[122] That would be $3,000 or so for every poor person in the country, which would be a very welcome sum.

The spoofing Golden Rule—those who have the gold, rule—suggests why governments are nasty tools for fixing social problems. Consider America's oil-driven foreign policy. Or consider its country-club designed income-tax system. Or consider its suburb-supported War on Drugs, destroying the lives of urban poor people, corrupting law enforcement agencies, and debasing foreign governments from Afghanistan to Colombia. Who doubts that the drug laws constitute a war by white suburbanites against people of color? As one expert on the use of controlled substances put it in 1995, "Too many whites are getting away with drug sales. Too many whites are getting away with trafficking in this stuff. The answer to this disparity is not to start letting people out of jail.... The answer is to go out and find the ones who are getting away with it, convict them and send them up the river, too."[123]

"It is vital," Ridley declares, "that we reduce the power and scope of the state." Yes. The freedom half of the Enlightenment Project can support in practical terms the reason half. "It is not to happiness alone," wrote Constant in 1819, "it is to self-development that our destiny calls us; and political liberty is the most powerful, the most effective means of self-development that heaven has given us."[124] Secret police and fixed elections and patriarchal oppression of women and unwise attempts to fulfill the two-centuries-old project of reason by regulation and state planning rather than by Adam Smith's "simple and obvious system of natural liberty"—to name some of the more important assaults on bourgeois human capital—do more damage to our goods and to our goodness than do conventional economic failings.

But is that true? How do I know? The experiments of the twentieth century told me so. It would have been hard to know the wisdom of Milton Friedman or Matt Ridley or Deirdre McCloskey in August 1914, before the experiments were well begun. But anyone who after the twentieth century still thinks that thoroughgoing socialism, nationalism, imperialism, mobilization, central planning, regulation, zoning, price controls, tax policy, labor unions, business cartels, government spending, intrusive policing, adventurism in foreign policy, faith in entangling religion and politics, or most of the other thoroughgoing nineteenth-century proposals for governmental action are still neat, harmless ideas for improving our lives is not paying attention.

In the nineteenth and twentieth centuries ordinary Europeans were hurt, not helped, by their colonial empires. Economic growth in Russia was slowed, not accelerated, by Soviet central planning. American Progressive regulation and its European anticipations protected monopolies of transportation like railways and protected monopolies of retailing like High Street shops and protected monopolies of professional services like medicine, not the consumers. "Protective" legislation in the United States and "family-wage" legislation in Europe subordinated women. State-armed psychiatrists in America jailed homosexuals, and in Russia jailed democrats. Some of the New Deal prevented rather than aided America's recovery from the Great Depression.

Unions raised wages for plumbers and autoworkers but reduced wages for the nonunionized. Minimum wages protected union jobs but made the poor unemployable. Building codes sometimes kept buildings from falling or burning down but always gave steady work to well-connected carpenters and electricians. Zoning and planning permission has protected rich landlords rather than helping the poor. Rent control makes the poor and the mentally ill unhousable, because no one will build inexpensive housing when it is forced by law to be expensive. The sane and the already-rich get the rent-controlled apartments and the fancy townhouses in once-poor neighborhoods.

Regulation of electricity hurt householders by raising electricity costs, as did the ban on nuclear power. The Securities Exchange Commission did not help small investors. Federal deposit insurance made banks careless with depositors' money. The conservation movement in the Western United States enriched ranchers who used federal lands for grazing and enriched lumber companies who used federal lands for clear-cutting. American and other attempts at prohibiting trade in recreational drugs resulted in higher drug consumption and the destruction of inner cities. Governments have outlawed needle exchanges and condom advertising, and denied the existence of AIDS.

Germany's economic *Lebensraum* was obtained in the end by the private arts of peace, not by the public arts of war. The lasting East Asian Co-Prosperity Sphere was built by Japanese men in business suits, not in dive bombers. Europe recovered after its two twentieth-century hot wars mainly through its own efforts of labor and investment, not mainly through government-to-government charity such as Herbert Hoover's Commission or George Marshall's Plan. Government-to-government foreign aid to the third world has enriched tyrants, not helped the poor.

The importation of socialism into the third world, even in the relatively nonviolent form of Congress Party Fabian-Gandhism, unintentionally stifled growth, enriched large industrialists, and kept the people poor. The capitalist-sponsored Green Revolution of dwarf hybrids was opposed by green politicians the world around, but has made places like India self-sufficient in grains. State power in many parts of sub-Saharan Africa has been used to tax the majority of farmers in aid of the president's cousins and a minority of urban bureaucrats. State power in many parts of Latin America has prevented land reform and sponsored disappearances. State ownership of oil in Nigeria and Mexico and Iraq was used to support the party in power, benefiting the people not at all. Arab men have been kept poor, not bettered, by using state power to deny education and driver's licenses to Arab women. The seizure of governments by the clergy has corrupted religions and ruined economies. The seizure of governments by the military has corrupted armies and ruined economies.

Industrial policy, from Japan to France, has propped up failing industries such as agriculture and small-scale retailing, instead of choosing winners. Regulation of dismissal has led to high unemployment in Germany and Denmark. In the 1960s, public-housing high-rises in the West inspired by Le Corbusier condemned the poor in Rome and Paris and Chicago to holding pens. In the 1970s, the full-scale socialism of the East ruined the environment. In the 2000s, the "millennial collectivists," red, green, or communitarian, oppose a globalization that helps the poor but threatens trade union officials, crony capitalists, and the careers of people in Western nongovernmental organizations.[125]

All these experiments of the twentieth century were arranged by governments against bourgeois markets. All of them were disasters. In short, the neoaristocratic, cryptopeasant, proclerisy, antibourgeois theories of the nineteenth century, applied during the twentieth century for taxing, fixing, resisting, modifying, prohibiting, collectivizing, regulating, unionizing, ameliorating, expropriating modern capitalism, failed of their purposes, killed many millions, and nearly killed us all.

VII.   Peroratio

By contrast: during the twenty-first century, if we can draw back from the unfreedom of anticapitalism and adopt instead the simple and obvious system of natural liberty, every person on the planet, in Vietnam and Colombia, India and Kenya, can come to have, complements of the bourgeois virtues, the scope of life afforded now to a suburban minority in the West. It's the Bourgeois Deal: leave me alone to buy low and sell high, and in the long run I'll make *you* rich.

If we will let people own things—their houses and businesses, for example; their labor power—and if we let them try to make profit out of the ownership, and if we keep out of people's lives the tentacles of a government acting as an executive committee of the country club or worse, we will prosper materially and spiritually.

We can have Aristotles, Wang Weis, Newtons, Austens, and Tagores by the dozens. We can have world science and world music and world literature and even world cuisine in richness unparalleled, a spiritual life untrammeled by need, a clean planet, long and happy lives. By the standards typical since Adam's curse we can have by the year 2100 another Eden. Well . . . all right: such utopian talk, I have said, has dangers. At least we can have material abundance, and the scope to flourish in higher things. And we can be virtuous about it.

Or we can try once again in our ethical confusion to kill it.

Appeal

Socrates: I count being refuted a greater good. . . . I don't suppose there's anything quite so bad for a person as having false belief about the thing we're discussing.
    —Plato, *Gorgias*

Audite et alteram partem (Listen also to the other side).
    —Medieval proverb, above the entrance to the town hall, Market Square, Gouda, the
        Netherlands

Regard not who it is which speaketh, but weigh only what is spoken. Think not that ye read the words of one who bendeth himself as an adversary against the truth which ye have already embraced; but the words of one who desireth even to embrace together with you the self-same truth, if it be the truth.
    —Richard Hooker, 1593

I beseech you, in the bowels of Christ, think it possible you may be mistaken.
    —Oliver Cromwell, 1650

It must be acknowledged that some of the following discourses are very abstruse and difficult; or, if you please, obscure; but I must take leave to add that those alone are judges . . . who will be at the trouble to understand what is here said.
    —Bishop Butler, 1725

Not all were grateful for his help, one finds,
For how they hated him, who huddled with
The comfort of a quick remedial myth
Against the cold world and their colder minds.
    —Robert Conquest, "George Orwell," 1969

It was just astonishing in those years [of Stalinism in left-wing circles in New York]—or any time—to come up against the absolute devotion of a true believer. There's no conversation you can have, no fact you can point out, no point you can make, because it's clear you're misinformed.
    —Jules Pfeiffer, on his play *The Bad Friend*, 2003

But I do have an apology to make in the ordinary sense, too. The present book I said is the first of a planned "Chicago/Amsterdam Quartet," each offering a separate portion of the apology for our bourgeois lives. Prudence Only is not enough. So volume 1, the present one. It has never in fact characterized the life of the bourgeoisie: volume 2. Yet bourgeois life, partly because the clerisy gave it after 1848 a cynical reason to ignore ethics, needs to be remoralized: volume 3. The attacks on bourgeois values are for the most part mistaken: volume 4. We should reconsider our stories of the bourgeoisie.

The four make complementary arguments. They lean on each other. Volume 1 has most of the philosophy and theology, volume 2 most of the economic and social history, volume 3 most of the intellectual history, and volume 4 most of the economics and the cultural criticism.

I apologize for imposing on you in this way. If I were more clever you would not have to scan four fat books to get the story. I apologize for not boiling the case for capitalism down to twenty or thirty wholly persuasive pages. If you've read the "Apology" preceding you've read my best shot at a shortish statement of the case. You see the problem. You say that it didn't entirely persuade you? I understand. I cannot in a jiffy prove in every single respect the case for bourgeois virtues as existing and important and desirable. After all, if it were so easy someone else would long ago have proven it, and there would be nothing left to prove—an argument economists will recognize.

Sometimes in this or that respect the optimistic case is hard to prove merely because it is wrong, in numerous senses of "wrong." Not everything the bourgeoisie does is wise and good. A myth of modern masculinity, for example, has tempted bourgeois men of late to act courageously when love or temperance or prudence is what is called for. The hero-imitating CEO is commonly a menace, and these days is paid rather a lot for his impersonation of Achilles. Further, a myth of Prudence Only has justified among *les bourgeois* certain policies lacking justice. Free trade is good, I strongly affirm. I am sworn to believe so as an economist. But my fellow free-market economists commonly spurn the claim of justice—namely, that we should right the hurt from creative destruction.

And you will hear economists saying that economic science "economizes on love." Neat. But the *economy* cannot actually get along without a good deal of love. Over half of consumer purchases at point of sale, for example, are on behalf of children and husbands and mothers and friends. Love runs consumption. Feminist economists have been noting for some time that without such love, and therefore without such altruistic purchases, the human race would promptly die out. A theory based on selfishness alone therefore cannot work scientifically. And if it *became* the way the social world actually worked, the social world would collapse. Some balance of virtues is in order.

Even in its four-volume completion, though, my project must leave many such matters at hints and summations, at one-sided cases and abbreviated examples. The subject is too big. There is barely time for me to be approximately fair to the defendant's case. The book is heavily footnoted precisely because of my inexpertise. You have some reason, I guess, to take seriously my unattested remarks about economics or economic history, and maybe the history of rhetoric—but not the ventures into philosophy or social psychology or Japanese history necessary to make the case. I will often irritate you, mistake facts out of ignorance, misunderstand the texts I am citing, choose the wrong grounds on which to argue, miss important texts and statistics and writers, fail to address all of your very reasonable doubts.

My excuse for trying is that for a century and a half, since the high-brow branch of the clerisy turned decisively against capitalism, the prosecution's case has been made over and over and over again, with fewer attempts to be fair in reply. No class in history has internalized such abuse as the Western bourgeoisie. Perhaps it's good for our souls. But the result is that most educated people's minds, such as yours, are thronged with unfavorable opinions of the way we live now. Time to listen to the other side.

In this connection I sometimes wonder why the Western clerisy doesn't grow . . . well . . . *bored* by the reiterated attacks on capitalism and the market and the bourgeoisie. How can they bear, I wonder, to hear yet another diatribe against the evil of profit, the curse of materialism, the insincerity of advertising, the scandal of excessive consumption, the irreligiousness of commercial dealing, the corruptions of corporations, the ruination of the environment, the inevitable poverty consequent on a system of market capitalism, the horrors of piano lessons and learning French and settling down to a quality job?

Since 1848, and in some versions back to the Hebrew prophets, it's "the same people making the same points about the same things to the same people," as the ancient Greeks said.[1] The book-length jeremiads come and come, unceasing waves every publishing season, from Dickens and Carlyle to William Gaddis's *JR* and Benjamin Barber's *Jihad* vs. *McWorld*. Each book presents itself as a fresh, brave unveiling of sin and hypocrisy, contrasting with the imagined purity of a lovely if counterfactual *non*capitalist and *non*bourgeois world. It must be, I mutter uncharitably under my breath, that people want to hear echoed and reechoed the anti-Daddy notions they picked up as college sophomores.

Daddy and his friends, I admit, have some actual crimes to answer for. For example, the execution of the Haymarket anarchists. The Congo. Oil *realpolitik*. But I am claiming that the anti-antibourgeois case is stronger than a lot of people think. The case is straightforward or complicated, reasonably persuasive or a trifle dubious, agreed upon by sociologists or assumed by economists, implied by historians or sketched by literary and social critics. But anyway it is extensive—four volumes of extent, actually—with a good deal of not wholly absurd reasoning and not wholly unbelievable evidence attached.

An open-minded opponent of capitalism would want to reflect on it, if only to achieve a more sophisticated opposition. Yet most of the opponents of capitalism, and its numerous lukewarm friends, are not acquainted with the case for the defense. They think the evidence is strong that capitalism is working badly right now, and has done in its past many bad works. My friend and colleague the prize-winning poet Anne Winters, for example, writes in the title poem of her recent book, the narrator sitting reading the *Times* in a café on Broadway:

> . . . . can I escape morning happiness,
> or not savor our fabled "texture" of foreign
> and native poverties? (A boy tied into greengrocer's apron,
> unplaceable accent, brings out my coffee.) But, *no*, it says here
> the old country's "de-developing" due to its mountainous
> debt to the First World. . . .[2]

Well, not so—though Anne's self-doubting "it says here" should be acknowledged. As Richard Lanham puts it to me, the opponents of capitalism make 2006 sound like 1933, or 1848, over and over again.

It has been a long time since 1933, or 1848. Personally speaking, I have been listening to imperfectly informed criticisms of capitalism all my adult life, from beloved classmates in college and from beloved colleagues in English, and even from some of my beloved fellow economists. Many people see every bad thing in our lives as being a result of capitalism, not being as a result sometimes, after all, of loss of Eden. Many are unwilling to see the material and ethical improvement since 1800 or 1900. Many still wax indignant at the very suggestion that our bourgeois life could be on balance ethically good. And the lukewarm friends of capitalism, who as I say are legion, are at least made uneasy by the notion of "bourgeois virtues." I am getting weary of this underreasoned disdain for bourgeois life. So should you.

I ask you at the outset, therefore, to forebear, and not to imagine that there is some quick, easy way that I could change your mind on these matters. I ask you not to think that I am merely bloviating or dissembling in not providing mind-transforming arguments in a jiffy. And I ask you for your own good not to become too quickly indignant when you encounter an argument that you think on its face to be implausible or incomplete. Please consider. Please suppose that I am of good will. Please, if only to improve your own case *against* capitalism, be at the trouble to understand what is here said.

Most people have opinions about the matter, and hold their opinions emphatically, often without having much considered. Perhaps it has to do with the age at which we equip ourselves with a politics, the romantic age of early adulthood. Like gender, settled in one's personal theories at age two or so, most people don't trouble themselves to rethink later their political opinions acquired at age twenty or so. Saul Bellow said of his early Trotskyism, "Like everyone else who invests in doctrines at a young age, I couldn't give them up."[3] People come as young people to hate the bourgeoisie or to love capitalism or to detest free markets or to believe passionately in the welfare and regulatory state. It becomes part of a cherished identity, a faith. I appeal to you to rethink your faith.

The case builds. Consider it possible that later chapters, or even later volumes, may extend the apology to advertising, say, by arguments not wholly intemperate—or to explanations of how capitalism has worked well for the poor, by arguments not wholly unjust. Think it possible you may be mistaken.

In the end even the full case may not persuade you. Go then in peace. But here at the outset I propose a bourgeois deal. I will try not to say unfair, untrue, partisan, idiotic, Fox-News, self-refuting, factually and ethically absurd things by the standards of a woman not wholly ignorant and not wholly malevolent. I will try to think it possible that even I myself may be mistaken. I will preach to *you*, the unbelievers outside the church, and not solely to my pro-capitalist friends singing now so beautifully in the choir. In exchange I ask you—you of the capitalist-doubting clerisy of the left, and even you of the capitalism-corrupted clerisy of the right—to exercise the virtue of patience.

In the main square of Gouda in the Netherlands stands its old city hall, built in 1448. Over the entrance is inscribed a Latin motto, a commonplace in the Middle Ages, if not always practiced then or now: *Audite et alteram partem,* "Listen even to the other side."

It was sound advice for the burghers of Gouda.

Commerce penetrates the secret places of the world, approaches shores unseen, explores fearful wildernesses, and in tongues unknown and with barbaric peoples carries on the trade of mankind. The pursuit of commerce reconciles nations, calms wars, strengthens peace, and commutes the private good of individuals into the common benefit of all.

    —Hugh of St. Victor, c. 1125

I don't know which is the more useful to the state, a well-powdered lord who knows precisely when the king gets up in the morning . . . or a great merchant who enriches his country, sends orders from his office to Surat or to Cairo, and contributes to the well-being of the world.

    —Voltaire, 1733

The progress of civilization, the commercial tendency of the age, the communication among the peoples, have infinitely multiplied and varied the means of individual happiness. To be happy, men need only to be left in perfect independence in all that concerns their occupations, their undertakings, their sphere of activity, their fantasies.

    —Benjamin Constant, 1814

In a community regulated by laws of demand and supply, but protected from open violence, the persons who become rich are, generally speaking, industrious, resolute, proud, covetous, prompt, methodical, sensible, unimaginative, insensitive, and ignorant. The persons who remain poor are the entirely foolish, the entirely wise, the idle, the reckless, the humble, the thoughtful, the dull, the imaginative, the sensitive, the well-informed, the improvident, the irregularly and impulsively wicked, the clumsy knave, the open thief, the entirely merciful, just, and godly person.

    —John Ruskin

Commerce is the name for free, mutual, and voluntary exchange among peoples. It is the normal activity by which interdependence is realized and the common good of all served. It is an activity typically more unifying than politics, nationalism, religion, or conquest. Its nature is social, as is its function, and as are the virtues it inculcates.

    —Michael Novak, 1984

1

THE VERY WORD "VIRTUE"

Bourgeois *virtues*? The question is whether virtues could be expected to flourish in our commercial society. Are there in fact bourgeois virtues? And what do they have to do with traditional talk about the virtues?

In 1946 the anthropologist Ruth Benedict wrote a book purporting to explain the ethical system of the Japanese to their former enemies. It perhaps said more, Clifford Geertz has noted, about a "look-into-ourselves-as-we-would-look-unto-others."[1] But never mind. With the substitution of "bourgeois" for "Japanese" her declaration of intent could serve here: "This volume . . . is not a book specifically about [bourgeois] religion or economic life or politics or the family. It examines [bourgeois] assumptions about the conduct of life. It describes these assumptions as they have manifested themselves whatever the activity in hand. It is about what makes [the bourgeoisie into an ethical one]."[2]

I'll use the words "ethical" and "moral" interchangeably, though favoring "ethical." In origin "ethical" is Greek and at the height of Greek philosophy leaned toward character and education, while "moral" is Latin and always leaned toward custom and rule. But this shadow of a difference was blurred even by the Greco-Roman moralists, and is not preserved in modern English, even in precise philosophical English. As happens often in our magpie English tongue, "ethical" and "moral" have became merely two words for the same thing, derived from different languages.

The newspapers restrict "ethics" to business practice, usually corrupt, and "morality" to sexual behavior, often scandalous. I opt for the ordinary, nonnewspaper usage that takes "morality" to be a synonym for "ethics," which is to say the patterns of character in a good person. True, the words have become entangled in the red vs. blue states and their culture wars. The left once embraced situational *ethics* and the right favored a *moral* majority. Now the Christian and progressive left wonders at the *ethics* of capital punishment and the Christian and neocon right wonders at *moral* decline. But at the outset let us have peace.

"Ethics" is the system of the virtues. A "virtue" is a habit of the heart, a stable disposition, a settled state of character, a durable, educated characteristic of someone to exercise her will to be good. The definition would be circular if "good" just meant the same thing as "virtuous." But it's more complicated than that. Alasdair MacIntyre's famous definition is: "A virtue is an acquired human quality the possession of which tends to enable us to achieve those goods which are internal to practices and the lack of which effectively prevents us from achieving such goods."[3]

A virtue is at the linguistic level something about which you can coherently say "you should practice X"—courage, love, prudence, temperance, justice, faith, hope, for example. Beauty is therefore not a virtue in this sense of "exercising one's will." One cannot say, "You should be beautiful" and make much sense, short of the extreme makeover. Neat, clean, well turned out—yes. But not "beautiful."

At the simplest level people have two conventional and opposed remarks they make nowadays when the word "ethics" comes up. One is the fatherly assertion that ethics can be reduced to a list of rules, such as the Ten Commandments. Let us post the Sacred List, they say, in our courthouses and high schools, and watch its good effects. In a more sophisticated form the fatherly approach is a natural-law theory by which, say, homosexuality is bad, because unnatural.[4]

In contrast, the other remark that people make reflects the motherly assertion that ethics is after all particular to this family or that person. Let's get along with each other and not be too strict. Bring out the jello and the lemonade. In its sophisticated form the motherly approach is a cultural relativist theory that, say, female circumcision and the forced marriage of eleven-year-old girls are all right—because they are custom.[5]

The "virtue-ethic" parallel to such college-freshman commandments or college-sophomore relativism is the vocabulary of the hero and of the saint. In its senior high-school version the two split by gender, at least conventionally, and at least nowadays. A man wants to be Odysseus, a woman Holy Mary, the one physically courageous, the other deeply loving.

The sharpness of the gender split appears to be only a couple of centuries old. By 1895 Oliver Wendell Holmes, Jr., could declare that "the ideals of the past for men have been drawn from war, as those for women have been drawn from motherhood."[6] "War is for men," said Mussolini some decades later, "what birth is for women."[7] Now at the beginning of the twenty-first century we still speak in our goodness talk mainly of courage and of love, the fatherly rhetoric of conservatives and the motherly rhetoric of liberals.[8]

The models are popular heroes and saints—Sergeant York was wonderfully courageous" or "Mother Teresa loved the poor"—and by analogy we praise the ordinary little virtues. We witness "Some village Hampden, that with dauntless breast / The little tyrant of his fields withstood," and we applaud. A local boy endures a football injury, courageously. Brave boy. A young almost-bride mourning for her soldier walks up and down, up and down, in her stiff brocaded gown, and we weep. A local girl volunteers at the retirement community, lovingly. Sweet girl.

Such talk is on its way to the virtues. But it's still high-school stuff. We can do better, getting all the way to graduate school, by being a little more philosophical. In particular we can enfold the street talk of manly courage and womanly love, fatherhood and motherhood, into the seven virtues of the classical and Christian world. This is my main theme. To the natural-law and cultural-relativist theorists we can reply that virtues underlie their theories, too, and that the virtues are both less and more universal than they think. That's what I propose to do, and then show you that a bourgeois, capitalist, commercial society can be "ethical" in the sense of evincing the seven.

The virtues came to be gathered by the Greeks, the Romans, the Stoics, the church, Adam Smith, and recent "virtue ethicists" into a coherent ethical framework. Until the framework somewhat mysteriously fell out of favor among theorists in the late eighteenth century, most Westerners did not think in Platonic terms of the One Good—to be summarized, say, as maximum utility, or as the categorical imperative, or as the Idea of the Good. They thought in Aristotelian terms of many virtues, plural.

"We shall better understand the nature of the ethical character [*to ethos*]," said Aristotle, "if we examine its qualities one by one."[9] That still seems a sensible plan, and was followed by almost all writers on ethics in the West, and quite independently of Aristotle in the East, until the cumulative effect of Machiavelli, Bacon, Hobbes, Locke, Rousseau, Kant, and Bentham at length killed it off. Thus Edmund Spenser in *The Faerie Queen* (1596) celebrated in six books Holiness, Temperance, Chastity, Friendship, Justice, and Courtesy.

Since about 1958 in English a so-called "virtue ethics"—as distinct from the Kantian, Benthamite, or contractarian views that dominated ethical philosophy from the late eighteenth century until then—has revived Aristotle's one-by-one program. "We might," wrote Iris Murdoch in 1969 early in the revival, "set out from an ordinary language situation by reflecting upon the virtues . . . since they help to make certain potentially nebulous areas of experience more open to inspection."[10] That seems reasonable.

Here are the Western seven, with some of their subvirtues appended. The

The Seven Virtues

HOPE
optimism, imagination, and
[with Courage] entrepreneurship

FAITH
identity, integrity,
loyalty, and [with Courage
and Justice] honesty

LOVE
connection, friendship,
affection, appreciation,
eros, agape

JUSTICE
social balance
and honesty [with Courage
and Faith]

COURAGE
autonomy,
daring, endurance,
steadfastness

TEMPERANCE
individual balance
and restraint, chastity, sobriety,
humility

PRUDENCE
know-how, foresight, *phronêsis*,
self interest, contextual rationality

system is a jury-rigged combination of the "pagan" virtues appropriate to a free male citizen of Athens (Courage, Temperance, Justice, and Prudence) and the "Christian" virtues appropriate to a believer in Our Lord and Savior (Faith, Hope, and Love).

Jury-rigged or not, the seven, I will argue, cover what we need in order to flourish as human beings. So also might other ethical systems—Confucianism, for example, or Talmudic Judaism, or Native American shamanism—and these can be lined up beside the seven for comparison. There are many ways to be human. But it is natural to start and for present purposes pretty much finish with the seven, since they are the ethical tradition of a West in which bourgeois life first came to dominance.

THE VERY WORD "BOURGEOIS"

Bourgeois virtues? Consider then that first word. Yes, we are bourgeois, we educated folk, not aristocratic or proletarian. We are businesspeople or bureaucrats, not kings or peasants. Yet for a century and a half now the word has been a sneer, as in "Oh, Daddy, you're so *bourgeois!*" or in Leadbelly's song "Bourgeois Town":

> These white folks in Washington, they know how:
> Treat a colored man just to see him bow.
> Lawd, in a bourgeois town,
> Hee! it's a bourgeois town.
> I got the bourgeois blues, gonna spread the news all around.[1]

At one time in French *bourgeois* meant without contempt merely "townsman-ly," from a Germanic (not Latin) word for a walled town. It shows up in Edin*burgh* and the New York *borough* of Queens and, with Latin *latro* added on, a *burg*lar, a thief preying on the town. It came itself from an Indo-European root, meaning "high." So "belfry" from the Old French *berfrei*, a high place of freedom from attack. The tribe of *Burg*undi came from the *high* country of Savoy. The Norse *berg*, "mountain," appears in *Bergen*, literally "the mountain," and ice*berg*. All of the Germanic words, it says here in *The American Heritage Dictionary of Indo-European Roots*, revised and edited by Calvert Watkins, are cousins through their Proto-Indo-European grandparents with Latin words in *fort-*, such as "fort" and "fortitude," or any strength.

Anyway *bourgeois* (boor-*zhwa*) is the adjective, describing Daddy, say, or the Long Island suburbs. It's also in the French the noun for the singular male person, a burgher. Benjamin Franklin was "a *bourgeois*." And strictly speaking in French, though odd-sounding in English, the plural men of the middle class go by the same word, those *bourgeois* trading news on the Bourse. The female burgheress, singular, adds an *e*, *bourgeoise* (boor-*zhwaz*). Madame Bovary was a bourgeoise, and she and her friends bourgeoises, plural, with again no change in pronunciation. The whole class of such people are of course that appalling *bourgeoisie* (boor-zhwa-*zee*), whence H. L. Mencken's sneering label, the "booboisie."

Got it.

But consider this: in sociological fact you are probably a member of it. You may therefore still be using the word as a term of self-contempt, like the f-word for gays or the n-word for blacks. As Mencken also said, the businessman "is the only man who is forever apologizing for his occupation."[2]

After the Second World War the self-scorning of the middle class became a standard turn among even the non-Marxist clerisy, from C. Wright Mills to Barbara Ehrenreich. Ehrenreich wrote in *Fear of Falling: The Inner Life of the Middle Class* (1989) of the bourgeoisie's "prejudice, delusion, and even, at a deeper level, self-loathing."[3] She would know about the self-loathing. Her father started as a copper miner (Ehrenreich was born in Butte) but became a corporate executive. She herself got a Ph.D. in biology, but was radicalized by Vietnam. So was I, incidentally, before my Ph.D. in economics took hold.

Self-loathing among the bourgeoisie has for a century and a half been a source of trouble. We need to rethink together the word and the social position. Guilt over success in a commercial society is for a victimless crime. Yet the children of the bourgeoisie seek an identity challenging that of their elders. The clerisy by which the children are taught accuses the middle class of inauthenticity, and plays on pseudoaristocratic contempt for "middle" construed as "mediocre." None of this makes very much sense. A commercial life can be as authentic and virtuous as that of a philosopher or priest. We need to recover its wholeness and holiness.

A reason to keep here the dishonored word "bourgeois" is to distinguish the rethinking from the statistical inquiries evoked by "middle class," or the older "middling sort." My focus is not mainly on how large the middle class actually was, numerically speaking, in 1600 or 1800 or now. Places where the middle class was exceptionally small, such as Russia in 1800, would perhaps be poor places to study bourgeois virtues. I'm not so sure. Certainly such places are interesting tests by absence. And a bourgeois ideology could I suppose be active without an objectively large middle class. A Marxist attributing false consciousness to the majority of American working-class people who call themselves "middle class" would say so.

The townly and businesslike ideology evoked here by "bourgeois" occurs anciently in any city of trade, whether or not such attitudes come to rule the place. On the other hand a large and ill-defined middle class such as America's can *dilute* bourgeois virtues, contrary to expectations, importing dangerous nostalgias like the cowboy and detective myths. The samurai myth has done similar mischief in Japan.

The middle class is divided into three parts, which by no means always get along with each other. The *haute* or *grande bourgeoisie* is the class of the big bosses, the owners of large factories and department stores, the directors and other denizens of corporate boardrooms, the bankers and merchants of the grander sort. In Europe they have long run the cities. In Holland the urban upper class from the fifteenth century on was called the *de regenten*, the regents. By the seventeenth century some 2,000 bourgeois ran the Dutch Republic.

In the United States the regents become in a few generations America's so-called aristocracy and send their children to Andover and Yale—thus the Vanderbilts, descendent from a ferry-boy on Staten Island, or the Kennedys, from gangsters and ward bosses; or the Bushes from a more distinguished family, containing Princess Diana, George Washington, FDR, Hugh Hefner, Benedict Arnold, John Hinckley, Jr., and, of all people, John Kerry. Eventually a few thousand of the American "aristocracy" came to run the country, too, a power elite.

But "aristocracy" is a European word and concept. The United States never had a literal feudalism and therefore was unusually open to Lockean ideas of equal access to life, liberty, and property.[4] The power elite runs things, I repeat. But it is partly open, unlike the class of regents in eighteenth-century Holland. In the virulently anti-Irish time of 1860 in America who would have anticipated that from 1960 every American president except Ford would have some Irish ancestry?[5] With no feudalism, except for a while a real Dutch version in the Hudson Valley and briefly a faux version in the South, the U.S. of A. has had no literal nobility. Never mind the pretensions of Park Avenue and Newport, Rhode Island.

The admirable Theodore Roosevelt, whose mother came from slaveholders in Savannah and whose father came from two centuries of Knickerbocker merchants and landowners in New York, was America's closest approach to a real aristocrat among modern presidents, with his fifth cousin Franklin. Before that, presidentially speaking, you have to go back to the Adams clan or maybe William Henry Harrison for even a whiff of aristocracy. Almost all American presidents in the nineteenth century were members of the clerisy—lawyers, mainly, like Nixon or Clinton in our day.

In thoroughgoing republics like America and Switzerland even the most haute of the bourgeoisie never quite make a true aristocracy.[6] Contrast England well into the twentieth century, with hundreds upon hundreds of Teddy Roosevelt figures, but ones who were actual dukes and marquises, owning much of the country's land rents, running company boards and staffing the empire. The undertow of feudal privilege and the angry resistance to it can be felt now even in social democracies like Holland, which in fact never had much of an aristocracy. Some of Europe's most social democratic parts still have kings and queens: Britain, Sweden, Norway, Denmark, Belgium, the Netherlands. The late Queen Mother Princess Juliana of the Netherlands said, "I come for the people, *not* for the directors." And yet, compliments of the directors of Shell Oil, she was among the richest women in the world.

The second part of the bourgeoisie is the Coleridgian "clerisy," what German historians have called the *Bildungsbürgertum*, the "education bourgeoisie," and what has been called in Eastern Europe since the nineteenth century the intelligentsia. That Europeans and their heirs kept making up praising or damning names for it—*philosophes, Bildungsbürgertum,* professionals, preachers, intelligentsia, intellectuals, Brahmins, mandarins, progressives, literati, illuminati, experts, brains trust, highbrows, eggheads, pointy heads, the best and the brightest, the chattering class, the talented tenth, the new class, the symbolic analysts, the creative class—testifies to its uneasy relation with the rest of society. The state bureaucrats of eighteenth-century Prussia or the lawyers of nineteenth-century Massachusetts or the college professors of twentieth-century California were neither aristocrats nor peasants nor proletarians, and so by a baggy definition they were bourgeois.

Eric Hobsbawm disputes that in England there was in the nineteenth century such a thing as a *Bildungsbürgertum*.[7] What is persuasive about his case is that the English clerisy was then small and, as he notes, did not follow party lines, as the Continental clerisy tended to do. England did not have until the twentieth century very many of the numerous high-status civil servants, among them party-line professors, that Germany and France honored and multiplied in the nineteenth century.

But even in England the clerisy was at least talky. In their study of the English middle class 1780–1850 Leonore Davidoff and Catherine Hall observe that "lawyers, teachers, doctors, and above all the clergy and writers spent their lives manipulating words, explaining the middle class to itself." They quote a writer on legal matters in the middle of the nineteenth century asserting that "the professional classes . . . form the head of the great English middle class, keep up to the mark its standard of morality, and direct its intelligence."[8] The clerisy overwhelmingly originated from the economic bourgeoisie—and from the literal clergy. Increasingly the "standard of morality" was critical of the fathers of the owning and managing bourgeoisie, to the advantage of the clerical sons wielding the pen.

We have a paradox at the outset here. Marx's father was a lawyer, Engels himself a factory owner. French painters in the nineteenth century were almost all from the bourgeoisie—with only an occasional Renoir from the working class or a Toulouse-Lautrec from the aristocracy. Yet the clerisy in its Romantic mood claimed a separate perch in the class system, separated especially from its parents of the bourgeoisie, a virtual papacy from which it issued bulls and excommunications. "How did it happen," asked César Graña looking back on the mid-nineteenth-century treason of the clerisy, "that while one section of the bourgeoisie was efficiently gathering profits with unbending matter-of-factness, another was giving itself over to philosophical despair, the cult of sensitivity, and the enthronement of the nonutilitarian virtues?"[9]

By now the "creative class"—Richard Florida claims it is 30 percent of the American workforce, up from 10 percent in 1900—includes occupations once viewed as working class or, if especially profitable, mercantile. Think, for example, of painters in seventeenth-century Holland, who were apprentices or masters, poor or rich, but anyway mercantile.[10] Contrast the clerical and antimarket cast of modern painters. They chatter as much as they paint. Language is often as important in modern art as is the artwork itself. One is always a little surprised at the smooth articulateness of modern painters, selling, selling. Often language becomes the art: *Ceci ne pas une pipe.*

American and British journalists once thought of themselves as workingmen, mostly, right through World War II: *Scoop* or *Front Page.* Journalists on the Continent had a higher tone, and therefore priestly claims. A famous radical poem of Holland in the 1930s, written on a slow news day by such a journalist—Jan Gresshof; he was fired for printing the poem in his newspaper—speaks of the conservative wing of his colleagues of the clerisy, "de dominee, de dokter, de notaris," the minister, the doctor, the lawyer-notary, who together strolled complacently on Arnhem's town square of an evening. "There is nothing left on earth for them to learn, / They are perfect and complete, / Old liberals, distrustful and healthy."[11]

Whether conservative or radical they are the experts, of whom Harry Truman said, "An expert is someone who doesn't want to learn anything new, because then he wouldn't be an expert." They are the chattering artists and the preaching intellectuals, too, experts in arts and ideas—though the average artist or professor after 1930s radicalism would be appalled to be classed with *de dominee, de dokter, de notaris.* That is the historical paradox, and the main worry: a class genetically part of the bourgeoisie, and before 1848 sympathetic to it, has in its radicalism for a century and a half damned . . . the bourgeoisie.

The third part of the middle class is the petite bourgeoisie, the lower-middle class, the owner of the corner grocery store, the lower-middle manager, in former times the small but not subsistence farmer. Most Americans, as Europeans did not, put the upper-*working* class in the bourgeoisie, and invited them into the bourgeois fraternal societies: the head clerk in the office, the electrician, the freight conductor, the chief sawyer.[12]

In his book *The Radical Middle Class: Populist Democracy and the Question of Capitalism in Progressive Era Portland, Oregon* (2003) Robert Johnston argues that the lower-middle class has been tagged wrongly with the label of reaction. His Portland heroes such as Harry Lane, a U.S. senator who defended Joe Hill and voted against American entry into the Great War, or Lora Little, editor and an activist against conventional medicine, had all of them a touch of the clerisy. You can't be an advocate without being easy with pen or speech. But they were advocates for the small proprietor against the expert, and did not join in the Progressive and *bildungsbürgertumlich* enthusiasm for top-down social engineering. Lane, for example, was eloquent against the Bureau of Indian Affairs. Johnston's middle-class radicals wanted the little man and his wife to run things.

They were more hostile to the upper-middle class, the "moneyed interest" above them, than to the blue-collar workers below them, from whom they often came. Such lower-middle-class folk were working stiffs. It was the *non*working bond holders and the boodling politicians and the arrogant bureaucrats, the parasites on all working people, who evoked their wrath, à la Michael Moore. Damned right. Johnston notes that in the survey of Akron, Ohio, residents in 1941 by Alfred Winslow Jones the lower-middle class "sought a 'middle ground' between collectivism and absolute property rights." The majority of Akron's small business owners "believed that unemployed miners should steal coal to keep warm, that the Flint sit-down strike was proper, and that neighbors should prevent farm auctions and eviction of renters."[13]

La grande bourgeoisie, the clerisy, *la petite bourgeoisie*: objectively bourgeois all.

One can be in science a lumper or a splitter, talking about chest and hip structures of the great apes in general or of humans in particular. Johnston is right that you can for some purposes usefully split the lower-middle class from the rest, and study it comparatively. But of course the choice is pragmatic, depending on your purpose. If your purpose is Johnston's, to rescue the lower-middle class of our great-grandparents from demonization by historians of Nazi Germany like Arno Mayer, who on slender evidence have assigned fascism to shop owners, then you split.[14]

If your purpose is mine, to begin "redeeming the middling folk," as Johnston puts it, all of them—though especially the *non*intellectuals despised since 1848 by the clerisy—then you lump everybody from sweating assistant managers to glittering CEOs.

There's no permanent thing out there in the world for all times and all purposes called "*the* middle class." Social categories, no less than the anatomy of great apes, evolve, and furthermore what will matter about the categories to the social scientist depends on time and on human purposes. Statistics and other facts are relevant, but never come supplied with their own interpretation. Johnston cites on this point the great British student of the working class, E. P. Thompson, who argued that over a generation or two there are changes in its definition.[15] Likewise one can see in English history a bourgeoisie of subordination to the charter-granting power c. 1249 evolving into a bourgeoisie of confidence c. 1649, beheading an anointed king, and then c. 1949 evolving into a bourgeoisie of generality and even of honor.

We are all bourgeois now, a bourgeois apologist would say, or we should work on becoming so, because work after all is a good thing. Not a dishonor.

That is the common element in any bourgeoisie, the honoring of work apart from manual drudgery or heroic daring. The European aristocracy delights rather in haughty idleness. As Stephen Greenblatt notes, in Shakespearean England "there was virtually no respect for labor; on the contrary, it was idleness that was prized and honored."[16] Bourgeois work is dealing, managing, advising. It is verbal work, the speaking of ideas, the calculating of amounts, what you and I are doing now, for example. Note that well into the twentieth century in England the word "gentleman" meant "often, a man whose means enable him to live in easy circumstances without engaging in trade," a man who did not need to work at anything.[17] "As for gentlemen," writes one of them in Shakespeare's time, "whosoever . . . can live idly and without manual labor . . . he shall be called master."[18] The shift in the meaning of the word follows the spread of work-admiring middle-class values.

Unsurprisingly, the word "gentleman" shifts away from the prizing and honoring of idleness first in bourgeois America. Everyone in the American middle class from the small-town plumbing contractor to the captain of industry admires purposeful, energetic work with words, and in a democratic spirit does not disdain helping out occasionally with the manual labor, either. Get busy! Even professors in America are businesspeople, as for instance Morris Zapp in David Lodge's early academic novels, or Stanley Fish in real life. Busy, busy, busy. An American professor does the job, he says to himself proudly, whether the work is of brain or of hand. Get the Job Done. Henry Ford inspects the line. Sam Walton stocks the shelves.

The pretensions to leisure among the wives of the upper-middle class has therefore been an embarrassment and a disability, cordoning them off from power. In the old days if the wife worked hard at housewifery or charitable works she was somewhat redeemed, at any rate in her own sphere, though still an object of fun in the style of Helen Hokinson cartoons in the old *New Yorker*. But eating bonbons has never been honored by the American bourgeoisie. Among the bourgeoisie a job of work is figured as autonomy and identity, adulthood and masculinity. In 1898 Charlotte Perkins Gilman celebrated "the demand in [even bourgeois] women not only for their own money, but their own work for the sake of personal expression. . . . Human labor is an exercise of a faculty, without which we would cease to be human."[19] Or at least we would cease to be bourgeois humans, self-defining workers.

Victoria Thompson argues that in nineteenth-century France the bourgeois women were excluded by convention from making money in order to make that work honorable for their men. The bourgeois men were worried about their lack of aristocratic standing. Women's production, the pride of French style, perfectly illustrated later by Coco Chanel, and still later in our New World versions by Julia Child or Martha Stewart, was supposed to arise only from their devotion to consumption: *les doigts de fée*, the "fairy fingers," of the woman "constituted an extension of her 'natural' feminine attributes rather than incursion into the [male, market, bourgeois] world."[20] Hers wasn't real work, though a fine, fine thing, you understand.

The economist Everett Hagen saw the high valuation of work as arising from the status anxieties of (male) English Dissenters and Lowland Scots in seventeenth- and eighteenth-century Britain and of impoverished samurai and prosperous merchants in late Tokugawa Japan. An aristocrat is the duke of so-and-so regardless of whether or not he has a go from time to time at soldiering or at estate management. The very word "aristocrat," by the way, is a French Revolutionary coinage, out of the older and classical "aristocracy" and "aristocratic." *Homo ludens,* the species of "playing man," is an aristocratic or a peasant ideal of a life, weekends of aristocratic hunting and drinking chronicled in a novel by Woodhouse, or equally alcoholic weekends of proletarian soccer rioting in Amsterdam by yobs from Millwall or Sheffield United. Carefree. The aristocrat or proletarian is often portrayed in bourgeois fiction, which is most fiction, as unworried. At least that's how it looks to a bourgeois worried about the next deal or the next deadline.

The proletarian or peasant sometimes feels driven to his work by the lash. He would rather not. And even when he exercises the proud excellence of a Silas in New Hampshire c. 1915 making a load of hay—"He bundles every forkful in its place, / And tags and numbers it for future reference, / So he can find and easily dislodge it / In the unloading"—he is merely the hired man.

The bourgeois dream is different—to "be my own boss," he says, working harder than when bossed by others. The owner-managers of American restaurants or American farms earn low pay per hour because they value so highly their busy autonomy on the job, 5:00 in the morning to 11:00 at night. In 2003 Robert Johnston pointed out that, after a long decline, the rate of self-employment in the American economy was growing. He quoted George Steinmetz and Erik Wright on its emotional significance: "At least a quarter of the total labor force, and a third of the male labor force, either is *or has been* self-employed."[21]

And never mind the large additional percentage who have never in fact been self-employed and never actually will be, but have an unreasonable hope they will be self-employed in the future. The bourgeois thinks of himself as entrepreneurial, and especially in America he admires such go-getting, even if he has had in fact a routine career as an employee in a great corporation or a big government office. Napoleon is supposed to have said that his ordinary soldier carried the baton of a marshal of France in his kit bag. Thus a military career open to talents. The American middle manager thinks the same way, and has only a slightly larger chance of actually putting his baton to use. Jack Sparks of Whirlpool began on the line.

Property, too, is admired and sought among the bourgeoisie, of course. Acceptance of property rights is shared with the aristocracy. No trespassing. This is mine. I get to use it up if I wish. It has been noted often, from Virgil in his *Georgics* to Thomas Jefferson in his letters, that having property lends respect, and even self-respect. "Cultivators of the earth are the most valuable citizens," wrote Jefferson. "They are the most vigorous, the most independent, the most virtuous, and they are tied to their country, and wedded to its liberty and interests, by the most lasting bonds."[22] Owning is a good thing. Thus Bush II and his "ownership society," at least in its words.

Great-souled gestures of consumption, giving to the church, a granite countertop for the remodeled kitchen, a summer home in Wisconsin, that third car, the Republican Party, are shared with the aristocrats, too. Since most of the bourgeoisie do not actually know how the aristocrats spend their wealth, the symbolizing of prestige is imitated mainly from other, somewhat grander bourgeois. This is Pierre Bourdieu's point in his exploration of class and consumption in France, *Distinction: A Social Critique of the Judgment of Taste* (1979). Spending property on hobbies and education and status-affirming toys helps make bourgeois people who they are. Everyone of means, they will say to themselves, has an elaborate gas grill under a green cover for the rain. We must have one, too. Everyone of means gives to the church. We must give, too.

But *bourgeois* property is different from that of the aristocrat or peasant. It is neither the easy inheritance claimed by the aristocrat nor the overused commons claimed by the peasant. It is not a given, zero-sum lump, as these two are. It is bound up, again, with a vision of freely chosen work. Bourgeois property is at least in fable remade every generation, like the tools of a guildsman. "Human capital" is a modern bourgeois' idea of skill. When

Theodore Schultz, the inventor of the concept in economics, visited an Alabama farm family in the late 1940s, he wondered to the mother and father about their poverty in run-down hog pens and an unpainted house. He told me that the mother replied in effect, "No, you are mistaken, Professor Schultz. We are not poor. We are rich: we purposely ran down the farm in order to invest in the education of our four children, all the way through college. That's where our treasure is."

Like a college education, property in home ownership is a sign of middle-class status in the United States, a modern version of the Jeffersonian and Roman republican idea of farm ownership as citizenship. The education and the home are not literally inherited, at least (again) in fable. They are bought during each bourgeois life, working for the mortgage, paying off the loans.

With the workers the bourgeoisie shares a resentment of the Great and Good, as they are called jeeringly in bourgeois England, and shares an eagerness to read about their fall. The petite bourgeoisie especially, most of all in egalitarian places like Australia or America, regards the political or corporate bosses as mafia dons, warlords, smooth-skinned thieves. Thus a shopkeeper in Santa Fe describes the sales tax, as he calculates it, as "5 percent for the governor." The hostility to their betters among the bourgeoisie is sometimes matched by a contempt for their inferiors, and such a mix does have fascist possibilities. But the better angels of the bourgeoisie are genially populist, like Clarence the angel to George Bailey the savings-and-loan banker in *It's a Wonderful Life*.

Equality, property, and honorable verbal work, helping out with the manual work at the crisis, these three abide. But the greatest of these is honorable work.

ON NOT BEING SPOOKED BY THE WORD "BOURGEOIS"

It does not seem on its face such a terrible way to live. It does not seem inconsistent with the virtues. Yet the very word "bourgeois" has been for a long time, I repeat, an embarrassment. In 1935 the Dutch historian Johan Huizinga noted that "in the nineteenth century, 'bourgeois' became the most pejorative term of all, particularly in the mouths of socialists and artists, and later even of fascists."[1]

We should try to redeem the word, and through it rediscover a virtuous middle class. In actual fact middle-class people have not been monsters. Their sworn enemies, from Lenin to Pol Pot, Abimael Guzman, and Osama Bin Laden, commonly have been. Middle-class virtuousness arises not merely when an occasional saintly bourgeoise overcomes the entailments of her social position and joins the Communist Party. A bourgeois social position, if properly tutored by education, draws out the virtues.

But the trouble is that "bourgeois" is used by the left to evoke the alleged ethical bankruptcy of the middle class. On some tongues it has come to mean "bossy, greedy, selfish, vulgar, sexist, patriarchal, fascist, snobbish, elitist, common, American, Midwestern, small-town, philistine, ignorant, uneducated, unethical, conventional, self-satisfied, uncharitable, hypocritical, imperialistic, undemocratic, militaristic, authoritarian, materialistic, and inegalitarian." The word therefore makes nonleftists uneasy. They worry that they are accepting in the word some nasty conclusions in no way obviously correct about owners and managers of the means of production.

The uneasiness of nonleftists, or of others merely puzzled by a phrase such as "the bourgeois virtues," shows up in Simon Schama's book, *The*

Embarrassment of Riches: An Interpretation of Dutch Culture in the Golden Age (1987). On page 6 he announces his ambition to "rescue the Netherlands from its ancient stereotype as quintessentially bourgeois." He has in mind Huizinga, and behind him the irritated assessments of the place by aristocratic foreigners, starting with Philip II's Duke of Alva and Elizabeth's Earl of Leicester.

Using the word "bourgeois," Schama writes, perpetuates "the deadening cliché that tells us at once too much and not enough. . . . The result is a kind of depressing historical perennialism by which the Dutch, being bourgeois, were whatever the modern mind supposes bourgeois to be," which is to say, bossy, greedy, selfish, vulgar, etc. He therefore wants another word for his beloved Nederlanders. "At the center of the Dutch world," he declares, "was a burgher, not a bourgeois." Rousseau in 1762 put it similarly, distinguishing a *citoyen* from a *bourgeois*.[2]

That is, Schama wants a word uncorrupted by the sneers of the left, beginning with Rousseau. Schama wants to honor the northern-lowlandish townspeople of the seventeenth century without implying that they were "bourgeois" in the corrupted sense of the word. "The burgher was a citizen first," you see, "and *Homo economicus* second. . . . If any one obsession linked together the [*burgerij's*] concerns . . . it was the moral ambiguity of good fortune," that embarrassment of riches.

The word "bourgeois" in its Marxist dress is to be rejected because it has become merely a synonym for *Homo economicus*, the man of untroubled selfishness which by now left and right agree in believing is the essence of middle-class life. The bourgeois in this belief is a machine for making (as it is always put) endless profit—profit by blessed invention if you are of the right, or profit by damned exploitation if you are of the left.

Early in the last long chapter in the book, Schama lets himself go. The word "bourgeois, after all, belongs to the classifying vocabulary of nineteenth-century and twentieth-century materialist social science that assumed systems of belief to be appendages of social power. Those frameworks of cultural analysis are notorious for their reductive insistence on a social continuum that extends from the division of labor to the destination of the soul."[3]

Schama can't bring himself to utter the word "Marxist." Ideas are not to be reduced to Marxist social class. "If my view is somewhat idealist, the opposite view is often unreflectingly materialistic."[4] Schama is right to reject the theory shared by left and right in which, for example, the "realism" of

Golden Age painting is supposed to be "some sort of clodlike bourgeois adhesion to the concrete."[5] If the supposition were true, it would be hard to explain the bourgeois enthusiasm for impressionist, or for that matter postimpressionist, or for that matter abstract expressionist, painting. Being bourgeois, Schama and I agree, is not the same thing as being stupidly literal and ethically corrupt. That's the point of my own book, too, as of Schama's: to celebrate the "bourgeois virtues"—if Schama would but accept the word.

Buying, selling, owning and operating, managing, planning, advising, persuading, inventing, designing, inquiring, reporting, educating, research-ing, exploring, calculating, accounting, defending, prosecuting, judging, curing, helping, regulating, governing in Amsterdam and in New Amster-dam, in market work and in housework, in the seventeenth century and now, do not automatically produce ethical salvation. But neither do they automatically produce ethical damnation. It is a life of navigating between the sacred and the profane.

"To be a Dutch burgher," Schama declares, "meant avoiding being either godless or helpless."[6] I agree. "Money-making, which the Calvinist Church so detested, was tolerated by distinguishing between proper and improper ways of making fortunes, and the concept of wealth as stewardship."[7] The left could here note sarcastically, and accurately, that in the seventeenth cen-tury "proper stewardship" included piracy, slave trading, and colonial exploitation. "To be Dutch," he concludes, "still means coming to terms with the moral ambiguities of materialism," now as in the Golden Age.[8] Yes.

But coming to terms with the moral ambiguities of materialism is the life of *any* bourgeois person, Dutch or Florentine, American or English, Japa-nese or South Asian. The early Medici bankers, two centuries before Schama's Dutch, writes Tim Parks, faced the same problem in ethical mechanics. "Precisely because [Cosimo il Vecchio] cares about his eternal soul he is aware of a fierce tension between the competing demands of the sacred and the secular. A rich and powerful man who is also a devout Christian must needs be anxious."[9] Such a bourgeois anxiety, Parks notes, would not describe the late Medici, by that time aristocratic dukes rather than high-bourgeois bankers.

You can't be rich and be loved, they say. The superstition is that to get rich you have to steal. Even the rich believe it. The anxiety of the rich middling sort has been famous in social theorizing for a century, since Max Weber's *The Protestant Ethic and the Spirit of Capitalism*, as Schama notes. It was lively in eighteenth-century writing on social ethics, too, such as that of Montesquieu and Adam Smith commending the bourgeoisie. And the anxiety-producing tension between the sacred and the profane has been an obsession in Christianity since the Sermon on the Mount.

A hungry peasant or a well-heeled aristocrat has, as we say, no issues with money and consumption. It's "eat black bread every chance you get" or "endow St. Paul's with stained glass." No issues there. But the *middenstand* live with the moral ambiguities of materialism. They have so very much of that matter, after all, and know how it was earned. Should a tithe for my church be reckoned before or after taxes? Is it hubris for Silas Lapham to build a vulgar house in the Back Bay? Should Emma Woodhouse persuade Harriet not to marry a mere farmer?

If the bourgeois Dutch nowadays excuse their wealth with good works such as the expedition to Srebrenica, so do bourgeois Americans now, who attend church for this purpose in startling numbers, and who like the Dutch embark on errands of mercy abroad which they sometimes do not have the aristocratic courage or peasant faithfulness to finish. In the great days of bourgeois Florence and Venice the churches themselves were lusciously decorated in expiation for the taking of interest and the taking of advantage. Parks instances the tomb and old sacristy in the Church of San Lorenzo commissioned from Brunelleschi and Donatello by Cosimo's father, the founder of the bank.[10] The guilt and pride of the bourgeoisie has festooned our cities.

As Schama himself conceded, "The tensions of a capitalism that endeavored to make itself moral were the same whether in sixteenth-century Venice, seventeenth-century Amsterdam or eighteenth-century London."[11] That is the right tactic for reforming our discussions about the rise of the bourgeoisie: namely, to note and analyze its ethical tensions. The mistake is to flee from the very word "bourgeois" because some people use it to mean "bad bosses," or indeed from the word "ethics" because some people use it to mean "inessential rules of business just short of indictable crimes," or "morality" because some people use it to mean "puritanical, sex-obsessed hypocrisy."

Schama has a fascinating chapter on housewifery. Why do the Dutch scrub their stoops? Why in Dutch but not in other Germanic languages is the word for "clean" the same as the word for "beautiful"? The Japanese, by the way, are similar. Among both people, and not among their neighbors, "cleanliness" = "beauty," and so "be beautiful" makes sense as an ethical command: be clean, which anyone can achieve. Such an aesthetic can perhaps be traced in the restraint of Japanese domestic architecture and the similarly "clean" lines of high modernism, in which the Dutch came to excel.

Schama notes that the importance of the home to bourgeois society was "not of course peculiar to the Netherlands."[12] "The family household," he writes, "was the saving grace of Dutch culture that otherwise would have been indelibly soiled by materialism."[13] Note the image of soiling by contact with the world. The moral ambiguity of compromise in the market is seen as dirty, touching a hundred hands. The Dutch home has soap and towels and moral clarity. The market entails carefully judged degrees of trust, orders of ability, the relativity of a price. At home the man retreats to the sacred absolutes of love, obligation, power. We say it is his castle, *Het Slot,* where he is no longer required to calculate and deal.

In 1652 Owen Felltham stood amazed at the houses of Flanders, "the best eye beauties of their country," of which "their lining is yet more rich than their outside; not in hangings [that is, tapestries] but in pictures, which even the poorest are there furnished with." In probate inventories we learn of deceased Netherlanders of quite ordinary bourgeois status leaving *hundreds* of paintings. A blacksmith would literally hang oil paintings on the wall beside his forge. Over a million paintings, it has been reckoned, poured out of the workshops of Holland in the Golden Age.

"Their houses they keep cleaner than their bodies," Felltham notes with disdain, and then adopts a Cavalier and Anglican Protestant and English haughtiness in asserting further that the Catholic Flemings keep "their bodies [cleaner] than their souls."[14] No: the cleaning of bodies and houses and front stoops is soul-cleansing, too, said the Dutch and Flemings. The northern European bourgeois home is not in truth a "castle." It is a temple. Compare the spiritual character of personal hygiene and housecleaning among the Japanese—though there the custom is not at all of modern or bourgeois origin.

"The effort to moralize materialism" is told in the Netherlands, of course, in characteristically Dutch ways, which Schama persuasively illustrates. The word *overvloed,* for example, means "abundance, *copia.*" But the literal meaning, "over flood," put Dutch people in mind of seawater surging onto the rich but low-lying provinces of Holland and Zeeland—"Zeeland" means "sea land" claimed from and bravely facing the waves. The image reminded self-critical Calvinists of overwhelmed dikes every ten years or so, now here, now there, with gigantic regional disasters remembered for generations every century or so, Saint Elizabeth's Day in 1421, for example, seventy-two villages in Zeeland abruptly engulfed in a night, over 100,000 people drowned; or latterly, January 31, 1953. A famous modern poem speaks of *de stem van het water met zijn eeuwige rampen / gevreesd en gehoord*, "the sound of the water, with its eternal disasters, is feared and heard." Flooding of water figures repeatedly in worries about an over-flood of *riches*.

Material abundance seems like such a force of nature, crushing all. Nothing is more abundant than the sea. To be deprived by overflooding riches of the necessity to work was bad, not good, because these were bourgeois, work-admiring people. Dutch has a terrifying word, *kwelwater*, the water that quietly seeps under an apparently sound dike. It is related in folk etymology to *kwellen*, "to torment, to torture." A Calvinist, at any rate the rigorist *predikant* who after 1619 claimed precedence in religious affairs in the Republic, would readily extend it to the seeping corruptions of the soul. The Netherlanders' "fear of drowning in destitution and terror [from water] was exactly counterbalanced by their fear of drowning in luxury and sin [from wealth]."[15] The Dutch stole the land from the sea, and worried about the counterclaim of nature, or of human nature. "Let us clean our stoops, and our souls," they repeated uneasily as they worked.

But is the moral effort especially Dutch? *Ik denk het niet*. I don't think the Dutch moralized their riches and other bourgeois do not.

The American bourgeoisie, for example, moralizes its riches as just rewards for cowboy courage, or as a gospel of philanthropy of the Carnegie/Mellon type, or as a democratic creed of opportunity seized. The Hindu bourgeoisie moralizes its riches as the favor of Ganesha or the expression of spiritual worth from a previous reincarnation or as provisioning for those pesky cousins. As behavior, of course, a sheer materialism without sincere reference to the transcendent is common enough in all societies, bourgeois or not. But it is the official theory of none. Official theories are about the transcendent, a beyond. Every human yearns for it.

Schama does not compare enough with other countries to make his case for Dutch exceptionalism. The same problem is seen among historians of the United States trying with exclusively American evidence to make a case for American exceptionalism. The very phrase "American exceptionalism," it appears, arose in the 1920s in discussions among Communists as to why America did not respond to socialism in a manner comparable with Europe.[16] The exceptionalisms are founding myths.

The Dutch were not in fact exceptional in character, merely a little early compared to the English or the French and a little late compared with the Florentines and Venetians. The Low Countries north and south were the earliest northern European regions to be thoroughly citified.[17] In 1467 Charles, Duke of Burgundy, ruled over a town-rich region, matched only by northern Italy. In 1600 the northern Netherlands had nineteen cities of over 10,000 population, as against only six in a Britain five or six times larger in total population.[18] One in four Dutch northerners, Jan de Vries reckons, lived in towns of 10,000 or larger in 1600, one in five in the Spanish Netherlands, that is, Belgium. Only one in seventeen Englishmen did.[19] The Low Countries were the first bourgeois society in the north. *Bourgeois*, I say—to preserve the comparison with other societies, such as our own.

That is one reason to keep the word "bourgeois." It does not have to mean "egotistical wretch." God or nature or Humpty Dumpty does not determine what words mean. We do. "Bourgeois" can mean, if we wish to use words this way—and can get over being spooked by Marx—"city dweller practicing an honored profession or owning a business or functioning at a managerial level in someone else's enterprise, including governmental and non-profit enterprises."

Such a person faces a particular set of ethical problems. He has the anxious ethical task of learning how to be a counselor yet self-prudent, a salesman yet other-loving, a boss yet just, a bureaucrat yet courageous, a scientist yet faithful. Schama is right to emphasize the ethical tensions of capitalism. But the Dutch are merely an early instance, as the Venetians and Florentines and Genoese were still earlier, with the Hanseatic League in attendance, and Osakans and Singaporeans later, of a by-now worldwide social class and a by-now worldwide ethical problem, namely, the tensions of bourgeoisness ascendant. Avoiding the very word in fear of its historical-materialist accretions doesn't help. The way to refute historical materialism is to examine the material and spiritual facts, as Schama does. Avoiding the b-word is no help.

Still, why not bow to the common prejudice and use instead "middle class" or "middling sort" or "the managerial/professional/upper-bureaucratic/

upper-entrepreneurial class" or "SES I, II, and the higher-status members of III and IV," or even Schama's "burghers," which is all I mean?

Well, I admit to a contrariness here, a wish to slow down the corruption of meaningful words. The word "rhetoric," for example, which for two millennia meant "the offering of good reasons," has been corrupted since the seventeenth century to become in English—less so in other European languages, I think—another of the very numerous English words for *false* speech. Let's recover it. "Anarchism," which means in Greek "without a ruler," that is, without an all-powerful state, has been corrupted in American English since the late nineteenth century to become just another word for nihilistic bomb-throwing. Let's recover it. And "feminism," which meant at its coinage an advocacy for the flourishing of women, has been corrupted in some minds since the 1970s to become just another word for bra-burning man hating—thus the late Bob Hope: "Feminists burn their bras, then complain about lack of support." Let's recover it, too.

I want to recover the word "bourgeois" by taking it back from its enemies. The word "capitalist," referring in the opinion of Communists in the 1880s to greedy monopolists of the means of production, was taken back in the 1980s to mean "advocates for and actors in free markets." "Quaker" and "Tory" originated as sneers, but were calmly appropriated by the victims and made honorable.

In April 1566 two hundred armed and Protestant-sympathizing aristocrats from the Low Countries presented a petition to Margaret of Parma, Catholic Philip's regent in Brussels, urging her to grant religious tolerance. She was advised by one of her counselors to pay them no heed. They were merely, said he in his aristocratic French, *gueux,* that is, "beggars." Never mind that the petitioners were themselves French-speaking aristocrats.

The Netherlandish noblemen seized upon the word, and called themselves proudly thereafter Beggars, Dutch *Geuzen.* Baron Henry Brederode, their leader, was called Le Grand Gueux. That summer the new word was claimed too by the Protestant iconoclasts. "Vivent les Gueux," the rioters cried in Antwerp, or perhaps "Leven de Geuzen," as they trashed centuries of religious art.[20]

The word has remained alive in the Dutch language. A group in 1568 devoted to the murder of Catholic priests called itself the Bosgeuzen, Forest Beggars. The pirate navy which took Brill from the Spanish in 1572 called itself the Watergeuzen, Sea Beggars. The orthodox Calvinists marching to kill off toleration in 1616 called themselves the Mud Beggars. One of the illegal newspapers during the German occupation of the Second World War was *De Geus*, The Beggar. The normal Dutch word for such reversals of a sneer became *geuzennamen*, beggars-names.

I hope to make "bourgeois" a *geuzennaam*, to remake a word of contempt into a word of honor.

PART ONE

The Christian and Feminine Virtues: Love

I HAVE LOVED, GOD KNOWS,

I'VE DONE MY SHARE OF THAT.

AND SOME OF THEM

HAVE LOVED ME BACK.

AND SOME HAVE NOT.

LOVE, I'VE FOUND,

IS ANSWERABLE ONLY TO ITSELF.

Helen McCloskey, "The Flow"

THE FIRST VIRTUE: LOVE PROFANE
AND SACRED

Love can be thought of as a commitment of the will to the true good of another.[1] Love is identified conventionally with the "feminine," which would not have recommended it to Nietzsche or to Aristotle. Of the seven virtues—courage, temperance, justice, prudence, faith, hope, and love—courage is, I repeat, stereotypically male, love stereotypically female. "Love is the general name of the quality of attachment," said Iris Murdoch, something which sounds to a man suspiciously cloying.[2] "The disdain for . . . words like 'love' and 'giving,'" the literary critic Jane Tompkins notes, "is part of the police action that [male] academic intellectuals wage ceaselessly against feeling, against women, against what is personal."[3]

The gendering of the virtues makes even Christian males a little nervous. It has troubled Christian ethics since the beginning. As Basil Willey once wrote, "There has always, perhaps, been a latent contradiction between our official lip service to the Christian standard in all its rigor, and the pagan ideal of 'the gentleman' which is what we [men] have really admired and sought to practice."[4] The French Jansenist Pierre Nicole wrote in 1671, "There are an infinity of small things which are extremely necessary for us to live, and can be given for free; and which cannot be traded so that they can be purchased only by love." He sounds like a modern male economist, thinking of love as an exchange. And said so: "Human civility . . . is only a sort of commerce of self-love, in which one endeavors to arouse the love of others by displaying some affection towards them."[5] No, dear.

A large group of philosophically savvy women, such as Elizabeth Anscombe, Philippa Foot, Judith Shklar, Iris Murdoch, Carol Gilligan, Nel

Noddings, Mary Midgley, Martha Nussbaum, Sissela Bok, Amélie Rorty, Susan Wolf, Nancy Chodorow, Joan Tronto, Virginia Held, Annette Baier, and Rosalind Hursthouse, have since about 1958 turned a woman's eye on ethical philosophy. They have noted that love is *not* self-love. (Ethical theory had been for a long time, oddly, a guy thing. I suppose that's an entailment of "theory" in general having been for a long time a guy thing. Women from Sappho to Virginia Woolf did their ethical thinking in poems and stories, not in philosophy.)

This program of Aristotle in modern dress, I say, has been strikingly feminine. Its leaders have been women, though, as Kathryn Morgan observed, none of them is a "star" in the style of John Rawls or Robert Nozick. "The community of feminist theoreticians is calling into question the very model of the individual autonomous self presupposed by a star-centered male-dominated tradition. . . . We experience it as common labor, a common task."[6] Let's get this kitchen cleaned up. No quarterbacks. Speak of thee, not me: "tuistically," from Latin *tua,* thy.

The theology and ethics and science of love is not that of bodice-ripping romance novels. It is hard nowadays to get beyond the Romantic idea of love, according to which one "falls" into it with no ethical restraint. Stendhal, for example, wrote a long treatise on the subject in 1822, *De l'amour,* in which love other than an adolescent version of *eros* is neglected. Alice Munro calls *eros* "a tingling contentment in the presence of the other person"; Nick Hornby, "the mad hunger for someone you don't know very well."[7]

Such "love" is, as C. S. Lewis put it, one of God's little jokes, "that a passion so soaring, apparently transcendent, as Eros, should thus be linked in incongruous symbiosis with a bodily appetite. . . . [W]e are composite creatures, rational animals, akin on one side to the angels, on the other to tomcats."[8] To give free rein to the tomcat in us would hardly be a virtue. It would be the vice of lust, a "love" unbalanced by other virtues, a yielding to passion.

Yet *eros* is not an ethical zero. As Lewis noted, it can touch the transcendent. *The Song of Songs* is erotic yet religious, loving yet Loving. The version of *eros* that Jane Austen's novels study, for example, is hardly animalistic. It is ethical, that is, it is concerned with the education of the will to the end of good character, and indeed is precisely about coming to know someone's character.

Mr. Knightley (note the name) rebukes Emma for her making merry of poor Miss Bates. Emma is instantly ashamed, and at length in love. As John Casey puts it, "Emma's love for Mr. Knightley has something to do with her sense of his moral rightness and authority."[9] The result is a marriage of true ethical minds, not mere bodies locked. The same can be seen in homosexual unions, the Boston marriage, for example, of Stein and Toklas, or the liaison of Socrates and Charmides. The special, deep friendship between lovers, a hunger that evolves into admiration, is not sinful.

The folk anthropology of "the traditional marriage" makes we moderns feel superior by imagining an alien Other. Modern romantic marriage is widely imagined to have superseded supposedly loveless arranged marriages in "traditional" societies—though, by the way, if you speak to women with arranged marriages they will often give you a different opinion.

The lovelessness of traditional society appears anyway to be a myth. Loving marriage and economically independent women were widespread, for example, in Europe. Aquinas in the thirteenth century attacked polygamy precisely because it makes the wife into a slave, a mere possession.[10] Aquinas classifies conjugal love as superior even to the manly friendship so much admired in his tradition, the tradition of Cicero especially.[11] Jews had a little before Aquinas outlawed polygamy on similar grounds. The historical anthropologist Alan Macfarlane finds "companionate marriage" in English society "as far back as we can conveniently go" in English history, expressed repeatedly as the union of souls reminiscent of Plato's metaphor in the *Symposium*. Macfarlane quotes a "Wife's Lament" translated from Old English as "we have vowed / Full many a time that naught should come between us / But death alone, and nothing else at all."[12]

In short, love and marriage / Going together like a horse and carriage is not a modern bourgeois invention, as, for example, Marx and especially Engels believed. In Macfarlane's account the English have always been in this sense bourgeois. Macfarlane finds agreement on the point from a surprising quarter, again from E. P. Thompson, who wrote in 1965 of a "bourgeois arch, which stretches [in England] from the twelfth century to our own time." "The central ideology" of English society, writes Macfarlane, has *always* been "a [nuclear] family pattern [focused on husband and wife, not children or ancestors or clan] and individualistic philosophy," to achieve the "ends . . . [of] equality of the sexes, physical comfort rather than misery, and responsibility for one's own decisions."[13] Bourgeois virtues.

One would expect the same from the Dutch, who in the eleventh and twelfth centuries were pioneers in an empty, tide-flooded swamp, to be taken for cultivation by busy dike-building, unlike the Muslim gardens of Iberia to be taken by heroic *reconquista*. Wives on a nonmilitary frontier are too useful to devalue, which may perhaps explain the autonomy of Dutch women compared with the Spanish women of the seventeenth century or even the French.

The alleged novelty of modern love runs parallel in recent scholarship to that of an alleged break in the sixteenth and seventeenth centuries in European conceptions of childhood, first claimed in 1960 by the French historian Philippe Ariès, and reaffirmed by Edward Shorter for the American case and Lawrence Stone for the English. The bourgeois family against which the young men of the 1960s were rebelling was seen, as Eamon Duffy described it in a recent review, as "oppressive; it de-eroticized children and women; it turned wives into baby machines, children into subordinate versions of their parents."[14] But the 1960s antibourgeois interpretation of the old and new family appears now, like the lovelessness of traditional marriage, to have been mistaken. "As far back as we can tell," writes Linda Pollock (note the similarity to Macfarlane's words), "most parents loved their children, grieved at their deaths and conscientiously attended to the task of child-rearing."[15] The historian of Roman social life, Richard Saller, makes a similar point.[16] Love is continuous, even, one might speculate, hardwired. Thus in England the *Pearl* poet of the late fourteenth century longed for his dead daughter, though as in *The Song of Songs* the longing is refigured as Love for God.

Love's expressions vary by culture and era, that is, but are not lacking anywhere. Parents love children, spouses love one another. The Puritan settler in Massachusetts, Anne Bradstreet, writes in 1656 of the loss to migration of her children, imagined as birds ("Four cocks there were, and hens the rest"). She comforts herself with her utility in their own utility: "Farewell my birds, farewell adieu, / I happy am, if well with you."[17] One can try to read her as utilitarian or conventional in expression, but it seems a misreading. Likewise for conjugal love. Puritans were in fact well known for insisting on a loving, unslavish relation between husband and wife. "To My Dear and Loving Husband" expresses more than Puritan patriarchy:

If ever two were one, then surely we.
If ever man were loved by wife, then thee;
If ever wife was happy in a man,
Compare with me, ye women, if you can.[18]

Love rules.

Love can also be called a "peasant" virtue, the modern label being
"proletarian." Courage is claimed to be above all the virtue of the aristocrat. As prudence is of the bourgeois. Love, courage, and prudence. When
she witnessed a religious procession one night in the late 1930s in a Portuguese fishing village it was suddenly plain to Simone Weil, a French secular Jew on her way to Christianity, that "Christianity is preeminently the
religion of slaves, that slaves cannot help belonging to it, and I among
others."[19] Love—even in its social forms as an abstract solidarity—is
pacific, Christian, and yielding. It is Nietzsche's "slave morality," subordinate to the Greek and aristocratic virtues he admired. So did Aristotle
admire them, and disdain any love but a friendship among men. Alasdair
MacIntyre notes that "Aristotle would certainly not have admired Jesus
Christ and he would have been horrified by St. Paul," with all their
embarrassing talk of love.[20] The pagans were not lovelorn, at least not in
their philosophies.

The feminine side of the stripped-down, two-virtue, love-or-courage
way people speak of exercising a will to do good might, I say, also be called
"Christian." I mean the word "Christian" here as evocative, not exclusive.
I do not mean to praise Christianity or attack non-Christians. I am well
aware that Christendom has not always been a feast of love, as Muslims and
Albigensians, Jews and Hussites know. A Buddhist nun of my acquaintance
has shown me centered virtues similar to those of the best of the Christian
monks. And I've seen the virtue of love in many a loving atheist and anticlerical. Nor am I, though a Christian—a progressive Episcopalian, if you
care, the quasi-Quaker branch of the Frozen Chosen—willing to claim that
Christianity brought new ethics into the world. Yet some of the virtues have
acquired a spin in the talk of literal Christians, carrying over into the minds
and hearts of *non*believers in the bourgeois West, loading faith with doubt.[21]
Bear with me, then, exercising if you please a Christian charity, when I use
the loaded word.

In the West before Christianity the most admired virtues, the "pagan virtues," were manful and military, not feminine and loving. In Plato's opinion, elaborated by other pagans and by Jews and Christians, with parallels in Chinese and other traditions, they were four, named by St. Ambrose in the fourth century AD the "cardinal" virtues: first physical and other varieties of that courage; then temperance, justice, and prudence.[22] Thus the Wisdom of Solomon (8:7) "teaches self-control [viz., temperance] and prudence, / justice and courage; / nothing in life is more profitable for men than these." And 4 Maccabees, an instance as Luke Timothy Johnson has put it, of "Jews thinking like Greeks," reinterprets Jewish law as expressions of a natural law of prudence, justice, courage, and temperance (for example, 1:2–4, 18).[23] "Cardinal" means "hinge-like" or by extension the imagined corners on which the earth turns. So the four virtues made the pagan world go round, absent Christian or romantic love.

The so-called Christian virtues, what St. Thomas Aquinas and his tradition called the "theological" virtues, are three. Thus St. Paul: "And now abideth faith, hope, and charity, these three; but the greatest of these is charity," agape, spiritual love, "the divine friendship of graced human beings."[24] St. Paul was already accustomed before he wrote 1 Corinthians to bundle them, for example, 1 Thessalonians 1:3, 5:8, as perhaps were still earlier Christians. The word "charity" is the King James Bible's attempt, and that of some translations in other languages, such as that of Louis Segond's La sainte Bible of 1910, to distinguish a higher Love from lower loves. "Charity" or charité translates Greek agape, spiritual love, distinguishing it from eros, physical love, or philia, friendship.

Most people read 1 Corinthians 13 as recommending love for your husband or your girlfriend, and for this purpose the passage appears on many Hallmark cards. That's not what St. Paul had in mind. Modern European languages—to the confusion of Romantics in love with love—use the same word "love" for both agape and eros. Until the gender anxieties of recent modernity interfered with the usage, indeed, French and English and Italian and German used it also for philia, friendship of men for men and women for women. That is, "love" signified all four—God's love for us, our love for God, sexualized love between humans, and nonsexualized love between humans. Amour, for example, seems to have about the same range of meaning in French as "love" has in English.

In Latin on the other hand *amor/cāritas/amicitia* parallels the Greek distinctions *eros/agape/philia*. *Cāritas* at Rome was from *cārus*, "dear," as in "expensive" or "beloved," and signified "esteem" or "high valuation," what C. S. Lewis called "appreciation love," as against *amor*, desire.[25] But modern languages blur the distinctions in their word "love." In French too the attempt to make *charité* into the word for "agape" did not take, as "charity" for this purpose did not in English. Later revisions of Segond's Bible gave in and used *amour*, as in modern English translations: "love," with its vulgar ambiguities.

Love, charity, *cāritas*, agape is the greatest virtue of the three theological virtues in Christianity because it is the essence of the Christian God, so unlike his predecessors, at any rate in his opinion. Hope and faith have no purpose in a god, foresighted and immortal. Only beings who can die need those virtues. And the Christian God does not "need" agape. By grace he gives it. No one would have accused Zeus of *loving* humans, except on occasion in a cheaply erotic sense. (The female gods like Athena seem to take a more motherly and less sexually dominating approach to their favored humans.) Yahweh demanded sacrifice of others' sons, Abraham's for example, but revealed no loving plans for sacrificing his own, except in tendentious readings by Christians of what they call the Old Testament. Yet the Christian God so loved the world, said John the Evangelist, that his only begotten son was ordained from the beginning of time to suffer, really suffer a human death, without sure knowledge of his Godness. Norman Mailer, of all people, has written a gripping novel on this theme, *The Gospel According to the Son* (1997), turning on Jesus' doubt, quoting the Twenty-second Psalm: "My God, my God, why hast thou forsaken me?"

The Christian or theological part of Love can be brought down to earth, but keeps a whiff of the transcendent. Love is not merely the earthly itch of lust, *eros*. The Romantic poets *loved* nature. Giacomo Leopardi in 1819 begins his most famous poem with "Always dear to me was that lonely hill." He adopts in this as in many other cases the high Romantic arrangement nature-reflection-nature.

William Wordsworth, on the other hand, as the critic Geoffrey Hartman observed, knew at the beginning of "Tintern Abbey" (1798) one thing only: "the affection he bears to nature *for its own sake*."[26] Nature is not to be *used* as an input into a utility function, as the modern economist would wish. Nor even is nature to be used in moral illustration, as poets before and after

Wordsworth did so freely—Shakespeare's sonnets or Housman's lyrics, for instance. Matthew Arnold begins "Dover Beach" (1851) with the cliffs of England glimmering and vast, turns then to reflections about the Sea of Faith, and ends with a battlefield, in pointed disruption of the tranquil bay and the sweet night air with which the poem begins. The traditions of the pastoral are disrupted for intellectual use.

But Wordsworth's nature in "Tintern Abbey," I say, is not to be *used* at all. It is simply a thing to be loved, *amandum,* sheerly. Note the parallel with love of God. "These waters . . . / With a soft inland murmur . . . / a wild secluded scene" do not raise the poet's blood pressure or bring into his mind the turbid ebb and flow of human misery. They merely "impress / Thoughts of more deep seclusion; and connect / The landscape with the quiet of the sky." Nothing *follows*. It is pure appreciation-love, earthly agape.

As the theologian David Klemm puts it, "material grace" is the experience in the world that "restores me to my own being" by being the presence of God.[27] "I, so long / A worshipper of Nature, hither came / Unwearied in that service." "Worshipper," not "enjoyer" or "user" or "national-park customer." Hartman writes, "This dialectic of love makes up his entire understanding. . . . Wordsworth's understanding is characterized by the general absence of the will to obtain relational knowledge."[28] No wonder that early Wordsworth was Mill's crutch when his Utilitarian life began to feel crippled.[29]

A modern Green Party member can give a utilitarian, consequential, instrumental, scientifically knowledgeable reply to an inquiry into *why* she loves nature. She can claim, for example, that the snail darter has a use as, so to speak, a canary in the world's coal mine, presaging a disaster that even a nonlover of nature would want to avoid. But had the snail darter no earthly use, the environmentalist would nonetheless go on loving it. You might as well ask why your mother loves you. She just does. Such love has no outside use. It is a sacrifice, a making sacred.

The archangel Raphael admonishes Adam in his love for Eve not to make her his god. Milton combines the Aristotelian doctrine of the mean with Augustine's and the neoplatonists' doctrine of human love as that spark off a transcendent flint. Raphael speaks:

> In loving thou dost well, in passion not,
> Wherein true love consists not; love refines
> The thoughts, and heart enlarges, hath his seat

In reason, and is judicious, is the scale
By which to heavenly love [viz., agape] thou mayest ascend,
Not sunk in carnal pleasure, for which cause
Among the beasts no mate for thee was found.[30]

Note the other, pagan virtues preventing the corruption of love into lust: prudence ("reason"); justice ("judicious"); and temperance ("not sunk in carnal pleasure"). And note the characteristically Miltonic ambiguity in the line-ending "scale." The reader is surprised, led from "scale" as temperance and justice to "scale" (*scalae*) as a staircase ascending to divine love.

Adam should see Eve as a spark *of the divine*, as one sees it in Vermeer's *Woman in Blue Reading a Letter*, or in Newton's *Principia*, or in *Paradise Lost*. The priest, novelist, and sociologist Andrew Greeley wrote, in line with Aquinian and Miltonian theology, and against Pauline, Augustinian, Cartesian, Spinozan, and Kantian theology stressing the nastiness of *eros*, that "God lurks in aroused human love and reveals Himself to us through it."[31]

5

LOVE AND THE TRANSCENDENT

Love reaches up to God.

In *The Four Loves* (1960) C. S. Lewis contrasts "need-love" like that of a small child for its mother with "gift-love" like that of a mother for her small child and "appreciation-love" like that of a mother and child for each other in maturity. Need-love expresses a need and dependency; gift-love a desire to serve in fulfillment of one's identity; appreciation-love an admiration, satisfied to view the face forever. Lewis observed that *eros*, one sort of love for human beings, "transforms what is *par excellence* a Need-pleasure [that is, mere lust or chemistry] into the most Appreciative of all pleasures," as the lover grows to see the beloved as desirable in himself.[1]

But the point would apply to the love of any need-pleasuring thing that one comes to savor in a nongluttonous way, as one "appreciates" wine. Such elevation of the form of love can accompany market-using consumption. Not all consumption is unloving. Even a consumption-scorning academic can get a sense of this if she will fondly bring to mind her variorum edition of *Paradise Lost* in her professional library, or her new centrifuge in her laboratory.

Yet the need-love for earthly things is of course dangerous. The theologian David Klemm summarizes Augustine so: "Most people . . . become attached to their objects of desire, and in this way are in fact possessed by them," needing and dependent.[2] It is, Klemm says elsewhere, "a window-shopping of the soul in which I lose myself in desires for shallow and untrue goods."[3] But "those who use their private property for the sake of enjoying God become detached from their goods and thereby possess them well," paradoxically.[4] The attachment we have to the world, the need-love for a fur coat or a trophy wife, is the source of our misery, not of our fulfillment, quite contrary to the tempting glow of pleasure on first acquisition. We arrive in the end at So What? . . . and pack last season's designer dresses off to the resale shop.

In such a system of love, however, the opposite of attachment to earthly pleasures is not detachment, a mere apathy following a rude version of Stoicism. "It is the feeling," Lewis puts it, "which would make a man unwilling to deface a great painting even if he were the last man alive and himself about to die."[5] In the 1950s a little boy threw mustard on a Rembrandt print, and the rich, sophisticated father was amused. Someone who loved God's world would have scolded him.

Love calls us, said Richard Wilbur, to the things of this world. It is a love appreciating the world, yet not dependent on it, which sees the spark of the divine in presentness, the sacred in the profane, the lovingly exercised "pressure" of which Chesterton spoke that keeps worldly things in existence continuously. And Hopkins: "He fathers-forth whose beauty is past change: / Praise him."

The modern, post-Romantic, stoic-materialist impulse is to set aside Augustine, C. S. Lewis, and Richard Wilbur, that God stuff, as superstitious nonsense—after all, the real point is the secular loving of others, right? We are put on this planet to help other people, yes? Surveys inquiring into the meaning of life regularly evoke that one as a response. You can be a good person, entirely loving, without loving something transcendent, yes?

No, not in the Christian view of love, or even in a non-Christian philosophy beyond altruistic hedonism. The theologian William Schweiker notes that "overhumanization," the modern urge to "subdue any 'outside' to the human project," undervalues transcendence.[6] "High modernity aims to dignify human existence and yet, ironically, dislodges human worth from any source other than the mechanisms of social power."[7] In 1942 Weil wrote,

> The collective is the root of all idolatry. This is what chains us to the earth. . . . It is only by entering the transcendental, the supernatural, the authentically spiritual order that man rises above the social. . . . The service of the false God (of the social Beast under whatever form it may be) purifies evil by eliminating its horror. Nothing seems evil to those who serve it except failure in its service. . . .

A Pharisee is someone who is virtuous out of obedience to the Great Beast [of the collective]. . . . Rootedness lies in something other than the social.[8]

In other words, the problem with setting aside "*God* is God" is that then the Great Beast of Society, or My Holier-Than-Thou Self, not to speak of SUVs and antique houses and young lovers, become god substitutes. In the Christian view, from Roman to Quaker, pride is the problem. It is the same, by the way, in Islam, which regards *shirk,* idolatry, as the master sin. The god (al-Lah) is god, not wealth or al-Uzza the Mighty One of Nakhlah. To engage in idolatry is to be separated from the true God, which is the point of the terrible punishments for setting up idols discussed in the Pentateuch. What distorts New Age spirituality in its merely therapeutic forms is this apotheosis of the self, what is good for the self-esteem of moi and my friends in Marin County. It sets up Moi as a proud little god. To put to a new use the old tag: in materialism *Homo homini deus.* Man becomes to Man a god.

But on the contrary *God,* that primal Thou, that Holiness immeasurably different from humanity yet immanent in the universe, and always the proper object of striving, is God. Erasmus of Rotterdam did not lack a sense of humor, but remarked soberly of the Latin tag, *Homo homini deus,* "Among Christians the name of God ought not to be given to any mortal man even in jest."[9] The original import of "man is to man a god," Erasmus explains, is to give "divine honors to those who conferred benefits." Gods are, so to speak, ring-givers, and so a human ring-giver is to be called a "god." In monotheism this will not do. As Schweiker says, his (and my) "teleological humanism specifies that the source of goodness is wider than human projects and powers and so [wider than the modern] nightfall of values."[10]

Monotheism is not merely numerical. What seems to us the bizarre practice of Roman emperors declaring themselves divine is no theological problem at all when gods are *N*. What Karl Jaspers called the "axial" faiths did bring something new during the millennium before and around the time of Christ, among them Christianity itself. They recommended ethical universalism, they rejected the me-centeredness of magic, and above all they emphasized the difference between the ordinary world and a truer realm of faith and hope. Our Father who art in heaven, *hallowed* be thy name. Dreaded, and different and detached from us. The word translated into English as "holy"/ "hallowed" is the Hebrew Bible's *kadosh,* meaning also "set apart." Christianity in its various forms is sociologically speaking merely one of these faiths, along with Islam and Judaism and Zoroastrianism and some versions of Hinduism, and even Buddhism and Taoism and Confucianism (the last three god-absent but universalistic and certainly antimagical).

The nonaxial, "archaic," nonuniversalistic faiths make ring-giving people—chieftains, ancestors, politicians, priests—into gods-to-be-worshiped. Thus the three Japanese generals who founded in the late six-teenth century the Tokugawa shogunate were all literally worshiped afterward, in elaborate temples at which one can still pray. Likewise the first restored Meiji emperor has a gigantic shrine in Tokyo, and his General Nogi, who with his wife committed hara-kiri when in 1912 the emperor died, has a smaller one. Robert Bellah remarks after recounting these facts that "there is nothing surprising in the divinization of human beings in an archaic cul-ture," by which he means a nonaxial culture, that is, one "affirming the world as it is rather than holding it in tension with ultimate reality."[11]

A nonaxial culture lacks attachment to a spiritual ultimate. Well short of the ultimate, a society without an ultimate has many gods to tend each piece of the world and the heavens. By contrast to such polytheism or ancestor worship or a civic religion such as Confucianism, the god of monotheists is jealous. God is on one view of the matter separated from the world, and bids us look upward. What starts in Judaism perhaps as an early nationalism of the Jews trapped between Philistines and Egyptians and Assyrians, and was certainly in Islam a later nationalism of the Arabs trapped between Byzan-tines and Persians, becomes theological. *Our* god is *The* God, *al-Lah.* In the beginning was the Word.

And to our good, it is said. The chief sin against the Spirit, Augustine declared, is indeed pride. "Pride" does not here mean ordinary self-respect, or even self-love in a modest, God-fearing way, or else there would be no justice in "love thy neighbor *as thyself.*" The sinful sort of pride is making oneself into a proud little god.

Even a saintly person can fall prey to "theological pride," the worst and last temptation. An old *New Yorker* cartoon shows two monks walking in the cloister, one declaring to the other, "But I *am* holier than thou!" The Angli-can divine of the late sixteenth century Richard Hooker put the joke this way: "The fall of angels doth make it almost a question whether we might not need a preservative still, lest we should haply wax proud that we are not proud."[12] The Anglicans of Hooker's day were complaining of two prideful doctrines. The Puritan said proudly that he was among the saints elected by

God at the beginning. Whence proud Cromwell guilty of his country's blood—and proud reborn Christians now, waiting for the Rapture. The Papists held a doctrine of perfect justification by the soul's infusion with righteousness and therefore salvation not from the continuing grace of God but salvation earned and merited. Whence proud priests, as meritorious purveyors of merit, from which simony and child abuse.[13]

In the making of a nonprideful character the central step is to love *God*— not moi or Heathcliff or any other treasure on earth, where moth and rust doth corrupt, and where thieves break in. Art or the revolution or science cannot really "serve the function of religion," as nonreligious people are always supposing, though of course they do serve similar psychological functions. "No," declares James Wood, an apostate but someone who understands religion; "the great 'strength' of Christianity is not that it offers medicines, but that it is true."[14]

Worshiping idols here below is bad for our souls. And it is impractical, a fragility of goodness. "There are false suns," writes Iris Murdoch, "easier to gaze upon and far more comforting than the true one."[15] The problem is that such things pass. The realest of things are in this sense mirages. "Man is in love and loves what vanishes," said Yeats. As Martha Nussbaum puts it, "By ascribing value to *philia* [love as friendship] in a conception of the good life, we make ourselves more vulnerable to loss."[16] Lovers leave, friends move away, riches get spent. And then what? If your life plan consists of accumulating SUVs and antique houses and young lovers, what *is* the point?

The great thief is death itself. It is a fearful thing to love what death can touch.[17] Whom do you love and who loves you? He will die, or you will, and therefore in one of you each bit of love will be redeemed in sorrow. "These lovely [earthly] things," wrote St. Augustine, "go their way and are no more; and they rend the soul with desires that can destroy it. . . . But in them is no repose, because they do not abide."[18] The other side of mortal love is mortal loss, every time.

One solution is to deny the fragility of love. And one way of denying it is not to have love in the first place, not to care about the lovely things and the beloved people. It is said that this is the Buddhist solution, the rejection of worldly attachment. It is an element in much Western thought as well, influenced by Stoicism. An alternative way of denying the fragility is to imagine a heaven, as the Abrahamic religions do. Its popular if theologically unsound form is a tale of benevolent dead people acting as angels to the living, such as Marley's ghost in *A Christmas Carol*. The more sophisticated Christian's attitude toward love is tragic. The tragedy of God crucified stands for all the impermanences of our loving lives.

Nussbaum admires the solution of pagan Aristotle. "There is a beauty," she says, "in the willingness to love someone in the face of love's instability and worldliness that is absent from a completely trustworthy love."[19] One accepts the tragedy and goes on loving nonetheless. But then isn't one's god beauty, or perhaps endurance, or flexibility? The later, Christian step, at least in its theologically sophisticated forms, is to bring out into the open what is implicit in the noblest pagan solutions, an implicit love of God—or, to address the growing unease of my dear nonbelieving readers, an implicit love of some other transcendent and undying goal, such as art or science or evolution or the environment or the life force or the revolution or baseball. A love for the spark of the divine translates the lover into a higher and permanent realm.

Dylan Thomas on the contrary refused to mourn the death, by fire, of a child in London. "I shall not murder / The mankind of her going with a grave truth" is a pagan and anti-Sunday-school declaration, noble and humanistic, admiring of the masculine virtues. It finds a transcendent in stoic humanism. But it lacks a theology, the grave truths, the truths of the grave. Salvation requires the transcendent and a theology, that is, a purpose to life that includes an account of why it should matter. I believe this is as true of a modern bourgeois life as it is of any other. Maybe more. You rich person in a modern economy have time to think.

Think then of this: Paul of Tarsus, and before him Jesus of Nazareth, and a little before him Rabbi Hillel, and long before them all Moses himself said, "Thou shalt love the Lord thy God with all thy heart, and with all thy soul, and with all thy mind. This is the first and greatest commandment." It is literally: "I am the Lord thy God," amplified by the second, "Thou shalt have no other gods before me"; and by the third and fourth about graven images and the Sabbath. "And the [new] second is like unto it, Thou shalt love thy neighbor as thyself." That is a summary of commandments five through ten, relating to other people rather than to God. "On these two commandments hang all the law and the prophets."[20]

The commandments of Moses are in summary (1) God is god, which is to say there *is* a transcendent, a sacred, a *kadosh*. And (2) Love thy neighbor as thyself, which is to say that a transcendent entails an ethical universe applying to the level of the nonsacred, the profane. The sacred and the profane in Abrahamic religions are connected by God's creation—they are separated but they are not alternatives. Your neighbor, too, is in the community of God's creatures, to be loved on this account if you love God. That is the transcending secular.

At least so people think who are unwilling to adopt the twentieth century's nihilistic materialism. Add even to the materialism a dash of Stoicism, as the most proudly materialist among us do, and you find yourself back to a transcendent, a free man's worship.

In 1952 Paul Tillich called Stoicism "the only real alternative to Christianity in the Western world."[21] (Well . . . Judaism? Buddhism? Socialism? Art?) Noble in its way, Stoicism can freeze into a sentimental posture of antisentimentality, being tough, Hemingway's "grace under pressure." Weil called such an attitude "the Roman caricature of [Greek] Stoicism."[22] In its modern American form, which is influenced by the Christian evaluation of the individual soul but is not in other ways Christian, such Stoicism has dropped even the classical elitism of the Wise Man. *Any* American can be a stoic hero, because, as Tillich the immigrant to the New World explains, "the individual is an infinitely significant representation of the universe."[23] The Romantic I in America contains multitudes. But there it is again, suddenly—a transcendent, the People.

Even in a wholly secular way of thinking, love of sublunary persons or things is good or bad depending on its association with the other virtues. This is the point Raja Halwani makes in discussing Nel Noddings's ethics of "care," that is, the argument that love is primary. Critics of Noddings have argued that ethics cannot be collapsed into care—or else the justice of universal ethics or the courage of autonomy necessary for human flourishing are damaged.[24]

Similarly, Adam Smith writes in a well-known passage that if love for our fellow humans were all we had to depend on, then the extermination of the Chinese would trouble us less, really, than the loss of a little finger.[25] It takes a sense of abstract justice, a virtue separate from love and not translatable into it, to care for a strange people you have never seen and can never love. The moral sentiment of justice impels the man within to scold a self that is so selfish as to save the finger rather than the entire race of Chinese. "What is it," he asks, "which prompts the generous upon all occasions and the mean upon many to sacrifice their own interests to the greater interests of others?

It is not ... that feeble spark of benevolence. ... It is reason, principle, conscience, the inhabitant of the breast. ... The natural misrepresentations of self-love can be corrected only by the eye of this impartial spectator."[26] It is the bundled virtues in a soul which ascend. I say "ascend" to my fellow believers in a loving and living God.

But to you others I have at least a practical suggestion, that love without other virtues is sin and simulacrum. An absorbing love of a child without the virtue of justice, for example, makes the child into a mere source of satisfaction for its mother. You know mothers like this. She "loves" her child, doubtless. But she loves him rather in the way that Screwtape—the imagined middle-management devil giving advice to a junior devil in C. S. Lewis's *The Screwtape Letters*—describes the "love" his fellow devils have for human souls: "To us a human is primarily food; our aim is the absorption of its will into ours, the increase of our own area of selfhood at its expense."[27] Such increasing of the area of selfhood—in a word, pride—changes love into domination.

"A love relationship," Murdoch observed, "can occasion extreme selfishness and possessive violence, the attempt to dominate the other ... so that it is no longer separate; or it can prompt a process of unselfing wherein the lover learns to see, and cherish and respect, what is not himself."[28] The political theorist Joan Tronto warns likewise about unbalanced and absorbing "love." She criticizes the communitarians like Nel Noddings and Elizabeth Fox-Genovese for imagining that love conquers all. "Without strong conceptions of right, care-givers are apt to see the world only from their own perspective and to stifle diversity and otherness."[29] Mother knows best. Yet on the other hand, "justice without a notion of care is incomplete."[30]

SWEET LOVE VS. INTEREST

So-called Samuelsonian economics is the main sort at American universities today. The only way it can acknowledge love is to reduce it to food for the implicitly male and proud lover, on a par with the other "goods" he consumes, such as ice cream or apartment space or amusing gadgets from Brookstone. Screwtape in fact is suspicious of the very existence of "love," and reinterprets it as interest. God's "love" for human beings "of course, is an impossibility.... All his talk about Love must be a disguise for something else—He must have some *real* motive.... What does he stand to make out of them?"[1]

A Samuelsonian economist will say, "It's easy to include 'love' in economics. Just put the beloved's utility into the lover's utility function, $U_{Lover}(\text{Stuff}_{Lover}, \text{Utility}_{Beloved})$." Neat. Hobbes, who seems to have had in his own life little to do with love, wrote in this economistic way in 1651: "That which men desire they are also said to Love.... so that desire and love are the same thing.... But whatsoever is the object of any man's appetite or desire, that is it which he for his part calleth Good."[2] Or, the modern economists say, "goods." But to adopt such a vocabulary is to absorb the beloved into the psyche of the lover, as so much utility-making motivation. Aquinas called it "concupiscent love"—"as when we love wine, wishing to enjoy its sweetness, or when we love some person for our own purposes of pleasure."[3] It can be virtuous or not depending on its object. But it is not the highest love unless it ascends: "Rare is the love of goods," David Klemm remarks, "that remains true to the love of God as the final resting place of the heart's desire."[4]

The philosopher Michael Stocker notes that a psychological egotist of the sort commended in modern economics could get the pleasure from the things lovers do, "have absorbing talks, make love, eat delicious meals, see interesting films, and so on, and so on," but would not love: "For it is essential to the very concept of love to care for the beloved.... To the extent that I act ... towards you with the final goal of getting pleasure ... I do not act for your sake.... What is lacking in these theories is simply—or not so simply—the person. For love, friendship, affection, fellow feeling, and community all require that the other person be an essential part of what is valued."[5] And the beloved must be a living value in himself. If you love him out of pride or mere vanity he is reduced to a thing, a mirror, no person. Love is therefore not the same thing as mere absorbing altruism. You need to explain this to the economists and other utilitarians.

Your mother loves you, in one restricted sense, for the altruistic pleasure you provide to her. When you graduated from college she got utilitarian pleasure in two ways. First, she got some pleasure directly—that she is the mother of such a brilliant child. It reflected on her own brilliance, you see, or on her own excellence in mothering. It added to her utility-account some points earned, straightforward pleasure, like frequent-flyer mileage.

And, second, she got some pleasure indirectly, because you did so well—for yourself, to be sure, *yet as a pleasure to her*. It is not for your sake. It is as though you were happy and accomplished *for her*. Even if no one else knew that you had graduated, she would know, and know the material pleasure and higher satisfactions your education would give you, and would be glad for *her* sake. It was "on her account," as the revealingly bourgeois expression says. That is, she absorbs your utility into hers. If you are happy, she is happy, but derivatively. It is a return on her capital investment in motherhood. It's still a matter of points earned for her utility.

Economists think this is a complete description of your mother's love. Hallmark could make a card for the economist to send to his mother: "Mom, I maximize your utility." The great Gary Becker of the University of Chicago, for example, seems to think in this fashion, as do his numerous followers. "We assume that children have the same utility function as their parents," Becker wrote in a classic paper with Nigel Tomes, "and are produced without mating, or asexually. A given family then maintains its identity indefinitely, and its fortunes can be followed over as many generations as desired. Asexual reproduction could be replaced without any effect on the analysis by perfect assortative mating: each person, in effect, then mates with his own image"[6] Well. So much for happy and loving families, Tolstoy be damned.

Becker is rather more careful than his followers, actually, noting in an earlier paper that "loving someone usually involves caring about what happens to him or her." He realizes that love—or as he usually styles it, with embarrassed male scare quotes, "love"—entails more than "caring" in his restricted sense: "If M cares about F, M's utility would depend on the commodity consumption of F as well as on his own." This is a attempt to acknowledge the evident truth that much of consumption and income-earning is *on behalf* of someone not the direct purchaser or income earner. After all, in the average American family with children about 35 percent of expenditure is directed at the kids.[7] Moms are not buying all those frozen pizzas to feed *themselves*.

But anyway, Becker in this paper is willing to reduce a family to the husband's—sorry, I mean "M's"—utility, using a methodological twist characteristic of Chicago economics: "If one member of the household—the 'head'—cares enough about other members to transfer resources to them, this household would act *as if* it maximized the 'head's' preference function."[8] That's nice so long as you're not worried about reinventing the common-law doctrine of *feme covert* in mathematical form.

Believe me, as myself a Chicago School economist, I attest that such a strange view has its uses for science. Really, it does. I've written whole books, scores of professional papers, going further, triumphantly concluding that *all* you need for historical explanation is "maximum utility."

But I was wrong. The economist's theory is not complete. For one thing, the behaviorism and positivism that often go along with utilitarianism are an unnecessary narrowing of the scientific evidence. Whitehead remarked in 1938 that "in such behavioristic doctrines, importance and expression must be banished and can never be intelligently employed." He added cleverly: "A consistent behaviorist cannot feel it important to refute my statement. He can only behave."[9] In 1982 Stuart Hampshire declared that our knowledge of our own minds, including ethical intentions, "deserves the title of knowledge no less than the kind of knowledge of past, present and future states of the world we derive from perception, from memory and from inductive inference."[10]

As the feminist philosopher Virginia Held notes, relationships "are not reducible to the properties of individual entities that can be observed by an outsider and mapped into a causal scientific framework."[11] She may be giving too much away: the *meaning* of a relationship, I repeat, is just as "scientific" as is a budget constraint. We do not have to go on forever and ever accepting the definition of "scientific" that happened to be popular among certain English and Austrian academic philosophers around 1922. Your love for your son is real and scientific and motivational, though in some circumstances a behaviorist psychologist watching you from a great height might have quite a lot of trouble "observing" it.

More important, treating others as "inputs into a self's utility function," as Becker and Tomes put it, is to treat the others as means, not as ends. Immanuel Kant said two centuries ago in effect that your mother, if she is truly and fully loving, loves you *as an end, for your own sweet sake.* You may be a rotten kid, an ax-murderer on death row. You're not even a college graduate. You give her "nothing but grief," as we say. In all the indirect, derivative ways you are a catastrophe. And yet she goes on loving you, and stands wailing in front of the prison on the night of your execution. Economists need to understand what everyone else already understands, and what the economists themselves understood before they went to graduate school, that such love is of course commonplace. It is common in your own blessed mother, and everywhere in most mothers and fathers and children and friends.

You see it, too, in the doctor's love for healing, in the engineer's for building, in the soldier's for the fatherland, in the economic scientist's for the advance of economic science, down in the marketplace and up in the cathedral. As the economist Andrew Yuengert puts it, "Without ultimate ends, there is no reason to be an economic researcher: economics is *for* ethics."[12] To be sure, there is routine form-filling in being a doctor and insincere uses of statistical significance in being an economics scientist. But without loving and transcendent ends such lives would have no point. Alasdair MacIntyre makes a distinction between goods "internal to a practice," like being a good scientist, and external, such as getting the Nobel Prize or getting rich. He notes that utilitarianism, even in so saintly a utilitarian as John Stuart Mill, cannot admit the distinction.[13]

Such loves, or internal goods, defeat the economistic view that all virtues can be collapsed into utility. Utility is the measure of an ends-means logic, what I am calling Prudence Only. *Loving* an end goes beyond means. Whatever happiness of identity a painter earns may be measured by the income he gives up. But that does not make the happiness the same thing as the income.[14] The happiness is comparable to the happiness of identity a skillful truck driver earns or a skillful tennis player, whether poorly or well paid.

The economist Amartya Sen speaks of a "duality" in ethics between what he calls "well-being," which is the utilitarian idea of people as pots into which pleasure is dumped, and "agency."[15] Agency is "the ability to form goals, commitments, values, etc." It "can well be geared to considerations not covered— at least not *fully* covered—by his or her own well-being." But I would call this "agency" the virtues of faith and hope and justice and, above all, love.

The philosopher David Schmidtz likewise speaks about two separate "rational" sources of altruism. He means "economistic" when he writes "rational." One source he calls "concern" for others, "which is to say [that the beloved's] welfare enters the picture through our preference function," that is, through our tastes for pleasures. It is the Beckerian notion of "caring." Schmidtz observes that there is quite a different altruism, too, a nobler one on its face, which he calls "respect," by which we constrain ourselves in regard to the beloved. "We manifest *concern* for people when we care about how life is treating them (so to speak), whereas we manifest *respect* for people when we care about how *we* are treating them, and constrain ourselves accordingly."[16] An economist would say that one has preferences over bundles of goods to be consumed ("concern"), but also over the constraints to be observed ("respect").

But to these usefully distinguished sources of caring I would add a third and a glorious one—one Schmidtz would acknowledge, of course, if he were not intent in the article on showing a "selfish" rationale for love. The third is *sheer* love, appreciation for the beloved, the expression here below of agape/*caritas*/holy charity. That it is sheer does not make it unanalyzable. Joan Tronto analyzes the ethics of care as politics, seeing in the ethical use of sheer love an attentiveness, a responsibility, a competence, and a responsiveness.[17] Attentiveness is temperance and humility in the face of the plight of others. Competence is a species of prudence. Responsibility arises from human solidarity, keeping faith with who we are. And responsiveness is the justice of attending to others. That is, love is not reducible to utility, and is a virtue only when in context with other virtues: temperance, humility, prudence, justice, solidarity, faith.

Of course. Only an economist or an evolutionary psychologist would think otherwise, and put embarrassed quotation marks around the very word "love," and then reduce it to gain. The most extreme of the evolution-ary psychologists claim that love itself is an evolutionary result of Prudence Only, this time of the very genes themselves. Consider Steven Pinker in 1997 on the rationality of friendship: "Now that you value the person, they should value you even more . . . because of your stake in rescuing him or her from hard times. . . . This runaway process is what we call friendship."[18]

No, Steven, it is what we call self-absorption. The cognitive philosopher Jerry Fodor remarks of Pinker's one-factor theory: "A concern to propagate one's genes would rationalize one's acting to promote one's children's wel-fare; but so too would an interest in one's children's welfare. Not all of one's motives could be instrumental, after all; there must be some things that one cares for just for their own sakes. Why, indeed, mightn't there be quite a few such things? Why shouldn't one's children be among them?"[19] He quotes Pinker on the evolutionary explanation for why we humans like stories, namely, that they provide useful tips for life, as, for example, to someone in Hamlet's fix: "What are the options if I were to suspect that my uncle killed my father, took his position, and married my mother? Good question." Star-tlingly, Pinker does not appear to be joking here. It's unintentionally funny, this "scientific" attempt to get along without sheer love, or sheer courage, or to get along without the aesthetic pleasure of stories reflecting faith and hope.

Even the admirable Robert Nozick falls prey to the reductionism of socio- and psycho- and evolutionary- and brain-science-biology. But char-acteristically he has wise doubts. "Someone could agree that ethics origi-nates in the function of coordinating activity to mutual benefit, yet hold that ethics now is valuable because of additional functions that it has acquired."[20] She certainly could.

In the analysis of the philosopher Harry Frankfurt this sheer love has "four main conceptually necessary features."[21] It must be "a disinterested concern for the well-being or flourishing of the person who is loved." That's the main point, and the way the utility-driven mother imagined by econo-mists is less than perfectly loving. Her utility function reflects precisely, and only, self-interest.

Frankfurt, by the way, equivocates between "love" as love of persons and "love" also of nonpersons such as the Revolution or Art or God. Thus he adds that love is "ineluctably personal," which I believe would be better expressed as "ineluctably particular." Anyway, the person (or transcendent thing) "is loved for himself or for herself, and not as an instance of type." One loves Harriet particularly, not incidentally as a type of "woman" or "Vermonter," however much one might admire those types. As Nozick puts it, "The love is not transferable to someone else with the same characteristics. . . . One loves the particular person one actually encountered. . . . Love is historical."[22]

And "the lover identifies with his beloved." The two share so much that the line between their selves is forgotten. A friend, said Aristotle, is another self. And finally "loving entails *constraints* on the will. It is not simply up to us." Our love for our children, though involuntary and often enough unreciprocated, is glorious. But it must be a give-and-take, acknowledging the constraints imposed by the children. "No, Ma. We'd better have Thanksgiving this year at my mother-in-law's house." The constraining is not *simply* up to us, observe, though it can and should be *self*-disciplined, too, if it is to be a virtue rather than merely an unrestrained and animal passion.

So: disinterested, particular, identifying, and constraining. None of these four fits an epicurean, utilitarian, pleasuring definition of love. The economist's Maximum-Utility Man, Mr. Max U, is above all self-interested. He couldn't care less if the item satisfying his interest is this particular one. He has no identity himself to project onto the beloved. And he regards all constraints on utility maximization as bad. "The hedonistic conception of man," Thorstein Veblen thundered in 1898, "is that of a lightning calculator of pleasures and pains, who oscillates like a homogenous globule of happiness under the influence of stimuli that shift him about the area, but leave him intact. He has neither antecedent or consequent. He is an isolated, definitive human datum."[23]

If the kid cries too much, declares our Max, the isolated, self-interested man, regardless of whether he is the father, let us send him to probable death in an eighteenth-century orphanage, since this particular kid is fungible with others. A house "filled with domestic cares and the noise of children" would make a poor place for discoursing on social justice and the raising of children. Thus on five occasions did Jean-Jacques Rousseau act, that great pre-Romantic teacher of good behavior in love and education.

Samuelsonian economics takes need-love, or more narrowly goods-and-services-concupiscence, as all love, and calls it pleasure or utility. But, as has been repeatedly discovered in experimental and observational studies, the argument fails even in its own terms. For example, suppose a Samuelsonian economist says that contributions to public goods—say, the British Lifeboat Service—is utility-based, in the sense that it is motivated *altruistically,* by a desire to make sure there are enough lifeboats. That is, the economic agent gives to the lifeboat fund *not* to cover the highly unlikely event that he himself might otherwise drown—*pace* Steven Pinker—but because many *other* people will. He is public spirited, altruistic.

Yet he is still a Max U fellow: he gets utility from contemplating the ample provision of lifeboats. It's like your mother Maxine U getting pleasure from your graduation. If she could get the graduation without spending a dime on you, all the better, right? Such an attitude is an ethical improvement over screw-you individualism of a Steinerian or Randian or Pinkerian sort. But it seems to be empirically false. In 1993 Richard Sugden, for example, noted that a plain implication of Max U altruism is that a pound note given by Max U would be a perfect substitute for a pound given by anyone else, at least in Mr. U's opinion. So Max U would *of course* free ride on other people's contributions to lifeboats. Every time. According to Sugden's empirical work on the lifeboat fund, however, people in Britain do not so free ride.

Which is evident: there *is* such a fund, and it does very well in bequests and in coins dropped into collection jars in pubs. Evidently British people feel that free riding in such a case would be bad—which is not a sentiment that would motivate a Max U-er. Sugden and others have shown repeatedly that people do not view the contributions of others as fungible pound for pound with their own contributions. People take the view that there is something ineluctably particular about *their* giving. So also in blood donations and in going over the top at the Somme. Altruistic hedonism does not look like a very good explanation of human solidarity and courage.[24]

You could reply that the lifeboat-givers or the blood donors or the voters down at the polling place get utility from the sheer act of giving their money or time without recompense. The love for God, in the altruistic hedonist view, is no different from satisfying an itch or buying a rugby shirt. Therefore economists studying the economics of religion, even if they are themselves believers, sometimes stop their concerns at explaining church attendance with the same tools one would use for explaining visits to the mall. But it is merely a pointless renaming of love—or justice or faith or some other virtue of steadfastness. As Lewis remarks, "one must be outside the world of love, of all loves, before one thus calculates."[25]

Lewis offers a ladder of love. The four loves human and divine are, climbing upward: affection, human sexual desiring (*eros*), human friendship (*philia*), and finally charity, that is, agape. The lowest is one's love for nonhumans, such as a dog or a thing. The highest includes, Aquinas says, a sacred version of friendship, the astonishing friendship between unequals of humans and God. Agape is God's gift, notes Lewis, following orthodoxy since Augustine, for God "can awaken in man, towards Himself, a supernatural Appreciative love." The proud blasphemy that we are loved for our evident merits dissolves into "a full, childlike and delighted acceptance of our Need. . . . We become 'jolly beggars.'"

The other three loves for humans, and I suppose also the best love for nonhumans, Lewis would group under "natural loves." These are not to be disdained. But they need to have that touch of transcendent agape, transcendent "charity," if love "is to be kept sweet."[26] "Whatsoever love elects to bless," says Richard Wilbur, "Brims to a sweet excess / That can without depletion overflow."[27] The overflow gives a point to a virtuous life, whether medieval or socialist or bourgeois.

7

BOURGEOIS ECONOMISTS AGAINST LOVE

Ah, yes. Bourgeois virtues. Remember them? At this juncture the male, prudent, scientific, economistic, and materialist stoic breaks into indignant rhetorical questions: "Who cares about sweetness? 'Sour' tastes fine to me. Point, schmoit. What possibly could love have to do with the hard world of a commercial economy? Let's get practical here. Can't we do just fine in a world of bourgeois business without love? Isn't that the, uh, point of economics? Isn't love something for weekends and the Home?" Or as Yeats said in 1909, "The Catholic Church created a system only possible for saints. . . . Its definition of the good was narrow, but it did not set out to make shopkeepers."[1]

Economics since its invention as a system of thought in the eighteenth century has tried to "economize on love," that is, to get along without it, that is, to justify shopkeepers far removed from saintly or poetic love. Economics has elevated prudence, an androgynous virtue counted good in both men and women as stereotypically viewed, into the only spring of action. Tracing it back to Epicurus, Alfred North Whitehead complained in 1938 that "this basis for philosophical understanding is analogous to an endeavor to elucidate the sociology of modern civilization as wholly derivative from the traffic signals on the main roads. The motions of the cars are conditioned by these signals. But the signals are not the reason for the traffic."[2]

The way most economists do their job is to ask, Where's the prudence? "The rudimentary hardheadedness attributed to them by modern economics," as Sen puts it, is the only virtue in the economist's world.[3] When in the 1960s I wanted to show that Victorian Britain did not fail economically I used

Prudence Only calculations of productivity to calculate that there was no residual to be accounted for by causes other than Prudence. When in the 1970s I wanted to show that medieval English open fields were insurance in an age of terrifying uncertainty I used Prudence Only calculations of portfolio balance to show that Prudence sufficed to explain the scattering of a peasant's plots of land. When in the 1980s I wanted to show how to teach economics through applied examples rather than useless theorem-proving—which unfortunately has since then triumphed in advanced and some elementary economic education—I used Prudence Only arguments throughout, though I was beginning in that decade to worry that they might not suffice.

Adam Smith asserted in 1776 that "what is prudence in the conduct of every private family can scarce be folly in that of a great kingdom."[4] A splendidly useful principle. Hardheaded. No talk of love, or of any other virtue than prudence. Smith, however, understood well what later economists have gradually come to forget. After all, said Smith as early as 1759, we want people to have a balanced set of virtues, including even love, not *merely* prudence, and this for all purposes, sacred, profane, business, pleasure, the good, the useful, the wide world, and the home, too. All. Annette Baier argues in "What Do Women Want in a Moral Theory?" that love and obligation, which are both necessary for a society to survive, arise from "appropriate trust."[5]

The economist and historian Alexander Field has based a similar argument on biology. He notes that on meeting a stranger in the desert with bread and water that you want, you do not simply kill him. Why not? Sheer self-interest implies you would, and if you would, he would, too, in anticipation, and the game's afoot. Once you and he have chatted a while and built up trust, naturally, you will refrain. But how does trust get a chance? How did it originate?

Field argues that it originates from "modules inhibiting intraspecific violence," that is, from a very long evolution of a taboo on hurting one's own kind.[6] The "failure to harm" nonkin is hardwired into animals. It evolved from selection at the level of the group, Field argues, not the individual. It's better for you as a behavioral egoist to kill the man you meet in the desert. But of course you are inhibited in doing so, because you are not in fact such an egoist: that's best for the human species.

I remember driving once in Amherst past a woman walking toward me on the verge, and the strange thought entering, "Suppose I run her down?" I didn't, I'm very glad to report. But there it was, the potential for intraspecific violence even in a very peaceable and law-abiding woman. André Gide's novel of 1914, *Lafcadio's Adventures*, turns on the utterly point-less murder of a stranger, pushing him off a speeding train, just to see it done. It happens.

But Field's point is that usually it does *not* happen. Considering the opportunities to harm, the inhibitions to doing so must be powerful indeed. For my purposes it doesn't matter whether the inhibitions come from socialization or from biology. Anyway—and perfectly obviously—we are equipped with desires for both the sacred and the profane, mutually rein-forcing and completing. One of the sacred computer chips in our brains or one of the sacred virtues in our characters is "being nice and trusting."

Adam Smith was not, it seems, a particularly religious man. But he was, in his only regular academic job, at Glasgow University ages 28 to 41, a pro-fessor of moral philosophy, and took his assignment seriously. After his death, however, his followers came to believe that a profane Prudence, called "Utility," rules. Jeremy Bentham and his followers, and especially his twentieth-century descendents Paul Samuelson, Kenneth Arrow, Milton Friedman, and Gary Becker, are to blame. These are good men, great scien-tists, beloved teachers and friends of mine. But their confused advocacy of Prudence Only has been a catastrophe for the science that Adam Smith inaugurated. No need, declare the economists of the late twentieth century, for the non-Prudent virtues—well, maybe a little Justice and Temperance on the side to keep the Prudence on track, but certainly not any need for the sacred, transcendent virtues, such as spiritual love. As Field writes, "To build a discipline on the proposition that [behavioral egoisms] exhaust the range of essential human predispositions is to lead to the unsustainable conclu-sion that there are no cartels, no racial discrimination, no voting, no volun-tary contributions to public goods, and no restraint on first strike (defect) in single play Prisoner's Dilemmas."[7] And no nationalism, no honor, no love, no courtesy between strangers.

In our time the Prudence Only ethic has become, "Maximize stockholder wealth, and by the way make sure that you as the CEO or CFO have a good chunk of it, and a little inside knowledge about its present value." You will find some ethicists in business schools arguing that the reason to be just or loving or temperate is precisely that it is prudent. Your stock options will be worth more if you do not sexually abuse your employees and cheat your customers. Virtue makes more money, doing well by doing good.

This is to miss the point of being virtuous. The point of a life exercising the virtue of love, for example, is its transcendence, not the stock options conferred on one who successfully lies about his commitment to the transcendent. In a famous article Milton Friedman argued, as the title put it, that "the social responsibility of business is to increase its profits."[8] Milton argued that a society with more wealth can better pursue its transcendent goals, and more wealth is produced by maximizing profits. That's right, and is one crucial argument for capitalism. He further argued that a hired manager for Boeing who improves his social standing in Chicago by getting the corporation to give to the Lyric Opera is stealing money from the stockholders. That's right, too, though there is a contrary economic argument, namely, that the ability to play the noble lord with the stockholders' money is part of executive compensation. The stockholders would have to pay the manager more in cash than they do if they insisted that he not be allowed to give away the corporation's money to worthy causes. But most people who have expressed shock or pleasure at Milton's article have not noticed that he adds a side constraint to the manager's fiduciary duty to the stockholders: "Make as much money as possible *while conforming to the basic rules of the society, both those embodied in law and those embodied in ethical custom.*"[9]

The opposite argument, I just said, is that being honest makes money. As it was expressed in a book on managerial economics, "Unethical behavior is neither consistent with value maximization nor employee self-interest."[10] Wouldn't that be nice, if it were true? The journalist Bennett Daviss wrote in 1999 in the magazine the *Futurist* an article entitled "Profit from Principle," with the subheading "Corporations Are Finding That Social Responsibility Pays Off." "In the new century," Mr. Daviss believes, "companies will grow their profits only by embracing their new role as the engine of positive social change."[11] Image ads spread the Good News.

It's a tough-minded, American idea. A study in 1999 by the Conference Board found that 64 percent of American codes of ethics in businesses are dominated by profits. By contrast 60 percent of the European codes are dominated by "values."[12] When many years ago the Harvard Business School was given more than $20 million to study ethics, it initiated courses that collapsed the virtues into the one good of Prudence, the utility of "stakeholders." Harvard has since then taught thoroughly all the virtue that money can buy.

The point is that Smith got it right and the later economists and calcula-tors have got it wrong. You can't run on prudence and profit alone a family or a church or a community or even—and this is the surprising point—a capitalist economy. In far away Japan some decades before Smith one Miyake Shunro (also known as Miyake Sekian), the director of a newly formed academy for 90 bourgeois students in the merchant city of Osaka, gave his inaugural address on the theme. Tetsuo Najita explains that in Miyake's discussion a profit is "nothing other than an extension of human reason. . . . Indeed, merchants should not even think of their occupation as being profit seeking but as the ethical acting out of the moral principle of 'righteousness' [gi]. When righteousness is acted out in the objective world, Miyake went on, 'profit' emerges effortlessly and 'of its own accord' without passionate disturbances."[13] In 1726 Japan, as only a little less urgently in Europe at the time, the task was to elevate the status of merchants, the lowest of the four classes of the Tokugawa regime. The elevation entailed leveling.

In Europe the priesthood of all believers cast doubt on God-given hier-archy in general, and yielded the radical egalitarianism of, say, Smith or Kant, with precursors a century before in the literal Levelers. One's position in the great chain of being came to be seen as a matter of nurture, not of nature. Thus Smith in that egalitarian year of 1776:

> The difference of natural talents in different men is, in reality, much less than we are aware of. . . . The difference between . . . a philosopher and a common street porter, for example, seems to arise not so much from nature, as from habit, cus-tom, and education. . . . [F]or the first six or eight years of their existence . . . nei-ther their parents nor their playfellows could perceive any remarkable difference. . . . [T]hey come to be employed in very different occupations . . . till at last the vanity of the philosopher is willing to acknowledge scarce any resemblance. . . . By nature a philosopher is not in genius and disposition half so different from a street porter as a mastiff is from a greyhound.[14]

Similarly in Japan, Conrad Totman notes, the seventeenth and especially the eighteenth century witnessed a nascent if minority "belief in universal human potential" and a "defense of callings other than rulership." The mer-chant's son Itō Jinsai (1627–1705) declared in 1683 that "all men are equally men." Another scholarly merchant's son, Nishikawa Joken (1648–1724), wrote even more startlingly, "When all is said and done, there is no ultimate principle that establishes superior and inferior among human beings: the distinctions result from upbringing."[15] Obvious, yes? Not to the men of the seventeenth century, in Europe or Japan.

As also for Smith and the other probourgeois intellectuals of the Enlightenment, the philosophical elevation of the bourgeoisie in Japan was achieved by showing business to be consistent with ethical behavior. As in Europe, it took two centuries or so to become widely accepted. From small beginnings in the late seventeenth and early eighteenth centuries the Japanese gradually reversed the ancient Confucian contempt for merchants, as the Europeans at about the same time reversed their own classical and Christian anticommercial prejudices.

At length in the new East and in the new West you did not need to be a Chinese general or a Confucian bureaucrat, a Buddhist priest or a samurai, a Christian monk or a duke, to be honorable. Najita explains that *gi* (recall Benedict on *gi-ri:* social obligation) meant in Western terms "justice," but with a prudent emphasis on its calculative side, "the mental capacity to be accurate and hence fair, principled, and thus non-arbitrary, . . . the human capacity to know external things, evaluate them, and make intellectual judgments as to what was, or was not, just."[16] A few decades after Miyake Shunro had lectured on bourgeois virtues to the school in Osaka, its new leader declared that "human beings are endowed by heaven at birth with a virtuous essence consisting of compassion, righteousness, propriety, and wisdom." It was a Confucian-based egalitarianism, from which Miyake had deduced—as Confucius himself, hostile to merchants, did not—"Like the stipend of the samurai and the produce of the farmers, the profit of merchants is to be seen as a virtue."[17]

Adam Smith, had he known of these contemporary developments in Japanese thought—though it was, I repeat, a minority movement there—would certainly have agreed, as his latter-day followers in the business-ethics movement do, Robert Solomon, for example. Business requires, Solomon declares, "both ethics and excellence," a motto that would serve for Japanese and American business nowadays on its sweetest behavior. No greed. No crony capitalism. "Less money, fewer clients," as Tom Cruise says in *Jerry McGuire.* No avarice.[18]

A hardened Chicago economist, or just a Chicagoan, might reply, "So? Call me 'greedy' or 'avaricious' if it makes you feel better, but I like my SUV and my mink, and if screwing other people gets me such toys, fine. What do I care about my so-called soul?" To which Zeno the Stoic replied, as Gilbert Murray put it, "Would you yourself really like to be rich and corrupted? To have abundance of pleasure and be a worse man? Apparently, when Zeno's eyes were upon you, it was difficult to say you would."[19] Zeno's Roman-Greek follower Epictetus said, "No man would change [honorable poverty] for disreputable wealth."[20]

It seems so, by the Deathbed Test: what would you wish to remember on your deathbed, more diamond rings consumed or more good deeds done in the world? Drek or mitzvoth? Aristotle wrote that things good by nature are those that "can belong to a person when dead more than alive."[21] "Although therefore riches be a thing which every man wisheth," wrote Hooker in 1593, "yet no man of judgment can esteem it better to be rich, than wise, virtuous, and religious."[22] Unto death.

Leave off if you wish the religious part or the death talk. "The virtuous person's reward is . . . an entire life of satisfying actions," writes Daryl Koehn, "while the vicious person's punishment is a life of actions that produce both unexpected and unintended consequences for himself and others."[23] Even in consequentialist terms, in other words, an instrumental and materialist view of love is a scientific mistake. A loveless economy would not work. And it would be hell. The secular meaning of the Christian word "hell" is personal corruption, which in truth makes ruling in such a figurative place worse, not better, than serving in heaven. "We must picture Hell," writes C. S. Lewis, "as a state in which everyone is perpetually concerned about his own dignity and advancement, . . . where everyone lives the deadly serious passions of envy, self-importance, and resentment."[24]

David Schmidtz sees again into the core here. He notes a mental experiment imagined by another philosopher that we could "pull a lever" to decide whether or not to have scruples. "Many of us would pull a lever that would strengthen our disposition to be honest." But as we actually are after Eden, we are weak. If you profess an Abrahamic religion you can call the weakness "original sin." Or you can argue as Schmidtz does that natural selection has made people, alas, "built to worry about things that can draw blood, not about the decay of their characters."[25]

In *The Invisible Heart* (2001), a finely crafted "economic romance" (*sic*), Russell Roberts makes a similar point about the limits of instrumentalism.

He improves upon a famous mental experiment of Nozick's in which you are asked whether you would like to be hitched up to an "experience machine."

"Superduper neuropsychologists," Nozick had posited, in a tradition going back through Huxley's *Brave New World* and Descartes' thought experiments to Plato's cave, "would stimulate your brain so that you would think and feel you were writing a great novel, or making a friend, or reading an interesting book. All the time you would be floating in a tank, with electrodes attached to your brain. . . . Would you plug in?"[26] In other words, "what else can matter to us, other than how our lives feel from the inside?" Apparently there's something more than instrumental feeling, more than what our good friend Max U cares about. As Nozick remarks in another book, "We are not empty containers or buckets to be stuffed with good things."[27]

Or imagine a "transformation machine," which would make us at the flick of a switch into the lives and characters of Albert Einstein or Queen Elizabeth I, "really." If you were starving on the streets of Calcutta you would instantly agree. But among you, oh comfortably bourgeois readers, any takers?

Roberts sharpens the questions by making clear, in his economist's way, the opportunity cost. His character Sam Gordon is discussing the matter with his class of high-school seniors:

> But there's one detail that I neglected to mention. This imaginary life that you get to experience while on the Dream Machine *must replace your actual life*. You will never wake up. You enter the room today as the teenager you are. You win the Masters, the Nobel Peace prize, surpass the popularity of the Beatles, then you grow old and die. It can be a painless death, preceded by [the dreamt experience of] a glorious old age. . . . But after they unhook the last electrode, . . . they put you into the ground. . . . They cart you away and bring on the next.[28]

"Still interested?" Sam asks his kids. Of course not. Max U would leap at such a chance to achieve—well, at least to "experience"—utility. But you as your actual self would not do so, because you intend to go on being *you*. "While a cat will be satisfied leading an animal's life of sensation and appetite," remarks Daryl Koehn, "a human being needs something more."[29]

The difficulty of life, within limits, is its charm. Sen makes this point with the use of his somewhat veiled term "agency."[30] He speaks of an "agency achievement" that is not reducible to "enhancement of well-being" in a utilitarian sense. His way of putting it sounds like David McClelland's old idea of "need for achievement," that is to say, the need for an identity that strives. No striving, no identity. You would agree to a magic spell to stop a cancer, surely.

If you could repeat your life you might do so, especially if this time you had a chance to get it right. In stories in books and TV you temporarily enter into imagined lives, perhaps not temporarily enough for your own good.

But scarcity in your own life seems essential for a real human life. Imagine you were an Olympian god. Being immortal, you would have no need for the virtues of hope, faith, courage, temperance, or prudence. These make no sense if you, like the Devil, cannot die. Othello stabs Iago, who replies in defiance, referring to the Devil's immortality, "I am cut but do not die." Though then he does. Most virtues are useless to someone who really cannot die. Even on Olympus, admittedly, the virtues of love and justice might have political rewards. But what gives human love its special poignancy, and gives human justice its special dignity, is the limit to life. You love a man *who will die*. You help a woman *who is a mere mortal*. Not being either a cat or an Olympian god you want a real life with real hazards and rewards, not an experience machine. You wish to retain an identity, a Faith and Hope, as you might put it, named You.

You might as well give in and call it a soul.[31]

The late eighteenth-century impulse and especially the utilitarian impulse was to force ethics into a behaviorist and naively scientistic mode, reducing it to some "immensely simple" formula, as one of the virtue ethicists put it. For example, many utilitarians and some Kantians do not want to acknowledge the force of words and free will and inner light. I myself acknowledged these unbehaviorist motivations late, finally realizing that the meaning of a human action, not merely its external appearance, is important for its scientific description.

Virginia Held argues that in ethics "we should pay far more attention . . . to relationships among people, relationships that we cannot see but can be experienced nonetheless."[32] We would not call a mother "virtuous" who felt no emotion in carrying out her duties toward her children. Nor would we call a good Samaritan "good" who saved the drowning victim in order to achieve fame.[33] Or call a business person "ethical" who followed the law out of fear of jail time. Virtue is not merely a matter of observable action. It is dispositional—feeling, for example, love and regret and anguish and joy for our acts of will.

That is, it is a matter of character, *ethos*, exercising one's will to do good, to *be* good. It is a matter of one's soul.

8

LOVE AND THE BOURGEOISIE

At the risk of sounding a bit uncool, I say to the graduating class that your success in life, and the success of our country, is going to depend on the integrity and other qualities of character that you and your contemporaries will continue to develop and demonstrate over the years ahead. . . . I could urge you all to work hard, save, and prosper. And I do. But transcending all else is being principled in how to go about doing those things. . . . And beyond the personal sense of satisfaction, having a reputation for fair dealing is a profoundly practical virtue. We call it "good will" in business and add it to our balance sheets. Trust is at the root of any economic system based on mutually beneficial exchange. . . . Our system works fundamentally on individual fair dealing.
  —Alan Greenspan, 1999

Love figures in any human group, even a capitalist group, understanding "love" in an expanded sense to include more than Aristotle's lower friendships for pleasure and profit. We do not have to be Hobbesians or utilitarians and reduce "love" to self-interest. We can be Stoic or Christian, or followers of Grotius or Adam Smith, and suppose that people care. In fact I'd claim we had better, if we want to be scientific about it.

Disinterested solidarity is necessary for any human activity—even, to take what would seem to be the hardest case, for the playing of a game. It has been discovered mathematically that games such as those contemplated by John Nash, that beautiful mind, cannot be played to mutual profit with Prudence Only rules. For one thing, if the game is finite—even as long as ten moves—it unravels into selfishness. For another, if it is not finite, it has an infinite number of solutions. The second point is known as the Folk Theorem, because no one knows who first devised it—and perhaps because it is so destructive of game theory that no game theorist now will claim it.

As some of the theorists remarked in 1994, "[Infinite] game equilibrium models of rational play lead to an outcome set where players can do almost anything and still be consistent with the theory. The prediction that individuals might do anything from a large set of feasible strategies is neither useful nor precise."[1] Such discoveries were logical, not factual, but they devastated the blackboard claims of Prudence Only to rule the world as we know it. Clever stuff.[2]

And anyone can understand that, say, chess players must adopt this or that rule of the game, such as the rook's move, which is not itself derivable from the prudent pursuit of victory inside the game. Even to play the game, much less to achieve mutual profit, there has to be an outside. To play chess you must have at least the minimal amount of fellow-feeling needed to perform the Alasdair-MacIntyre-like "practice" called "playing a game of chess according to accepted rules." It would wreck the game if, noticing that you would win if you could move your rook diagonally, you announced, "This time I'm going to move my rook as though it were a bishop."

Playing the board game Monopoly under a rule of no side deals, with children who have no grasp of the importance of building houses quickly, is a quite different experience from playing it with adults sophisticated in the game who live in a commercial culture accustomed to contingent contracts. "You sell me New York Avenue for $2000 and I'll throw in two exemptions from rent if you land on any of my properties . . . all right, *four.*"

Alexander Field argues persuasively that "the willingness of substantial numbers of humans to violate the unambiguous predictions of game theory in both cooperating and in engaging in third party punishment underlies our ability to initiate and sustain social order."[3] As noted from far outside the mathematical theory of games, by the philosopher John Searle and the literary critic Stanley Fish, any game depends on interpretive communities, all the way down.[4] And interpretive communities are just that—communities, commonalities, fellow-feeling, solidarity. That is, they are spheres of love.

One can object that disinterested solidarity is not "love." But the stretch is not so great, and it has a purpose. I mean by "solidarity," besides the intense engagement of true love, the mere trust, good humor, neighborliness, respectfulness, cooperativeness, decent intentions of our daily lives.

These can be self-interested in part, just as Aristotle said. When a neighbor becomes bad company we walk away. When a beloved does, we try harder. It is as though love—or any virtue—is a gravitational force weakening with distance from the core. Admittedly, people can be courteous to neighbors and good-humored with fellow game-players merely because they recognize they will be punished if they are not. That's only Prudence.

The question here is whether the gravitational force of Prudence is enough to account for *all* of solidarity, or whether solidarity has an influence from the sphere of Love, or Justice, or Faith. Plainly, as a scientific matter, it does. The solidarity expressed in cheerfully greeting a neighbor is a kind of love. The fleeting solidarity of the deal agreed is a kind of justice. The solidarity of sports fans is a kind of faith.

Off the blackboard and the game board it is becoming increasingly clear that real economies depend on real virtues. If one performs economic experiments on students and other hired victims, the love, justice, temperance, faith, hope, and courage come tumbling out even from the laboratories. A pioneer in the field, Vernon Smith, puts it this way: "laboratory experiments also support reciprocity in two person extensive form games under very unfavorable conditions in which we give the self-interest its best shot: *complete anonymity*. Hence these norms are so strong that half the subjects cooperate without ever knowing the identity of their matched counterpart. Moreover, we can show that this depends on the second mover seeing the payoffs foregone by the first, and therefore knowing what he/she has done for me lately."[5]

Experimental economists are, with economic historians, among the minority of reliably scientific economists—the others tend on their bad days to wander off into meaningless speculation and arbitrary tests of "significance," and they have a lot of bad days. The economic experimentalists would do well to test explicitly for virtues other than Prudence. Substantively speaking, they would then merge with social psychologists, as economic historians have merged with historians.

An economic actor must have a social stage, since no contract can be explicit about every aspect of a complex transaction, or even of a simple transaction. In selling a newspaper to me the newsagent trusts that I won't at the last minute snatch back the money and run out of the store with the paper he has just handed me, or take out a loaded Magnum .45 when he opens the cash register. It's not exactly because I love the newsagent, though a weak form of love develops if I buy from him every day. But it shows a form of justice, surely, and a faithful identity as a law-abiding citizen who does not rely on stealing, who pulls her weight.

A classic paper in 1963 by the legal sociologist Stewart Macaulay studied firms that did business in Wisconsin. He confirmed what everyone in business knows, that business normally depends on a state of trust, not on explicit contracts to be enforced in courts. One large manufacturer of cardboard boxes looked into how many of its orders had no agreement on exact terms and conditions that would satisfy a lawyer looking for a "contract." The manufacturer found that in the mid-1950s the percentage ranged from 60 to 75 percent of the orders, in an industry in which an order canceled means you end up holding a lot of useless boxes shaped and printed to the particular customer's specifications.[6]

It drove the company lawyers crazy. One said, "Often businessmen do not feel they have 'a contract'—rather they have 'an order.' They speak of 'canceling the order' rather than 'breaching the contract.'"[7] Another lawyer declared that he was "sick of being told, 'We can trust old Max,' when the problem is not one of honesty but one of reaching an agreement that both sides understand."[8] The nonlawyer businessmen didn't see it that way. "You get the other man on the telephone and deal with the problem. You don't read legalistic contract clauses at each other if you ever want to do business again. One doesn't run to lawyers if he wants to stay in business because one must behave decently."[9] One uses the courts only when someone defects. But few defect. There's a purely prudent reason, to be sure—that it's bad for business. But there's a just, faithful, loving ("good old Max") reason, too.

People want to be virtuous in business as elsewhere in their lives. Macaulay concluded that "two norms are widely accepted. (1) Commitments are to be honored in almost all situations; one does not welsh on a deal. (2) One ought to produce a good product and stand behind it."[10]

In 1912 before a House committee on the money trust, J. P. Morgan was being questioned by a hostile Samuel Untermyer:

> *Untermyer:* Is not commercial credit based primarily upon money or property?
> *Morgan:* No sir; the first thing is character.
> *Untermyer:* Before money or property?
> *Morgan:* Before money or property or anything else. Money cannot buy it . . . because a man I do not trust could not get money from me on all the bonds in Christendom.

Of course. If you want to be frightfully sophisticated about people's *real* motives and claim that these are not the rules of bourgeois life, you will need to explain why you get indignant when they are violated, and why in your daily transactions you assume they will be obeyed.

That does not mean you need to abandon tough-minded economic reasoning. Here, for example, is some tough-minded economic reasoning: the more people in the game, the easier it is to cheat, a new sucker coming along every minute. But the incentive to cheat is balanced by love, by shame, by the Man Within. That's sociology. *Both* prudence and solidarity rule. Here's some related economic reasoning: solidarity is especially, though not exclusively, powerful in small groups; prudence, in large. But such reasoning is also classical sociology, the point of Ferdinand Tönnies' book of 1887, *Gemeinschaft und Gesellschaft,* natural community and unnatural society, loving family and associational firm. And it is also, for that matter, classical political philosophy, the point of Aristotle's *Politics.*

Moving in 1980 from Chicago to Iowa City, I was startled by the reduction in the cost of doing business, and noticed the cost going up again when I moved back to Chicago in 1999. Even in near-suburban Oak Park, where I lived for a few months before I moved downtown, a store selling Irish merchandise would not take back the same afternoon a cloak bought, but not worn, which I had decided after a couple of hours I didn't want at the price. No way, the owner said. Tough luck, dearie. The virtue I thought we shared had disappeared once money changed hands. We had a contract, not an order. In Chicago in 2003 trying to sell a car, before finding CarMax and plain dealing in the suburbs, I spent half a day swimming through commercial slime on Western Avenue. "Your car, ma'am? That Toyota Avalon outside? I'll give you $2,500."

I love commerce and I love Chicago. I love even my newly established identity as a tough urban girl who can take it as well as dish it out. But every transaction in Iowa City or Schaumburg was easier. Checks passed, grocery clerks smiled, auto mechanics did what they said they were going to do, clothing stores and Toyota dealers wouldn't think of treating you in any fashion but by the Golden Rule. When I visited for a number of weeks at Denison University in little Granville, Ohio, after three years of Chicago rehardening, with episodes in tough old Amsterdam as well, there it was again, like taking off tight shoes. I *knew* the local jeweler in Granville would do a good job of resizing my rings. He did. In tough old Rotterdam in 1996 the jewelers needed close supervision, and often took advantage—well, not Marianne and Trees's jeweler on Mauritsweg, whom we had grown to trust.

You can't run human groups on Prudence Only, not well. And "well" means not merely prudently and profitably—though the Iowa City/ Schaumburg/Granville monetary gain is not trivial, *Gemeinschaft* in aid of *Gesellschaft*, J. P. Morgan's test of character in aid of smart loaning. But humans want more. Depending on Prudence Only makes it harder to achieve a transcendent, sacred goal such as communal love or social justice or scientific progress. And such a transcendent goal, I repeat, is necessary to make the prudence have a point.

On the other hand, when I moved back to Chicago from Iowa City and later from Granville, I noted also a rise in the richness of the *gemein-schaftlich* attachments I could form in the big city: thirty Episcopal churches within easy driving distance instead of four or five; seventy ethnic groups in bulk instead of two; twenty Irish pubs instead of one. Iowa City is a little jewel, and so is Granville on an even smaller scale. But they *are* little, SMAs of perhaps 100,000 all told in Iowa, 20,000 in Ohio, as against millions within a similar travel time in Chicago.

Tönnies, with many sociologists since, predicted that the big places such as Chicago would be soulless. He and the others have claimed that over time the soulless *Gesellschaft* replaces cozy *Gemeinschaft*. What is wrong in Tönnies is just what is wrong with most German social thought in the nineteenth century, a belief in historicism before the facts had been ascertained by professional historians—although professional history, too, was a nineteenth-century German planting, which bore its fruit in the twentieth century outside Germany. True, a big city has of course more businesslike *Gesellschaft*—admittedly or splendidly depending on how you feel about "unnatural" human projects. But it has more *Gemeinschaft*, too, more loving human connection, and that in enormous bulk. In consequence it has more of that third thing, the invisible-hand specialization that makes for a rich life. A big city has more of everything. That's why there are so many people there.

The historian Wilfred McClay praises another historian, Thomas Bender, for arguing that "the most influential of all sociological dualisms—*Gemein-schaft* and *Gesellschaft*—[is] to be understood, not as designating strictly discrete and sequential phases in the evolution of human social relations, but as signifying two kinds of relations that, particularly in a modern society, coexist and contend with each other." McClay observes that "one benefit of this approach is that it helps us account for the ways that premodern, traditional, and *gemeinschaftlich* ways and values coexist with, and even interpenetrate, the characteristic ways of the modern world, contrary to a more monolithic understanding of modernization."[11]

Brian Uzzi in an elegant 1999 paper in the *American Sociological Review* showed that borrowing firms did best—saving 3 percentage points on their borrowings, which is very large on loans costing 6 or 10 percent—when they *mixed* strong-tie relations with bankers ("*X* has been our bank for fifty years") and arm's-length ties. The firms mixed love/faith with prudence.[12]

You can do this in a big city. Focusing on the alienating, disintegrative results of big scale is a problem with the focus, not with the scale. And anyway a French peasant in the twelfth century was as "alienated" from the goings-on of the upper levels of European Christendom as much as is a modern bourgeois from the goings-on of the upper levels of global capitalism. Yet both the peasant and the bourgeois live in families, have friends, have projects. All human communities work with prudence and solidarity. Both.

A balanced set of virtues within prudent, economical, capitalist, market-oriented behavior is not merely a supplement, a nice thing if you happen to have a taste for it. It's virtuous, and necessary for a good life. It's necessary for transcendence, which gives life its worldly *and* its otherworldly value. Business, Michael Novak argues, is a "morally serious enterprise."[13] By contrast, the Prudence Only behavior celebrated in recent economic fable is bad. Bad for prudent business—consult on this point Arthur Andersen. Bad for a just and faithful life. Bad for children and other beloveds. Most important, bad for the soul. We call it greed.

The ethical wholeness matters. When the unionized teachers of Philadelphia quarreled with the superintendent in the 1990s about reward-by-result, their anger came from the insult as much as from a prudent regard for their tenure. Are we—we professionals—to be trained with incentives like seals? Their indignation cost the school system millions of dollars and its chance to teach the children to read.

Professionals are educated to consider something other than pocket-book prudence. It's the very meaning of the word "profession," as distinct from "racket." I recently was introduced to an architect and told him I was an economist. He replied, only half joking, "I *hate* economics," and explained amiably that what he meant is that all day long he has to ask if Prudence is worth this or that sacrifice of Quality. A friend who is a professional lighting designer says that the pressure of Prudence Only is something he has to resist all day. He *could* get a little more profit by doing a little worse job, using the wrong wattage here or there, cutting this or that corner. But he won't. He's a lighting designer, not a crook.

It's a matter of identity, and makes society possible. We tell jokes about doctors performing surgery on our pocketbooks and about lawyers closing the curtains and asking us how we want it to come out. But most people would reject a career of doctoring or lawyering if they actually credited the jokes, since most people do not want to be thieves or con men. Law and health would collapse if the only careers were such dishonest versions. Politics threatens to, always. Cynicism about careers on the Cook County Board or in the Italian Parliament means that the government is in fact left to the crooks, and republican virtue is put under siege.

Blair Kamin, an architecture critic for the Chicago *Tribune*, rails often against a local architect named Loewenberg for his cookie-cutter skyscrapers. The buildings are so notorious that they have spawned a noun to describe how they "blight" a neighborhood, "Loewenbergization." The other Chicago architects are scandalized that Loewenberg will put up a high-rise a mere twenty blocks from another that reuses the very same blueprints. Goodness. In Chicago such economizing at the expense of Art matters because the place fancies itself the architectural capital of the known universe. According to Kamin the offending Loewenberg buildings exhibit a "sterile symmetry and unarticulated surfaces that recall the old housing blocks of East Berlin," "dismal themes," "overgrown and under-detailed," "comically bad."[14]

You can see that Mr. Kamin does not like Mr. Loewenberg's work. To which Loewenberg calmly replies, "We design to a budget." Kamin in turn fumes, "That attitude is as cynical as it is lamentable, an abrogation of the architect's responsibility to design for the broader public." Kamin is trying to shame Loewenberg, and any architect who might think to imitate Loewenberg, into being professional beyond Prudence Only. Loewenberg and his clients aren't buying. Kamin and I think they should.

The conflict pervades our culture. *Zen and the Art of Motorcycle Maintenance* is still assigned in the business schools as a deliberation about quality and rhetoric. But *most* of what the students are taught there is a variation on Prudence Only.

The English aristocracy defended itself in a democratic age as a service class, going to Eton the better to serve king and country. Dedicated to loving England, and incidentally getting employment in politics and the Empire, they viewed themselves as upholding an alternative to a bourgeois ethic imagined as Prudence Only. Remember John Gielgud as Master of Trinity College in *Chariots of Fire* scolding the Ben Cross character for transgressing the code of the *amateur*, the lover. Now the children of the aristocracy go to Eton and thence to careers as chartered accountants in a global economy— nothing so quaint as England, my England. Prudence Only reigns, it is said. Love is devalued, at least in capitalist theory.

But love in the extended sense is necessary for a company, or England, or any human project. Love *does* make the world go round. Robert Frank has argued at length that the trustworthiness necessary for business "is motivated not by rational calculation," which would reduce all virtues to Prudence, "but by emotions—by moral sentiments, to use Adam Smith's term."[15] True. But there is a deeper argument available. Harry Frankfurt points out that "love makes it possible . . . for us to engage wholeheartedly in activity that is meaningful."[16] Humans want meaning. They just do, and they do not make an exception for capitalism.

C. S. Lewis composed a paean to male friendship—he wisely realized he had a less-than-reliable understanding of women's friendships—in which the friends sit side by side looking at a beloved object, trading remarks about it. Aristotle also thought this third thing to be looked at together was essential for friendship. So it is with the project at the office this week, or the Super Bowl on TV, or Shane and Starrett in the movie bonding in work, "their minds . . . on that old stump."[17] "Friendship must be about something," writes Lewis, "even if it were only an enthusiasm for dominos or white mice. . . . Friends . . . are all travelers on the same quest."[18] Such male friendship is how a company of men works wholeheartedly to make deals or automobiles.

A woman would say that friendship is about the friend or, still better, about the relationship. She or it, not the Super Bowl, is the object. The female version of friendship is how a company of women works wholeheartedly. Think of women cleaning up after a meal, the point being to help Jane. I have a friend who founded a small publishing company, and at first she tried an exclusively motherly style of leadership. She found she had to bring in some of the father. Her company works on loving relationships, prudently judged, balanced in style between male and female. A company or a market runs partly on Love.

Of course a company and a market work also on Prudence. But the modern academic theory of market capitalism, that Samuelsonian economics I studied so passionately in the 1960s and 1970s, goes astray in imagining that the *only* character we need in understanding capitalism is Mr. Maximum Utility, the monster of Prudence who has no place in his character for Love—or any passion beyond Prudence Only. Recall Steven Pinker's analysis of love as Max U—or Max G[enes]. Max U does not work scientifically, the only terms the Samuelsonian economists profess to care about, for which see the economists Frank and Frey and George Akerlof and many others.[19] And in terms that the rest of us can appreciate, he is a menace. Iris Murdoch describes Max U as "the agent, thin as a needle, [who] appears in the quick flash of the choosing will."[20]

Such a fellow would view friendship, *philia*, as an exchange, and would never achieve what Aristotle saw as the highest stage of friendship, love for the friend's own sake.[21] Another's "own sake" is meaningless in a Max U view of the social world. Things in such a world are valued for their capacity to yield utility, with the result, as Michael Stocker has noted, that people disappear.[22] The so-called "man" Max U does not value even himself as a person, and leaps at the chance to hitch himself up to an Experience Machine. Impulsive, manipulative, shallow. How many sociopaths can there be? Max U is a chimera conjured by the clerisy, left and right. They portray a world impossible for most actual human beings.

This is the point of a famous paper by Amartya Sen in 1977, just as Sen was working his way out of a Max U intellectual world, "Rational Fools: A Critique of the Behavioral Foundations of Economic Theory." The founder of modern Max U reasoning, Francis Y. Edgeworth, had acknowledged in 1881 that such a fellow as Max U depended on "unsympathetic isolation abstractly assumed in Economics."[23] But as you can see, economists think that "sympathy"— literally in Greek (which Edgeworth knew well) "fellow feeling"—is all there is to relations among humans. I am sad because you are sad. "Behavior based on sympathy," Sen writes, nice though it is, "is in an important sense egoistic, for one is pleased at others' pleasure and pained at others' pain, and the pursuit of one's own utility may thus be helped by sympathetic action."[24] In virtue-ethical terms, sympathy is a matter of prudence and lower-level (that is, not transcendent) love. Or maybe it is a matter of mere prudence, since this "love" is itself derivative, a sympathy *because* it gives prudent pleasure. Recall your mother getting derivative utility from your graduation from college.

Sen argued that important realms of our lives are governed instead by "commitment." Unlike sympathy, a commitment *reduces* your utility, at any rate your first-order utility in the manner of ice cream eaten or son's college degree attained. In Kantian terms commitment is a duty. In virtue-ethical terms, commitment is a matter of justice, faith, and transcendent love. Recall Adam Smith on Justice for the Chinese. Not prudent. Commitment involves "counterpreferential choice, destroying the crucial assumption [in Max U, Samuelsonian economics] that a chosen alternative must be better than . . . the others for the person choosing it."[25] Acknowledgment of the virtues beyond prudence and passion, in short, "drives a wedge between personal choice and personal welfare." "Much of traditional economic theory relies on the identity of the two."[26] In doing so, economics assumes a world without ethical commitment: "The *purely* economic man is indeed close to being a social moron."[27] Come to think of it, no "close" about it.

To speak instrumentally against instrumentalism, actual human businesses would collapse into dissembling and advantage-taking à la Dilbert if the businesses did not practice friendship and other forms of non–Prudence Only virtue. Look round at your own workplace. How does your office actually operate? Really, now. As a hell? With monsters of prudence running around taking care of Numero Uno? No, not really. Admittedly in some departments of economics you will meet one or two such people, who declare candidly that "our model in economics proves" they should act like jerks. But outside economics everyone knows that a well-functioning corporate office runs in part on love.

Everyone also knows that the love can be trumped. In this and other contexts you will see people who think that greed is good or that the story of My Brilliant Career trumps ethical considerations or that maximizing stockholder value settles every ethical question in business. In his commencement address at Berkeley in May 1986, the year before he was jailed, Ivan Boesky told the kids that "Greed is all right, by the way. I want you to know that. I think greed is healthy. You can be greedy and still feel good about yourself."[28] The kids cheered. Now most of us laugh sardonically.

We find the cartoon strip *Dilbert* funny, if we do, because the avaricious behavior of its central characters is over the top, crazy-funny, unacceptably and indeed imprudently Prudent. True, when an office is led badly it becomes a bit Dilbertian. I've been in such organizations, and so have you. But usually it is not actual prudence, the good of the company, that is served by on-the-job jerkness. As *Dilbert* itself shows, ego-tripping and irrational obsession run a bad business into the ground, and some of the good ones, too. Likewise in *Doonesbury*, what is funny about Duke, the recurrent Hunter Thompson figure, is his single-minded if drug-addled pursuit of self-interest, set off against the selflessness of his girlfriend Miss Honey.

The point is that actual workplaces are not often really like Dilbert's or Duke's. Robert Solomon puts it this way: "Is the community we work for a white-collar version of hell, or is it a community where (despite the early hour) we are glad to see our colleagues and get on with the work of the day?"[29] More so as capitalism enriches its workers, and as its worker-consumers require to be treated like free citizens, the workplace becomes a home place. More's the pity, some have said, for it tempts people away to a comfortable place, the job, the office, to the loss of the home.

I say again: look around at your own workplace. In the capitalist West now the chances are that it is not a satanic mill in which you labor in noise and dust and isolation for twelve hours a day. It's not the carding room of a Yorkshire woolen mill in 1830. A recent survey finds that even in I'm-All-Right-Jack Britain half of the workers "look forward to going to work." In the Tough-Guy United States, two-thirds do, and elsewhere in the developed world still higher percentages.[30] Such employees go to work expecting to be treated like human beings, expecting to be even a little loved. An employee of modern capitalism is ethically offended when her boss complains about the harmless decorations festooned on her cubicle. Who does she think she is? Doesn't she love me? A wholly prudential worker, the economist's monster of prudence, or a preindustrial slave accustomed to abuse would be incapable of such indignation and sorrow.

The writer Don Snyder tried construction work to survive one winter in Maine: "There were six of us working on the crew, but the house was so large that we seldom saw one another. . . . Once I walked right by a man [without greeting him] in my haste to get back to a second-story deck where I had been tearing down staging. [The contractor] saw this, and he climbed down from the third story to set me straight. 'You can't just walk by people,' he said. 'It's going to be a long winter.' "[31] Consultants on workplace politeness emphasize that saying hello to people is basic. Not saying hello is of course imprudent—you alienate your coworkers by failing in this elementary acknowledgment of solidarity. But why are people so offended? On the vending-machine characterization of others that the Max U model assumes, no offense would be taken. But people do take offense. Even in a workplace of tough-guy American men, the avaricious, competitive, Dilbertian, "businesslike" Prudence can't be all there is.

In other words, it's not the case that market capitalism requires or generates loveless people. More like the contrary. Markets and even the much-maligned corporations encourage friendships wider and deeper than the atomism of a full-blown socialist regime or the claustrophobic, murderous atmosphere of a "traditional" village. Modern capitalist life is love-saturated. Olden life was not loving; communitarian life was not; and actually existing socialist life decidedly was not. No one dependent on a distant god such as the Gosplan or Tradition can feel safe. Paradoxically, a market linked so obviously to our individual projects makes us safer and more loving.

As the libertarian Catholic economist Jennifer Roback Morse puts it, a capitalist business partnership is like a marriage, not like a temporary contract: "The contract between the partners does not govern every detail of the relationship's functioning. The partners do not attempt to specify every duty of each party during the course of their relationship: only the most basic duties are so specified. The contractual relationship between partners is not the end of the relationship or the method for how the parties relate to one another. The parties expect to do a great many things of mutual benefit that cannot be included in the set of legally enforceable promises."[32] She argues that contract-like marriages, and contract-like business partnerships, do not work very well. A lack of committed love "undermines the self-giving required at the heart of the committed marriage: we practice holding back on our partners; we practice calculating."

9

SOLIDARITY REGAINED

Now of course in the view of classical social science in the nineteenth century, repeated by many otherwise skeptical scholars down to the present, the coming of capitalist modernity has meant a loss of solidarity. The sociologist Philip Selznick, for example, writing in 1992, rehearses the tragic story of a rural *Gemeinschaft* lost, to be contrasted with the cold modern world of rationality and contract, at the limit of a townly *Gesellschaft*. "These benefits [of modernity]," he writes, "are purchased at the price of cultural attenuation. The symbolic experiences that create and sustain the organic unities of social life are steadily thinned and diminished."[1]

Who says? Really, now, how d'you know? In common with most social scientists, Selznick assumes without inquiring much into the evidence that modernization has these effects, and that they do go to the limit, organic unities terminally thinned and diminished. Selznick and the others rely mainly on the repeated assertion without evidence in canonical works by Marx, Tönnies, Weber, and Durkheim, followed by twentieth-century ethnography before the generation of Clifford Geertz and twentieth-century history before the generation of Peter Laslett—in the 1960s Geertz and Laslett challenged the pieties of 1950s modernization theory, which assumed that Marx, Tönnies, Weber, and Durkheim had got the history right. "In almost every sphere of life," Selznick asserts, "there has been a movement away from densely textured structures of meaning to less concrete, more abstract forms of expression and relatedness."

We are asked to believe that a graduate student in Professor Selznick's law and sociology courses at Berkeley, the descendent of, say, Chinese peasants, has access to less densely structured textures of meaning, a thinner, less love-filled life, than his ancestors. The student reads, let us say, English perfectly and French and German very well, and can understand a little spoken Cantonese. He is married and has a three-year-old daughter—whose feet, by the way, he wouldn't think of binding. He needs only to complete his Ph.D. dissertation on "The Abstract Forms of Expression and Relatedness in Modern Life: A Study of Tönnies and Durkheim" to take up a satisfying career of teaching and research. He has fellow graduate students he will keep as beloved friends for a long life. He stays in touch with his college classmates, and with some of his friends from the neighborhood where he grew up, in Rio Linda, north of Sacramento.

In what feature exactly, one might ask Professor Selznick, is the graduate student able to enjoy less texture, structure, concreteness in his expression and relations than his male ancestors? One of his male ancestors was his immigrant great-great-grandfather working as a coolie on railway construction in Nevada—he died in a tunnel collapse at age thirty-one. Another great-great-great grandfather lived in a village in southeast China. He could not read a single character, and left the village once only, feet first, when he died at age forty-four.

On the face of it, the graduate student has a more textured, structured, concrete life, *and* a more uniform, flexible, and abstract one than these men. He has wider experience, a life twice or three times as long, more friends, longer-living relatives, more interesting work, and access to the world's best in spiritual experiences—advanced Buddhist thought, for example, or the piano sonatas of Beethoven.

True, he cannot go back to the ignorance of his ancestors. None of us can, after innocence. We know that the earth is round ($p < .05$), we know that cholera is caused by sewerage in the drinking water, we know that people with good advanced degrees in the humanities are capable of serving as SS officers. We cannot forget so by an act of will. But what of it?

Selznick says that "the fundamental truth is that modernity weakens culture and fragments experience." Does this mean that moderns don't have a culture? That can't be right. Does it mean that the moderns participate in more villages, so to speak, than their home village alone? Yes: they participate in the village of work, the village of an extended family in which relatives surviving into their eighties are commonplace, the village of a church or temple, of a professional association, of a square-dancing club, of local

politics, of a women's reading group, of a bridge club, of a service organization, of hospital volunteers, of a local coffee house, of Giants fans, of Berke-
leyites, of Californians, of Americans, of world citizens passionately aware
of our shared big blue marble. What is wrong with that?

What exactly has humanity lost from such "fragmentation"? It should be
easy to gather actual evidence on the amount of fragmentation and especially the amount of "loss" if it is so very pervasive a feature of modern capitalist life. The evidence needs to be comprehensive in its accounting and
serious in its history. It should not be a notion generalized from Durkheim's
anomie or from a professor's whinge against his bourgeois neighbors.

The century-and-a-half-old premise among anticapitalists is that we
have through capitalism lost a good world worth keeping. But evidence
has in fact been assembled by generations of social historians since 1900
against the German Romantic idea of a Black Forest homeland for a noble
peasantry—a peasantry which allegedly benefited from more densely textured structures of meaning than we moderns can muster.

The evidence is overwhelming. The historians have found that the
Gemeinschaft of olden times was defective. The murder rate in villages in the
thirteenth century, to take the English case, was higher than comparable
places now.[2] Medieval English peasants were in fact very mobile geograph-
ically, "fragmenting" their lives.[3] The imagined extended family of "traditional" life never existed in England.[4] Or, to turn to other instances: The
sweetness of the old-fashioned American family has been greatly exaggerated.[5] The Russian *mir* was neither ancient nor egalitarian, but a figment of
the German Romantic imagination.[6] Vietnamese peasants did not live in
tranquil, closed corporate communities.[7]

Love, in short, is arguably thicker on the ground in the modern, Western,
capitalist world. Or at any rate it is not obviously thinner on the ground
than in the actual world of olden and allegedly more solid times. The feminist Nancy Folbre remarks that "we cannot base our critique of impersonal
market-based society on some romantic version of a past society as one big
happy family. In that family, Big Daddy was usually in control."[8]

Robert Bellah and his coauthors of *The Habits of the Heart* (1985) repeat
the tale of lost solidarity. It is one of their main themes. "Modernity," they
say without offering evidence—why seek evidence for so obvious a truth?—
"has had . . . destructive consequences for social ecology . . . , [which] is
damaged . . . by the destruction of the subtle ties that bind human beings to

one another, leaving them frightened and alone."[9] They worry that "the first language of America," individualism, "may have grown cancerous."[10] They give aesthetic and moral meaning to their everyday lives as social scientists by detecting through traditional forms of scrutiny of their neighbors a "weakening of the traditional forms of life that gave aesthetic and moral meaning to everyday living."[11]

Everyone believes it. Everyone does, that is, except the historians who have actually looked at the comparative evidence. Except them, everyone believes in "the extreme fragmentation of the modern world."[12] After warning about the misleading nostalgia for a "romantic vision of one big happy family," Folbre retails the usual critique of modernity based on it. "Social critics like Karl Polanyi," she writes, "have long warned that the growth of market-like behavior . . . might encourage selfish calculation." So they have, but with not much evidence. "Economic development seems to lead to a decline in the importance of close personal relations." I don't think so; if anything, it seems to lead to the opposite. "Our culture has almost certainly become more materialistic." By comparison with Roman civilization or medieval European civilization? I don't think so. "Adam Smith believed that we would become . . . more civilized. I haven't seen much evidence of this."[13] You haven't? Not in the rights of women, the extent of higher education, the number of books published, the attendance at museums and orchestra halls worldwide? Such pessimism appears to have more to do with the alienation of academics from the society around them than with the historical or sociological facts.

Intellectually speaking the claim of "fragmentation," I say, descends from German suspicion of French Enlightenment, which around 1800 emerged as Romance, and later in the century was intellectualized as the particularly German theme in professional folklore, history, anthropology, theology, and at last sociology. One finds many central-European intellectuals and their followers early in the twentieth century repeating what they learned about the modern world's lack of solidarity from Marx, Weber, and the rest, accented by the passing bells of 1914–1918: thus Karl Mannheim, Martin Heidegger, Karl Polanyi, Arnold Hauser, Herbert Marcuse, Theodor Adorno, Max Horkheimer, and many others after the Great War declaring themselves to be hollow men.

The German sociologist and Fascist enthusiast Hans Freyer (1887–1969) wrote in 1923 that "we feel ourselves to be unconfirmed, lacking in meaning, unfulfilled, not even obligated." No commitment, no Faith or Love. The Hungarian literary critic and Marxist revolutionary and later Communist state functionary Georg Lukács (1885–1971) wrote in 1913 about the lack of "totality" in modern culture.[14] The implied premise, borrowed from the philosophical history of the German Romantics, is that former times *did* have such a totality. The decades following 1914 were to show what could be accomplished by making the antiliberal search for "totality" into an "ism." The evidence has always been weak for a new "fragmentation." But the claim justified in Europe 1914–1945 a violent assault on liberal democracy. "Everything in the State, nothing against the State, nothing outside the State" is one version. And in its milder echoes nowadays the nostalgia for an alleged unity justifies at least a disdain for the way we live in Middletown or the San Fernando Valley.

Bellah and his fellow authors defer to Robert Putnam on the evidence for a rise in "bowling alone." *Habits of the Heart,* they note in the introduction to the updated edition of 1996, "was essentially a cultural analysis, more about language than behavior."[15] Putnam, they say, assembled the real evidence of behavior. The behavioral evidence is not persuasive. They quote Putnam in the 1990s, for example, as predicting that the Internet would probably "not sustain civic engagement." That behavioral prediction by now does not seem to have been a very good one. Look at the "civic engagement" of Howard Dean's Internet-based campaign for the Democratic presidential nomination in 2003–2004, or the new unionism built on e-mail mobilization.[16] Look at the hundreds of thousands of little communities worldwide that now gather every evening in the ether to chat and court and opine and quarrel, a virtual stroll along an electronic boulevard.

The new social forms do not constitute an "obligation" or a "totality" in the sense that twentieth-century Fascists and Communists understood the terms. They are not that "terrestrial paradise," as Isaiah Berlin described the myth that has long haunted Western thought, "an ideal state of affairs which is the solution of all problems and the harmonization of all values."[17] But what is the evidence that there ever was such a totality, or that it would be a good idea if it ever were achieved? The idea is Rousseau's general will and its dismal spawn. "The Fascist conception of the State," wrote Mussolini and Gentile in 1932, "is all embracing; outside of it no human or spiritual values can exist, much less have value."[18] Swell.

And in any case, the notion that "social capital" has declined appears to be misleading. Richard Florida conveniently summarizes the recent criticism of

Putnam's work by Dora Costa, Matthew Hahn, Robert Cushing, and others.[19] The decline of social solidarity that worries Putnam seems to be exaggerated.

In particular the numerous "weak ties" of the modern world, as Mark Granovetter put it, have, taken together, great strength. They are like a rope made of many strands. At the beginning of modernity Bishop Butler used the same phrase as the sociologists now use looking back on it: "Anything may serve . . . to hold humanity together in little fraternities and co-partnerships: *weak ties*, indeed, and what may afford fund enough for ridicule, if they are absurdly considered as the real principle of that union; but they are in truth merely the occasions."[20] The occasions of work group-ings and hobby clubs and NASCAR races is the "natural principle of attrac-tion in man towards man" which one finds in 2006 as much as in 1725.

Putnam yearns for the one-strand rope of an invented tradition. Florida challenges him gently:

> I am not advocating that we adopt lives composed entirely of weak ties. . . . But most Creative Class people that I've met and studied do not aspire to such a life and don't seem to be falling into it. . . . They have significant others; they have close friends; they call mom. But their lives are not dominated or dictated by strong ties to the extent that many lives were in the past. . . . Interestingly, people seem to prefer it this way. Weak ties allow us to mobilize more resources and more possibilities for ourselves and others, and expose us to novel ideas that are the source of creativity.[21]

Richard Sennett, in *The Corrosion of Character: The Personal Conse-quences of Work in the New Capitalism* (1998) is, like Bellah and other com-munitarians, nostalgic for strong ties, the "social bonds [which] take time to develop, slowly rooting into the cracks and crevices of institutions."[22] He has particular nostalgia, as many on the left and right do, for the 1950s in Amer-ica: "Strong unions, guarantees of the welfare state, and large-scale corpora-tions combined to produce an era of relative stability."[23] I remind my communitarian and neocon friends—who share more than they realize a love of "stability"—that if you were not male and white and straight and a suburbanite and a union member, those 1950s were not in fact very nice, even in America. They were nice only by comparison with still earlier times of still stronger ties, still greater stability, and still tighter social bonds rooted in institutions. *Enracinement* sounds nice. But the real glory is the flower, the human flourishing, not the roots.

Somehow we have traveled from the sunny realism of Bishop Butler and Adam Smith in the eighteenth century to a dark and unrealistic pessimism in the twentieth century, at just the time that liberal capitalism is succeeding. We've traveled from Butler's belief that "it is manifest fact that . . . the generality are frequently influenced by friendship, compassion, gratitude; and even a general abhorrence of what is base, and liking of what it fair and just" to Christopher Lasch's assertion that we live in a culture of narcissism.[24] We've traveled from Smith's belief that "the uniform, constant, and unmitigated effort of every man to better his condition . . . is frequently powerful enough to maintain the natural progress of things towards improvement" to Georg Lukács' assertion in his old age (the 1960s) that "even the worst socialism is better than the best capitalism."[25]

I suggest that German Romanticism was the detour. German Romanticism still seems attractive to many, against the Scottish and liberal idea of letting people alone in their marketplaces to fashion a varied culture. I follow Berlin in observing that one strand in Romance led to modern racism, by way of myths of *Kultur*. Another strand, he says, led to modern revolution, by way of myths of Action. And a final strand led to some of the best of modern liberal values, by way of Romanticism's novel notions of sincerity and authenticity.[26] Jerry Muller notes that there was a liberal counterargument to the bad strands in Romance even in Germany—such as Walter Goetz in 1919 making "an extended critique of the notion that there existed some ongoing essence of the German *Volk*."[27] Muller, or for that matter Goetz, could have cited another German, Franz Boaz, working in America to the same liberal and antiracist end.

When Bellah and his coauthors venture to illustrate the modern fragmentation, they do not persuade. The only example they give of the fragmented character of modern solidarity is "the euphoric sense of metropolitan belongingness" that comes "when a local sports team wins a national championship." These are "rare moments," they claim, which happen "briefly."[28] They view them as fleeting episodes of trivia.

That doesn't seem right. Sports championships are rare and brief, of course, aside from the New York Yankees since Ruth, and in Chicago for a while during Michael Jordan. But the belongingness in the big city and its hinterland that sports teams nourish is not rare. To some in the clerisy it seems trivial, I realize, but loyalty to sports teams creates for millions in America and Holland and Japan an enduring belonging. It's nicer, actually, than war. And it's not brief. Ask a New Englander about 1918–2004. Ask a sixty-year-old Englishman today about the World Cup win over Germany in 1966, or a Dutchman about the loss to Germany in 1974. My ninety-eight-year-old grandmother wore a Cubs cap while she watched on television her beloved team of Ernie Banks, Ron Santo, and Billy Williams trying and failing, yet again.

Yes, I know: such stuff is so silly, so unacademic, so characteristic of the alienated lives of moderns. It is so much less dignified than the densely textured structures of meaning that came out of the villages of English *Volk* c. 1300 playing, uh, football.

The five-person *Habits* team interviewed about 200 Americans. They concede that they found no one among the 200 who was fragmented. "Most are seeking in one way or another to transcend the limitations of a self-centered life."[29] But that's what people have been doing since the invention of language—at least in the brief episodes in which their material circumstances have given them time to think. "If there are vast numbers of a selfish, narcissistic 'me generation' in America, we did not find them." That's right: there are not *actually* in very large numbers the sociopaths and *Dilbert* characters who are supposed in some theories to be generated by capitalism.

What the *Habits* team did find is that people could not articulate a theory, usually, beyond a naïve ritualism or a naïve individualism provided to them by the less thoughtful of the local clerisy, the parish priest, say, or a village philosopher who has read Ayn Rand. But are Americans actually moved by the worst of these, and in particular by radical individualism? Some Americans say it. But do they do it? Is Prudence Only, Screw You, Mac, *really* the operating system of capitalism? The clerisy has believed so since 1848. Is it right about this?

Habits of the Heart begins with a relentless if polite criticism of one of the interviewees, called "Brian Palmer," a businessman who holds two full-time jobs to support his family. The main complaint against Brian seems to be not that he has no values—which would be a strange assertion under the circumstances—but that he can't say what they are. "Apart from the injunction not to lie ['integrity is good and lying is bad'], he is vague about what his values are."[30]

Gosh, that's terrible. Palmer is a poor *theorizer*. He can't say what his values are. Another interviewee, "Wayne Bauer," is a community organizer.

Apparently it is not only the business bourgeoisie who have this characteristically modern American problem of ethical disfluency. When grilled about his ethical theories, the college professors note, "Wayne becomes strangely inarticulate." Liberated people "will make society 'better,' he says." The exasperated professors quiz the student: "What does he *mean* by 'better'?"

Only a group of intellectuals would regard as a grave problem such a failure to articulate. One is inclined to respond uncharitably: "If even the glorious Immanuel Kant found it challenging to articulate the meaning of life, what do you expect to get by way of such theories from 200 ordinary Americans, untrained in German philosophy and sociology and theology? I suppose that in the 200 ordinary Americans not even one could articulate the categorical imperative, much less give its three alternative formulations. So bloody what?" I said uncharitably.

The unspoken premise of the *Habits* method is that under the "traditional" forms that gave aesthetic and moral meaning to everyday living in olden times, the results of conversations with 200 people would be quite different. But that's not likely. If you asked 200 American fundamentalists nowadays or 200 of Hester Prynne's fellow Puritans what their values or their ethical theories were, you would get a predictable set of allegedly Bible-based formulas. Hester's Puritans would be articulate, all right, wonderfully so. Words would spill out with King James eloquence. But the words would give little or no scientific insight into the actual state of love and justice in Boston or Springfield c. 1680. The formulas would not be the actual sociological rules of seventeenth-century Massachusetts.[31] Ditto for a sample of ordinary modern fundamentalists. There would be theorizing, all right, but bad theorizing, bad in every sense: mistaken, superficial, insincere, uninsightful, often enough concealing a hatred for others under a theory of a hateful God. And certainly you would get little or nothing by way of *independent* theorizing, except perhaps from a rare Anne Bradstreet. The Puritans would get a bare C+ in the professors' examination. The 700-Club fundamentalists would get a C–. To be sure, these are better than the well-deserved D– assigned to the appalling Brian Palmer and Wayne Bauer, but certainly not the honor-roll level of theorizing the professors seek.

My argument is in some ways the opposite of that in *Habits of the Heart*, though the *Habits* authors and I agree on many things. We agree that ethical matters are important, that Prudence Only is a poor ethical theory, that what they call "Biblical" values are not to be disdained. But I would argue that bourgeois and capitalist and modern American life in fact participates in the transcendent as much as life anywhere has. I'm willing to stipulate that bourgeois life does not participate in the transcendent any more than earlier and noncapitalist life—though I wish that my friends of the clerisy who despair of modernity would concede in turn that because of capitalist economic growth many people in capitalist countries, for example, my friends of the clerisy who despair of modernity, have now the time and mental equipment to push beyond What Dad Said.

Doubtless the booboisie doesn't push hard enough. Doubtless it views artists and academics as something like inessential entertainment. But at least some of the booboisie try to reach the transcendent, in their contemptibly naïve ways. And the rest at least pay willingly for someone else to try. American Babbitts save for their children's college educations on an impressive scale, educations in which the children are taught to despise the values of their parents.

When the political philosopher Harvey Mansfield noted to his colleague Judith Shklar in the Government Department at Harvard that virtue in America is *bourgeois* virtue, she replied, "Is there any other kind?"[32] That's right, and more professors need to acknowledge it. Americans, bourgeois and working-class, in fact exhibit an integrated set of virtues, though present-day, nonclerisy, nonfundamentalist people have no ready formulas for describing it in a way that would satisfy a panel of professors.

This is not the interviewees fault, the rhetorical subtext of *Habits* to the contrary notwithstanding. It's the clerisy's job to provide articulations that illuminate our lives. Artists and intellectuals provide the images and the theories articulating a transcendent. For a century and a half a good part of the clerisy has been off duty, standing in the street outside the factory or office or movie studio hurling insults at the varied workers there.

On this, Bellah, Madsen, Sullivan, Swidler, Tipton, and I do agree: "Individuals need the nurture of groups that carry a moral tradition reinforcing their own aspirations."[33] Time for members of the clerisy, such as we six, to articulate a moral tradition more useful than Down with the Bosses or To Hell with the Poor or Back to the Church or Reverse the 1960s or Prudence Only.

PART TWO

The Christian and Feminine Virtues: Faith and Hope

THE LORD IS MY SALVATION SINCE I CAN THINK
NO OTHER THING TO THINK FOR WHEN THE EARTH
BECOMES A DREAM AND VANITY THE BUTT OF STARS
AND PAIN FORGOT IN COUNTLESS SPACE.
THE LORD IS MY SALVATION FROM PILGRIM'S ROAM
AND LONELINESS, FROM MAN'S FAILURE TO SAVE
THE DREAMER FROM THE DREAM, FROM LIFE
IN DISILLUSIONMENT, FORGETFULNESS AND DUST.

—*Helen McCloskey, "Out of Desperation"*

10

FAITH AS IDENTITY

Nihil aliud scio nisi fluxa et caduca spernenda esse, certa et aeterna requirenda. [Nothing else I know except that things perishing and transitory should be spurned and things certain and eternal should be sought.]
—St. Augustine, *Soliquia*

The theological virtues are above the nature of man, whereas the intellectual and moral virtues belong to the nature of man. . . . Therefore the theological virtues should be distinguished. . . . The intellectual and moral virtues perfect the human intellect and appetite in proportion to human nature, but the theological virtues do so supernaturally.
—Aquinas, *Summa Theologiae*

To speak then of the profane world, the self-regarding virtues are prudence, temperance, and sometimes courage—since the courage sometimes is directed to self-preservation. And the other-regarding virtues are love, justice, and sometimes courage, the courage sometimes being on the behalf of others. Let's be quantitative about it. The individual and the social virtues are by this reckoning $2\frac{1}{2} + 2\frac{1}{2} = 5$. To do the sum the other way, they are the pagan four of courage, temperance, justice, and prudence, with the Christian virtue of love added to them, reaching up to the transcendent, making five.

Something's missing. In the analysis of Aquinas and of other Western ethical thinking before Kant, and now sometimes in the revival of virtue ethics, there are seven: $5 + 2 = 7$, the pagan four plus that Christian virtue of love, *eros, philia,* agape . . . and two more: faith and hope, virtues six and seven. They complete the traditional ethical psychology of humans. Hope and faith are the other transcendent. "They have God not only for their end, but for their object":[1]

The Three Theological Virtues

HOPE
- Martin Luther King -

FAITH
- St. Peter -

LOVE
[Peasant/Proletarian/Saint]
- Emma Goldman -

In spiritual terms faith, as St. Paul said in part, is "the argument for things not seen" (Heb. 11:1). St. Thomas Aquinas wrote a hymn defining faith:

Quod non capis, quod non vides,	What you do not grasp, not see,
Animosa firmat fides	A lively faith affirms,
Praeter rerum ordinem.	Beyond the order of [material] things.[2]

Even to look at nature one must affirm an order beyond the mere things. Facts without precepts are blind, a blooming, buzzing confusion. "No argument," the political philosopher J. Budziszewski notes, "can be so completely drawn as to eliminate its dependence, conscious or unconscious, on undemonstrable first premises."[3]

The discovery in the nineteenth century of non-Euclidian geometries and in the twentieth of undecidable propositions should have taught the most scientific among us that faith grounds observation. The mathematicians Philip Davis and Reuben Hersh note that "underlying both mathematics and religion there must be a foundation of faith which the individual must himself supply." Mathematicians, they observe, are practicing neo-Platonists and followers of Spinoza. Their worship of mathematics parallels the worship of God. Both God and the Pythagorean theorem, for example, are believed to exist independent of the physical world; and both give it meaning.[4] Faith in what Aquinas called the "eternal" law is nonetheless a faith. Admittedly the faith of the Christian has more. It comes from the grace of God.[5] But who is to say that scientific faith is not also God's grace in action?

The physicist Stephen Barr puts it this way: "Even the atheist . . . asks questions about reality in the expectation that these questions will have answers. . . . It is not because he already has the answers. . . . [I]f he [did] . . . he would not be seeking them. Yet he has the conviction. . . . This is a faith."[6] And a great faithman, Thomas Merton, once wrote, "Faith is first of all an intellectual assent. But the assent of faith is not based on the intrinsic evidence of a visible object. . . . The statements which demand the assent of faith are simply neutral to reason. . . . Faith brings together the known and the unknown so that they overlap: or rather, so that we are *aware* of their overlap. . . . The function of faith is not to reduce mystery to rational clarity, but to integrate the unknown and the known together into a living whole."[7] Faith is not an attack on science or a turn to superstition. Like the assent to the enterprise of science as a whole, as against particular scientific propositions embedded in the enterprise, it is not based on the visible. Physicists affirm that "God is a mathematician" or "God does not play dice." Such faiths are not against rationality, but complete it.

The faith, in other words, need not be faith in God. Many secular folk believe in a transcendent without God, though approaching him. "I think all poets are sending religious messages," declared Richard Wilbur, "because poetry is, in such great part, the comparison of one thing to another; or the saying, as in metaphor, that one thing *is* another. And to insist, as all poets do, that all things are related to each other, comparable to each other, is to go toward making an assertion of the unity of all things."[8]

But why then is faith a virtue? Why isn't it sheer epistemology, a matter of how we know, though concerning things not seen, such as a faith in the orderliness of the universe or in the power of reason or in a god of love? Because, C. S. Lewis explains, faith is a kind of spiritual courage, a willed steadfastness against the times when "a mere mood rises up against it." Faithfulness is necessary for epistemology, "thinking with the giving of assent," as Augustine put it. "Belief" in Germanic origin is cognate with "beloved," from Indo-European *leubh-*, whence "love." It connoted faithfulness, and only later acquired the meaning of giving credence to a proposition. A physicist who was, as Lewis says, "just a creature dithering to and fro" about whether in designing the universe God, figuratively speaking, is a mathematician would be a poor physicist. A historian who has nothing of "the art of holding on to things [her] reason has once accepted, in spite of [her] changing moods" is going to dither to and fro about whether or not history is caused (figuratively speaking) by the class struggle or by a horseshoe nail. She will not really have tested the class struggle or the horseshoe nail. As a historical scientist she will not be wholly virtuous, because as Lewis observes, she will change her mind unreasonably.[9]

Faith is a backward-looking virtue. It concerns who we are; or, rather, italicized, who we *are*, "the mystic chords of memory." In personal and modern terms it is called "integrity" or "identity." "If we create a society that our descendants will want to hold on to," writes Kwame Anthony Appiah, "our personal and political values will survive in them."[10] The faith needs to be instilled, "because children do not begin with values of their own." Though Appiah does not attach his notion of "identity" to religious "faith," perhaps he should. In social and ancient terms it is the virtue of insisting on belonging to a community, such as a polis or a church. As Tillich put it, faith is "the courage to be a part of," to share a social purpose. "I have fought a good fight, I have finished my course, I have kept the faith," says the Christian, and does keep the faith steadfastly against many contrary moods.

The political scientist James Q. Wilson uses "duty" instead of faith, though he speaks of duty also as "fidelity," from of course *fides*, faith.[11] That is: adhere to one's commitments; do your duty in the face of temptations to take a free ride. As Wilson says, and Lewis said, faithful duty is akin to courage.[12] Indeed all the virtues require courage in the face of attack. But all courage requires faith, in turn, so that the courage is exercised for something enduring. Wilson's leading example is Admiral James Stockdale's leadership of the American POWs in the hands of North Vietnamese torturers. But he notes that the signs of faith lie all about. Faith is the who-you-*are* that finds you contributing to public radio, conserving water in a drought when no inspector will spot a defection, turning up to vote against George W. Bush when your vote was after all of no consequence.

Wilson adopts the view of the Scottish Enlightenment, and the Aristotelian tradition before it, that ethics is a matter of habit and character, not continuous decisions under a rule of reason. Like other virtues, he argues, faith is behaviorally instilled, working in tandem with genetic predispositions. Once instilled, it is a feeling, a complaining conscience, what Smith called the Impartial Spectator. That is why Hutcheson and Hume and Smith in eighteenth-century Scotland claimed that virtues arose from "moral *sentiments*": virtues are matters of a prepared feeling rather than a decision on the spot.

You begin, though, with a decision to cultivate the moral sentiments. You enroll with a free will at Annapolis and train your ethical muscles. Like a body trained to a sport, the present performance is both forward- and backward-looking, hopeful and faithful, both. The rule of reason, by contrast, insists on disowning the past, extracting you from your history. Utilitarianism insists on faithlessness.

Fides was the term by which the Romans described their relationship with allies. In the Roman wars against Carthage, Inc.—so bourgeois as to distribute annually the "profits" of the state to its citizens, in the style of Alaska with its oil revenues—the rule of Faith repeatedly overcame a rule of mere Prudence. In the last stages of the first of three Punic Wars, for instance, the prudent Carthaginians decided to economize on their navy, in the very years in which the extraordinarily faithful if previously not very nautical Romans built and staffed additional war galleys to the number of two hundred. In the Second Punic War the Romans were defeated again and again in Italy by Hannibal, losing 50,000 dead in a few hours at Cannae. But they never ransomed captives, nor hesitated to free slaves to staff fresh legions. They kept the faith in Rome.

The Dutch have a somewhat heavy word expressing the tug of the past through faith, *lotsverbondenheid,* solidarity. It means the sharing with solidarity of a common fate, those *bonden,* bonds, to the *lots*—compare English "lot," as in "your lot in life." Aristotle's phrase for it is "another self." Such friendship is a combination of love and faith directed here below. Love without faithfulness would be called "inauthentic" or "phony" or at best "inconstant, flighty," the crushes of adolescents or the serial polygamy of adults. In some families faith without love would be called "having relatives."[13] Friends of mere use or amusement, Aristotle's first two types, do not have *lotsverbondenheid:* "Such friendships . . . are easily dissolved if the parties become different; for if they are no longer pleasant or useful they cease loving each other."[14]

Friends of the third type, who care for one another as for themselves, do have a bonded lot. The Dutch university students portrayed in Paul Verhoeven's movie *Soldier of Orange* (1979) go through the Second World War in different ways, one dying as a German officer on the Eastern Front, another sitting peacefully at home and passing his exams to become a lawyer, another escaping to England and becoming an RAF pilot, while several others die in the Resistance to the German occupation. The hero of the movie, played by Rutger Hauer, keeps faith with them all, even with the traitor and the shirker, embodying *lotsverbondenheid.* In a scene on the beach at Scheveningen, for example, the others walk away from the fellow student who has traitorously joined the German army. The Hauer character, although himself by then leaning toward the Resistance, will not abandon him. Later the two *verbonden* friends, even though they have taken politically opposite paths, exchange postcards. Their lots are bound. You go to your high-school reunion. You say to yourself, "I have nothing in common with these people." But you do, if you are a person, theologically speaking. You have faith.

Lotsverbondenheid is made evident in the technique of psychological intervention called family-constellation therapy. The participants play roles of mother or son or cousin or dead grandfather or anyone else bound by life's lottery to the person who is the main subject of the therapy. Even someone who murdered a former spouse may have a place in the constellation. It is not a drama viewed in detachment. Faith is called upon, performing a sort of public oath. The exercise of one's will toward *lotsverbondenheid* is faith, *geloof.*

We are told by the *Habits of the Heart* authors that nowadays "The rules of the competitive market, not the love of families or the practices of the town meeting or the fellowship of the church, are the real arbiters of living."[15] Bourgeois society is supposed to have undermined faithful friendship. The claim has been a theme in European thought since Bacon, perhaps an echo of the aristocratic and classical disdain for the bourgeoisie. But recent sociology has shown Bellah and Bacon and Plato are mistaken. Markets are consistent with real friendship.

An economistic way to make the point is a paper by Paul Ingram and Peter Roberts in the *American Journal of Sociology* in September 2000, "Friendship among Competitors in the Sydney Hotel Industry." They find that the friendships among competing hotel managers in the forty Sydney hotels in their study generate about $2.25 million more of gross revenues per year per hotel—for example, through recommendations of the competing hotel when fully booked—than would be generated by a hotel with friendless managers.[16] They add "the critical caveat that the instrumental benefits of friendships are inextricably tied to the affective element," that is, you can't successfully fake friendship.[17] The faithless ones get found out.

Considering the depth of skill among primates in performing and detecting falsehood, this is not surprising. Both prudence and solidarity work. "Individuals who try to form and maintain friendships solely as a means to material gain will fail to evoke trust and reciprocity." That is, Prudence Only will not work, and so "those who would limit the intrusion of society into economy by . . . characterizing embedded relationships between buyers and suppliers as predictable outcomes of a repeated, noncooperative game" are mistaken.[18]

One can show it historically, too. "Far from traditional society being suffused with brotherly *gemeinschaftlich* virtues," the sociologist Ray Pahl has concluded, "the reverse appears to be the case. Counter to what the classical sociological tradition appears to suggest [Simmel, for example], Aristotelian styles of friendship ["for the friend's own sake"] re-emerged with the coming of commercial-industrial society in the eighteenth century.... Counter to what is assumed in much modern social theory, it was precisely the spread of market exchange in the eighteenth century that led to the development of new benevolent bonds."[19]

Pahl believes, rather less persuasively, that friendship between men flourished unusually in twelfth-century Europe. Peter of Blois declared in the 1180s, "Are not my friends my inner self, whom I cherish and who take care of me in a sweet commerce of services, in an identity of affection?"[20] But what is clearer than his medieval evidence from monks and heretics is that in *early modern* Europe people were by modern standards extraordinarily feckless. Shakespeare's plots are filled with betrayals—far above the frequency in Ibsen's or O'Neill's, which on the contrary are often grim illustrations of *lotsverbondenheid* in a bourgeois society. Even in a Shakespeare comedy everyone is fooling someone else, lying, disguising, dissembling. Stephen Greenblatt traces the theme of perfidy in Shakespeare to his supposed secret Catholicism, in a world in which exposing such a secret was fatal.[21] Shakespeare is not alone in portraying an exceptionally shifty world in England around 1600. Lawrence Stone concluded that "so far as surviving evidence goes, England between 1500 and 1660 was relatively cold, suspicious and violence prone."[22]

Pahl cites the ironically named Boncompagno da Signa, who in his *Amicitia* of 1205 paints a similarly grim picture of faithless friends in Italy. One Paolo da Certaldo wrote a *Book of Good Practices* around 1360 with 388 precepts for merchants, among them "test [a purported friend], not once but a hundred times," a sentiment repeated in the same words a half century later by Giovanni Morelli, another Florentine businessman and moralist.[23] Certaldo quotes a proverb, "He who trusts not, will not be deceived," and Morelli advises the novice merchant, "Above all, if you wish to have friends or relationships, make sure you don't need them.... Cash ... [is] the best friend or relative you can have."[24]

But Pahl argues, following Allan Silver, that the economistic exchange model beloved of tough-guy sociologists and anthropologists in the early twentieth century fits even modern history poorly. And it was not favored by most of the ancients in theory. Cicero lambastes the Epicureans—the ancient Mediterranean's version of Max U economists—as "those men who in the manner of cattle [*pecundum ritu,* literally, "by the rite of the cattle"] refer everything to pleasure" and who "with even less humanity . . . say that friendships are to be sought for protection and aid, not for caring." He calls them "men abandoned to pleasure," who "when they dispute about friendship have understanding of neither its practice nor its theory."[25]

Adam Smith, allegedly the inventor of a theory that made do without love, did not in fact follow such an odd theory in his work or in his life. Smith and his friends thought of sympathy as creating a trusting society as by an invisible hand, in the way that prudence created an efficient one, an argument stressed by the economist Jerry Evensky.[26] As Daniel G. Arce M. put it, citing Evensky, "It is the coevolution of individual and societal ethics that leads to the stability of classical liberal society."[27] Pahl concludes that "sometime in the eighteenth century friendship appeared as one of a new set of benevolent social bonds."[28] It was not in modern times but in the olden times that the life of man was solitary, poor, nasty, brutish, and short.

This is no paradox. When a poor man can buy as much for his penny as a rich man, though he have fewer pennies, he is not required to doff his hat to get his daily bread. He does not need to pretend to be an ally of the butcher or the baker. This frees him when the occasion arises to be a real friend, an equal. Allan Silver notes that "the intense loyalties, coexisting with the frank expectation of reward, found in codes and cultures of honor before commercial society" were not nice and were not good for real, that is, bourgeois, friendship. Samuel Johnson described an aristocratic "patron" in his *Dictionary* as "a wretch who supports with insolence, and is paid in flattery," in the fashion of Lord Chesterfield. Johnson found the relationship with his paying bourgeois readers more satisfactory: "No man but a blockhead ever wrote, except for money."

In a world governed by honor one makes friends to keep from being assaulted, Cicero's "protection and aid." In a world governed by markets one buys protection, one hopes, anonymously with taxes or with fees to one's condominium association, and then is at leisure to make friends for the sake of real friendship. Modern capitalism—though we must not suppose, as many people do, that markets did not exist before 1800—was supported by, and supported in turn, a trust in *strangers* that still distinguishes prosperous from poor economies. The division of labor in the modern world, as Paul Seabright has emphasized, is achieved through "honorary friends."[29]

Trust and friendship, further, make possible speculative bubbles, from the tulip mania of the 1630s to the dot-com boom of the 1990s. The very fact of capitalism's speculative instability, therefore, argues for an entirely new prevalence of belief in strangers. "Credit" is from *creditus*, "believed." A business cycle based on pyramids of credit was impossible in the distrustful sixteenth century. The macroeconomy could in earlier times rise and fall, of course, but from harvest booms and busts, not from credit booms and busts. In those premodern-capitalist days God's hand, not human beliefs, made for aggregate ups and downs. Medieval and early modern people trusted only allies, and had wise doubts even concerning some of them: "How smooth and even they do bear themselves! / As if allegiance in their bosoms sat, / Crowned with faith and constant loyalty."[30] Premoderns had to keep faith with God and with their lords temporal. Late moderns keep faith with the market and with their friends.

On this theory the episodes of disorder and unemployment in capitalism from the 1630s in Holland and from 1720 in northern Europe arose from the virtues of capitalism, not from its vices, from its trustworthiness, not from its greed. To be more exact: the business cycle arose from trustworthiness breaking down suddenly in an environment of quite normal human greed for abnormal gain, the *auri sacra fames* which has characterized humans since the Fall. What is novel in capitalism is the faithful trust, *lotsverbondenheid* writ large.

11

HOPE AND ITS BANISHMENT

Man doth seek a triple perfection: first a sensual . . . then an intellectual. . . . Man doth not
seem to rest satisfied . . . but doth further covet . . . somewhat divine and heavenly, which
with hidden exultation . . . [such desire] rather surmiseth than conceiveth. . . . For although
the beauties, riches, honors, sciences, virtues, and perfections of all men living, were in the
present possession of one; yet somewhat beyond and above all this there would still be
sought and earnestly thirsted for.
  —Richard Hooker, *Of the Laws of Ecclesiastical Polity*, 1593

Hope is, by contrast to faith, forward-looking, the virtue of the energetic
saint or entrepreneur who seeks "a future, difficult, but attainable good."[1] It
is the opposite of *acedia*, spiritual sloth, despair, hopelessness, the "desperation" (< *de + sperare*, to be separated from hoping) that the seventeenth of
the Church of England's Thirty-Nine Articles warns against, "a most dangerous downfall, whereby the Devil doth thrust [curious and carnal per-
sons] into desperation."

Hope is of course essential for eternal life, and for humdrum life, too, as
one can see in the lethargy that comes over a human who, as we say, "has
nothing to look forward to." Carol Shields, the modern novelist of psychological health, calls hope "the slender handrail."[2] Richard Wilbur, the modern poet of psychological health, repeatedly surprised by joy, puts it this
way: "Joy for a moment floods into the mind / Blurting that all things shall
be brought / To the full state and stature of their kind."[3] The secular, or "natural," version of hope is an egalitarian version of Aristotle's aristocratic and
favorite virtue, "great-souledness," *megalopsychia*, translated literally into
Latin as "magnanimity."[4]

Christian doctrine and so-called "Austrian" economics agree in stressing that hope is about that ever-unseen future. It cannot be reduced to a mechanical prediction in the style of positivism, or to some easy dream of fey or elf, the assurance of indulgences purchased or chantries financed. "By hope we are saved," says St. Paul in Romans 8:24, "But a hope seen is not a hope, for why hope for something you already see?" It is a notable oddity of non-Austrian, "neoclassical," Samuelsonian economics that it imagines that we *already* have the information to make accurate judgments about the future. In such a case we would be in heaven, or hell, and hope would not exist: "Neither the blessed nor the damned can possess hope," as the theologian Romanus Cessario puts it. Hope is a virtue, Aquinas said, of the wayfarer, not of a person in command of all he is ever going to get.[5] It is, he said elsewhere, "the movement of a spirit aiming at great things."[6]

I am thinking, to change the image, of backward-looking faith as the rootedness of humans, in their identity as Dutch or female or psychologists or mothers. Then hope is the forward-looking flower growing from the roots. Lacking roots, one is faithless, having no place from which to grow. Rootlessness is the characteristic American failing, at any rate by comparison with the heavy rootedness of much of the rest of the world. But without the flower one is stuck in the soil. That is the characteristic failing of Asia and Europe, an excess of faith, at any rate by comparison with the crazy, uprooted hopefulness of America.[7]

Globalization has put faith and hope out of balance. The Marxist geographer David Harvey has noted that the "time-space compression" of modernity has eroded identity.[8] Or at any rate it can. It happened in the Europe of old. One can watch the cozy world of self-satisfied and rooted Franks being challenged by successive others in the Crusades, the age of discovery, the confrontation with the primitive, the shocks to European provincialism administered by Atlantic capitalism, imperialism, world wars, and finally globalization. Marshall Berman writes, "To be modern is to find ourselves in an environment that promises adventure, power, joy, growth, transformation of ourselves and the world—and at the same time threatens to destroy everything we have, everything we know, everything we are."[9] Hope can erode faith.

Ceaseless travel, made cheap to moderns, is exhilarating. But it is disturbing, too. Dilip Gaonkar points out to me that the dream of "retirement" in modern America has become a parody of the word. The oldsters do not "retire" to Innisfree. They change residences compulsively, looking for a new life, indulging a hope at the sacrifice of faith. The ultimate in such itinerant retirees is someone who owns a condo of the latest kind—on a cruise ship. "Wake up in a new harbor every couple of days" says the teaser in the eBay ad for a $70,000 ocean-going condo on the Norwegian Star. "Living on a ship circumnavigating the globe or catching your ship for a few days when it reaches your selected vacation spots, will raise a few eyebrows. You can hear it now: 'You live *where?*' It is a well deserved opportunity, but not for everyone. You have to love travel, be adventuresome, accept challenges with aplomb and enjoy exploring new places and meeting interesting people."[10]

Yet the American or European gazing at other cultures as a conqueror or anthropologist, or for that matter a condo owner on a cruise ship, presents a pathway for non-Europeans out of the tribe or village. Move to metropolitan France, as Ho Chi Minh did after working on a French ocean liner, living in London and the United States. Work as a pastry chef in Boston's Parker House—baking, one supposes, Parker House rolls. Then use the capitalist economy of Paris to remake yourself into a founding French communist.

Mobility in space, in other words, offers hope of a new identity. An American folk song from the early nineteenth century asked, "Oh, what was your name in the States? / Was it Thompson, or Johnson, or Bates? / Did you murder your wife and fly for your life? / Say, what was your name in the States?"—that is, the organized states admitted to the Union, as against the territories. Lighting out for the territories, of course, is the American myth of freedom through movement away from the faith-based oppressions of one's born class or region. It is Ben Franklin moving from fraternal domination in Boston to autonomy in Philadelphia, disembarking at the Market Street wharf carrying three great puffy rolls under his arm; it is the Frontier Hypothesis, the road movie. It is the blissful literalization of freedom.

Mobility does make for freedom. That's why Adam Smith, the egalitarian advocate for freedom, was so outraged by British and in particular English restrictions on the mobility of workers. A sharecropper who can move to another Southern county, or north to Bronzeville, cannot be exploited *in situ* by the country store. He's not in place. He's in the wider world. He can yet hope.

The rise of a secular hope and the fall of a spiritual faith, in other words, is nothing like always bad. A faith rooted in the economic importance of land made elders and imagined ancestors powerful, for good or ill. You can see it in the twists of eighteenth-century plays and novels right through Jane Austen, in which the elders control inheritance and therefore the hopeful young. The displacing of land by human capital as the main source of wealth sharply devalued faith, the past, the dead hand, the mortgage, the family line, the ancestors. And it upvalued hope, the future, the children, the individual.

Religious versions of faith and hope and love have been banished from the list of virtues in the West twice, during two waves of anti-Christian revision, what William Schweiker calls the "banishment of religious resources."[11] Or, if you wish, there was one long banishment interrupted in the late eighteenth century by a surprising revival of religious enthusiasm, at any rate in Protestant Europe.

The first banishment happened among the clerisy of Europe in the late seventeenth and early eighteenth centuries. The new philosophers reaped the harvest of seventeenth-century natural philosophy. Having learned that comets were not portents and tides were not miraculous, they generalized to a rejection of "particular providence": a rejection of God's restless agency in the world. Prayer, for example, has no efficacy if God is a remote prime mover.

A founding figure is Pierre Bayle (1647–1707), a French Protestant heretic and skeptic who found refuge in Rotterdam to write his *Dictionnaire historique et critique* (1696, 1702), the "arsenal of the Enlightenment."[12] Bayle and other deistic or even atheistic theoreticians, culminating with Voltaire, Holbach, and Hume, were reacting to excessive faith and hope in the wars of religion.

The deists and neo-Stoics of the age of equanimity were therefore eager to banish the transcendent. "The words 'taste' and 'politeness,'" J. G. A. Pocock notes, "for most of the eighteenth century, were freighted with a heavy ideological load. To latitudinarians and *philosophes* they connoted that reasonable and civic [faith] . . . with which it was hoped to replace the enthusiasms and fanaticisms of Puritanism or Christianity."[13] And for a time it did.

Take England, for example. The political settlement in 1660 and especially in 1689 had parallels in arts and manners. "After the Restoration the time had come," Matthew Arnold observed, "when our nation felt the imperious need of a fit prose, . . . of freeing itself from the absorbing preoccupation which religion in the Puritan age had exercised. . . . The needful qualities for a fit prose are regularity, uniformity, precision, balance. . . . But an almost exclusive attention to these qualities involves some repressing and silencing of poetry.[14] "Regularity, uniformity, precision, balance": he might as well have said "literary Prudence and Temperance in their bourgeois expressions." It is no surprise to find Arnold the nineteenth-century Hellenist commending poetry for an aristocratic expression of the virtues, its "glory, the eternal honor, . . . this noble sphere."[15] Arnold is not exactly contemptuous of the literally prosaic virtues of the bourgeoisie. He is not a proud aristocrat, not actually. But in judging poetry he takes his stand on the plains of Ilium or in the courts of Shakespeare's imagined age of Lancaster and York, not in the coffeehouses of Addison's London, or the London of Chaucer, either, that hive of the bourgeoisie before its greater time.

The second banishment of religious faith and hope gathers force among secularizing intellectuals around the middle of the nineteenth century. A. N. Wilson attributes the odd hiccup in the banishment—on in the eighteenth century, then off, then on again in the mid-nineteenth—to "Hume's time bomb," that is, *Dialogues Concerning Natural Religion*, published in 1779, three years safely after Hume's death and three years, too, after the publication of another anti-Christian bomb with a long fuse, Gibbon's *Decline and Fall of the Roman Empire*. In Wilson's view these sat on library shelves until the new seriousness of religiosity in England in the 1820s and 1830s caused them to be taken down and examined. In their own time, Hume could logic-chop and Gibbon sneer and the cosmopolites of 1776–1779 could laugh along with them. Not the sober and intellectually serious late Georgians and early Victorians.[16]

Arnold himself, though a deist and a devout student of the Bible, said it ("Dover Beach" was composed about 1851):

> The Sea of Faith
> Was once, too, at the full, and round earth's shore
> Lay like the folds of a great girdle furled.
> But now I only hear
> Its melancholy, long, withdrawing roar. . . .

Or Edward FitzGerald in 1859, though the sentiments are of course also ancient and Epicurean and indeed secularly Persian of the early twelfth century:

> Myself when young did eagerly frequent
> Doctor and Saint, and heard great argument

> About it and about; but evermore
> Came out by the same Door as I went in. . . .

> Into this Universe, and *Why* not knowing
> Nor *Whence*, like Water willy-nilly flowing;
>   And out of it, and Wind along the Waste.
> I know not *Whither*, willy-nilly blowing.

Or Thomas Hardy in 1866:

> If but some vengeful god would call to me
> From out the sky, and laugh. . . .
> But not so. How arrives it joy lies slain,
> And why unblooms the best hope ever sown?
> —Crass Casualty obstructs the sun and rain.
> And dicing Time for gladness casts a moan. . . .

Wilson has given a lively and touching portrait of the European and especially British men and women of the clerisy—and often enough of the clergy—who lost their faith then. John Maynard Keynes, writing in the 1920s, portrayed the late 1860s as "the critical moment at which the Christian dogma fell away from the serious philosophical world of England, or at any rate of Cambridge."[17] Early in the 1860s the soon-to-be economist Alfred Marshall was preparing for holy orders; by the end of the decade he and his fellows could not, Keynes writes, be called Christians. In praising the passage, Joseph Schumpeter notes that in the 1860s "Christian belief, gently and without any acerbities, was dropped by the English intelligentsia."[18]

Wilson takes his title, *God's Funeral*, from another poem by Hardy, a poem written fifty years after "Hap." Hardy in 1910 envisions Christians, as Feuerbach had some seventy years before, projecting their anxieties into their God:

> I saw a slow-stepping train—
> Lined on the brows, scoop-eyed and bent and hoar—
> Following in files across a twilit plain
> A strange mystic form the foremost bore. . . .

> Yet throughout all it symbolized none the less
> Potency vast and loving-kindness strong. . . .

>   "O man-projected Figure, of late
> Imagined as we, thy knell who shall survive?"

This was a quarter century after the sad doubt in England had begun to spread beyond the clerisy. In the 1880s "the loss of faith which had hitherto tormented only a few of the better-informed," Wilson reports, "had reached the suburbs" through among other routes a best-selling novel *Robert Elsmere* (1888), by Mrs. Humphrey Ward (née Mary Augusta Arnold: her uncle was Matthew Arnold; her nephew was Aldous Huxley).[19] Not that everyone became a skeptic. The Great War was still on the British and the German sides a religious crusade. By the Second World War, though, Christianity had been squeezed even out of war.

Also in the middle of the nineteenth century one sees the sharper French turn of the clerisy against the clergy in, say, Flaubert, or in Baudelaire. Progressive thought in France was from the time of Voltaire and Helvétius anticlerical, reinforced by the reactionary stance of the church during the Revolution. It was therefore anti-Christian and in the end antitheist. Progressives in France were and are dismally existentialist in their celebration of Crass Casualty. Wilson attributes the harsher anticlerical turn in Catholic Europe also in part to the reaction of former seminarians, "kept in genuine ignorance of biblical scholarship or of the developments of modern philosophy . . . who therefore suffered easily explicable crises when, in later life, they started to read books."[20] Compare Catholic Ireland, as in *Portrait of the Artist as a Young Man.*

In Britain, as in Germany and the United States, advanced thinkers often kept a worshipfully Christian tone even in their plans for the new society. Schumpeter attributes the tone to the Englishmen "having started their intellectual travels with a thorough grounding in Anglican theology (and, owing to the constitutions of Cambridge and Oxford colleges, with definite obligations towards it)." In consequence they "arrived at their final positions by way of conscious wrestling rather than by a growing agnosticism through indifference."[21] Note the contrast with Wilson's hypothesis of crisis in Catholic countries. In any event, there is a quasi-Christian cheerfulness about, say, George Bernard Shaw's English socialism which one does not find in Bertolt Brecht's Continental version.

12

AGAINST THE SACRED

In their official Christian vestments, that is, hope and faith were often unwelcome after 1848 in the salons and ateliers of European and especially Continental sophisticates. So still. Even the excellent Rosalind Hursthouse seems embarrassed by the Transcendent Two. Her exposition of virtue ethics in 1999 mentions in its index the virtue of love ninety times under various headings: benevolence, charity, compassion, generosity, kindness, loyalty, friendship.[1] The last two, I've said, have perhaps an element of faith in them. The virtue of justice, the male philosophical obsession, she mentions twenty-eight times. Temperance (and self-control) eighteen. Courage twenty-four. Moral wisdom, *phronēsis,* that is, prudence, which underlies all the virtues, twenty-six times. The typically modern and bourgeois philosopher's virtue of Honesty (= Justice with Faith and Courage) twenty-two times. That covers five of the classical seven, reproducing the secular pentad analyzed by Adam Smith and others in the Scottish Enlightenment.

But where *are* the other two, sacred hope and faith? Hursthouse ends her book with an appeal to "Keep hope alive." Her only other mention of the two is a page attacking "piety" as irrational, not characteristically human, "based on a complete illusion" from an atheist's point of view.[2] One wonders: is the physicist's pious but entirely atheistic faith in the orderliness of nature, which Hursthouse elsewhere notes is essential for a scientific worldview, therefore also irrational? Is science, then, "based on a complete illusion"? Hursthouse's own project—of justifying the virtues piecemeal from within a cultural set of them—is likewise undercut. It depends on philosophical faithfulness and hopefulness that such a procedure makes some sense, which she herself says are not justifiable philosophically, a mere piety.

That is, we humans live on air. My suggestion to my good colleagues of the modern clerisy is that they get used to it. The most characteristic virtues of humans are not a rationality or a persistence that one can see plainly in ants and bacteria as well. They are hope and faith. So late in the age of banishment, I wish that the advanced members of the clerisy would recover from being embarrassed by the most characteristically human virtues.

In his recent, elegant book, *A Small Treatise on the Great Virtues* (1996; English ed. 2001), the French philosopher André Comte-Sponville, for example, explicitly rejects both Faith and hope from a place among his eighteen virtues. The pagan tetrad of prudence, temperance, courage, and justice he acknowledges as cardinal, and these begin his book.

In the last chapter he deals also with love, along lines similar to mine, in fact—he draws heavily there as I do on Simone Weil, and elevates agape to primacy, though skirting uneasily its religious content. His attempts to distinguish love from Compassion, Mercy, and especially generosity are not wholly persuasive. He quotes his master the philosopher of music at the Sorbonne (d. 1985), Vladimir Jankélévitch, as admitting that "though the two are not the same, love and generosity, 'at its most exalted,' are hard to separate one from the other."[3] And so they are. Distinguishing true generosity from possibly self-interested indulgence of family and friends, the care of children, for example, depends in Jankélévitch and Comte-Sponville precisely on generosity being exercised "at its most exalted." The logic of classification would seem to require therefore that generosity be viewed, as it is in Aquinas, for example, as a subspecies of love.

But with the other two of the theological virtues, faith and hope, Comte-Sponville has no patience at all. He attempts to exclude incense-smelling faith from his virtues entirely. One device is to call it instead "fidelity," with a prominent chapter of its own, with no mention that faith in the transcendent might possibly include faith in God. The device does not work very well, since it merely substitutes the one faith-word for another, both derived from *fides* by longer or shorter etymologies.

Comte-Sponville writes wisely that "where there is mind there is memory. . . . Fidelity is . . . memory itself as a virtue."[4] He quotes Montaigne on fidelity as "the true basis of personal identity." But in the very quotation Montaigne declares a "fidelity to the *faith* [*foi*] I swore to myself," which seems a sound way to think about it. "The past," Comte-Sponville writes, "is in need of our compassion and gratitude; for the past cannot stand up for itself."[5] That too seems right. The towering dead are indeed owed some backward-looking faith, or else we are nobodies ourselves, disloyal pleasure-machines with no sacred identity. We are not worthy of self-love if we have not faith.

Fidelity, Comte-Sponville writes beautifully, is "an always particular presence within us of the past," our father, dead, our grandmother, the three men with the same last name from a village in southwestern France, whose dates on the wall of the parish church record them killed successively in the very first month, a middle month at the time of Verdun, and the very last month of the Great War.[6] We should preserve, Comte-Sponville puts it, "love for the sake of what once took place."[7]

But all this is precisely faith, *foi, fides*. It's too bad—too bad at least according to the faith of French anticlericals—that it's gotten mixed up with faith in God. But there you are. "Faith," writes A. N. Wilson about the decline of the Godly version of it in the nineteenth century, "was not something which could be gradually eliminated from the human scene. It was a vital component of the human make-up—personal and collective."[8]

The plainest exercise of antitheism in Comte-Sponville, however, is reserved for hope. Having taken occasional jabs at it in the previous 287 pages, he finally admits the reason for his distaste: "Faith, hope, and charity are traditionally the theological virtues (because they have God as an object). The first two I have not included in this treatise because they have no plausible object, it seems to me, other than God, in whom I do not believe." Yet Comte-Sponville *has* included faith, as fidelity. He continues, "Moreover, one can do without these two virtues: courage suffices in the presence of danger or the future." One might think that the second, forward-looking part of courage, "in the future," is precisely hope. But he is determined not to let the word in. He thinks hope is a fool's "virtue," suitable for the soft-minded who merely hope and pray when a tough, masculine, existentialist courage is what is called for.

He is not here reading Aquinas very carefully. Aquinas makes plain that courage is about fear (in the present) but hope is about imagination (about a future)—which analysis Comte-Sponville himself concedes during his chapter on courage: "*The future* is . . . an object of our imagination."[9] *Précisément.* The courage to face a present pain is one thing. It is akin to Temperance in its presentness. Courage resists pain now, temperance pleasure now. The hope to face imagined *future* pains for some imagined *future* purpose is distinct from these.

A woman can have a stoic courage in the face of the pain of chemotherapy yet lack the hope that makes it work. Physicians are finding that encouraging a lucid, realistic hope is therapeutic. The mind and body are connected. Jerome Groopman of Harvard Medical School argues that "Hope . . . does not cast a veil over perception and thought. In this way, it is different from blind optimism: It brings reality into sharp focus."[10] Hope is not about fooling ourselves—or at any rate no more about fooling ourselves, after innocence, than are any of the other virtues. Hope, though a religious virtue, is not necessarily about religion.

Comte-Sponville is quite correct to note that "all the barbarities of this [twentieth] century were unleashed in the name of the future, from Hitler's thousand-year Reich to Stalinism's promise of brighter and better tomorrows."[11] But such a remark contradicts his assertion that the only plausible object for hope is God, and shows the illogic in his case against counting hope among the great, if dangerous, virtues. *La révolution* or *das deutsche Volk* were plainly objects of hope. Yet they are equally plainly not God. That is one reason we need to keep hope firmly in view, because when unbalanced by the other virtues, it produces evil, such as revolutionary socialism or revolutionary fascism.

Comte-Sponville attacks hope, then, as utopian, "the seductions of hope and the dangers of utopia." One can certainly agree that damage has been done in the world by hopeful "utopic" theorists, as the tenth Federalist Paper skeptically put it. And the theorists did so especially after 1789. In the same way a hopeful religious utopianism did damage in Europe for a thousand years before 1789.[12] Such, for example, was Oliver Cromwell's rejection in the 1650s of the faithful precedent of the rule of law in favor of a hopeful vision of a city set upon a hill, and his arbitrary rule. But Hope does damage precisely because it takes all the future as its imaginative object and its ethical end. When unbalanced it justifies any number of broken eggs to make the imagined omelet. Hope is one of the characteristically human virtues—and when alone and unbalanced it is one of the characteristically human vices, too. The barbarities of the twentieth century were hopes granted. Be careful what you hope for.

Comte-Sponville declares that "faith and hope have left us; we live without them."[13] I do not think so. He and you and I do not in fact live without faith and hope. No one does for long, not really, or else she goes off and hangs herself. Comte-Sponville confuses God with the numerous other possible objects of Hope and Faith, showing in particular the atheist's stony inability to grasp that these other objects, in which he does believe, are psychologically the same as the God in which he proudly does not. Similarly in 1902 Bertrand Russell declared that a free man's worship was to be erected on "the firm foundation of unyielding despair."[14] One wonders why; but especially whether: Russell was miserable as a child, but as an adult gave few signs of despair, yielding or not.

In a similar Schopenhauerian vein, Romantically attractive now for nearly two centuries but still dubious, Comte-Sponville declares that politics is a matter of "will ... not hope."[15] I think not. Will and prudence act to *balance* and *complete* hope, as do faith and the other virtues. Politics, like the economy, is a field for the exercise of all the virtues together, and the vices. The will itself is a mixture of courage and temperance. The unsystematic and one-by-one conception Comte-Sponville has of the virtues shows up here. He does not see how virtues talk to each other.

Comte-Sponville in the end simply doesn't want hope and faith in his book. But after all they are part of human life, and keep barging in. The reason they do so—and here is something to be learned from the French clerisy's three-century-old distaste for religion—is that faith and hope are the *verbal* virtues. They require the symbolism of words. The invention of language and with it metaphor and other art made theorizable an imagined past and an imagined future. "The peculiar power of the human mind," wrote Stuart Hampshire, following his master Spinoza, "is the power to think about its own states and processes, and, by this reflective thinking, to modify them."[16] The cave painters of Lascaux, or the earlier painters of rocks in Ubirr in northern Australia, to give the usual interpretation, made hopeful images of the animal bodies they hoped to kill and the animal spirits they kept faith with. We cannot be sure of the details of their hope and faith precisely because we lack their words.

The other virtues can flourish without speech, even in nonhumans. Think of White Fang in the team, or finally at home in California, exhibiting canine courage, justice, prudence, love, and even perhaps temperance, though I suppose that one is a little hard to see in a dog. Aristotle noted that "in a number of animals we observe gentleness or fierceness, mildness or cross temper, courage, or timidity, fear or confidence, high spirit or low cunning, and, with regard to intelligence, something equivalent to sagacity."[17]

But not faith or hope. We say a dog is faithful, and is hopeful for the bone. But in a dog these are reducible to solidarity with the pack and pleasure in the marrow. Is human faith or hope so reducible? Marx and Freud to the contrary, I think not. The aborigine's Dreaming or the tales of the Great Spirit, the holy text, the Johnny Cash song, the language in our lives spin out and out. Humans can't leave ideas alone.

"The animals do not live in the world," sang Edwin Muir,

> Are not in time and space
> From birth to death hurled.
> No word do they have, not one
> To plant a foot upon,
> Were never in any place.
>
> For with names the world was called,
> Out of the empty air,
> With names was built and walled,
> Line and circle and square. . . .[18]

Think of a human mother before language who courageously overcomes her fear of bears and so with prudence finds some berries close to the bear's cave, which she shares lovingly with her child, exercising temperance in not gorging on them all herself, and then gives some to her child's playmate, too, in justice. Yet without a language in which to symbolize the transcendent, she cannot be said to exercise faith in the historical identity of her Clan of the Cave Bear, or hope for an afterlife in the sky. And she can't pass on her faiths and hopes. Perhaps this is why recognizably modern customs of burial and art appear rather suddenly together, after 50,000 BC, worldwide, when language appears to have spread rather suddenly out of Mother Africa, worldwide.

The heroine of the David Lodge novel *Thinks . . .* (2001) faces a conference of confidently positivist and behaviorist brain scientists. She gently notes to them the literary axiom they may perhaps have overlooked, "that human consciousness is uniquely capable of imagining that which is not physically present to the senses," instancing Marvell:[19]

> The mind, that ocean where each kind
> Does straight its own resemblance find;
> Yet it creates, transcending these,
> Far other worlds and other seas,
> Annihilating all that's made
> To a green thought in a green shade.

There could be no religion without language. That is clear enough. What is not clear is the outcome of our two- or three-century-old experiment in language without religion. Perhaps the two are inseparable. I talk; therefore I believe.

From the aborigines of the songlines and the cave painters of Lascaux to the plastic present, then, people have not lived without the transcendent. We are unique in this. Or at least so we imagine, lacking access to the spiritual world of whales and gorillas.

"If [faith] was not directed towards the true God," A. N. Wilson points out, noting the logic of the first commandment, "it would be directed towards idols."[20] And therefore the modern Westerners rejecting God found other gods, in will or despair or history or spiritualism or science or the environment. Giuseppe Mazzini had declared in 1835 that "the republican party is not a political party; it is essentially a religious party," and he declared again in 1848 that Young Italy "was not a sect but a religion of patriotism. Sects may die under violence; religions may not."[21] In the same revolutionary year he wrote: "Young men of Italy, it is time that you should comprehend how grand, how holy and religious is the mission confided to you by God."[22] By the end of the century Puccini's Tosca, who "lived for art, lived for love," and her lover Cavaradossi, similarly motivated—and somewhat accidentally a nationalist revolutionary, too—explore the limits of these substitute religions among the Italians.

The Age of Substitution begins, as I have noted, among a handful of advanced European souls as early as 1700, is widespread among them in 1800, is a passion among a wider clerisy after 1848, and takes hold among the newly educated masses after 1880 and especially after 1968. Interestingly, Japan embarked on the first part of this history a little earlier. In the late seventeenth century it had its own secular phase, in a Japanese version of the Enlightenment, against Buddhism. And in the mid-eighteenth century, somewhat in advance of similar Romantic nationalisms in Europe, some Japanese substituted National Learning for a China-worshipping and classicizing Confucianism.[23]

In Europe for about two centuries now, for example, a secular religion of Beauty has been fashioned out of one or another Art. Wagner's remark that "I believe in God, Mozart, and Beethoven" is not merely a secular witticism. It is a serious invitation to beatitude through Art, a faith reaching its height in the early twentieth century. It persists. Lucy bothers Schroeder over his piano with an earnest question: "I'm looking for the answer to life, Schroeder. What do you think is the answer?" Next panel, he replies with screaming capitals: "BEETHOVEN!" Next panel, more screaming: "Beethoven is it, clear and simple!! Do you understand?!" The fourth panel fills with notes from a piano piece, presumably by Beethoven, and Lucy's subdued "Good grief!"[24]

And it is new. The musicians in Mozart's time, or the painters in Vermeer's, or the poets and playwrights in Shakespeare's, had viewed themselves as crafts- and businesspeople, not as secular saints. All those craftspeople, further, were, most of them, believing Christians, if only because believing in Christianity was not viewed as optional. They did not need Art, capital A, or screaming block capitals, because they already had a transcendent, called God, capital G.

The shift comes with radicalism and Romance. Consider, for example, the modern public art museum, which begins in 1793 with the opening of the Louvre to all citizens. The Vatican had started occasional public exhibitions in 1773. But the Louvre was an aggressively populist project, a project transferred by the Bonaparte brothers to the Accademia of Venice in 1807 and to the Rijksmuseum in Amsterdam in 1808.[25] The museum was transformed in a revolutionary age from a plaything for aristocrats into a democratic temple to Beauty, replacing God. In the early twentieth century the museum came to be devoted to the admiring of genius and in the late twentieth century to the anticipation of shock. But anyway "devoted."

That is, museums since the late eighteenth century have been temples for the worship of some God-replacing transcendent. One is quiet in them, contemplative, worshipful, impressed by the presence of the Sacred. One carries home trinkets from the museum gift shop like crucifixes from the shops around St. Peter's. "As people desert the churches to fill the galleries," writes Nathalie Heinich, "art is no longer an instrument, but instead an object of sacralization. . . . Widely circulated reproductions are but substitutes . . . in those places where the ordinary person can experience the presence of the originals, preserved as relics."[26] Indeed the literal churches of Christianity have been turned into museums, especially in Italy. The skeptical tourists swoon before Christian frescoes. How odd / Of God / To be crazy / About Veronese. But not so crazy / As those enticed / By Christian Veronese / Who spurn the Christ.

Charles Hutchinson, one of Chicago's pork kings, and Martin Ryerson, a lumber baron, made the Art Institute in the 1890s a democratic cathedral of culture. The bourgeois Chicagoans acquired European paintings by the square yard—for example, El Greco's *Assumption of the Virgin,* urged on the Paris agent of the institute by Mary Cassatt. Hutchinson replied to sneers at such bourgeois virtue, "We have made our money in pigs, but is that any reason why we should not spend it on paintings?" Hutchinson in fact spent fully half his large annual income from meatpacking on civic projects, such as the Art Institute, and on Jane Addams's Hull House.

Addams herself is sometimes said to have used art to raise the immigrant poor of Halstead Street. That was a typically Progressive project, the bourgeoisie bending down to impart bourgeois values to the poor. In truth Addams was skeptical of the notion favored at Toynbee Hall in London (1884–) that art was elevating. But a mile away from Hull House and far up the social scale, Hutchinson certainly did have in mind civilizing the millionaires of Prairie Avenue with the Art Institute.[27] Neither project in the short run would achieve its end, since art is not so powerful in the short run. But the point is that they tried, viewing art as their god.

It is hardly surprising nowadays to find art museums very common in, say, the progressive Netherlands. Bookstores in the sophisticated neighborhoods of Rotterdam or Amsterdam or Gouda shelve their many books of poetry next to their few books on God. Until the 1960s half of the titles issued by Dutch publishers were religious. No longer. But the old stock of cultural capital, formerly religious, is reappropriated now for nonreligious ends of a secular and yet still transcendent Faith and Hope.

The Noorderkerk was the first church built in Amsterdam for specifically Protestant worship. It is still used sometimes as a church in the sober fashion of the North Hollanders. But mainly it is now a meeting hall to celebrate secular faith and hope. On the day of remembrance for the Amsterdam Jews, at 8:00 p.m. exactly, a little band outside the Noorderkerk in the yuppified neighborhood of Amsterdam's Jordaan plays a few songs, the hymns, so to speak, for the largely gentile congregation, and then God's service moves inside for communion with transcendent Faith and Hope, the reading of secular poems, and the playing of classical music.

13

VAN GOGH AND THE TRANSCENDENT PROFANE

We are in a transition stage between a mechanistic concept of man and an amalgam of both the rationalistic and what you could call the mystical or spiritualistic concept of him. . . . The work of art, the great work of art, is going to be that work which finds space for the two forces to operate.
—Arthur Miller, 1958

The Wagnerian replacement of religion with Art is typified by a Dutchman: Vincent van Gogh. He has become a Christ-figure of art appreciation, tormented for the bourgeois' sin of not buying his paintings when he was alive, and now redeemed in dollars. Vincent was a poet in paint, a self-educated sophisticate. He read novels and journals of opinion ravenously in four languages, taking themes for paintings directly from them, and wrote letters in three of the languages often and well, especially to his equally sophisticated art-dealer brother, Theo. Thanks to his literary bent, he is the most word-described of nineteenth-century painters, at any rate per year of artistic activity.

The van Gogh of popular myth is the tortured artist, his allegedly chronic madness and his actual suicide casting a shadow back on his art, as he feared it would. Had he not started to have attacks of a supposed mental illness in December 1888, and especially had he not committed suicide in July 1890, but lived out a normal span like Monet or Cézanne, we would have more of his art, with the same qualities—which were technical developments, not effusions of madness—at a lower price per painting, unhyped by the Romance of his illness and death. The productions of Virginia Woolf, Ernest Hemingway, Sylvia Plath, and Anne Sexton have suffered, and in

Romance benefited, from a similar overemphasis on their alleged or actual mental illnesses. According to modern psychiatric dogma, suicide just *is* crazy. Anyone in the United States who threatens suicide can be committed to a mental institution against her will.

In van Gogh's case the overemphasis of his alleged mental illness began six months before his death with an article in *Le Mercure de France* by the young critic Albert Aurier, who saw madness and greatness in "the isolate." Van Gogh wrote to Aurier thanking him for praising the paintings, though trying to show him that this was no isolated madman holding the pen, or the brush, but a man of normal mind who was a competent and thoughtful artist.[1]

The myth, however, has been unstoppable. It fits well the late-Romantic, wannabe-aristocratic notion of the mad artist, as in Kirk Douglas's riveting but nutty performance in the movie *Lust for Life*. Saul Bellow, speaking of Delmore Schwartz in *Humboldt's Gift*, attributes the attitude to the prestige of business and technology in America: "The weakness of the spiritual powers is proven by the childishness, madness, drunkenness, and despair of these martyrs. . . . So poets [and other artists] are loved, but loved because they just can't make it here."[2]

But the mad-artist idea is not confined to capitalist America. Herbert Read in *The Meaning of Art* (1931) spoke of van Gogh's letters: "Here is a veritable Painter's Progress, but with no Celestial City at the end of it, only chaos and dark despair—the madness and self-inflicted death of a genius in a cold and uncomprehending world."[3] A sidebar in the section about the Van Gogh Museum in the *Eyewitness Guide to Amsterdam* (1995) gives "An Artist's Life" in seventy-two words: fully forty of them concern his illness.[4] Among the Dutch, speaking to themselves, it is a similar tale. *De Millenium Top-40*, giving sketches of the forty "greatest" Dutch people of all time, ranked Vincent thirteenth and entitled the sketch *Zelfmoordenaar die bleef leven*, "a suicide who continued to live." It devotes over half of its 360 words to a bizarre comparison of van Gogh with Nietzsche gone mad allegedly from syphilis, a comparison said to be *minder gek dan het lijkt*, "less crazy than it seems," and a still more crazy one with the "suicidal artist-politician" Adolf Hitler.[5]

If a great novelist died at age thirty-seven of heart disease brought on by lack of temperance in diet, no one would think to retell 55 percent of her artistic story as a battle of the waistline. Dylan Thomas did die at thirty-nine, apparently from drinking. But no one interprets his poetry as being a result of his boozing. Indeed, from age thirty-one to thirty-nine he wrote a total of eight poems.[6] No doubt the myth of audacity added to his fame, postmortem—his last words are supposed to have been, "I have just drunk eighteen double whiskeys in a row. I believe that's a record." We seem to want these cults to flourish.

Van Gogh's main illness was said at the time to have been epilepsy, which has not been classed with paranoia and the like for quite a while. He did also appear to have a few psychotic breaks, though it is easy in psychiatric diagnosis to be wrong. A Dr. Peyron wrote in May 1889 that van Gogh had "acute mania with hallucinations of sight and hearing." Peyron was the same doctor who the following autumn told Vincent's brother Theo that the disease was a form of epilepsy.

Van Gogh's troubles are more consistent with George III's disease, that is, inherited porphyria, an accumulation in the body of self-produced porphyrin, a chemical involved in the transport of oxygen to the cells, exacerbated by his drinking, especially of absinthe. Acute attacks sometimes bring on anxiety and other behavior disturbances, and are painful. Whatever van Gogh had during that year and a half, it was episodic, with long intervals of quite ordinary health in which he continued, as he had done before the illness came on, to develop his art with his usual thoughtfulness.

Vincent was a difficult person, lonely yet enthusiastic, inclined to turmoil in relationships. But in seeming contradiction he was a cheerful and enterprising Dutchman, too. Everyone "knows" he sold only one painting in his lifetime, "The Red Vineyard" (1888), though an economist observes that in fact he "sold" a great many more—to other painters in trade for their paintings, which did have a cash value in the market. In 2004 a collective of artists chosen by critics initiated just this scheme for old-age insurance: give to the collective a few works when you're unknown and then get a pension on the basis of all the artists' more valuable work when you're old. Nonetheless van Gogh's lack of worldly success would have depressed anyone so hopefully intent on "the art of the future," a phrase he drew from a manifesto by the commercially more savvy Wagner.

The myth classifies Vincent with lunatics, or at best with suffering humanitarian poets romanticized, and sees in his controlled swirls of impasto in his late works the mad artist. But to believe this you have to believe a psychiatrism finding madness everywhere. He was ill for only those last nineteen months, and then, I repeat, only from time to time. Vincent's sister-in-law, who knew him well, believed that "fear of the illness that was threatening him, or an actual attack" precipitated his suicide.[7] Suicide was in 1890 a reaction *minder gek dan het lijkt* to a dread disease without a cure, increasing in severity.

He was prudent about the illness except for his continued heavy drinking. He cooperated in finding asylums that would protect him so that he could work in peace between attacks. Psychiatrists have a name for such cooperativeness, "insight," commonly lacking in people attracting their attentions. From the depths he never writes letters or tries to paint. People with epilepsy describe a fog on the brain persisting long after an attack. Porphyria, to repeat, is also episodic. After each recovery, Ronald de Leeuw the former director of the Van Gogh Museum notes, "he writes clearly, rationally and with a marked lack of sentimentality about his illness." Above all "he studiously refuses to grant mental illness any positive influence on artistic creation."[8]

Van Gogh's illnesses did not make his art. They blocked it.[9] In his estimation, sex did, too. He declared in a letter of June 1888 to his young artist friend Émile Bernard: "Painting and fucking a lot don't go together, it softens the brain. Which is a bloody nuisance."[10] His art certainly did not derive from his madness, or from his sexual activity, or from his bodily pains, or from his drinking. He painted when he was well and sober. His art had nothing to do with being sick.

What *is* this insistence on the mad, alcoholic artist? Such a man (always a man) is above all imprudent. He does not plan. He can't handle money. He injures himself. The bourgeois is known as a seeker of safety—this against the fact of risk in a commercial life. The mad artist rejects safety. The myth is an antibourgeois faith in the autonomous human spirit—this against the opportunities for expression in a commercial life. Who is in love with the myth? Sons and daughters of the bourgeoisie.[11]

Compare the attitude toward van Gogh the antibourgeois bourgeois with that toward the most despised artist of modern times, Norman Rockwell—despised that is by the clerisy. Rockwell's scenes of middle-class life are loathed for their warmth. Sentimental? Of course, rather like the sentimentality reflecting a loving regard of El Greco's *Assumption of the Virgin* or of van Gogh's *Irises*. What outrages the clerisy in Rockwell is his embrace of bourgeois American life—that and his commercial success and his long, sober, boring life: he is the opposite of van Gogh in every way except his sentimentality and his bourgeois values and his lack of esteem among his high-art contemporaries.

In his painting van Gogh was not foolish or mad. There is even doubt, by the way, about the circumstances of the ear-cutting-off. A German art historian, Rita Wildegans, claims that Gauguin did the ear-cutting, and that van Gogh was covering up for his friend by claiming that he himself did it. Vincent, as nonreligious people say, was spiritual. He sought faith and hope, but substituted art for religion. Van Gogh was canonized, I have noted, at the peak of Art as religion, the age of high modernism, Picasso to Pollock.

By the time of his best painting he was no longer the intense young Christian seeking after sainthood he had once been. Yet he was still, de Leeuw writes, a "struggling seeker after God": "Whether his particular concern was religious or artistic, he invariably cultivated his inner universe and confidently sought the eternal in the temporal."[12]

Explaining in the letter to Bernard in June 1888 mentioned above how he painted one of his many studies on Millet's *The Sower*, he speaks of the technical details ("the rest of the sky is chrome yellow 1 and 2 mixed"), noting that "I couldn't care less what the colors are in reality." Postimpressionism came to be more and more about the arrangement of colors on a flat surface. He then declares to Theo his search for faith and hope, tying them to a particular aesthetic project: "I am still enchanted by snatches of the past [his faith], have a hankering after the eternal [his hope], of which the sower and the sheaf of corn are the symbols. But when shall I get around to doing the *starry sky*, that picture which is always in my mind?"[13] "I keep hoping," he wrote to Theo in September, "to express hope by some star."[14] Hope, hope, hope. Thus his *Starry Night* (June 1889). The very painting that is supposed to show him as the mad artist turns out to have been not a crazy effusion but a project long conceived, worked on repeatedly, planned carefully before his first illness, and achievable only when well.

One of his two last paintings was *Wheatfield with Crows*, which, "hankering after the eternal," is shadowed by birds of ill omen. Yet, write Denise Willemstein and the staff of the Van Gogh Museum, "this theory is probably incorrect as the subject is traditional. . . . Moreover, in his final letter to Theo, dated 25 July, Vincent ordered new paint, suggesting that he still had many plans for new paintings."[15] He shot himself two days later. Vincent was not the sort of nonbourgeois, non-Dutch brother to waste long-suffering Theo's money on a gesture.

Johan de Meester wrote a newspaper article about the painting six months after Vincent's death. It emphasized, as he put it in a letter to Andries Bonger, Vincent's brother-in-law, "the side that interested me most as a pessimistic psychologist." Bonger wrote back politely but firmly, "I have not considered Vincent 'a sick man.'" He rejected de Meester's comparison of Vincent with Claude, the painter and suicide in Zola's novel *L'oeuvre* (1886).

Zola was advancing the theories of the doctor and criminologist Cesare Lombroso that men of genius were mentally ill—for example, epileptic.[16] Medicine in its initial decades of real science seemed to wish to redefine virtually everyone as sick. It is the theme of Freudianism. In April 1887, before Vincent had fallen ill, Theo himself had written of the Zola novel, "Before I read it, I also thought according to the criticism that Vincent had much in common with the hero. But that is not so. That painter was looking for the unattainable, while Vincent loves the *things that exist* far too much to fall for *that*."[17] A later Dutch painter, Jan Sluyters, wrote about it this way in 1953: "His paintings have nothing strange, mysterious, or abstract about them. They are the most natural impressions of a perfectly healthy temperament. . . . People—how well I know it—have often written about mental disorders, etc., etc., but of these so-called nervous disorders I have discovered no trace in his entire *oeuvre*. . . . He shows . . . the usual things of daily life . . . fanatically, yes!—but naturally."[18]

In another letter to his brother in the year of miracles, 1888—again *before* the attacks—van Gogh confessed to "a terrible need—shall I say the word—of religion. Then I go out at night to paint the stars."[19] His art became Art, a simulacrum of religion like others put forward as the sea of faith receded. The simulacra since Keats's *Ode on a Grecian Urn* have been more or less in sequence, I have noted, beauty, literature, history, the nation, spiritualism, science, progress, evolution, the future, the race, the revolution, struggle, the suburban family, technology, peace, Wall Street, and the environment. Van Gogh's was the movement of a faithful spirit aiming at great things, as humans keep faithfully hoping.

"I can well do without the good Lord in my life and also in my painting," van Gogh wrote a few weeks before the paint-the-stars letter, "but, suffering as I am, I cannot do without something greater than myself, something which is my life—the power to create. . . . I want to paint men and women with a touch of the eternal, whose symbol was once the halo, which we try to convey by the very radiance and vibrancy of our coloring."[20] He suffered spiritually, not mentally: he had no attacks yet.

The other of his last two paintings, *Tangled Roots*, could equally have been a suicide note. But the putative illness of his suicide, or the rational plan of his suicide, or the momentary impulse of his suicide in the face of a new attack of porphyria, is of no help in understanding the bulk of his art, for example, *Starry Night*. Sometimes a suicide note is just a suicide note.

And van Gogh was of course bourgeois. An educated Dutchman who worked from age sixteen like his brother as an art dealer could be no other. He wrote in French when in France, as he did to Theo. In the usual businesslike Dutch way with commercial languages he was also completely fluent in English—he gave his first sermon in England in English—and could read German well. He was the son of a Dutch Reform pastor and the nephew of three other art dealers. Holland's pastors are dealers, too. His father managed the farms of pioneering Protestants in the Catholic south of the Netherlands.

And so Vincent made the case for his sacred ends in profane terms, expressing as simple prudence his hopes for a very grand Studio of the South. To his brother, who supported him apparently gladly and was paid in pictures to obviate the appearance of a peasantly handout, he wrote with prudence that if Gauguin were to join him in Arles the enterprise would have low costs and would make money. "You always lose by being isolated. But you might think it's a good idea that we share expenses, set an amount of, let's say, 250 francs per month, if every month, besides and apart from my work, you get a Gauguin. Provided that we do not exceed that sum, wouldn't it mean a profit?"[21]

Compare his scheme for the leading Impressionists to pool some of their market-valued paintings to support "a whole battalion of artists who have been working in unremitting poverty," for example, that same V. van Gogh.[22] These are natural terms to use in pitching an idea to a businessman in 1888. An aristocrat in the same activity, like Henri de Toulouse-Lautrec, only son of the Comte de Toulouse and on his mother's side as well coming from one of the grandest families in France, would deign to talk this way to no one. And a peasant would merely beg the noble lord's indulgence, or claim his due, inarticulately. Only a bourgeois would offer *words* and *reasons* and *calculations* in support of transcendence. The Vincent of Romance is above all antibourgeois, "making no concessions to his bourgeois surroundings."[23] But that's not Vincent van Gogh.

In other words, we humans, even we bourgeois humans, cannot get along without transcendence—faith in a past, hope for a future, justified by larger considerations. If we don't have religious hope and faith, we'll substitute hope and faith in art or science or national learning. If we don't have art or science or national learning or Anglicanism, we'll substitute fundamentalism or the Rapture. If we don't have fundamentalism or the Rapture or the local St. Wenceslaus parish we'll substitute our family or the rebuilt antique car. It's a consequence of the human ability to symbolize, a fixture of our philosophical psychology.

We might as well acknowledge it, if only to keep watch on transcendence and prevent it from doing mischief, as did once a Russian hope for the Revolution and as now does a Saudi Arabian faith in an Islamic past. The Bulgarian-French critic Tzvetan Todorov, who has seen totalitarianism, warns that "democracies put their own existence in jeopardy if they neglect the human need for transcendence."[24] Michael Ignatieff put it well: "The question of whether . . . the needs we once called religious can perish without consequence . . . remains central to understanding the quality of modern man's happiness."[25] Evidently the answer is no, religion cannot perish without consequences. There are bad consequences and there will be more. That is not a reason to return to the older sureties. It is a reason to take seriously the transcendent in our bourgeois lives.

14

HUMILITY AND TRUTH

I cannot conceive the necessity for God to love me. . . . But I can easily imagine that he loves that perspective of creation which can only be seen from the point where I am. . . . I must withdraw so that he may see it.
  —Simone Weil, *Gravity and Grace*

According to one standard English translation of St. Thomas Aquinas's *Summa Theologiae,* the humble person "in respect of that which is his own ought to subject himself to every neighbor, in respect of that which the latter has of God's."[1] It's a cloudy sentence, and not any clearer in the Latin. But it seems in context to mean merely this: we should respect in other people what God, after all, has created. To scorn listening to others is to commit the chief theological sin against the Holy Spirit, pride. The sparks of perfection in people are to be esteemed, "that we may know the things that are given to us by God," as St. Paul put it.[2] Or, as St. Augustine wrote—also quoted approvingly by Aquinas—"We must not esteem by pretending to esteem, but should really think it possible for another person to have something that is hidden to us and whereby he is better than we are."

The founding Quaker George Fox urged us to listen quietly and "answer the witness of God in every man, whether they are the heathen . . . or . . . do profess Christ."[3] Father Peter Maurin was described by Dorothy Day after his death in 1949 as "truly humble of heart, and loving. . . . He . . . saw all others around him as God saw them. In other words, he saw Christ in them."[4] And Rabbi Jonathan Sacks (since the point is not merely Christian) wrote in 2002, "Truth on the ground is multiple, partial. . . . Each person, culture and language has part of it. . . . The [Jewish] sages said, 'Who is wise? One who learns from all men.'"[5]

To put it academically and economically, humility enjoins listening to one's colleagues for the sake of Truth's message in them. Shut up and learn something. The wisdom books of the Hebrew Bible are full of such advice, as in the proverbs of Solomon:

> Wise men lay up knowledge, but the babbling of a fool brings ruin near (Prov. 10:14).

> He who belittles his neighbor lacks sense, but a man of understanding remains silent (11:12).

> If one gives answer before he hears, it is his folly and shame (18:13).

Or Jesus son of Sirach: "The tongue of man is his fall. . . . But if thou love to hear, thou shalt receive understanding" (13, 33). "Some people without brains," says the Scarecrow in the movie of *The Wizard of Oz*, "do an awful lot of talking." Harry Truman, I have noted, defined an expert as "someone who doesn't want to learn anything new." Such pride is the opposite of humility, the humility to listen and learn.

The philosopher Amélie Oksenberg Rorty once described the habit of intellectual humility, rare among academics eager to speak and reluctant to listen. What is crucial is "our ability to engage in continuous conversation, testing one another, discovering our hidden presumptions, changing our minds because we have listened to the voices of our fellows. Lunatics also change their minds, but their minds change with the tides of the moon and not because they have listened, really listened, to their friends' questions and objections."[6]

Humility is part of the cardinal virtue of Temperance, which in turn is the internal balance essential for a good life. Humility, said Aquinas, answers among the Christian virtues to the pagan virtue of great-souledness, which Aristotle the pagan teacher of aristocrats admired so much. To be humble is to temper one's passions in pursuing, as Aquinas put it, *boni ardui*, goods difficult of achievement. To be great-souled, which in turn is part of the cardinal virtue of Courage, is to keep working toward such goods nonetheless.[7]

We appear to need both. Think of the balance of hope and temperance, and in particular the balance of great-souledness and humility, that is necessary to sustain good work in science and scholarship, or in sports or crafts, or in any difficult good. Your high-school driving instructor said, "Aim high in steering." Words to live by, a great-souledness. But the skepticism of humility is also needed, to listen to the hints of the highway. If we are not to end in foolishness, or in the ditch, we need to aim high but also to listen, really listen.

The goods difficult of achievement must to be "goods" in the noneconomic sense in order for humility and great-souledness in pursuing them to be ethical. Scholarly excellence in understanding actual economies, for example, or the use of one's wealth in proper stewardship, are good goods, and proper objects therefore of a paired humility and great-souledness in their pursuit. Scholarly excellence in understanding imaginary economies, or wealth used in projects of gluttony, is not such a good. It is not surprising to find people bound up in such bad goods exhibiting an idiotic pride and lack of temperance. They sin boldly, but do not believe in or rejoice in Christ, or any other good Good. Humility would resist such presumption, as Aquinas's Christian version of great-souledness resists despair.[8]

To be prideful in the bad, un-Christian, boyish sense is to will to defy God, which is to say to make oneself the object of striving, a very god, violating the first through fourth commandments. God is God, said the commandments, not little moi: *Sh'ma Yisrael adonai elohaynu adonai echad*, Hear, O Israel, the Lord our God is one Lord.

Thus Lucifer, who even when he was light-bearer among the angels was not given to humble listening, is described in *Paradise Lost*:

> he of the first,
> If not the first archangel, great in power,   660
> In favor and pre-eminence, yet fraught
> With envy against the Son of God, that day
> Honored by his great Father, and proclaimed
> Messiah King anointed, could not bear
> Through pride that sight, and thought himself impaired.   665
> Deep malice thence conceiving and disdain.[9]

"Impaired" turns on the usual sort of Miltonic ambiguity. Lucifer thinks, that is, falsely imagines, himself to be a "pair" with Christ, thus "impaired," but immediately the reader is surprised to see that Lucifer thinks himself impaired, that is, damaged. And Lucifer thinks himself into actual damage, indeed "conceives," that is, generates, himself, by way of the double meaning of "conceive" = "think up" and "conceive" = "create a child." He could not "bear," that is give birth to, the sight of Christ; he was fraught with, that is, bearing, envy, coming "through" the master sin, pride.

Such word games seem impossibly cute. But that was how Milton worked.[10] For example, the number of the last line, 666, known in numerology as the

Devil's number, is exactly where Lucifer becomes Satan (Hebrew "enemy"). The year 1666 was a culmination of disasters for Restoration England, a plague year (1665) followed by the Great Fire (1666). But it was a year of triumph for Milton the Puritan and embittered Cromwellite, who in it appears to have fin-ished the first editions of *Paradise Lost* (published 1667) and *Paradise Regained*, though blind. Michael Lieb points out to me that 999 is important, too, the line in book 9 of Adam's Fall in *Paradise Lost*. It is the result of turning upside down that 666, again the number of the beast (Rev. 13:18). From Milton's viewpoint one could say that 666 + 999 = 1665, the beginning of apostate England's well-deserved troubles.

Satan in Milton is a great speaker, and no humble listener, which has led Romantics such as Blake and Goethe to imagine that Milton was of Satan's party. But he is utterly incapable of shutting up and learning anything, as Milton shows most clearly in the Satan-Christ colloquies in *Paradise Regained*. His pride is the opposite of a proper humility that could balance his undoubted great-souledness.

The theologian Stephen Pope emphasizes that "humility should not be confused with humiliating self-abnegation before others."[11] "Some strands of Christian piety and theology," writes another theologian, Ellen Charry, "suspect that enjoying life is somehow impious." She notes that humility as interpreted by medieval monasticism— "because of poor theological education of monastics"—was interpreted as requiring self-abnegation."[12]

St. Catherine of Siena (1347–1380) never learned to write—she would dictate as many as three texts simultaneously to three scribes, in the style of St. Thomas—but became a diplomat in the chaotic Italy of the Schism and was proclaimed at last a doctor of the church. She starved to death at the age that Jesus was crucified by insisting on eating nothing but the eucharist. Dorothy Day said that reading a hagiography of St. Catherine inspired her to her own life of radical abstention in the name of Christ. The outcome, Charry notes, "looks to many of us like defiant pride rather than obedient humility. Humility, perhaps now the most despised of Christian virtues, is, nevertheless, essential to happiness." But in Catherine "we see how easily it slips over into pride."[13]

Simone Weil, too, in her proud self-abnegation seems like a literate ver-sion of St. Catherine. Weil declares in her notebooks that "humility is the refusal to exist outside God," as she so refused. "It is the queen of virtues."[14]

But as Thomas Merton put it, "Humility is a virtue, not a neurosis. . . . A humility that freezes our being and frustrates all healthy activity is not humility at all, but a disguised form of pride."[15] That's Satan's repeated error. He thinks humility before God is self-abnegation, and a prideful self is his little god. Better to rule in hell than serve in heaven, says he. No, Satan, wrong again. Humility is seen erroneously as the opposite of a world-enjoying spirit. Satan thinks of it as merely an inconvenience to the questing will. Confusion about humility is widespread. If you are a candidate for the priesthood in the Episcopal church, you will fear that your "discernment committee" assigned to test your calling will turn out to be itself a site of envy and pride, engaging in hazing under a demand that you be "humble."

What may be bothering Satan is the feminine quality of humility. Feminist theologians such as Valerie Saiving, Judith Vaughan, and Rosemary Ruether have been observing for decades that humility has a womanly cast, and that the corresponding sin of excess against the spirit is precisely self-abnegation—as Saiving put it in 1960, "triviality, distractibility, and diffuseness; lack of an organizing center or focus; dependence on others for one's own self definition; . . . in short, underdevelopment or negation of the self."[16] It is a point that John Stuart Mill made in his feminist blast of 1869: "I believe that equality of rights would abate the exaggerated self-abnegation which is the present artificial ideal of feminine character."[17] Excess in self-abnegation is to humility as excess in pride is to great-souledness. Together the two virtues balance and complete each other. On their own, without the other, they are not virtues at all, but rather the characteristic female sin against the spirit and the characteristic male one.

True humility is not undignified. Uriah Heep is most umble, but of course has merely the semblance of the virtue. He esteems, or more accurately feigns to esteem, only rank. *That* is undignified. "But how little you think of the rightful umbleness of a person in my station, Master Copperfield! Father and me was both brought up at a foundation school for boys. . . . They taught us all a deal of umbleness. . . . We was to be umble to this person, and umble to that; and to pull off our caps here, and to make bows there; and always to know our place, and abase ourselves before our betters. And we had such a lot of betters!"[18]

True humility on the contrary is democratic, looking for the best in people, and often finding it. In theological terms, it is to answer the witness of God in any other person, whether he is the heathen or does profess Christ.

Uriah does not honor the God's Truth in the least high-ranking of us, which is to say that he embodies the error that rank and truth are identical. He defers unreflectively to rank. In similar fashion, to give examples from the theory of prudence, misled "Austrian" economists will defer unreflectively to, say, Ludwig von Mises or misled MIT neoclassical economists to Paul Anthony Samuelson. Like a bad scientist, Uriah does not listen, really listen, to anybody or anything.

In his *Autobiography* Benjamin Franklin makes a characteristic joke about the matter, noting of humility, "I cannot boast of much success in acquiring the reality of this virtue; but I had a good deal with regard to the appearance of it."[19] Yet in fact—a point which applies to most of his self-descriptions, and is part of his craftiness in appearing umble—he understated his ethical achievement here. The mature Franklin was well known as never giving an answer before he had heard out the other person. He acted as though he had read and taken careful note of the medieval motto, Listen even to the other side.

In an age of orators Franklin was a listener. In the Constitutional Convention he hardly spoke, not out of pusillanimous fear of failure—this diligent printer had stood before kings, and had all the great-souledness a man could require—but out of a proper and habitual humility toward his fellows. To be humble in this sense, from the Christian and doubtless other perspectives, is merely to have a decent respect to the opinions of humankind, because other men and women sometimes reveal God's Own Truth. As Iris Murdoch expressed it in 1967, "Humility is not a peculiar habit of self-effacement, rather like having an inaudible voice. It is selfless respect for reality and one of the most difficult and central of all virtues."[20]

A striking example in my own experience—I myself cannot boast of much success in acquiring the reality of this virtue—is the late Don Lavoie (1951–2001), a professor of economics at George Mason University. His very name reflects it: officially "Don," in French-Canadian style, not the full Hibernian Donald, which means in Old Irish "world ruler," and was indeed once my own name.

He was humble, a most startling quality in a profession not known for showing it. When a physicist some time ago attended a conference about economics and chaos theory he remarked that he had once thought that *physicists* were the most arrogant academics around.[21] Lavoie was not umble. His respect for the opinions of humankind was not deference to mere rank. He was a democrat, small *d*. He embodied the great-souledness that Aquinas viewed as paired with humility. He ventured on great, hopeful projects, such as bringing the humanities to economics, seriously, or bringing the computer to economics and to its teaching, seriously. He satisfied in full the Aquinian definitions of a humble and great-souled venturer, being as well a Christian with a telos of approach to God.

"The good man," writes Murdoch, "is humble; he is very unlike the neo-Kantian Lucifer. . . . Only rarely does one meet somebody in whom [humility] positively shines, in whom one apprehends with amazement the absence of the anxious avaricious tentacles of the self."[22] Murdoch points out that humility is one of the chief virtues in a good artist and in a good scientist. In his *Justice as Translation* the legal scholar James Boyd White put it in terms of humble reading, "a willingness to learn the other's language and to undergo the changes we know that will entail."[23]

Among the contending schools of economic science there is one which does at least theoretically recommend humility, listening, really listening, scientifically speaking—not certainly the Marxism I started with, nor the Harvard Samuelsonian economics I was trained in, nor the Good Old Chicago School economics I then practiced, but the NYU-Auburn-George-Mason-University-Austrian economics that Lavoie discovered young as a student of computer science and improved in his work. Austrian economists are the free-market followers of the literal, ethnic Austrians Menger (1840–1921), Mises (1881–1973), and Hayek (1899–1992). They have now for about a century been explaining to us other economists that the economic scientist cannot expect to outguess the businessperson.

We should *listen* to the mystery of entrepreneurship, the Austrians say, not airily assume as my fellow Samuelsonians tend to do that nothing whatever is to be gained by actually talking to economic "agents," because after all such "agents" are completely determined by such-and-such a Max U model. As a noneconomist professor at the business school of the University of Chicago put it to me once, the Samuelsonians, especially at Chicago, believe a contradiction: that everyone is rational; and that everyone who doesn't believe so is an idiot.

I said Lavoie improved Austrian economics, and this is one way he did it, by uncovering a hermeneutics in economics, and by listening for the hermeneutics inside the actual economy itself. Hermeneutics is the listening side of a speaking rhetoric, as Lavoie said.[24] It is the art of understanding what you have listened to—really listened to, an art of close listening. Austrian economics is the natural home for a humanistic approach to the economy, which acknowledges, as economics after Smith mainly has not, that humans are speaking and listening and interpreting animals. Smith believed that the propensity to truck and barter was based on the faculty of reason—so much for Max U and the reason half of the Enlightenment project. But he added, and believed, "and the faculty of speech," which is the other, freedom half, ignored after his death.[25]

The habit of listening, really listening in Lavoie's academic life was strictly paralleled, that is, by his belief that hermeneutics worked also in the economy. Adam Smith was again wiser than his followers. Smith's butcher and baker are not merely Max U folk who treat the rest of the world as a lamentable constraint on their own willfulness, a sort of vending machine, as I have said.[26] A person in business depends on an imaginative engagement with the customers and suppliers, to guess what they are thinking, to see the witness in them. The Quakers were good businesspeople. The rigorously humble Amish are well-known as brilliant farmers, within their self-imposed constraints of no tractors and no electricity. An alert businesswoman "subjects herself to every neighbor." She listens and learns from other people and from the world, through that selfless respect for reality. The businesswoman's goods are difficult of achievement, requiring great-souledness, but depend also on listening to what people want and the world will allow.

The business section of the *Chicago Tribune* has a feature on Mondays called "My Biggest Mistake," in which managers of small businesses confess to this or that expensive failure to answer the witness of reality: not listening to customers here; not listening to employees there. It is hard to imagine a similar column in a publication directed at the clerisy: "My biggest scientific mistake" in running an experiment on oxidative phosphorylation or "my biggest artistic mistake" in wrapping a building with cellophane. The clerisy chooses never to stoop. Considering the allegedly modern temptations to pride in capitalist enterprise it will seem odd to say so, but Lavoie believed, as I do, that a capitalist at her pretty-good best is humble. McDonald's offers a humble meal for working people at half an hour's minimum wages. Wal-Mart listens closely to what its customers want.

A proud, modern, secular member of the clerisy, on the contrary, declares that he can get along without such stuff, and scorns the humility of religion, or of capitalism. But he accepts the cornucopia of a capitalist society. And he is himself in thrall to a faithful or hopeful vision of, say, art or science or progress or hap or even merely to his proud self-image as the village atheist: "I thank whatever gods may be / For my unconquerable soul."

"The man who has made his choice in favor of a profane life," noted Mircea Eliade in 1957, "never succeeds in completely doing away with religious behavior. . . . [E]ven the most desacralized existence still preserves traces of a religious valorization of the world."[27] Humans symbolize, and symbolizing entails hope and faith. The atheist treats as sacred the scenes of his youth, the graves of his ancestors, the loves of his life, the blessed hope for his career, for his science, for his family. "The issue between secularists and believers," writes J. Budziszewski, "is not whether to have faith in a god, or faith in something other than a god; it is whether to have faith in this or that kind of god."[28]

H. L. Mencken admired in himself and in Joseph Conrad and in Theodore Dreiser—at least in Dreiser's more aristocratic moods—the "ability to look into the blackness steadily." He detected backsliding on this matter even in his hero Nietzsche, who, "shrinking from the horror of that abyss of negation, revived the Pythagorean concept of *der ewigen Wiederkunft* [the eternal recurrence]—a vain and blood-curdling sort of comfort. To it, after a while, he added explanations almost Christian—a whole repertoire of whys and wherefores, aims and goals, aspirations and significances."[29] Theodore Dreiser, too, labored sometimes under "the burden of a believing mind," lapsing into "imbecile sentimentalities." He was after all "the Indiana peasant."[30]

Such a pose as Mencken's is dissected by Murdoch: "The atmosphere is invigorating and tends to produce self-satisfaction in the reader, who feels himself to be a member of an elite, addressed by another one. Contempt for the ordinary human condition, together with a conviction of personal salvation, saves the writer from real pessimism. His gloom is superficial and conceals real elation."[31] Mencken admitted as much. He was cheerful right to his major stroke in 1949, which left this great writer penless. In 1922 he had declared himself the happiest of men, elated to live in a nation so filled with boobs, clowns, morons, and Methodists— "the Ku Klux Klan was, to all intents and purposes, simply the secular arm of the Methodist Church"—that he could earn a comfortable living making fun of them.[32]

The agnostic and especially the atheist, unaware of the god he believes, is as uncritical in his faith as a Sicilian widow lighting a candle before a statue of the Virgin. Oliver Wendell Holmes, Jr., had been annealed in the fires of the Civil War. He was seriously wounded three times, and saw his best friend die. Before the war he had been a devout and peaceable Emersonian, an abolitionist who joined up on principle. In the war he lost his principles, adopting instead a hard faith of mere duty. No God for him—except the Romantic H*ms*lf of the Stoic materialist. "The faith is true and adorable," he wrote in "A Soldier's Faith," delivered on Memorial Day in 1895, "which leads a soldier to throw away his life in obedience to a blindly accepted duty, in a cause which he little understands, in a plan of campaign of which he has no notion, under tactics of which he does not see the use." Small comfort the words must have been to the widows and orphans in attendance. But Holmes was a hard man.

The mere, eloquent assertion of his Faith was as far as Holmes could get in defending it. "Truly courageous persons," Daryl Koehn argues, "do not fight to death simply because ordered to do so. . . . They consider whether a . . . situation demands such a stance."[33] But Holmes did not consider ethics to be a matter of consideration. He did not bring a theology to bear, no repertoire of whys and wherefores, aims and goals, aspirations and significances. Theologies are denied to the nonfaithful by their faiths.

Yet note the title, "A Soldier's Faith," thirty years after the war, and listen to the religious words pouring out. The man who with Captain Holmes has known "the blue line of fire at the dead angle of Spotsylvania . . . [knows] that man has in him that *unspeakable something* which makes him capable of a *miracle*, able to lift himself by the might of his own *soul*, unaided, able to face annihilation for a blind *belief*."[34] While sick with dysentery behind the lines at Fredericksburg, a younger Holmes wrote to his mother with what was already a mixture of an aristocratic and a shadowy Christian view: "It's odd how indifferent one gets to the sight; of death—perhaps. because one gets aristocratic and don't value much a common life—Then they are apt to be so dirty it seems natural—'Dust to dust.'"[35] Holmes planned his last words: "Have faith and pursue the unknown end."

So likewise the Nobel laureate in physics and learned theologian Stephen Weinberg accepts invitations to appear on television to attack the very notion of God. He defends his own god, Physics, against the heresies of relativism and postmodernism professed over in the departments of English and sociology, about which, thank God, he knows nothing at all. Weinberg has no need for the hypothesis of a Jehovah. Not for him, this proud physicist, humility before what Kant called the two most astonishing facts, astonishing after thinking about them for a lifetime: "the starry skies above [compare Vincent] and the moral universe within."[36]

No religion. No theology. No transcendent. No love or faith or hope. The abyss of negation. Glorious and brave.

ECONOMIC THEOLOGY

The only ethical judgment an economist is supposed to be able to make is a wholly uncontroversial one. If every person is made better off by some change, the change—which is then called "Pareto optimal," after the Italian economist who formalized the notion—should take place. Even philosophers like John Rawls and Robert Nozick have adopted this bland criterion. They have tried and tried to pull a decently detailed ethical theory out of the Paretian hat.

So-called welfare economics has recently shown some faint stirrings of complexity in ethical thought, as in the works by the economist and philosopher Amartya Sen, and more in the works of younger economists and philosophers inspired by his forays. But most academic economists continue working the magician's hat. The hat does not contain a living theory of moral sentiments. Sen complained of the "lack of interest that welfare economics has had in any kind of complex ethical theory," and added, "It is arguable that [utilitarianism and] . . . Pareto efficiency have appealed particularly because they have not especially taxed the ethical imagination of the conventional economist."[1] Truth be known, this "welfare economics" and what passes for "ethical" theorizing among economists and economics-loving philosophers is a Victorian, utilitarian parrot, stuffed and mounted and fitted with marble eyes.

An economist named Robert Nelson has tried in two amazing books to give the stuffed parrot back to the pet store. The books have puzzling titles: *Reaching for Heaven on Earth: The Theological Meaning of Economics* (1991) and *Economics as Religion: From Samuelson to Chicago and Beyond* (2001). The theological meaning of . . . economics? Economics as . . . religion?

Nelson, who now teaches at the University of Maryland, was for a long time a "policy analyst" working on zoning and property rights, federal coal policy, and the case for abolishing the U.S. Forest Service.[2] Though trained in the arcania of academic economics, he uses economics for practicalities. He therefore knows a dead parrot when he sees one. He is not, as many economists are, devoted to finding out what can be drawn out of a hat if you assume you have stuffed it backstage with parrots.

Economics and theology are usually believed to be opposites. According to Nelson, who leans against a presumption since Goethe and Coleridge, they are not. Economics is the doppelganger of theology. Like Veblen, though with a different politics, Nelson takes seriously the newspaper cliché that economics is "mere" religion, voodoo economics. But he drops the "mere." Theology is a serious business, the discussion of ordering principles.

Economics, he argues, has become the theology of a new religion of abundance. "Almost all the leading schools of economics have had more impact on the world by virtue of their religious authority" "than by the specific technical knowledge . . . they have provided."[3] Joseph Schumpeter and Robert Heilbroner both called it "vision." Economics is the vision thing of the ordinary.

Nelson detects two theological traditions, which he calls the Roman and the Protestant. His "Roman" means ancient Roman but also Roman Catholic, and his "Protestant" means Lutheran/Calvinist but also rebellious and cantankerous. The issue between the two schools, the optimistic Romans and the pessimistic Protestants, has always been the perfectibility of humankind. The Romans emphasize the four cardinal virtues, courage, temperance, justice, and prudence, and think they are attainable in the works of this world. By their works shall ye know them. The Protestants emphasize the three "theological" virtues, faith, hope, and love, and count on amazing grace to save a wretch like me.

The United States is famously a Protestant country, given to gathering under tents in which sinners declare for Christ. On Sundays even Catholic Americans nowadays partake of the Protestant spirit. But during the rest of the week, says Nelson, even Protestant Americans are Romans. "Of all nations, the United States exhibits a characteristic national outlook that matches most closely the Roman tradition. Americans typically believe that reason guides the world, showing a deep faith in progress."[4] Contrast Italian people. An American soldier was asked if he "hated" his Iraqi enemy. "No,

of course not. I reckon I'm here to do a job, and so is he." A centurion standing uneasily between Jesus and the Pharisees could not have better expressed the Roman view.

Ancient Rome, especially under its republic, had a civic religion, depending on the reading of entrails and the interpretation of the flights of birds
among other sensible precautions. The civic religion of the modern world is
social engineering, which depends on a similar divination, called "time
series econometrics." The new religion promises material salvation, yielding, as Nelson points out, spiritual salvation as well. For better or worse,
economics is the theology of the new religion of this-worldly progress and
problem solving.

But it doesn't work very well, partly because it's not recognized as religious. Religion, I've said, is not something that can be dispensed with. We
need religion just as much as our ancestors did, which is to say that we need
an account of the transcendent, the meaning, the faith, the hope, the love.
Nelson believes that the American civic religion needs renewal. His own
suggestion is a merger of two of the churches, the environmentalist and the
libertarian, the tree-worshipers and the market-worshipers. Save the earth,
by all means—by getting our engineering off it. Take the tools away from
the Army Corps of Engineers, who failed in 2005 at New Orleans. Prevent
the ranchers from using government land at a subsidized price. Abolish the
U.S. Forest Service. Get Washington out of the business of running the
country from a nice office on K Street. Nelson's new theology is anti-
Roman, that is, anti-imperial and anti-social-engineering. It is Protestant in
Nelson's wide sense—wary of bishops and centralization, unpersuaded by
time-series econometrics.

The Political Economy Research Center in Bozeman, Montana, is an example of the new faith, showing how the wilderness can be protected by capitalism rather than by a capitalist-influenced government. PERC's manifesto is
"Private property rights encourage stewardship of resources. Government
subsidies often degrade the environment. Market incentives spur individuals
to conserve resources and protect environmental quality. Polluters should be
liable for the harm they cause others."[5] The magic word there is "stewardship,"
a theological term of long standing. Nelson, PERC, and I are suggesting that
a true stewardship comes from ownership, not collectivism.

The contrasting, Roman faith shows in the views of Robert Reich, the
famously short professor of government at Brandeis. Reich appears to be a

charming, intelligent man: how can you dislike a short man who writes a book called *I'll Be Short: Essentials for a Decent Working Society* (2003)? But in 1991 he sounded the alarm against what he called the "succession" of the educated classes. He worried that taxable income would move out from under the taxing authority—precisely the program, at least in words, of Bush II. Why does it matter, according to Reich? Because without taxes the lobbyists on K Street cannot spend your money to make a community.

The economist Albert Hirschman speaks of the three social options of exit, voice, and loyalty. If you don't like the environmental policies of your town, you can either love it or leave it, exercising loyalty or exit; or else you can go down to City Hall and complain, exercising voice.[6] The Roman tradition in social thinking, represented on the left by Reich and on the right by George Will, wants to create fresh reasons for loyalty. It wants to block the exits. Nelson, by contrast, views exit as just the ticket, the most basic of political and religious rights. The Protestants—or the ecumenical Rome of John XXIII—regard exit as making for a freer world. Only an established church, says Nelson, views the splintering of religious power as bad.

Though he has his opinions, Nelson preaches "tolerance of diverse economic theologies." This is not the present situation in economics, which is dominated by a theology "from Samuelson to Chicago and beyond." Nelson is unimpressed by the claims of the Samuelsonian Chicagoans to a monopoly of scientific method. He doubts in fact, as many students of the matter since Thomas Kuhn have, that there is really such a thing as "scientific method." "To abandon the [so-called] scientific method . . . is to undermine a basic faith of the American welfare state, a faith as deeply embedded in Western civilization as the Roman tradition of thought." He proposes instead a "postmodern economic theology," as I do here, and Don Lavoie did, and Arjo Klamer does.

"Postmodernism" does not mean what you may have gathered from the outrage of conservative cultural journalists. It means merely dropping the artificialities of high modernism, and in particular dropping the fact-value split in its cruder forms and the established church of social engineering. "The new world of the welfare state and of economic pursuits would have to be placed within the context of a broader understanding of the meaning or purpose of human existence." Nelson's hero, Frank Knight, would have detested the word, but of course Nelson is calling exactly for an economic theology.

PART THREE

The Pagan and Masculine Virtues: Courage, with Temperance

NO LONGER WEEPING FOR ONE ANOTHER
AS ACHILLES DID IN PASSIONATE GRIEF,
MODERN MAN HAS TAUGHT HIMSELF
THAT TEARS ARE TO BE STEELED AGAINST
IN MUTE ACCEPTANCE OF HIS GRIEF.
THUS, HE GROWS LESS LIKE ACHILLES,
AND MORE LIKE A MAN WHO MAY, HIMSELF,
BE CAUSE FOR GRIEF.

—*Helen McCloskey, "The Right Stuff"*

16

THE GOOD OF COURAGE

I am preaching, as everyone should, in favor of "virtue." I commend it to you. But in its etymology it contains a worry: "virtue" is constructed in Latin from *vir*, "adult male human."[1] True, even in Roman times *virtus* had widened beyond "manliness" to include pretty much what we mean by it now. But as late as Tacitus around AD 100 it was still the normal word for manly valor on the battlefield. One of the bizarre features of the *Germani*, Tacitus wrote, is that their women were valorous in this sense: "The [German] woman should not think herself exempted from valor [*virtute*]," since women accompanied their men to the battlefield, as cheerleaders and sometimes as active participants. A woman's "virtue" in the male and modern sense among the Romans was *pudicitia*, "modesty, purity."[2]

In non-Christianizing works through the Renaissance the Latin word and its Romance derivatives kept this whiff of the men's locker room. Machiavelli especially had in mind men, and violent, proud ones, not women, when he praised the *virtù* of the prince or of a republic. Thus Milton's Satan in *Paradise Lost*, back from his mission to Eden, addresses the hosts of hell: "Thrones, dominions, princedoms, *virtues*, powers."[3] What made *Il Principe* so scandalous for centuries after its posthumous publication is that in a religious age it praised no feminine virtue. In all his writings Machiavelli associated Christianity with effeminacy, and with states that failed. In return the men of the Roman Church kept his writings on the index of forbidden books from 1559 until 1850.

In modern Italian *virtù* has lost its association with men. The historian Carlo Ginzburg thinks that Machiavelli's usage was in its breadth idiosyncratic, meaning "forcefulness," and that other Renaissance Italians did not use the word this way.[4] Leo Strauss gives the same reading: "This obscurity is essential. . . . [because] the reader is meant to ascend from the common understanding of virtue [namely, Christian goodness] to the diametrically opposite understanding [namely, manly aggression]."[5] The modern *Nuovo Zingarelli* gives the manly, aggressive meaning, *forza d'animo*, force of spirit, only as definition 6 of 12 of *virtù*, "by extension, literary," and cites Machiavelli. In *Il Principe* the successful prince's virtue was reduced to a manly forcefulness, the good citizen's to a manly loyalty. Machiavelli drew on Greek or Roman examples of the best—or at any rate the winning—emperors, popes, and generals, the thrones, dominions, and princedoms, exemplars of old Spartan or old Roman "virtue." The team showing such *virtù* coheres, and scores touchdowns—whatever the point might be of such "winning," note the women from the sidelines. Nowadays we make jokes about testosterone; or lament the forcefulness of Osama bin Laden.

Harvey Mansfield denied once that "manliness" is the right translation, and argued that an assertive, showy, violent self-interest is what Machiavelli had in mind. Yet "such virtue," Mansfield wrote, "is prudence inspired by glory and thus combined with the kind of manliness that is *comfortable with ferocity* and capable of acquisitiveness."[6] And elsewhere he and Nathan Tarcov define it as "a new conception of virtue as the willingness and ability to do whatever it takes to acquire and maintain what one has acquired."[7] *Virtù* in Machiavelli is not a cool, just, dignified, republican manliness; it is more like *machismo*: proud, unjust, unloving, intemperate, adolescent, the worst qualities of manliness. But manly, or at least adult male, nonetheless.

We have had a long run of our virtue talk dominated thus by a male idea of courage, three or four thousand years of writings, with many eons doubtless before the writing. Where men rule, courage rules. Where battlefield courage is at a premium, as in the Spain of the Reconquista, I have noted, women are devalued.

Masculine identity depends on success in a field of play. The aristocracy and gentry look down on mere tradesmen having no claim to military courage. In truth, trading had its own dangers, of course. But the dangers were emasculating, not a glorious death in battle. They were merely nasty threats to masculine identity. As Jeremiah James Colman, seed-merchant of Norwich, of Colman's mustard, remarked bitterly about his worries over bankruptcy, in business "I may be a man one day, and a mouse the next."[8]

The task of bourgeois ideology in the nineteenth century was to up-value—that is, to masculinize—*economic* success. It only partly worked. "Courage" defined in the pagan and heroic way still crowded out more balanced or bourgeois views of the virtues, at least in the minds of some men. Justice Holmes in 1895 addressed the men: "Who is there who would not like to be thought a gentleman? Yet what has that name been built on but the soldier's choice of honor rather than life?"[9] The sports-and-war talk still dominates the airwaves and the boardrooms and the cabinet rooms, to our woe.

Paradoxically, the sweet universalism of axial religions devised 800 BC to AD 632 was accompanied by a reinforcement of male governance, and therefore by an intensification of the honoring of courage. To paraphrase Henry Kissinger on academic life, modern politicians (that same Henry, for example) are obsessed with physical courage because in their lives so little of it is really at stake.

Courage is a necessary and splendid human virtue; and certainly battle-field courage is especially so, the last full measure of devotion. Its pathologies arise only from an absence of *other* virtues to complete it, such as prudence and temperance and justice, those pagan virtues, or love. The stories told to boys hold up an aristocratic ideal of courage in battle. The problem is: merely in battle.

The world praised by the pagan virtues is in mythic origin that of a military aristocracy, free males of rank battling. Slaves and women do not count, unless a Spartacus or a Jeanne d'Arc assumes the habit of an aristocratic male. "In a rude society," Adam Smith explained to his middle-class students at Glasgow in 1766, as the society was changing, "nothing is honorable but war."[10] The aristocrat is courageous and honorable, great-hearted in hospitality, quick to anger. Achilles derides the king, who proposes to take Achilles' concubine seized in war, "You wine sack, with a dog's eyes, with a deer's heart. Never / once have you taken courage in your heart to arm with your people," and swears to leave Agamemnon's quarrel with the Trojans. Agamemnon has his "mind forever on profit," no honorable purpose in such a society.[11]

Achilles himself, though, is imperfect in pagan virtues. He has physical courage aplenty, the central virtue of a society of quarreling chiefs, but not enough temperance or justice or even the fourth and least aristocratic of the pagan virtues, prudence. He is what the Vikings called a berserker, in the end angering the gods with his *eros*-unhinged violence against the corpse of Hector. Simone Weil viewed the *Iliad* as "the poem of force," force being "that *x* that turns anybody who is subjected to it into a *thing*."[12] Forcefulness in humans is Machiavelli's *virtù*, or *forza d'animo*.

A more balanced model for pagan virtues in Homer is wily Odysseus, a man "of many turns" like a merchant, shown most completely in his name-poem of travel and ingenuity. Zbigniew Herbert says of his "collective hero, the Dutch bourgeois of the seventeenth century," that "if the Dutch modeled themselves on the heroes of the great epics, surely Odysseus was closer to them than Achilles."[13] Yet honesty of a modern and bourgeois sort would not be prudent in someone leading his men by guile and *virtù* out of, say, the Cyclops's cave. Athena remarks affectionately (for "two of a kind, are we") that "even a god / might bow to you in ways of dissimulation."[14] In fifth- and fourth-century drama, in an Athens at the height of its commercial power, Odysseus comes across even more as a crafty merchant type, and especially a false speaker, as in Sophocles' *Philoctetes*.[15]

Anyway, the other three pagan virtues—temperance, justice, and prudence supplementing mere forceful courage—typify the Homeric Odysseus, or the Virgilian Aeneas, or, from Icelandic tales, Gunnar Hamundarson in *Njal's Saga*, "extremely well-bred, fearless, generous, and even-tempered, faithful to his friends but careful in his choice of them. He was prosperous."[16]

The problem is that aristocratic stories of courage in battle, even of battlefield courage balanced by the other three pagan virtues, are not the stories of our lives. We do not live nowadays in military camps drawn up before the walls of new Troys, even temperate, just, and prudent camps, most of us at any rate. The We of modern times includes nonaristocrats and nonmen, to give us "heroes" in the literary sense such as Anne Elliot or Erin Brockovich. Anyway, nonsoldiers.

The stories of courage-above-all were always already mythological. After the archaic times of an Odysseus or a Gunnar the little communities jostling with Sparta or Clusium still required occasionally in the ideal citizen the four pagan virtues, defined for a real man. *Vir* in Latin, like "man" in English, but not *andros* in ancient Greek, means "soldier," too, especially a foot soldier, as in "officers and men."

But the virtues are to be exercised in a democratic phalanx, not in an aristocratic duel. Horatius and his two comrades at the bridge point the moral, at any rate according to Macaulay's poem about the event composed in the 1830s and early 1840s. The courageous three are supposed in 508 BC to have held off an entire Etruscan army at the Sublician Bridge to Rome by being permitted, according to Macaulay's version, to challenge the enemy three at a time, sportingly:

> But at his haughty challenge
> A sullen murmur ran,
> Mingled of wrath, and shame, and dread,
> Along that glittering van.[17]

The aristocratic conventions of the duel are imposed on the history. Maybe the aristocratic duel was real behavior in archaic societies carried into more bourgeois city-states. More likely, Macaulay is simply using the fair-play conventions of the ruling class in nineteenth-century England. Macaulay's source, Livy, writing in the first decades of the empire, five centuries after the alleged event, imagines the Etruscans throwing spears in a decidedly unsporting way "from every side."[18] Even the beneficiaries of ancient freedom, in other words, were not Homeric heroes dueling one on one.

The citizen armies of the early Western city-states from the seventh century BC on were not highly trained duelers like Odysseus or Horatius—or, in that bizarre parody of aristocratic dueling, dating at Rome from the third century BC, gladiators. In a bench of rowers or a phalanx of hoplites they were nonetheless disciplined—that is, temperate. The ideal citizen of the polis was courageous *and* temperate—rather more temperate in fact than courageous, the beginning of a long devaluation of battlefield courage in actual social behavior, if not in story. The oarsmen in Athens' wooden wall were paid, free citizens. They were not, as was typical of non-Greek fleets in the Mediterranean for the three millennia of rowed warships, slaves or convicts. A significant exception to the servile propulsion of galleys was Venice, at least until 1571. Venice was the other republic holding the gorgeous East in fee.

And ideally the landsmen, the volunteer hoplites—literally, "shields-men," from the *hoplon*, Homeric "tool," Attic "heavy shield," the main tool of their kind of war—were small owners with something to lose in their wheat fields from the depredations of invaders. As Victor Hanson has pointed out, though, unlike their wheat fields, their vines and olive trees were too deep-rooted to destroy with fire—and even wheat, as a grass descended from wild grasses in often-burned plains, would regrow next year. He concludes that it was not plants the hoplites were mainly defending, but the honor of men not to be trifled with.[19] Such men were at first recruited from the free male farming population, taking down their arms from the place of honor in the late spring season for campaigning—that is, after wheat planting—and usually surviving to tell the tale around their hearths. In Greece the Spartan aristocrats alone were full-time soldiers, and correspondingly powerful out of proportion to their numbers.

At Athens in Periclean times the system of widespread physical courage augmented by temperance was breaking down. Hanson notes that "in place of agrarian protocol and phalanx fighting, city-states in search of absolute victory applied capital and technology [for example, siege machinery] without ethical restraints." Athens anyway had by then fewer free farmer/hoplites than outsiders, slaves, and especially free tradesmen living on sea-borne grain—with no special stake in preventing damage to crops beyond the city walls. During the Peloponnesian War "military service of all types became divorced from social status."[20] The armies were infused with mercenaries. Prudence ruled.

The legions of the early Roman Republic by contrast showed a special courage combined with a special love/faithfulness for the fatherland, and more training under temperance than non-Spartan Greeks would tolerate. The Romans remasculinized courage, exhibiting an altogether new level of citizenly *virtù*. Even the tiny group of early Romans, and all the more so that steadily larger group up to at last the millions who could say "I am a Roman citizen," were hard to beat. At any rate they were hard to beat permanently. They were in fact beaten by nearly everyone they faced—by Etruscans, Gauls, Greeks, Carthaginians, Germans, Samnites, Parthians, Dacians, Picts—but would come back to the task with mad courage again and again.

Until the century-long Roman Revolution after 133 BC, the legions were drawn literally and exclusively from the middling citizenry led by the richer citizenry of Rome itself or of its carefully chosen allies. The *equites,* or knightly, upper class, for example, had to pay for their horses. Before the Second Punic War, 218–201 BC, the more heavily armed foot soldiers were drawn in fact from the more well-to-do, since a legionnaire under the republic in its prime paid for his equipment, like the Athenian hoplite, or the wealthy Athenian citizen sponsoring a warship. But as early as about 400 BC the rank and file of the Roman legions were beginning to get some cash payment. And in 107 BC property qualifications for service in the army were dropped entirely. The armies of the late Republic were not occasional citizen-levies, but professional and prudent, serving for decades in Rome's shocking aggressions.

The armies of the late republic and the empire were literate, too. All legionnaires were required to learn to read, and were able therefore to act as quasi-bourgeois bureaucrats after the war was won. The occupied provinces run by republics like Athens and Rome, and later Venice or America, and then the literal empires of Alexander and Augustus, had replaced the earlier citizen foot- and horse-soldiers with bureaucratic professionals, and had replaced citizen oarsmen with slaves.

The individualistic Courage of the hero in a duel, therefore, and the collective Temperance of the polis in arms, were not much in demand. In second-century AD Rome it has been calculated that a mere 2 percent of the male population was under arms, only 160,000 men. A democracy in crisis, such as France in the First World War, armed many millions, 43 percent of its males of all ages; and similar percentages for preliterate societies in wartime—those peaceful primitives such as the Tahitians, or the less peaceful Zulus in the War of 1879.[21] But usually not. Prince Maurice of Nassau's armies in bourgeois Holland c. 1600, which engaged in such unheroic and effective tricks as carrying field shovels for trenching, were small relative to the Dutch population.[22]

In empires and democracies, in other words, a steadily lower percentage of the male population has needed to be physically courageous, ever. Only 5 or so percent of the male labor force in the United States bear arms on the job. Or in other terms, 3 percent of the male population age fifteen or over do. Or, to compare with the earlier figures, under 2 percent of the entire male population, adults or children, eerily similar to the share in imperial Rome.[23] By now, that is, a lower percentage than in early democratic Athens or early republican Rome need be aristocratically Courageous in an arms-bearing way, whether actual or imitative. The profession of arms has become specialized and small, like all professions in a large society, if the society is not fixed on one mad goal of conquest or defense—contrast Frederick the Great's Prussia, with routinely 15 percent of the adult men in the army, and his blue-uniformed recruiters scouring the streets to seize more.

Modern armies in democracies therefore sometimes look like corporations—prudent rather than courageous. We imagine the soldiers still acting like Odysseus, saving Private Ryan. But as they themselves reply when praised for heroism, they are merely doing the job.

Or not doing it. At Srebrenica on July 15, 1995, it seems from popular accounts, a Dutch force abandoned its job of protecting the Bosnian Muslims and fled to safety in Zagreb, with Dutch politicians to greet it and plenty of Heineken beer. The elite Air Mobile Brigade suffered two deaths, both by accident, not battle. Seven thousand Bosnian men and boys were immediately executed by the victorious Serbs—not all of them "under the noses of the Dutch forces," as newspaper accounts had it. Only a few hundred were executed literally under their noses, according to the English translation of the summary report by the Netherlands Institute for War Documentation in 2002.[24]

A small minority of Dutch public opinion has viewed the episode as shameful, and in particular as a betrayal of the aristocratic ideal of Courage entailed in being a soldier. The minority feels that the intervention by the Dutch battalion created a *lotsverbondenheid* with the people of Srebrenica which cannot now be tossed away.

Most Dutch people, though, regard the event as a necessary, bourgeois compromise with disaster—a triumph of Prudence, so to speak, getting almost all of the Dutch boys home without a scratch. The soldiers were sent to Srebrenica from "a mixture of compassion and ambition": the traditional modern Dutch compassion for victims of war and famine (the Netherlands ranks second only to Norway in proportional contributions to international charities), and the ambition of politicians and generals to "demonstrate the capabilities of its showpiece Air Mobile Brigade at a time of cut-backs."[25] The Canadians had originally garrisoned Srebrenica, and when they went home none but the Dutch were courageously willing to take their place. In the crisis, further, when the enveloping Serbian army tested the resolve of the Bosnian irregulars and of the Dutch soldiers, the French refused to provide air support. The Serbian army was overwhelmingly more powerful than the few hundred Dutch soldiers at Srebrenica. In the words of the report, the Dutch force "had effectively become a defeated battalion in the power of the [Serbian army]."[26]

Yet physical courage is demanded from specialists in it even in a bourgeois society. The battalion was "defeated" without a fight. The Dutch offered no resistance to probes, took up static positions easily evaded by the Serbs, who it appears from their evasions were afraid to bring down the wrath of the United Nations by killing Dutchmen on a UN mission. Then the Dutch accepted the Serbian proposal to "screen" for "war criminals" the Bosnian men and adolescent boys still in Srebrenica, whether armed soldiers or merely refugees. Most of the Bosnian men with weapons and with hostile intent had in fact already escaped the enclave.[27] The remaining, defenseless Bosnian males were handed over to the Serbs, and were all promptly shot, though only some of the Dutch soldiers, as I mentioned, were aware of this activity, about which many later received psychological counseling.[28]

The Institute for War Documentation, which had been set up long before to give a balanced accounting of Dutch heroism and cowardice, resistance and collaboration in the Second World War, believes that the Dutch general was "forced" to accept the Serbian deal. Hand over the men and boys, the Serbs are said to have offered in effect, and we will leave the women and (small) children alone. The frame for the story recounted by the historians of the institute is a bourgeois prudence, a utilitarian calculation of cost and benefit, some thousands of men and boys—*whose fate was not suspected*, the report implies—in exchange for many more thousands of women and small children.

The trouble is that the context was not one of enforceable quasi contracts in the flower market of Alsmeer or the offices of Royal Dutch Shell. It was a context of peasant/aristocratic warfare, not bourgeois business. The Dutch force left the battlefield without fighting, having got a "promise" that the women and children would not be disturbed, a promise by someone who had repeatedly broken his promises. On this occasion the Serbs did not actually kill the women and small children. But the outcome does not justify the claimed assumption at the time that the deal would hold. The Serbs had shown what they were capable of. The "deal" looks a lot like an excuse for saving the skins of the Dutch in exchange for putting those of the seven thousand men and many thousands of women and children in mortal danger.

Why indeed did the Dutch force not fight and die, as was its aristocratic duty? Why does an army—a part of bourgeois society sworn to putting itself aristocratically in harm's way, like firefighters running up burning twin towers or police exchanging gunfire with criminals—not exhibit Courage? The report from the institute offers the practical, Prudent reason:

"Armed resistance was not an option here because the [Serbs] would have probably slaughtered [everyone, including also the women and children among] the refugees." That is the explanation for why an elite force of combat-ready soldiers did not fire a shot.

But if the slaughter of the women and children was seen as probable at the time, then of course it would have been still more probable that the Bosnian men and adolescent boys placidly handed over were due for a similar fate. One cannot offer "protecting the women and children from racial cleansing" as an explanation for the Dutch general's unwillingness to risk his own life yet simultaneously claim that the same Dutch general did not realize that the Bosnian males over fourteen were going to be racially cleansed.

And as the report admits, "it is not impossible to imagine that, on a political and psychological level, the [Serbs] would have baulked at a fight that would have resulted in [UN, that is, Dutch] casualties."[29] Yes, it is not impossible to imagine. The tactical point, foremost in the mind of every UN soldier on assignment anywhere—the triggering function being commonly the point of UN forces—is offered as just barely within the range of imagination. On the other hand the fate of the betrayed Bosnian men and boys—unlike that of the women and small children, who "probably would have been slaughtered"—is said to have been *un*imaginable, a surprise.

If the Dutch soldiers had been courageous, it is possible to imagine that the Serbs would not have attacked them. If so, then on grounds of prudence, putting courage aside, the Dutch should have taken action. As Napoleon said to one of his regiments two days before the battle of Jena, "My lads, you must not fear Death; when soldiers brave Death, they drive him into the enemy's ranks."[30] In the aristocratic theory of warfare the Dutch should have offered themselves as a sacrifice to the gods of courage. It is the telos of soldiers to do so. No deals. And probably—but not certainly, for the gods of courage do not offer certitude—the Dutch would have driven Death into the Serbian ranks; or, better, in fear of him they would have persuaded the Serbs to refrain from racial cleansing.

Or so say the small minority of Dutch public opinion that continues to be ashamed of Srebrenica. The minority has a larger complaint, the grounds for which are exhibited in the institute's report. The complaint is that the historians who worked on the report, and the bulk of the Dutch people, are *not* ashamed. They do not acknowledge the *lotsverbondenheid*. They do not accept, for example, any present-day ethical responsibility toward the survivors of Srebrenica. They view the slaughters as an unhappy event caused mainly by the other Westerners implicated, such as the homeward-bound Canadians or the perfidious French, an event from which the Dutch, fortunately, extracted themselves. A bad business deal. Let bygones be bygones. The Dutch historians have found a balanced, prudent view, perhaps an outcome of the *Ja, maar . . .*, the "Yes, but . . ." style of consultation in Holland. It is a bourgeois rhetoric applied to war.

There is a time for aristocratic courage. Courage, not prudence or love or faith, is sometimes what is called for. François Jullien wrote in 1996 a remarkable book in praise of the ancient (and modern) Chinese notion of achieving success in war or other imperium by "upstream" manipulation of the incipient—not waiting until heroic virtue is necessary, downstream, with events tumbling by then with unstoppable force. He notes that such a way of life is prudent, effective—but unheroic.[31]

Western businessmen are fascinated by Sun Tzu's *The Art of War*, busily reading it on airplanes. It does not elevate to the chief virtue of a general/CEO heroic Courage but rather a bourgeois Prudence:

11. What the ancients called a clever fighter is one who not only wins, but excels in winning with ease.
12. Hence his victories bring him neither reputation for wisdom nor credit for courage.
13. He wins his battles by making no mistakes.[32]

This is not about heroic gestures but, as Jullien puts it, "efficacy."

For this lack of heroism, however, "there is a price to pay. . . . To confront the world [in the Greek and Western style] is a way to free oneself from it. . . . [It provides] the substance of heroic stories and jubilation [and, he notes elsewhere, tragedy, absent from Chinese tradition.] . . . [T]hrough resistance, we can make our way to liberty."[33] Jullien argues that the Chinese sages on the art of war were explaining, in more detail than Machiavelli, how to be a successful tyrant. From this point of view it is no accident that the culture providing stories of Prometheus, Achilles, Antigone also gave us an idea, if an imperfect practice, of freedom. Tragedy, hopeless courage, Roland at the pass of Rencesvals, the Dutch if only they had acted so at Srebrenica, is the choice of the free man.

ANACHRONISTIC COURAGE

IN THE BOURGEOISIE

I am not a king, have laid no kingdoms waste. . . .
Should I not hear, as I lie down in dust,
The horns of glory blowing above my burial? . . .
Tell me, as I lie down, that I was courageous.
Blow horns of victory now.
   —Conrad Aiken, "Tetélestai"

We talked of war. JOHNSON: "Every man thinks meanly of himself for not having been a soldier, or not having been at sea. . . . The impression is universal: yet it is strange." . . . Such was
his cool reflection in his study; but whenever he was warmed . . . he, like other philosophers,
whose minds are impregnated with poetical fancy, caught the common enthusiasm for splendid renown.
   —*Boswell's Life*, 1778

When the old tales of Western courage got written down, their values were
already antique. This is another problem with the Western and masculinist
focus on gut-checks and violence; a problem, that is, beyond its actual, sociological antiqueness. The accounts of it that throng our Western culture are
phony from the start.

After all, it is mainly the civilized—the "citizen-ized," those of high
standing living in town—who can read and write, and can record the
alleged deeds, not the illiterate and rural aristocracy itself, which leaves such
stuff to priests and bards and especially to posterity. The writings of the
civilized Mediterranean had of course audiences mainly nonaristocratic,
the Many of the Greek city-states and the plebs of the Roman Republic.
And yet the writings taught in the schools to the boys patrician or plebeian

represented as I have noted an archaic, physically courageous, wholly aristocratic virtue. For the Greeks it was Homer and for the Romans it was
translations and then imitations of Homer such as Ennius and Virgil. Cicero
was a lawyer, not a soldier. Yet he told his brother that his "childhood
dream" was expressed in the lines from *The Iliad*, Glaucus telling what his
father had said to him in sending him off to Troy, "Always be the best [*aris-
teuein*, compare "aristocratic"], my boy, the bravest."[1]

Which is to say that our cultural vocabulary for the chief pagan virtue in
the West isn't fresh news from the front, any front. The vocabulary of courageous heroism is sociologically inauthentic, reworked over centuries, belated, secondary, not based, as historians say, on primary sources. Homer
was imagining a warrior society long gone, about five centuries gone. He
himself lived in an eastern Aegean culture radically less knightly and more
workaday than the one he imagined. "The resulting picture," writes Hanson,
"is an amalgam-mosaic spanning five hundred years . . . ; it may not reflect
an actual historical society at all."[2]

So usually. A little after Homer wrote, in the sixth century BC, a redactor
in the style of Deuteronomy looked back on Joshua the berserk nomad
marching up to the walls of Jericho back, far, far back, in the thirteenth century BC, a little before Troy fell. The mythical Aeneas, counting from the
actual date of the fall of Troy, would have died more than a thousand years
before he was imagined by Virgil as a model of archaic piety. Beowulf of the
Spear-Danes lived if he did centuries before his literate cousins in far-off
Saxon England set down a version of his tale. Geoffrey of Monmouth in the
twelfth century crafted the knightly stories, and in the fifteenth Thomas
Malory perfected them, about a King Arthur who flourished, if ever, perhaps in Wales around AD 540.

The Icelandic sagas prove the rule, at its edges. The historical Gunnar was
killed in a siege of his house about (perhaps exactly) AD 990 and his ally
Njal burned in a similar siege about 1011 (the site can be visited still). But the
saga writer, though he creates in the Hemingwayesque restraint of saga
prose an impression of reporting from the scene, was looking back on the
events from 1275 or so, from an Iceland thoroughly Christianized and commercial. The Icelandic sagas "must be thought of as historical novels rather
than histories," R. I. Page warns. "Their authenticity must be continually
questioned. The Viking historian must feed on more austere fare."[3] Some
think that the sagas can be fed on, still, as documents of an oral tradition

carrying fact. To the contrary, Jesse Byock points out, the "bookprosist" view of the sagas was to some degree a result of nineteenth-century Icelandic nationalism eager to see the century and a half of saga writing not as merely the writing down of traditions but as "one of the most powerful literary moments in recorded history," in the words of the leader of this view.[4] Compare the two-hundred-year dispute over the authorship of Homer.

The stories of Joshua or King Arthur are still more clearly "historical novels." The days of yore are doubly so:

> Miniver cursed the commonplace
> And eyed a khaki suit with loathing;
> He missed the mediaeval grace
> Of iron clothing.

Nor of course do we postmedievals live in societies led by literal aristocracies of fighting men. So why, one might ask, should we go on being governed in our ethics by aristocratic virtues characteristic of such men? True: only Walpole among eighteenth-century prime ministers of England was without literally aristocratic blood on a mother's or a father's side.[5] And true: the last British cabinet still having a majority of aristocrats was surprisingly late, Gladstone's of 1892. Thirty years later in Bonar Law's, there were still equal numbers of aristocrats and commoners. Thatcher's of 1979 still contained nearly a quarter from the "landed establishment," though some quite recently recruited to it. But even in that class-haunted nation it is by now a long while since real aristocrats mattered. Harold Macmillan's cabinet of 1957, it was said, had more "old Estonians" (émigré politicians) than old Etonians.[6]

Centuries earlier the English and then the Scottish aristocrats had stopped their Homeric bloodletting and had turned to farming, court masques, and the gaming table. The proportion of violent deaths for males over age fifteen in English ducal families—"the king's brothers," so the very top of the social order—is an astonishing one-half for the cohort born 1330–1479, dying courageously in the Hundred Years' War and the Wars of the Roses. It falls to about a fifth for those born under the Tudors and Stuarts, then to about one in twenty for those born under the Hanoverians, fighting in the ethically restrained wars of the eighteenth century. The mortality rate from war comes back, startlingly, to its medieval levels for sons of dukes of an age to serve in World Wars I and II. So compelling is the faith in an aristocratic courage; and so ethically unrestrained is modern war.[7]

Most of us in modern democracies therefore have forgotten what an "aristocracy" literally is. American university students believe "upper class" is merely a fancy word for "rich." European and especially British students have less difficulty understanding caste-like classes. The young Americans begin to understand if they are urged to think of European "class" as equivalent to American "color."

Most Americans therefore think of the Kennedys as "aristocrats," though the older ones are only two or three generations from proletarian origins— Senator Edward's grandfather Kennedy grew up poor—and none are professional soldiers. It's a metaphor. Professors and artists since the late nineteenth century have preened themselves as a "new aristocracy," though of merit (they modestly say) rather than of birth, as though there were such a thing. Such a category mistake among democrats would have puzzled a Renaissance duke with a nine-hundred-year-old name.

When in the sixteenth century the new Dutch Republic threw off Spanish and other dukes and kings, its aristocracy lost the mechanisms of refreshment by new ennoblements. The aristocratic rump, now an entirely closed class, remained somewhat influential in the affairs of the republic, though continuing to shrink. But no one in the Netherlands mistook the nouveau-riche merchant class, the regents, with a training in accounting and classical languages, for literal aristocrats, with a training in violence and leadership.

Income had nothing to do with it, and still doesn't. There persists in places like Holland and Sweden, now five or more centuries after the sanguinary deeds that elevated it, an aristocracy consisting of a few folk living in modernized castles behind hedges. Though democrats now, they still possess the self-confidence of hereditary rulers, often taking up military careers. My friend the economist Axel Leijonhvufvud (literally, "lion head") comes from such a family, ranking high in the Swedish aristocracy, a descendent of Norse kings. It causes an American peasant of Norwegian descent like me to swoon.

We all need to be courageous in life. But even our physical courage cannot be merely aristocratic *virtù*, if we wish to stay out of jail. It cannot be Homeric or even old Roman, certainly not olde-tyme as filtered through the stories from Homer to Hollywood. "How much longer," asked John Stuart Mill in 1869, "is one form of society and life to content itself with the morality made for another?"[8] It is my main concern here. We ordinary, unarmed citizens in the West, as against our fellows who volunteer to fight as imitation aristocrats at Srebrenica or the Somme or the local crime-or-fire scene, are urban and democratic and liberated and pacified and bourgeois and even female now. Perhaps we should acknowledge the fact.

That is, the word and ideology of courage has been corrupted. Bourgeois men have adopted instead the mythical histories of knights and cowboys as their definition of masculinity. Stories help construct identities and, as William Reddy argues, even emotions.[9] We, and especially the men among us, keep turning, turning over in our minds aristocratic stories of virtue in the line of the *Iliad*. You would think that bourgeois men of Europe or Japan or America were actual kings of Ithaca, or of Engelond verray, parfit, gentil knights.

Take the professions of arms c. 1800 in England. England was to be sure "une nation de boutiquiers," in Napoleon's well-worn phrase (well-worn even before Napoleon: I quoted Adam Smith's use of it in 1776). Yet Napoleon was the son of a businessman and bureaucrat, and himself a genius of prudence. He was affecting to scorn the *other* bourgeois nation that at last defeated him. The British navy in the age of Lord Nelson, if one looks merely at the origins of the officers, was ordinarily in fact nonaristocratic, Nelson himself the son of a parson, Captain William "Bounty" Bligh the son of a customs officer. The equally eminent Dutch navy of the previous century had been equally egalitarian, drawing its *admiraals,* its Tromps and van Dorps, from sons of common sailors and of aristocrats, both.

William McNeill observes that navies possess an analogy in merchantmen that armies do not. There is no civilian analogue to an army. The British navy therefore required habits of mind natural to commercial ventures, such as double care in provisioning a ship before setting sail, or never missing a tide, or manning the pumps with energy in a crisis.[10] Work, work, work. No laying about merely waiting for the wild charge. Like engineers in the Royal Navy under steam, below-decks with the black gang monitoring pressure gauges, an eighteenth-century British naval officer had to know quite a lot and do all sorts of jobs and was therefore permitted to be less than genteel—a nonaristocratic Scot, for example. Being Jack Aubrey is not just a matter of aristocratic courage.

Indeed, as Jack is always saying, it is a matter, too, of bourgeois profit from prizes. Captain Wentworth in Jane Austen's *Persuasion* (1818) reminisces about the sloop *Asp*: "I knew that we should either go to the bottom together, or that she would be the making of me." And then about his frigate: "Those were pleasant days when I had the *Laconia*! How fast I made money in her!"[11]

But England expected its sailors, whether of bourgeois origin or not, to do their duty, which was defined peasant-wise for the men and aristocratically for the officers. Not bourgeois-ly. Admiral Lord Nelson died at Trafalgar because he chose, as was his nouveau-noble duty, to stand on the quarterdeck in full view of French snipers, with medals flashing in the smoke. Those are the traditions of brave men at sea, as a postaristocratic Lord Jim ruefully apprehended. Jane Austen's ideal potential husband, acknowledged to be in want of a wife, is a naval officer, honorable offstage doubtless in a very gallant way, though never so lofty as an actual aristocrat. Two of Jane's much-beloved brothers ended as admirals; another was for a time in the army. Even bourgeois Carthage would literally crucify admirals and generals who came home empty-handed. The Dutch behavior at Srebrenica would have earned a British admiral in the nation of shopkeepers a court martial and speedy execution—"to encourage the others," as Voltaire described the execution in 1757 of a British admiral for not doing his utmost.

The army of the Duke of Wellington was even more rigidly tied to aristocratic myth, and unlike the navy was sociologically speaking an aristocratic preserve. The *echt*-aristocratic officers at Waterloo were expected to sit nobly on their horses and face decapitating cannon fire while their peasant or proletarian soldiers were permitted—no, ordered—to lie down.

John Keegan points out that by the time of the Napoleonic Wars the army officers, unlike their Homeric or medieval models, were not supposed to engage directly in slaughter. The sailors still did, with cutlasses issued in a crisis indifferently to seamen and admirals. An English captain at Waterloo, doubtless a crack shot of deer and grouse, spotted a French common soldier climbing into the farmyard he was under orders to defend, and "instantly desired Sergeant Graham, *whose musket* [the captain] *was holding,* . . . to drop the wood [that the sergeant himself was carrying], take [back] his [musket *from the very captain*] . . . and shoot the intruder." Yet the captain would gladly have dueled to the death man-to-man with a French fellow *officer*. "The only feats of arms worth the name were those conducted between men of gentle birth, either one on one or in nearly (ideally exactly) matched numbers," like cricket teams.[12]

The point is that bourgeois men still take their models from aristocratic warriors, or cricket teams. By 1914 the British and other European armies had evolved beyond the literal aristocracy of eighteenth-century officer corps. The evolution made the Great War possible. By then the officers, though aristocratic in imagination, were bourgeois in origin. Thorstein Veblen had this point right: that aristocratic values survived in the imaginations of the bourgeoisie.

In her profound study of the rise and fall of the American western, Jane Tompkins quotes the inventor of the acceptably middle-class version of the genre, Owen Wister, writing in 1895, seven years before *The Virginian*: "In personal daring and in skill as to the horse, the knight and the cowboy are nothing but the same Saxon of different environments." Tompkins notes, "Wister's identification of the cowpuncher with the Anglo-Saxon knight-at-arms is a way for an upper-class composer-turned-short-story-writer with doubts about his independence to claim a robust masculinity."[13] The predominately Norman knighthood of England would have been amused by Wister's concept; and King Arthur was if anything a Celt, not a Saxon. Yet still, the purpose is clear: to appropriate for use today our stories of old courage.

Wister, like his friend and fellow enthusiast for heroism Teddy Roosevelt, knew the West as scenery, but could not have known the samurai warriors of his imagination, because they did not exist. His model was not "reality" but the elaborate fictions developed in the workingman's dime novel. *Buffalo Bill, King of the Border Men* appeared first in December 1869 as a magazine serial. The author of the Deadwood Dick series, Edward Wheeler, who described his occupation on his letterhead as "Sensational Novelist," lived in Philadelphia and never ventured much further west than that.[14] Wheeler wrote thirty-three dime novels from 1877 until his death in 1884, and after his death ninety-seven more novels appeared under his name, petering out finally in 1897. The author of *Shane* (1949) admitted that when he wrote the novel he "had never been west of Toledo, Ohio."[15]

The cowboys inspiring the myth early and late did actually make the Long Drive in Texas and Kansas and the Indian Territory briefly in the 1870s and early 1880s before the southern rail lines were extended west, and later herded dogies in the draws as employees of the cattle barons of Wyoming and Montana. There were only some 35,000 of them. The number is uncertain, but anyway it was a very small share of the 17,000,000 or so Americans working for a wage at the time. The western cattle industry was some small fraction of 2 percent of national income in 1880. After all, beef was not a very large share of the nation's expenditure—ask yourself how much even you in your early twenty-first-century prosperity spend out of your annual income on the farmer's share of the proceeds from beef. Only a small part of the beef had seen the Wild West. Corn-fed cattle from Iowa pens, not grass-fed from Montana open ranges, dominated the industry from 1900 at the latest. The workers who took care of the grass-fed cattle were buried in the occupational category at the bottom of the proletariat, farmhands. They were proletarians, not aristocrats. They were commonly teenagers, not men. Upwards of a quarter were people of color.

The bourgeois real-estate men who governed the cow towns kept their boys under strict control, by taking their guns away. Gun control is not a recent idea. The actual gunfight at OK Corral, October 26, 1881, for instance, was about Doc Holliday and the three Earp brothers, as the law in Tombstone, trying to take away the pistols the McLaurys and Clantons were illegally displaying in town.

A classic study of the extent of violence in the cow towns of Kansas discovered that all the murders 1870–1885 came to a mere one and a half per town per trading season, and few of these were the outcome of *Shane*-type duels.[16] It's hard to duel with pistols to the death when the city fathers have disarmed you. Less than a third of gunshot victims in the non-Hollywood cow towns returned fire. Many were not armed, as for instance the Caldwell wife shot dead in 1884 by her drunken husband. The fictionally terrifying Bat Masterson, for example, killed no one while resident in Dodge City. The cowboy, like the samurai and the knight and the Homeric hero, is a belated fiction.

"Fiction" does not mean "an utterly pointless fantasy without the slightest reference to the actual world," at least not in the minds of the male audiences for such tales of courage. As Norris Lacy and Geoffrey Ashe observe in *The Arthurian Handbook*, "Medieval storytellers . . . and their audiences viewed Arthur's kingdom rather as people now regard the Wild West. . . . Like the Wild West, [Arthur's Britain] was a realm of the imagination, but its creators would have denied that they were simply inventing out of nothing."[17]

The assertion that a fiction is about something that once actually happened is important to the men who read it, as to the men who read Tom

Clancy novels about spies and use them to interpret the day's headlines, or to make their next business deal. In his introduction to an edition of *The Ox-Bow Incident* (1941) by Walter Van Tilburg Clark, the literary man Clifton Fadiman declared that "we should remember that the background out of which the Western came was once a reality, that there *was* a Wild West, that gunplay *was* a habit."[18]

Not really. The blood spilling out of the dime novels, carried into the mature western novels and then into the western movies, most profusely in the spaghetti westerns at the very end of the genre, was a literary and economic device, not a sociological statistic. The boys and men of the 1870s, and the 1970s, had to be enticed to turn the page, and to buy the next novel in the series, or to go to the movie. "A hundred dead in two chapters," the *Atlantic Monthly* sneered in 1879.[19]

On the last page of his first Deadwood Dick novel, set in contemporary (1877) South Dakota, Wheeler—remember, he lived in Philadelphia—adds "a few words to end *this o'er true romance* of life in the Black Hills." He reports on the after-plot life of the characters, such as Calamity Jane, Dick's sometime fiancée and fight mate, who "is still in the Hills." "And grim and uncommunicative [note this: no talk], there roams through the country of gold a youth in black, at the head of a bold lawless gang of roadriders, who, from his unequaled daring, has won and rightly deserves the name—Deadwood Dick, Prince of the Road."[20]

As Robin Hood was to feudal lords, so Deadwood Dick and Jesse James and Bonnie and Clyde and other outlaw heroes were to American capitalism. Or they were at least in song and in story. In sociological fact James and his gang were the sons of rich Missouri slaveholders, continuing after the war the guerrilla resistance to Union and abolition they had learned before and during it. The historian James McPherson notes that "the unromantic truth is that Jesse spent much of his ill-gotten gains on fine horseflesh and gambling," not paying off the mortgage of poor farmers or engaging in other proto-socialist gestures.[21]

It's unclear what Wheeler meant by claiming his roadrider story was "o'er" true. But despite the reportorial rhetoric, it wasn't. The men and boys reading the dime novels did not want pure fantasy, science fiction, so to speak, because they wanted to imagine themselves into the fictions, and so the fictions denied their fictionality. The black cowboy, Nate Love, later claimed to be the "real" Deadwood Dick, but this is an instance among many, from James Fenimore Cooper to the urban cowboys of suburban Dallas, of life imitating art.

Some dueling did go on, exceptionally rarely, in the streets of Dodge City. The medieval knights did joust from time to time, though not much, or they would have killed themselves off Monty Python–style. The samurai did refuse on their honor to perform executions in anger, usually. And even in commercial Florence in the sixteenth century, Cellini the sculptor, no aristocrat, had to the credit of his *virtù* numerous victims in duels and other affrays. Yet it is not a true history of olden times to portray lethal dueling as how Real Men spent their days, a habit.

Do the math. If a population of male aristocrats engaged in lethal duels on N occasions over some period, by the end, of course, only $(1/2)^N$ would survive. I said "lethal" duels, one-on-one. If such duels happened weekly, for example as one might infer from watching *Gunsmoke* on TV, then an aristocracy of 10,000 courageous cowboys would be reduced by the end of a ten-week TV season to merely 10 (very) quick-draw sharpshooters still standing.

You get the point. Fights literally to the death, above once every eighteen years or so, it turns out, would overwhelm even preindustrial birthrates of 4 percent of the existing population in a year. And since people die for other reasons, too, a much less frequent rate of heroic killing—once, say, over an entire career of noble sword-fighting or gunslinging—would destroy the social class that indulged in it. This is why challenges male-on-male in the mammalian world are ceremonial rather than lethal. If bucks actually killed each other each spring at the rates their faux aggressions seem to promise, there would be no species of deer surviving. The same argument in reverse was Darwin's crucial insight, derived from the economist Malthus, that in a world of scarcity a proliferating class *needs* to be cut down, somehow; and so it must compete for food and sex to the death.

Class suicide in fact does seem to characterize gang members in Philadelphia nowadays, who take their models from the television art, and was nearly so of the English dukedom during the Wars of the Roses. Shakespeare's Bishop of Carlisle prophesies accurately in imaginary 1399, "the blood of England shall manure the ground / . . . and this land be called / The field of Golgotha and dead men's skulls."[22] But the mathematics shows that death-defying courage can only in romantic theory be the virtue primarily called upon in any society, except in the emergency services or in a literal military camp, and then only at the rare, looming crisis.

Such a fiction does of course a cultural job. Especially it fueled in an age of democracy the occasional explosions of mass armies, 1861–1865, 1914–1918, 1939–1945. In peacetime it gave the overcivilized man of the late Roman Empire or of Enlightened Europe before the Revolution or of late nineteenth-century America a way out, at least in imagination, from under the skirts of women and the domination of priests—and an escape from under an urban, unheroic, international market which took his manhood in a moment's beastly roaring on the floor of the Bourse.

Like the highwaymen or the Rob Roys of earlier British romance, "Deadwood Dick and [the fictionalized] Jesse James," writes Bill Brown (agreeing in this with Michael Denning), "contested the dominant ideology, the encroachment of advanced capitalism. . . . The James brothers achieved iconic status as a force that could interrupt the success of capitalists (the banks) and the institutions of modernization (the train)"—though the hero of the later *bourgeois* version of the Western initiated by Wister's *The Virginian* breaks a strike and protects the owner's capital, in the style of John Wayne in *Red River*.[23]

TACITURN COURAGE AGAINST
THE "FEMININE"

Beauvoir articulates the process whereby women, by agreeing to live in comfort inside the fantasies of men, put themselves in a permanently false position. . . . Men are forever feeling betrayed, not supported, . . . because when fantasy is governing perception, the truth appears as a blasphemy. . . . Woman as Object may be spared the heavy burden carried by primary Subjects only by suffering the dishonor of constant two-way self-betrayal. . . . [She] often meekly accept[s] every form of raw deal in punishment for representing falsity and weakness.
  —Anne Hollander, 1999.

Jane Tompkins argues that one enemy is language itself: "Westerns treat salesmen and politicians, people whose business is language, with contempt."[1] This is the case even though the occupation of the implied reader of the westerns is in fact a man who earns his living in talk-work. The comical Rebel in the movie of *Shane* boasts loudly, drunkenly, with a courage lacking temperance; and we know, Tompkins observes, that he is doomed (in the book from which the movie derived he is less central, and his lack of taciturnity is less emphasized). "It's Shane," she writes, "the man who clips out words between clenched teeth, who will take out the hired gunman."[2]

Taciturnity is not noticeable in Homeric heroes. After all, they are Hellenes, addicted to persuasive talk. The index of speeches in Stanley Lombardo's translation of the *Iliad* contains about six hundred items, and these not mere bright quips ("A crippled newsie took them away from him"), but full-blown exercises in persuasion, about twenty-five per book, a long interlude of yammering every thirty lines or so.[3] The knights of the Round Table, according to Mallory, yammered a good deal, too. Maybe it is specifically Roman, and romanizing, revived in a particular sort of haut-bourgeois gentleman in the nineteenth century, to demand as it were laconic behavior from our heroes.

Mary Beth Rose suggested that a new and bourgeois and even feminine "heroism of *endurance*" takes the place in early modern times of the aristocratic heroism of action.[4] She notes, with Norbert Elias, that the nation-state required a monopoly of violence. Just as the cow towns of Kansas disarmed their cowboys, the Tudors and Valois disarmed their barons. In Milton's *Paradise Regained* (published 1671), Rose observes, Christ is not the venturing warrior of book 6 in *Paradise Lost*, but a hero of taciturnity. His victories against Satan tempting him in the wilderness consist of *not* engaging in speech making, as at the end of book 1, in three lines of in effect a Valley girl "Whatever" dismissing a loquacious twenty-five-line appeal by Satan to "talk at least." After Christ's brevity Milton himself adds an amazing half-line: "He added not" (1.497), embodying Christ's noble—that is, Roman—unwillingness to talk. Satan, the great talker and venturer-forth, is thoroughly puzzled: "What *dost* thou in this world?" (4.372, emphasis supplied); and elsewhere:

> Perplexed and troubled at his bad success
> The Tempter stood, nor had what to reply,
> Discovered in his fraud, thrown from his hope,
> So oft, and the persuasive rhetoric
> That sleeked his tongue, and won so much on Eve,
> So little here, nay lost.[5]

Milton, eloquent for the Commonwealth and English poetry, here disdains rhetoric, joining in this many seventeenth-century men of ideas and letters, from Bacon attacking metaphors with metaphors—thus too Descartes, Pascal, Hobbes, Spinoza—to Newton spinning one eloquent hypothesis after another while declaring "Hypotheses non fingo," I do not [deign merely to] spin hypotheses.

By the end of the eighteenth century, in, for example, *The Magic Flute*, taciturnity has been raised to the very essence of masculinity. The one and only test of the opera's hero to join the men's club of Freemasonry is to keep quiet in the face of temptations from loquacious women. No heroic action; no swordplay: just endure like a tight-lipped Roman man. Mozart's librettist stresses over and over that silence is Tamino's badge of heroism, one which his comically talkative, less-than-aristocratic sidekick Papageno fails repeatedly to display. Tamino is a prince of the blood, again emphasized. By contrast, a man of mere commerce *must* talk if he is to do business.

Shane a century and a half after Mozart still looks longingly back to an imagined aristocracy of taciturn and noncommercial Romans. E. Countryman and E. von Heussen-Countryman note that the movie "renders commerce problematic." The lone knight Shane himself is willing to join the farmer Joe Starrett, a Cincinnatus finally driven to take down his weapons, in a stirring scene of stump-removing, "bonding on Joe's ground, literally." But it is honest, wordless toil—direct production for subsistence, not the schemes and weaselwords and endless bargaining of Ryker and his capitalist gang.[6]

To Ryker's suggestion early on in the movie that Shane join the commercial side, the knight replies, No deals. Jack Schaefer's novel of 1949 is on some points less anticapitalist than George Stevens's movie of 1953. The offer from Ryker to Shane comes later in the novel than in the movie, in chapter 12 out of sixteen, and therefore is less temptingly corrupt: Shane has long since become a Lancelot for the homesteaders. Starrett in the novel is more persistent than in the movie about his economic schemes for the farm, and as a petit bourgeois man is more critical of the Ryker figure. Ryker, by the way, is called "Fletcher" in the novel. One wonders if the Dutch word *rijker*, "richer," spelled in handwriting exactly *ryker*, is being evoked by some sly script doctor of recent Dutch ancestry. Anyway, Ryker/Fletcher engages, says Starrett, in "poor business" and is "wasteful," the sort of prudential talk that would be read with pleasure by an American bourgeois in 1949.[7] Compare John D. MacDonald's detective novels, with their obeisance to the businesslike.

Middlemen are featured in both novel and movie. The owner of the saloon and general store is a Good Bourgeois. But there are bad ones, too. The novel has a five-page scene of the aristocratic Shane and the petit bourgeois Starrett outwitting "a peddler or trader" who tries to overcharge for a new plow. The peddler in cruder novels would have had a Jewish name or would have been from the East, or both.

Shane is uninterested in becoming permanently a laborer for wages, or what is perhaps more to the point, temperately restrains his desire to become an adulterous Lancelot to Marion Starrett's Queen Guinevere. In the end he rides on to further knight errantry—he tells Joey, "A man has to be what he is"—leaving the peasantry in possession. So do the surviving three in the Japanese cowboy movie, *Seven Samurai* (1954), based, the director Kurosawa said, on American westerns such as *Shane*. So do the surviving three in the American remake returning the favor to Kurosawa, with American cowboys/samurai, *The Magnificent Seven* (1960). The director of *Shane*, George Stevens (it was his only western), once declared outright that his hero had overtones of medieval knighthood.

All the westerns had it, as, for example, Stanley Kramer's *High Noon* (1952). The bourgeoisie pursues Prudence Only, economic goals, to "keep the town decent, *keep it growing*," as the Thomas Mitchell character puts it emphatically. In Mitchell's fluent, climactic speech in the church he argues—we are surprised by the argument, considering the conventions of the genre—*not* that a man's gotta do what a man's gotta do, which is the aristocratic, ducal formula, but that investors from the northern part of the state are thinking of investing in the town, and therefore to keep things quiet and commercial the Gary Cooper character, the outgoing sheriff, should leave town without dueling with the villains.

The Gary Cooper sheriff cannot then or at any other point in the movie find much eloquence to explain his knightly duty to stay and fight—not to the church people, not to a bourgeois town, not even to his new Quaker wife, the Grace Kelly character. His wife does fight in the end, lethally. In the cold war we all needed to, even Quakers. Contrast the reversal of such roles before anti-Communism took hold. The John Wayne of *Angel and the Badman* (1947) becomes finally a pacifist under his wife's influence. In 1947, after all, Americans were still laying down their weapons. Thomas Dewey, confident of victory in the 1948 elections, nobly refrained from using the anti-Communist card, which swiftly thereafter developed in American politics into the only winning card.[8] Though it is complicated: *High Noon* was designed as an anti-McCarthyite movie, inspiring right-wing replies from that same John Wayne.

But like noble Tamino and noble Shane, Gary Cooper scorns using the persuasive words. He is not a politician. It is revealing that *High Noon* is the favorite movie of U.S. presidents, measured by actual showings at the White House (Clinton saw it thirty times). The Gary Cooper/president figure is an employee of the bourgeoisie, but he is quite different from them, as are the taciturn hired swords/guns in *Seven Samurai* and *The Magnificent Seven*, impoverished aristocrats. The folklorist John Lomax had set the tone in 1910, as the western myth was becoming bourgeois and respectable: "Dauntless, reckless, as gentle to a pure woman as King Arthur, [the cowboy] is truly a knight of the twentieth century."[9] That "reckless" should worry Americans. Anyway, not a capitalist.

For the self-dubbed knights of the bourgeois world the other enemies, aside from the talk-talk capitalists, were those tiresome, Bible-reading, churchgo-ing, water-drinking, talk-talk *women.* As Peter French notes, "Women do a lion's share of the talking in westerns," and gain no honor for it.[10] Tompkins observes that the female lead in the 1957 version of *The Gunfight at the O.K. Corral,* the Jo Van Fleet character, is merely an absorber of dishonor to purify her male lovers in preparation for battle, Burt Lancaster as Wyatt Earp and Kirk Douglas as Doc Holliday. "Her [pacific] words are always in vain, they are chaff, less than nothing, another sign of her degradation."[11] Words and women, say the cowboys, are a lethal combination. Guns first, talk later.

The sentiment is old, right from the beginning of the modern story of emancipation alternating with reaction. *The Magic Flute,* again, is relent-lessly misogynistic on this score. The gendering of aristocratic nostalgia could not be more explicit in the scripting of low-born Papageno's failure as a man, except as one of inferior appetites. Papageno is unable to meet the Masonic/*Shane* standard of being "steadfast, tolerant, and *discreet*": at one point he blurts out, startlingly, "Ich wollt, ich wär ein Mädchen": "I wish I were a girl." Later he asks Tamino plaintively, "Can I not be quiet when I must? Yes! When it comes to business [*Unternehmen,* undertakings], I'm a man."[12] But he's not. Compare Sancho Panza—though the nonaristocratic character in Mozart carries no hint of antiaristocratic irony, and Sancho in 1614 certainly has nothing feminine about him. By 1791 the gender world of Europe had shifted.

A century later it had shifted again. American literature after 1900 embodies a bourgeois and masculinist reaction to female religiosity and female rights. You can see it in the westerns, the hard-boiled detective sto-ries, the literary imitations of journalistic pith: Zane Grey, Dashiell Ham-mett, Ernest Hemingway. "I don't like eloquence," says Hammett's first hard-boiled hero in 1924, the Continental Op (operative, that is, for the Continental Detective Agency). "If it isn't effective enough to pierce your hide, it's tiresome; and if its effective enough, then it muddles your thoughts." An antirhetorical rhetoric was the imagined tough guy's way of eluding, as Claudia Roth Pierpont puts it, "the feminine imperative against which Hammett defined himself: the tireless urging to feel, to connect, to talk, talk, talk."[13]

Talk, talk, talk is an American black imperative, too, against an aristocratic Roman and bourgeois American ideal of taciturnity. In Ralph Ellison or Zora Neale Hurston the men are very Attic Greeks in their eloquence, "big picture talkers . . . using a side of the world for a canvas." In *Their Eyes Were Watching God* (1937) Jamie complains about her husband Jody being the mayor: "You'se always off talkin.'" He replies, "Ah told you in de very first beginnin' dat Ah aimed tuh be uh big voice. You oughta be glad, cause dat makes uh big woman outa you."[14] Women form in the book, until they get their own voices, a Greek chorus to the men's eloquence.

Talk of prohibition and the vote for women—never mind blacks—stuck in the craws of a lot of American men, as had earlier the domestication of the bourgeois male, subordinate to the angel in the house. "For most of the nineteenth century," Tompkins notes, "the two places women could call their own in the social structure were the church and the home. The Western contains neither. . . . [M]en gravitated in imagination towards a womanless milieu."[15]

Think of Teddy Roosevelt, the fragile (and "aristocratic") child who adopts the strenuous western life with grim manliness. After his first wife and his mother died suddenly in the same week, he took his sorrowful exercises far away from home and church, a New York Dutchman in Dakota with other splendid fellows shooting everything that moved. Roosevelt had been in fact a Harvard classmate of Owen Wister—*The Virginian*, 1902, is dedicated to Roosevelt. H. W. Brands writes that Roosevelt's "great good luck was to come of age when America had a particular weakness for romantic heroes."[16]

Roosevelt was a prolific writer about his self-created romances, like his younger contemporary Winston Churchill. Churchill was of course an actual aristocrat, first cousin of the 9th Duke of Marlborough, nephew of the 6th Earl of Airlie, witnessing with dismay in Britain, as TR did in America, the decline of "a small and serious ruling class."[17] Roosevelt wrote a six-volume *The Winning of the West* (1889–1896), which with Frederick Jackson Turner's presidential address to the American Historical Association at the Chicago World's Fair of 1893 helped set the tone of nostalgia for a lost frontier of real men. Roosevelt's history of the American navy of John Paul Jones and Oliver Hazard Perry remained a classic for decades. In the second year of his presidency a fourteen-volume *oeuvres complètes* appeared—fourteen thick and self-authored volumes, not merely bureaucratic papers written by others. He was a man of many words. He wrote about ten letters a day, 150,000 in total, while Holmes, whom he appointed to the Supreme Court, managed a mere 10,000. A war-monger, then a peacemaker, a threatener, then a deal maker, a strike settler, Roosevelt talked, talked, talked from whatever pulpit he could command.[18]

Literary men of action early in the twentieth century, especially in America before Hemingway masculinized American fiction, were caught uneasily between feminine words and masculine action, speaking softly but wanting to be known for carrying a big stick. William Carlos Williams writes in 1913:

> First he said:
> It is the woman in us
> That makes us write—
> Let us acknowledge it—
> Men would be silent.
> We are not men
> Therefore we can speak
> And be conscious
> (of the two sides)
> Unbent by the sensual
> As befits accuracy.[19]

"Male poets born in the Gilded Age," writes Guy Rotella about Robert Frost, who masculinized American *poetic* style, "confronted . . . a business-dominated society [judging] their chosen work not to be work at all, and certainly not manly work."[20] About the same time, quoting an imagined manifesto for the Writer in *Death in Venice* (1912), Thomas Mann wrote, "We poets . . . may be heroic after our fashion, disciplined warriors of our craft, yet are we all like women, for we exult in passion, and love is still our desire—our craving and our shame."[21]

In the minds of literary men less subtle than Frost or Mann, such as Teddy Roosevelt, the nonwork work was all supposed to come out gloriously in the end, this quasi-manly, poetic yammering leading to undeniably manly violence, women cheering from the castle window, like a knightly tale of olden times, the splendid little wars of imperialism, the white man's burden, the charge up San Juan Hill—successful of course, with the bold colonel on horseback surviving, like a boy's game. All four of Roosevelt's sons served in France—as did the sons, I've noted, of British ducal families, noblesse oblige—and one got the Croix de Guerre.

The ageing Roosevelt was crushed when his youngest son, beloved, troublesome Quentin, met his fate somewhere among the clouds. Is *this* what war is like, a courageous son actually dying? In August 1918, still three months from Armistice, he wrote, "It is rather awful to know that he paid for his life, and that my other sons may pay for their lives, to try to put in practice what I preached." TR's luck held, though. His other sons survived the war, and he himself died in 1919, before the apparent failure of the peace had devalued the romantic sacrifice.[22]

After 1916, after Verdun and the Somme, the highbrows at least had started to doubt the old lie. Middle-brow culture held onto it. As you go up the stairs to the reading room of Harvard's Widener Library, you come on the landing to a gigantic, Rubenesque double mural painted by John Singer Sargent a little before his death in 1925. One panel is inscribed, "They crossed the sea crusaders keen to help the nations battling in a righteous cause"; the other, "Happy those who with a glowing faith in one embrace clasped death and victory." Sweet and proper is it to die for the fatherland.

The romance of the Homeric hero spreads in American literature in TR's time. It has roots of course as far back as Cooper's *Leatherstocking Tales* (1823–1841). Think of Daniel Day Lewis's luscious performance in the movie of *The Last of the Mohicans*. It persists to the present in the middle- and low-brow reading of bourgeois men. Early in Zane Grey's *Riders of the Purple Sage* (1912; it has since then never been out of print), Bern Venters rejects the voluble peacemaking by Jane Withersteen, and demands she return his guns, after a gunslinger who happens along has saved him from a humiliating beating: "Hush! Talk to me no more of mercy or religion—after today. Today this strange coming of [the gunslinger] left me still a man, and now I'll die a man! . . . Give me my guns." Venters disarms the woman by stopping her *talk*. Quoting the passage, Tompkins remarks, "In Venters, American men are taking their manhood back from the Christian women who have been holding them in thrall."[23] With words.

19

BOURGEOIS VS. QUEER

In almost no American movie before the 1960s does a man fail to use violence on a woman. The gesture of preventing a woman from leaving the room by grabbing her arm is routine in movies into the 1950s even from gentlemanly types like Fred Astaire and Spencer Tracy. Imagine an American bourgeois man doing that now. Less temperate overmastering of women in the movies was practiced frequently, for example, by John Wayne, as when in *The Quiet Man* (1952) he carries off over his shoulders a kicking and screaming Maureen O'Hara. The gentlemen sometimes allow themselves a little date rape. Even sweet Gary Cooper rapes Patricia Neal in *The Fountainhead* (1949)—though, you know, she really wanted it. The gentle and bourgeois among early twentieth-century American men appeared to be unhappy about the feminine, and authorized themselves therefore to master and manhandle it.

All the more did they authorize themselves to master and manhandle apparently "feminine" men. These taciturn, tough, pagan, fishing, hunting, boxing, misogynistic, Boy Scouting, antimollycoddle, and above all courageous men became increasingly obsessed with homosexuals, especially gay men, and most especially flamboyantly talkative, effeminate gay men. Recent scholarship on gender history in the United States, summarized by John D'Emilio and Estelle Freedman, has located an "early-twentieth-century crisis in middle-class male gender identity."[1] The story is paralleled in Britain after the trials of Oscar Wilde (1895) and in Germany after the scandal of Philipp von Eulenburg (1906), though in America the turn against homosexuality took a more violent character. Fag bashing is an especially American sport.

No one before the late nineteenth century thought of same-sex affection as defining a whole class of human beings. Homosexual acts even in culturally backward America were never, after the totalitarianism of the early Puritans, viewed with enough distaste to evoke the Biblical penalty—the penalty in Leviticus (18:22 and 20:13) is, of course, death, as it is there for other appalling crimes, such as cursing your parents or committing adultery (20:9–10). Abraham Lincoln, it now seems somewhat plausible, was gay; Walt Whitman was without any doubt. Nobody cared much. In fact during most of the nineteenth-century, homosexual acts in America were ignored, until the turn after the Civil War to purity in the Comstock Law and the like, putting the United States in the van of antisex countries. Consenting sodomy was not against the law in New York state until the 1890s. Until 2003 it was illegal in Texas. We have emerged from one hundred years of virulent homophobia, comparable to a similar episode in the thirteenth century. St. Thomas was in this matter conventional, ranking homosexual acts just below murder.[2] As John Boswell shows in detail, the thirteenth century was a local maximum of such attitudes, and Aquinas was going along with them, illogically.[3] Likewise the modern hysteria about unnatural acts.

Public attributions of *passive* homosexuality in Western societies were shaming always, at any rate for an adult. See, for example, Catullus 57's smirking commentary on the sex life of Julius Caesar. But to be ashamed of an *active* role was something new in the late nineteenth century. Wilde was led into the first of his three disastrous trials by a manly desire to challenge for this reason the Marquis of Queensbury, a wretchedly bad choice of sparring partner. In France at about the same time Marcel Proust, though notoriously gay, was ashamed of it, and in order to defend what he imagined was his good name against the charge of unusual tastes, engaged repeatedly in courageous if stylized dueling with pistols. No one was ever hurt. Compare bucks in spring. He went to lengths in *Remembrance of Things Past* (1913) to recast the good loving by a man as love for a woman ("Albert" → "Albertine"), which unfortunately, as he explained to an indignant André Gide, left all the bad loving to the many homosexual characters in the novel.

In France, however, homosexuality was merely a matter of social shame, and of occasional high-handedness by police and judges, not of explicit legal sanction. The sole exception was the law passed under the Vichy government, repealed in 1982, raising the legal age of consent to twenty-one for homosexual liaisons; for heterosexuals it was fifteen. As Scott Gunther puts it, except for this one, fascist exception, French law, unlike American or British or German, simply did not mention homosexuality.[4] The French have long been amused by the Anglo-Saxon, Dutch, and German fixation on queers, just as the northerners have long been amused by the French and Italian fixation on being cuckolded.[5] In Shakespeare the balance is Latin in this matter, obsessed with cuckoldry yet relaxed about homoeroticism. Homophobia is modern, in the north.

Simon Schama notes in the Dutch Republic a startling outbreak in 1740–1742 of "a hysterical persecution of homosexuals in a culture that had virtually no history of witchhunts of any kind since the Anabaptists had swung on the gallows two hundred years before."[6] The laws under which some hundreds of prosecutions were brought in these few years, resulting in some score of executions, dated to the same 1530s, with extensions in 1570. In the Golden Age prosecutions were rare. Schama suggests that up to 1740, during a long time of peace—which is not how one would characterize the earlier Golden Age—"there were time and space for the Dutch to brood over their own identity and the unsettling discrepancy between a heroic past and a prosaic future."

In Britain the modern law criminalizing male homosexual acts under which Wilde was prosecuted was passed only in bourgeois and long-peaceful 1885, the Labouchère amendment, and was not seriously used for ten years. In America, as typically, the initiative was local, not national, and therefore varied greatly, though it started at about the same time, in the 1880s. Something about those 1880s.

It took decades during the very late nineteenth and early twentieth centuries for modern gender hysteria to build in the northern countries, though this time the Netherlands was not a part of it. Michael Quinn's startling *Same-Sex Dynamics among Nineteenth-Century Americans: A Mormon Example* (1996) establishes that Mormon leaders who came to maturity in the nineteenth century "looked upon sodomy as less serious than other sexual sins."[7] A focused faith that God hates fags, the laserlike focus on merely two of the hundreds of prohibitions in Leviticus, took hold even in conservative American Christianity only in the mid- and especially the late twentieth century.

It's puzzling, this anxiety about homosexuality. Why did a bourgeois courage seem to require such an angry reaction to the encroachment of the (alleged) feminine? The change toward fear of fags becoming so apparent around 1900 and accelerating thereafter was sometimes said to have happened because modern life for the bourgeois man allowed too little scope for his physical courage. That is, the men just had to land violent hands on women and gay men because the women and their gay brothers had taken away the other opportunities for manly play, such as gunplay. In any event that's what real American men like Owen Wister and Zane Grey and Jack London and Teddy Roosevelt seemed to be hinting in their gun-happy, feminine-excluding fictions.

In Europe between the wars, Richard Vinen notes, "political styles become more aggressively masculine." "In spite of, or perhaps because of, the enfranchisement of women . . . uniforms and clenched fists dominated demonstrations, and speeches were about 'struggle,' 'battle,' and 'the enemy.' "[8] Dating the gender crisis as late as the 1930s, George Chauncey links it to the Depression: "As many men lost their jobs, their status as breadwinners and their sense of mastery over their own futures, the central tenets undergirding their gender status, were threatened."[9] But in some advanced male imaginations, as I've said, homophobia or gynophobia constituting the dark matter to courage appears a good deal earlier. Before 1914 one can see already, for example, in Roosevelt the elder and in the strange death of Liberal England the masculinization of political rhetoric and the appeal to military metaphors of struggle—that is, to *Kampf*.

Wilde's conviction and jailing for gross indecency in 1895, I say, was a turning point among educated English speakers in the matter of homosexuality, a model application of the Labouchère amendment. The very word "homosexuality" was just becoming known. It appears to date from 1869; though the first quotation in the *Oxford English Dictionary* is 1897. Only with Wilde, argues Alan Sinfield, were effeminacy, arty tastes, love of other men, and those acts of gross indecency bundled together in the bourgeois mind and viewed by straights as horribly dishonorable. For decades afterward in England the euphemism for sodomy was "unspeakables of the Oscar Wilde sort." That was the phrase for example, in E. M. Forster's posthumously published coming-out novel, *Maurice*, written in 1914.[10] "All these years [since the trials of 1895]," Wilde's eldest son Cyril, once wrote to his brother Vyvyan, "my great incentive has been to wipe that stain away; to retrieve, if may be, by some action of mine, a name no longer honored in the land. . . . The more I thought of this, the more convinced I became that, first and foremost, I must be a *man*. There was to be no cry of decadent artist, of effeminate aesthete, of weak-kneed degenerate. . . . [I wish] nothing better than to end in honorable battle for King and Country."[11] On May 9, 1915, King and Country arranged to wipe away the stain.

The eagerness of American, British, and German doctors after the 1870s to get into the business of social engineering, a half century in advance of their total victories in drug and licensing laws, played a role in the strange rise of homophobia. Lucy Ann Lodbell, who in the 1850s passed as Reverend Joseph Lodbell without arousing the interest of the legal or medical authorities, and wrote a memoir, was by 1883 reclassified as mentally ill, justifying incarceration in a madhouse. "It is reasonable to consider true sexual perversion," wrote one Dr. "Wise" about the reverend's case, "as always a pathological condition and a peculiar manifestation of insanity."[12] The turn against same-sex intimacy—intimacy practiced among males in armies and navies always, and praised in Hellenizing and Romantic literature through Walt Whitman and A. E. Housman—led to a succession of laws prohibiting gender deviation, something like a men's version of the women's push for Prohibition, with likewise a reign of terror half-enforcing the laws.

D'Emilio and Freedman note that the medicalization of homosexuality worked two ways. Especially in a purity-minded America fearful of contagion from immigrants and blacks and other untouchables, it made people think that the unspeakable of the Oscar Wilde sort was a disease that could be spread by contact, or perhaps "recruitment," as to a fraternity. Why do young men become gay? Because the parties are better.

Yet at the same time medicalization encouraged Americans to think that homosexuality was an inherited identity rather than a vicious moral failing. Thus Kinsey's research from the late 1930s on. Certainly the psychiatrists, whose American branch dropped homosexuality as an "illness" only in 1973, though not finally in all versions of the illness until 1986, deserve full credit for a long and manly history of torturing homosexuals. For transsexuals the American, Canadian, and British psychiatrists are still at it, bless 'em, at, for example, the Clarke Institute in Toronto, named after a famous Canadian eugenicist, and at Johns Hopkins University Hospital, and especially the rat psychologists and psychoanalysts among them.

As the second European war approached, the fear of the feminine climaxed. In Britain in the twenty years of increasing state power after 1931, prosecutions under Section 11 of the Criminal Law Amendment Act of 1885 quintupled. In the 1930s the Nazi state was using with enthusiasm the notorious Paragraph 175—inherited by the German Empire in 1875 from the unusually harsh Prussian code. The Bolsheviks at first legalized homosexuality, in accord with their progressive ideas. But by 1934 they had decided it was just another sign of bourgeois decadence, and did what they usually did with bourgeois decadents.[13]

Alan Turing, the British mathematician of the computer and breaker of the German military code, was homosexual. He was fictionalized as heterosexual, by the way, in the movie *Enigma*; compare Proust's technique. In 1952, just before the strange business of legal ramifications for private acts began its long unraveling, Turing was sentenced by a court to take female hormones. He reckoned gaily that the sentence was better than the judge's alternative of prison; or, as he did not say, the psychiatrists' of electric shock therapy or lobotomy.[14]

During the early twentieth century in American culture as in other Germanic countries one can see the gynophobic and homophobic hysteria of a bourgeois Courage spreading like an oil slick. In the first lines of *The Sea Wolf* (1904) Humphrey van Weyden, the narrator and victim, introduced as an effete writer of essays on "Poe's place in American literature" for the *Atlantic*, "scarcely knows where to begin." His last name means in Dutch "of the meadows," *van der weyden,* and in London's time evoked the racial degeneration of the Eastern, Hudson Valley Dutch "aristocracy"—such as Roosevelt ("rose field"). Van Weyden is a derivative writer, and starts out as an evident pansy, implies Jack London of the West, quite another breed of man-writer.

The scene of the sinking ferry which opens the book is dense with gender anxiety. London spends a page recurring to Van Weyden hearing the "screaming bedlam of women." So when Van Weyden is swept away by the tide ripping out of the straits from San Francisco Bay, he himself recalls, "I shrieked aloud *as the women had shrieked.*" The Cockney cook from a fatefully passing ship who helps fish him out is "weakly pretty, almost effeminate," as Cockneys apparently always are. In a transvestite gesture, he gives some of his clothes to Van Weyden, who recalls, "I shrank from his hand, my flesh revolted"—whether from the taint of the "hereditary servility" of the Cockney race or from "his effeminate features" is unclear.

And yet the Cockney assigns effeminacy to Van Weyden himself, a literary gentleman, unproletarian: "You've got a bloomin' soft skin, that you 'ave, more like a lydy's than any I know of." When the captain Wolf Larsen appears, it is with a great noise of "not namby-pamby oaths," of which Van Weyden writes with ladylike delicacy, "It should not be necessary to state, at least to my friends, that I was shocked." The first words Larsen says to Van Weyden are, "You're a preacher, aren't you?" The world of women, preachers, and homosexuals recedes as the schooner *Ghost* speeds toward the seal-hunting grounds and a masculine rebirth.

The novel ends with the formerly effete Van Weyden jury-rigging an entire ship—"I did it! I did it! With my own hands I did it!"—and being swooned over by Maud Brewster ("My man"). The former aesthete queer, practically a woman for God's sake, is redeemed for the manly cult of courage.[15]

Again, in Dashiell Hammett's *The Maltese Falcon*, first published in 1929, Joel Cairo, whose very name evokes myths of the love of boys in Araby, is introduced in a page of effeminizing clichés. He was "small-boned," "his black coat, cut right to narrow shoulders, flared a little over slightly plump hips," he "came towards Spade with short, mincing, bobbing steps. The fragrance of chypre came with him." He spoke "in a high-pitched thin voice, and sat down. He sat down primly, crossing his ankles . . . and began to draw off his yellow gloves. . . . Diamonds twinkled on the second and fourth fingers of his left hand. . . . His hands were soft and well cared for." Cairo pulls out a little gun to frisk Spade: "His dark eyes were humid and bashful and very earnest." It's hard to imagine anyone but Peter Lorre in the movie role.

"He lifted Spade's coat-tail and looked under it. Holding the pistol close to Spade's back, he put his right hand around Spade's side and patted his chest," a mistake in the world of tough heterosexual men: Spade disarms Cairo with a swift turn, and then, for the insult, calmly knocks him out. In the novel (not in the movie) when Cairo wakes, he demands with powder-puff indignation, "Why did you strike after I was disarmed?" " 'Sorry,' Spade said, and grinned wolfishly."[16] Compare the courageous and intemperate Wolf Larsen. Jack London's friends called him "Wolf," and his mansion in California was the Wolf House.[17] *All* the male villains in *The Maltese Falcon* are queer, which Hammett's editor tried to get him to change. Hammett wouldn't.[18]

Such passages are impossible in nineteenth-century literature in English before Wilde, even in the working-class dime novels and penny dreadfuls, or indeed nowadays outside of the club comedian's homophobia in search of an easy laugh. In nineteenth-century American fiction, for example, cross-dressing and the like are common enough—recall Jo in *Little Women*;

or Huck Finn trying to pass in drag—but are not particularly sexualized or scorned.

The dime novels referred to gender bending with a calmness that startles the modern reader. Deadwood Dick and pals, male and female, jumped with abandon into and out of drag.[19] The *Adventures of Buffalo Bill* around 1882 in Beadle's Boy's Library of Sport, Story, and Adventure, chapter 18, "A Clever Disguise," claims that our hero captured a road agent by posing as a girl rider. "Buffalo Billy got the reward for his capture, and a medal from the company, and he certainly deserved all that he received for his daring exploit in the guise of a young girl, and a pretty one too, the boys said he made, for he had no mustache then, his complexion was perfect, though bronzed, and his waist was as small as a woman's."[20] The actual Wild Bill Hickok, too, it appears, was notably androgynous in behavior. But the book taking special, disdainful note of Hickok's queerness is not contemporary. It looks back from the gender-anxious date of 1930.[21]

Something special, in other words, happens in the half century of middle-class but tough-guy fiction in America after Owen Wister and Jack London. The fictional shift is especially American, not French or British, though I understand that Argentina at the same time developed in Spanish a similar tough-guy fiction.

In *The Sun Also Rises* (1926) Hemingway's narrator and alter ego is a figure of ethical seriousness, practicing his American bourgeois ethic in which one pays the price, working for the one true sentence. He observes "a crowd of young men," homosexuals, coming into a Parisian dance hall, and almost permits his fears to arouse his manly skill at boxing: "I could see their hands and newly washed, wavy hair in the light from the door. The policeman standing by the door looked at me and smiled. . . . I was very angry. Somehow they always made me angry. I know they are supposed to be amusing, and you should be tolerant, but I wanted to swing on one, any one, anything to shatter that superior, simpering composure."[22]

Hemingway was always interested in gender roles, and was sophisticated for his time about homosexuality. He was even sophisticated about transvestism and transsexuality, which was extremely unusual. Aside from the implied transsexuality in his novels, especially his posthumous last, his mother dressed him quite late in girl's clothing and in the 1920s and 1930s the works of the pioneering sexologist Havelock Ellis were among his favorite books. It seems like something out of his novels, but is true, that his youngest son Dr. Gregory Hemingway—though well after his father's death—became Gloria.[23] The narrator's homophobia in *The Sun Also Rises* toward "the crowd of young men" cannot simply be assigned to the author. But Hemingway was representing a reaction common then even among sophisticated American men.

The violent fear of being approached by homosexuals is strange when you think about it. What exactly is the big, strong, heterosexual man so terrified of? It's the *talk* of the effeminate homosexuals that seems to arouse the violence, just as for white men in America it was the talk of blacks or the talk of women. Or the talk of trade union organizers—in *The Grapes of Wrath* it is the agitators, the talkers such as Jim Casy the ex-preacher, whom the growers' cops swing on.

In *The Naked and the Dead* (1948) Norman Mailer's alter ego jokes to his Harvard classmates in fictional 1941, "You know when nothing else is left I'm going to become a fairy, not a goddamn little nance, you understand"—one imagines college juniors swinging drunkenly, anxiously on a talkative little nance behind Copley Square—"but a nice upright pillar of the community, live on green lawns. Bisexual. Never a dull moment, man or woman, it's all the same to you, exciting."[24] Compare Cary Grant playing Cole Porter in 1946, just before even a little gentle, veiled jesting about homosexuality became taboo in Hollywood. The Motion Picture Code had already in 1934 forbidden anything more explicit. Published casting directories for American stage and film in the first decades of the twentieth century had routine categories for "nance" or "pansy" actors. Edward Everett Horton, for example, backed up Fred Astaire in *The Gay Divorcee* (1934), *Top Hat* (1936), and *Shall We Dance* (1937), apparently in order to make the less-than-macho Astaire believable as a leading man.

The fear that femininity would take over, emasculating the bourgeois man, a fear to be resisted by boxing or going fishing or watching bull fights or even indulging an occasional urge to swing on the talkative, less-than-macho men, or by manhandling women, is a theme in every Hemingway novel from *The Sun Also Rises* to the very posthumous *The Garden of Eden* (1986, drafted 1948–1958). Though, I repeat, considering how he toyed always with gender-crossing themes, Papa is not quite so simple as this. Kathy Willingham argues ingeniously, for example, that the woman Brett Ashley in *The Sun Also Rises* is not merely a fearful man-eater, as contemporary critics uniformly said, but a matador, the most admired man in

Hemingway's mythology—pretty and small and coy and dressed in smooth silks, taunting the bull.[25] She's not called "Mary" or "Jane," after all, but the highly gender-ambiguous "Brett." But if Hemingway's gender talk is not quite so simpleminded as it first appears, it encompasses the simplicity, and the swinging on gays and women, too.

The white male bourgeoisie seemed to fear an improbable alliance among women and gays and blacks, who before the 1960s had all been nicely silenced. In Ralph Ellison's *The Invisible Man* (1952) the black hero, a mild and studious boy, is saved from the machinations of his (black) college president and the president's (white) tycoon trustees by the . . . wait for it . . . *homosexual* son of the last tycoon.

20

BALANCING COURAGE

Nonaristocratic men, at least the non-goddamn-little-nancy ones, imagined themselves in butch tales of whitened, imperialist, macho, womanless, taciturn, WASPish, aristocratic courage, and if the men were bourgeois, the intelligentsia began in the 1920s to be amused. A bourgeois man did not in his own opinion have the moral luck to be a real hero, that is, aristocratic and weapon-wielding.

In 1922 Sinclair Lewis savagely spoofed in six pages the morning drive to his real estate office by George Babbitt, a manly head filled with boyish tales of Courage: "To George F. Babbitt, as to most prosperous [male] citizens of Zenith, his motor car was poetry and tragedy, love and heroism. . . . The office was his pirate ship but the car his perilous excursion ashore. . . . Babbitt . . . devoted himself to the game of beating trolley cars to the corner . . . a rare game, and valiant. . . . [Even parking his car] was a virile adventure masterfully executed."[1] Lewis for all his cruelty and intellectual snobbery was on target. He regularly was on target in mimicking attitudes and language he was making fun of. The characters who speak woodenly in Lewis are his alter egos, the intellectuals. It is rightly said that Lewis was himself entangled in those risible bourgeois values. Modern male writers, especially American male writers, allow themselves aristocratic poses, but are highly amused by other people taking them.

Twenty years after *Babbitt*, James Thurber (ditto for his class values) was still making fun of the bourgeois man's dreams of glory, to always be the best, my boy, the bravest:

"We're going through!" . . . *"We can't make it, sir! It's spoiling for a hurricane, if you ask me." "I'm not asking you, Lieutenant Berg," said the Commander. "Throw on the power lights! Rev her up to 8500! We're going through!" The pounding of the cylinders increased: ta-pocketa-pocketa-pocketa-pocketa-pocketa. . . .*

"Not so fast! You're driving too fast!" said Mrs. Mitty. "What are you driving so fast for?"

"Hmm?" said Walter Mitty. He looked at his wife, in the seat beside him, with shocked astonishment.[2]

Such fantasies motivate business and military and political leaders as much as their calculations of profit and loss. Frank Knight writing in 1923 on the ethics of competition claimed that "the competitive economic order must be partly responsible for making emulation and rivalry the outstanding quality of the character of the Western peoples who have adopted and developed it." He contrasts it with "the religious ideals to which the Western world has continued to render lip-service—a contrast resulting in fundamental dualism in our thought and culture."[3]

The historical sociology here is perhaps a bit dubious. Knight was the first American translator of Max Weber, and one can see the Weberian influence. Competitiveness after all is no less the life of Afghani tribesmen and other decidedly nonbourgeois types. And bourgeois life is in fact largely a matter of cooperation, not competition: thus the Kiwanis Club mentality that Lewis spoofed; or the cooperation c. 1700 of traders in lumber and tobacco across oceans worldwide. The philosopher Jennifer Jackson asks how a capitalist life can be reconciled with moral virtues. The two temptations to vice in such a life, she supposes, are the encouragement of intemperance in consumption and the "avid competitiveness" of the businessperson, "the seeming unremitting need to be doing others down."[4] One would like to know the society of men, capitalist or not, that did *not* exhibit an unremitting need to do others down. Or, while we're on the point, one would like to know too the society of men or women that did not exhibit intemperance in consumption. As a system, capitalism, on the contrary, in modern times is a great triumph of cooperation. The play of competitiveness in the souls of businessmen does not seem to be essentially bourgeois. It reflects more often the jousting values of an aristocracy, or more accurately a neo-pseudo-aristocracy, and the male roles governed in fantasy by them.

But Knight observes acutely that "economic activity is *at the same time* a means of want-satisfaction, an agency for want- and character-formation, a field of creative self-expression, and a competitive sport. While men are 'playing the game' of business, they are also molding their own and other personalities."[5] Joseph Schumpeter had given in 1912 a similarly sociologized analysis of why capitalists played the game, a step beyond the naïve assumption in Marx and Veblen and many more recent critics of the bourgeoisie that "endless accumulation" is the game. Accumulation, Schumpeter said, was for social status, not only for itself. "For itself," business-people "delight in ventures," "exercising one's energy and ingenuity." And the macho "will to conquer," "akin to sport," is motivating, too. Yes—though none of the games is peculiarly capitalistic, and only for the status-taking motive "is private property as the result of entrepreneurial activity an essential factor in making it operative."[6] At the funeral games of Hector, too, the men raced, exercising their energy and skill, and proudly won, and nobly lost.

Yet Schumpeter, too, was influenced by Weber, and by Marx. He writes in 1942 that "capitalist civilization is rationalistic, and anti-heroic. . . . The ideology that glorifies the idea of fighting for fighting's sake and of victory for victory's sake understandably withers in the office among all the columns of figures."[7] I don't think so: the younger Schumpeter had it more right. It is not the case that the industrial and commercial bourgeoisie dislikes a "warrior ideology that conflicts with its 'rational' utilitarianism." It was not the case that bourgeois Europe had put aside aristocratic values in, say, 1914. Rather the contrary: the bourgeoisie had been reanimated by heroic values. And still.

An aristocratic myth, in other words, still animates the men of the middle class. It peaked in the Greatest Generation, who grew up reading the boys' books of a fading Romance. Alexander Gerschenkron (1904–1978) was a Russian émigré professing economics at Harvard 1948–1975, famously learned in two dozen languages, a student of Shakespeare, of statistics, of chess problems, of the Boston Red Sox, an expert in Russian and many other histories and literatures. Nicholas Dawidoff, the author of a best-selling biography of the baseball catcher and spy, Moe Berg, describes his grandfather's aristocratic and Russian temper as "charging the most ordinary events in his life with conspicuous moment" (ta-pocketa-pocketa-pocketa). Gerschenkron "never wanted to be associated with anything likely" (a rare game and valiant). He "never felt right if he was not feuding with someone" (wanting to swing on one, any one, anything to shatter that superior, sim-pering composure). "He believed that a gentleman does not say unflattering things out of another man's hearing" (you wine sack, with a dog's eyes, with a deer's heart). "My grandfather was a life-long champion of what he called 'French manners'" (extremely well-bred). "You were more generous with a friend than you were with yourself" (fearless, generous). "Any form of self-pity was anathema; he was someone who never wanted to be seen as a vic-tim" (today this strange coming left me still a man. Give me my guns). "Over and over again he had to win [his wife's] favor" (as gentle to a pure woman as King Arthur).

Like a Greek aristocrat in the *Iliad*, Gerschenkron's most unbelievable thing was courageous talk. On April 11, 1968, at a tumultuous meeting of the Harvard faculty in the face of a student takeover of University Hall, he gave a twenty-minute oration without notes calling his colleagues to arms—well, at least to action (in a rude society nothing is honorable but war). Always be the best, my boy, the bravest / and hold your head high above the others. "My grandfather didn't command armies or lead governments or win pennants," Dawidoff concludes, "but he was big, big in his qualities."[8] A bourgeois aristocrat.

Gerschenkron was, as we say, quite a guy. His aristocratic courage looked better than the cowardice of many of his colleagues at the time. The next year he was visiting the Institute for Advanced Study at Princeton. A Prince-ton administrator gave a seminar at the institute suggesting that the univer-sity grant all the demands of the black students. When the institute fellows pressed him on the point, the administrator burst out in vexation, "Well, after all, the black students have the guns." Into the stunned silence follow-ing this remark, Gerschenkron, with more learning than originality, dropped, in his Russian accented basso profundo, "Ven I hear the vord 'gun,' I reach for my culture."

But there can be ethical mischief as well as good in the gendered fantasy of courage. Screwtape explains,

> Think of your man [whom we devils are trying to corrupt] as a series of con-centric circles, his will being the innermost, his intellect coming next, and finally his fantasy. You can hardly hope, at once, to exclude from all the circles every-thing that smells of the Enemy [viz., God]: but you must keep on shoving all the virtues outward till they are finally located in the circle of fantasy, and all the desirable qualities [that is, desirable to devils, therefore sins from God's point of

view, for example, pride, covetousness, envy, anger, gluttony] inward into the Will. It is only in so far as [the non-sins, the virtues] reach the will and are there embodied in habits that [they] are really fatal to us [devils].[9]

The CEO who dreams himself an artist of war, a samurai or general, is thereby encouraged not to notice that in the boardroom his actual will behaves habitually in the service not of real ethical courage, in taking a prudent risk, say, or in standing up to the latest accounting trick, but in the service of pride and envy and covetousness.

It is said perhaps in jest that men think of sex every fifteen seconds. What is true is that they think of courage every minute of their lives. It's entailed by their gender identity, and is encouraged by an age nostalgic for aristocratic virtue. Maybe it's biological, but certainly the biology can be muffled or amplified by social arrangements—by the laws of wife-beating, for example, or the stories we tell. Women, it is said, dream of love, men of courage. The bourgeois men dream themselves back to cowboys and knights, to Horatius at the bridge, to the plains of Ilium, to tall Hector, breaker of horses, to Odysseus the resourceful, and to swift-footed Achilles, son of Peleus, and his aristocratic rage.

Yet the best among the best, *hoi tōn aristōn aristoi,* must show a balance of virtues. Courage isn't enough, even for a full-time hero. Even noble Gunnar of *Njal's Saga* violates the temperate, just, and prudent rules worked out in Iceland for the resolution of blood feuds. He carries on killing, with disastrous results.[10] Philippa Foot wrote that "nobody can get on well if he lacks courage, and does not have some measure of temperance and wisdom, while communities where justice and charity are lacking are apt to be wretched places to live, as Russia was under the Stalinist terror, or Sicily under the Mafia."[11]

You need *all* the pagan virtues in play—prudence (what Foot calls wisdom) *and* courage *and* temperance *and* justice. Even an institution specialized in courage, such as an army or a fire department or a police force, must exercise the other virtues, too. "A man who places honor only in successful violence," wrote Dr. Johnson of the Western Islands of Scotland, "is a very troublesome and pernicious animal in time of peace."[12] It was the problem of the late Roman Republic, as of many disordered times, that Roman men sought aristocratic glory in violence rather than bourgeois wealth in peace.

The Danny Glover character in *Lethal Weapon* inquires of the Mel Gibson character, also a policeman, "You ever met anyone you *didn't* kill?" A courageous institution or society or person lacking temperance and justice and prudence will not last, or work.

So at least we wish. We need a criterion for the virtue of virtues, an answer, not necessarily a simple one, to the question "Why is *this* a virtue?" It is not the case, as opponents of virtue ethics sometimes believe, that an answer has to reduce virtue ethics to duties or to utility. Edmund Pincoffs has suggested that we could decide which characteristics are virtues by asking whether we could approach or flee the person having them.[13] The moral philosopher Hursthouse identifies four ends, in two dimensions, survival/flourishing of the individual/group: the mere survival of the individual or of the group, or the flourishing of the individual or of the group.[14]

Alasdair MacIntyre is one among the male philosophers, among them Bernard Williams and John McDowell, who have contributed to virtue ethics. His answer to the question is a "social teleology." You test virtue *X* by asking how *X* contributes to the purpose, end, telos of the society, what Knight called "the moral habitability of the world."[15] The ancient theorists of the virtues applauded that balance and completion of virtues, worth having of course in a little community. What sort of person suits best the telos of democratic Athens or republican Rome? Well, of course a person having the four virtues courage, temperance, justice, and prudence. Jean Bethke Elshtain puts Aristotle in the postheroic camp. She too uses the movie *Shane* as an example: in the end Shane himself must leave, she writes, because "he is as out of place in the placid, settled kingdom of a tamed town on the American frontier as was Achilles' gory glory in Aristotle's list of civic virtues."[16]

Unfortunately, as Elshtain well understands, the question about the virtue of virtues can't really be answered as it typically was before the game was spoiled by Machiavelli and Hobbes. The old question and the then-obvious answer was in effect, "What does a society need to be virtuous? Well, that's obvious: a throng of virtuous chaps." The new social sciences of the eighteenth century came to realize, a century or two after the Terrifying Italian and the Angry Englishman had first said it, that social virtue, and certainly *virtù sociale,* does *not* require personal virtue in every one of a society's citizens, or perhaps in any of them. A self-interested mob of corporate-raiding, asset-stripping Gordon Gekkos might result, for example, in a rich economy, thank you very much.

The ancients and medievals by contrast argued about politics in a less social-scientific way. They were less aware that what is true of individuals might not turn out to be true of a group composed of such individuals. As Isaiah Berlin put it, Machiavelli's juxtaposition of the private, Christian world of personal virtues and the public, pagan world of political *virtù* raised for the first time a disturbing question:

> What reasons have we for supposing that justice and mercy, humility and *virtù*, happiness and knowledge, glory and liberty, magnificence and sanctity, will always coincide, or indeed be compatible at all? . . . Machiavelli . . . undermines one major assumption of Western thought: namely that somewhere in the past or the future, in this world or the next . . . there is to be found the final solution to the question of how men should live. . . . The very search for it becomes not merely Utopian in practice, but conceptually incoherent.[17]

In Plato's *Republic* the balance within the individual called temperance is taken as a parallel, even a cause, for the balance within the polis called justice. "And isn't he moderate because of the friendly and harmonious relations between these same parts?" asks Socrates. Glaucon replies (and Socrates evidently approves), "[Temperance] is surely nothing other than that, *both in the city and in the individual.*"[18] In Aristotle's *Politics* it was an explicit principle, says Sir Earnest Barker in his gloss, "that what is true of the felicity of individuals is also true of communities."[19]

Well, no, sadly, it is not. But set aside for a long while the problem that Plato and his graduate student Aristotle were perhaps overenthusiastic for the parallel between individual and civic virtue. Set aside that a later tradition known as civic humanism or civic republicanism looking back to the polis has the same problem. It has the problem, namely, that virtue in each person is strictly speaking neither necessary nor sufficient for the virtue of and certainly not for the survival of the whole community.

I will never fully resolve the social/private dilemma. At least I am in good company—for example, the company of all social observers since the dilemma first became clear in the eighteenth century. Alasdair MacIntyre, to pick a modern example, argues persuasively in his "social teleology" that "the essential function of the virtues is clear. Without them, without justice, courage, and truthfulness, practices could not resist the corrupting power of institutions."[20] Think of a scientist who is not committed to telling the truth, or a judge not committed to justice. Yet one can argue—people have—that institutions like competitive pressures in science or the procedures for recalling judges will result in social virtues regardless of the dishonesty of scientists and the corruption of judges. It may be. Smith, Tocqueville, and Marx each had invisible-hand explanations of why good or bad in people can lead to bad or good in the system. But observe that they held on to their non-invisible-hand indignations, about mercantilists corrupting the British state or *intendants* overcentralizing prerevolutionary France or Mr. Moneybags engorging the national income.

The dilemma is that private good is neither necessary nor sufficient for public good. The dilemma shows among the American Founding Fathers, as David Prindle among others has noted. John Adams doubted "whether there is public Virtue enough to support a Republic"; yet James Madison expected political competition, like economic competition, to make it "more difficult for unworthy candidates to practice with success the vicious arts by which elections are too often carried."[21] Adams stands for a civic republicanism depending on individual virtue, Madison for a liberalism depending on constitutional structures. Either individual virtue is necessary for the polity to thrive, or else ingenious structures can offset the passions with the interests.

Set aside for the present book, that is, the potentially paradoxical details of "social teleology." I will return to it in *Bourgeois Towns: How a Capitalist Ethic Grew in the Dutch and English Lands, 1600–1800.* I hope. At least we can agree, following Aristotle, that person-by-person the whole set of pagan virtues is desirable for the telos of the person herself: "No one would call a man happy [*makarion*] who had no particle of courage, temperance, justice, or wisdom."[22] You are not going to be a fully realized woman if in your mad courage you lack temperance and justice and prudence. You are going to be swept with animal passions. The jails are filled with people of undoubted physical courage. Their problem is that they have been too courageous, Thelma and Louise–style, Bonnie and Clyde–style, willing to take risks that noncriminals will not or cannot take.

The virtues are distinct. An ethic that elevates manly courage to the only virtue will speak of suicide bombers as "cowardly," since there is only one unified antivirtue if there is only one unified virtue. If you have only one word for the Good Man you are led to unhelpful locutions. Adolf Hitler was not merely "crazy," or in pursuit of some unanalyzable goal of "evil." A man with personal courage beyond doubt, and charming and witty in company, what he lacked in the end were the *rest* of the pagan four. Having one of them is not enough.

Or three out of four. When in 1937 Winston Churchill praised Mussolini as having "amazing qualities of courage, comprehension, self-control, and perseverance"—that is, Courage, prudence, temperance, and courage again, with faith—he was praising, as an aristocrat raised at Harrow and Sandhurst would, an almost balanced set of the pagan virtues. Churchill said once that if he had been an Italian he would have become a Fascist. Yet presumably even he found the Justice of Italian Fascism a trifle deficient.[23]

In other words, courage needs other virtues to be a virtue. Temperance, for example, self-control. From Achilles the berserk warrior to Tony Soprano the New Jersey mob boss, any society needs its men to exercise "impulse control." The problem with men, especially young men, is the excess of courage. Cardiff City's football hooligans are of all social standings, including at least one millionaire and one former professional footballer. The lads who on the day of the game mob the Swan and Anchor, surrounded by British police on the alert, are not always young and unemployed. What they share is an addiction to courageous violence, admittedly more common among young men with time on their hands than old men with jobs. What Eric Hoffer called true believers are the young, courageous men who make up the stormtroopers in every violent upheaval, good or bad.

Perhaps it's biological. In any case the *virtù* of young males requires elaborate socialization to check and channel. In East Africa not long ago a group of young male elephants, orphaned by poachers, engaged in what can only be described as gang banging. There is film of one particularly bold teenager tossing clumps of grass and mud at a rhinoceros, over and over again, challenging him to unequal battle. The teenagers became a nuisance also to the humans in the neighborhood, and the problem was solved at last by laboriously moving the worst offenders hundreds of miles into a herd led by mature female elephants, as elephant herds are. The boys stopped their *Rebel Without a Cause* behavior and became temperate members of the elephantine community. Doubtless they were happy, too, *makarioi*, and well favored, flourishing, *eudaimonikoi*.

Temperance itself is not an unalloyed good. "In some people," Foot reminds us, "temperance is not a virtue, but is rather connected with timidity or with a grudging attitude in the acceptance of good things."[24] A related sin is literal hopelessness, acedia, spiritual sloth, not caring. It is the second-to-the-worst in the deadly list. The virtue of temperance in Christian thinkers like Aquinas is not about mortification of the flesh, but on the contrary the moderate yet relishing use of a world charged with the grandeur of God. The characters in Grant Wood's painting *American Gothic* seem on one reading to show an excess of temperance. Only the wisp of hair over her right shoulder betrays the woman's passion.

Paul Dombey in Dickens's first antibourgeois novel, *Dombey and Son*, published in installments between the year of the repeal of the Corn Laws and the revolutionary year of 1848, "was not a man of whom it could properly be said that he was ever startled, or shocked; but he certainly had a sense within him, that if his wife should sicken and decay . . . he would find a something gone from among his plate and furniture . . . which . . . could not be lost without sincere regret. Though it would be a cool, business-like, gentlemanly, self-possessed regret, no doubt."[25] In truth, Mrs. Dombey's status in law, like that of any bourgeois woman in England in 1848, was little better than his plate or furniture. As we expect from the passage, Dombey is in for a lesson about letting one's life be ruled by temperance and prudence without courage or justice, and especially without Dickens's favored virtue, a secular and sentimental version of Christian Love.

The point is that to last like bronze the virtues must be alloyed with each other. A personality governed wholly by temperance is bad, as is one governed wholly by courage, or wholly by justice. It's the "wholly" that's the problem. Imagine how dangerous it would be to be in a platoon filled with Medal of Honor types or how tiresome to be in a nunnery filled with Mother Teresa types. As Susan Wolf puts it, "If the moral saint is devoting all his time to feeding the hungry . . . then necessarily he is not reading Victorian novels, playing the oboe, or improving his backhand. . . . A life in which *none* of these possible aspects of character is developed may seem a life strangely barren."[26]

PART FOUR

The Androgynous Virtues: Prudence and Justice

THE BRICK IS FALLING INTO PLACE
ROW AFTER ROW. SOON I WILL SIT
ON A PATIO DESIGNED BY

A MASON WHO KNOWS HIS CRAFT.
MY NEIGHBORS QUIT THEIR WALKS TO WATCH

A SKILLED MASON LAYING BRICK.
DILIGENCE IN LEARNING HOW

A THING IS PUT TOGETHER
TURNS A MAN INTO A MASTER,
TURNS HIS WORK INTO ART.

—*Helen McCloskey, "The Making of a Patio"*

21

PRUDENCE *IS* A VIRTUE

A person or a society must have also the last of the four pagan virtues, prudence—last in heroic value, first in political and economic and bourgeois value. I mean by "prudence" all the words following on the ancient Greek *phronēsis*, translated as "good judgment" or "practical wisdom." Oddly in modern Greek *phronēsis* has been specialized to good judgment in the upbringing of children. In the Latin of Cicero and Aquinas ancient *phronēsis* is *prudentia*. In plain English it is "wisdom" in its practical aspect or "know-how" or "common sense" or "savvy"—French *savoir-faire* and fancy-English "rationality" or "self-interest."

"Prudence" seems a reasonable long-period average of such words. The Germanic languages less frenchified than English cannot translate exactly the English/French/Romance/Latin word "prudence," lost in connotation among foresight (Dutch *voorzichtigheid*), caution (*omzichtigheid*), policy (*beleid*), good sense (*verstandigheid*), knowledge, saving, caretaking, management, calculating. In Dutch a possible translation of prudence is the neologism *berekendheid*, "calculating-ity," or, worse, *berekenendheid*, "be-reckoning-ness." Neither is recorded in compendious Dutch dictionaries.

Prudence is not academic knowledge, *sophia* or *scientia*, praised by the philosophers from Socrates to the Great Books as a knowledge of ends. The claim that philosophers such as themselves gain a special knowledge of ends—*phronēsis* or *prudentia* means "practical knowledge of *means*," the sense, writes Gadamer, "of what is possible, what is correct, here and now"—will seem optimistic to anyone who knows many philosophers, worldly or Academic.[1] As Aristotle observed, "If [the Platonic idea of the

Good] were so potent an aid, it is improbable that all the professors of the arts and sciences should not know it," as they appear not to.[2]

Prudence as practical know-how *is* a virtue. This was once a commonplace, in Aristotle, for example, the obligation to self-development, or in Aquinas the obligation to use God's gifts. The Christian version is reformulated in 1673 by Joseph Pufendorf of Leipzig, Heidelberg, and Lund thus: "It seems superfluous to invent an obligation of self-love. Yet . . . man is not born for himself alone; the end for which he has been endowed by his Creator with such excellent gifts is that he may celebrate His glory and be a fit member of human society. He is therefore bound so to conduct himself as not to permit the Creator's gifts to perish for lack of use."[3] Thus Milton's Comus tempting the Lady in 1634 argues that by a niggardliness in using God's gifts "th'All-giver would be unthanked, would be unpraised / Not half his riches known . . . / And we should . . . live like Nature's bastards, not her sons."

One can detect in Pufendorf's "it seems superfluous" a hint of the modern substitution of prudence as mere behavior for prudence as an ethical obligation. We have been inclined for some centuries now in the West to relegate prudence to an amoral world of "mere" self-interest—especially so since around 1800, with the "separation of spheres" into a male market and a female home. "By allocating selflessness to women," notes Joan Williams, "domesticity helped legitimate self-interest as the appropriate motivation for men."[4] Or in Stephanie Coontz's formulation, "Men learn their roles and values best in places women cannot go."[5]

The inclination to demoralize prudence is not simply stupid, though it has had some bad outcomes. Wise philosophers such as Michael Oakeshott have erected systems on the distinction between "prudential" (or "enterprise") associations such as business firms on the one hand and "moral" associations on the other such as families. I am saying that in this matter Oakeshott was mistaken. It may be that such a distinction is the typically modern ethical mistake, the mistaken assumption that homely *Gemeinschaft* is the exclusive site of virtue and that businesslike *Gesellschaft* is an ethical nullity. It is certainly Machiavelli's and Hobbes's mistake.

"The virtues nowadays thought of [as] especially worthy to be called moral virtues," writes Philippa Foot, "are often contrasted with prudence." But she shows this is wrong. "A reasonable modicum of self-interest" is also an "Aristotelian [necessity] for human beings."[6] It is not surprising to find women criticizing a separation of spheres that makes prudence into a mas-culine realm of action and the rest of the virtues into matters for the clois-ter. The theologian Ellen Charry notes that "happiness" has come to mean "prudent utility," what she calls "a state of mild euphoria." The modern sup-porters of such a view, such as Peter Singer or Shalom Asch, "would say that the 'things other than happiness'" are indeed more important, because "happiness, having been privatized, is thought to be self-serving."

> This attitude is socially disastrous, because on its terms there is no reason for people to want to contribute to the common good, since they assume that it will not make them happy. . . . Seeking happiness, which ancient philosophy recog-nized to be a universal and proper desire, now opposes being good. Concern for the loss of civility, the triumph of "autonomous individualism" so bemoaned in recent sociology—as in the writings of Robert Bellah—is partly the result of an assumed enmity between goodness and happiness.[7]

This is the crucial difference between a virtue ethics that focuses on the good life and a neo-Kantian, academic ethical philosophy that focuses on good intentions toward other people—leaving mysterious the desire to do such good deeds in the first place. Virtue ethics, by contrast with neo-Kantian ethics, attends also to the self and the transcendent, giving a reason to seek goodness. Kant himself was in 1785 more to the point: "Act to use humanity, *both in your own person* and in the person of every other, . . . as an end."[8]

Among moderns before virtue ethics, in other words, only a habitual disposition to take care of others was construed as "virtue," and then for its intentions rather than for its practical effect. Having such other-directed good intentions in one's heart was said to be virtuous. This is pure Kant, not merely neo-Kantian, and evangelical Protestant, too. The intentions are vir-tuous even if, when carried out, as in high-rise public housing along the Dan Ryan Expressway, or the war on drugs brought onto the streets of Watts and East L.A., or the First and Second Iraq Wars, they do not quite deliver. And surely, we in European culture have been saying for a long while, know-ing how to take care of oneself is hardly a *virtue*?

Yes, it is. And so is the correlated carefulness in "helping" others. The love or Justice moving us to help others is a vice, not a virtue, when unalloyed with prudence. The good Samaritan who ignorantly if unintentionally kills the person he is trying to help is properly held responsible in law. Knowing that one must put out a candle before leaving the room is a good thing, even if you didn't mean to burn the place down, even if your intentions were pure, even if it was your own room to dispose of. The school of Plato defined prudence (that is, *phronēsis*) as "the ability which by itself is productive of human happiness; the knowledge of what is good and bad; the knowledge that produces happiness; the disposition by which we judge what is to be done and what is not to be done."[9]

Aquinas declares that "any virtue which causes good in reason's consideration is called prudence," and observes that prudence "belongs to reason essentially whereas the other three virtues [viz., courage, temperance, and justice] . . . apply reason to passions."[10] And elsewhere he says, "One needs to deal rightly with those things that are for the sake of the end [*finis*], and this can only come about through reason rightly deliberating, judging, and commanding, which is the function of prudence. . . . Hence there can be no moral virtue without prudence."[11] Or still elsewhere, the job of such practical reason is "to ponder things which must be done . . . but it is through prudence that reason is able to command well."[12]

It is the executive function. Executive, not technical. In his book urging an Aquinian ethic on economics, Andrew Yuengert points out that the adjusting of means to ultimate ends that is "prudence" is not merely the adjusting of means to intermediate ends of "technique."[13] In Rosalind Hursthouse's textbook of virtue ethics the word "prudence" is rare. But the equivalent phrase, "practical wisdom," occurs repeatedly, because reason must rightly deliberate about any virtue if the intended act of justice or temperance or faith is to do the job.

Prudence is so to speak the grammar of the virtues. Robert Hariman writes that it "fulfills an executive function in respect to human flourishing."[14] A faithful Roman Catholic who believes imprudently—that is, unwisely in practical terms—that going to mass regularly suffices for resurrection at the Last Judgment is making a dreadful mistake. A federal judge who believes himself a just man fails in his project if he is ignorant of the law, or if he entertains a theory of it that no one else regards as just.

Amélie Oksenberg Rorty neatly encapsulates the Aristotle behind Aquinas as requiring that "the virtuous person perform the right action in the right way at the right time on the right objects."[15] Clearly, such a person must be a *phrónimos*, a person of practical reasoning, "really knowing what one is doing, being aware of the circumstances and consequences of one's actions, with the right conception of the sort of action one is performing."[16]

He is, Aristotle said, "able to deliberate well about what is good and advantageous to himself"[17]

A person notably lacking in prudence is, we say, a loose cannon. Think of the nautical image, Jack Aubrey–style: an iron cannon weighing two tons gets loose from its lashings and hurtles with thirty feet of momentum toward the battened porthole on the other side of a man-o'-war lurching with every wave deep to port and then to starboard in a force 7 gale off Cherbourg. *Of course* prudence is a virtue. Try living in a ship or a family or a polis, or for that matter as a Crusoe on a desert island, without it.

Prudence fits, for example, all of Alasdair MacIntyre's requirements for a virtue: "an acquired human quality the possession and exercise of which tends to enable us to achieve those goods which are internal to practices [such as statecraft]." A virtue is acquirable in part only, since people are admitted as having from early childhood varying gifts for common sense, as for lovingness or even justice-giving. MacIntyre himself accords "practical reasoning" (that is, prudence) the status of a virtue when it is understood as a "capacity for judgment . . . in knowing how to select among the relevant stack of maxims and how to apply them in particular situations. Cardinal Pole possessed it [in statecraft]; Mary Tudor did not."[18] Sir Thomas More said that Pole, a sixteenth-century Englishman loyal to the pope, was as learned as he was noble and as virtuous as he was learned.

Imagine a community filled with imprudent people, Mary Tudors in bulk, and you'll see the social virtuousness of prudence. The imagining is not difficult. A community of schoolchildren would fit the bill, as in *The Lord of the Flies,* or a community of adolescents such as the Latin Lords. Or indeed—and this is a crucial point—a community of moral saints would fit, too, if "moral" is taken to mean "improving the welfare of others or of society as a whole" without considering one's *own* flourishing. There is a private virtue in prudence, too.

The exclusively public, social, altruistic definition of "virtue" is implicitly adopted by Susan Wolf in her essay mentioned, "Moral Saints."[19] The implicit definition introduces a flaw into her case. In the style of many Anglophone philosophers she leaves out privately self-interested prudence as a virtue, and so lets her moral saints behave badly toward themselves.

This is not good. And indeed showing its badness is Wolf's point, by a reductio. It's the Jewish-mother version of goodness: "Oh, don't bother to replace the bulb. I'll just sit here in the dark." But the mother, after all, is

God's creature, too, and benevolence therefore should include a just benevolence toward herself. Being wholly altruistic, and disregarding the claims of that person also in the room called Self, about whose needs the very Self is ordinarily best informed, is making the same mistake as being wholly selfish, disregarding the claims of that person called Other. In both cases the mistake is to ignore someone.

Oddly, selflessness—note the word—is unjust, inegalitarian. "There is a manifest negligence in men of their real happiness or interest in the present world," said Bishop Butler in 1725. People are "as often unjust to themselves as to others."[20] The more optimistic Earl of Shaftesbury took in 1713 a social view to arrive at praise for prudence:

> The affection toward private or self-good, however selfish it may be esteemed, is in reality not only consistent with public good but in some measure contributing to it. . . . [It is] for the good of the species in general. . . . So far as being blamable in any sense, . . . it must be acknowledged absolutely necessary to constitute a creature good. . . . No one would doubt to pronounce so if he saw a man who minded not any precipices which lay in his way, nor made any distinction of food, diet, clothing or whatever else related to his health and being.[21]

Just as humility is not self-abnegation, prudence is not self-centeredness.

As Michael Stocker puts it, "modern ethical theories would prevent each of us from loving, caring for, and valuing ourself."[22] Max U does not value Max the man. He values himself and others and ice cream only for its utility-producing capacity, not for his sweet, or his not-so-sweet, self. Such an ethical universe is not merely imperfect. It is, Stocker concludes, "devoid of all people."

No wonder we agree so readily with Wolf in finding her sort of moral saint obnoxious. They are unjust toward themselves, monsters of altruism. No wonder actual monks and nuns watch carefully for prideful and imprudent excesses in their mortifications of the flesh. No wonder Gandhi makes us more than uncomfortable. George Orwell noted that Gandhi was literally, and on three occasions, willing for his wife and children to die rather than eat animal food. He exhibited an inability to love friends and family in particular, exclusively, as against the for-all-we-know-perfectly-sincere universal love he exhibited to an unusual degree. Thus too Erasmus complains about saintly Socrates that he was "a man completely deaf to all human sentiment," and Gregory Vlastos notes Socrates' "frigidity."[23] The average moderately good human being," writes Orwell, is not "a failed saint." To be like Gandhi or Socrates, as admirable as they are in some dimensions, is to miss part of humanity, the caring for oneself and for one's best beloved. Saint-hood, too, like tobacco and alcohol, Orwell affirms, "is also a thing that human beings must avoid."[24]

We labor to teach our children and adolescents and our dogs and, yes, ourselves the practical wisdom that keeps them and us from injuring or impoverishing or failing to develop themselves and others and ourselves. In the selling of retirement homes the salespeople speak of the "Benjamin Franklin close."[25] The salesperson lists with the older person the costs and benefits, or the balance sheet, of buying into the Scottsdale Royale Retire-ment Community. It has been found that people now old, who have lived through the Great Depression or the war or are just old and well off, are focused, not unreasonably, on prudence. Provide, provide. To close the deal the salesperson has to acknowledge in the style of an imagined Franklin—it is not the real Ben, by the way—that life is a calculation.

The selling technique here is not some improper trick. An imprudent person, someone who doesn't know the value of money and how to keep accounts, is a menace to his friends and family, and to his own developed self. And certainly he is a menace to his need in old age to provide, provide. He may be chivalrous in some sense, courageous and temperate and just, even great-souled, as Aristotle wished, or loving, as did St. Paul. Yet without prudence he is a particular kind of fool, not virtuous as a whole. He is trag-ically or comically flawed, as most of us are, more or less, short of King Arthur or Cardinal Pole.

Catalunya, around Barcelona, politically in Spain but culturally au-tonomous, and having its own language and literature distinct from Castil-ian, is in its own view a nation of sensible businesspeople enchained by fate these many centuries to a government of aristocratic madmen in Madrid. Catalunya praises above all the virtues *seny* ["SEHN-yuh"], the local version of prudence. The great Catalan historian Jaume Vicens Vives (1910–1960) declared famously that his region evinced *seny,* prudence or common sense, combined with *rauxa* ["RAU-shah"], passion or madness, the two "punts cardinals del temperament català."[26]

In medieval times, when Barcelona was the chief port of the Western Mediterranean and Catalan was the lingua franca of the Christian fleets, a Catalan poet could think of no higher praise of his beloved than that she was "plena de seny," full of common sense. Robert Hughes tells of a

Catalan country priest anxious to get to dinner rushing to set out *another* wooden Jesus whose feet could be kissed when the line of worshipers in front of the first one, brought in earlier with all slow solemnity, appeared to the priest inefficiently long. "Perhaps only in Catalunya," Hughes observes, "the first industrial region of Spain, could time-and-motion study be so quickly and instinctively applied to piety."[27] It's *seny*, as against the Castilian lack of it.

Consider, for example, that noble Castilian, Don Quixote de la Mancha. His courage is unquestionable, though exercised against phantasms, as when he meets a cart filled with actors and takes it to be Death and company. "The knight's spirit mounted with the belief there was some new and perilous adventure presenting itself." And he is of course exacting in justice, too—his lady Dulcinea del Toboso, in sober fact a milkmaid, must always receive her just due, as surely will by way of just revenge any foul giant or contemptuous knight who balks at acknowledging her excellence. (Likewise in a gesture to knightly manners in the cowboy myth the Walter Brennan/Judge Roy Bean character in *The Westerner* [1940] extracts obeisance to posters of Lillie Langtry put up behind his bar.) And the Don is disciplined by temperance, his cowboy-like willingness to live a hard life: "Labor, unease, and arms alone were designed and made for those the world calls knights errant," he declares, willing with the other Shanes of the world to bed down rough in the barn, weapon at the ready.

Sancho Panza is a peasant or a bourgeois (one imagines that he must have had Catalan blood)—anyway, a practical man, *pleno de seny*, a man of prudence, ready with proverbial wisdom, ever articulating profane value: "I renounce the governorship of the promised isle [which glory the Don supposes throughout is Sancho's true goal], and all I want in payment . . . is . . . the recipe for that marvelous liquor . . . worth more than two *reals* an ounce"; or, lovingly, "The well-being of a single [self-appointed] knight errant is worth more than all the enchantments . . . on earth." Don Quixote, whose mind is on higher things, hushes him, as he does always when prudence breaks in—though even a knight errant feels practical wisdom somehow necessary, as he shows by offering crackpot rationalizations for his adventures, prudence within a world of madness.

No *seny*.[28]

∞

Because aristocratic and slave-owning members of city-states first discussed the pagan virtues systematically, the pagan four of courage, temperance, justice, and prudence are often supposed to be especially suited to the ancient polis, and irrelevant therefore to the sick hurry of modern life. But the supposition cuts economics off from virtue, which is a mistake.

In view of the highly commercial character of Greek culture from at the latest the seventh century on, the anticommercial construal of the Greek-labeled virtues seems strange. After all, the urns from which we learn so many details of Greekness contained olive oil bound in profit for a startling array of places, from Phoenicia's strand to where the Atlantic raves outside the western straits. The old idea that the aristocracy of Greece and the senatorial class of Rome were nobly landholding, and wouldn't think of lending money at interest or investing in a scheme of apartment building for profit, is of course nonsense.[29] Athens and Rome were great *commercial* empires. When Aristotle is struggling to make justice fit his formula for virtue as a mean between deficiency and excess, he turns with enthusiasm to the marketplace for examples.[30] As Thomas Carney observes, "The history of antiquity resounds with the sanguinary achievements of Aryan warrior elites. But it was the despised Levantines, Arameans [for example, Jesus of Nazareth], Syrians, and Greeklings who constituted the economic heroes of antiquity."[31]

The aristocracy, however entangled in the economy, affected to disdain it. Plato's Socrates declares in *The Republic* that "the more men value money-making, the less they value virtue."[32] Aristotle says of retail trade that it is "justly to be censured, because the gain in which it results is not natural made, but is made at the expense of other men."[33] By "natural made" he means grown from plants and animals. Aristotle is exhibiting here a hardy physiocracy that views only agriculture as "productive." Late in the *Politics* he says that, of course, "the life of mechanics and shopkeepers . . . is ignoble and inimical to goodness."[34] In 44 BC Cicero declares to his son Marcus that "trade, if petty, is to be considered vulgar; but if wholesale and on a large scale . . . it is not to be greatly criticized. . . . But of all the gainful occupations none is better than cultivation of the soil, none more fruitful, none more sweet, none more appropriate to a free man."[35]

It was such aristocratic, or wannabe-aristocratic, snobbishness about urban production in the ancient world, rehearsed in the Hellenic revival of nineteenth-century divines and schoolmasters, that made the three nonprudence pagan virtues of justice, temperance, and courage seem *non*bourgeois virtues, thankfully not seared with trade, bleared, smeared with toil. After all, toil was for slaves and women, and trade for ill-bred shopkeepers. Free men of landed wealth, the leisured citizens of the polis, or the boys at Eton and Rugby, were to do the great-souled stuff.

For all their actual immersion in a market economy, the two founts of virtue-talk in Athens—Plato the literal aristocrat and his graduate student Aristotle, the son of a physician in the Macedonian court and himself tutor to royal Alexander—did not view businesspeople as capable of true virtue. Julius Caesar likewise attributes the bravery of the Belgians to their distance from cultivation and refinement and to their lack of commerce with merchants whose goods tend to the effeminization of the spirit (*ad animos effeminandos*). Seneca the Stoic in a commercial Rome was contemptuous of the idea that businessmen could have honor, though it is among his many self-contradictions that he was born into an extremely rich family and himself lent money at interest.

Businesspeople in this aristocratic view, I have noted, did not have the moral luck to be in a position to show their mettle. The Homeric, the political, and even the Stoic versions of pagan virtue were explicitly antibourgeois. A hero or a landed gentleman or a philosopher unmoved (*apathes*) by earthly desires should be hostile toward any suggestion of *pleonexia* (excess, greed). The founder of Stoicism, Zeno of Citium [335–263 BC], was, it appears, the son of a Phoenician businessman, which is perhaps why he took a little broader view, though nonetheless antibourgeois. The dual heroes of Roman Stoicism were a Greek slave and a Roman emperor, in their luck as differing as could be. Aristotle did not even admit that the citizen-soldier's feats were real courage. The hoplite "seems to face dangers because of the penalties imposed by the laws and the reproaches they would otherwise incur"—so unlike, one might retort sarcastically, the Homeric hero obsessing about his reputation.[36]

The exclusion of commercial prudence from the highest virtues becomes absurd in the late Roman Republic and early Empire, and caused endless theological difficulties in the Christian Empire, especially in the West, right through to Luther and Calvin. It still haunts our talk of virtue.

THE MONOMANIA OF IMMANUEL KANT

The ancients Plato and Augustine and the moderns Immanuel Kant and Jeremy Bentham, on the contrary, wanted to find some elemental, single Good that could be poured into useful shapes whole, unalloyed. Kant called it "pure reason" (*reinen Vernunft*), Bentham "utility." Their intellectual program, attempted over the next two centuries by hundreds of ethical philosophers down to John Rawls and Robert Nozick, and still going strong, was to reduce the virtues to *a* virtue. Here is all of virtue, the Platonic idea of the Good, the virtue of virtues, here on my convenient pocket-sized card, with no stories or traditions behind it, no culture, merely universal Reason.

Thus Kant, with a pocket-sized, three-by-five-inch card inscribed "Imagine the action you propose to take would be elevated to a general rule for all society." Or Rawls: "Imagine you are a risk-averse person making rules for society behind a veil of ignorance about your own location in the society." Such metarules are as applicable to creatures on a planet circling Proxima Centauri as to us humans.

From its beginnings in Plato's writings such ethical monism did not work very well. As Aristotle said—he apologized for thus refuting his teacher—"it is not easy to see *how* knowing the same Ideal Good will help a weaver, . . . or how anybody will be a better physician or general for having contemplated the absolute Ideal."[1] The neo-Aristotelian and anti-Kantian turn in recent ethical philosophy can be put this way: it's no good talking like Plato or Kant of the ultimate when most of the ethical issues we face are matters of practice as a weaver or a physician or a mother. Or to put it more strongly, as people like Alasdair MacIntyre and Richard Rorty and Stanley Fish do, the ultimate never comes up.

In the preface to his *Grounding for the Metaphysics of Morals* (1785) Kant declared, "The ground of obligation must be looked for, not in the nature of man nor in the circumstances of the world in which he is placed, but solely a priori in the concepts of pure reason."[2] We are to study how people are supposed to behave without reference to their psychologies or their customs or their histories.

He offers in the *Grounding* only two reasons for this on-its-face bizarre assertion about the proper method of ethics—which on Kant's authority was then followed scrupulously for nearly two centuries by ethical philosophers in the West. First, he says, there is and should be a division of labor between theorizers and observers "if we are to know how much pure reason can accomplish." He means that we are to set aside actual human culture, in the manner so to speak of a controlled experiment. And second, "morals themselves remain exposed to corruption of all sorts as long as this guiding thread is lacking, this ultimate norm."[3]

A virtue ethicist is moved to respond, a trifle impatiently, "Why, dear Immanuel, 'must' a division of labor govern ethical philosophy, why 'must' there be an ultimate norm, why does it seem plausible to you that we will be corrupted by a lack of such a norm, why 'must' duty be derived as though by geometric proof from an axiom of a hypothetically 'pure' rational creature, who never was a child, never had a mother or father, never walked the actual streets of an actual Königsberg?" Kant in the *Grounding* suggested no reply, or merely the Platonic/Cartesian reply that we "must" turn our minds to an ideal rather than to the "merely" ordinary. In *The Critique of Practical Reason* the method is defended as separating "ought" from "is," following Hume in this. But why would it seem plausible that "ought" sentences would have no contact with "is" sentences? They don't in life.

Kant entirely separated ethics from anthropology and psychology, indeed from any empirical claim whatsoever. Ethics in his view was to take place in its own realm. After him, therefore, ethical thinking in the West was haunted by the fear that to justify ethics in actual humans is to fall prey to a "naturalistic fallacy," as G. E. Moore came to call it in attacking Bentham, Mill, and Sidgwick for their utilitarianism. One ought not to derive an Ought from an Is, an ethical precept from a factual statement. Thus, "free trade is desirable because it causes happiness in humans as they actually are" is an error.[4] A fallacy. Illusion.

"When we run over libraries persuaded of these principles, what havoc must we make?" Hume asked in the peroration of *An Inquiry Concerning Human Understanding* (1748): "If we take in our hand any volume; of divinity or school metaphysics, for instance, let us ask, *Does it contain any abstract reasoning concerning quantity or number? No. Does it contain any experimental reasoning concerning matter of fact and existence?* No. Commit it then to the flames: for it can contain nothing but sophistry and illusion."[5]

No theology; no natural law; no ethics. We are to have only mathematics on the one hand and on the other the "sciences"—though in the wide, non-post-1850 English sense, that is, systematic studies of the world, human or natural: *Wissenschaften.*

But no philosophy either, whether academic or worldly, is to survive the flames. It does not seem to have occurred to Hume that his *Inquiry* would be among the first to go, and shortly thereafter his theoretical essays on economics advocating free trade. Nor does it seem to have occurred very often to the philosophers in Kant's train that in saying "You *ought* not to derive Ought from Is" they were engaging in a natural human ethical activity.[6] Nor does it seem to have occurred to them that a Greek-admiring ethics or the Roman equivalent of morality would lack point unless based on philosophical psychology (*ethos*) or philosophical anthropology (*mos*).

Kant helped create the glorious yet mischievous utopianism of the Enlightenment project; but by fiat, not by reasoning. He had one implicit reason, though not mentioned in the *Grounding*, which must as ordinary politics be given weight. It is that we "must" strip social status from ethics. Universal, unparticular reason, he seemed to reason, would apply to a miller as much as to a marquis. Writing in a world of 1785 in which status most oppressively ruled, the egalitarian axiom of Kant, and of Bentham and Smith and Locke and Richard Hooker and John Knox and for that matter St. Thomas of Aquino, St. Augustine of Hippo, and Jesus of Nazareth, was revolutionary stuff. "A man's a man for a' that" is an explosive idea.

I say it had been foreshadowed in soul-focused religions, especially in Protestantism and it appears in early-church Christianity, such as in the democratic governance of John Knox's Presbyterianism or Calvin's Geneva, or among the still more radical Congregationalists or Quakers or Baptists—who in some eras would let even women preach—or among the Lutheran Pietists of Kant's ancestry. As it was put at the dawn by a Presbyterian soldier, "I am sure there was no man born marked of God above another, for none comes into the world with a saddle on his back, neither any booted and spurred to ride him."[7]

Kant's notion that status is an accident but that the human duty to reason is an essence echoes his own absolutist king, Frederick the Great. Frederick wrote an *Anti-Machiavel* in 1740, published in French under Voltaire's auspices at the Hague in the same year that Frederick ascended the throne. It was the year Kant entered university as a student at the former Prussian capital. Kant's own book on ethics was published in his old age, a year before the end of Frederick's long reign. In the *Anti-Machiavel* Frederick forswears personal gain from kingship, thus contradicting, as he imagined, Machiavelli's supposedly self-profiting prince. He declares famously that "the ruler is far from being the arbitrary master of his people; he is indeed, nothing other than the first servant."[8] In 1842 Thomas Macaulay the Liberal noted sarcastically that Frederick had nonetheless "studiously kept up the old distinction between the nobles and the community. In speculation, he was a French philosopher, but in action, a German prince."[9]

In 1785, aged sixty-one, and with increasing rigor as he grew older, Kant scornfully rejected an "anthropological" approach to ethics. Kant was not scornful of anthropology itself as a subject. Indeed, he taught it every Saturday morning in term, as Manfred Kuehn tells us in his recent, splendid biography.[10] But Kant thought it was to be impaled on Hume's Fork to include facts of actual human life in *ethical* philosophy. Hume's *Inquiry concerning Human Understanding*, Kant said, had awakened him from his dogmatic slumber. But, oddly, he did not appear to know of Hume's other, ethical treatise, of human nature.[11]

For instance Kant rejected as a maxim of a true and therefore universal ethics the "honor" (*Ehre*) that, as Kuehn notes, "may even have been more important to the citizens of the larger towns and cities of Prussia" than to the literal and *Ehre*-regarding aristocracy. Thus Kant's father was of the honorable guild of harnessmakers, if poor; and Kant himself of the honorable guild of scholars.[12] Kant appealed rather to an egalitarian psychology reminiscent I repeat of the Pietism of his parents—Kuehn, though, does not think that Pietism was the source. "Honor is something entirely conventional," Kant wrote. "By contrast, the representation of right lies deep in the soul of everyone, even of the most delicate child."[13] Find the maxim within the soul and we can construct a pure, ultimate, nonanthropological universal ethic.

There was another, personal reason for Kant's fascination with ethical maxims and his increasing rigor in hedging them off from the life world. This was his intimate friendship from age forty-one to age sixty-two with Joseph Green, an English trader in timber, fruit, and spices, a Hull man who lived most of his adult life in Königsberg. Kant had many friends within the bourgeoisie of Königsberg, as did Adam Smith at the same time in Glasgow and Edinburgh. The parallels between Kant/Green and Smith/Hume are striking; and Mr. Green was in fact a conduit for Humean ideas to Kant. As the Kant scholar Lewis White Beck expressed it in his brilliant parody of 1979 (an alleged manuscript of Boswell's account of a [nonexistent] visit to the Königsberg group in 1785), "Dr. Smith had told me of an English merchant here resident, a Mr. Green, a man of prudence & virtue."[14]

Green was "the most intimate friend Kant ever had."[15] Like Kant a life-long bachelor, Green spent every single afternoon and early evening for fully twenty-one years in Kant's company, supplying the philosopher with detailed criticism. The criticism, Kuehn notes, seems to have resulted in a comparative lucidity in Kant's writing style, lost after Green's death in 1786. Kant's writings during the friendship contained "many phrases and idioms . . . that can be traced back to the language of merchants, such as 'borrowing,' 'capital,' and so forth."[16] One might guess that Kant refused offers from the universities at Erlangen and Jena in 1769–1770 in part because his special friend of by then three years' standing was attached by business to Königsberg. Kant did mention his "very wide circle of acquaintances and friends" in the letter awkwardly taking back an initial acceptance of the offer from Erlangen.[17] He also declined a call to Halle in 1778.

Green's influence on Kant was psychologically profound and philosophically important. According to Kuehn, Green's example transformed Kant's character. Mr. Green was above all a "Man of the Clock," the title of a comedy in 1765 by the famous progressive Königsberg playwright and member of their set, one of Kant's followers and later his benefactor, Theodor Hippel, spoofing Green.

Mr. Green was not difficult to spoof. Kuehn recounts that Kant and Green had arranged one day to take a carriage ride together the next morning at exactly 8:00. Kant was a little late. He had not yet become the Professor Kant by whose comings and goings one could adjust one's watch. Yet Green, true to his maxim of following the clock, set off in the carriage anyway. Passing Kant hurrying along the road toward the house, he drove past him, "with Kant vigorously signaling for him to stop." He did this not because he was angry at Kant's tardiness, but merely because "it was against Green's maxim" to deviate from any prudent plan.[18] In the play Hippel has his Green character declare, "I do not get up because I have slept enough, but because it is 6:00 a.m. I go to eat not because I am hungry, but because the clock has struck 12:00."[19]

The case shows vividly the force of a bourgeois and even a specifically English and nonconformist version of reason in the Enlightenment. Besides Kant and his English merchant and Smith and his Scottish ones, there is Voltaire, who himself made a fortune in finance before he was thirty—he added to it throughout his life, and died one of the richest commoners in Europe—and the English merchant to whom he dedicated in 1732 his play *Zaïre*.

In Hippel's play an academic character, based it seems on Kant as he was in 1765, age forty-one, before Green took entire charge, complains that in his own, nonbourgeois work, prudence and plan cannot rule: "A dissertation . . . is not a bank draft. With such work one cannot keep hours." Kuehn remarks that "little by little [Kant] learned to write philosophy like a bank draft," until in the year before Green's death he produced *The Grounding*:

> Green's effect on Kant cannot be overestimated. . . . [Kant] gave up playing cards to please Green. His visits to the theatre became rarer, and late in life they ceased almost altogether. Green was completely tone deaf. . . . Kant, "at least in his early years" [wrote a contributor to the memorial lectures for Kant in 1804] "listened to good music with pleasure." He gave up that custom as well. . . . The elegant *Magister* [that is, a German academic before his professorship] with a somewhat irregular and unpredictable lifestyle changed into a man of principle with an exceedingly predictable way of life. He became more and more like Green. . . . The days of the whirlpool of social diversions were coming to an end—not suddenly, but slowly: maxim by maxim. . . . Kant's view of maxims, as necessary for building character ["morals themselves remain exposed to corruption of all sorts as long as this guiding thread is lacking, this ultimate norm"], was, at least in part, indebted to Green's way of life. It was not an accident that in the lectures on anthropology in which Kant spoke of maxims, he often claimed that the English had the most solid understanding. He himself relied on the judgment of his English friend.[20]

The Kantian tradition in ethical philosophy, then, begins with a mono-mania for Prudence Only—a prudence worthy of Jeremy Bentham and the modern economists. In a not charming sense it is bourgeois. That such intemperate lunacy lies at the heart of the modern and anti-Aristotelian theory of ethics should give pause.

Bernard Williams, another of the pioneering virtue ethicists since the 1950s, concluded that "the resources of most modern moral philosophy are not well adjusted to the modern world." "Its prevailing fault, in all its styles, is to impose on ethical life some immensely simple model," such as contract behind a veil of ignorance, rationality as European bourgeois men might define it, or utility, which seems so *measurable*.[21] An intellectual revolution was initiated 1690 through 1785, dethroning the thick, storied, pagan-Christian account of the virtues, plural, and erecting one or another universal monism in their place. Reason was to become a new monotheism, demanding sacrifice and promising salvation in return, either here below or in the Good Society by and by.

It was an admirable effort, courageous and prudent and hopeful, worth the attempt. Perhaps it had something to do with the rise of the bourgeoisie, uneasy in a system of the virtues which had classically talked of heroes and saints. It certainly had to do with the contractarian idea so obvious to the bourgeois that, in the words of Richard Rumbold (the Presbyterian soldier I mentioned) before he faced the hangman in 1685, "the king having . . . power enough to make him great; the people also as much property as to make them happy; they being, as it were, contracted to one another."[22] No saddles and spurs. And the scientific revolution must have made ethicists strive for a similar rethinking.

Yet on the whole, except as I say as a historically contingent rhetorical tool of liberals against status, Locke's and Kant's and Bentham's systems have failed. They succeeded negatively as a political expedient, thank God. But afterward they failed positively as an ethical guide. They have not given us guides to action and they have not matched how we live.

THE STORIED CHARACTER OF VIRTUE

"When I was young," said Clovis, "my mother taught me the difference between good and evil—only I've forgotten it."

"You've forgotten the difference between good and evil?" gasped the princess.

"Well, she taught me three ways of cooking lobster. You can't remember everything."

—Saki (Hector Hugh Monro)

An ethic of the virtues gives a guide. It does not solve every ethical problem slam-bang, which as Rosalind Hursthouse notes is no special problem—because after all neither does any other serious ethical theory.[1] Even as straightforward an ethical theory as "follow the 613 commandments of the Torah," Hillel's count, has not proven to be slam-bang, not even close.

Deciding whether a certain act "would be the object of choice of all rational beings" (as Hursthouse summarizes Kant) or "maximizes happiness" (as one might summarize Hume and Bentham) or "would be chosen at the social contract" (Ockham, Suarez, Hobbes, Locke, Rawls, Nozick) is no less difficult than deciding whether the act entails cowardice or hatred or injustice. Ethics "after virtue" was commonly more difficult to apply, not less. The stories of our culture give us models for acting courageously or lovingly or justly. The virtue-words with stories attached appear anyway to be how humans reason ethically. "A [Greek] tragedy," Martha Nussbaum declared, "does not display the dilemmas of its characters as prearticulated; it shows them as searching for the morally salient; and it forces us, as interpreters, to be similarly active."[2]

The point applies to less elevated stories than *Orestes* and *Antigone*. In my thirties and forties I used to jog long distances. I did not then tell myself

Kantian or utilitarian ethical reasonings, though neither was entirely irrelevant, I suppose. The Kantian duty to step out the door on a cold morning or the utilitarian reasoning that after all it was good for me did help, a little. Kant's maxim would not acknowledge any pleasure in the run, and Bentham's calculation would not acknowledge any identity in it. Virtue ethics combines the two. The unity of ethical thinking was torn apart by the analysts of the eighteenth century. It is somewhat harder to see a contractarian motive in a lone daily run. The fact casts light on a fault of contractarianism such as Nozick's, namely, that it reduces ethics to the improvement of *other* people, ignoring self-improvement, and ignoring also the transcendent—unless we think, as monotheists in fact do, of making covenants with God, or with ourselves.

To actually keep putting one foot in front of another I told myself, as we do, little character stories, of Pheidippides running from Athens to Sparta, say, or of the game of making it to the next bridge, or of my identity imagined and actual. I was in a sense fooling myself, though aware. I learned from running how to make a change from a very overweight smoker to a somewhat overweight nonsmoker. In my fifth decade, that is, I learned that the combination of temperance plus courage we call persistence can achieve with small steps quite a lot. As they say in Alcoholics Anonymous, choose not to drink one day, or one hour, at a time. *Beginnen is ondernemen,* the Dutch say. Literally, "to begin is to undertake"—a journey of a thousand miles.

I had of course "known" such an obvious truth long before in the intellectual sense sufficient for Kantian or Benthamite reasoning. But to little good for weight control. That's what's wrong with Kantian or Benthamite reasoning. It is *reasoning,* not a cause for action. "Moral knowledge, unlike mathematical knowledge," Hursthouse notes, "cannot be acquired merely by attending lectures and is [therefore] not characteristically to be found in people too young to have much experience of life. A normative ethics should not aim to provide a decision procedure which any reasonably clever adolescent could apply," like the chain rule for derivatives.[3] But an adolescent's head is of course filled with stories and characters to imitate, for good or evil.

Both Kant and Bentham were sweet but notably inexperienced men. As Mill said of Bentham, "He was a boy to the last."[4] Kant and Bentham had seen little of life. Neither of them had been married or had run a business or had carried a spear in the phalanx. Both of them supposed, with

Socrates—who I have to admit had had all these experiences of life—that knowledge of the good is enough for the will to achieve it. I am not against sweet, inexperienced, and unmarried men. After all, my hero Adam Smith was one. One of my other heroes, Aquinas, was another. But, unlike Kant or Bentham, Adam Smith managed somehow to restrain the impulse to theorize much beyond human life as actually lived. And Aquinas surpassed in intellectual flexibility and a sense of lived life many a neo-Thomist.

My running, so to speak, changed my character to long, slow distance. I stopped thinking of my economic scholarship as a matter of the next article and started to think of it as a marathon. "Running," said Sir Roger Bannister to the BBC cameras on the fiftieth anniversary of his first breaking the four-minute mile, "is only a metaphor for life." A certain kind of life, actually. And your life becomes a metaphor for running itself. I applied the narrative of running to other parts of my life, such as slowly, slowly acquiring small Latin and less Greek, or learning to read a smattering of difficult books in the humanities. Reading *The Grounding for the Metaphysics of Morals*, you see, is like a marathon, or at least like a run from Iowa City to the Lake McBride Dam and back.

Guides to ethical life, to repeat, are achieved mainly through story and example. As Robert Hariman puts it:

> What to do? One typical [modern] response is to look for rules: what would any rational person do in this situation? . . . There was another approach familiar to the classical thinkers, however, which was to look to exemplars: how have other individuals managed situations such as this one? The attention given to the particular wise person—the *phronimos*—is not merely a heuristic device. . . . Prudential theory [which is Hariman's name for the Ciceronian program of virtue ethics in action] requires a bifocal perspective that alternates between impersonal norms and individual circumstances, a perspective that is similar to the reading strategy for understanding a persuasive text.[5]

Hariman is here referring to the fruitful notion of the rhetorician Richard Lanham that we should "toggle"—Lanham was using the computer term—between surface and depth, rhetoric and philosophy, practice and theory.[6]

The theoretical precepts are not useless. In baseball: "Keep your eye on the ball." In writing: "Don't overload your sentences." But they are like a coach offering commentary, not the achievement itself. There are no formulas, or else such activities would not be valuable arts. They would be mere skills, easily acquired by anyone, like typing or using econometrics.[7]

Indeed, coaching itself has no formulas, or else great coaches would be a dime a dozen.[8] Ted Williams's book, *The Science of Hitting*, offers precepts for life as much as for "the single most difficult thing to do in sport"— hitting a major-league fastball.[9] To achieve in hitting you need to witness and then to imitate Williams's swing, among the wonders of mid-twentieth-century sports. But you need to do it, and keep doing it, supported by a boy's myth of excellence. It was a story Williams told to himself, a story of his ethical character, not a decision-making formula. The story kept him at batting practice until his hands bled.

The character thus formed I say applies to more than baseball. In 1995 at a conference organized by the rhetorician Herbert Simons I heard a paper by Linda Brodkey about teaching writing called "Writing on the Bias." Brodkey told how she learned to write by watching her mother sew. Her mother was a gifted seamstress and could cut cloth "on the bias" to give a dress a graceful drape. The daughter learned to write—and she writes well—by translating the virtues of dressmaking into the virtues of writing.[10]

Likewise I learned how to do academic tasks—actually any task—by watching my mother do carpentry or sewing or cooking or learning Greek irregular verbs, witnessing the virtues of hope and courage operating in them. Try learning to sew or write or hit a major-league fastball by following the categorical imperative, or the greatest happiness of the greatest number. Try learning with those ideas to be "good" in any sense. They don't work.

We build our characters story by story. In the romantic comedy written and directed by Harold Ramis, *Groundhog Day* (1993), the Bill Murray character, a self-centered jerk of a TV weatherman, is condemned to relive his February 2 of 1992 over and over and over again. At first he sins deliciously, indulging in tablefuls of food for example, three hot fudge sundaes, a big stack of pancakes, a plate full of bacon. "Don't you worry about love handles?" Not if after the intemperance the clock is always turned back to a new 6:00 a.m. of the very same Groundhog Day, to the same bright chatter of a wake-up show predicting c-o-l-d in Punxsutawney, PA. Phil's motto is to eat, drink, and be merry, for tomorrow will be today all over again.

He is the only person on the scene who remembers all his yester-todays. So by reliving the day he can correct each false move in achieving pleasure, as in his attempted seduction of his TV colleague, the Andie MacDowell character. He learns, for instance, that she always orders sweet vermouth on ice with a twist of lemon and always toasts to world peace. He therefore can craftily ingratiate himself by anticipating just these, getting better and better at concupiscent "love," for his pleasure late in the day. Tomorrow won't do, because it never dawns. The seduction fails, of course, because McDowell is pure. It *is* a romantic comedy.

After many hundreds of iterations of his February 2, having indulged every sin, he enters a dark night of the soul, killing himself in every conceivable way. One time he kidnaps the groundhog-of-honor and drives off the edge of a quarry. But to no avail. The curse of waking up again and again on the same February 2 in the same bed-and-breakfast hangs on, and he repeats yet again the day he knows to perfection. He knows the exact second at which the waiter will drop the tray of dishes or where exactly the slush-filled hole is located in the street or the identities and histories of every single actor in the little drama on the *n*th day of its run. He has the time—all the time—to learn French, ice-sculpting, pop piano, dazzling by evening his colleagues who knew the Phil of the day before as a talentless piece of TV talent.

But having tried to make his pleasures of lust and gluttony into his gods, and having reached despair, he begins to shift, to grow in character. "I am *a* god," he says at the midpoint, puzzled, "not *the* God, I think," an angel, perhaps, able by repetition to know every way to prevent unhappy accidents. That he now gives a damn is evidence of his ethical growth. Phil arranges, for example, to arrive every morning exactly when a little boy falls out of a tree, exactly in time to catch him, the ungrateful brat. "Maybe God is just someone who's been around for a long time." Yet he discovers, too, the limited power of an angel-not-God. Despite repeated shots at that same February 2, he is not in fact able to save the life of an old derelict fated then to die. By such spiritual exercises Phil's character evolves, gradually. Bill Murray's craft is on display here, as when he conveys even failed acting, the Phil character playing a role mechanically to some end not consistent with true character. Virtue is character, not rational maxims or parlor tricks of good-deed doing—"when someone's *watching* you," Tom Lehrer warbled long ago.

Phil becomes truly virtuous. By experimenting on a big scale he discovers, in other words, the best life for a human, the ethical laws of our nature. "There is not," said Shaftesbury, "the least degree of certainty wanting . . . concerning the preferableness of the mental pleasures [in Phil's case, mastery of French] over the sensual [three hot fudge sundaes] . . . and even of the sensual accompanied by good affection and under a temperate and right use [jazz piano] to those which are no ways restrained" [plotting to seduce the MacDowell character].[11] Phil discovers the balanced virtues of love and courage and the rest, and even a humility quite inconceivable in Phil the Jerk.

He is able for the first time to love in the higher sense, that is, to care for someone for her own sake instead of merging her utility into his own. MacDowell therefore falls for him, he is redeemed by love, the curse is broken, a February 3 dawns, and they live happily ever after. I said it was a romantic comedy.

The conventions of the genre in a secular age make it impossible for him to find God in the last reel, but the story otherwise persuades. People really do prefer to be virtuous rather than vicious. Exiled tyrants like the late Idi Amin of Uganda, retired in luxury to Saudi Arabia, believe to the end of their days that what they did for their people was good—eating them, for example. Plato's (or Socrates') error was only in believing that sheer intellectual information about the Good would suffice. Plato was correct that if we know, *really* know, virtue, on our pulse, after thousands of repetitions of Groundhog Day, then we will prefer it to evil.[12] Satan's facile formula, "Evil be thou my good," doesn't work in human lives any more than in angelic lives.

The movie asserts that, regrettably, most of us need experience, quite a lot of it, to become ethically educated, to be led out of lives of big and little evils. If we have the short lives of the preindustrial world, for example, there's no second, third, fourth act in which to set aside alcohol or violence, acquisitiveness or cruelty, in favor of the really good life. Seneca made this point. For many of us it takes fully three score years and ten to get even close to the ethical life. Or it takes many good movies. Unsurprisingly, there opened in early 2004 an Italian remake of the *Groundhog Day* plot, called *È già ieri*, "it's still yesterday," and an Adam Sandler vehicle with a similar theme, *50 First Dates*. There's a TV movie on the theme called *Christmas Every Day* (1996). Over and over and over again.

Or good autobiographies—or inspiring stories of any form in our culture, if we haven't the wit to see the ethical in our own lives. Hursthouse observes that "we do not always act as 'autonomous,' utterly self-determining agents," the way the masculinist version of ethical reflection supposes. We "often seek moral guidance from people we think are morally better than ourselves," or at any rate have gone through annealing experiences we think relevant to our own lives.[13] In a womanly way we are fascinated by ethical stories, finding them in literature, in autobiography, in gossip.

It is a fault in Hursthouse's philosophically sophisticated exposition of virtue ethics that she does not acknowledge the river of narrative in which humans swim. She argues persuasively that an adolescent cannot be wholly ethical, that the writing of a complete ethical Code Napoléon is an unattainable goal, that in short an educated judgment must be exercised.[14] Yet how then are we to grow into such ethical wisdom? Breadth of actual life experience is clearly relevant, though commonly not sufficient. But so is breadth of hearing and watching and reading the images and stories of our culture.

A story: The prison-hardened gangbanger and thief Carl Upchurch had been in solitary confinement at the federal penitentiary of Lewisburg, Pennsylvania, for two months before he noticed the little paperback book propping up one leg of the table. "I pulled it out, excited to have found something to alleviate the monotony. I turned it over and stared at the cover in disgust. It was Shakespeare's sonnets." He put it back. But his time in solitary was long, and "after three more days of staring at gray, I pulled it out again, muttering that Shakespeare was better than nothing."

> I don't pretend that Shakespeare and I immediately connected. I must have read those damn sonnets twenty times before they started to make sense. . . . I had almost always been contemptuous of intellect. That book of sonnets didn't just change my opinion—it quite literally changed my mind. . . . I wanted to ask for more books, but I didn't have a clue where to start. At least I knew that Shakespeare had written other stuff besides the sonnets, so I requested anything else they had by him. I . . . started plowing my way through thirty-eight plays and some other poetry. . . . Caught up in the first flush of literary exploration, I was pretty impressed with myself. In retrospect, it was lucky I was in the cell alone. . . . [The] guys would have burst my bubble mercilessly.[15]

He burst it often enough himself, in further explosions of macho violence. But gradually he emerged, through what he calls "de-niggerization." Story by story he remade his character. For example, this very tough guy wept his way through Les Misérables.

Religious ritual, which seems so idiotic to the secular mind, has the same feel as Carl's nth chance to go straight or Phil's nth repetition of Groundhog Day. The words and motions of the mass give the faithful repeated chances to get it right. At the *n*th repetition of "this is my blood, the cup of salvation" you for the first time grasp, really grasp, the meaning of redemption through Christ's sacrifice. Well . . . part of it at any rate.

If Kantianism, and its vulgar British cousin, utilitarianism, did not in fact provide guides to an ethical life, they do provide cool poses to assume, neat stories the man espousing them can tell himself.

The utilitarian can pose as practical, a numbers man. I have said why I think this modern myth of practical prudence is sometimes phony or dangerous. But when the issue is in fact a matter of numbers, and the fix is not in, the practical man is a useful guy to have around. He can tell you very properly that this particular design of a highway off-ramp implies a certain value of human life, whether or not you are comfortable with such numbers. Grow up, he says. Face facts. If we spend thousands of dollars investigating each airline fatality and only scores of dollars investigating each highway fatality, the result will be less safety. The economist says, "Shift some money from airline to highway investigations." When you want to be practical and consistent and not waste money, the utilitarian should be listened to. Really.

The uses of Kantianism are more spiritual. The ideal Kantian is, as Iris Murdoch put it, a combination of Romantic and Puritan, a man who chooses never to stoop, but always does his duty. Compare Alexander Gerschenkron. Gerschenkron was, surprisingly to those like me who knew him only superficially, a believing Christian. But he was also the best, my boy, the bravest. Kant helps bourgeois men without a god feel nonetheless proud of who they are.

In the *Grounding* Kant denied such ethical pride to women, almost explicitly: "There are many persons who are so sympathetically constituted that, without any further motive of vanity or self-interest, they find an inner pleasure in spreading joy around them. . . . In such a case an action of this kind, however dutiful and amiable it may be, has nevertheless no true moral worth."[16] This is the kind of analysis, in which womanly people cannot be virtuous, that annoyed Carol Gilligan. "How recognizable, how familiar to us, is the man so beautifully portrayed in the *Grundlegung*," Murdoch writes. He is "with us still, free, independent, lonely, powerful, responsible, brave, the hero of so many novels and books of moral philosophy. . . . He is the offspring of the age of science, confidently rational and yet increasingly aware of his alienation. . . . He has the virtue which [the bourgeois men of] the age requires and admires, courage."[17]

How noble, how glorious, above all how manly to face damnation without illusions. I called it "secular stoicism," that god-absent *virtù*. Murdoch notes that from Kant to Nietzsche is "not such a very long step," and thence to existentialism and "the Anglo-Saxon ethical doctrines [of ethics, in the early twentieth century, 'emotivism' in particular,] which in some ways closely resemble it." The central doctrine of secular stoicism is that ethics is not a matter of the nature of imperfect human beings, much less of transcendent ethical realism, and certainly not of God. The post-Kantian secular stoic believes that ethics is merely a matter of steady, manly, secular, human will. "In fact Kant's man," Murdoch observes, "had already received a glorious incarnation nearly a century earlier in the work of Milton: his proper name is Lucifer."[18]

EVIL AS IMBALANCE, INNER AND OUTER:

TEMPERANCE AND JUSTICE

In the new alternative to Platonism and its descendents Kantianism and Benthamism, Bernard Williams wrote, "Morality is seen as something whose real existence must consist in personal experience and social institutions, not in sets of propositions."[1] It is an alternative as new as Aristotle, Cicero, and Aquinas, with parallels in Chinese and Indian philosophy.

The classical virtue ethicists believed they had spotted the seams in the universe, the essence of prudence or the substance of justice. In reusing their words now, in an expanding universe, we do not have such ambitions. The ethical, we believe, is local, not universal, knowledge. It is contingent and fallible, not universal and necessary. "It is a contingent fact," writes Hursthouse, "that we can, individually, flourish or achieve *eudaimonia,* contingent that we can do so in the same way as each other, and contingent that we can do so all together, not at each other's expense."[2]

Such a notion of the ethical, Kant would have said with a sneer, is only anthropological or psychological or historical, not pure and rational. Alasdair MacIntyre characterizes the monistic tradition of Hobbes, Bentham, and Kant as asserting without much evidence—or on the evidence, as MacIntyre notes, of a misunderstanding of how geometry proceeds—that "there is a way of founding adequately the first principle or principles of right action by appeal to considerations which they take to be equally available at the commencement of enquiry *to every rational person as such.*"[3] Any rational person just knows that we "must" imitate Euclid in method and "must" come to the categorical imperative in substance. There's no grounding to the "must" in *The Grounding.*

And the method assumes its conclusion in another way, too: that we are discussing a person possessing practical wisdom already. No need to learn to cut cloth on the bias by watching one's mother, to take batting practice, to run marathons. No need to grow in practical or ethical experience. The representation of right lies deep in the soul of everyone, says Kant, even of the most delicate child, an axiom, an assumption. One is reminded of the joke about a physicist and an economist on a desert island finding a can of beans. They only lack a can opener. The physicist says, "Let's build a fire and heat the can. By the laws of physics, it will explode, and that way we can get into the beans." The economist says, "What a messy solution! I have a much neater one, which uses the laws of academic economics. First step: assume as an axiom that we have a can opener. . . ."

The ethics of the virtues asks insistently of the universalizers, though always politely, "Do you have a reason for seeking the universal? What guidance, when all is said, can such a priori generalities give to actual lives?" Talk of the local, contingent, nonuniversal virtues has the virtue at least of preserving how we actually talk, and therefore might help us talk—and behave. And there is a worry in the actual behavior of people who, as Alasdair MacIntyre puts it, "identify what are in fact their partial and particular causes too easily and too completely with the cause of some universal principle." "They usually behave," he notes, "worse than they would otherwise do."[4]

Factually speaking, as Alan Wolfe found in his surveys and interviews about American ethical views in the 1990s, "virtue," singular, as a word means little to ordinary Americans, except to arouse annoyance at the conservative churches and their recent obsession with sex, sex, sex. But to Wolfe's Americans the particular named virtues, plural, mean a great deal, provoking calm yet committed discussion. Americans admire especially, for example, loyalty, that blend of faith, love, justice, and temperance, and honesty—courage, justice, and faith; and in a broader sense a bourgeois blend of all the virtues.[5]

The way we actually talk does not depend on the Golden Rule or the categorical imperative or even the vaguer maxim of maximizing utility, at least not much. It depends on the particular virtues, straight from the *Girl Scout Handbook*, on the testaments old and new, and on the songs, poems, stories, family histories, and public dramatizations which give them life. Go and learn the commentary.

But the virtues do not work one-by-one. Murdoch observed that

> as we deepen our notions of the virtues we introduce relationship and hierarchy. Courage, which seemed at first to be something on its own, a sort of specialized daring of the spirit, is now seen to be a particular operation of wisdom [including what I am calling prudence] and love. We come to distinguish a self-assertive ferocity from the kind of courage which would enable a man coolly to choose the labor camp rather than the easy compromise with the tyrant. It would be impossible to have one virtue unless it were a very trivial one such as thrift.[6]

Or unless it were in fact a vice. Mary Midgley speaks of the treacherous Iago in the play Othello: "Iago's envy . . . has taken him over. It swallows up every other motive. . . . All attempts at inward balance have ceased. . . . There are no more conflicts."[7] Iago lacks temperance: "I do hate [Othello], as I do hell's pains," he says in the first scene, using a proverbial exaggeration, though also an ironic foreshadowing of his ultimate destination. As an economist would say, he is "specialized" in one or two virtues, showing courage in venturing and prudence in completing his somewhat haphazard plan against Othello, but showing none of that inward balance in acknowledgment of the conflict between one virtue and another that would make room in a good person for love or justice or hope: namely, temperance.

You are moved to hate the boss who passed you over in favor of some insipid Cassio, and for all you know slept with your spouse. But you draw back from hatred, anger, envy, with a mild reflection that after all it would be unjust to indulge your feelings, or that after all the Lord has laid down that "vengeance is *mine*," not thine. But Iago courageously and unbalancedly does not draw back. His "motiveless malignity," as Coleridge put it, arises from his character, not from the "motives" he offers, now one, now another, "the mere fictions of his own restless nature, distempered by a keen sense of his intellectual superiority, and haunted by the love of exerting power, on those especially who are his superiors in practical and moral excellence."[8] Iago's sin, like most sin, originates in the master sin of pride.

Likewise in *Paradise Lost* Satan declares courageously and single-virtuedly, "So farewell hope, and with hope farewell fear, / Farewell remorse: all good to me is lost; / Evil be thou my good." Of course it's not so simple as he claims. In seeing with Stanley Fish how Milton works, one should remember that theologically speaking Satan must be wrong about almost everything of importance.[9] C. S. Lewis writes, "What we see in Satan is the horrible co-existence of a subtle and incessant intellectual activity with an incapacity to understand anything."[10] Satan is not just a liar, "with calumnious Art / Of counterfeited truth." He is an idiot savant of unbalanced *virtù*.

Satan is not some Other to God, a force of pure Evil as against pure Good. We must rid ourselves, wrote Lewis in the midst of the Second War, "of the absurd fancy that devils are engaged in the disinterested pursuit of something called Evil (the capital is essential)."[11] Devils have goals like our own—honor, affection, nourishment, dominion—and being like us creatures (that is, created by God) have the usual virtues and vices. Their chief lord is shown by Milton as gloriously courageous, accepting as great a share of hazard as of honor. I have noted that his courage has mislead romantics from William Blake to Jack London into imagining that Satan is admirable even in Milton's secret heart. London took the proud words of Milton's Satan as his personal motto: "To reign is worth ambition, though in hell: / Better to reign in hell, than serve in heaven."[12]

Courage, in other words, is a virtue, but in a bad man or a fallen angel or a CEO gone off the ethical rails it is a virtue uncompleted by other virtues, such as Temperance or Justice or Love. Iago is courageous and, especially, prudent, but intemperate and, especially, unjust and unloving. The result is unchecked Envy and Hatred.

The classical and now revived analysis of virtues involves such balance and completion among the incommensurate virtues. The virtues cannot simply be added up into one sovereign Good, using that handy pocket-sized card. Aristotle or any typical recent Aristotelian, as Alan Ryan puts it, "approaches human nature more as a biologist than a mathematician, willing to recognize a variety of goods and ills [which suit different kinds of being] and a variety of ways of life which promote" the goods and ward off the ills.[13] That's right: the long experiment in ethics of emulating Descartes and Newton, with their mathematical axioms and rigid proofs, has failed. We neo-Aristotelians want to try instead to emulate Darwin, Mayr, and Gould, with their biological classifications and their stories.

That is to say: being good—lowercase *g*, no single Platonic ideal—always involves alloyed virtues, tin with copper, each a distinct element, to yield the more durable bronze. In fact sin—evil being sin institutionalized—merely is some one or two virtues unalloyed with the rest. St. Gregory the Great classified the sins into the seven deadly ones. In matters of money an excess of virtuous Prudence unalloyed is sinful Greed, and its character is the miser. In matters of the body an excess of love is gluttony or lust, and its character is the sybarite. Sin is a condition. Sins, plural, are acts. In Christian terms, sin is distance from God. Sins push one further away.

To think of sin or evil as a unified essence of its own, a contagion easily spotted in the very face of the person infected by it, is a Romantic and suburban Manichaeism according to which most of us believe ourselves to be—for all our admitted weaknesses, you see—on the good and light side of the Force. As Sartre once noted, "Manichaeism conceals a deep-seated attraction towards Evil . . . a curiosity fascinated. . . . In Berlin I knew a Protestant in whom sexual desire took the form of indignation. The sight of women in bathing suits aroused him to fury; he willingly encouraged that fury and passed his time at swimming pools."[14]

On account of our after-knowledge of its evil fruit we are now rather more ravished, if we allow ourselves, by *Triumph des Willen,* Leni Riefenstahl's film celebrating will-and-art politics in 1934 Germany. Listen to one Archibald Q. Stanton, a lay viewer of the film in 2002, about what he calls this "Feel Good Movie of the Century": "Set aside your preconceptions, notions of political correctness, kick back with some nachos and enjoy the spectacle, pageantry, patriotism and just plain ole unmitigated evil of a bygone era."[15] We cannot pretend to be much superior to Mr. Stanton, having ourselves felt the sexiness of evil, with or without nachos. We thrill to horror movies like *Jaws* or *Friday the Thirteenth.* It is therefore erotic as well as comforting to imagine Evil, though very interesting, as a rare case and therefore mainly irrelevant: Hitler or Darth Vader or Osama bin Laden.

Ethical questions are then corralled off as transfixing oddities. They are not how in the next minute or so you treat your husband or the clerk at the store or your fellow driver on the Kennedy Expressway. They are about how you decide, after consulting newspaper editorials and presidential commissions, the exceptional Bill Moyers/Charlie Rose issues of abortion and cloning and bombing and other titanic wrongs and rights.

The problem for such a modern, secular, post-Holocaust, and Romantic view, in other words, is the banality of evil. As the philosopher John Doris puts it, in his book arguing that situations matter more than the character assumed in virtue ethics, "It takes a lot of people to kill . . . 6 million . . . human beings, and there just aren't enough monsters to go around. Unfortunately, it does not take a monster to do monstrous things."[16] Doris cites the famous experiment by Stanley Milgram in 1960–1963, in which ordinary citizens of New Haven were persuaded to (as they believed) torture other people to extreme pain and death.[17]

The *ordinariness* of the Germans—and let it be noted, the Austrians and Poles and Hungarians, among others—who served as Hitler's willing executioners, for example, disappears if we are looking for some essence of evil. Albert Speer, Hitler's official architect and from 1942 minister of production, was a very saint of Prudence Only, an *echt* efficiency expert. But he was merely a more extreme version of ordinary Germans. He resembled ordinary Dutch and French people watching placidly out the window at Jews and Gypsies, homosexuals and socialists, being marched efficiently away. Compare ordinary Swedes trading peacefully with Hitler. Or ordinary Danes working with their usual efficiency in Hitler's war machine. Or ordinary Swiss accommodating the banking needs of Nazi officials. Or, when it comes to that, ordinary Britons and Americans supporting their governments' refusal to accept Jewish immigrants.

If we search always for the titanic we miss the banal evil, the unbalanced, uncompleted virtues, of our own, small, ordinary, local lives. In mainline churches nowadays the very words "evil" and "sin" are taboo, except on Sunday mornings, and then they appear not in the sermon, but only in the older hymns and rituals—and for special occasions in the rhetoric of conservative politicians. The *Oxford English Dictionary* notes dryly that evil as "the antithesis of good" is "now little used." "Deliver us from evil," you say in prayer—but you certainly do not mean *your* participation in the institutions of sin. You in such a pageant are (surely) a sweet old Dr. Jekyll, and far away and far below is some terrifying, alien, evil, and above all rare Mr. Hyde.

In the view of virtue ethicists from Aristotle to Annette Baier, on the contrary, we are all capable of sin, and get into it daily. This is the secular meaning of the Christian conviction that we are born in sin. It is the Greek and Christian sense of tragedy persisting in our culture—opposed recently by an evangelical enthusiasm for a rapture in which *we*, at least, will be saved. Sin in the Greek and orthodox Christian view is not radically foreign, something Satan made me do just this once, or something that only satanic people from the red or the blue states do, Anthony Hopkins playing Dr. Hannibal Lecter. Compare in this connection, by the way, *Dr. Faustus*, *Dr. Frankenstein*, *Dr. Strangelove*, *Dr. Roger Chillingworth*, the learned if evil physician, husband to Hester Prynne of *The Scarlet Letter*; or, in Charlotte Perkins Gilman's "The Yellow Wallpaper," the "scientific" *Dr. John X,* the scorning and confining husband, and *Dr. Y*, the wife's complicit brother—thus are the learned honored in Protestant Europe.

Anyway, sin is domestic. We actual, suburban humans are imperfect. We do not have, for example, perfect temperance. We chicken out, overindulge, harden our hearts, can't think it through, remain confusedly ignorant. And so a courageous gesture with our SUV at 70 miles per hour on the Kennedy Expressway, a banal, unremarkable aggression against a too-slow driver, a mini-heroic act, will once in while produce a looming, ramifying catastrophe.

The need for balance in the virtues, lest they be specialized into sin, is tragic. In *Democracy and Social Ethics* (1902) Jane Addams spoke autobiographically, as a woman would, about the conflict between the "family claim" which kept her from going to Smith College as she had planned and the "social claim" which later drove her life: "The collision of interests, each of which has a real moral basis and a right to its own place in life, is bound to be more or less tragic. It is the struggle between two claims, the destruction of either of which would bring ruin to ethical life."[18]

"Most merciful God, we confess that we have sinned against you, in thought, word, and deed, by what we have done, and by what we have left undone." We are to confess our ordinary inability to balance our virtues in a world of scarcity, failing to exercise, for example, a properly Christian, cheek-turning love toward someone who has hurt us. Justice alone is not enough. Justice alone, unbalanced, will morph into the sin of anger. One must have love, and courage and temperance and the rest.

Bishop Butler in 1725 viewed temperance as the crux, as one would naturally in an eighteenth century very conscious of its progress over the chaos of religious war. Self-interest was a matter of prudence and courage, benevolence of love and justice. But neither could flourish without temperance restraining the passions. "Men daily, hourly sacrifice the greatest known interest to fancy, inquisitiveness, love or hatred, any vagrant inclination. The thing to be lamented is not that men have so great a regard to their own good or interest [even] in the present world, for they have not enough."[19] "The greatest known interest" is eternal salvation. But in Butler's way of arguing it could be any great secular end, too. The problem is to control passion, to balance virtues, as temperance does.

"The existence of inborn tendencies to evil," Midgley writes, "need not puzzle us too much. It only means that our good tendencies are not complete or infallible."[20] Philippa Foot calls vice a "natural defect" in a living thing, as a tiger would be defective without teeth or an oak tree without leaves and a human without love or locomotion. For example, people who habitually free ride on the efforts of others "are just as *defective* as those who have defective hearing, sight, or powers of locomotion."[21] But perfection is as rare in ethics as in body.

As St. Augustine and later Aquinas thought of it, sin is not a thing in itself but an absence, a hole in the fabric.[22] The holes are original and ordinary. Or as Milton thought of it, sin is not a thing in itself, since after all nothing but God exists. It is rather a mistaken love for and loyalty to the imagined holes—again ordinary, for God loves and respects us so much that he gave us the free will to make such a mistake, to make nonentities our gods. And after loss of Eden we do.[23]

Justice, the giving of dues, said St. Augustine, is the social parallel to temperance. Temperance speaks of inner, justice of outer weather. Temperance is the management of the self, justice the management of society. The one is a balance of passions, the other a balance of citizens. "Just as a man is well-ordered in himself by virtue [namely, temperance]," says Aquinas, "so too is he well-ordered to his neighbors [by justice]."[24] As John Rawls noted, justice is the characteristic virtue of institutions, and of the people running them. Justice is the characteristically social virtue among strangers, because as Aristotle observed, "if men are friends, there is no need of justice between them," which is to say that from someone who loves you as he loves himself you have no need to claim your due.[25]

What is due depends. Before the Protestant and egalitarian and bourgeois sentiments of the eighteenth century in northwestern Europe flowered into a passion for equality, a just balance meant what we and the reactionaries would now call "order." The *ordines,* the classes, of Roman society were enforced by law and by the customs of the ancestors with bewildering precision, such as the details of seating at the games, the senatorial *ordo* in front, knights next, plebs in the back. *And this was just.* Justinian's *Institutes* of 533 begins by defining justice as "the constant and perpetual will to acknowledge the right of each."[26] But "right" (*ius*) varied with social condition. And this was just.

Pliny the Younger declared that nothing is more unequal than equality itself. Shocking injustices as we now believe they are such as slavery or pedophilia could therefore survive millennia of ethical scrutiny, or rather a blithe lack of scrutiny. Thus too the inequality of women; or of children subject to a *pater familias*; or more recently the inequality of homosexuals abused by law and custom in Germanic countries; or of black bodies swinging in the Southern breeze; or of young black or Hispanic men imprisoned for selling coke to suburbanites slumming.

Humans have shown repeatedly that they can imagine almost any injustice—at any rate an injustice by the most elevated egalitarian standards of bourgeois Europe—as fit, decorous, natural, what we do, nothing-to-be-done-about-it-anyway; in a word, as "just." Consider the Germans of the Third Reich, or the Germans rehearsing for the Third Reich in East Africa in 1904. Consider Hotel Rwanda. We have shown ourselves capable of imposing almost any indignity on Iraqis or Tutsis or *barbaroi* or any inferior.

Dignitas in Latin is from an Indo-European base **dek-* meaning "receive, be fitting," from which also *decus* (ornament) > *decōrus* (proper) > decorous. What is decorous depends in a hierarchical society of course on the dignity of rank. It is the free adult male Roman citizen, not a slave or woman or child, for whom it is *dulce et decorum* to die for the fatherland. Aristotle declares that "justice between master and slave and between father and child is not the same as absolute and political justice. . . . A chattel is . . . a part of oneself."[27] Well, of course. An *ancilla*, a female household slave (from which we get the word "ancillary"), was recommended by ancient ethical writers as a sexual object useful for preventing *real* adultery. Never mind her admitted humanness. Galen the doctor warns an owner not to hit slaves with his fist, to avoid injury to *his*—the owner's—fist. Wait until the passion subsides, he counsels, then apply the rod of justice. Never mind the slave's humanness.

One waxes indignant about past slavery. But the point here is that its justice was until the late eighteenth century entirely unquestioned. Souls in such a view are of course equal before God, the "of course" applying, for example, to Greek and Roman Stoicism, and to the Abrahamic religions of the Near East. It does not seem to apply to Hinduism, where a higher rank in the orders of the world must be earned in successive incarnations. Little wonder that over the millennia the castes of India have been sociologically hardy. The equality before God that distinguishes monotheism from rank-preserving polytheism is ancient.[28]

But as Samuel Fleischacker points out, a this-world egalitarianism was not imagined until Rousseau and especially Adam Smith. Equality of souls did not imply anything like equality of condition in this life.[29] On the contrary, fallen man must take up his burden as God's test. The poor are to be relieved because charity is a Christian duty and a Jewish *mitzvah,* not because the poor servant is entitled to a comfortable life. Until the bourgeois ethicists of the late eighteenth century, whose new policy was carried out in the nineteenth century, every Stoic, Jewish, Christian, and Muslim society placidly accepted slavery, on the principle, for example, of rendering unto Caesar in this life what is Caesar's. And rendering unto quite a few other people, too: my lord, my master, my owner, my boss, my priest, my husband, my father, my older brother.

And until the bourgeois ethicists of the late nineteenth century, whose new policy was carried out in the twentieth century, almost every society enforced the subordination of women, on the principle, for example, that a woman is an imperfect man. And until the bourgeois ethicists of the late twentieth century, whose new policy is being carried out in the twenty-first century, Christian societies among others adopted the persecution of homosexuals, on the principle, for example, that anything that causes anxiety to young heterosexual men is to be assaulted. Whatever the conception of justice, an orderly ancient one or a Protestant modern one, justice is the virtue of treating with respect whomever *should* be treated with respect. The rule of justice is: no dissing. It is not a rule of prudence or love or any of the other virtues.

Bourgeois societies from ancient Jerusalem to modern Hong Kong have been notably, if never perfectly, free. This is because two people doing business must deal with each other, not overawe or submit to each other. So bourgeois society developed a historically unique notion of justice. Samuel Fleischacker in recent books has noted that Adam Smith, the theorist of bourgeois virtues, was a radical egalitarian, quite unimpressed with the claims of philosophers (say) to superiority over street porters.[30] An old notion has survived scrutiny: eighteenth-century liberal philosophers did abandon an appeal to status in favor of an appeal to contract, and the European society surrounding the philosophers was changing this way, too. So Henry Maine said in 1861, and Tocqueville, too, in *The Ancien Régime and the French Revolution.*

By contrast, everyone in Elizabethan England believed in a great chain of being from God through kings to lords to masters to apprentices to women to slaves. You can see it vividly in Shakespeare. David Cannadine argues that in Britain "the Elizabethan world picture did not die with the Elizabethans."[31] By now in America only certain members of the country club believe it. Whether we like it or not, we liberals, and even we radicals and conservatives in our less bloody-minded moods, are entangled in a bourgeois conception of justice.

THE PAGAN-ETHICAL BOURGEOIS

The Royal Palace on the Dam Square in Amsterdam began its life in 1648 not as a monument to royalty—Holland was officially a republic until Napoleon—but to the *burgerlijk* virtues that had triumphed in war and commerce over Spain during the Eighty Years' War.[1] It was raised on the mud by the Amstel on a forest of Norwegian logs, proverbially 13,659 of them. So precise were these bourgeois. Dutch schoolchildren learn it as 1 followed by 365 followed by 9. It was among the largest nonecclesiastical buildings in Europe, the eighth wonder of the world, as Christian Huygens, the Dutch Sir Philip Sidney, and Joost van den Vondel, the Dutch Shakespeare, both proudly claimed. It was completed in 1665.

For a century and a half afterward it was the city hall, the *Stadhuis*. Its main room, judged one of the architectural jewels of Europe, was named *De Burgerzaal*, the (full, voting) citizens' hall. The hall and its building were designed on strict Vetruvian principles, an outsized Palladian villa, but built for the bourgeois citizens of Amsterdam rather than for an outsizedly rich patriarch of Aquileia or Venetian nobleman. The Dutch historian Pieter Geyl calls it "a real citizen's palace."[2]

Larger than the great New Church next door ("new" in 1385), contemporaries spoke of a contest between secular and ecclesiastical power. The alternative proposal for celebrating the peace was to supply the church with a magnificent new tower. The church-improving proposal was rejected, and the New Church to this day lacks a proper tower. The Stadhuis served no royal or religious purpose, no celebration of aristocratic or peasant/Christian virtues.

At the four corners of the building's principal roof façades, front and rear, were placed four large bronze statues, whose plaster casts were later put up in *De Burgerzaal* as well. The statues and casts may still be seen. They do not celebrate greed (is good) or avarice (above all). On the contrary, they celebrate as was usual in Dutch civic tradition on the front façade justice with her scales (*rechtvaardigheid*: "right-skill") and Prudence with her mirror. The prudence-word is actually *voorzichtigheid*, foresight, which again reflects the difficulty of rendering *prudentia* in Germanic languages except English. Similar ornaments placed in 1441 on the Ducal Palace at that older mercantile republic, Venice, are identified in Latin: *Justitia* preeminent, *prudentia, temperantia,* and *fortitudo,* with *charitas.*[3]

To get the pagan four entire, the Stadhuis celebrates temperance (*matigheid*) and vigilance, as was *not* usual in Holland until then—the original architect intended the fourth virtue to be, as classically, courage, but his successor for some reason made the substitution. Perhaps he thought vigilance (*waakzaamheid*: watchfulness) less belligerent than martial courage (*moed*) in a new—though as it turned out brief—time of peace. In any event, Amsterdam at the height of its success as a bourgeois republic spoke like Venice insistently of a balanced set of virtues.

And in fact it spoke of the pagan four, not merely of gain, gain, and gain—though gain, which is to say prudence, figures, too, with that fourth of the bronze statues, and inside and outside with reliefs and inlays celebrating the world-girdling commerce of the city. The wily Venetians were less candid in their celebration of gain.

Likewise at one end of *De Burgerzaal* the entrance to the Magistrate's Court is surmounted by Death and Retribution aiding Justice in trampling the sins of Greed, personified by King Midas, and Envy. The upper bourgeois are to eschew greed, and so they are to give to charities, for example, as they did with an open hand. In exchange the lower orders are not to envy the upper. Earthly possessions represented in the frieze and arch are restrained by the harness of Temperance and the sword of Justice, with Hercules' lion skin and club to complete with Courage the three non-prudential pagan virtues.

And on and on. As Blair Hoxby put it, the "decorative scheme [of the Stadhuis] was probably the most sustained exposition of mercantile ideals in the language of emblems, allegory, and classical allusion extant anywhere in the world."[4] It all sounds impossibly preachy. Surely "content," and "morals" in illustration of folk proverbs, cannot be the subject of serious art. Surely, like us, Dutch people must have thought of Art as being for Art's sake, yes? The MoMA rules, right?

No. Dutch people in the early seventeenth century read much of their art ethically: Rembrandt, Hals, Vermeer. That is why they had the century before stripped their churches of the lovely papist ornaments accumulated over centuries in one of the richest quarters of Europe. No non-Protestant messages, please. Images were ethically charged, and were not viewed as objects for Art's sake alone. True, sometimes a cigar is just a cigar.[5] But the "genre" paintings so characteristic of the Golden Age in the Netherlands, like the conceits of metaphysical poetry in early seventeenth-century England and Milton's "typologies" (a theological term for parallels and anticipations of history), were often heavily and ethically metaphorical. As R. H. Fuchs observed in explaining such a sensibility, arising out of a Protestant duty to read and understand God's texts oneself, "Had not Christ himself spoken in parables?"[6]

The theme of the four virtues honored by the city hall is repeated, in case you missed it, in the little room known in English as the Tribunal. A wooden public scaffold to where the fated victim was to adjourn would have been set up just outside the room, on the Dam Square. The judges handing down the sentence of death faced a large statue of Justice with sword and blindfold and another of Prudence with a self-reflecting mirror, as on the front façade. The condemned prisoner faced elaborate bas reliefs of Love and, again, Justice and Prudence. Left to right he could read, if he had been classically educated, sculptures showing a Greek father who lovingly volunteered to be punished in his son's stead; then Solomon's prudent judgment; and finally a Roman father, an early Brutus, who justly executed his own sons for treason. In other words, to repeat, in its icons the first bourgeois society in northern Europe dealt in the virtues of love, prudence, and justice as much as in rye and nutmeg. So we do still, though we have become embarrassed to say so.

As the Dutch of the Golden Age grasped, the ancient notion that courage, temperance, and justice could not flourish in a commercial society is wrong. Prudence, it was always realized, *could* certainly flourish among city folk, which made suspect a hero with too much of it. A coldly maximizing merchant is no Achilles. Remember that Odysseus was a trifle suspect on this score. One is not shocked to find Dante, no friend of commerce, assigning Odysseus, as a false counselor, to the next to the lowest of nine levels of Inferno, the place for those committing simple fraud (also in that eighth level, a little higher up, are astrologers and magicians, that is, in modern terms, economic forecasters).

Yet the courage to venture on the largest bourgeois building in Europe, the temperance to stick to the plans once formed, the justice to enforce business contracts on the delivery time of Norwegian lumber propping it up, all these are virtues withal. From the English side—the English were just then learning to restrain their penchant for noble gestures—Sir William Temple commenting on the Dutch Republic in 1673 contrasted the aristocratic soldier with the bourgeois trader: "One intends to make his fortune suddenly by his courage . . . the other slower, but surer, by craft. . . . This makes the first frank and generous, and [inclined to] throw away upon his pleasures what has been gotten in one danger, and may either be lost or repaired in the next. The other wary and frugal, and loath to part with in a day what he has been laboring [on] for a year, and has not hopes to recover but by the same paces of diligence and time."[7]

Temple uses throughout the chapter, sometimes acknowledged, the nobility-admiring turns of Tacitus concerning the Germans, among them the alleged ancestors of the Dutch. Here, for example, Temple shadows *Germania* 24: the noble Germans "will stake their personal liberty on a last decisive throw" of the dice, though Temple's rhetorical purpose is the opposite of Tacitus's. Of course Temple (or Tacitus, for that matter) is not to be taken as simply conveying facts to the page. But the opinion about the lack of nobility among the early modern Dutch was general, and foreigners accustomed to government by aristocrats therefore laughed at them—though Temple points out that the governing class, the rentier regents, were in fact bred up to government rather like an aristocracy.[8]

"Rather like"—but a real aristocrat, like the Earl of Leicester, who had been assigned ninety years earlier to meddle in Dutch politics, would sneer at the "Sovereign Lords Miller and Cheeseman" with whom they had to deal.[9] "Many foreigners," noted the liberal Huizinga in 1935, "believed that the policies of the United Provinces had but the one aim of flattering the greed of avaricious merchants." Well, yes: so the aristocrats have always believed about trade-enhancing policies. But "these very policies also benefited the country as a whole."[10]

The "pagan" virtues, when taken out of their heroic or Hellenic context, are after all merely human, good for business, good for life: the courage to venture, the prudence to venture aright, the temperance and justice to keep balance in doing so. The mother of a handicapped child, the manager of a company facing bankruptcy, the ordinary person rising daily to work in an ordinary job for her son or his daughter, need to be courageous, temperate, just, and prudent, "the better fortitude / Of patience and heroic martyrdom / Unsung." St. Thomas's teacher, St. Albert the Great, summarized Cicero's claim that every virtuous act has all four: "For the knowledge required argues for prudence; the strength to act resolutely argues for courage; moderation argues for temperance; and correctness argues for justice."[11]

In *On Duties* (44 BC) Cicero had declared that the four pagan virtues constitute a man's *honestas*, there meaning simply "rectitude, moral worthiness."[12] But in Latin *honestas* also meant "honor" in the aristocratic sense, that is, reputation, as does exclusively its reconstructed root **honos* without suffix and the usual *honōs* (genitive *honōris*) or simply *honor*. The Romans used rather the original of our "sincere," originally meaning "pure," for what we now call "honest." *Sinceritas* was not highly esteemed in a shame culture of aristocrats, and in fact this particular form is not attested before Augustus. At Rome and in its offshoots ethical goodness was what was worthy of esteem in a man of honor. "To live honorably" is the modern English translation of the advice in Justinian's treatise on Roman law in AD 533, *honeste vivere*, not our modern "live honestly."[13] Truth telling was distinctly secondary to this notion of *honestas*. Think of the haughty virtues, the *dignitas*, of an English lord or of a Mafia don.

Othello's characterization of "honest Iago" (1.3.298, 2.3.160) and "my friend, your husband, honest, honest Iago" at 5.2.162 just before he discovers Iago's lies are therefore not quite so crude cases of dramatic irony as they appear to us now. In *Othello* as most usually in Shakespeare the word means chiefly "honorable," as men still speak in jest of the purity of an "honest" woman. This sense with reference to women is also very common in Shakespeare—eight times, for example, in *Othello* about Desdemona ("I do not think but Desdemona's honest," 3.3.230).

Thus 5.1.32, "O brave Iago, honest and just / That hast such a noble sense of thy friend's wrong." Iago is here characterized as a warrior, *brave* and *noble* as a warrior should be, though, as it will turn out, having neither integrity nor justice. In *Othello* the word is used twenty-five times about dishonorable Iago, nine of these by Iago about himself and fourteen about Iago by the tragically misled Othello. The play mentions honest/honesty fully fifty-three times—as against only five times in *Macbeth*, ten in *Lear*, sixteen in *Hamlet*, or twenty-nine even in *Winter's Tale*, all of which like most of Shakespeare are centrally concerned with honor and falsity.[14] In 1713 Shaftesbury was still using "honest" to mean "honorable, virtuous." He inquired "what honesty or virtue is, considered by itself," and concluded piously that "it is impossible for an atheist to be virtuous, or share any real degree of honesty, or merit."[15]

The same happens in French—*honnête* has an obsolete sense of "civil, courteous"; and *honnêteté* an obsolete sense of "virtue, decency." Now it means "truth telling." It happens, too, in Germanic languages with an entirely different root word. The usual Dutch or German words for "honesty" now mean "truth telling," but in olden days, as in Latin-derived languages before the rise of the bourgeoisie, meant "noble honor." In modern Dutch *eerlijkheid* means simply "honesty." *Eerlijkheid duurt 't langst,* "honesty lasts the longest," that is, "honesty is the best policy." But it arises, as does "honesty" in French and English, from honor words in a very different society. The Dutch element *eer* itself still today means simply "honor," *eerbaarheid* "chastity," *eergevoel* [= "honor feeling"] "sense of honor," *eren* "to honor or revere," as in Dutch hymns to *de Heer*. And *erezaak* "a point of honor"; even old *eerverlies*, "corruption of blood lines."

The *OED* notes that in English "honest" in sense 1a, meaning "held in honor" or "respectable," from *honestas* by way of French, was obsolete after 1692. This is just about the time that England became as bourgeois as the Dutch Republic. The Bank of England in imitation of Dutch models was founded in 1694, for example; and the nation acquired like the Netherlands a public debt. The last citation of the meaning "commendable," sense 2a, is Pope's *Iliad* of 1715–1720, though still in use, as we have seen, in 1732. The year 1720 is the time England and Europe generally had its first fully capitalist financial crash. Financial crashes I have noted characterize capitalism precisely because a market society depends on the *honesty* of strangers, in the modern sense. The meaning of "honesty" as our usage of "sincere," says the *OED*, is "the prevailing modern sense," sense 3c, though used occasionally this way from Middle English. In *Othello* the two senses of it, honorable and sincere, mingle.[16]

It is no surprise that in a commercial democracy such as ours the word "honesty" has come to signify instead our master virtue, the egalitarian and bourgeois equivalent of an aristocratic and anticommercial "honor." John Casey is astonished that aristocratic honor "today . . . finds almost no place in the thought of moral philosophers," though it was central in the Renaissance and before.[17] But that is because it has been replaced by "honesty," which in a bourgeois society plays an identical social role. In *The Stones of Venice* (1851–1853) John Ruskin remarks after a long disquisition on the origin of virtue lists, "It is curious that in none of these [Italian] lists do we find either *Honesty* or *Industry* ranked as a virtue, except in the Venetian one."[18] Surely it is not so very curious, considering the frankly bourgeois and busy character of the Venetian Republic at its height, and the honor-obsessed cultures of contemporary feudal societies like France or England. As Ruskin notes, later the virtue of "Industry, in Northern [that is, proto-bourgeois French, German, Dutch, English] art and Northern morality, assumes a principal place."

The Japanese constitution was imposed in 1946 by Douglas MacArthur on his charges. In the course of her remarkable work on the linguistics of Japanese politics (1991, 2001, and especially 2002) Kyoko Inoue has noted that the English phrase "individual dignity" (as in Article 23, "Marriage shall rest upon . . . individual dignity and essential equality of the sexes") was quite innocently translated by the Japanese Diet ratifying the constitution as *jinkaku*.

The word was a Meiji Restoration coinage *jin* (individual) + *kaku* (rank), used in westernizing (specifically French-imitating) legal reforms in the late nineteenth century for "legal personality," as in corporate law. One might also translate it as "standing," as in "having standing to sue." But the root *kaku* means "rank" in a sense of justice that would have seemed completely ordinary to a seventeenth-century Frenchman or a fifth-century Greek. The dignity of an emperor or a samurai or a mid-twentieth-century free male Japanese comes from his rank, not from his humanity shared with commoners, women, slaves, Koreans.

Until the 1970s, when in the junior high school textbooks that Inoue takes as representative *jinkaku* began to be replaced by more egalitarian words meaning "humanity," ethical discourse in Japan had trouble digesting the emphatically nonhierarchical notion of "dignity" entailed in radical Christian and then radical bourgeois and finally radical democratic talk in the West. Indeed the two Japanese intellectuals Inoue discusses as beginning in the 1920s to drain *jinkaku* of its hierarchical meaning were among the 1 percent of the population professing Christianity. As Robert Bellah notes, in Japan "Christians played a role out of all proportion to their numbers in the cause of social reform in the period before World War II."[19]

In an aristocratic and hierarchical society of status and shame, the four pagan virtues lead up to honor = the courage, justice, and faith to take the front rank in the line of battle. In our bourgeois and egalitarian society of contract and guilt, they lead up to honesty = the courage, justice, and faith to be reliable in making a deal.

The ethical bourgeois can be seen in his enemies. Consider Jean-Paul Sartre, who remained a fellow traveler long after Khrushchev's destalinization speech, long after the Hungarian Revolution, long after the disappointments of actually existing socialism. "The philosopher of liberty," Raymond Aron wrote, "never managed, or resigned himself, to see communism as it is. He never diagnosed Soviet totalitarianism, the cancer of the century, and he never condemned it as such."[20] In his youth and in his age he was, with Simone de Beauvoir and that generation of French intellectuals, unthinkingly antibourgeois. It is ironic, by the way, that Sartre and Beauvoir both used metaphors of market dealings in describing their "open" relationship—well . . . open for Sartre—and the sexual ideal of free men and women.

The ethical content of Sartre's early work such as *Being and Nothingness* has been brilliantly drawn out by Ronald Santoni, in his 1995 book *Bad Faith, Good Faith, and Authenticity in Sartre's Early Philosophy*. Santoni sees the passage from "bad faith" (*mauvaise foi*) to Heideggerian "authenticity" as ethical—this against the popular parody of existentialism as amoral, a Valley Girl "Whatever." Bad faith is lying to oneself. Good faith attempts at least not to lie. The third and most noble state, authenticity, ascends to a still higher level, accepting the ambiguities and ethical responsibilities of a full life.

But Sartre seems to be importing a specifically political concern into his ethical thinking. Good faith, or sincerity, is (*hélas*, Sartre would add) a bourgeois virtue, that is to say, a virtue the capitalist system would honor, at least in its preachments. In this way of looking at it, bad faith would be the manner of life of the very worst of the bourgeoisie. In writing of good faith,

Sartre is considering, with distaste, the project of liberalism, by a European definition of the word, which tries to imagine and bring into being a good capitalism. Santoni observes that Sartre spends very few pages on good faith, but entire books on bad. Perhaps the explanation for his brevity is that good faith is precisely the best project—but withal he strongly feels an ethically inadequate project—of the detested bourgeoisie.

The probourgeois theorists, on the contrary, would claim that the best of capitalism is good faith, which in Santoni's words "pre-reflectively accepts rather than flees human reality. In short, it is self-acceptance as freedom." Sartre seems to be suggesting "Yes, good faith *is* the best from a bad lot. It is the best from *les bourgeois,* and therefore still very bad. What one should aspire to is authenticity, an altogether unbourgeois condition." This political concern would perhaps explain what Santoni calls "Sartre's baffling counterintuitive claim that good faith [or 'sincerity,' for that matter] shares the project and goal of bad faith."[21] Faith is bourgeois. If I've got this right, Sartre would fit also into the dogmatic secularism of French intellectuals at the time, against *foi* of a churchly sort. No *foi*, thank you, good or bad: we're French leftists.

The true best, that third thing above the plane of mere faith whether good or bad, is authenticity, that "self-recovery" or "deliverance." It is an aristocratic virtue, which would recommended it to the Marxist clerisy of Sartre's time. But in political theory it follows from the Revolution. Neither Sartre nor Santoni says this in so many words. Sartre claims that a cowardly reaction to the anxiety of being and nonbeing is the source of *in*authenticity. But my point is that the bad faith vs. good faith yielding finally to authenticity fits the dialectic structure of the philosophical argument and fits, too, Sartre's political beliefs.

Sartre's Revolution is to be led by philosophers. In this interpretation Sartre accords a glorious place to the clerisy, that embodiment of "reflection," to use the Sartrean vocabulary, because the clerisy leads humanity, with a self-consciously grasped "willed choice." One is tempted to note cynically: What other class would elevate a sheer intellectual activity to world-changing? And what other class would accord orthodoxy, upright opinion, such power?

In 1955 Simone de Beauvoir defended the Stalinist orthodoxy that she and Jean-Paul espoused in this way: "Truth is one, error is many. It is therefore no coincidence if the right wing claims to be pluralist."[22] The clerisy

alone can experience a "radical conversion"—note the revolutionary rhetoric here—maintaining nonetheless "ambiguity." Ambiguity, understand, is
not a bad thing in such a theology, so long as the proper clerisy is in attendance to interpret the signs. The blessed confusion gives the clerisy, whether
secular or religious, its leading role in the state. Ambiguity therefore is
beloved of Sartre.

The clerisy is uniquely positioned, says Sartre, to accept responsibility
and moral agency. One is here inclined to call the preacher of ethical
responsibility to account for "the cruel, duplicitous stratagems employed by
the polygamist Sartre in [sexual] love," as Santoni puts it. Or to wonder how
an advocate of moral agency could so long admire Communist tyrannies.[23]
Bad faith, Sartre claimed, is a flight from freedom, adopting, for example,
the absurd conventions of French bourgeois society. Bourgeois good faith
might be admitted as a stage "laying the foundation" for authenticity, as in
orthodox Communist thought the success of the bourgeoisie lays the foundation for the revolution and for Communism.

But that hopelessly bourgeois good faith or sincerity, Sartre is saying, is
in the end impossible. One cannot possibly, contrary to what Santoni hopes,
"rescue good faith from the controlling tentacles of bad faith" (p. xxxix).
The liberal project, which is Santoni's and mine but of course not Sartre's,
is ethically impossible. Sincerity, in Sartre's puzzling words, is a "phenomenon of bad faith." Only a faux-aristocratic authenticity is possible, for a
select few.

Sartre was wrong. The bourgeois project *is* on balance good and *has* in
large part succeeded. The Other, such as the working class, Sartre claims, is
"menaced" by capitalism (Santoni's word, p. xxxvi). I don't believe so. That
particular Other has for one thing become bourgeois. And the remaining
proletariat, and other Others, such as women, became free and prosperous
within capitalism, as well as ethically complete. The goal of a society in
which "each-for-itself affirms and promotes the freedom of the Other"
(Santoni again) is a good description of what bourgeois capitalism has in
sober fact accomplished.

In book 9 of *The Spirit of the Laws*, chapters 1–5, Judith Shklar observed, "Montesquieu attributed all the commercial virtues to citizens [of Athens]. . . .
Frugality, prudence, honesty, caution, these are the commercial traits of

character, and a democratic republic needs them especially."[24] Beyond these, commerce uses the cardinal virtues, too. As Aquinas and every theorist of the virtues through Smith concluded, the pagan and civic and "natural" four are an almost complete account—perhaps the masculine side of a complete account—of even the bourgeois virtues.

The Four Pagan Virtues

JUSTICE

Social Balance
- Gandhi -

COURAGE

[Aristocrat/Hero]
- Achilles/Shane -

TEMPERANCE

Individual Balance
[Priest/Philosopher]
- Socrates/Jane Austen -

PRUDENCE

[Bourgeois/Businessperson]
- Benjamin Franklin -
Know-how, Practical Wisdom,
Rationality, Max U-ism

PART FIVE

Systematizing the Seven Virtues

WE CRAVE AN EASY SYNTHESIS,
INFORMATION GATHERED, TESTED ON OUR PULSE,
DIGESTED INTO TRUTH.
A COGENT WHOLE, A SIMPLE KNOWING.
THAT'S WHY I CANNOT UNDERSTAND
WHY WE LEFT THE CHURCH.

—Helen McCloskey, "A Discarded Route"

26

THE SYSTEM OF THE VIRTUES

The principal ends of human acts are God, self, and others, since we do whatever we do for the sake of one of these.
  —Aquinas, *Summa Theologia*

Our life *consists in* this achieving of a pure relationship between ourselves and the living universe about us. This is how I 'save my soul.' . . . [If you view] love as the supreme, the only emotion worth living for, then you will write an immoral novel. Because . . . *all* emotions go to the achieving of a living relationship.
  —D. H. Lawrence, 1936.

The "moral universe within" has been described for 2,500 years in the West, then, in terms of the seven virtues, containing hundreds of particular virtues, among which are the virtues for a bourgeois life. In ethical space the bottom is the realm of the Profane, where prudence and temperance rule, the top the realm of the sacred—of spiritual love, and faith and hope. Moving from bottom to top is moving from self-disciplining virtues whose main object is the Self through altruistic virtues whose main object is Others (love of humans; justice) to the transcendent virtues whose main object is god or physics or the nation. That is, bottom to top is the axis of wider and wider ethical objects.[1]

The essentially transcendent virtues of faith and hope, I have noted, are essentially verbal. The others can be silently yet fully expressed. Prudence and justice are calculative and intellectual. They have been thought since Plato and the writers of footnotes to Plato to be the most characteristically human of virtues. Prudence and justice could be seen in a god-haunted society as gifts or laws from the Creator to humanity: "for which cause /

The Seven Virtues

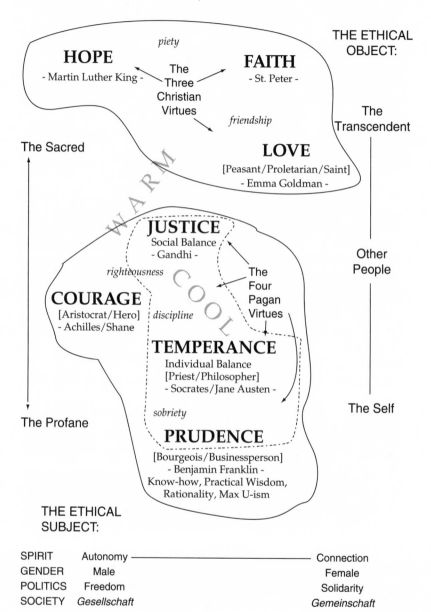

THE ETHICAL OBJECT:

HOPE
- Martin Luther King -

piety

The Three Christian Virtues

FAITH
- St. Peter -

friendship

LOVE
[Peasant/Proletarian/Saint]
- Emma Goldman -

The Sacred

The Transcendent

WARM

COOL

JUSTICE
Social Balance
- Gandhi -

righteousness

The Four Pagan Virtues

COURAGE
[Aristocrat/Hero]
- Achilles/Shane -

discipline

TEMPERANCE
Individual Balance
[Priest/Philosopher]
- Socrates/Jane Austen -

Other People

sobriety

PRUDENCE
[Bourgeois/Businessperson]
- Benjamin Franklin -
Know-how, Practical Wisdom,
Rationality, Max U-ism

The Profane

The Self

THE ETHICAL SUBJECT:

SPIRIT	Autonomy ——————————	Connection
GENDER	Male	Female
POLITICS	Freedom	Solidarity
SOCIETY	*Gesellschaft*	*Gemeinschaft*

Among the beasts no mate for thee was found." Animals were "dumb" in both senses.

By the grace of Darwin, however, we now see the calculative virtues in the least human of beings, in ants justly sacrificing themselves for the queen, or dandelions prudently working the cracks in the sidewalk. The terminology is figurative, note the scientists, a human attribution, not Nature's own way of putting it. But that is what we are discussing: human figures of speech. Natural history has taught us in the past three centuries to realize that the lion is not actually "courageous," ever, but merely prudent in avoiding elephants and just in acknowledging the pride's hierarchy. Courage and temperance are emotion-controlling and will-disciplining, and therefore, we now realize, human. Faith, hope, and love, above all, provide ends for a *human* life. The rest are means, and prudence is not the highest, God-given rationality but the lowest evolved strategies of these.

The triad of temperance-justice-prudence near the bottom and middle is cool and classical, and therefore recommended itself to theorists of the bourgeoisie such as David Hume and Adam Smith. The others at the top and edges are warm and Romantic, and came into their own in the nineteenth century. Hume called temperance-justice-prudence the "artificial" virtues, necessary for the artful making of any community whatever. They were of particular interest to men who had seen or vividly imagined communities collapsing in the tumult of religious war and dynastic ambition, of Jesuit and Presbyter, of Hapsburg and Bourbon and Stuart. Hume and Smith both, for example, had witnessed the Jacobite rising of 1745, and with nothing like sympathy—they were not wild Highlanders, and certainly not Catholics, but lowland Scots of a deist or atheistic bent who had made their peace with Englishry.

"Enthusiasm" was in the eighteenth century a term of abuse. Let us confine our discussion, most of the *philosophes* of France and Scotland agreed, to the cool, dignified, essential, and "artificial" virtues. Hume was using the categories and argument of Pufendorf, defending natural law against the intellectual and political chaos of the early seventeenth century. The categories became part of European classicism in the seventeenth and eighteenth centuries, reacting to the rhetorical charms of the Renaissance and the rhetorical excesses of the Reformation and Counter-Reformation.

The other, "natural" virtues of courage, love, hope, and faith impart warmth and meaning to an artfully made community. Sometimes too much warmth and meaning. The Scottish followers of Hutcheson admitted love, as benevolence, and admitted courage, as enterprise, but rather off to the side of their main concerns. They certainly had no patience with hope and faith, and Hume was fierce against their religious forms, "celibacy, fasting, and the other monkish virtues." Imparting warmth and meaning was decidedly not what the Scots of the Enlightenment had in mind. That is a Romantic project, and these were not Romantics.

That Adam Smith was a virtue ethicist for a commercial age is pretty plain. He escaped, as Hume did not entirely, from the "prison," as Hayek puts it, of the Greek categories *physei* (natural) and *thesei* (artificial). He emphasized a third category, the social interaction neither natural rock-like nor artificial painting-like, the invisible hand.[2] Hayek observes that the eighteenth century learned the third category from the appalling Dr. Mandeville. But Smith used it to support rather than attack conventional ethics.

Smith made his virtue-ethic purposes clearest at the end of his life, in a part 6 added to *The Theory of Moral Sentiments* thirty-one years after its first publication. Section 1 of the new part is an encomium on the Prudent Man. Section 2 is an analysis of love in an expanding circle outward from self to country. It concludes with a criticism of going still higher, to the faith and hope in transcendence that had been so troublesome to the Scotland of his grandfathers:

> The administration of the great system of the universe, however, the care of the universal happiness of all rational and sensible beings, is the business of God and not of man. To man is allotted a much humbler department, but one more suitable to the weakness of his powers, and the narrowness of his comprehension: the care of his own happiness, of that of his family, his friends, his country. That he is occupied in contemplating the sublime can never be an excuse for neglecting the more humble department.... The most sublime speculation of the contemplative philosopher can scarce compensate the neglect of the smallest active duty.[3]

One can hear him including the theologian or other advocate for the transcendent in that phrase "contemplative philosopher." Compare Hume's "divinity or school metaphysics."

And then Smith embarks on a concluding, climactic section 3, "Of Self-Command," the master virtue in his book. "The man who acts according to the rules of perfect prudence, of strict justice, and of proper benevolence [love, that is] may be said to be perfectly virtuous." That accounts for three of the seven virtues: prudence, justice, and love. But suppose he knows he should so act, but can't bring himself to it? "The most perfect knowledge, if it is not supported by the most perfect self-command, will not always enable him to do his duty." "Extravagant fear and furious anger," to take one sort of passion, "[are] often difficult to restrain even for a single moment." The "command" of fear and anger was called by the ancients "fortitude, manhood, and strength of mind," which is to say courage. "The love of ease, of pleasure, of applause, and other selfish gratifications . . . often mislead us." The command of these the ancients called "temperance, decency, modesty, and moderation," that is to say, temperance.[4]

So: in Smith there are the five virtues, of prudence, justice, love, courage, temperance. There is no room for faith and hope.

But this will not do. Alasdair MacIntyre—his name and Glasgow birthplace are not irrelevant, nor is his youthful Communism or his mature Catholicism—argues that the artificial and all the natural virtues including faith and hope are to be taken together: "The virtues that we need, if we are to develop from our initial animal condition into that of independent rational agents [viz., prudence, temperance, and justice], and the virtues that we need, if we are to confront and respond to vulnerability and disability both in ourselves [courage, hope] and in others [love, faith], belong to one and the same set of [seven] virtues, the distinctive virtues of dependent rational animals."[5] All three sets of virtues are drawn on for a full life. The Romantics after the eighteenth century understood this. The Christians before the eighteenth century did, too.

In particular, Prudence Only will not be a life worth living. As Ellen Charry observes, "The gratification of being a part of a larger reality [Tillich's 'the courage to be a part of'] that gives each experience a purpose beyond its momentary accomplishment buffers the soul against life's disappointments."[6] For "ye have your closes, / And all must die."

It is an obvious secular truth, too. Enjoy the White Sox game, by all means, in the present—the ballgame, the show, the peanuts, the Cracker Jack, in the lower region of prudence, sheer utility. Live as Nature's son, not her bastard. But enjoy also your own little son's delight in being there with his father, at the middle region of Love. And at the higher regions take joy in "being part of a larger reality," baseball or American fatherhood or the democratic tradition.

∞

The seven virtues in the diagram illuminate other ethical systems. William Schweiker, for example, quotes with approval Tzvetan Todorov's characterization of humanists, believing that "freedom exists and that it is precious, but at the same time . . . [appreciating] the benefit of shared values [such as hope and faith], life with others [such as love and justice], and a self that is held responsible for its actions [showing temperance, prudence, and moral courage]."[7]

The philosopher Harry Frankfurt starts with the usual definition of "virtue" as "altruism," confined to the middle region of the diagram. The ethical object at the bottom is a self, I have noted, and at the top is a transcendent; in the middle the object of ethics is other people. Like Susan Wolf writing about her obnoxious moral saints, Frankfurt uses terms like "morality," "moral principles," and "moral philosophy" as though they did not include either the self or the transcendent as objects of ethical action.

Such a definition appears to be a convention in mainstream, Kant-derived ethical philosophy. "Morality is most particularly concerned with how our attitudes and our actions," Frankfurt writes, "should take into account . . . other people."[8] Well, not in the view of Aristotle or the other virtue ethicists. Morality among them is about the good life for a human, which requires a character of prudence and temperance toward oneself, and faith, hope, and higher love toward the transcendent. And it requires justice and courage and lower love on behalf of other people—the Scots called it "benevolence." Thus *ethos*, character. Robinson Crusoe on his island, I said, had a good or bad ethical life, even before Friday. So virtue ethics.

But Frankfurt comes to the same view in the end, concluding that love must have a transcendent object for a human life to have a point. "A person may legitimately be devoted to ideals—for instance, aesthetic, cultural, or religious ideals—whose authority for him is independent of the desiderata with which moral principles are distinctively concerned; and he may pursue these nonmoral ideals without having his personal interests in mind at all."[9] The ideal of the transcendent, such as God or baseball, are independent of altruism. The transcendent is *defined* as "nonmoral," namely, not having in mind the self-interest of prudence and temperance. Frankfurt is saying that the transcendent, and in particular a notion of Love which includes what Christians would call agape, is necessary for a fully human life. In this way the ethics of the Enlightenment is sacralized.

He could have got to the conclusion by way of virtue ethics with less heavy lifting. "What we care about, what is important to us, and what we love" give point to a life, says Frankfurt. But these, I note, *are* faith, hope, and charity.[10] I expect that Frankfurt is well aware of all this, and is engaging in a crafty figure of argument necessary in a corner of the academic world dominated by Kant. He shares with Wolf and many other modern philosophers the job of clambering out of the rationalist hole that Kant dug so diligently.

Frankfurt here seems to be marshaling a reductio ad absurdum, to show that Kantianism or for that matter utilitarianism does not give a coherent account of an ethical life. The ethical life cannot in fact to be reduced, Frankfurt is saying, to formulas for deciding ethical dilemmas, formulas applicable to any rational creature as such. On the contrary, "it requires us . . . to understand what it is we ourselves really care about."[11] It depends on *ethos,* on agape and *philia,* on character, on moral sentiments, on a philosophical anthropology and psychology, on being a particular woman in Chicago at a particular time, with particular loves and faiths and hopes. As Philippa Foot put it, Kant went wrong in not realizing that "the evaluation of human action depends . . . on essential features of specifically human life."[12]

In fact, as I have noted, the Kantian program is self-contradictory, which among Kantians is judged the worst sin. The character of ourselves that we care about, a caring denied in pure rationalism, is what makes a Kantian moralist—or for that matter, if he reaches beyond ice-cream hedonism, what makes a utilitarian moralist. You have to want to be good. You have to care about what Frankfurt calls "ideals" and I and many others in Western ethical tradition call "transcendentals." Only then will you have an interest in following, say, the categorical imperative or the true happiness of all people in your dealings with others. The ethical-theorizing "constructed self" that the social psychologist Timothy Wilson speaks of *wants* to work with the ethical-behaving "adaptive unconscious." Being good, in Frankfurt's account and in mine, is a consequence of "what we regard as important to ourselves," not itself derivable from Kantian or utilitarian maxims.[13]

Left and right in the diagram exhibit the gendered character of the virtues, masculine and feminine in the conventional tales. Women of course are supposed conventionally to think of the world from the perspective of right-side love, or its corresponding vices, such as envy and jealousy. Men are supposed to think of the world from the perspective of left-side courage, or cowardice, vainglory, self-absorption, and so forth.

Another name for the right side in the diagram is "connection"; and for the left, "autonomy." Knight believed that even ordinary desires could be reduced "in astonishingly large measure to the desire to be like other people, and the desire to be different."[14] Tillich called them "participation" and "individualization," and noted that there is a "courage to be as a part," that is, to participate. Michael Ignatieff called the one side "connection and rootedness" and the other side "freedom": "a potential contradiction . . . arises between our need for social solidarity and our need for freedom." We have rights, which is good, allowing us to achieve our left-side projects of hope and courage regulated by justice. But we need "love, respect, honor, dignity, solidarity with others," Ignatieff notes, on the other, upper-right-hand side, and these cannot be compelled by law.[15] Hence Hume's vocabulary of "natural" as against "artificial," law-enforced virtues.

Whether or not men in general do actually fall on the left, autonomous side, the male non-Scottish, non-virtue-ethics ethical philosophers of the eighteenth century certainly did. The Kantian and Benthamite men, for example, are just that, men deciding ethical issues without regard to connection, men fiercely autonomous, adults always in their primes, rational beings never dependent. So they believed. They are, as the feminists put it with irritation and amusement, "separative selves."

The third fresh option in seventeenth- and eighteenth-century ethical philosophy, contractarianism, is likewise gendered as masculine. A Hobbesian/Lockean/Rousseauian "contract" is not the usual metaphor with which women describe their lives. Rather: love, caring, obligations of affection, "a view of the self as relational."[16] Women in fact find themselves with children and parents and friends and husbands and lovers to take care of. Men seem to think of such connections as optional, wholly contractual, even relationships of exchange. Thus Marcel Mauss, a leading male anthropologist of the early twentieth century, encouraged people to think of the gift, too, as a sort of exchange.

The feminists such as Carol Gilligan and Virginia Held resist. Annette Baier, following them, observes that not all male ethical philosophers take the side of autonomy. She gives passing grades on the matter to Aristotle (connection in the polis), Marx (class), Mill (progressive sympathy), and

MacIntyre (dependent rational animals, and practices), and then she studies Hume from the feminine, connective perspective in detail. Hume is, she
argues, "uncannily womanly" in emphasizing the role of sympathy as
against higher law, having others to share experiences with, and the love of
children as the exemplum for ethical theory. She finds in Hume a stress on
"the inescapable mutual vulnerability and mutual enrichment . . . [of] the
human conditions . . . [which] make autonomy not even an ideal."[17]

A socialist like Paul Tillich would have viewed the right side of love, justice,
and faith as commendably anticapitalist, as against the left-side enterprise of
courage and hope. Capitalism is, after all, the system supporting the virtue of
enterprise, and that is the left-side virtues—though I have emphasized that in
fact even capitalism depends of the loving right side, too. Tillich among others
would have quarreled with placing courage only on the left, masculine side.[18]

The pioneering feminist economist/philosopher Julie Nelson would
argue that any ordering has the danger of privileging one over the other. I've
said why I think all the virtues work in any serious ethical life. So by placing them high up I am not saying that hope and faith are superior to prudence and temperance, or that love trumps courage every time. Nelson
would use positive and negative versions of each virtue, deconstructing the
geometry of a "top" thought superior to a bottom, or a "left" sinister.[19] So
love of others can be negative as love of others only, without sufficient self-
love: self-abnegation, the womanly sin.[20] Or one could use Aristotle's notion
of a mean splitting the difference between excess and deficiency.

And indeed the placement of the virtues in the diagram is that of mythical convention, not God's truth, or even science's. Thus upper-and-right
pertains to the past, lower-and-left to the future: well . . . perhaps. The four
virtues in bold are the signature virtues of the mythically ancient social
classes: warrior (courage, daring), peasant (love, loyalty), merchant (prudence, know-how), and priest/brahmin (temperance, wisdom). More mythical convention. But that is how we talk.

There is no reason why the number of sins should equal the number of
virtues, though of course in Western tradition, thanks to Pope Gregory,
there are also seven, and deadly. In modern English they are lust, gluttony, avarice, anger, envy, sloth—that is, acedia, from Greek, spiritual sloth,
a lack of hope, replacing "sadness" in the seventeenth century—and pride

mastering above all. They can be paired off by social class, pride being the characteristic sin of the rich, such as the Florida woman in her mink who on TV in 2004 while clinging to her husband said about the poor, "*We* aren't *losers.*" Acedia is the corresponding sin of the poor and hopeless. Avarice-gluttony are again sins of the rich and envy-anger of the poor, similarly paired. And lust, after the Fall, is ubiquitous.

Sin or vice, I have argued, is the notable lack of any one or more of the virtues, and so the seven virtues lead to seven single lacks, imprudence, injustice, intemperance, and so forth. But as Hursthouse notes, "Although our list of generally recognized virtue terms is, I think, quite short, our list of vice terms is remarkably—and usefully—long."[21] She notes that the list far exceeds the number of rules that Kantians imagine might be formulated to summarize ethical ideas. The list of vices shows how we actually reason ethically. We call people names. Hursthouse instances "irresponsible, feckless, lazy, inconsiderate, uncooperative, harsh, intolerant, indiscreet, incautious, unenterprising, pusillanimous, feeble, hypocritical, self-indulgent, materialistic, grasping, short-sighted, . . . and on and on."

Take down your *Roget's International Thesaurus*, the third edition of 1962, for example. Virtue itself (category number 978) takes up about half a column of words; the two opposites that follow, vice (979) and wrongdoing (980) take up two full columns. Asceticism (989), temperance (990), fasting (993), and sobriety (995) fit handily into about two columns, interlarded with seven and a half columns on intemperance, gluttony, and intoxication (which last by itself accounts for five and a half columns). Respect (962) has a column of words, followed by two and half columns on disrespect, contempt, and ridicule. Courage (891), in two columns, is surrounded by anxiety, fear, cowardice (888–889) and rashness, totaling six and a half columns. Cut the six and a half in half to allow for Roget's habit of alternating opposites and it still works out to 3.25 pusillanimous vices to every two virtues of courage.

The richness of our vocabulary of abuse comes from the stories and images that ground ethical thinking. We remember Billy in kindergarten who would not lovingly and justly cooperate, and he becomes our exemplar for the lack of those qualities. Judas Iscariot becomes the exemplar of intemperance and faithlessness.

If there are seven virtues and if the lack of any combination constitutes a vice, then the combinatorial mathematics implies that there would be . . . let me see, 7 items taken 6 at a time plus 7 taken 5 at a time plus 7 taken 4 at a time . . . exactly 126 vices. I jest. Seriously, there's no guarantee that every language has a word for any random failure, such as a lack of faith, justice, and prudence in the presence of the other four, love, hope, courage, and temperance. A man like this would have no rootedness or identity, would not give people respect, or even their due, and would be careless and uncalculating. Yet he would be affectionate, brightly hopeful about something turning up, courageous over present fears, and modest in his needs. Not a Mr. Micawber, precisely. But it's Arthur Miller's Willy Loman to a T. The play lets us reflect, then, about this uncategorized vice.

Such a system for reflection has behind it a library of philosophizing, which is one reason for taking seriously the particular septet. Plato, Aristotle, Cicero, Aquinas, and at the very end, before Kant, Adam Smith, and now the women and men exploring virtue ethics, did not merely copy each other. They built on each other's thought a great engine of analysis.

Hursthouse argues, following Gary Watson and Neera Badhwar, that "we believe the virtues form some sort of unity."[22] To put it in an economist's terms, the separate virtues are complements; or to put it statistically, they are not independent. That is, we are startled when on some occasion a bad man behaves well, apparently, and tend to doubt the claim that he did in fact behave well on this occasion. And we expect good men never to behave badly. So as academics we are surprised when a "good" economist behaves badly in other ways, a Nobel laureate at the University of Chicago expressing a virulent homophobia, for example. At least we are a little surprised.

27

A PHILOSOPHICAL PSYCHOLOGY?

If the seven are good, common places to start a philosophical psychology, then they should show up in the works of psychologists. They do.

A startling new book, published under the auspices of the American Psychological Association, edited and largely written by Christopher Peterson and Martin E. P. Seligman, *Character Strengths and Virtues: A Handbook and Classification* (2004), lends empirical support to the seven, at any rate within the European tradition in which they were theorized. It seeks, as the philosopher Peter Danielson says in another connection, the "ethical genome."[1] In 644 big-format text pages, using 2,300 citations to the technical literature in clinical and social psychology and related fields, the forty drafters of the chapters (which Peterson and Seligman then rewrote) present a "manual of the sanities," that is, the "positive psychology" of healthy people. Studying sanity is an idea that the psychologist members of the board for the Values in Action Institute of the Mayerson Foundation, which sponsored the volume, such as Mihaly Csikszentmihalyi (which is pronounced "CHICK-sent-me-high") and Howard Gardner, have been especially known for.

Peterson, Seligman, and the others detect twenty-four "strengths of character," on the basis of ten criteria, not all of which are satisfied for every strength (about half of the twenty-four do satisfy all ten).

The ten criteria on the left side of the figure are on their face useful reflections on the virtues. Yet if they were merely speculative, the exercise would be much less interesting. The authors, however, take seriously the matching of the criteria with the psychological literature, quantitative and

Ten Criteria for Twenty-Four Strengths of Character

Contributes to the good life, as for example:	1. Curiosity, 12. Social Intelligence
is valued in its own right,	8. Integrity, 17. Humility,
does not diminish other people,	11. Kindness, 22. Hope, 5. Perspective
does not have an *admirable* opposite,	7. Persistence, 20. Appreciation of Beauty and Excellence, 21. Gratitude
can be assessed (that is, observed),	9. Vitality, 14. Fairness, 15. Leadership, 7. Persistence
is embodied in human exemplars,	10. Love, 24. Spirituality, 1. Creativity
shows sometimes in children as prodigies,	4. Love of learning, 19. Self-Regulation,
shows sometimes in total absence,	23. Humor, 3. Open-Mindedness 6. Bravery
and finds support in human institutions.	16. Forgiveness and Mercy, 13. Citizenship

Source: Peterson and Seligman, *Character Strengths and Virtues*, 2004, pp. 29–30 and throughout.

qualitative. In other words, the twenty-four strengths of character not mere assertions but findings, summarizing a gigantic scientific literature.

The twenty-four species of strengths are clustered into the encompassing genuses of: courage, humanity, justice, and so forth—that is to say precisely the "virtues [,] . . . the core characteristics valued by philosophers and religious thinkers."[2] The authors number them as six rather than seven, but this is mainly because they lump hope and faith together in one virtue named transcendence, that is, "strengths that forge connections to the larger universe and provide meaning."[3] Five of these "High Six" virtues they identify lay down with ease on the classical seven—transcendence (that is, faith and hope), courage, humanity (that is, love, which appears in their classification as a "character strength" within what they view as the wider virtue), justice, temperance.

The only lack of fit is their genus of wisdom-and-knowledge, which is *not* prudence seen as practical wisdom, Aristotle's *phronēsis*, but *intellectual* strengths of character, namely, creativity, curiosity, open-mindedness, love of learning, and perspective. These are desirable strengths, surely. But in the classical definitions they would not be virtues at all, but aptitudes ethically indifferent—such as having a high percentage of fast-twitch muscles, the better to run a record mile. Or they would be subspecies of prudence, not a genus substituting for it. Or perhaps they would be subspecies of love of learning or of hope for a touch of the transcendent in art and science. Aquinas in fact did not believe that such "habits," as he calls them, are properly classified as virtues.[4]

The psychologists instead put their version of what they call "prudence" under the cardinal virtue of temperance, and define it narrowly as "being careful about one's choices; not taking risks." This is a tiny part of the wider classical or Aquinian or Smithian concept of prudence, and *is* in fact more naturally placed under temperance. It's the virtue of proper caution. Psychologists are likely to identify such a thing as "not taking risks" with what they call "impulse control," which is rather easy to measure in experiments and questionnaires, and can even be found in a part of the brain. The drafting author of the chapter directly on prudence, Nick Haslam, spends two pages worrying about such a reduction.

But in the classical definitions it is temperance, not prudence, which is the virtue of controlling impulses. Haslam, as revised by Peterson and Seligman, states flatly that "Aristotle does not . . . equate *phronēsis* with . . . impulse control," which is correct. Aristotle and Plato and the rest had another word for self-control, *sophrosynē* (from *sophron*, "sober"), which Cicero translated as *temperantia*.[5] Prudence in the classical definitions is intellectual and calculative, like justice, not emotion-controlling, like temperance and courage. Prudence belongs with the intellectual virtues, not with temperance, and indeed could be said, as all writers from Plato to Adam Smith did say, to be the chief of the intellectual virtues.

Having criticized the Peterson and Seligman psychologists on this score I should admit the great truth underlying their work: that emotion and intellect are intertwined, not always to be distinguished—the book has four citations to Antonio Damasio's thinking on the matter; though none to Martha Nussbaum's. But that is precisely why, as the team asserts and as Aristotle, Aquinas, Adam Smith, Martha Nussbaum, and Deirdre McCloskey also assert, the virtues do make a coherent system, and not merely a fungible list of good things you might want to get hold of.

Aquinas's definition of prudence, for example, is that prudence is "any virtue which causes good in reason's consideration."[6] Prudence deals "rightly with those things that are for the sake of the end." It is "reason rightly deliberating, judging, and commanding." "There can be no moral virtue without prudence."[7] Prudence as know-how, that is, figures in the exercise of *any* virtue. It should not be sorted away as a minor aspect of temperance.

I agree with Peterson, Seligman, and their collaborators that the exact sorting of strengths into the wider virtues is not very important to their project, since their empirical work goes on always at the level of "strengths" or at the still lower level of "situational themes." Yet the sorting *is* important for my own project, namely, finding how the classical virtues lie down on capitalism. The team appears to me to have sorted mistakenly here, mainly because it has not looked closely enough into the meaning in Western ethical history of "prudence" as against "wisdom" and "temperance." That's no great sin in a splendid project. After all, even a well-regulated team of over forty people can't do everything, and they are to be congratulated for their just and prudent gestures toward the history of ethics.

One side of the problem, I would argue, is that the authors have confused *phronēsis*, practical wisdom, with *sophia*, theoretical wisdom. This at any rate is the way Aristotle typically used *sophia*, as a supreme and scientific knowledge. According to Liddell and Scott, earlier *sophia* does refer in fact to "skill" or indeed "practical wisdom." You could contrast *phronēsis* instead with *episteme*, the usual Greek word for knowledge.[8] But anyway *phronēsis* is devalued by the prestige of Theory. Aquinas, as I've noted, did not think theoretical, *speculativus* wisdom was a virtue at all, but a gift of the Holy Spirit, though he himself possessed the gift to a miraculous degree. Aquinas distinguished, for example, the theoretical "knowledge" of chastity, the kind, say, a philosopher might have, from the prudential "knowledge by connaturality" that a truly chaste person has in her life.[9]

The definition of wisdom given in chapter 2 of the Peterson and Seligman book, "Universal Virtue? Lessons from History," drafted by Katherine Dahlsgaard, depends revealingly on a German source, namely, certain researchers at the Berlin Max Planck Institute. It is "revealing" because, remember, all Germanic languages except English have difficulty in translating Latin *prudentia* = Greek *phronēsis*. The Berliner Max Planckers speak of wisdom as "good judgment and advice about important but uncertain matters of life."[10] Yes. But this is precisely *phronēsis*, or Latin practical *prudentia*, not Germanic *Weisheit* or wisdom, which mixes the practical and the theoretical. The Dutch word for philosophy is *wijsbegeerte*, wis[dom] desire, a calque on the Greek literal meaning, *philo-sophia*, "love of theoretical wisdom." English/French/Latin "prudence" is not Aristotle's theoretical *sophia*,

which Cicero translated as *scientia* and *sapientia*. *Phronēsis/prudentia/*
prudence is a knowledge of means, not of ends, good judgment in practical
matters, not a command of theories.

The Dahlsgaard-drafted chapter quotes the Yale psychologist R. J. Sternberg (1998), another prominent psychologist on the board of the Values in
Action Institute. Sternberg writes about one of his three sorts of intelligence: wisdom "is involved when practical intelligence is applied to . . . a balance of various self-interests . . . with the interests of others."[11] Sternberg is
here precisely not speaking of *scientia* or *sapientia* but of *prudentia* mixed
with *justitia*. Note that he even uses the phrase which translates Aristotle's
phronēsis: "practical wisdom."

And so the Peterson-Seligman book later repeatedly elides theoretical wisdom and practical prudence. The Haslam-drafted chapter on Prudence does
a better job sometimes, because he has evidently troubled to read Aristotle, if
not perhaps Aquinas. But even Haslam gets entangled in *sophia*, maybe
because he was saddled with the group's too-wide definition of "Wisdom."[12]

The group have also, on the other border of the word "prudence," as
I said, confused prudence with temperance. Haslam in particular seems to
struggle honorably with it. The confusion is important because most of the
psychological measures of prudence mix it with other virtues. Thus the five-
factor model of personality traits developed by Costa and McCrae speaks of
"conscientiousness" as a prime trait. It is said to be made up of classically
prudential facets such as "competence, order, and deliberation," but then
also justice, in "dutifulness," hope, in "achievement striving," and temperance, in "self-discipline."[13]

Haslam himself says that "Prudence therefore implies a balance and har-
mony . . . play[ing] a mediating role, . . . ensuring that hope is *tempered* by
realism."[14] This is temperance, not prudence. Or rather, as his unconscious
use of "tempered" suggests, it is an amalgam of the know-how to plan and
the willpower to carry out the plan. The one is prudence, the other temperance. Haslam speaks of "the components of prudence having to do with
balance," but immediately admits that they "fall under Aristotle's concept of
moderation"—*sophrosynē* is the word Aristotle used for the virtue; and *to
metron*, the [golden] mean, for the corresponding method.

The ethical tradition of the West, in short, would shuffle some of the
character strengths the psychologists have examined under other headings.
In particular it would place under a *virtue* of prudence some of the

strengths now under "wisdom and knowledge," such as open-mindedness, love of learning, and perspective, and under "humanity" the strength called "social intelligence" and under "justice" the strength called "leadership." It would rename the strength now called "prudence" as "caution," or "impulse control," and leave it under "temperance," where it appears to belong.

But no matter. What is anyway striking is that a group of modern clinical and social psychologists, using largely Western evidence, have on the whole confirmed what ur-Westerners such as Aristotle and especially Aquinas discerned by other means: that the virtues among us Westerners (at least) are these particular seven, and that they work as a system in the best of our lives and the best of our communities.

The philosopher John M. Doris has challenged such systems, calling them the theory of "globalism," the notion that people "have" characters, "robust traits or evaluatively integrated personality structures."[15] He points out the impressive body of evidence from experimental psychology that people are in fact highly sensitive to situation—that an ordinary Ukrainian can be made into an extermination-camp guard reasonably easily. He notes, too, that non-Western societies, such as the Japanese, "interpret behavior more in terms of situations and much less in terms of personal dispositions than is typical in the West."[16] Doris's book is a model of philosophical psychology, even more thorough, if such a thing can be imagined, than Peterson and Seligman, at any rate per person. But in the end he admits that our ethical stories in our culture and our notions of courage and faith are important for ethical judgment. He thinks that being realistic about the stories and the notions, noting how fragile and specifically Western the notion of character is, "tuning down" our virtues, will make us better.[17] Could be, and at any rate a philosophical psychology is one way to find out.

28

ETHICAL STRIVING

I have been claiming in various ways that the seven virtues, or some modernized, tuned down, or tuned up version if you wish—anyway, virtues—are more fundamental than the three strands of modern ethical thought inherited from the European eighteenth century that are still alive in academic circles in the English-speaking world, Kantianism, utilitarianism, and contractarianism.

The excellent little primer on ethics by the late James Rachels begins with a "minimum conception of morality" underlying any ethical system whatsoever. In describing "the conscientious moral agent" at which the analysis must begin, Rachels selects unconsciously from the seven virtues. The conscientious moral agent will be in part "someone who is concerned [love] impartially [justice] with the interests [prudence to discover these] of everyone who is affected [justice, love, faith] . . . ; who carefully sifts facts [prudence again] . . . ; who is willing to 'listen to reason' [justice plus temperance = humility] . . . ; and who, finally, is willing to act on the results [courage]. . . ."[1] Since this is quite an arduous task, a *bonum arduum,* he'd better have hope, too.

That is, ethics must start from an ethical person imagined as the Ethicist, who turns out to have all seven of the Western virtues. Think of how impossible it would be to come to Kantian or utilitarian conclusions if the Ethicist did not already have the character Rachels praises—of concern, impartiality, carefulness, humility, courage, and so forth. He wouldn't give a damn.

The economist Mark White has arrived at a similar conclusion. He says that a Kantian ethical theory posits a prudential and an ethical self, the choice between them being determined by a probability, *p,* that one has the strength of character to follow the ethical self. This seems to fit Kant, and as White points out it also fits John Searle's notion of a "gap" in decision making allowing for free will; one is reminded, too, of Stuart Hampshire's account of free will. But White realizes that something is fishy. "Is the probability distribution, representing one's character, exogenously given? Though that would make things much simpler, I should think not; it is crafted by our upbringing, and even to adulthood one can act to improve his character. Of course, this begs the question: to what goal or end does one improve character?" His reply is that "in the Kantian model . . . we assume that a rational agent's true goal is to be moral."[2] But that is the goal of being a virtuous person.

Annette Baier made a related point about characteristically male ethical theories. "Their version of the justified list of obligations does not ensure the proper care of the young and so does nothing to ensure the stability of the morality in question."[3] It is not merely a matter of demography. It is a matter of more fundamental reproduction, as the Marxists say. Somehow the conscientious moral agent assumed in the theories of Descartes and Kant and Bentham and Rawls must appear on the scene, and must keep appearing generation after generation. "The virtue of being a *loving* parent must supplement the natural duties and the obligations of [mere] justice, if the society is to last beyond the first generation." Imagine a human society with no loving parents. We have some approximations of this horrible prospect in children war-torn and impoverished, boy soldiers or girl prostitutes. One worries—perhaps it is not so—that the outlook for them becoming conscientious moral agents is not very good.

The main argument against an ethics based on God's commandments or psychological or ethical egoism is that they all assume, as Rachels shows, initial positions impossible within their own hypotheses. For instance an Ayn Randian advocate of "ethical egoism"—namely, the belief that one *should* be selfish, hurrah for the buccaneer capitalist, greed is good—will argue that "everyone would be better off if we acted this way." But the rhetoric violates the selfish premise, since it starts from an incongruous concern for "everyone." Epictetus made the same argument against Epicurus.

What is required for any ethics is, of course, a conscientious moral agent, a virtuous person. Kant himself said this. In his *Reflections on Anthropology* he praised "the man who goes to the root of things," and who looks at them "not just from his own point of view but from that of the community," which is to say (wrote Kant), *der Unpartheyische Zuschauer*, which as it happens is precisely the German translation of Adam Smith's ideal character from whom all virtues are said to flow, the impartial spectator.[4]

Kant is here undermining his own ethical program, since the impartial spectator is not *derivable* from maxims. His system is supposed to ground everything in maxims that a rational being would necessarily follow. It doesn't. What Peter Berkowitz said about Kant's political philosophy could also be said of his ethical philosophy, that he "makes practical concessions to virtue and devises stratagems by which virtue, having been formally expelled from politics, is brought back in through the side door."[5] Or as Harry Frankfurt puts it,

> There can be no well-ordered inquiry into the question of how one has to reason to live [such as Kant's], because the prior question of how to identify and to evaluate the reasons that are pertinent [that is, those favored by a conscientious moral agent, the impartial spectator] in deciding how one should live cannot be settled until it has first been settled how one should live. . . . The pan-rationalist fantasy of demonstrating from the ground up how we have most reason to live is incoherent and must be abandoned.[6]

I note a parallel in epistemology to this inability to hoist oneself as an ethical or political theorist up out of the horizon of character. In parallel with Rachels's conscientious moral agent, White's high *p* decision maker, Baier's well-raised ethical adult, or Kant's *Unpartheyische Zuschauer*, what is required for science is a conscientious scientist. This has been said recently by Hillary Putnam and others, and by me following them for economics.[7]

No mere method works. A good citizen of your own science requires ethics just as does a good citizen of your country or of your neighborhood or of your family. Nothing like what I have been calling a "pocket-sized card," such as the categorical imperative or the greatest happiness principle or contractualism or the alleged rules of scientific method, gets us to where we want to get by way of good scientific citizenship. What prevents us from being misled by other scientists is not the National Science Foundation or the referee system or the method of science, as splendid as these all are, but the courage, hope, faith, justice, love, temperance, and prudence of our colleagues.[8]

If the field of "science studies"—the children and grandchildren of Thomas Kuhn who have flourished in history, sociology, and philosophy since the 1960s—had to be summarized in a sentence, it would be "Scientists are human beings." Scientists are not parts of a machine, or functionaries in a house of intellect. They are socialized, moral agents, more or less conscientious, equipped more or less with prudence, temperance, justice, courage, love, faith, and hope.

It is still conventional among scientists themselves to cling to the idea that, say, the referee system mechanically assures good outcomes through Prudence Only—even while complaining under their breaths about the idiocy or the moral turpitude of their editors and referees. In his popular book about how he used mitochondrial DNA to trace the ancestry of Europeans, Bryan Sykes claims that "it is only during the review process prior to publication that the assumptions and interpretations are thoroughly checked." Uh-huh. Any scientist who has participated in such a "process" knows that it is okay, all right, on-the-whole-desirable, coming close to the standards of Ralph's Pretty Good Grocery—but quite far from the Baconian antirhetorical fantasy of "thoroughly checking the assumptions and interpretations."

Sykes's piety does not fit his own experience, at least as he recounts it. He describes in detail how one Erika Hagelburg challenged his technique. He calls her, by the way, "Erika" throughout. One is uneasily reminded of James Watson's calling Rosalind Franklin "Rosy," which nobody but Watson in *The Double Helix* ever called her. It was a rhetorical technique for downplaying the standing of a woman scientist with claims to rival Watson's. Watson doesn't call any male enemy "Chuck" or "Bob."[9]

Still, judging only from Sykes's account, it would seem that Dr. Hagelburg was perfidious. Sykes had hired her and trained her. Yet she turned on him, he claims, and then, he claims, would not show him the data she used to attack his technique. "I am sad to report"—more in sorrow than in anger, you see—"that my requests for [her] samples to verify . . . did not produce results."[10] But wait: isn't the referee process supposed to prevent all this, automatically, by Prudence Only? Isn't it a "process" without human and ethical intervention other than Max U? Erika Hagelburg's coauthored 1999 paper attacking mitochondrial methods after all was published in "the prestigious" *Proceedings of the Royal Society.* Wouldn't that automatically activate the scientific method?

The so-called scientific method—I speak as an economic scientist and as a partisan of the science-studies view—does not work. Good science like other good human behavior depends on virtues, on human character. The idea is Aristotelian. As Ralph McInerny puts it, "In the *Ethics*, Aristotle treats moral virtues first and sees them as dispositive to and presupposed by the intellectual virtues."[11] Thus we observe scientists with large ethical flaws, such as the great biologist James Watson or the great statistician Ronald A. Fisher or the great psychologist Cyril Burt or the great economist George Stigler, and are inclined to suspect their science. Our suspicions are sometimes confirmed. On the other hand we would be very surprised to find anything untoward in the work of great scientists we know to be good also in the ethical sense, whether or not we agree with them: in biology E. O. Wilson, for example, or in economics Thomas Schelling or Barbara Bergmann or Milton Friedman, or in history John Hope Franklin or William McNeill.

Since 1980 a small group of philosophers have been advocating in fact "virtue epistemology." Justified belief, as much as good behavior, they argue, depends on such virtues as "intellectual carefulness, thoroughness, humility, courage, trust, autonomy, or fairness."[12] Elizabeth Anscombe in 1958 suggested that we give up the notion of "moral duty." "It would be a great improvement if, instead of 'morally wrong,' one always named a genus such as 'untruthful,' 'unchaste,' 'unjust.'"[13]

Similarly in epistemology Richard Rorty suggested in 1987 that we give up "Truth," and substitute in a similar way the pragmatic reasons for believing.[14] In a later essay, "Ethics without Principles," he drew the analogy explicitly: "The trouble with aiming at truth [that is, Truth, capital *T*] is that you do not know when you have reached it, even if you had in fact reached it. But you can aim at ever more justification, the assuagement of ever more doubt. Analogously, you cannot aim at 'doing what is right,' because you will never know whether you have hit the mark. . . . You cannot aim at being at the end of inquiry, either in physics or in ethics."[15] You can make more and more persuasive arguments about physics or politics, and you can make yourself more and more virtuous as a physicist or citizen. The virtue epistemologists are combining the two projects of a pragmatic epistemology and a pragmatic virtue ethics.

My quantitative, economist's way of saying this is a little diagram. Imagine small-*t*, provisional truth in any field of inquiry measured on the vertical axis and our years of patient inquiry measured along the horizontal. At the Second Coming I have no doubt that all will be revealed, namely, the

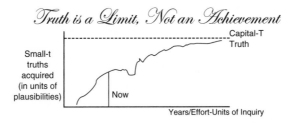

Truth is a Limit, Not an Achievement

capital-*T* Truth of human ancestry or colloidal physics or economic history. We await that day full of hope, Christ's reign of a thousand years.

But clearly we have not arrived there yet. I repeat: if the experience over the past century and a half with non-Euclidean geometry and Einsteinian physics and Gödel's Proof does not persuade you of this, you are not persuadable by reasoning or evidence. Repent, and remember William Thomson, Lord Kelvin, who scorned Darwin because physics in the 1890s was in his opinion finished, by that very Lord Kelvin. Using the rigid consequence of c. 1890 physical logic, the sun, he asserted on the eve of the discovery of atomic energy, could not possibly have had enough chemical energy to accommodate the eons necessary for Darwin's absurd theory.

So we are approaching Truth only asymptotically, if by some hopeful miracle we in fact are "approaching" rather than "unconsciously receding from" it. All we can do is to try out ways of keeping the curve tilting onward and upward. Or so we imagine for the nonce.

The Scientific Revolution, practiced as a messy mixture of ego and instrumentation and politics, appears to have been a lurch in the direction of Truth. The scientific method reported to you in high school, sad to say, often has not. For instance, it stopped progress in geology for fifty years after the first proposal in 1915 of plate tectonics. It has stopped progress in many fields of economics, by recommending for the past fifty years—on a mistaken view of how real science works, admittedly—existence theorems without calibration and statistical significance without loss functions. The phony economics thus generated is about to collapse, *deo volente*, and will leave the real stuff. The referee system, too, has ruined some areas of scholarship, by substituting dull normal science for intriguing and thought-provoking results. The fetish of the double-blind experiment in medicine has killed tens of thousands of patients in order to tidy up the publication records of medical scientists. That too must collapse, because it is hideously unethical.

We don't know the dimensions of the diagram. We do not know right now how close we are to God's Truth, because in order to know we would have to be already in possession of it. As Stuart Hampshire put it, "A thoroughly and consistently naturalistic account of the limits of human knowledge will stop short of making any inference from the actual structures of knowledge, now in our possession, to the permanent structures of reality."[16] Or of Reality. For the same reason we do not really know whether this or that argument or piece of evidence drives us closer to T, or away from it. But no matter. We toil on, and seek the light, and try to listen, really listen to the arguments of our fellows.

There's a similar asymptotic diagram for the Good. We have attained some level of small-g good, and struggle in our local, contingent ways to keep on some path plausibly pointed at the Good. Strictly speaking, as Rorty says, you cannot aim at it for sure, because you never know if you have hit it. Witch burners in the Rhineland in 1610 were quite sure that the Good was served by their activities, and most people agreed with them. Eugenicists in 1910 were quite sure that compulsory sterilization and the like were Good, and most people agreed with them. We are shooting at targets in the dark.

The two diagrams seem to be related. If we isolate one from the other, neither works. An immoral life in science drifts away from Truth and Good, *simultaneously.* The only rule of method is to toil and seek, honestly. Oddly, this rather obvious truth about the advance of knowledge was known at one time in Western culture. But it was then forgotten, indeed, spurned, at about the same time that rhetoric and the ethics of the virtues became deeply unfashionable. The theologian Ellen Charry argues that in the "modern, secularized construal of truth . . . knowing the truth no longer implied loving it, wanting it, and being transformed by it, because the truth no longer brings the knower to God but to [the] use [of] information to subdue nature."[17] Remember the etymology of "belief" as "beloved." Earlier Christian thinkers,

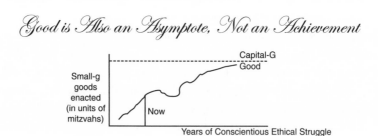

Good is Also an Asymptote, Not an Achievement

such as Aquinas, "could not envision a notion of truth that is not salutary, . . . for if something is harmful to us, it must be false and certainly cannot be the truth of God."[18] Charry recommends "the pre-seventeenth-century theologians, who wrote before the modern disjoining of truth, beauty, and goodness took hold."[19] So do I, and T. S. Eliot.

If you want a good career, of course, you can follow the script of James Watson in *The Double Helix*. "A generation of graduate students," wrote Anne Sayre about Watson's teaching, "learned a lesson: the old morality is dead, and they had . . . been told about its demise by . . . an up-to-date hero who clearly know more about how science was acceptably 'done' than the old-fashioned types who prattled about 'ethics.' "[20] To the contrary, said Ronald Coase, a Nobel prize winner in economics (b. 1910): "My mother taught me to be honest and truthful."[21] In the same volume James Buchanan (b. 1919), speaks of a teacher in graduate school who "instilled in me the moral standards of the research process. . . . [S]omething that seems so often absent in the training of economists of the post-war decades."[22] That's about all the method we can handle.

Beyond the academic analysis, for whatever the analysis is worth, each virtue has behind it a library of human stories. Robert Hariman notes that in answering the question What is to Be Done, one can answer with Aristotle and the philosophers up to Kant, "Look for rules." Or one can answer with Sophocles, Thucydides, and the sophists up to Jane Austen and Iris Murdoch, "Look for exemplars," that is, human models of prudence or justice or love.[23] Plutarch, for example, most of whose surviving work is ethical theorizing, was in his *Lives* steadily ethical, inspiring medieval saints' lives and modern mythologies of national heroes, William Tell to the Blessed JFK.

We are still writing them, filming them, singing them, retelling the stories in the women's gossip or the men's instant replays. It is not merely the abstract, Aquinian analysis of, say, courage that forms an ethical tradition of resistance to fear, of course. It is the stories of particular courages, in our particular faiths, Western or Eastern or Northern or Southern: anyway particular.

The old children's encyclopedia *The Book of Knowledge* (1911) had sections in each of its twenty big volumes called "The Book of Golden Deeds" focused on the faithful courage of, say, Father Damien, a Belgian missionary to the South Sea lepers, or the just courage of Sir Samuel Baker, "an intrepid

English traveler, who, with his brave young wife, went to the stronghold of the [slave] traffic in Africa, and grappled with it there," or hundreds of other tales of derring-do. It is 1911, remember, and the place is London for the British edition and New York for the American. In 1911 even sophisticated parents in the English-speaking world would not laugh out loud at the description of Sir Samuel's "British pluck," or of "the gallant Lady Baker, the first white woman ever to visit these parts, [who] supported him heroically in his determination."[24]

The volumes are drenched in ethical stories in the style of the violent, imperialist, muscular-Christian, and neopagan courage-worshiping world about to be blown to pieces at Verdun. "The Child's Book of the United States" in the same volume 14 reproduces a painting of Commodore Perry at Lake Erie, together with a sophisticated criticism of the painter's inaccuracies, since the painter was of course not there. The narrative ends with Perry's "We have met the enemy, they are ours: two ships, two brigs, one schooner and one sloop." "The Child's Book of Famous Stories" gives a vivid précis of *The Count of Monte Cristo*, ending with the novel's last sentence: "'My friend,' said Valentine, 'has not the count just told us that all human wisdom is contained in these two words—*wait* and *hope*?'" No wonder that the bourgeois boys and girls in the 1910s and 1920s who consumed such stuff grew up in the 1930s and 1940s to be saints of stoicism, and in the 1950s and 1960s the conquerors of suburbia.[25]

What makes "courage" applicable to us humans or to us Chicagoans or to us English-speaking bourgeois children 1911–1955—and not merely to abstracted rational beings from nowhere in particular—are such stories, our own stories, much beloved, "real" or imagined, the stories of Father Damien, of Lady Baker, of Shane, of Horatius at the bridge, of Jeanne d'Arc in 1431 refusing it is usually claimed on pain of death to reassume women's clothing, of Bishop Hugh Latimer in 1555 remarking calmly to his stake-mate as the torch was applied, "Be of good comfort, Mr. Ridley, and play the man. We shall this day light such a candle by God's grace in England as I trust shall never be put out." What makes someone South Asian is not merely an abstract belief in the doctrine of transmigration of souls but a cherished remembrance of stories from the Puranas, even if transmitted mainly through Bollywood. What makes someone Japanese is not merely a theoretical devotion to the doctrines of Zen but a familiarity with the stories of the Noh, Kyogen, and Kabuki theater, even if transmitted mainly through comic books.

William J. Bennett recognized correctly in *The Book of Virtues: A Treasury of Great Moral Stories* (1993) that we learn to be good or bad, of course, much, much less from philosophical precept or religious commandment than from example and story. For instance, the little children can learn from the example of that same William J. Bennett, who admitted to "going too far" in losing $8 million in a year gambling on slot machines. That's going too far, kids, gambling away the royalty income from *The Book of Virtues*.[26] Similar lessons can be learned from a distinguished line of American right-wing critics of 1960s morality, Jim Bakker caught embezzling, Jimmy Swaggart caught with prostitutes, Newt Gingrich caught lying about adultery with an aide while pressing Congress to punish President Clinton for lying about adultery with an aide, Rush Limbaugh caught with controlled substances, Bill O'Reilly caught falsifying his vita and abusing a female employee, Tom DeLay caught violating Texas election law and accepting bribes from foreign agents. Do what I say, little children.

Willy Loman the salesman asks of his flawed, beloved eldest son Biff, "Why is he stealing? What did I tell him? I never in my life told him anything but decent things."[27] But Willy told Biff the precepts in doubled proverbs, *A* and not-*A*: "Never leave a job till you're finished—remember that." *Looking toward the 'big trees':* "Biff, up in Albany I saw a beautiful hammock. . . . Wouldn't that be something? Just swingin' there under those branches. Boy, that would be," and his voice trails off.[28] Finish a job; but swing in a hammock. Work hard; but take it easy. Willy advises Biff as an adult how to ask for a big job: "A business suit, and talk as little as possible, and don't crack any jokes"; a few sentences later: "Walk in with a big laugh. Don't look worried. Start off with a couple of good stories to lighten things up. It's not what you say but how you say it—because personality always wins the day," though not for Willy. "And don't say 'Gee.' 'Gee' is a boy's word. A man walking in for fifteen thousand dollars does not say 'Gee!'"[29] Four pages later, at the end of the act, he says to Biff, "Gee, look at the moonlight moving between the buildings!"

Earlier the boys—Biff and the conventionally petit-bourgeois Happy—are in high school:

> *Biff:* Did you see the new football I got?
> *Willy, examining the ball:* Where'd you get a new ball?
> *Biff:* The coach told me to practice my passing.
> *Willy:* That so? And he gave you the ball, heh?

Biff: Well, I borrowed it from the locker room. *He laughs confidentially.*
Willy, laughing with him at the theft: I want you to return that.
Happy: I told you he wouldn't like it!
Biff, angrily: Well, I'm bringing it back!
Willy, stopping the incipient argument, to Happy: Sure, he's gotta practice with a regulation ball, doesn't he? *To Biff:* Coach'll probably congratulate you on your initiative![30]

Willy—unsuccessful, bourgeois Willy Low Man who aches for something big—can't coach his eldest son to the role that brother Happy accepts, unhappily, of minor, ethical functionary in capitalism. Biff remains an insolent serf stealing from the lord's barn, or from the lumberyard where the boys work summers. Yet Willy admires this in Biff. At least Biff lashes out, exercising a faux-aristocratic nerve:

Willy: You shoulda seen the lumber they brought home last week. At least a dozen six-by-eights worth all kinds a money.
Charley: Listen, if that watchman—
Willy: I gave them hell, understand. But I got a couple of fearless characters there.
Charley: Willy, the jails are full of fearless characters.[31]

To which Willy's faux-grand-bourgeois brother Ben, "success incarnate," a very Ben Franklin, speaking from Willy's imagination, adds, "And the stock exchange, friend!" They all do it, the big guys.

Willy can recommend the virtues only piecemeal: courage to steal boldly, but then separately, independently, in contradiction to that precept, justice to refrain from stealing; hope to venture on studying for the regents' exam, but then separately and unconnectedly the temperance to stick to it.

As the economist and feminist philosopher Irene van Staveren notes in a penetrating analysis of the play, "Willy's dream mixes up different values."[32] Willy and his son would do better if they could live the virtues as a system, out of a character good as a whole—as does indeed Willy's friend Charley, and Charley's studious son Bernard, who cannot persuade his friend Biff to study for the high-school exam.

Robert Hariman notes that the system comes also from formulating rules, but recommends with Richard Lanham, I have noted, a "toggling" between exemplars and rules.[33] It's like solving a differential equation or writing a sonnet or running an experiment. None are rule-bound to the point of automaticity, though rules are helpful here and there. Let's see: $y' + R(x)y = S(x)yk$; hmm: can it be made linear? Let's see: ninth line; time to start the sestet. Let's see: a delicate laboratory balance; uh-oh—will traffic outside the laboratory affect the result?

Van Staveren argues that "Willy invested in the capabilities of freedom but did not invest in the capabilities belonging to the domains of justice and care. . . . Without a commitment to care Willy is no longer able to sustain relationships with his clients."[34] That seems right. But she does not think, and neither do I, that the economistic vocabulary of "investing" is going to reduce ethical growth to a formula. The search for rule-bound certitude became an intellectual obsession in Europe as faith receded. The ancient case for a full theory of the separate virtues, as against a pocket-sized card, is that the named virtues are the lives of humans.

29

ETHICAL REALISM

The virtues in the moral universe within really do exist, as much as those starry skies above. We claim to be "realists" of whatever sort because we want to be able to use against others the rhetorical turn of declaring that "such and such [which we wish to hold] is really the case, True." For example, we will want to if we are German pioneers of scientific history *wie es eigentlich gewesen*, "as it actually was."

There is no known test for whether we as historians of, say, the Battle of Gettysburg are in possession of the battle's Reality, that *Wesen*. We can test whether we have this or that fact right—Lee was suffering from a heart problem, Longstreet had a cold, a professor of rhetoric was in command at Little Roundtop. But the number of particular facts about the battle is infinite. As John Keegan observes, the history of a battle has a "rhetoric" that involves choosing from the infinitude of particulars some few facts considered important.[1] The only test for importance is our human rhetoric. There is no standpoint outside of humanity from which we can view the truth. The freshman who wrote on the final exam that "all history is bias because we can't get outside our human point of view" was, as freshman often are, unconsciously wise.

We are all in this sense realists. The warrant for Reality is that the statement "*X* is really true"—for example, the truth that Lee did not go right because of his illness—amounts to saying that "in our rhetorical community one *should* at least admit *X*." For example, among us serious students of the battle, Marse Roberts is agreed to have been ill in July 1863, and his illness is agreed to have been crucial.

The kind of realist I am, and am recommending that you admit you are, is an ethical realist. By this I do not mean that I am good, and you, if you do not agree, are bad. I mean that these agreements about Reality, such as the reality about the Battle of Gettysburg, are ethical judgments, things that we assert together we *should* believe in.

We all admit, whatever our philosophical convictions, that the table before us is real (small *r*) and that if we step heedlessly into the Oostzeedijk in Rotterdam on a busy Monday morning we are likely to get run down by a bicycle or a car or a tram. I don't think that serious philosophical disagreements are really—there it is again, signaling again a feature of our speech community—about such matters. The material realists, opposed to the ethical realists, are fond of invoking the solidity of the table or the dangers of the Oostzeedijk Straat to criticize other philosophers. They say, "You would not for a moment survive out there without believing in our kind of Realism." But notice that material realist philosophers are not any better at surviving the Oostzeedijk than are relativists and postmodernists like me. So it must be that the anti-material realists *and* the material realists themselves are really talking about something other than tables and trams.

I say they are talking about ethics, and I say it's a good thing. An *ethical* realist says that what we know is not the objective world. She points out that there is no known test, to repeat, for whether we have correctly attached our words to the reality of Gettysburg. To put it philosophically, there is no known test for ultimate ontology. And in any case, as literary critics note, the notion of "attaching" words to reality is a metaphor, since words are words, not "reality." The statement "the cat is on the mat" is not the same thing as the fact of the cat being on the mat. The ethical realist therefore wants to give up the 2,500-year-old project of finding the test for attachment between ways of saying things and Reality. It has not worked out, the hopeful project to find "Reality with the big R, reality that makes the timeless claim, reality to which defeat can't happen," as William James put it.[2] As Richard Rorty puts it, "It might, of course, have turned out otherwise. People have, oddly enough, found something interesting to say about the essence of Force and the definition of 'number.' They might have found something interesting to say about the essence of Truth. But in fact they haven't."[3]

To this the material realists reply that their claim of True statements on the one hand and Real existence on the other, and a Brooklyn Bridge of epistemology between the two, are necessary to prevent "permissiveness" and, as they invariably put it, "anything goes." They fear a "lack of discipline." Their fear is neurotic and authoritarian. As James observed, "The rationalist, radically taken, is of a doctrinaire and authoritative complexion: the phrase 'must be' is ever on its lips."[4] The material realists sound like a Monty Python skit on sado-masochism. John Cleese as the philosopher. And look: when the material realists become indignant about the terrible sophists like James and Rorty and McCloskey they are making an *ethical* claim that it is bad not to be a material realist. As I said.

I have been saying so for quite a while, but have only recently grasped what I was saying. In the first edition of *The Rhetoric of Economics* (1985) I wrote,

> You are more strongly persuaded that it is wrong to murder than that inflation is always and everywhere a monetary phenomenon. . . . To deny the comparison is to deny that reason and the partial certitude it can bring applies to nonscientific subjects, a common but unreasonable opinion. There is no reason why the . . . pseudoscientific [assertion such as that] "at the .05 level the coefficient on M in a regression . . . is insignificantly different from 1.0" . . . should take over the whole of persuasiveness, leaving moral persuasiveness incomparably inferior to it.[5]

I was reflecting Wayne Booth's demonstration that to make ethics into "mere" opinion is a mistake.[6] Then I discovered that other people had said approximately the same thing. The philosopher Hilary Putnam, for example, declared that "to claim of any statement that it is true . . . is, roughly, to claim that it would be justified were epistemic conditions good enough" and that "in my fantasy of myself as a metaphysical super-hero, all 'facts' would dissolve onto 'values.' . . . To say that a belief is justified is to say that it is what we ought to believe; justification is a normative notion on the face of it."[7]

Realism is a social, that is, a rhetorical, that is, an ethical necessity for any science. "Men demonstrate their rationality," wrote Stephen Toulmin in 1972, "not by ordering their concepts and beliefs in tidy formal structures, but by their preparedness to respond to novel situations with open minds."[8] Compare the virtue of humility. Such a definition of "rationality" casts in a new light the conventional philosophy of science about "rationally reconstructed research programs." The philosopher and social psychologist Rom Harré wrote in 1986 that "knowledge claims are tacitly prefixed with a performative of trust."[9] Compare the virtues of justice and good faith. The economist Marc Blaug, who in other moods and in the same book supports the conventional philosophy of science, agrees: "There are no empirical, descriptive is-statements regarded as true that do not rely on a definite social consensus that we 'ought' to accept that is-statement."[10]

The claim of neopositivists like Blaug, however, is that we can hedge off the ethical claims of scientific practice from ethics more generally. The philosopher Daniel Hausman and the economist Michael McPherson assert that answers to questions of fact in science can be given by a social consensus "in which the answers are not influenced by any values apart from those which are part of the science itself."[11] As Andrew Yuengert puts it in quoting them, "This is a claim that economists who disagree on 'ethical' goals like commitment to the poor can still agree on shared standards of economic inquiry—parsimony, a commitment to mathematical formalism, and so forth." Yuengert and I do not think so. Indeed, as Yuengert notes, Hausman and McPherson themselves immediately criticize that version of the claim: "To speak of a 'value-free' inquiry," they write, "may be misleading. It suggests that the *conduct* of the inquiry is value-free. But the conduct of inquiry cannot possibly be value-free. Inquiring involves action, and action is motivated by values."[12] Justification is a normative notion on the face of it. Knowledge claims are tacitly prefixed with a performative of trust. Therefore a social consensus in a science, like a social consensus in a corporation or a marketplace or political community, is motivated by values. The science presupposes virtues. The values of parsimony, mathematics, and so forth are not "part of the science itself" in a sense independent of virtues. If we want a real science we are presupposing real virtues.

In the fall of 1997 as a new Christian I started to read C. S. Lewis again. As a bookish adolescent, at the recommendation of my agnostic father, I had read *The Screwtape Letters* (1942), and much later as an adult Lewis's autobiography, *Surprised by Joy* (1956). But in 1997 with more focused intent I read *Mere Christianity* (1952, based on lectures delivered during the war). Early in the book Lewis is arguing for the reality of ethics, a moral law beyond convention or evolutionary prudence: "There is one thing, and one only, in the whole universe which we know more about than we could learn from external observation. That one thing is Man. . . . In this case we have, so to speak, inside information. . . . And because of that, we know that men find themselves under a moral law, which they did not make, and cannot quite forget even when they try, and which they know they ought to obey."[13]

We do not know about Reality, the *Wesen*, in any way that would elevate it above mere pragmatic reality with a small *r*. But we do know, Lewis is arguing, the extrapositivistic fact about our ethical selves. I think, therefore I self-judge.

As you might expect, Lewis draws theistic conclusions from the fact. But a prejudice against belief in God need not stand in the way of admitting Lewis's observation: what we really know is ethical. Iris Murdoch, who was not a Christian, wrote that "the possession of a moral sense is uniquely human, . . . 'as if it came to use from elsewhere.' It is an intimation of 'something higher.'"[14] Her system of scare quotes suggests some unease not shared by Lewis. But the point, I repeat, can be given an entirely nonspooky rationale. As Stuart Hampshire put it, "There is a distinct kind of knowledge which a person normally has of her own conduct and intentions."[15] What we know together as reality is what we should agree on for practical purposes, such as crossing the Oostzeedijk. What we Know as Reality, if anything at that exalted level, is *only* ethical. We Know Ought, not Is.

In *The Critique of Practical Reason* (1788) Kant makes a similar point, most gloriously. Ask a man who claims that he operates only under material compulsion, and that he has no freedom to act ethically against, say, an opportunity for gratifying lust, "if a gallows were erected before the house where he finds this opportunity, in order that he should be hanged thereon immediately after the gratification of his lust, whether he could not then control his passion; we need not be long in doubt what he would reply." So far the behaviorist man is acting in a manner consistent with his behaviorist, antiethicist theory. He resists the lust merely because he is an Epicurean, merely because gratification-plus-hanging is materially unpleasant. He is a Prudence-Only economist.

> Ask him, however, if his sovereign ordered him, on pain of the same immediate execution, to bear false witness against an honorable man, whom the prince might wish to destroy under a plausible pretext, would he consider it possible in that case to overcome his love of life, however great it may be. He would perhaps not venture to affirm whether he would do so or not, but he must unhesitatingly admit that it is possible to do so. He judges, therefore, that he can do a certain thing because he is conscious that he ought, and he recognizes that he is free—a fact which but for the moral law he would never have known.[16]

Perhaps we know the starry skies above. Perhaps we know what we instrumentally prefer to consume. But we most assuredly know the moral law within.

30

AGAINST REDUCTION

The life of reason or utility or even contract or some versions of natural law would apply equally, I've noted, to six-headed creatures from a planet in another galaxy as they would to human beings. Contrary to the Cartesianism of eighteenth-century and some later thought, the alleged universalism of modern ethical thought from Kant to Rawls and Nozick is bad, not good. We do not need literally universal theories of ethics, any more than we need universal theories of cuisine, covering also food for silicon-based creatures, or of psychology, covering also the behavior of angels. We need—declare the feminist ethicists, for example—not a theory of rationally prudent agents, but a theory of French people and of Europeans and of moderns, who are prudent within other virtues and vices.

The trick is to find a useful middle ground—a golden mean, you might say—between on the one hand an ethical theory like "Act on the maxim which can at the same time be made a universal law," which, Kant asserted proudly, would apply to any rational creature whatever, and on the other hand an ethical theory like "When a calf, a lamb, or a kid is born, it must not be taken from its mother for seven days," which would apply only to followers of Moses after the thirteenth century BC. You can of course choose to carry on with every one of the 613 commandments of Moses, or some Conservative or Reform selection. But presumably you follow these only because you follow a higher and more general, *yet still specifically Jewish and human and nonuniversal*, law: for example, "I am the Lord thy God," the God who tells about himself in the Hebrew Bible, the God of Moses and the prophets, the one we Jews have been discussing now for three millennia, that one.

You can opt for the categorical imperative instead. But at such a high level of abstraction the justification flies off into interstellar space. It's too general. The laws of gravity were of course the inspiration for the law-seeking of Kant and Bentham and of practically everyone else in the West in the eighteenth century. The laws of gravity apply to Earthbound things but also to interstellar space. Amazing. So you can expect to get *something* from an ethical theory that claims to apply universally, as one can get something from thinking of the flight of a cannonball using $F = ma$. But in the ethical case, not much. And for actual artillery on a battlefield having on the very day air resistance at a pressure of 1025 millibars and 85 percent humidity and an 11 kilometers breeze from the north-northwest and a southern-hemisphere Coriolis effect, you are going to have to modify the ideal parabola derived from $F = ma$ in a vacuum quite a lot, too, if you wish to economize on cannonballs and avoid collateral damage. That has been the trouble with ethical theorizing in a vacuum since Kant (or Plato). A bit like epistemological thinking since Kant (or Plato). Or political thinking. Or metaphysical.

Benthamism is particularly hardy. Whole classes of professors find it impossible to think of the Good except as something reducible to an index that aggregates emotions (so-called love, courage, etc.) into one Utility. Mill said of Bentham that "no one who . . . ever attempted to give a rule to all human conduct, set out with a more limited conception either of the agencies by which human conduct *is,* or of those by which it should be, influenced."[1] Bentham and his modern professorial followers can't see why one would need, say, seven virtues, unless they are summed into one, and the one is then used to make choices. Pick the bundle of "virtues" that maximizes utility. Simple.

The more sophisticated among the mathematically inclined economists will speak of "Debreu's representation theorem," after the Nobel-winning economist who perfected the argument. We are back, they will say, to the completeness, transitivity, and continuity required of an ordering of baskets to allow the maximization. If we include empathy in the utility function of an otherwise self-interested actor, the economists put it, we are back in a world in which cost and benefit are easily calculated—easily at least in conception. Cooperation in a repeated prisoner's dilemma, Brutus dooming his sons, a child caring for dying puppies, or even suicide bombers in some higher cause, can all be explained simply with empathetic motives. Empathy is the omitted variable with which one could eventually mop up the omitted variable bias when acquiring the econometric dataset of one's dreams.[2]

So the modern mathematical and econometric economist. But it doesn't work. The economist has merely renamed as tastes, preferences, empathy the thing to be explained. As Robert Frank notes, "When a man dies shortly after drinking the used crankcase oil from his car, we do not really explain anything by asserting that he must have had a powerful taste for crankcase oil."[3] Amartya Sen puts it so: "If a person does exactly the opposite of what would help achieving what he or she would want to achieve, and does this with flawless consistency, . . . the person can scarcely be seen as rational."[4] Making "empathy" or "a powerful taste" or "consistency = rationality" into an all-purpose motive that explains everything else is unhelpful. We've renamed Love "empathy." And for what scientific gain? *Alors?*

But further: Love is not love, I have noted, not the best sort of love for another human and certainly not Aristotle's or Jesus' or C. S. Lewis's highest sort, if it is utilitarian. Brigid O'Shaughnessy has almost run out of arguments to persuade Sam Spade to let her go:

> She put her hands up to his cheeks and drew his face down again. "Look at me," she said, "and tell me the truth. Would you have done this to me if the falcon had been real and you had been paid your money?" . . .
>
> He moved his shoulders a little and said, "Well, a lot of money would have been at least one more item on the other side of the scales."
>
> She put her face up to his face. Her mouth was slightly open with lips a little thrust out. She whispered: "If you loved me you'd need nothing more on that side."[5]

That's right. Orderings and trade-offs of material things are irrelevant to True Love. It's not for sale.

But Spade will not be persuaded: "Dreading the role of the chump," says Robert Frank in making such a point in the general case, "we are often loath to heed our nobler instincts."[6] Or more exactly, we let one nobility trump another. Loyalty to his profession as a detective, faith in his identity as a *non*chump, Spade says, wins against putative love. True Love—or True Patriotism or True Courage or True Faith or True Anything—is not an input into something else, or else it is not True.

"It is in the nature of loving," Harry Frankfurt observes, "that we consider its objects to be valuable in themselves and to be important to use for their own sakes" (compare Aristotle's notion of friendship).[7] So says theology, literature, Patsy Cline, and all characterizations of humans that are not based on an analogy with accounting—one more item on that side of the scales—that is, prudence. "If a strength [of character, one of the twenty-four they identify] is recognized only when it produces a payoff," as Peterson and Seligman argue, "we do not need the notion of good character to account for human conduct. We can return to a radical behaviorism and speak only of prevailing rewards and punishments. But as Aristotle and other philosophers concerned with virtue persuasively argue, actions undertaken solely for external reasons cannot be considered virtuous, because they are coaxed or coerced, carroted or sticked."[8]

The impulse to find some prudential seed for so-called virtues is modern. Benjamin Franklin himself claimed famously to be governed by Prudence Only, a rhetoric popular by the time he composed the first part of his *Autobiography*. As Tocqueville said, "In the United States as . . . elsewhere people are sometimes seen to give way to those disinterested . . . impulses . . . ; but the Americans seldom admit [it]. . . . They are more anxious to do honor to their philosophy than to themselves."[9] Like that of his countrymen, Franklin's rhetoric was false. In his life he was a good friend and a good citizen, just and courageous, hopeful and temperate. He was not perfect, but he was not a Prudence Only machine, not at all. Max Weber, D. H. Lawrence, William Carlos Williams, and even the perspicacious Alasdair MacIntyre don't grasp this about their "pattern American."

Even very sensible philosophers want nowadays to deny such observations by reducing every virtue to prudence. In his last book Robert Nozick tried to argue that "ethics exists because at least sometimes it is possible to coordinate actions to mutual benefit."[10] Or: "Ethics arises when frequently or importantly there are situations offering opportunities for mutual benefit from coordinated activity." And a utilitarian—which Nozick was not—would say that "since cooperation to mutual benefit is the function of ethics, the only thing that matters is . . . the size of the social pie."

But after sixty-four closely reasoned pages, Nozick is left worrying that ethics must have something more. The reason he gets into trouble is that he makes the characteristically modern philosophical mistake of simply defining ethics as "concerning interpersonal relations."[11] That is, his main argument has no place for the virtues of self-improvement or of devotion to a transcendent. It is a middle-level ethics, neither at the hope-faith-love top or the temperance-courage bottom, but aimed at Justice implemented with prudence. It is entirely about economics, that is, about "Pareto optimality," about mutually beneficial deals. The ethical object is the other people in the deal, not ever oneself or God.

But I said Nozick was sensible. And it is hard to imagine a more intellectually honest person. So occasionally he breaks into praise for the alternative ethical objects, as though realizing uneasily that his reduction to prudent deals has not sufficed. He distinguishes four "levels or layers of ethics," referring to a treatment in his semipopular book, *The Examined Life* (1989).[12] The first, or lowest, is the mutual benefit on which Nozick spends most of his analytic effort in *Invariances* (2001), Pareto optimality, the ethic of respect. The next highest is an ethic of responsibility, discussed also in his 1981 book, *Philosophical Explanations*.[13] The next is an ethic of caring, Nozick's version of love. And the highest is an ethic of Light, "truth, goodness, beauty, holiness," or in other words the ethics of faith, hope, and transcendent love.[14]

Nozick admits that he has no account of how the levels relate, or why he should always refer to the ethics of respect as basic—except on the not unreasonable political grounds that it is the least controversial. He has no acquaintance with the virtue ethicists. They are never referred to by this most ethically obsessed of the analytic philosophers—the two references to Bernard Williams in *Invariances* are on matters of metaphysics, not ethics. Aristotle is discussed only briefly as an ethical theorist; Aquinas is not mentioned in any work of Nozick, nor are any other virtue ethicists.[15] He appears not to have read with any care Smith's *The Theory of Moral Sentiments*. *Invariances* speaks of Smith's favorite book on one occasion, as holding a theory of the "ideal observer," a misquotation placed in quotation marks—the phrase is the "impartial spectator," not the "ideal observer." And the passage construes the notion in Smith as being about "moral" matters having to do with other people, not the self-shaping temperance that is the chief theme of *The Theory*.[16]

Nozick, like Frankfurt and other mainline English-speaking analytic philosophers, finds himself trapped at the bottom of a Kantian well, unable to clamber up to the virtue-ethical fields of flowers lying round it.

Modern students of the economics of religion note that religious affiliation is like a social club.[17] Caught again attending to utility, eh, Mr. Churchgoer? Some part of behavior is explained this way, by accounting for cost and benefit. My grandmother religiously attended and generously contributed to the Congregational Church in St. Joseph, Michigan, for seven decades with, she claimed, no high motive of faith or hope in mind. She said, "I go to church for the social life." All right, Granny, I see. And what's the harm? Churches and synagogues and temples are vital institutions in America, standing between the individual and the state, said Tocqueville, providing social services if nothing else.

But the Congregationalists in England and Holland in 1620 who fled for the New World were not in it for the good bridge games. Nor indeed are piously believing Congregationalists now. Nor most of the Episcopalians attending Grace Place in Chicago. Not all motivation is instrumental. Some is identity. One cannot grant the economists that all of life is instrumental without descending into a Benthamite nightmare of corrupted purpose.

And anyway my grandmother's self-deprecating description of her motives need not be taken at face value. Being a church lady is an identity, too, after all. It cannot be reduced to networking for bridge games, not entirely. It has its own sacred part.

In India under the Raj in the 1850s it was thought by some misled Indians to be advantageous to convert to Christianity, for education at least, or government jobs. And "so"—you might say if you thought of religious conversion in wholly secular terms—South Asia has to this day some Christians descended from converts. Actually, most of the converts were untouchables, who being illiterates before and after conversion, got no benefit whatever in government funds for secondary schools or bureaucratic posts. The untouchables in the 1850s mistakenly believed that conversion to the Europeans' religion would raise their status. Alas, it did not.

But anyway it is by now highly *dis*advantageous to be an Indian Christian, unless you are an Italian Christian marrying a Gandhi. Indeed, the former untouchables, who comprise the majority of South-Asian Christians, are in India forbidden to get affirmative action for . . . untouchables. Becoming Christian was in the event, you see, a disaster for the children and grandchildren and great-grandchildren of the converts, not an advantage. As Jeffrey Cox, the chief student of these matters, puts it, "Such is the cunning of history." Christians are regularly murdered in India and especially in Pakistan, where they constitute the chief non-Muslim minority.

Yet the South-Asian Christians, whose ancestors might have been accused of (incompetently) maximizing utility or of (foolishly) joining what they thought was an advantageous club, now would not for a moment think of abandoning their faith. They have, as Sen would put it, a "commitment" to Christianity. They are not doing it for reasons of utility or of sympathy.

The fact is irritating to extreme Hindu nationalists, who interpret the faithfulness of the Christians as mere prudence. To which one replies in Yiddish idiom: Some prudence.[18]

The Jewish club, too, had prudential advantages, the assurance of credit, say. But, obviously, for merely a Prudence Only club its members would not have endured exile and worse from Spain, pogroms and worse from Russia, yellow stars and worse from Germany, discrimination and worse from America. This is not a club any "rational" person would want to join. It's a Groucho Marx club. Religious and intellectual and social and friendship groups we join or are born into can be analyzed in terms of prudence, a little. But not entirely. They have meaning, something that a Prudence Only academic field like demography or neoclassical economics or realist international relations does not acknowledge.

As the representative of my Episcopal church I went in 2003 to the installation of a new rabbi for the Chicago congregation of Makom Shalom ("peace place"), which shares our building on South Dearborn Street. It was very moving, Hasidic in its joyous frenzy, with those wonderful pentatonic tunes and the old words. *Sh'ma Yisrael. Baruch adonai.* An errant thought popped into my head: "Wow. This is fun! Heh, wait a minute: should I convert on the spot to Judaism?"

Well, no, not actually, dear. In the way of many arrant thoughts, it was exceptionally silly. It's not who Deirdre is. It would be utterly Faithless to do so. I approve of progressive Judaism—the new rabbi was "Reb Alicia," so you get the idea. And I think I can at least see the point of even an orthodox Judaism. Speaking of the progressive and nouveau-Hasidic type of a Jewish life, I would doubtless get a lot of utility of an instrumental sort from joining up—the respect for learning, the self-mocking Yiddish humor, the according of dignity to market activity, the mysteries of a Hebrew very, very far from Indo-European languages, and those tunes. Golly. Sounds like a gas. But no, say I, if I am who I am. Jehovah did not make a deal with my ancestors—or, rather, only with my spiritual ancestors, not with my literal northwestern European branch of the family, the daughters of Ursula, Helena, and Velda. Deirdre is from another part of the human circus.

Viewing humans as mere single preference orderings explains a lot of their behavior. I myself have written whole books showing how. You can even attempt—as David George, Albert Hirschman, Amartya Sen, George

Akerlof, Harry Frankfurt, Richard Jeffrey, Amitai Etzioni, Richard Thaler, H. M. Shefrin, Mark Lutz, Robert Frank, John Davis, J. S. Mill, and others have—to add a level of sophistication to the analysis by speaking of metapreferences for preferences, or conflicting selves.[19] That's an improvement, the same improvement as moving from simple utilitarianism to rule utilitarianism.

So I take a course in Shakespeare not because reading difficult texts is simply pleasurable first time around but because I wish to be the kind of person who enjoys *King Lear*. I commit myself therefore to a rule of attending class and doing the homework. Obviously the study of languages has the same structure. Learning the subtleties of meaning of the Dutch words *maar* and *nog* is quite interesting, actually. But it is not simply pleasurable, like eating white asparagus, new potatoes, and ham with melted butter while sitting in a back garden of Hilversum on a glorious day in late spring with dear Dutch friends.

But love and loyalty, I repeat, have an excess content missing even in sophisticated versions of maximum utility. To argue that one learns Dutch on utilitarian grounds is highly implausible, considering that nearly everyone in Holland speaks English. The beggars in Amsterdam are fluently quintilingual. One learns Dutch in order to honor a beloved land and people. Not utility.

The many economists advocating the simplest version of Max U doubtless enact love and courage and the rest perfectly well, as do all undamaged humans. When a young colleague and I discussed the matter, I replied to his Max U characterization of love so: "I advise you not to tell your wife what you've just claimed, namely, that you understand her love in instrumental terms." He got the point right away. Mrs. Economist would not react well to being told that his love for her was merely a function of the pleasure in his utility function. Not if their marriage has an ounce of love.

To such colleagues I say, hear, oh *Economici*, that someone like me, who was persuaded of precisely the position you espouse, and is not a total dope, has changed her mind. Let that play on yours. Read a few novels. Talk to your spouse. Go to temple. Praise His blessed name in the dance. Sing praises unto Him with timbrel and harp. Hear, oh Israel.

Courage, temperance, justice, prudence, faith, hope, and love. You might say of course that they are mere words, these seven virtues. I reply that $N = 7$ is a reasonable if not particularly golden mean between 613 and 1. It is rich enough to capture actual humanity, shining a light on a particular German or Chinese definition of courage as against temperance. It is neither so general as to be useless or so specific as to pertain only to a local tribe.

Each of the seven has that library of philosophy and fiction associated with it, the truth of reason and the truth of narrative. Each of them— prudence, justice, faith, and the rest—is an essentially contested concept. That's a merit, not a fault. It tells us that we are at the frontier where ethics matters. In the contestation is the work. If "courage" is taken to mean fortitude in battle and other manly exercise, it has one set of stories associated with it. If it means fortitude in childbirth and other womanly labor, quite another. Most of us are never tested for martial courage, and most of us enact justice in some less glorious way than from the bench of the American Supreme Court—before which, by the way, Biff's studious friend Bernard was privileged at last to plead. Yet we still have a character-building use for stories drawn from places high and low.

We need the words. It's useless, or very nearly so, to stay at the level of the Good, or the categorical imperative, or preference orderings.

A woman needs to know how to behave in detail when facing a big presentation tomorrow at the office. All the bosses will be present, and the main client. She is fearful. She says to herself, "Come on, girl: be courageous," and the very word evokes the stories of courage in our culture, giving her ethical tools for the job. "When Florence Nightingale faced the Purveyors of the military hospital during the Crimean War or the Army Medical Board in London," the woman recalls to herself, "she didn't snivel and whine. She courageously spoke out. I must be like Nightingale":

> It was not by gentle sweetness and womanly self-abnegation that she had brought order out of chaos in the Scutari Hospitals, that, from her own resources, she had clothed the British Army, that she had spread her dominion over the serried and reluctant powers of the official world; it was by strict method, by stern discipline, by rigid attention to detail, by ceaseless labor, by the fixed determination of an indomitable will.[20]

Stories like Nightingale's are, as we say these therapeutic days, "resources" for good behavior.

31

CHARACTER(S)

The Dutch economist Arjo Klamer puts it to me this way. A person needs to have this or that virtue on this or that occasion. Sunday mornings in church, for example, she exercises the virtue of spiritual love; Saturday nights on the dance floor (say) the virtue of self-asserting courage; Mondays through Fridays the virtue of careful prudence.

That's not to say that "everything's relative" or some other version of high-school nihilism. Acting like a prudent bourgeois on the dance floor, where risky courage is in order, or like a courageous aristocrat in church, where pious temperance is in order, would be contrary to the proprieties. The classical theory of the virtues depended heavily on "decorum," what is sweet and proper on the particular occasion. Adam Smith bases the system of the virtues on a balance of "propriety" among the contending virtues, which can be tested "nowhere but in the sympathetic feelings of the impartial and well-informed spectator"—"reason, principle, conscience, the inhabitant of the breast, the man within, the great judge and arbiter of our conduct."[1] We are each the exerciser of virtues and vices, and each of us is doubled by the judgment of "the man within."

We are all composed of differing characters, and have use at different times for different stories of good behavior, putting them in conversation, as Klamer says. I have used, maybe overused, the figure of "balance" among the virtues. Robert Hariman makes the same point against it as Klamer does: "The idea that the prudential person is balanced becomes an oversimplification, an easy metonymy for a much more dynamic process of alternating contradictory impulses within oneself."[2] He adds that one must sometimes be calm when a friend is angry, courageous when others are excessively prudent, if the society is to work well. One chooses the character of the aristocrat or the peasant in this situation or that, "not just to resolve [one's own] internal tensions but in order to counteract such alternations in others."

John Gray, following Isaiah Berlin, comes to a related conclusion:

> Justice and mercy, temperance and courage, may not be fully realizable together in any one individual since they evoke different moral capacities. . . . There is a thesis here of moral scarcity, . . . a matter of moral psychology or philosophical anthropology. . . . [Yet] value-pluralism of the sort Berlin espouses may be a thesis of abundance, not scarcity, . . . as it holds that there is a vast diversity of valuable options [of lives to be lived] . . . which are uncombinable and among which choices must be made, but which are also incommensurable, so that when one array is chosen in preference to another there is no sense in saying that any definite measure . . . of value has been lost.[3]

The philosopher Loren Lomasky makes a similar point, that people are varied "project pursuers," and Robert Nozick believed that envy's sting could be reduced by having "a diversity of different lists of dimensions and of weightings" of what mattered in a society.[4] The conclusion is that we have access—broader and broader access in the modern world—to multiple characters, at different times, as Klamer and Hariman put it, or in different lives, as Berlin and Gray put it, or in different projects, as Lomasky and Nozick put it.

The characters are specialized in the Indo-European social classes: the aristocratic warrior, the peasant herdsman and cultivator, the merchant, the priest. A rich, modern society calls upon us from time to time to play all the roles. But not formerly. "So great has been the influence within contemporary moral philosophy of Hume, Kant and the Utilitarians" (in advocating an egalitarian vision of the universally good person), Stuart Hampshire writes, "that it has been possible to forget that for centuries the warrior and the priest, the landowner and the peasant, the merchant and the craftsman, the musician or poet . . . have coexisted in society with sharply distinct dispositions and virtues. . . . Varied social roles and functions, each with its typical virtues and its particular obligations, have been the normal situation in most societies throughout history."[5]

Consider the corresponding virtues of the four classes, matched to their alleged character, aristocrat, peasant, bourgeois, and priestly. The "character" of a class will sometimes be its character in the eyes of others, sometimes in its own, sometimes even, though rarely, in sociological fact. To each virtue corresponds a vice of excess or deficiency, which might add another dimension, so to speak, behind and before the virtues. In Aristotelian fashion, as I said, one could take the virtue to be the golden mean, or in Julie Nelson's terms take it to be the positive of a positive/negative pair. Thus the aristocratic virtue of wit corresponds to the vice of its excess, mere mindless wordplay, or of its deficiency, oafish jests merely malicious.

Such a classification of virtues is a bit of a parlor game, though the four-way social classification has been a manner of talking since the Rig-Veda and so is not wildly arbitrary, and is richly storied. To be of some use the four-way classification need not match the seams in the universe. The part of each of us that is aristocratic supports our wit or our courage when we need each one. Thus Oscar Wilde to American customs agent: "I have nothing to declare except my genius"; Oscar Wilde in prison: *De Profundis*.

The Virtues and the Four Classes

ARISTOCRAT PATRICIAN	PEASANT PLEBEIAN	BOURGEOIS MERCANTILE	PRIEST ARTISTIC/INTELLECTUAL
hero	peasant/saint	merchant	priest
pagan	believer	secular/worldly	cloistered
Odysseus	Jesus	Benjamin Franklin	Picasso/Bertrand Russell
pride of being	pride of service	pride of accomplishment	pride of creation
gesture	action	deal	ritual
honor	duty	reliability	integrity
forthrightness	candor	honesty	accuracy
loyalty	faith	sociability	professionalism
courage	fortitude	enterprise	imagination
acceptance of fate	hope	foresightedness	ambition
wit	jocularity	humor	irony
courtesy	reverence	respect	appreciation
propriety	humility	modesty	self-criticism
magnanimity	benevolence	consideration	sympathy
justice	fairness	responsibility	accuracy
foresight	traditional wisdom	prudence	insight
temperance	frugality	**thrift**	discipline
love	charity	**affection**	agape
social grace	dignity	self-possession	self-awareness
subjectivity	objectivity	conjectivity	meta-theoretical-ness

The part that is priestly supports our temperance and proper pride of intellectual creation, when we need those. And so forth.

These are stereotypes, not always, I repeat, sociological facts. They are myths, self-images, ideologies, true or false class consciousness. C. S. Lewis, who was a close student of medieval literature, noted that "the Knights in Froissart's chronicles had neither sympathy nor mercy for the 'outsiders,' the churls or peasants. But this deplorable indifference was very closely intertwined with a good quality. They really had, among themselves, a very high standard of valor, generosity and honor."[6] Compare the Icelandic tales of the Vikings, such as King Harald the Stern, so nobly, courageously dying from a gold-tipped arrow lodged in his throat at Stamford Bridge—but with an appalling career behind him of mercilessness toward monks and peasants and women.

"The voice of the peasant," Lewis continues, should be discounted when it recommends for a knight a life as "cautious" and "close-fisted" as the churl. But "the habit of 'not giving a damn' grows on a class. To discount the voice of the peasant when it really ought to be discounted makes it easier to discount his voice when he cries for justice or mercy. The partial deafness which is noble and necessary encourages the wholesale deafness which is arrogant and inhuman." It's how an ethos is built, for good or ill. And note Lewis's own implied ethic of noblesse oblige: one is to attend to the voice of the peasant not out of an egalitarian humility that one should "answer the witness of God in every man, whether they are the heathen . . . or . . . do profess Christ," but out of a downward-looking pity.

But consider: any one of the four columns could be an ethical way for a human to live. Read the columns. An aristocratic and proletarian and priestly set of virtues is conceivable, and each has had a long run in our culture. Once each column was all the rage, the prestigious form of life to some group of opinion makers. But so also is the third, bourgeois set conceivable as a good way to live. And it matches better now who we mostly are, most of the time, 9–5, Mon–Fri—though since 1848 it has not had much prestige among those practicing the fourth column.

The bourgeois virtues, derivable from the seven virtues but viewable in business practice, might include enterprise, adaptability, imagination, optimism, integrity, prudence, thrift, trustworthiness, humor, affection, self-possession, consideration, responsibility, solicitude, decorum, patience, toleration, affability, peaceability, civility, neighborliness, obligingness, reputability, dependability, impartiality. The point of calling such virtues "bourgeois" is to contrast them with nonbusiness versions of the same virtues, such as (physical) courage or (spiritual) love. Bourgeois virtues are the townsperson's virtues, away from the military camp of the aristocrat or the commons of the peasantry or the temple of the priest or the studio of the artist.

For instance, what do you suppose is the rate of "nonperformance," as the bankers call it, on big loans to business in the modern world? Ten percent? Twenty? I mean, these are nasty, dishonest people, those businesspeople. Well. It's in fact 2 percent. A banker acquaintance in Chicago tells me that her bank, making loans for large real estate deals, has had *zero* nonpayment of debts for five years. Anyone who has dealt with college deans and professors knows that the comparable rate of nonperformance is a good deal higher in academic life. A promise from a dean is approximately worthless. A promise from *me* is merely a hopeful speculation. But a businessman's word is his stock-in-trade. Scholars and scientists and their administrators, the wordsmiths contemptuous of the businessman, habitually prevaricate. Who then is the gentleman?

Sometimes the distinction between bourgeois and other virtues is mere verbal shading. An aristocrat has wit, a peasant or worker jocularity. A businessperson must have humor of an amiable sort ("Walk in with a big laugh"). But it can be more than shading, too. Trustworthiness is a business virtue, paralleled in some ideals of a peasant or working-class community by a loving solidarity. But solidarity can have socialist or fascist outcomes, also bad for business, and for the rest of life.

Physical courage shown by aristocrats in war and sport resembles bourgeois enterprise. But collapsing the two into one virtue encourages warfare in business, which has led to shooting wars. Bad for business. Imperial Japan, for example, believed on the basis of a warlike economics, which had no support in academic economics, that it had to conquer places to get oil from them. American diplomats in the 1930s, if not economists at the time, believed the same theory, and resisted Japanese expansion. The result was Pearl Harbor and the Pacific war, with no gain to either side. After the war both sides achieved their aims by trade, benefiting rather than conquering the people with whom they traded.

The usual vocabulary of the virtues, persisting to the present, I have been saying, tells only of a world of heroes in war or of laborers in the vineyard.

Our ethical talk overlooks the ever-growing world of management, negotiation, leadership, persuasion, and other business. The eighteenth century began to construct an ethical vocabulary for merchants, especially in Scotland, and most especially in the writings and teaching of Adam Smith. As Michael Novak put it, "Smith saw his own life's work as moral teaching for the 'new class' of his era."[7]

You're part of it, probably.

32

ANTIMONISM AGAIN

As Stuart Hampshire notes, it has been conventional in the West since Descartes, Vico, and Kant to divide arguments between principle and history, reason and imagination, mathematics and story, and then to make principle, reason, and mathematics into the measures of humanity.[1] It has been a mistake. Closely reasoned, calculative logic is very nice. I am in favor of it, especially in designing buildings or tax laws. I practice it as an economic historian. Hurrah for calculation. And it's so universal.

But all that does not make it the only human virtue. As Hannah Arendt noted, "All that the giant computers prove is that the modern age is wrong to believe with Hobbes that rationality, in the sense of 'reckoning with consequences,' is the highest and most human of man's capacities."[2] The sociologist Harry Collins has driven the point home in his study of expert systems.[3] Darwin, similarly, as I've said, found a kind of rationality in the lives of finches and earthworms. Darwinism suggests that the rationalist fascination with calculative logic (*logos/ratio*) as God's unique gift to humanity might be misleading. Calculative logic is evolution's gift to *all* species.

Kant made a mistake in rejecting as a constituent of ethics the unreasoning particularities of philosophical anthropology or philosophical psychology. Likewise Pierre Ramus in the late sixteenth century misled the professors of Europe in thinking of rhetoric as merely a matter of style instead of the whole of human reasoning. And Plato misled us all in rejecting the mere opinion (*hē doxe*) that humans are the measure of all things. Ramus and Kant were pre-Kantians, not pre-Hegelians.

The problem lies with Kant's unifying of ethics under the banner of reason against imagination, or any excessive unifying of the virtues, a pursuit of monism, a formula of certitude, a quick little way of deciding questions free of culture, a trick acquirable by a reasonably clever adolescent after attending lectures.

And to be fair, it is the Kantians rather than Kant himself who seek algorithms for judgment, to "solve moral quandaries without recourse to moral wisdom," as Hursthouse puts it.[4] Jonsen and Toulmin are characteristically useful on this point, arguing that "not for nothing does Kant call moral and other practical imperatives 'maxims.' In so doing he places himself in the practical tradition of Aristotle, Cicero, and the casuists, rather than the theoretical inheritance of Plato and the moral geometers."[5] They argue in similar terms that Jeremy Bentham, too, was a casuist. "Taken in its social context, utilitarianism was not an abstract intellectual theory, but a powerful political weapon."[6] The scale would then range from at one extreme utilitarians and Kantians, who seek only algorithms, through deontologists of the middle ground like Kant himself and practical improvers like Bentham himself, to at the other extreme—extremism in the defense of virtue is no vice—the casuistic heroes of Jonsen and Toulmin (and Aristotle, Cicero, Aquinas, Juan Azor, and Jeremy Taylor) and virtue ethicists like Adam Smith, who identify "the impartial spectator within" as the guide to judgment.

A quick little formula, the pocket-sized card, does not acknowledge ethical dilemmas, which is to say two virtues tugging within one culture that values the virtues differently than some other culture does. It is among the commonest ethical experience of our lives. The Japanese—at least in Benedict's account; and the old Romans—got it right. There are "circles" of obligation, which can be thought of in a Western way as the competing claims of courage to venture and temperance to hold back. Make the witticism as it occurs to you at someone else's expense, or resist the temptation? Cicero never could resist the temptation. In the great and small ethical choices, we in fact daily face dilemmas with real tradeoffs, about which we discover only by living them or listening to stories about them in our culture: between the justice of the death penalty, in some people's view, and the love leading to mercy even to the one of the malefactors crucified on Golgotha; or between the prudence of cooking a meal tonight and the hope of someone calling to go out to eat.

Kant's most famous example to the contrary—claiming as he does that there are no real dilemmas, that the rule of Reason can resolve them all on the basis of universal and self-evident axioms—has been amazing people ever since he first gave it, in an essay of 1797, "On a Supposed Right to Lie Because of Love of Humanity." It was written, note, eleven years after Mr. Green's death and therefore by a Kant without the check of bourgeois prudence.

The logic of his categorical imperative, said Kant, requires that, if asked by a man who has told you he is on a mission of murder, you should reveal the location of his intended victim. The maxim, a "perfect duty": always tell the truth. You do not know for sure what the consequences will be if you tell the horrible truth, but you do know for sure that you will have lied if you fail to tell it.

Kant was anticipated by forty years in this line of argument by the Reverend David Fordyce of Aberdeen:

> Sincerity . . . is another virtue or duty of great importance to society. . . . It does not indeed require that we expose our sentiments indiscreetly, or tell all truth in every case; but certainly it does not admit the least violation of truth. . . . No pretense of private or public good can possibly counter-balance the ill consequences of such a violation. . . . It belongs to us to do what appears right and conformable to the laws of our nature, and to leave heaven to direct and over-rule events or consequences, which it will never fail to do for the best.[7]

Aside from the last Panglossian and theistic appeal, which Kant denied himself, and which *Candide* had anyway in 1759 made a catchphrase for idiocy in Europe, Kant could have written this. Fordyce's short book containing the passage, *The Elements of Moral Philosophy*, had been translated into French and German by 1757, and was described c. 1760 as "celebrated" in Germany.[8] Much of the book was reprinted well into the nineteenth century as the entry "Ethics" in the *Encyclopaedia Britannica*, the first through third editions of which Kant might also have seen. So perhaps the similarity is more than coincidental.

Kant and Fordyce believed you would not want the maxim "Lie when you imagine it might have good consequences" to be universal. One can understand the point: "Without [sincerity] . . . society would be a dominion of mistrust," as Fordyce put it. It is called by modern linguists "the axiom of quality." But to a murderer? Not the least violation of truth? Isn't the ethical act that is to be evaluated not the act of "lying" in general, which to be sure we would not want to generalize, but "lying to prevent a murder," which we would indeed wish to make a universal ethical law? If a lie could have spared someone from the gas chambers, as in fact it sometimes did—"He's only thirteen years old, Herr Commandant"—wouldn't you, my dear Immanuel, recommend it?

Alasdair MacIntyre puts the point this way: "Lutheran pietists brought up their children to believe that one ought to tell the truth to everybody at all times whatever the consequences, and Kant was one of those children. Traditional Bantu parents brought up their children not to tell the truth to unknown strangers, since they believed that this would render the family vulnerable to witchcraft. In our culture many of us have been brought up not to tell the truth to elderly great-aunts who invite us to admire their new hats."[9] "But each of these codes," he continues, "embodies an acknowledgment of the virtue of truthfulness." It's just that the exercise of truthfulness varies in detail with the internal goods achievable in being a German Pietist or a traditional Bantu or a Scottish bourgeois.

Ethical choices I say come up a hundred times a day, in the dilemma between doing X and doing Y, both goods. Go visit the friend in the hospital or finish grading the papers for tomorrow's class? Call Deb to go eat at Hackney's or finish another paragraph of writing? And then, too, one must make a choice about those portentous issues that the editorial page regards as the very meaning of ethical: protect the mother's choice or the embryo's life? Pull the feeding tube? Intervene in a mass slaughter?

Any monism denies the dilemmas. Thus economics of the Max U variety says: Come now, no dilemma; just do what maximizes utility. Or an evolutionary psychology of the we-brain-scientists-have-it-all-worked-out variety says: Face up to it, there's no dilemma; just do what your genes are telling you to do. Or a revealed theology of the we-already-know-God's-will variety says: Bless you, no dilemma; just do what God so evidently wishes. Or a natural theology of the early Enlightenment variety: Be calm, no dilemma; just be assured that all is for the best in the best of all possible worlds. Or the reason-loving-side-of-the-late-Enlightenment-project variety: Seriously, no dilemma; just follow the rule of reason, such as the categorical imperative.

The opposite side of the Enlightenment's love of reason, as I've said, is love of freedom. That side does not think dilemmas are so easily resolved. Aristotle treats the moment of choice as the result of a painful deliberation, personally and historically contingent, about "matters which, though subject to rules that generally hold good, are uncertain in their issue; or where the issue is indeterminate; and where . . . we take others into our deliberations, distrusting our own capacity to decide."[10] The Talmudic tradition from Hillel and Akiva down to Marx and Freud celebrates the indeterminateness of dialogue. The school of Hillel says such and such, to which the school of Shammai replies so and so. The Jewish tradition of interpretation has some of its origins in the Greek sophistic tradition, against which Plato the monist railed.

The Christians, too, like Plato, have preferred rather to settle things once and for all, and then have demanded that the government enforce with fire and sword what God so evidently wishes, in the Nicene Creed or the Augsburg Confession. But Aquinas himself, in the very method of dialogic argument in his *quaestiones*, exhibits the deliberative spirit, as does the great Jewish influence on Aquinas, Moses Maimonides.

In other words, "choice" in the system of the Western virtues since c. 330 BC, brought to some sort of perfection AD 1267–1273, active in Western thought up to the time of Adam Smith, and still underlying our culture, is made not by applying a formula, but by rhetorical and narrative reflection. The philosopher John McDowell wrote that "one knows what to do, if one does, not by applying universal principles but by being a certain kind of person: one who sees situations in a certain distinctive way."[11] And one comes to see situations that way by rhetorical and narrative reflection. The philosopher Jerry Fodor complained about the most recent of the monistic formulas which keep popping up, "The direct evidence for psychological Darwinism is very slim indeed. In particular, it's arguably much worse than the indirect evidence for our intuitive, pluralistic theory of human nature. It is, after all, our intuitive pluralism that we use to get along with one another. And I have the impression that, by and large, it works pretty well."[12]

Amos Oz said once that when he is sure of some ethical position he writes a nonfiction article. But when he faces a dilemma, as between Jew and Palestinian for example, he writes a story. Stories—the stories of those seven nonfungible virtues in our culture—give us reasons to be good, and to understand that we cannot be perfectly, monistically so. Some of what makes us human is precisely our stories and our languages. Some stories suit Chinese culture better than European or Indian. That's no scandal. As Isaiah Berlin wrote, "Forms of life differ. Ends, moral principles, are many. But not infinitely many: they must be within the human horizon."[13]

John Gray describes Berlin's "rejection of the species of rationalism for which the dilemmas of practice are in the end illusory" as "agonistic liberalism." In Berlin's thinking, Gray explains, "conflict and rivalry enter into the ideal of liberty itself."[14] Gray is perhaps overestimating Berlin's theoretical ambition, but anyway the Gray/Berlin point is a good one. No formula can summarize the stories of varied human lives, nun and soldier, French and Chinese. Even the Greek ideal of "human flourishing" is a little suspect, since it subordinates a person's choice to a universal judgment of what's good for her, and it was articulated by men who disdained and oppressed the non-Greek, the nonfree, the nonmale.

On the contrary, says Berlin, leave her alone to invent herself, as a square dancer or opera lover. The song "Achy Breaky Heart," words and music composed by Don Von Tress, might not be as Good from the point of view of a critique of judgment as the aria "Che gelida manina," composed by Luigi Illica, Giuseppe Giacosa, and Giacomo Puccini. An imperious Hellene would like to intervene, to resist the closing of the American mind, and impose taxes on square dancers to pay for subsidies to opera. But letting people alone to invent themselves in their music is a good in itself, said Berlin—Isaiah, or Irving.

Isaiah is not here advocating the Romantic commandment "Be thy essential, earnest, sincere self." Freedom is not merely an approach to a preexisting ideal self. On the contrary, such "positive freedom" has often excused tyrants helping us to find our ideal selves in front of the Inquisition or down in room 101. What is being recommended by agonistic liberalism is "the goodness of choice," as Gray puts it—not necessarily to be understood as autonomy, that is to say, courage, but as self-creation, that is, hope and faith.

The nun creates herself as cloistered and obedient, the opposite of an autonomous Romantic hero. Yet hers is in its own way a glorious life, a glory I have witnessed in five close friends among Catholic nuns. In a famous passage in *Anarchy, State, and Utopia* Robert Nozick lists thirty-six names together with "you, and your parents": Wittgenstein, Elizabeth Taylor, Casey Stengel, The Lubavitcher Rebbe, and so forth. He asks, "Is there really one kind of life which is best for each of these people?"[15] Gray declares similarly, "The virtues of the Homeric epic and of the Sermon on the Mount are irreducibly divergent and conflicting, and they express radically different forms of life. There is no Archimedean point of leverage from which they can be judged."[16] That's right.

A strange but powerful support for antimonism is Machiavelli. Berlin elsewhere argues persuasively that Machiavelli's originality—what alarms people about him nearly five centuries after his death—is precisely his uncovering of "an insoluble dilemma, the planting of a permanent question mark . . . that ends equally ultimate, equally sacred, may contradict each other, that entire systems of value may come into collision without possibility of rational arbitration."[17] The prudence and justice of the pagan virtues, which Machiavelli admired, may conflict with love and faith of the Christian virtues, which he regarded with contempt. I wonder if the belief that virtues could not conflict is as ancient as Berlin implies. Perhaps it is only a certain kind of Christian who believes that rational arbitration always works. Greek tragedy accepts the conflict, for example.

It's an Italian sensibility. If you and your friend are not playing the same language game, you will of course come to different evaluations, as Italians are always aware and usually calm about. The Italian film *La meglio gioventù* (2003) tells of the love that binds friends and family despite differences. Nicola becomes a progressive psychiatrist; his brother Matteo joins the police in the fraught times of the Red Brigade. Giulia involves herself in violent revolution; her sister in law Giovanna becomes a judge volunteering to put down the Mafia in Sicily. These are insoluble dilemmas, radically different forms of life. Yet without possibility of rational arbitration between their views, the Italians in the film keep faith, *lotsverbondenheid*. It is a grace that is often hard for theoretically equipped Americans, blue or red, to practice.

Sen has traced the surprising influence of this bit of Italian grace from Antonio Gramsci to Piero Sraffa to Ludwig Wittgenstein in the Cambridge of 1929 down to ordinary language philosophy in the 1950s.[18] Giacomo Leopardi, the early Romantic poet, shows often the usual displaced religiosity in his Romantic yearning for *L'infinito*. But he acknowledges too—indeed, states as an axiom of his reflections on life here below—that "the world is a league of scoundrels against men of good will."[19] Such talk is impossible from English transcendental monists like Coleridge and Wordsworth, or Shelley and Keats, according to whom truth is beauty, beauty truth, recollected in tranquility. Byron and Browning on the other hand talk like Leopardi, and often. But Byron and Browning, after all, were honorary Italians.

Ordinary, nontheoretical Americans understand the Italian point without philosophical instruction. The clerisy notes with puzzlement that Americans for instance are both liberal and republican, committed to both free contracting and to sacrificing for the community.[20] That is, Americans since the Founders have admired both modern freedom, the right to be left alone, and ancient freedom, the right to participate. Americans are both anarchists and busybodies, mountain men shooting at the FBI and politicians jailing marihuana users.

You see both the liberal and the republican virtues admired, for example, in the small cities of the Midwest. Is this because Americans, especially Midwesterners, and especially Babbitts in their Zeniths, are stupid and bourgeois and, worst of all, philosophically inconsistent? No, as the post-1929 Ludwig Wittgenstein would surely have said, had his attention been drawn to the philosophical problems of the Midwest. The historian Catherine Stock writes of how the "old middle class" in the Dakotas weathered the Great Depression. They held "fundamentally contradictory, but equally heartfelt, impulses." That is, they admired values that come into collision without possibility of rational arbitration, "rational" meaning "formulaic, single-valued, monistic, decisive, axiomatic, deductive, ultimate, solving all dilemmas" and all those other neatnesses admired so much by Cartesians and Kantians and Benthamites.

The notion that virtues have to be noncontradictory is a professor's logic. But it is not reasonable. It confuses, in the style of Wittgenstein before 1929, the logic of propositions with the "logic" of the world. In a famous debate in 1939 Wittgenstein Mark II attacked Wittgenstein Mark I in the person of the mathematical logician Alan Turing:

> *Wittgenstein*: Where will the harm come [from a logical contradiction]?
> *Turing*: The real harm will not come in unless there is an application, in which a bridge may fall down or something of that sort.
> *Wittgenstein*: . . . The question is: Why are people afraid of contradictions? It is easy to understand why they should be afraid of contradictions in orders . . . *outside* mathematics. . . . But nothing need go wrong. And if something does go wrong—if the bridge breaks down—then your mistake was of the kind of using a wrong natural law. . . . "I lie, therefore I do not lie, therefore I lie and do not lie, therefore we have a contradiction [namely, the Paradox of the Liar], therefore [because a contradiction implies in logic that any proposition whatever is valid] $2 \times 2 = 369$." Well, we would not call this "multiplication," that is all. . . .
> *Turing*: Although we do not know that the bridge will fall if there are no contradictions, yet it is almost certain that if there are contradictions [Turing is referring to the contradictions in pre-nineteenth-century calculus] it will go wrong somewhere.
> *Wittgenstein*: But nothing has ever gone wrong that way yet.[21]

Ethical life is like bridge engineering, not like mathematics. There is nothing desirable in axiomatizing ethics in order to make sure that it is consistent. Consistency, after all, is a minor virtue. *Pace* Plato, Hobbes, Spinoza, Kant. If you deduce from your axiom that you should inform a murderer of the location of his intended victim, well, we should not call this "ethics," that is all.

As the Midwesterner Jane Addams said, family and social claims struggle, tragically, but necessarily, and "the destruction of either . . . would bring ruin to ethical life." It sounds obvious to say that Americans are engaged in "contradictions" when they claim to value both liberal autonomy and republican connection. But that's how people of good will are.

Virtues are not to be subsumed under a monism free from "contradictions," that is, from the tensions and balances of any ethical life.[22] Stock herself gives a catalogue of the "impulses" in her Dakotans. A better word for them would be "virtues": "loyalties [faith] to individualism [courage] and community [justice, temperance], to profit [prudence] and cooperation [love, justice, faith], to progress [hope] and tradition [faith again]."[23] And bourgeois.

33

WHY NOT ONE VIRTUE?

The seven virtues of the Western tradition before Kant are ethical primary colors, the red, blue, and yellow not derivable from others but themselves able to form other colors. "The cardinal virtues," Aquinas notes, "are called more principal, not because they are more perfect than all the other virtues, but because human life more principally turns on them and the other virtues are based on them."[1] Blue plus yellow yields green. Love plus faith yields loyalty. Courage plus prudence yields enterprise. Temperance plus justice yields humility. Justice, courage, and faith yields honesty.

Various moderns have tried to make up a new color wheel, with integrity and civility or indeed honesty as primary. Thus a *New Yorker* cartoon in 2002: a man who looks like he's just returned from a grilling by a Senate committee about Enron and other accounting disasters says to his little son, "Honesty is a fine quality, Max, but it isn't the whole story." Making up new primaries is like depending on purple and green, or chartreuse and aquamarine—good and important colors, among my favorites, but technically speaking, "secondary," or even "tertiary," the palette of Gauguin and Matisse against that of late van Gogh and late Piet Mondrian. In this ethical case the made-up primaries are accompanied by no tradition of how to mix or array them.

And they are, I repeat, all derivable from the older primaries. Thus honesty is courage, justice, and faith combined: the courage to speak out great-souledly; the justice to give the due answer; the faith to adhere to one's true identity. And so on, using St. Thomas or a modern virtue ethicist as a guide.

Take down your *Roget's Thesaurus* again. In the 1962 edition the categories were still those that would have occurred to an English physician, scientist, and secretary of the Royal Society, bilingual in the French of his father, in 1805, categories improved over his career, and published first in 1852, with numerous subsequent editions until his death in 1879. Examine the main headings of "Class Eight: Affections." You get the following. Note where the seven virtues fall:

859	Patience: tolerance, forbearance, endurance, stoicism
868	Cheerfulness: geniality, good humor, buoyancy, liveliness, vivacity, spiritedness
878	Humorousness: wittiness
879	Wit and Humor: jocularity, cleverness
886	**Hope**: trust, confidence, **Faith**, reliance, optimism
891	**Courage**: boldness, valor, confidence, fortitude, hardihood, resolution, daring, venturesomeness, enterprise
893	Caution: care, **Prudence**, discretion, judiciousness, deliberateness, forethought, foresight
895	Taste: elegance, grace, refinement, cultivation, discrimination, decorousness, decency, propriety, restraint, simplicity
900	Simplicity: naturalness
903	Pride: self-esteem, self-respect, dignity, courtliness, gravity, sobriety
904	Humility: modesty, plainness
920	Sociability: affability, friendliness
923	Hospitality: cordiality, amiability, friendliness, neighborliness, generosity, liberality
925	Friendship: amiability, peaceableness, congeniality, neighborliness, fellowship, staunchness, [loyalty]
929	**Love**: affection, ardor
934	Courtesy: politeness, civility, affability, graciousness, respect, courtliness, refinement, cultivation
936	Kindness, Benevolence: affability, geniality, gentleness, mildness, consideration, thoughtfulness, solicitude, regard, concern, obligingness, charity, altruism, good will, generosity
939	Public Spirit
942	Pity: mercy, ruth, charity, forbearance, compassion
944	Condolence: sympathy
945	Forgiveness: forbearance, magnanimity
947	Gratitude: appreciation
962	Respect: regard, consideration
972	Probity: rectitude, uprightness, integrity, honesty, reputability, highmindedness, conscientiousness, candor, openness, forthrightness, trustworthiness, reliability, dependability, fidelity, faithfulness, loyalty, faith, constancy
974	**Justice**: fairness, impartiality, disinterestedness, unbiasedness
977	Unselfishness: magnanimity, generosity, liberality

986   Chastity: purity, decorum, propriety
990   **Temperance**: moderation, forbearance, restraint, self-discipline, sobriety
1026   Piety: **Faith**, reverence

Neither Faith nor Prudence have major headings of their own, a comment on the intellectual world of 1852. In Aquinas's of 1252 they most certainly did.

The point is that any random virtue in this table can be related to the seven. But the seven cannot be derived from the other virtues. Take for instance one virtue important to medievals especially, Chastity. In Aquinas, as the theologian Diana Fritz Cates observes, it is "the species of temperance that concerns sexual relations."[2] Or as Aquinas himself said more delicately, "A person is said to be chaste because he behaves in a certain way as regards the use of certain parts of the body."[3] Aquinas rejects the notion that chastity is a "general virtue" (as he argues temperance is), because in that wider sense it is merely metaphorical, comparing the proper spiritual union with God with the proper physical union of people.

Or take the virtue of liberality, put by Roget under hospitality and unselfishness. Aquinas argues that it might be considered a part of justice, quoting St. Ambrose (*De Offic.* i): "Justice has to do with the fellowship of mankind. For the notion of fellowship is divided into two parts, justice and beneficence, also called liberality or kind-heartedness." Aquinas objects to Ambrose's analysis, observing that justice is about what is due whereas liberality is precisely about what is *not* due. "The giving of liberality arises from a person being affected in a certain way towards money, in that he desires it not nor loves it: so that when it is fitting he gives it not only to his friends but also to those whom he knows not. Hence it belongs not to charity, but to justice, which is about external things."[4]

Think of a tree of life, Ygdrasil, so to speak, from which branch out the individual virtues. I am thinking of a tree viewed from above. From this viewpoint the most easily seen and lived level is the story of particular virtues, the top canopy of leaves on the tree. See Roget's list. The particular major virtues, the scores of virtues that Aquinas analyzes, for example, would be the leaf-bearing branches just discernable. The seven abstracted Western virtues are the main branches further down. The rational good life is the trunk.

In saying that the seven are sensible places to begin I am not declaring them universal or permanent from here to Proxima Centauri, merely widespread and persistent from here to ancient and modern Jericho and Timbuktu. The union of three Christian and four pagan virtues is of course historically contingent. A. Th. van Deursen writes, "European culture of the seventeenth century rested on two pillars: Christianity and the classics of Graeco-Roman antiquity. They were inseparable, not because they cannot be separated, but because European history had bound them together."[5]

Kant and Bentham tried to separate them. The result has been, you might say, existential angst and ethical chaos. Maybe those old European theorists of the virtues were onto something. I do not speak of their practice of virtues, of course, considering the long history of European religious fanatics and royal murderers. I speak merely of their theory.

The argument I am making is philosophical, but supplemented by some anthropological and historical and literary arguments: anyway, un-Kantian. There's no essence, I suppose, of "courage" in God's eyes—though, by the way, if anyone has found it, I would lay odds on Aquinas.[6] The ethics here have their origin in Aristotle, but we have the advantage over the Philosopher and his follower the Divine Doctor that we know more—though the "more" we know is, as T. S. Eliot once remarked . . . Aristotle and Aquinas. "Courage" does not mean just the same thing to a Roman knight as to a Christian knight, or to a samurai as to a cowboy, or to a free man in the Athens of 431 BC as to an adult woman in the Paris of AD 1968.

Ideas change even under the same rubric, the intellectual historian observes. Words are emptied out of content and refilled. Witness "justice," as I have noted, in a society of routine slavery as against a successor society horrified at the very idea; or a little boy's idea of playground fairness as against his adult self's belief in the justice of markets. You are in molecules different from the child you once were. For certain purposes of, say, microbiological investigation of the accumulation of heavy metals, that is the salient fact. But for many other purposes the child is the parent of the adult. So too the history of temperance or justice can matter to their present meanings.

One might ask what lies "behind" the virtues—it is the question that Plato and Kant asked so very persistently. It is the question of what makes the virtues virtuous. By now many philosophers and even more undergraduates believe that ethics is "just a matter of opinion," "a flag used by the questing will," as Iris Murdoch described the modern view, "a term which could with greater clarity be replaced by 'I'm for this.'"[7] Murdoch and I do not approve of such "emotivism," as it is called. On the contrary, "excellence has a kind of unity and there are facts about our condition from which lines converge in a definite direction."[8] Murdoch, a persuaded Platonist, argued that Good is "that in the light of which the explanation [of any particular excellence] must proceed," and she retold for these purposes Plato's allegory of the sunlight beyond the fire in Plato's cave. The Sun of Good illuminates our path.

Murdoch was an atheist, too, and would have resisted respelling "the Sun of Good" as the "Son of God," which a persuaded Christian would prefer. Yet Murdoch, like all Platonists, seemed to flirt with theism, and writes in 1969 a characteristically brilliant essay "On 'God' and 'Good.'" "If we say that Good is Reason, we have to talk about good judgment," she writes, and so we end standing in the light cast by the Good anyway. "If we say that Good is Love, we have to explain that there are different kinds of love," bad and okay and good.[9] You see what I mean by her flirtations with theism, even Christianity. If you are a determined Platonist, then the root of Ygdrasil is the Good, period; or, again, with one letter left off—I earnestly invite you to do so—God, period.

Another and Platonic image for the unity of the virtues (for example, *Phaedo* 100c) is to think of it as the locus or asymptote or envelop or limit, to use again mathematical imagery that Plato would have liked, of all sequences of bad-okay-good-better-best. All these, declares the Platonist, "I better in one general Best."

The Platonic Limit:
The Good is the Tendency of Particular Betterments

			Bad soldiering			
			Okay soldiering			
			Good soldiering			

Bad art	Okay art	Good art	Go(o)d	Good science	Okay science	Bad science

			Good mothering			
			Okay mothering			
			Bad mothering			

But in answering the question "Why Virtue?" you can if you wish stop short of the Platonic form of the Good. Doing so has the virtue—note the word—of saving you from a collapse into a formula for goodness. In Aristotelian fashion you can satisfy yourself with particular virtues that seem to have something to do with a good life. The Aristotelian woman gazes at the ring of good art (evincing, say, the virtue of hope), good soldiering (courage), good science (justice), good mothering (love) encircling the good. She stays at the level of the main branches of the tree.

The question of the rooted, ultimate Good, as the strong anti-Kantian and anti-Platonic argument puts it, never comes up. Certainly that is Aristotle's claim. In the first sentence of the *Nicomachean Ethics* he praises without citation the Platonic commonplace that "the Good [*t'agathon*] is that at which everything aims." But then he at once notes the variety of life's aims. "Since there are many practices, arts, and sciences, varied are their aims," and spends the rest of his book detailing them.

Aristotle and Aquinas viewed choice as agonizing—quite unlike the brisk formulas of utilitarianism, for example, with which we economists say we approach life. The protagonist of *An American Tragedy*, Clyde Griffiths, faces as a young man "for the first time in his life . . . a choice as to his desire." Will he fit into the drinking and whoring of his fellow bellhops in the Kansas-City hotel, or will he keep faith with his mother and father and their street-preaching temperance? The particular virtues and vices struggle inside him for a paragraph. Hope: "Strange, swift, enticing and yet disturbing thoughts raced in and out of his consciousness." Courage: "And through it all he was now a little afraid. Pshaw! Had he no courage at all?" Love as social solidarity: "These other fellows were not disturbed by the prospects." Love as family: "His mother!" Justice as rule-following: "But what would his mother think if she knew?" Faith and justice as backward-looking identity: "He dared not think of his mother or his father either at this time." Temperance abandoned: he "put them both resolutely out of his mind."[10] And so he decides, though he lives to regret his decisions.

Regret and tragedy are impossible in Max U's world. Ralph McInerny summarizes utilitarianism so: "If every action is for the sake of an end, and every end taken to be good, and there are no mistakes in the matter, then anything anybody does is good and everyone is as he ought to be." That's not Clyde. Scientifically speaking, "remorse and regret prevent this easy solution."[11]

Murdoch, though no Aristotelian, agreed that the virtues short of the Good are indeed separable and rankable. They form an interlocked system, not to be reduced to one, and certainly not to something like "Utility." "The good man," she wrote, "knows whether and when art or politics is more important than family. The good man sees the way in which the virtues are related to each other."[12]

Related, not absorbed. For example, a good life is not to be understood as pleasure, or else we have simply absorbed all virtues into prudence. J. Budziszewski, though he admires Adam Smith's book *The Theory of Moral Sentiments*, argues that "for Smith, the criterion of human flourishing is a pleasurable activity of the soul rather than a rational activity of the soil: his doctrine of virtue rests on a hedonic foundation."[13] I am not so sure. I admit that one can give a hedonic reading to such remarks as "What so great happiness as to be beloved, and to know that we deserve to be loved?" But note the "that we *deserve* to be," "because it excites these sentiments in other men." Smith disagrees with the Hume of *A Treatise on Human Nature*, single-mindedly emphasizing a self-interest utility and the control of passions; he agrees with the later Hume of the *Inquiry Concerning the Principles of Morals*, admitting sheer love, called "sympathy." Such love, approbation, sympathy is a matter of solidarity with others, not utility.[14]

And the good that Smith seeks is not merely other-directed. The Impartial Spectator inside the Smithian soul embodies the rational activity of a soul. Smith divides your soul theatrically into an actor and a spectator, and assigns you responsibility for both within you. You are not merely a utilitarian enjoyer. You are the backstage producer as much as the customer at the ticket window. "To be amiable and to be meritorious: that is, to deserve love and to deserve reward, are the great characters of virtue" is not a sentence that a Bentham could have written.[15] "Deserving" an ice cream cone this afternoon may increase your utilitarian pleasure. But the deserving part is itself a separate ethical construction. It's not made from pleasuring. Not in Smith.

But anyway Budziszewski is correct that reducing virtue to pleasure can't be allowed. After all, a highly specialized hero or saint could be having a jolly good time, achieving pleasure in the exclusive exercise of his or her single-minded virtue. Heroism or sainthood, however, or for that matter the maximizing utility of the wholly prudent man, is not in any of its extreme forms a full human life, rationally speaking.

Some good scholars in economics and literature and even some philosophers believe that the study of ethics is best pursued with a mind uncluttered with such ethical philosophy and its history in our culture, not to speak of philosophical psychology or philosophical anthropology. They hack the tree of life to pieces, so to speak, and then cheerfully reassemble the decultured leaves and branches that result into arrangements pleasing to them, affixing a cardboard label, "A Tree."

As Hobbes, who was a leader in this tree surgery, said in 1640 of "those men who have written concerning . . . moral philosophy, . . . whereof there be infinite volumes," "[no] man at this day so much as pretend[s] to know more than hath been delivered two thousand years ago by Aristotle. And yet every man thinks that in this subject he knoweth as much as any other; supposing there needeth thereunto no study but that it accrueth to them by natural wit."[16] The thought resembles the evangelical Protestant belief in the efficacy of grace alone. It was no tedious course of study, but "grace that taught my heart to fear / And grace my fears relieved," recommending *The Good News Bible.*

DROPPING THE VIRTUES, 1532–1958

The system of the virtues developed for two millennia in the West had been widely dropped by the end of the eighteenth century, starting earlier with Machiavelli, then Bacon, then Hobbes, then Bernard Mandeville as isolated but scandalous precursors of Kant and Bentham, who then rigorously finished off the job. It was not dropped because it was found on careful consideration to be mistaken. It was merely set aside with a distracted casualness, perhaps as old-fashioned, or as unrealistic in an age with a new idea of the Real, or as associated with religious and political systems themselves suddenly objectionable.

Francis Bacon, for example, who in his old age employed the young Hobbes as a secretary, spoke a great deal about ethics in his *Essays*, on which Hobbes worked. But he spoke with contempt for ethical tradition. A Victorian editor quoted with approval an apology by one Dean Church, who wrote of the *Essays* that "they are like chapters in Aristotle's *Ethics* and *Rhetoric* on virtues and characters; only Bacon takes Aristotle's broad marking lines as drawn, and proceeds with the subtler and more refined observations of a much longer and wider experience."[1] Ah, yes: such as Bacon's own "long and wide experience" in betraying his friend and benefactor Lord Essex at the behest of Elizabeth; in corrupting judges while a crown officer; and, when at length he became Lord Chancellor of England, in extorting bribes for favors not delivered. Bacon was the last man in England (wrote Macaulay) to use the rack for official purposes. This is our ethical guide. One is reminded of William Bennett.

Bacon's text in fact gives no hint of viewing Aristotle or Aquinas or any-one else as his ethical guide. He never mentions them and never gives analy-ses similar to theirs. He needed no study but what accrued to him by natural wit. His "refinement" in ethics is behavioral, in the manner of Machiavelli or Hobbes, not philosophical: this is how to succeed in life, "success" mea-sured by proud titles, the Lord Chancellor's mace and the corresponding opportunity to solicit bribes. I do not know why these hard men of the sev-enteenth century were so unwilling to build on the ethical tradition of the West. Perhaps they wished merely to put away everything the Middle Ages took from the classical world, rather like the scientific contempt for reli-gious tradition in our own times.

It's no hot news to observe that Machiavelli was the pioneer in such a new ethics. Ethics in Aristotle or Aquinas or Adam Smith concerns what people are and how they act, tested against a higher standard of the good of the polis or the approach to God or the simple and obvious system of nat-ural liberty. Ethics in *The Prince*, by contrast, concerns the will of the prince. There is no other test. The test is so to speak aesthetic, the prince as artist of the state. The book is a manual for painting a "successful" state, success measured by the fulfillment of the prince's artistic will. What do you wish to paint, young master? Here, let me show you the techniques. Hold the brush thus.

Isaiah Berlin sees Machiavelli as a hinge in Western thought, as realizing suddenly in his consideration of *l'arte del stato*, statecraft, that Christian or any other comprehensive system of ethics is one thing and Prudence Only is another. Machiavelli is followed centuries later by a wider movement making the same argument, Romanticism, with its turning of everything, including politics, into Art.

The historian Carlo Ginzburg has developed some startling evidence for this claim about Machiavelli.[2] He notes that the phrase usually translated simply as "politics" in *Il Principe* is in fact as I said "the art of the state."

What of it? This: Aquinas had noted in his commentary on Aristotle's *Politics*, which did have to do with the art of a polis, that the Latin transla-tion from the Greek has two words in play: *agere*, to do, as against *facere*, to make. These relate to the Greek *praxis/phronēsis* for the doing-word and *poesis/techne* for the making-word. Aquinas (who did not read Greek, by the way) preferred *agere*, "to do"—precisely because it related to ethics. Art, *ars*, *techne, poesis*, "the making of objects," the Divine Doctor noted, does not have to do with ethics. A sculpture is well or badly made, and is not in itself a good or bad deed—though one can of course dispute such an Oscar Wildean point. As Aquinas said in the *Summa Theologiae*, "Art is right reasoning about what is to be made whereas prudence is right reasoning about what is to be done."[3]

Ginzburg claims that in reading Aquinas it occurred to Machiavelli just then to take the other route, there rejected by Aquinas, and make politics instead a matter of *ars regium*. Ginzburg notes that other people have read Machiavelli this way, in a chain back through Charles Singleton in 1953 to Jacques Maritain in 1942 to Pierre Bayle in 1702 quoting earlier authorities. All of them pointed to how Machiavelli appeared to be taking the other side of Aquinas's distinction between doing and making, *agere* and *facere*. Machiavelli abandoned the analysis of action as good or bad in favor of creating *uno stato*, beautiful or ugly, well or poorly made—but like a poem or a statue or a symphony ethically neutral.

Ginzburg has found two textual reasons to believe this tradition. For one thing, the edition of Aristotle's *Politics* that Machiavelli probably read was printed together with that commentary by Aquinas in which the make/do distinction for politics was drawn. For another, there was in the library of Machiavelli's father, in which it can be shown the young Niccolò browsed energetically, a Latin commentary by Donato Acciaioli on the other relevant Aristotle, the *Nicomachean Ethics*. Acciaioli explicitly notes that in Aristotle's first paragraph (1094a10) he could have chosen the word *aretēn* (virtue) rather than *dunamin* (ability, capacity, power). *Aretēn*, in its Homeric version of the word, by the way, is cognate with Ares, the god of war; compare *vir* > *virtus* = manly virtue in battle. Ginzburg suggests that Machiavelli, who like Aquinas did not read Greek, leapt at the notion that ability in the sense of the power to create, *facere*, being an artist of the state, is one kind of "virtue," but a virtue drained of the conventional ethics applying to practice or *phronēsis*, precisely in fact the Machiavellian *virtù* of *Il Principe*.

Whatever the reason, a century and half later we find Hobbes providing a list of virtues which contrary to the force of his sneer quoted above has learned not a thing from Aristotle, Cicero, Aquinas. Nothing at all. It is a pile of chopped-up good and bad passions unsystematized.[4] Earlier in *Leviathan* he had again sneered at the very idea of ethics, much in the style of logical positivists and their descendants nowadays: "Such as are the names of virtues and vices: for one man calleth wisdom what another calleth fear; and one cruelty what another justice; one prodigality what another magnanimity; and one gravity what another stupidity, etc. And therefore such names can never be true grounds of any ratiocination."[5]

Hobbes and Machiavelli nowhere take the virtues seriously as a system. They were early in that strange belief that a serious political philosopher had no need to be serious about ethics. Ancient rhetoric is scornfully dropped by the same people at the same time. After the seventeenth century in the West a serious ethical or epistemological philosopher had no need to be serious about persuasion. With Richard Lanham and Robert Hariman, I suspect a connection, and note that virtue ethics and rhetoric revive in academic circles at about the same time, the 1960s.[6]

Albert Jonsen and Stephen Toulmin have suggested a connection between the two histories. The "moral geometry" that people like Pascal and Spinoza demanded in the seventeenth century revived a Platonic project.[7] And along with it went an antirhetorical frame of mind. Plato was of course contemptuous of the lawyers of sophistry, as he was of all democratic institutions. Aristotle was less persuaded that we could do without persuasion, and wrote sympathetically about the art of honest rhetoric. I have noted that Aquinas, who wrote just after the *Nicomachean Ethics* had been rediscovered in the West, has a highly dialogic and rhetorical method. This is contrary to the anachronistic modern view of Aquinas as a handbook of settled judgments. Jonsen and Toulmin argue that in the late sixteenth and early seventeenth century Roman Catholics and Anglicans needed guides to judgments recently unsettled by political and religious turmoil, and found it in casuistry—"case ethics," to use the less dishonored term. "No rule," observe Jonsen and Toulmin," can be entirely self-interpreting."[8] How to interpret? Persuade. It was a revival of thirteenth-century scholasticism, which had replaced a rural and monastic focus on fixed rules with a rhetoric "based on disputation," as Lester K. Little notes.[9] "Classical rhetoric," write Jonsen and Toulmin, "provided the elements out of which later casuistry developed."[10] How to persuade? Be a *vir bonus dicendi peritus,* a good man skilled at speaking, as Quintilian had put it in the late first century AD. How to be good? Be, as Aristotle and Aquinas suggested, a student of the separate virtues in their system. Pascal killed casuistry, and Descartes and Bacon and Hobbes killed rhetoric, along with other scholastic traditions. Little wonder that an ethics of the virtues, brought to a climax in Aquinas, began to die then, too.

Europeans in the early modern times when this atheoretical attitude toward the virtues got underway had not literally forgotten the Platonic root of the Good, or the Aristotelian branches. After all, they read Latin well, and sometimes Greek, and were raised on Cicero, that clear-headed popularizer. Until the seventeenth century, in fact, and aside from the Italian books of Dante, Petrarch, Boccaccio, Ariosto, and Tasso, with French romances, there was in Europe not a great deal in the way of non-Latin or non-Greek literature to be read. The readers were anyway Christians steeped in the pagan and theological virtues, 4 + 3 = 7. Until the twentieth century the prestige of the classical languages kept the books analyzing the pagan virtues alive, as until the twentieth century the prestige of Christianity kept the books analyzing the theological virtues alive. Every literate person from Machiavelli to Bertrand Russell knew the seven virtues and was even acquainted to some degree with the body of reflection that supported their system. Adam Smith, a late writer in the tradition, stands four-square on five of them—trimmed, as I said, of faith and hope.

What appears to have intervened rather is not sheer ignorance but a dropping of the system as a system, replaced by a new habit of making up virtues on the spot out of social theories or social graces. The authority of the Philosopher and of the Divine Doctor was challenged. The New Sciences, certainly, encouraged Europeans to retheorize the social and philosophical world as Galileo, Descartes, and Newton had retheorized the physical. Every self-respecting theorist became his own Aristotle or Aquinas.

Perhaps too the new practice has to do with traditions of medieval courtly love or Renaissance courtliness. Social grace (Castiglione's *sprezzatura*) or nonchalance (*disinvoltura*) of a distinctly non-Stoic and non-Christian sort becomes at court the master virtue.[11]

Take Jane Austen. Austen was an ethical writer, very far from an easy aestheticism that says there is no such thing as a moral or an immoral marriage, that marriages are simply well or badly arranged. Remove ethical evaluation from an Austen novel and you have removed its movement. All her novels are tales of ethical development. And ethics for whom? Surely for the class of middling landed wealth she came from and which she described, you might say. Her books are in fact notably undescriptive of these lives—the servants present in modest numbers around every character, for example, are never given voice and are indeed hardly ever mentioned; nor the children. A room or a country prospect is never fully characterized in the way of a Scott. She is not engaged in social science or the production of handbooks for the lesser gentry or the making of Romantic myths for the nation.

The class work of an Austen novel is not done by portrayal of the rural middle class, but by the effect on the implied audience.[12] Austen is a reader-response writer of an especially astringent sort. Virginia Woolf remarked that Austen's writing, like indeed any writing, but hers strikingly, "stimulates us to supply what is not there," since in a form of words no physical thing can be literally "there." Words are words, to repeat, not objects. Austen is especially canny at this, endowing "with the most enduring form of life scenes which are outwardly trivial."[13] The critic Wolfgang Iser remarked in turn that " 'the enduring form of life' which Virginia Woolf speaks of is not manifested on the printed page; it is a product arising out of the interaction between text and reader."[14]

So. The virtues recommended by Austen's free, indirect style playing on the reader's mind are not those of aristocrats or even—more surprising in a devout, if nothing like Enthusiastic, daughter of an Anglican clergyman— of Christians. The virtues recommended could even be called the best of the bourgeoisie, the rural bourgeoisie we call the gentry. Marilyn Butler notes that the best people in the novels exhibit goodness as "an active, analytic process, not at all the same thing as passive good nature."[15]

But Austen's ethical thinking stops short of system, as though from a principle: No Systems. John Casey summarizes the Austenian ethic so: "Moral goodness requires the disciplining of our imagination by objective truth. It implies judgment and analytic skill. . . . Practical wisdom, which is a necessary condition of moral goodness, is undermined and rendered nugatory by selfishness, insincerity, dishonesty, and pride."[16]

In 1814—her third published novel, *Mansfield Park*, had just sold out its first printing—Austen advised in a letter her twenty-one-year-old niece Fanny Knight about a suitor. John Plumtre is admittedly not "the creature you and I should think perfection, where grace and spirit are united to worth, where manners are equal to the heart and understanding." That is the ideal in the novels. Austen's heroines learn by an active, analytic process of just the sort that Aunt Jane is exhibiting. What do they learn? That young men with polish do not always have depth, and those with depth do not always have polish.

But Plumtre is "the eldest son of a man of fortune, the brother of your particular friend, and belonging to your own country" [that is, your own rural neighborhood]. Considerations of prudence, the variables of property and pocketbooks and the profane, are never far from the scene in her novels or in the actual lives she lived and watched—though in this case Fanny was an heiress in her own right, and "much above caring about money," Aunt Jane remarks, a little tartly. But variables of solidarity and the Sacred dominate. We are dealing with a beloved niece, not a minor character exhibited as a Max U-er obsessed with prudence.

Plumtre has an "amiable mind, strict principles, just notions, good habits. . . . All that really is of the first importance," though Fanny is worried that he needs to get "more lively"—but married to you, Aunt Jane suggests, he will. "And as to there being any objection from his [religious] goodness, from the danger of his becoming even Evangelical," well, that is no proper objection, is it, Fanny? Not among us daughters and nieces of Anglican clergymen, though we ourselves of course are not inclined to enthusiastic religiosity. "Don't be frightened by the idea of his acting more strictly up to the precepts of the New Testament than others." Later, Fanny rejected John, as indeed "if his deficiencies of manner, etc. strike you more than all his good qualities" Aunt Jane had urged her to do."[17]

Jane talks of virtues up and down, back and forth, on all sides. But not from a theory. Her English suspicion of theory allows for ethical complexity. Complexity, but not coherence: grace, understanding, manners, amiability, good habits; each gives its set speech, and then withdraws from the scene.

Take, for example, ten pages (1, 22, 65, 70, 125, 207, 228, 233, 241, 244) chosen literally by random number table from her last novel (published posthumously), *Persuasion*, and consider the ethical loading of the language. The Good: admiration, respect, interest which never failed [thus Sir Walter Elliot as he read in the pages of *The Baronetage* about himself and other worthy knights], precisely, most accurately, ancient, respectable [all ironic, as so often in Austen], very handsome [fortune], explicit, responsible, eligible, of a gentleman's family, most consoling, [his profession] qualified [him], the commonest civility, once so much [to each other], attached, happy, gentle, formidable, right to be done, judged so well, simple, better than nothing, renewed spirit, a little smile, a little glow, agreeable, in very good style, the appearance of a gentleman, finest, most generous, the law of honor, sincere, from the heart, favorably, sensible, agreeable, advantage in company, so pleasantly, so much respect. The Bad: not suited him, cold, suspicious, a little weather-beaten [ironic, of the admiral], shyness, reserve, pretense, equal pain, now nothing, horror, in an agony of silence, despair, in the bitterest agony, [a] slight [curtsey], late, reluctant, ungracious, inferior [in circumstances], [the] poor [one], [my] poor [Charles], inferior situation in society [ironic, in free indirect speech, as so often in Austen], disrespectful, hypocrite, unkind, ignorant, giddy, desirable, affected, poor [man], hard-hearted, cruelty, so alarmed. It is an ethical world in which the two principles of private worth and social standing sometimes clash and sometimes dance together across the Octagon Room at Bath.

Look at the density of ethical evaluations, about eight on each small-format page, implying about 2,300 in the 290 pages of this edition. This is not naturalism, a Zola or an Ibsen or a Frank Norris or a Louis Couperus examining characters as "human beasts." It is the opposite, an ethicism in literature, emphasizing choice. The author sits always at our elbow urging us with gentle irony to look on this person or that behavior with or without approbation. Social virtue, as exhibited in Anne Elliot of *Persuasion*, requires one to be amiable, comforting the afflicted and allowing for fools. In *Emma* the ethical turning point comes when the heroine lashes out at the tediously garrulous but harmless fool Miss Bates. And one must have or acquire also some modest standing by rank or fortune, a competency. Private virtue, as also in Anne Elliot—the most loveable, literally "amiable," it is said, of Austen's heroines—is to have both sense and sensibility. Anne's, and Austen's, concerns are steadily ethical.

But, I repeat, the ethical evaluations, though exhibiting a balance of autonomy and connection, moral courage and sociable love, are not systematic. In the daughter of a clergyman in an officially Christian age and society one is very surprised not to see more concern with the transcendent. In an Austen novel, as a friend put it to me, you can't spit without hitting a clergyman. But God or his system of virtues is literally never present.

Or take George Orwell. Again it's hard to name a more ethically concerned writer:

> A curious cunning virtue
> You share with just the few who don't desert you.
> A dozen writers, half-a-dozen friends.
> A moral genius.[18]

Orwell praises Charles Dickens, for example, as "generously angry," and takes sides with him. Dickens, like Orwell himself, was "hated with equal hatred by all the smelly little orthodoxies which are now [March 11, 1940] contending for our souls."[19] Dickens's "good-tempered antinomianism" is not quite a self-description accurate for Orwell. I mean the "good-tempered" part. Orwell was very fierce against party lines, which is why he has been so easy to appropriate for left and right and middle, since he was against all of them, and in favor of all of them, selectively. It reminds one of Austen updated. No systems, says Orwell, for we have in the 1930s and 1940s seen the consequences of ethics subordinated to systems. In August 1944 one finds him blasting away at right-wing Colonel Blimps who find war lovely always. But at the same time he blasts away at war resisters who find even a war against fascism objectionable.[20]

The ethical word continually on Orwell's lips—compare Austen's "amiability," combined with "serious reflection"—is "decency," especially the "common" kind, combined with social criticism. He found "decency" in all manner of common folk, down and out in Paris and London, in the miners or workless workers on the road to Wigan Pier. Such a democratic thought would never have occurred to Austen, who was no Romantic.

It seems to Orwell that "in the chaos in which we are living"—no intemperate view of the early 1940s—"even the prudential reasons for common decency are being forgotten."[21] Saying the obvious was the first duty of an intelligent person. What enrages him about the Left Book Club in London and the Stalinists in Spain, and everywhere the fascists and imperialists and Colonel Blimps, is precisely their cynical or stupid advocacy of something higher by way of ethics. The revolution must be served, said the Communists, for reasons of higher hope. Therefore we can run show trials in Spain to execute anarchists and other enemies of Comrade Stalin. King and country must be saved, said the Establishment, for reasons of higher faith. Therefore we can run wars and empires to tame and slaughter the wogs, who begin at Calais.

Transcendent hope and faith were the problem. Austen seems to take a similar view. Bad transcendentals lead in Austen's view to risible foolishness, as in Sir Walter Elliot's faith in family and blood lines. In Orwell's more serious world they lead to totalitarianism, as in the Spanish Communists' hope for a Stalinist revolution.

Though Orwell remained true to the label of socialist, he admired people like Arthur Koestler who converted from party-line Stalinism when they realized that it entailed the rape of decency. Orwell was defending Dickens, but he might as well have been defending himself when he wrote that "it is not at all certain that a merely moral criticism of society may not be just as 'revolutionary' . . . as the politico-economic criticism which is fashionable at this moment. . . . Two viewpoints are always tenable. The one, how can you improve human nature until you change the system? The other, what is the use of changing the system before you have improved human nature? . . . The moralist and the revolutionary are constantly undermining one another."[22]

Charles Dickens himself had been of course nothing like a socialist—the idea and the word barely existed—and was ignorant of how an economy worked except in publishing and the theater. His ideal, notes Northrop Frye, "would have to be an intensely paternalistic society, an expanded family."[23] Marx called his sort of view Feudal Socialism, "half lamentation, half lampoon; half echo of the past, half menace for the future," with "total incapacity to comprehend the march of modern history."[24] Orwell the socialist asserts that Dickens "had not the vision to see that private property is an obstructive nuisance." Orwell, like Marx, was at least consistent in his disdain for property, being notably, even self-destructively, careless of creature comforts.[25]

But Orwell approves of a Dickensian ethic of decency. "'If men would behave decently the world would be decent' is not such a platitude as it sounds."[26] Orwell's word "decency" can be thought of as justice, with a little hope, a modicum of love, a nonfanatical faith, a temperance restraining one from using guns and torture to get one's way. Lionel Trilling noted that Orwell praised, too, aristocratic virtues in their bourgeois dress c. 1910, the *Boy's Own* magazine ideals of sportsmanship, gentlemanliness, duty, and physical courage, though Orwell the socialist "must sometimes have wondered how it came about" in a capitalist society.[27] No systems, and certainly not the system of the seven virtues.

35

OTHER LISTS

Yet "few have resisted the temptation," says chapter 2 in Peterson and Seligman's *Character Strengths and Virtues*, "to articulate a definitive list of the virtues that constitute the well-lived life."[1] So true. It's a Great Books impulse. (See *The Great Ideas: A Syntopticon of Great Books of the Western World* [1952], pp. 925–1009.) Peterson and Seligman's chapter 3, which the two editors wrote by themselves, examines among the less serious lists William Bennett's, the Boy Scouts', Benjamin Franklin's, Charlemagne's, and the wizard Merlin's, taken from a Web site. And then it reviews more respectfully the scientific literature in psychology on the matter in Erikson's stages (1963), Maslow's hierarchy (1970), Norman's Big Five (1963), Greenberger et al.'s psychosocial maturity (1975), Marie Jahoda's concepts of positive mental health (1958), Ryff et al.'s dimensions of well-being (1989), Piaget's (1932) and Kohlberg's (1981) moral reasoning of the child, Schwartz et al.'s universal values, Buss et al.'s desirable characteristics in a mate (1990), Kumpfer's resilience factors (1999), Vaillant's defense mechanisms (1971), Gardner's multiple intelligences (1983), Leffert et al.'s internal development assets, and the vocabulary lists of virtues by Allport, Oddbert, Cawley, Martin, and Johnson.[2]

But even this admirable project overlooks most of ethical philosophy, and most of what ethics says about such lists. Hursthouse's textbook on virtue ethics has 126 items in its bibliography, Peterson and Seligman over 2,300. The forty-odd psychologists contributed on average about 60 citations each. They are polite toward ethical philosophy. Yet their and Hursthouse's bibliographies overlap in a mere five items: two from Aristotle;

L. Blum's *Friendship, Altruism, and Morality* (1980); Elizabeth Anscombe's "Modern Moral Philosophy" (1958), and Linda Zagzebski's *Virtues of the Mind* (1996). That's it. Ethical inquiries seem often to take place so, in nonoverlapping conversations.

Even moderns with self-consciously ethical projects, in other words, seem spooked by the history of ethics, and resist reading it. The only book of Simone Weil that appeared in something like the form she intended, *The Need for Roots: Prelude to a Declaration of Duties towards Mankind* (1943 [1949]), was a tract explaining the strange defeat of France and imploring her countrymen to recover their rootedness in the mysticism of work and Jesus. It begins with a list of thirteen needs of the soul—a small step or two away from a list of virtues: order, liberty, responsibility, equality, hierarchism, honor, punishment, freedom of opinion (a ten-page Rousseauian appeal to introduce censorship in obedience to the general will), risk, private property, collective property, truth (with more censorship, this time a "special court . . . for publicly condemning any avoidable error," with powers of imprisonment over people like Jacques Maritain saying such silly things as that the ancients never questioned slavery).[3] The rest of the book concerns number 14, the need for taking root, *enracinement*, expressed as transcendent virtues of love and hope and especially faith approaching God. (Or expressed as the vice of Romance and anti-Semitism.) In accord with her distaste for the unmystical St. Thomas Aquinas—"perhaps on insufficient acquaintance," T. S. Eliot notes dryly in his preface to the English translation of 1952—her list has no system and no connection to the traditions she recommends.

Even my beloved Simone Weil. Who in 1928 placed first in the entrance examination for the Ecole Normale Supérieure—Simone de Beauvoir was second that year: two women. The Simone Weil who in preparing for her final exams in moral philosophy at the Ecole assigned herself to study "thoroughly" Aristotle, Bentham, Schopenhauer, Nietzsche; "carefully" Machiavelli, Hobbes, Leibniz, Bergson, Schelling, Fichte, Hegel, and Lenin; and "systematically" the pre-Socratics, the Sophists, Socrates, Plato, Locke, Hume, Berkeley, Spinoza, and Kant.[4] When applicable, in Greek. Even, I lament, this admirable Weil assembles virtues in Hobbesian style from branches ripped from the tree. Homer nods.

The University of Chicago economist and historian Robert Fogel, to take a more recent example, is a great historical scholar of economic and

How Fogel's Fifteen Virtues Lie Down on the Classical Seven

sense of purpose	Hope, Courage
vision of opportunity	Hope
sense of the mainstream of work and life	Prudence
strong family ethic	Love, Faith
sense of community	Love, Faith
capacity to engage with diverse groups	Justice, Love, Prudence
benevolence	Love, Justice
work ethic	Temperance, Prudence, Justice
sense of discipline	Temperance, Prudence
capacity to focus	Temperance, Prudence
resisting hedonism	Temperance
capacity for self-education	Prudence, Hope
thirst for knowledge	Prudence, Hope
appreciation for quality	Temperance, Faith
self-esteem	Prudence, Faith

Source: Fogel, *Fourth Great Awakening*, 1999, pp. 205–207.

demographic matters, among the best in the late twentieth century, and has a serious interest even in the history of religion. But at the climax of his interesting book of 1999 on the ethical poverty of poor Americans and the "fourth great awakening," he suddenly proposes a set of fifteen virtues which he reckons would be good for the poor of Watts and Appalachia to cultivate.

On its face there is nothing objectionable about Fogel's list—except perhaps that fifteen seems a large and insufficiently analyzed number. It sounds like the strange number of dimensions that physicists these days believe they need for a unifying theory of everything, as they modestly put it. Certainly anyone, especially someone who is not doing well in bourgeois America, would be wise to develop "a sense of purpose," "a sense of community," "a capacity to focus," and so forth. The historically black colleges have been very busy at making their students bourgeois in this way.

But by grabbing this or that virtue intuitively from around the color wheel, instead of disciplining oneself to the old primaries, you lose the old analyses and the old stories for improving your thinking. Sticking with ethical categories you already know from their stories in your culture will permit you, for example, to pick apart the bourgeois man's notion of Courage,

to see what is bad or good in it, silly or proper. In Fogel's list, certain bourgeois versions of the virtues come striding in by the kitchen door unan-
nounced—a "work ethic" that serves the Man, eh, Professor Fogel? And
some Christian versions burst into the front parlor without proper intro-
ductions—a "benevolence" sprung from bourgeois considerations of status?

Fogel's list, to be frank, is a criticism of poor urban black Americans—
name the poor urban Korean American community of your acquaintance
that is conventionally thought to show insufficient "work" ethic or the poor
urban Hispanic American community that is conventionally thought to show
insufficient "strong family" ethic. His list is derived uncriticized because unac-
knowledged from the traditions of white, northern European, Protestant, and
haut bourgeois culture. Quite uncharacteristically in such a great scholar, but
typical of the casual way ethical theorizing has been handled in the West since
the decline of a religion giving it force and focus, he hasn't done his homework. Even my beloved Bob Fogel, who revolutionized the study of economic
history. Who hired me in 1968. Who continued to develop intellectually into
his old age. Even, I lament, this admirable Bob. Homer naps.

Similarly, William Bennett, who is not a great French mystic or a great
American economic historian, and certainly not Homer, in *The Book of
Virtues* (1993) proposes, it seems again without a great deal of thought, a list
of ten virtues, which seem to map into the classical seven so. It reminds one
of Gene Autry's "Cowboy Commandments" of 1939: "1. The Cowboy must
never shoot first, hit a smaller man or take unfair advantage. 2. He must
never go back on his word. . . . 10. The Cowboy is a patriot."[5] Autry's list in
fact coheres rather better than Bennett's. I do not know why a professional
philosopher—which is Bennett's academic training: political philosophy—
would bypass the literature on the virtues when writing a book about the
virtues. But Bennett is not the only or the most prominent philosopher in
the English-speaking tradition to skimp thus on work, loyalty, honesty, self-
discipline, responsibility, and perseverance.

A French and altogether more perseveringly philosophical work along these
lines is *A Small Treatise on the Great Virtues* (1996) by the teacher of classical
philosophy at the Sorbonne I have mentioned several times, André Comte-
Sponville. His list has eighteen virtues, shades of Fogel, not all of them "great"
ones, and including a number of rather minor ones (Purity, for example).

Bennett's List

Self-discipline	Temperance
Compassion	Love
Responsibility	Courage, Justice
Friendship	secular Love
Work	? Temperance, Justice, Courage
Courage	Courage
Perseverance	Courage
Honesty	Courage, Justice
Loyalty	political Faith (patriotism),
[Love	Love]
Faith	religious Faith

Source: William J. Bennett, ed., *The Book of Virtues*, 1993

What system there is in his book is provided by occasional references to his three masters, Spinoza and two French philosophers, his former colleague, Vladimir Jankélévitch (d. 1985) and "Alain" (the nom du plume of Émile-Auguste Chartier, 1868–1951, a philosopher long at the Ecole Normale Supérieure; he was Simone Weil's mentor in left politics during the 1920s).

There is much to be learned from Comte-Sponville—such as that Spinoza needs to be read by anyone serious about ethical philosophy; and that Messrs. Jankélévitch and Alain need some looking into as well. The chapters on politeness and gratitude are very fine. But the book has the feel of a closed lecture hall at the Sorbonne, redolent of Gauloises. It's French provincial.

In particular Comte-Sponville has sealed himself off from English-language influences, as though to resist Disney and McDonald's. The text and footnotes are overwhelmingly francophone in their reference. Even German and Italian figures get short shrift. *Le centre est Paris.* London and especially New York and Chicago barely exist. Comte-Sponville's translator, Catherine Temerson, did an amazingly thorough job of giving English editions and page numbers to replace the original French ones for Montaigne, Pascal, La Rochefoucauld, and other heavily used writers, which reduces the francophone impression of the notes. Jankélévitch and Alain had not then been translated, so for them the French editions had to suffice.[6]

I am not criticizing Comte-Sponville for relying excessively on the language of his birth. That would be unpersuasive coming from someone who, you will note, when she very learnedly cites Montaigne, Nicole, Molière, Bayle, Thomassin, Montesquieu, Voltaire, Frederick's French, Rousseau, Bonaparte, Constant, Tocqueville, Baudelaire, Renan, Rimbaud, van Gogh's French correspondence, Albert Aurier, Proust, Gide, Weil, Sartre, de Beauvoir, Aron, Bourdieu, Todorov, Jacques Le Goff, Nathalie Heinich, François Jullien, and indeed Vladimir Jankélévitch and Comte-Sponville themselves, uses English translations. I am not *quite* being as Anne Elliot put it to herself in *Persuasion* "like many other great moralists and preachers . . . eloquent on a point in which her own conduct would ill bear examination." I am criticizing rather Comte-Sponville's, and Weil's and Fogel's and Bennett's, lack of scientific care in collecting the data. The slapdash scholarship, I've noted, is typical of how ethical inquiry has been handled in the West since the rise of emotivism c. 1900, or since the receding sea of faith c. 1848, or even in some circles since Machiavelli and Bacon and Hobbes recommended that we toss away two millennia of study of the virtues.

Among about 150 citations to authors in the index of *The Small Treatise* a bare 15 write in English, the German-born Arendt and the Austrian-born Popper among them. Rawls, Arendt, and Popper—that is, one born American, a naturalized American, and a naturalized Briton—are the only twentieth-century English-writing philosophers cited. None of the virtue ethicists, therefore, get into Comte-Sponville's lecture hall, not one, not Foot or MacIntyre or Nussbaum or Williams or Anscombe or McDowell, though Comte-Sponville is without doubt of their company and his treatment would have been improved by listening to them.

I have already noted how Comte-Sponville's anticlericalism denies him specifically Christian systems of the virtues, though to his credit he does make occasional raids into Aquinas. And it must be admitted that the English-speaking virtue ethicists themselves, with exceptions such as MacIntyre, do virtue ethics with even less engagement with Christian ethical thinking.

More generally, the various fields of ethical scholarship don't much talk to each other. On ethical and scientific grounds, I think, something should be done. The recent book I mentioned on "virtue epistemology," for example, is courageous. But it is narrow in its intellectual conversation. That does not seem a good plan for a group advocating ethical intellectuality. Its list of references is ungenerous on virtue ethics itself, and does not contain Feyerabend or Lakatos or much of anything from the social criticism of epistemology, and cites (this in a 2003 book) none of Hilary Putnam's recent work.[7] About a quarter of the citations are to works by one or another of the thirteen authors of the essays written for the book—though admittedly self-citation is after all characteristic of any small and beleaguered academic movement.

But Comte-Sponville goes a step further: he writes on virtue ethics without reading any books or articles about it. *Pas un seul.* The deafness in Comte-Sponville to recent English and older Christian talk of the virtues would be as though a French jazz musician made no musical reference to Charlie Parker or Thelonious Monk, and refused even to listen to Armstrong or King Oliver. There is no citation to virtue ethics after Aristotle and Aquinas, I say, in a treatise on the ethics of the virtues. This is jazz relying on Jelly Roll Morton.

It could make one indignant, if one were inclined that way. The seven citations in Comte-Sponville's index to English-language humorists outnumber his citations to all English-language moralists of any description before the twentieth century except Hume (Hobbes 3, Bentham 1, Locke 1, Mandeville 1; no Sidgwick, Mill, Smith, Hutcheson, Butler, Shaftesbury). Of the thirty-one page citations to English-language writers a fifth are to Woody Allen and Groucho Marx. One is disappointed not to see more engagement with the ethical thought of Jerry Lewis.

36

EASTERN AND OTHER WAYS

But after such criticism, doubtless very well deserved, one must in justice give credit where credit is due. Austen and Orwell, with Weil and Fogel and Bennett and Comte-Sponville, or even Gene Autry, the Boy Scouts, Shun-chih (the Six Maxims), Rotary International (Four-Way Test), Dante (circles of hell), and the management of the Yomiuri Giants (the Gaijin Ten Commandments) deserve gold stars, full credit, extra points even, against self-described ethicists who leave their case at Max U or the categorical imperative or, in vulgar mode, the adding up of "stakeholders." The people I have been so churlishly complaining about at least use some list of unfungible, complexly interacting, and above all storied virtues. Good on them.

The alternative is to search for a unified ideal, a formula, a three-by-five-inch card for the Good—that mad if noble project of Aristotle's thesis supervisor. The Talmud tells of Rabbi Hillel's most famous remark. A certain heathen challenged Hillel to teach him the entire Torah while standing on one foot. Hillel replied, the heathen standing on one foot, "What is hateful to you, do not do to your neighbor: that is the whole Torah, while the rest is commentary; go and learn it." Conveniently short. But notice the coda, "go and learn the commentary." It is emphatically not a three-by-five card, such as "Maximize utility" or "Follow the categorical imperative." It's a library card. As Murdoch says, "A reflection [on the virtues] requires and generates a rich and diversified vocabulary for naming aspects of goodness. It is a shortcoming of much contemporary moral philosophy [she wrote in 1969] that it eschews discussion of the separate virtues."[1]

The Chinese sages understood this well, beginning a century before Aristotle noticed it. The Confucian virtues are not obviously identical to the Western seven. "Confucius" (551?-479? BC) is the Latinized name from the Chinese for "Kung the great teacher." Kung reflected on moral charisma or moral power and its connection to the proper rites, but his method of teaching, gathered in *The Analects*, is not systematic. It proceeds by parable and by often obscure proverb and by quotation from a preexisting body of poetry, somewhat in the manner of the Nazarene five centuries later offering strange little fables to his followers and quoting Hebrew scripture back at the Pharisees. The stories and proverbs of *The Analects* and other writings that contained the sayings attributed to Confucius were referred to again and again in the twenty-five centuries of Confucian philosophy, as the writings about the Nazarene and the writings of the Philosopher have been in the West. Like Christianity and Aristotelianism, too, Confucianism is no mere static body of thought.

Philip Ivanhoe, from whom I have mainly learned the little I grasp of all this, notes that Chinese ethical philosophy concerns itself much more with education and cultivation of character than with Platonic explorations of the Good. And so, like virtue ethics (and like the schools of Greco-Roman ethics after Plato, and like existentialism c. 1950, too), it is more likely to focus on what Kant called "anthropology" or "philosophical psychology."[2]

The lack of interest in ethical development, as against the ethical action of already formed adults, is a fault in the footnotes to Plato that constitute Western ethical philosophy. Hursthouse commends Aristotle for never forgetting that we were all once children, noting that "to read almost every other famous moral philosopher is to receive the impression that we, the intelligent adult readers, sprang fully formed from our father's brow."[3] From Zeus's brow, note, not Hera's. Hursthouse does not make the feminist point, and also, by the way, seems unacquainted with the famous moral philosophers of the East, who as I say focus on development.[4] Western moral philosophy is peculiarly masculinist and, so to speak, adultist, taking an autonomous, finished adult, preferably a middle-aged and childless bachelor, as the site of philosophizing. Feminists such as Carol Gilligan and her many followers and critics do not forget that we were all once children, and feminists such as Nel Noddings and Annette Baier do not forget that we all came from families.

Neither I say do the Chinese. "Mencius" (391–308 BC) was Meng Tzu, and thus his epithet was "Mengzi," Meng the teacher. This Meng was contemporary with Plato and Aristotle, and was, so to speak, the St. Paul to Confucius, analyzing what the master had left in storied form. He identified the four "sprouts" of good ethical character, the inborn characters of humanity from which a good person can grow: benevolence, righteousness, propriety, and right-and-wrong. We are in another ethical world, it seems. But Mencius's botanical metaphor is simply a psychology, the human plant for a flowering of virtue. The flowers themselves springing from the sprouts look a good deal like Western virtues. Courage, for example, is of course prominently mentioned. The "flood-like energy" (*hoaran zhi qi*) of ethical courage, the prudence and temperance shown in heart-and-head (*xin*, pronounced in this Latinization as "shin"), the mental courage and temperance of "focus" (*si*) do not sound all that far from habits of the heart and of the ethical mind admired in the West. "Right-and-wrong" is in fact merely prudence, common sense.

There is a price to pay in the motherly, developmental sprouts of Confucian ethics. Remember François Jullien's exposition of the devaluation of courage by the "upstream" strategy in Chinese thought, and its cost in freedom. The case is similar here. The emphasis on development implies a hierarchy of full adults supervising presumed children—for example, the Confucian bureaucrat supervising the "small men" of mere commerce. There's a similar tension in Western thought on the left. James Boyd White criticizes the market-loving school of law and economics, which posits a fully competent adult, mysteriously produced. "Our lives [in fact entail] . . . the development of wisdom, judgment, taste, and character."[5] I agree. The autonomous man may be a myth. Yet isn't it sometimes a politically good myth? And doesn't participation in markets in which you are treated as though you were an adult—admitting that very few of us actually are—help you to fuller competence? I think so; Jim White is doubtful.

In any event, the virtues of grownups admired in the Confucian tradition are, unsurprisingly, pretty much those admired by Greek pagans—and by French Christians, too, and doubtless by the Bushmen of the Kalahari. The three leading virtues according to Confucius himself are prudence (wisdom, *chih*: here it would seem a mix of *sophia* and *phronēsis*), love (benevolence), and courage: "Wisdom, benevolence, and courage, these three are virtues universally acknowledged in the Empire," and anywhere else you might mention.[6] For example, they were acknowledged in *The Wonderful Wizard of Oz* (1900): the Scarecrow lacked prudent brains, the Tin Man a loving heart, and the Cowardly Lion imperial courage.

And Confucius is repeatedly characterized as exercising temperance as well: "Even when there was plenty of meat, he avoided eating more than rice. Only in the case of wine did he not set himself a rigid limit. He simply never drank to the point of becoming confused."[7] And he also speaks of *eros*, as in quoting a compact poem of a lover pining:

> The flowers of the cherry tree,
> How they wave about!
> It's not that I do not think of you,
> But your home is so far away.

"The Master commented, 'He did not really think of her. If he did, there is no such thing as being far away.'"[8]

Similarly in Buddhism one can pick out the Western seven virtues if you work at it a little. Buddha said, "Evil deeds are committed from partiality, enmity, stupidity, and fear."[9] That is to say, evil comes from a lack of justice, love, prudence, and courage. Temperance and hope are easily discerned in the very discipline of a "noble lay-disciple," who can expect if he follows it to be "fortunate both in this world and the next, and when his body breaks up on his death he is reborn to bliss in heaven." Only faith is absent from the master's words, at any rate in its backward-looking form, though of course his followers practiced it.

So elsewhere east of Suez. *The Vimalakirti Sutra* presents a vivid portrait of a rich, mercantile, bourgeois Buddhist. The text we have is the Chinese translation of AD 406 of a lost first-century Sanskrit original. A chapter entitled in its English translation by Burton Watson "Expedient Means" explains why Mr. Vimalakirti was blessed. Each attribute can be assigned to a Western virtue or antivice:

> If he was among rich men, they honored him as foremost among them because he preached the superior Law [that is, proper prudence] for them. If he was among lay believers, they honored him as foremost because he freed them from greed and attachment [that is, improper prudence and improper love]. If among warriors . . . he taught them forbearance [temperance, justice]. If among Brahmans . . . he rid them of their self-conceit [pride]. The great ministers . . . because he taught them the correct law [justice]. The princes . . . because he showed them how to be loyal [faith] and filial [love, justice]. . . . The common people honored him as first among them because he helped them to gain wealth and power [prudence again, and hope].[10]

The Japanese are in some ways an easier case than the Chinese and the South Asians, in other ways harder. Westerners have no trouble recognizing the heroic stoicism of the samurai as parallel to the character of a Christian knight. Check off the virtues: courage, temperance, faith as integrity, prudence in the skills of the swordsman, though brought to what seems to a Westerner an insane degree of perfection, with a sword so repeatedly tempered that it can cut in half a Western sword at a stroke. The parallel allows for profit in such odd cultural exchanges as the importation of Japanese children's cartoons, and Tom Cruise in *The Last Samurai* with Japanese and English subtitles.

But Ruth Benedict argued in 1946 that the Japanese, unlike the Westerners or the Chinese, do not have a notion of an invariant character, called by the Greeks and their Christian and Muslim admirers a "soul," *psyche, anima.* Most official Buddhisms worldwide, for example, do not recognize a *pudgala,* a soul resistant to change from one reincarnation to the next. Japanese Buddhism is on this matter orthodox. The tragic Mizoguchi film, *The Life of Oharu* (1952), from a seventeenth-century novel, tells the story of a woman's social descent. But it tells it in long shots. Japanese morality lies on the surface of society, not inside the person. It is a matter of *mos* in the Roman sense, not *ethos* in the Greek.

Benedict argued that Japan was a "shame" culture, as against the modern Western "guilt" culture. To avoid shame one must follow the "circle of *chu,*" the infinite duty to the emperor or to the nation, or the "circle of *giri,*" the finite yet precise duty to others or to one's honor. Either set of duties is external. They are both about social honor, not about the state of one's soul. Compare the similar duties of personal sacrifice at Rome, the early Brutus I have mentioned executing his two sons for treason, or Roman mothers telling their boys to go and die for the *patria.* A table of Japanese virtues, Benedict claims, is not a description of a courageous, just, hopeful, loving person. That would be Greek, not Roman. The Japanese/Roman virtues derive from the social circles of obligation.[11] They sound, indeed, Kantian, which is perhaps another objection to Kant's strange system, since he is recommending it for modern Europeans, not Japanese or ancient Romans. "Each circle," Benedict explains, "has its special detailed code and a man judges his fellows, not by ascribing to them integrated personalities [good or evil], but by saying of [bad men] that . . . 'they do not know [the code of the circle of] *giri.*'"[12]

The Japanese who before August 1945 were eager to die repelling the American invasion switched immediately, when the emperor announced the surrender on the radio, to wholehearted solidarity with the American occupation.[13] An American wishes that the Vietnamese or the Iraqis had had the same ethical tastes. A similar reassertion of the claims of *chu* had happened in Japan a decade before in the other direction. The Fascist government had jailed radicals. In 1933, under torture by the police and pleading letters from their mothers, the anti-Fascist radicals commenced "returning to Japan," as it was put, reaffirming in the circle of *chu* their loyalty to the emperor.[14] By 1936 fully three-quarters of the convicted radicals had actually done so.

It strikes a modern Westerner as perfidious, in the line of Churchill's crude jibe at the Germans, "The Hun is either at your throat or at your feet." Iago or Richard III did no worse, a Westerner would say indignantly. Even the extorted confessions at show trials in the Soviet Union were recognized at the time, by the Russians at any rate, as shameful, and recognized as shameful even by the Russians running the trials, who made efforts to conceal the methods by which the confessions were extracted. Their guilty efforts managed to mask the nature of the trials from a good many Westerners, if not, I repeat, from any Russian. A victim who miraculously escaped from Stalin and his gang 1936–1938 would instantly repudiate his "confession."

But the switches in Japan, however achieved, were on the contrary high moral deeds following the circle of *chu*. Japanese tragedies are not generated by internal contradictions of character, but by competing claims of differing circles, as though Hamlet's indecision were on account of a sacred loyalty to his uncle. In this respect the Japanese appear more Greek than Roman, at least the Greek of Sophocles or Euripides as against the opposed Greek tradition of the philosophers, especially of the Stoic philosophers and their Roman followers. Antigone faces the competing claims of family loyalty to her brother and civic loyalty to her king. She is not a modern individualist. She is so to speak Japanese.

The Japanese, according to Benedict, "do not see human life as a stage on which forces of good contend with forces of evil. They see existence as a drama which calls for careful balancing of the claims of one 'circle' against another."[15] The Japanese equivalent of *Shane* or *High Noon* is the eighteenth-century *Tale of the Forty-Seven Rōnin*. A *rōnin* is a "floating man," a masterless samurai, a sword for hire. Taken from an actual event in 1701–1703, the play tells how the forty-seven elaborately avenged an insult to their dead master. So much is Western, if from the modern Western point of view startlingly thorough. In order to get into a position where they could strike back, for example, some of the *rōnin* pretended to be honorless, inconsequential, not-to-be-feared men for nearly two years. That's not quite the quick Romantic revenge followed by quick Christian remorse, diluted at last to quasi apologies, "if I have offended anyone," which the average American nowadays takes as good behavior.

And the *rōnin*, after redeeming their honor on the one account, and becoming wildly popular with the masses, then submitted to the collective suicide ordered by the shogun. They satisfied the claims of the circle of *giri* and then also of *chu*, honoring their master and then also obeying their nation. Strange stuff from the perspective of Western notions of heroic/bourgeois/Christian/Romantic individualism—though again one can see a parallel in Greek tragedy and Roman tradition.

In the end, though, the virtues are not precisely universal. The thoughtful chapter in Peterson and Seligman on the matter concludes that "there is a strong convergence across time, place, and intellectual tradition about certain core virtues."[16] I am of course very ready to believe this. But the chapter—and the rest of the book, which is light on psychological data outside the here and now in the West—does not entirely persuade.

William Reddy has made a persuasive case against universality, with applications to non-Western societies and to the Sentimental Revolution in Europe itself after 1770. He says that emotions, at least, if not virtues exactly, are "overlearned cultural habits," like language or customs, varying radically from place to place and from time to time.[17] George Washington, for example, wept on many public occasions, as when he took leave of his army in 1783. Yet in 1972 Edward Muskie lost his bid to become the Democratic nominee for president because he wept in vexation at a Nixon-inspired calumny on his wife. Different times, different definitions of manly virtue.

Ethics is a local narrative. Well, so what? In science generality must sometimes be sacrificed to applicability. It makes no sense to try to explain the fauna of a pond in Vermont always at the mechanical and atomic level when an evolutionary story about that particular sort of pond serves us better.

In 1985 Richard Rorty put it well, in defending what he calls "postmodern bourgeois liberalism." He distinguished two strands in post-Enlightenment thought, the Kantians and the Hegelians. The Kantians are people like John Rawls and Ronald Dworkin "who think there is such a thing as . . . an ahistorical distinction between the demands of morality and those of prudence."[18] By contrast, the Hegelians, such as John Dewey, Alasdair MacIntyre, Richard Rorty, Stanley Fish, and Deirdre McCloskey say that there is "no appeal beyond the relative merits of various actual or proposed communities. . . . The Hegelians see nothing to be responsible to except persons and actual or possible historical communities."[19]

37

NEEDING VIRTUES

Or one can take the view of Machiavelli interpreted on the contrary as a monist advocating Prudence Only—the Prudence Only view of Callicles or Thrasymachus in Plato, Hobbes (again, on a narrow reading of certain famous passages), Mandeville (no narrowing required), Bentham (throughout), Bonaparte, Talleyrand, Bismarck, Nietzsche (popularized), Justice Holmes, Bertrand Russell, H. L. Mencken (see Nietzsche), Sigmund Freud, Henry Kissinger, Steven Pinker, and Judge Richard Posner of the United States Seventh Circuit Court of Appeals.

These men declare that the long tradition of virtue talk is mere blather. To its decline: good riddance. What we do not need: more preachers and other hypocrites. How to decide: power; or power's democratic cousin, utility; or power's other, natural cousin, evolution. As Knight wrote in 1923, "The nineteenth-century utilitarianism was in essence merely the ethics of power, the 'glorified economics' to which we have referred before. Its outcome was to reduce virtue to prudence."[1]

The turn in the past four centuries away from the virtues toward "realism" about the vices has orphaned the good. As Michael Polanyi put it, each philosopher since Descartes has worked "with the whole force of his homeless moral passions within a purely materialistic framework of purposes."[2] Thus in 1640 Thomas Hobbes announced the new antiethical dispensation: "Every man, for his own part, calleth that which pleaseth, and is delightful to himself, GOOD; and that EVIL which displeaseth him: insomuch that while every man differeth from others in constitution, they differ also one from another concerning the common distinction of good and evil. Nor is there any such thing as *agathon aplox*, that is to say, simply good."[3] If virtues cannot be connected to self-interest or genetics, to utility or power, they are, in the early twentieth-century philosophical term of Vienna and Cambridge, simply "meaningless," which is to say undiscussable.

Most academics and other intellectuals by now adhere to this chocolate-ice-cream theory of ethics, articulated philosophically out of the late logical positivism of the mid-1930s to the postpositivist present by A. J. Ayer, Moritz Schlick, Charles Stevenson, Richard Hare, John Mackie, Allan Gibbard, and Simon Blackburn, namely, that ethical arguments are mere preferences, like an uncriticizable preference for this or that flavor of ice cream. You prefer chocolate to amaretto. I prefer on the other hand amaretto to chocolate. No point in arguing.

It is also called the "hurrah-boo" theory. Ethical and aesthetic preferences, Holmes wrote in 1902, are "more or less arbitrary. . . . Do you like sugar in your coffee or don't you?"[4] Hurrah. In the same year: "Our tastes are finalities."[5] Boo. In the fourth year of the Great War he wrote to Harold Laski, "When men differ in taste as to the kind of world they want the only thing to do is to go to work killing."[6] The problem is the word "taste," with its invocation of considerations more or less arbitrary, sugar in your coffee, hurrah-boo. Perhaps Holmes was merely expressing that he was appalled by the war and hopeless, as many were in that year. But here he is in 1920 writing to Pollock: "I think that the sacredness of human life is a purely municipal ideal of no validity outside the jurisdiction. I believe that force, mitigated so far as may be by good manners, is the *ultima ratio,* and between two groups that want to make inconsistent kinds of worlds I see no remedy except force. . . . Every society rests on the death of men."[7] And here is he is again in 1918: "Deep-seated preferences cannot be argued about—you cannot argue a man into liking a glass of beer—and therefore, when differences are sufficiently far reaching, we try to kill the other man."[8] To settle the matter of south Slav nationalism or German naval ambitions or the Eastern question we need to go to work killing.

Jeffrey Masson describes the psychoanalytic branch of this modernist rejection of ethics. In becoming an analyst he was himself to be analyzed by a Dr. Irvine Schiffer of the Toronto Psychoanalytic Institute. Masson describes Schiffer's behavior ("Lie, cheat, steal, it's all the same to me," said Schiffer), and offers its theory:

Since he seemed to believe that a good person can do no harm, anything he did to me was by definition good, since he considered himself a good person. Since I was not yet a good person [that is, not yet a Schiffer-certified analyst], anything I did was by definition bad, and wrong. He had no need of ethics, since he automatically did the right thing. He quoted a phrase that Freud had used in a letter to the American psychiatrist James Putnam, about ethics being self-evident. Freud claimed that he had never done a bad thing in his life.[9]

Concerning the blessed Sigmund: never mind humility.

For example, it was not bad of Freud to violate Justice, as Masson documents in another book, by lying about the actual sexual abuse of girls by their fathers in fin-de-siècle Vienna in order to go on collecting money from the fathers to have their daughters analyzed as having the "false," "imagined" memories of abuse. Never mind justice. And it was not bad of Freud to abandon his principle that mental patients must be voluntary, and to approve of compulsory analysis of patients at a Swiss mental hospital, in order to spread the fame of psychoanalysis. Never mind faith. Never mind. Our prudential tastes are finalities.

The central dogma of modernism, the literary and ethical critic Wayne Booth has noted, is "the belief that you cannot and indeed should not allow your values to intrude upon your cognitive life—that thought and knowledge and fact are on one side and affirmations of value on the other."[10] Note the ethical self-refutation embodied in such a rule of method. He instances Bertrand Russell as one in whom "passionate commitment has lost its connection with the provision of good reasons."[11] As Russell himself noted in quite another connection, self-reference leads to cycling self-contradiction. "All Cretans are liars," quoth the Cretan.

Russell the aristocrat and mathematical philosopher applied low and sometimes no standards to his opinions about ethics and politics and economics. His friend Santayana describes Russell during the Great War exploiting his retentive memory without ethical reasoning: "This information, though accurate, was necessarily partial, and brought forward in a partisan argument; he couldn't know, he refused to know everything; so that his judgments, nominally based on that partial information, were really inspired by passionate prejudice and were always unfair and sometimes mad. He would say, for instance, that the bishops supported the war because they had money invested in munitions works."[12] George Orwell noted once that only intellectuals could believe such a hare-brained "realism." "The ordinary people in the Western countries," he wrote, "have never entered, mentally, into the world of 'realism' and power-politics."[13] They believe in decency, in virtues, and in urging them on each other. That such virtues may sometimes come into collision, especially if the clerisy neglects its task of thoughtful arbitration, is not in such untutored minds decisive evidence that power or utility should take over the show.

Economists and calculators have long led the attack by the new clerisy on preaching the virtues. The economist Marc Blaug, for example, in many other respects a surprisingly sensible member of his profession, asserted in 1980 that "there are no . . . methods for reconciling different normative value judgements—other than political elections and shooting it out at the barricades."[14] When men differ in taste, go to work killing. By "methods for reconciling" Blaug appears to mean "airtight proofs such as the Pythagorean Theorem." Neatness reigns. The sort of amiable, casuistic reasoning together that Booth and others in the rhetorical tradition recommend, the trading of "more or less good reasons," such as the stories of good or bad lives, ranging from the Hebrew Bible and Plutarch to the latest movie, is spurned by such a theory.

Schumpeter of Vienna and Harvard had earlier expressed an ethical philosophy similar to Blaug's: "We may, indeed, prefer the world of modern dictatorial socialism to the world of Adam Smith, or vice versa, but any such preference comes within the same category of subjective evaluation as does, to plagiarize Sombart, a man's preference for blondes over brunettes." Hurrah-boo. Thus also Lionel Robbins of the London School of Economics: "If we disagree about ends it is a case of thy blood against mine—or live and let live, according to the importance of the difference, or the relative strength of our opponents. . . . If we disagree about the morality of the taking of interest . . . , then there is no room for argument."[15] And a fount of this attitude, again, Bertrand Russell: "As to ultimate values, men may agree or disagree, they may fight with guns or with ballot papers, but they cannot reason logically."[16]

The theory is that of "emotivism." Emotivism was believed by very many twentieth-century people, some under the influence of logical positivism, some under the influence of a falling away from religious faith. It is "the doctrine that all evaluative judgments and more specifically all moral judgments are *nothing but* expressions of preference."[17] Or as Hobbes wrote in 1651, "Good and evil are names that signify our appetites and aversions."[18]

Emotivism, observe again, taken as a doctrine one should believe, is of course self-contradictory, since preaching against preaching is preaching. But logic is not the strong point of logical positivism or of those who have fallen away from religious faith.

Undergraduates and many of their professors become uneasy and start giggling when an ethical question arises. They regard such questions as having mainly to do with sex—thank *you*, fundamentalists of the late twentieth century—or with unargued authority, such as the Baltimore Catechism and the nuns to enforce it. The agreement to disagree that ended the wars of religion in Europe can be traced in their unease and in their stock remarks expressing it: "That's just a matter of opinion"; "Religion should not be mentioned in polite conversation"; "If we disagree about ends it is a case of thy blood against mine"; "The only methods for reconciling different normative value judgments are political elections or shooting it out at the barricades." According to the chocolate-ice-cream theory, to be caught making statements about shameful behavior is to be caught in meaningless burbling. Shame on you.

Aristocratic or peasant virtues elevated to universals have not given an ethical home for the bourgeoisie. A theory of virtue transcending our actual behavior and a theory of knowledge transcending our actual rhetoric of inquiry have put ethics and science beyond argument. The itch for a transcendent objectivity has had the result of turning the answers to important questions into unargued pronouncements. Thou shalt not commit adultery. Light is a particle. The bishops support the war because the Church of England owns the stock and bonds of munitions manufacturers.

In 416 BC, rejecting all appeals by the hitherto neutral island of Melos to justice, temperance, hope, and faith, the Athenian envoys in Thucydides' account applied relentlessly the logic of prudence (with courage) alone:

> We shall not trouble you with specious pretenses. . . . In return we hope that you . . . will aim at what is feasible . . . since you know as well as we do that right, as the world goes, is only in question between equals in power, while the strong do what they can and the weak suffer what they must. . . . If any [other cities] maintain their independence [from the Athenian Empire] it is because they are strong, and . . . if we do not molest them it is because we are afraid. . . . We know . . . that by a necessary law of their nature [men] rule wherever they can. . . . You will show . . . great blindness of judgment unless . . . you can find

some counsel more prudent [*sōphronesteron*, lit. more temperately, more soberly].[19]

The Melians demurred and the Athenians besieged them.

The Athenian envoys were articulating a bracing, tough-minded philosophy of value, attractive to *übermenchen* and especially *überherren* everywhere. A lot of intellectual men really like it. In the 1950s it reached a sort of climax among intellectual men, especially American professors and writers worried about the masculinity of intellectual work. It reduces in Benthamite style all other so-called virtues to one, prudence—with a nicely macho courage in attendance. Prudence rules.

If one takes the courageous, realpolitik view, the theory of numero uno, the belief that nice guys finish last, then prudence in turn reduces to power. It reduces, that is, to the will of the strong. It is aristocracy in action. If one takes on the other hand a more Enlightened, universalist and utopian view, then prudence reduces to utility, that is, to the summed wills of everyone. It is peasantry in action. If one takes finally a more Scientific, eugenic, just-the-facts view, then prudence reduces to selection, that is, to the summed wills of nobody. In the first two cases it is *will* that counts, not mutuality or affection or other merely bourgeois sentiments. In the third it is nature's own will. The strong do what they can. And so in the next winter after the dialogue the Athenians broke through the walls of Melos, executed all the men, and sold all the women and children into slavery.

The political rhetorician Robert Hariman has noted that "realism" in politics is not a stance outside of ethics, as it claims to be, but is on the contrary the adoption of a very particular *ethos*. Realists in international relations following George Kennan and Hans Morgenthau, such as Henry Kissinger, like to think of themselves as tough guys dealing with reality. As the philosopher James Rachels put it, one reason so many people adopt "psychological egoism"—the realistic notion that after all everyone is selfish—despite overwhelming evidence that it is factually wrong, and logically incoherent besides, is that it "appears to be a hardheaded, deflationary attitude toward human pretensions."[20] It's a pose, and a masculine one at that.

The guys get the pose from the Machiavellian line in Western culture, and before Machiavelli from the Melian Dialogue, or the stories of King Saul persecuting David. "Real peace," they say proudly, "will be the down-to-earth product of the real world, manufactured by realistic, calculating leaders whose sense of their nations' self-interest is diamond-hard and unflinching." Richard Nixon was here putting on what Hariman calls "the strategic temperament," the ideal character of prudence and courage with a bit of temperance necessary to be a successful prince, according to Machiavelli. Machiavelli's ideal leader is not colorless. By no means. He is colored manly, or at any rate macho, and disciplined. "The Machiavellian writer," Hariman observed, "persuades by appeal to this distinctive political personality. . . . The Machiavellian prince . . . would have been quite 'idealistic' when compared to the many overgrown children holding court throughout Italy" in his time, indulging their love and anger without prudent purpose.[21] You can see the alternative imprudence in King Lear, or in Leontes, King of Sicily, in *A Winter's Tale.*

"Realism is a characteristically modern political style that crafts an aesthetically unified world of sheer power and constant calculation."[22] Not actual calculation, you understand, but the pose of being calculating. It is the silent, tough-guy pose of Henry Bolingbroke, soon to be Henry IV, against Richard's eloquent defense of eloquence in *Richard II.* As Katharine Eisaman Maus observes, "The view of politics associated with Bolingbroke, a view that initially seems hardheaded and realistic, begins to seem not very practical after all. An acceptable social order requires more than the brute force he deploys so expertly. It requires a common set of ideas and practices, a common language and attitude, a set of rituals—all the immaterial abstractions Henry had originally been inclined to disregard."[23]

Of course the neoaristocratic neo-Machiavellians scorning the softness of justice or love and other immaterial abstractions turn out on inspection to have in their lives if not in their theories a reasonably full set of ethical convictions. The economist Andrew Yuengert notes that "most economists are already struggling to integrate the practice of economics into their lives as goal-oriented humans, even though the tenets of positivist method discourage them from doing so."[24] They have a sense, if unexamined and therefore a trifle sentimental, of love, justice, hope, and so forth. Above all they walk about with a sense of masculine and aristocratic pride in their courage.

If they could see a video of their own funny walks they might spot the ethical self-contradiction. But these are not men given to self-examination. As Bernard Williams said about the temptations facing the amoralist, "He must resist, if consistent [in claiming that ethics is bosh], . . . [a] tendency

to think of himself as being in character really rather splendid—in particular, as being by comparison with the craven multitude notably courageous,"
standing alone against the soft and bourgeois conventions of ethics.[25] Or as
the conservative political philosopher J. Budziszewski puts it, describing his
youthful and nihilistic self, "Like Nietzsche, I imagined myself one of the
few who could believe such things—who could walk the rocky heights
where the air is thin and cold."[26]

"The idea," said Judge Posner to a interviewer, describing the rocky heights
on which he walks, "is that a person is responsible for his own life. . . . We have
no right to blame anyone else for the result because it was ours to make or
muff. This is a philosophy, or psychology . . . of self-assertion, of liberation
from oppressive frameworks such as that created by religion or other dog-
mas."[27] Note Posner's uneasiness about the word "philosophy," and the
concession in the two-wordedness that he does not have an examined
"psychology," either. Such a life is indeed one of "assertive," that is, masculine, courage, that most willful of virtues. When alloyed with the other
virtues it constitutes the Kantian/Nozickian regard for the self-ownership of
people that Posner and I both admire. But when not alloyed with love or justice it is precisely a life, as Posner says, of self-assertion, and of self-assertion
alone, psychological egoism, one courageous guy against the world, no religion but that of the self. Consult your local sociopath.

Or consult Justice Holmes, whom David Luban summarizes as even in
his legal judgments delighting in force or will "because he sees in it the vital-
ity and joy that is our salvation from despair," laughing as a young man
laughs.[28] Albert Alschuler speaks of Holmes's "aftershave virtues."[29]
Remember Holmes on the true and adorable faith which leads a soldier to
senselessly throw away his life. "I believe the struggle for life is the order of
the world, at which it is vain to repine," said he on that occasion, and then
carried the Calliclesian/Spencerian/Sumnerian/legal-realist idea into his
court.[30] As Trotsky put it in 1921, " [We Bolsheviks] were never concerned
with the Kantian-priestly and vegetarian-Quaker prattle about the 'sacredness of human life.'"[31] Such self-assertion in the face of existential angst is
the choice of the antiliberal, the Bolshevik, the Fascist, the faux-despairing
Romantic wandering on the rocky heights.

Such a politics is, scientifically speaking, sinful. It is the unbalanced *virtù*
of a Satan, and its systematic, institutionalized advocacy by modern Hobbesians or Nietzscheans is evil. Evil, remember, is systematically institutionalized

sin. You cannot get more systematically institutionalized than the United States Supreme Court, 1902–1932, or for that matter the Seventh Circuit Court of Appeals, 1981–present.

I mean the terms "sin" and "evil," you understand, in their technical senses. Justice Holmes is always amusing to read, as, for example, in *Buck v. Bell*, 274 U.S., 200, 207 [1927]. And Judge Posner and I go back a long way, agreeing on many points of economics, and are on distantly friendly terms. I learned Latin as an adult partly because I was so impressed that Dick, who was a colleague from 1969 at the University of Chicago, had as an adult learned Greek. In a brave and dutiful spirit similar to Posner's in learning Greek, Holmes explained to Frederick Pollock why at age seventy-eight he was reading Machiavelli: "I don't remember that I ever read Machiavelli's *Prince* [a surprising confession in one so attached to a Machiavellian theory of society]—and I think of the Day of Judgment. There are a good many worse ignorances than that, that ought to be closed up."[32] Holmes learned to ride a bicycle at age fifty-four.[33]

It's merely that in their legal theories, though not always in their lives, or even always in their legal judgments, my father's hero, the Yankee from Olympus, and my distantly friendly acquaintance, Dick Posner, are not advocating virtues. Associate Justice Holmes declared in the *Buck v. Bell* opinion of 1927 that "it is better for all the world, if instead of waiting to execute degenerate offspring for crime, or to let them starve for their imbecility, society can prevent those who are manifestly unfit from continuing their kind. The principle that sustains compulsory vaccination is broad enough to cover cutting the Fallopian tubes. Three generations of imbeciles are enough."

So sterilization laws remained on the books another fifty years in thirty-three states, with over 60,000 operations performed.[34] The United States, by the way, was not the worst offender, even excepting Germany. Sweden sterilized 63,000 people 1935–1975, tiny Norway 40,000.[35] The legal theory, backed by the best science at the time, is that people like Carrie Buck—who, incidentally, was not promiscuous but was raped by the nephew of her foster parents and was not feebleminded but poor—should be prevented from damaging other people in their offspring. It is a utilitarian argument. People are not to be treated as ends but as means. Carrie Buck is to be used for the putative good of the community.

Posner's theory is similar, namely, that the law, the police, the prisons, with the judges of the Seventh Circuit Court of Appeals, are to enforce prudence . . . and *nothing more*. Dick doesn't believe in backward-facing justice, or the rights-talk and Quaker prattle that goes with such a faith. For similar reasons, though appealing to racial science instead of economic science, Holmes dismissed Buck's pretended right. That is, Holmes's intellectual descendent Judge Posner puts his faith in forward-looking, Prudential considerations alone. Rights, schmights. The lawyers who practice in Posner's court in Chicago say that there are three bodies of law: state, federal, and Posner.

In Posner's theory, for example, rape is to be allowed under license by the state, at least hypothetically, *if it would result in greater future utility to the rapist than disutility to the victim*. After all, the perpetrator of a rape gets utility from the very fact of its involuntary character, so there is no market in which he can lawfully purchase it. And after all the rapist is a person, too. His utility should weigh in the utilitarian balance.

As the economist Mark White puts it, the wealth-maximizing, "Hicks-Kaldor" criterion of improvement that Posner advocates has no basis in Kantian or any other than utilitarian ethics.[36] Posner declares that "if transaction costs are positive . . . the wealth-maximization principle requires the initial vesting of rights in those who are likely to value them most, so as to minimize transaction costs. This is the economic reason for giving a worker the right to sell his labor and a woman the right to choose her sexual partners."[37] And it is the only reason Judge Posner will acknowledge in his court.

It follows that if employers develop a very great and wealth-enhancing desire to get their cotton crop in and if transaction costs are high, then slavery is all right. If a rapist develops a very great desire to have sex with Ms. Citizen, given that transaction costs for rape *are* high, then rape is all right. There's no such thing, you see, as that nonsense upon stilts of a worker's "right" to freedom or a woman's "right" to say No. There's no backward-looking justice under Posner law. In the tradition of Bentham's and Holmes's disdain for the very idea of "rights," Judge Posner insists on looking forward, prudence-style. His divergence from them is only that he adds wealth to the criterion of power. So unlike Bentham and sometimes Holmes, Posner is not an egalitarian.

The reader may think I am exaggerating Posner's views. She should examine *Economic Analysis of Law* (4th ed., 1992), p. 218, and almost identical passages in subsequent editions (for example, the 6th edition, 2003, p. 216), in which he makes the argument about rape. It is a page that by itself would keep this crushingly learned and prolific jurist off the Supreme Court. Posner is intelligent—though persistently and stubbornly misled. As he himself acknowledges, "That any sort of rape license [or slavery license or any-takings license] is even thinkable within the framework of the wealth-maximization theory that guides so much of the analysis in this book will strike many readers as a limitation on the usefulness of that theory." It might.

Holmes wrote similarly, with lips curled in disdain: "From societies for the prevention of cruelty to animals up to socialism, we express . . . how hard it is to be wounded in the battle of life, how terrible, how unjust it is that any one should fail."[38] Rights, he wrote to Harold Laski in 1925, are merely "what a given crowd . . . will fight for."[39]

The Athenians spoke likewise, enjoining the preachy Melians "to let 'right' alone and talk only of interest." As the Melians had predicted, though, the tough, willful, efficient, assertive, courageous, economistic, plutocratic, rights-ignoring, future-oriented, sociopathic Athenian guys soon found in 413 at Syracuse and finally in 404, utterly defeated by their now very numerous enemies, that their tough words had for themselves, also, vacated "what is our common protection, the privilege of being allowed in danger to evoke what is fair and right." King Lear protests to Regan and Goneril to "reason not the [forward-looking and utilitarian] *need*" but rather what is *owed* in justice to a king and father. But the evil sisters, like the Athenians, are unmoved by such ethical appeals. "One day," writes Michael Ignatieff of the passage in the play, "the look of entreaty will be met by the stare of force."[40]

As a theory of ethics, this macho talk of Prudence Only, diamond-hard and unflinching, with the stare of force and the most recent scientific backing, has weaknesses.

PART SIX

The Bourgeois Uses of the Virtues

I'M TIRED OF THE MARKET, MATT.
TIRED OF OPTIONS. THAT'S THE LONG
AND SHORT OF IT NOT TO MENTION
THE ABSENCE OF CASH WHEN THE BILLS COME IN.
I'VE COUNTED IT UP ON MY ADDING MACHINE.
CAPITAL LOSS AGAINST CAPITAL GAIN
LEAVES ME RIGHT IN THE MIDDLE
WITH NO TICKET TO SPAIN.

—Helen McCloskey, "To Matt of Merrill"

38

Prudence is the central ethical virtue of the bourgeoisie, in the way that courage is of the aristocrat-hero or love is of the peasant-saint. But the point is that it is not the only one. In Adam Smith's book about prudence, *An Inquiry into the Nature and Causes of the Wealth of Nations* (1776), he embedded it among the other virtues, such as justice and especially temperance. Smith himself provided the details of the embedding in his only other book, *The Theory of Moral Sentiments* (1759). More people nowadays are reading Smith this way, as an ethical philosopher.

If Smith had been also a modern econometrician he would have put it as follows. Take any sort of willed behavior you wish to understand—brooding on a vote, for example, or birthing children, or buying lunch, or adopting the Bessemer process in the making of steel. Call it *B*. Brooding, buying, borrowing, birthing, bequeathing, bonding, boasting, blessing, bidding, bartering, bargaining, baptizing, banking, baking. It can be put on a scale and measured; or perhaps seen to be present or absent. You want to give an account of *B*, a little story about what causes it to happen, with quantitative weights on the causes if your ambition is scientific rather than philosophical.

What the hard men from Machiavelli to Judge Posner are claiming is that you can explain *B* with Prudence Only, the *P* variables of price, pleasure, payment, pocketbook, purpose, planning, property, profit, prediction, punishment, prison, purchasing, power, practice, in a word, the Profane.

Smith and Mill and Keynes and Hirschman and quite a few other economists have replied that, no, you have forgotten love and courage, justice and temperance, faith and hope, that is, social Solidarity, the *S* variable of

speech, semiotics, society, sympathy, service, stewardship, sentiment, sharing, soul, salvation, spirit, symbols, stories, shame, in a word, the Sacred.
The two-level universe of the axial religions are these, the Profane and the
Sacred. The two summarizing commandments, I have noted, refer to the
two levels: (1) love God and (2) love your neighbor. As the historian of religion Mircea Eliade put it, "Sacred and profane are two modes of being in the
world."[1]

Or at least they are two modes of being in a God-haunted world, especially the world of Abrahamic religions. A world without al-Lah is magical
or materialist, merging the sacred and the profane into a single plane of
technical tricks. The shaman's tent and the local Brookstone store have a lot
in common. In both you get gadgets for dealing with life piecemeal, trick by
trick. The special holiness of a J*H*W*H separated from mere humans,
I repeat, is reflected in the Christian's Lord's Prayer, "Our Father who art in
heaven, *hallowed* be thy name," and in other parts of monotheism.

The gods of polytheism are less sacred and less apart from us because
they are competitive. For example, in the Cantonese Temple of the Five
Hundred Gods, destroyed in the Cultural Revolution, the supplicant could
choose a diverse portfolio of gods to which to offer incense, the way one
lights a candle before the shrines of the Blessed Virgin *and* of St. Thomas
and of St. James.[2] The Protestants were protesting such residual polytheism

The P and S Variables

PRUDENCE	SOLIDARITY
Price	Sympathy
Payment	Service
Pocketbook	Soul
Purpose	Spirit
Planning	Sentiment
Property	Stewardship
Profit	Salvation
Prediction	Semiotics
Punishment	Shame
Purchase	Symbol
Privacy	Society
Power	Speech
Practice	Stories
THE PROFANE	THE SACRED

among the Romans, "the Romish doctrine concerning . . . worshipping and adoration . . . of images as of relics, and also invocation of saints, . . . a fond thing vainly invented, and grounded upon no warranty of scripture; but rather repugnant to the word of God." Of *al-Lah*, the One, *echad*, that is.

The Japanese, lacking gods, especially a jealous, monopolizing, single God, mix the sacred and the profane in ways that startle a Westerner accustomed by a monotheistic culture to a strict separation.[3] Favors of friendship or clientage in the West are supposed to be granted with the free hand of a proud aristocrat or a charitable Christian. They have value precisely because they are not accounted for in a bourgeois way. Ruth Benedict claimed to see in Japanese life up to the American Occupation "a postulate of indebtedness" which reduced the sacred to the profane. The Japanese, she said, view favors as exchanges, for which written records are kept and even a species of interest charged if the redemption is long in coming. "Americans are not accustomed to applying these financial criteria to a casual treat at the soda fountain or to the years' long devotion of a father to his motherless child," but "in Japan they are regarded quite as financial solvency is in America and the sanctions behind them are as strong as they are in the United States behind being able to pay one's bills." The truly virtuous are those who pay their ethical bills, "like our stories of honest men who pay off their creditors by incredible personal hardships."[4]

Whether this is an accurate description of the Japanese is not here important. It is in any case a tale of *P* taking over from *S*. Economists have specialized in the profane *P*, anthropologists have specialized in the sacred *S*. But most behavior, *B*, is explained by both:

$$B = \alpha + \beta P + \gamma S + \varepsilon.$$

To include both *P* and *S* is only sensible. Sociologists call it "multiplex." It is not wishy-washy or unprincipled. Of the neorationalist claim that everything can be reduced to *P*, Jerry Fodor remarks:

> I suppose it could turn out that one's interest in having friends, or in reading fictions, or in Wagner's operas, is really at heart prudential. But the claim affronts a robust, and I should think salubrious, intuition that there are lots and lots of things that we care about simply for themselves. Reductionism about this plurality of goals, when not Philistine or cheaply cynical, often sounds simply funny. Thus the joke about the lawyer who is offered sex by a beautiful girl. "Well, I guess so," he replies, "but what's in it for me?"[5]

Amartya Sen is not abandoning economics when he calls for "a remedial expansion of the set of variables and influences that find room in economic analysis."[6] In analyzing the bargaining power of women in various times and cultures, for example, it is simply true, and no disgracing betrayal of one's identity as a quantitative social scientist, to admit that norms, laws, and the obligations of love matter. Nor on the other side is it a betrayal of the interpretive turn to admit that the P-variables of the relative economic productivity of women and the relative physical strength of men matter for a society's rate of wife-beating. Both work.

The equation including both P and S is a figure of speech, not a program for literally quantitative research. I do not mean to suggest by it that the Sacred can be made into the same units of influence-on-B as the Profane. Identity is not the same as prudence, and recent attempts to absorb the sacred into the profane as a sort of exalted commodity are of limited value, limited by the very sacredness in question. There are *some* prices at which *some* women might be induced to become prostitutes. But we are not talking here only about the price. Wilfred McClay quotes an apposite remark by Kant: "In the realm of ends everything has either a *price* or a *dignity*. Whatever has a price can be replaced by something else as its equivalent; on the other hand, whatever is above all price, and therefore admits of no equivalent, has a dignity."[7]

On the other hand, I do not wish to offer comfort to the followers of Karl Polanyi, such as the late, great classical historian Moses Finley, who believe that because the ancient world had views of S which devalued businessmen it was not subject to the ordinary economics of supply and demand. That's mistaken, too, serving merely to exempt the "substantivists," the economic anthropologists rejecting modern economics, from having to learn the wearisome mathematics and statistics that go along with P factors in the economy. Modern economies are just as embedded with multiplex virtues as were ancient ones. John Stuart Mill wrote that "the creed and laws of a people act powerfully upon their economical condition; and this again, by its influence on their mental development and social relations, reacts upon their creed and laws."[8] Any society operates with both P and S.

Let me use the metaphor of an equation, nonetheless—though I do realize it will tempt some of my economist colleagues to put S into dollar terms. I just want to remind them of a technical point. It is that econometrically speaking, unless the P and S variables are orthogonal, which is to say unless they are entirely independent, or unless the covariance of *P* and *S* is zero, or unless there is reason to believe that a variable such as *PS* multiplied together, say, has no influence, then an estimate of the coefficients α and β that ignores *S* or *PS* will give biased results. An increase in sample size will not solve the problem. Technically, the estimates will be inconsistent. The bias and inconsistency are important to the degree that the *S* variable is important. The experiment is not properly controlled. Its conclusions are nonsense.

There has to be a transcendent goal to a career in business. Economics professors who doubt this should ask themselves why *they* work. If solely for the paycheck, perhaps they should seek another line of work. They are unlikely with such a utility function to perform well the MacIntyrean practice of being an economics professor—"practice" in this sense being "any . . . co-operative human activity through which goods internal to that form of activity are realized . . . with the result that human powers to achieve excellence . . . are systematically extended."[9] In business the case is the same.

The pseudo or actual transcendent goal can be as profane as merely the keeping of the score in a macho game of acquisition. He who dies with the most toys wins. But it can also be devotion to workmanship, duty, calling— being an apartment manager who provides the tenants with a decent place to live or a dentist who fends off gum disease in her patients. Or providing goods for poor people, in Wal-Mart. Or enlarging the life opportunities for one's family. These are devotions, too.

The particular sacred goal will commonly change the workings of prudence. That's what's right about Moses Finley's view of the ancient economy—though the market for grain in ancient Greece and Rome would still have worked, and did in fact work, pretty much as it does now. Again, the modification of pure prudence has been discovered to be powerfully influential in laboratory experiments, as Elizabeth Hoffman and Robert Frank and many others have noted.[10] If you allow the subjects to talk to each other, or even allow yourself to recruit subjects who are already friends, the *P*-Only behavior falls toward zero. People cooperate "irrationally" in aid of sacred solidarity—or in its transcendent spelling, Solidarity.

As the economist Frank Knight noted in 1934, "Rigorously speaking, there is no such thing as an economic interest, or a material interest," no human with *P*-Only motivations, because "economic interest is never final; it is an interest in the efficacy of activity, and the use of means, in promoting . . .

final interest. And these final interests do not inhere in particular physical things . . . but are all, at bottom, social interests. Even the food interest, the 'most' material of all, is in concrete content overwhelmingly a matter of social standards."[11] Knight, who was philosophically sophisticated for a modern economist, would have been aware that "final" is the Latin for Aristotelian "having to do with the telos, the end or purpose." The professor of law James Boyd White notes that " 'exchange,' upon which economics focuses too much, is a secondary rather than primary mode of life. It presupposes another world, in which it is embedded and which it can strengthen or weaken."[12] The economic historian John Nye explores the logic of P Only in the last thousand years of ruler and ruled in Europe—but he starts, as any discussion of literal or tax slavery must, at the S value of freedom: "Individuals value that freedom more than anyone else," and therefore are willing to make deals with their ruler to buy it.[13] We desire, said Aristotle at the beginning of the *Nicomachean Ethics*, some end for its own sake, some S. It is mistaken to think that P Only can be a life for a human.

But the myth of *Kapitalismus*, to use the German word in honor of its German origin, is that capitalism consists precisely in the absence of any purpose other than accumulation "for its own sake." Thus Robert Heilbroner: "Capitalism has been an expansive system from its earliest days, a system whose driving force has been the effort to accumulate ever larger amounts of capital itself."[14] Thus Weber, too, in 1904–1905: "The *summum bonum* of this ethic [is] the earning of more and more money. . . . [A]cquisition . . . [is] the ultimate purpose of life."[15] The argument is straight Marx, money-to-capital-to-money.

At the level of individuals there has never been any evidence for Marx's argument. The chief evidence that Weber gives is his humorless and literal reading of Benjamin Franklin's *Autobiography*. Of course Weber modified the pointlessness of the Marxian impulse by claiming that "this philosophy of avarice" depends on a transcendent "*duty* of the individual toward the increase of his capital."[16] But his Franklin, who after all was no Calvinist, at age forty-three abandoned forever the life of "endless" accumulation and devoted the rest of his long life to science and public purposes. So much for "ever larger amounts of capital itself."

Many fine scholars believe the claim that modern life is unusually devoted to gain. It is mistaken. "The unlimited hope for gain in the market," writes the political theorist Joan Tronto, "would teach people an unworkable premise for moral conduct, since the very nature of morality seems to dictate that desires must be limited by the need to coexist with others."[17] Running a business, though, would teach anyone that gain is limited. Dealing in a market would teach that desires must be limited by the need to coexist with others. The tuition in scarcity, other-regarding, and liberal values of a market society works as an ethical school. Pagan or Christian preachments, absent capitalism, did not.

Even so fine an anthropological historian as Alan Macfarlane believes the Marxist/Weberian lore: "The ethic of endless accumulation," he writes, "as an end and not a means, is the central peculiarity of capitalism."[18] If it were, the miser would be a strictly modern figure, and not proverbial in every literature in the world. "In this consists the difference between the character of a miser," wrote Adam Smith in 1759, "and that of a person of exact economy and assiduity. The one is anxious about small matters for their own sake; the other attends to them only in consequence of the scheme of life which he has laid down for himself."[19] "Scheme" of life, an S-variable.

At the level of the society as a whole there *is* "unlimited" accumulation. Corporations, with supposedly infinite lives—though in truth 10 percent die every year—are indeed machines of accumulation. The individual economic molecules who make up the river of capitalism may not always want more, but the river as a whole, it is said, keeps rolling along. True, and to our good. The machines and improved acreage and splendid buildings and so forth inherited from an accumulating past are good for us now.

But there is no case for accumulation being peculiar to capitalism. Infinitely lived institutions like "families" or "churches" or "royal lineages" existed before modern capitalism, and were sites of accumulation. Thus improved acreage spreading up the hillsides under the pressure of population before the Black Death. Thus the splendid building of the medieval cathedral, a project of centuries. Accumulation is not the heart of modern capitalism, as economists have understood at least since the calculations by Abramowitz and Solow in the 1950s, and before them the calculations by G. T. Jones in 1933.[20] Its heart is innovation.

Richard Posner has long advocated "wealth maximization" as the standard for good law. If judges arrange the laws of liability so that the economic pie is made as large as possible, then our wealth—"our" meaning the society's as a whole—is maximized. Good. You can see the merit of the argument, a utilitarian one. It goes along with "unlimited" accumulation. But in

1980 Posner was checkmated in two moves by another eminent legal scholar, Ronald Dworkin, who made the same observation as Knight had, that wealth is a means, not itself an end.[21]

The observation is ancient. Aristotle said in the *Nicomachean Ethics,* "Clearly wealth is not the Good we are in search of, for it is only good as being useful, *a means to something else.*"[22] Ends of justice, themselves for the sake of love or faith or hope, can be served by greater social wealth, to be sure. But they can be corrupted by greater social wealth, too. It's an empirical matter whether the historical balance has been positive or negative, an empirical matter we are exploring in this book. And in any case an economist would say, "If you want justice or faith to prosper, you should pursue them directly, not indirectly and uncertainly through another, allegedly correlated means, such as wealth."

The economist Robert Frank has been arguing this for years. His version of P and S is to show in detail that "the most adaptive behaviors will not spring from the [direct, simple, short-run] quest for material advantage."[23] By this he means that people love or leave tips or build reputations *out of their characters*, and that what is "adaptive" about forming a character is not instant profit but very long-term survival. This is also the vision of Ferguson and Hume and Smith: we build a successful commercial society out of love and justice, too; trust spreads, as it in fact did in the eighteenth century. The contractarian philosopher David Gauthier is the modern master of this sort of sweet reasoning.

Yet I doubt that Frank is right to cling to "survival" as the goal of human life, and therefore to cling to the just-so stories of evolutionary psychology. What about human flourishing, beyond bread alone? What about the spandrels of San Marco and other accidental results of evolution that Gould and Lewontin showed can undermine the retrospective claims of functionality? Love surely is not only a "commitment mechanism," a way of keeping people from wasting time in looking for new mates when the ones they have are pretty good already. Frank's argument here is cute, and parallels nicely, as he points out, the requirement of a lease in rental property. Swell. But he wouldn't say, I think, and certainly never to his wife, that it's a full account of love.[24]

In any case, "the self-interest [P-Only] model," Frank argues with numerous tests and examples, "provides a woefully inadequate description of the way people actually behave."[25] Frank wants to offer a "friendly amendment" to *P* Only, namely, that people commit at a higher level to having a good character *S*-style, which is then advantageous.[26] I'm not so sure his suggestion is "friendly" to the belief of most economists that *P* Only rules. If one admits *S* in the thorough way that Frank does, and as a few other economists such as George Akerlof and Bruno Frey do, you end like Adam Smith speaking of the values and relations of a particular form of life, that is, the transcendent and the self-disciplining. You do not remain like Jeremy Bentham or Gary Becker or Richard Posner fixated on the single virtue of prudence for pleasure.

39

SACRED REASONS

The sacred and the profane are woven together. Take, for example, the characteristic transcendent commodity of modernism, the sacred work of high art. Olav Velthuis, a young Dutch scholar and journalist who worked with Arjo Klamer of Erasmus University, has studied the pricing in first-time sales of high-art paintings in New York and Amsterdam, interviewing hundreds of dealers. Among art dealers and among the economists watching the art dealers, Velthuis notes, prudence has a rhetoric. The economist-observer would wish to find that the pricing of art is profane, a matter of wealth maximization. Yet the dealer-participant wants to play both roles, *both* sacred and profane. He or she wants to be the pater/materfamilias in a sacred imitation of the family *and* the smart cookie in a profane imitation of the stock exchange. *P* and *S*, both, rule.

How dealers in the first-time purchase and sale of art negotiate such a contradiction with their *talk* is crucial: "The highly ritualized way in which contemporary art is marketed is not just a matter of cultural camouflage but is the heart of what the art market is about. Therefore it makes sense to study how dealers talk when they do business."[1] Indeed it does. Economists and some sociologists want to stick with an eighth-floor view. Velthuis wants to get down also into the rhetoric of the life world, "to supplement Bourdieu's structural reading of the market for symbolic goods with a symbolic reading." It does seem natural to read symbols symbolically. Late Pollocks, and the market talk about late Pollocks, anything to do with Pollocks, are certainly symbolic.

But the economist wants to read all prices as prudence, and the anthropologist wants to leave that to the economist. The anthropologist want to read high art as solidarity, and the economist wants to leave *that* to the anthropologist. All this leaving-of-that to the other leaves the first-time pricing of art underexplained.

The avant-garde circuit which is the focus of Velthuis's research creates literally two spaces, the front room of the private art gallery in Soho or the Museum Quarter and the back room—the sacred museum out in front and the profane office behind. He contrasts the dual ritual of the avant-garde circuit with a third, "commercial" circuit, of more accessible art, sold at high prices on Michigan or Seventh Avenue or at lower prices on Hilton Head Island, or at still lower prices at the local mall. The dealers on the commercial circuit "bring out their own straightforwardness and honesty." The commercial dealer is bourgeois, the avant-garde aristocratic, and each defines herself by contrast to the other.

The reigning duchess of the avant-garde circuit, Marian Goodman, prefers to be called a "gallerist" rather than a "dealer." She was asked by a journalist what the difference was, but would not say. The journalist speculated: "The French-sounding 'gallerist' signals . . . an old-fashioned cosmopolitan ethos, for which the Atlantic Ocean is a lake shared by aspirants to transnational culture."[2]

The avant-garde dealers give the art museums discounts precisely because the work will not therefore enter into the profaning world of auction houses or commercial dealers. The auction price is higher, but the gallerist spurns it. The gaps between gallery and auction prices which Velthuis observes are large, explained by the steady effort of the gallery owners to keep their circuit separate from the other. From an economist's P-Only point of view their efforts are crazy, as though sellers of wheat in Chicago just detested the idea that some of their lovely red winter product would end up getting sold in, of all vulgar places, Liverpool. "Dealers actively seek to control the 'biography' of artworks that leave their gallery." "Selling to the highest bidder was considered 'immoral,' 'very unethical,' and 'extremely controversial.' "[3] Getting a higher price is "controversial"? We are not in a bourgeois ethical world.

In particular, for S-reasons, the dealers want their artists to have shapely careers, with an impoverished bohemian start, a vigorous middle age, and an honored and wealthy old age, in the style of Monet. One dealer put it this way: "Young artists deserve a grace period in which what they do can be viewed as a work of art, not a price tag."[4] The price for the same work is about the same across the various avant-garde galleries, but insulated from commerce, family-style. The gallery owner is "an educator and confidant."[5] Marian Goodman declared that "the choice of whom to work with goes to one's spiritual core. It starts with intuition, but it's important to reflect on how deep a commitment one feels before one gets involved."[6] The Profane is enabled by the Sacred, and the Sacred is the end. The Marxist cycle of money-capital-more money is not correct. What is correct is the cycle of Sacred-Profane-More Sacred.

Arjo Klamer himself gives another example of how P and S interact. The charitable organization Doctors Without Borders (*Médecins Sans Frontières*) was asked whether it would accept a large cash contribution. Well, why not? The P-Only logic of economics says that a contribution relaxes the budget constraint, making more of the organization's good works possible by paying more doctors to work for it. But in fact Doctors Without Borders turned down the contribution. The problem was that the very meaning of the organization was the grace of the gift *from the doctors*. To make them into merely paid employees would transform the enterprise into just another hospital.[7] Likewise a couple of weeks after the Indian Ocean tsunami the organization outraged some by turning down further contributions to its relief work. "As you know, it is very important to MSF that we use your contribution as you intend it to be used," *Médecins Sans Frontières* said on its Web site. "This is why we want to let you know that at this time, MSF estimates that we have received sufficient funds for our currently foreseen emergency response in South Asia."[8]

Some doctors laboring in the same needful fields sneer at such purity, pointing out that MSF therefore puts its or its contributors' sacred identity rather than the health of patients at the center of its concern. But the sneer is itself an expression of sacred identity: we are not those moral aesthetes at Doctors Without Borders, but practical, high-volume care providers who understand that money is money.

Similarly, the Cooperstown museum of baseball will only accept *donations* of memorabilia—it never buys them. The Salvation Army in Naples, Florida, returned a $100,000 donation from the winner of the $14.4 million Florida Lotto in 2002, since it believes gambling is a sin. The Salvation Army will not employ even highly competent gays and lesbians, if they are out, since it believes homosexuality is a sin, on the sacred grounds of two prohibitions in the Hebrew Bible and one in Paul's letters. The Salvation Army, and the conservative Anglicans unhappy with the gay bishop of New Hampshire, and the parents who push gay children out onto the streets, follow strictly these two thou-shalt-nots in Leviticus 10:13 and 20:13, with the routine five in the Ten Commandments. They do not follow the 358 other thou-shalt-nots of orthodox Judaism. Whether this odd selection has any rationale, the gift or the principle or the identity is Sacred. "Sacred" here does not mean the same thing as "admirable" or "following Jesus' example of love" or even "based on competent biblical scholarship familiar with the Hebrew and Greek texts." The point is that the Salvation Army's beliefs on these matters are not for sale.

Arjo Klamer draws out the moral with a personal example. Suppose you go in distress to a good friend, who spends an hour over coffee comforting you. At the end of the hour the friend says, "All right: time's up. That'll be $100, for counseling." Because the consultation happened as "friendship" such a demand is impossible, friendship-destroying. As the sociologist Allan Silver put it, "Friendships are diminished in moral quality if terms of exchange between friends are consciously or scrupulously monitored."[9] Yes, true, at any rate in an axial culture maintaining a large gap between the Sacred and the Profane. Never mind that the counseling services would be more prudently allocated among competing uses if a price system were introduced, as it already has been in the allocation of donuts and movie tickets. Friendship at Aristotle's highest level is transcendently Sacred. At its lower levels it is more like trade, accepting each other in spite of what we know. Yet even lower friendship has an element of transcendence, in that it goes beyond Prudence or Justice, and is something higher than literal, priced trade.

Likewise you would not run your home entirely on prudential principles, requiring your children to pay for their meals. *That does not mean that* P *variables play no role whatever in friendship or in families.* As Sen puts it, "Normal economic transactions would break down if self-interest played no substantial part at all in our choices."[10] It means merely that both P and S are at work. Of course the S variables are the conditions under which the P variables work, and of course the P variables modify the effects of S variables. "The confounding of the sacred and the profane," says the literary critic Stephen Greenblatt, "are characteristics of virtually the whole of Shakespeare's achievement as a dramatist."[11] No wonder. The store clerk from whom you buy your glazed donut every morning can become a "friend," then a friend, then perhaps a Friend. It's the human dance of Sacred and Profane.

John Stuart Mill put it well in a classic definition of political economy as "the science which traces the laws of such of the phenomena of society as arise from the combined operations of mankind for the production of wealth, *in so far as those phenomena are not modified by the pursuit of any other object.*"[12] Yes: P-objects are the usual object of economic analysis, but the analysis is modified by S-objects such as an imprudent love for Harriet Taylor, or a disinterested and highly unpopular advocacy of rights for women, or a high-minded sentiment of unity and solidarity with other human beings. It is how we get star-crossed lovers and political martyrs.

Even within economics itself there is no such thing as a pure P-Only, production-side phenomenon. At about the time of Mill's last edition of *The Principles of Political Economy* the younger economists decided that whatever value a product has depends on S variable tastes. There is no labor that resides in a commodity and explains its value. Taste-value, and the opportunity cost of being unable to have some other taste-value such as amaretto if you select chocolate this time, is all the economy runs on, said the generation of 1871.

David Hume had hinted at a similar consumption-oriented economics in 1751, when the forces were gathering in Scotland to constitute the non-French Enlightenment. P variables, that is self-love, rationality, utility, labor costs, production, he argued, come to be experienced only because of the exercise of an S variable. "If I have not vanity," he wrote, "I take no delight in praise.... Were there no appetite of any kind antecedent to self-love, that propensity could scarcely ever exert itself because we should ... have felt few and slender pains and pleasures."[13] Before him Bishop Butler had noted that "the very idea of an interested pursuit necessarily presupposes particular passions or appetites.... Take away these affections and you leave self-love absolutely nothing at all to employ itself about."[14] And before him Cicero had noted that "everyone loves himself, not with a view of acquiring some profit for himself from his self-love, but because he is dear to himself on his own account."[15] The P variable of profit means nothing without a S variable of Sentiment.

The S variables themselves are more than vanity of vanities. You do of course get some ponderable and perhaps vain pleasure from your family. True. And you get ponderable pain as well. But the family sprung in the first instance from love. Given love, a child is to its parent a unit of pain or pleasure in a utilitarian calculus. But neither would weigh without being at the outset, as Cicero says, "dear" (*carus*). The *P* and *S* intertwine.

That is: even the character of the purely prudent, pleasure-loving person, an apparent Shallow Hal of instrumentalism, depends on characters and on loves false or true formed somewhere else than on the Profane side of human character. The philosopher David Schmidtz puts it this way: "If there was nothing for the sake of which we were surviving, reflection on this fact would tend to undermine our commitment to survival," like an Oblomov or a Bartleby: amotivational.[16] The "something for the sake of which" is our identity, our faith. It can be as good and profound as a true love for a merciful God or as bad and superficial as an unreflective "love" for being cool. But if it's not there, if you have not love, if you lack the striving for the transcendent, you dither—and wither. Another philosopher, Harry Frankfurt, says, "Suppose we care about nothing. In that case, we would do nothing to maintain any thematic unity or coherence in our desire or in the determination of our will." Such a man "would be uninvolved in his own life."[17] He would have no identity.

That's the deepest problem with a *P*-Only view of human motivation. Such people would not be human. Without Knight's "final interest" even the business of prudence would not work. Practical reason does not come with its own motivation. And thinking requires emotion. So the pure rationality of the dream of Descartes is impossible.[18] The psychologist Nico Frijda noted that "with cognitive judgments [alone] . . . there is no reason . . . to prefer any goal. . . . Cognitive reasoning may argue that a particular event would lead to loss of money or health or life, but so what?" Gordon Bower put it this way: "Emotion is evolution's way of giving meaning to our lives."[19]

Even a "mere" self-regard is not automatic, Schmidtz points out. "It may be standard equipment, so to speak, but even standard equipment requires maintenance."[20] I knew a man once who delighted in exercising the character of the Prudent Man. I was with him when he bargained in Italian for an entire hour off and on about the price of a big can of olive oil from a store in the North End of Boston. The year was 1966, before the neighborhood was yuppified. Now the prices are fixed, and higher, even discounting for inflation. My prudent friend had three levels of motivation. For one thing, he was interested in the prudent saving on the oil, perhaps a dollar or so.

That can't explain much, even in 1966 dollars. More important was his pleasure in enacting so audaciously—to the point of an embarrassing display of intemperance—the character of the Prudent Man. Another *P* variable? No: *S* in aid of *P*. And, third, he was keeping faith with the indubitably *S*-ish variables of his Lago Maggiore Italian speech, birth, society, and the stories that honor such a character. It was his identity, his *S* variables, his sacred faith. It required maintenance, and he worked at it. As Hume said, to repeat, "Were there no appetite of any kind antecedent to self-love, that propensity could scarcely ever exert itself."

Emerson speaks of Napoleon's attachment to the character of the supremely Prudent Man, which, I say again, not always means "cautious," which certainly would not characterize Napoleon, but always "having know-how, *savoir faire,*"

> that common-sense which no sooner respects any end than it finds the means to effect it; the delight in the use of means; in the choice, simplification and combining of means; the directness and thoroughness of his work; the prudence with which all was seen and the energy with which all was done, make him the natural organ and head of what I may almost call, from its extent, the *modern* party. . . . [He] showed us how much may be accomplished by the mere force of such virtues as all men possess in less degrees; namely, by punctuality, by personal attention, by courage and thoroughness. "The Austrians," he said, "do not know the value of time."[21]

The aristocrats who led the Austrians, in contrast to bourgeois Bonaparte and his ragtag of talents, were careless of such an ignoble value as exact calculations of time. True, Napoleon was always impatient, which was not bourgeois of him; and he was physically courageous, which the average shopkeeper has little need of. Yet Emerson says, wisely, "I should cite [Napoleon], in his earlier years, as a model of prudence." And one could say the same of George Washington, in all his years.

Napoleon had pretensions to status in the gentry of his native Corsica. This got him into military school, but not into the regiments of the real aristocrats. Paul Johnson sees the origins of Napoleon's bourgeois behavior in his head for figures and his training in the unfashionable but calculative artillery. "Bonaparte began to pay constant attention to the role of calculation in war: distances to be covered; speed and route of march; quantities of supplies and animals, rates at which ammunition was used. . . . Asked how long it would take to get a siege train from the French fortress of Verdun to the outskirts of Vienna, most officers of the day would shrug bewildered shoulders or make a wild guess. Bonaparte would consult a map and give the answer in exact days and hours."[22]

A French historian said of Napoleon that after he abandoned Josephine in pursuit of marital alliances he became lazy and "bourgeois." No: he became lazy and *aristocratic*. His earlier mad energy was precisely that of the consummate bourgeois engaged on a piece of business—in his case, depending on how you value Napoleon, raping Europe or protecting the Revolution. My Italian American friend was in these respects a Napoleon on a little stage, ruthlessly skilled at cards and baseball and coaching girls' basketball, delighting in the exercise of Prudent means. But it was in aid of a Sacred identity. It was his faith. No dithering.

NOT BY *P* ALONE

Humans live through both *P* and *S*. That is to say, a good person is motivated by prudence, but also by other virtues, such as love, faith, courage, temperance, justice, and hope. Michael Novak observes that in the modern world "a strictly economic, business language has grown up without including within itself the moral, religious, even humane language appropriate to its own activities."[1] That's the problem.

I know a woman with exquisite taste, whose home is full of graceful objects meaningful in her life—a reproduction of a sculpted head from Greece, in honor of her study years ago of the ancient Greek language; a black abstract painting owned by a dear friend who died too young; numerous books of poetry, which she studies to set a standard for her own. Her home is a temple to Memory. Her possessions are not mere corrupting "consumption," so many bags of Fritos or cases of Coke. Her objects are a species of worship, a touch of transcendence. They are reminders of the love and pain that anchor most women's lives.

And yet this woman can remember the price of everything she owns, every deal she has made since girlhood, and is prudent in other ways as well, saving money, making it with care and courage. She does both *P* and *S*. Bourgeois people do.

Laurel Thatcher Ulrich, in her biography of Martha Ballard, wife of a miller and surveyor, mother of nine children, but especially a midwife delivering over eight hundred babies in the Maine of the Early National period, reflects on why Martha did it: "What took Martha Ballard out of bed in the cold of night? Why was she willing to risk frozen feet and broken bones to practice her trade? Certainly midwifery paid well." There's the prudence, and she had no saintly abnegation about it: "Martha cared about her 'rewards,' and she kept her midwifery accounts carefully." Yet she was not a creature of *P* Only. Faith mattered. Her diary is full of conventional praises to God, and often more than conventional. "She interpreted her work, as all her life, in religious terms." But "even more [midwifery] . . . was an inner calling, an assertion of being." "Martha Ballard's specialty brought together the gentle and giving side of her nature [thus love] with her capacity for risk and her need for autonomy [thus courage]."[2] Both *P* and *S* work in bourgeois lives.

A master-word in Dutch culture is *zuinig,* meaning thrifty, frugal, economical.[3] Nothing peculiar about that, you might say—all cultures, of course, have to deal prudently with the fact of scarcity—until you note how very far the Dutch take it in practice. An American would be ashamed to go to the lengths of *zuinig* behavior that are seen as compulsory scripts in Holland.

The candle culture of the country, for example, is a nice offset to a wet, dreary climate. But a Dutch housewife, regardless of income, would be ashamed to light candles unless it was after sunset. Her shame is a cultural memory of a time in which saving candles mattered. Classrooms in Dutch and other European universities depend on natural light unless the sun has gone down. No waste of lighting at midday, whether or not the atmosphere is gloomy and the blackboard indiscernible, as in the Department of Philosophy at Erasmus University it often is. A well-to-do Hollander will subject himself to an extra hour of shopping in order to get the hoped-for bargains at the periodic vegetable market in the town square, muttering to himself one of the scores of Dutch proverbs exalting thrift. *Zuinigheid met vlijt bouwt huizen als kastelen*—literally, "Thriftiness with diligence builds houses like castles"; freely, "Take care of the pence, and the pounds will take care of themselves."

I have a Dutch friend, from a prosperous family, now himself even more prosperous, who is a generous, openhanded man in friendship. Yet in his student days he literally gave himself jaundice by insisting on eating only bread with tomato sauce while on a long vacation in Italy—because it was a *zuinig* diet, and was by the low standards of Dutch cuisine tasty enough. Dutch CEOs take a lunch of one piece of cheese slapped between bread, with a glass of milk, and then exclaim to each other how *lekker* (good tasting) it is. Dutch people of whatever income routinely put their once-used teabag in a little dish set out for the purpose of using the bag a second time. Some even reuse their coffee grounds. The bourgeois mother of another Dutch friend washes out the plastic bags she has used and hangs them out to dry.

The *kaasschaaf*, the cheese parer, for slicing very thin slices off the block of cheese, is picked up by Americans as a novelty as they leave Schiphol airport. But they don't use it once they get home. Instead they go on as before cutting off whole big chunks to eat. It would scandalize a Dutch housewife.

In truth, hard cheese does taste better when pared, so the paring could be explained as rational in a cheese-eating nation. But there are less easily evaded cases. All Dutch kitchens are supplied with a utensil for scraping out the last little bit of yoghurt or spaghetti sauce from a jar. It is called by the Dutch a *flessenkrabber*, a bottle-scraper, consisting of a tiny rounded rubber edge attached to a foot-long plastic handle. Dutch people cannot believe that other nations don't have it—well, except for New Englanders of an earlier generation, among perhaps a few others, which makes again the point of its strangeness in a rich world. Even poor Dutch people could get along without the fraction-of-a-cent's worth of sauce sacrificed if the unscraped bottle were thrown into the trash—no, I'm sorry: into the recycling bin. And the Netherlands has been one of the richest countries in the world for centuries.

People scrape not out of Prudence Only, not for *P* values, but because that is what a Dutch person *should* do, *S*-style, like scrubbing the front stoop, or skating the Eleven-Town Tour when the canals in Friesland ice up. It is a "sacrifice," literally "making sacred," the *S*-holy deed of paying homage to one's Dutchness. And that is what the Dutch say when you laugh at their *flessenkrabbers*. They retort that food is God's gift, and it is therefore sinful to waste it. Or in a more socialist vein they say that to waste it is to insult the labor that went into producing it. Or, such theologies aside, they declare that they were raised anyway as Dutch people to do so. Their identity is sacred.

To most Americans the cheese paring and sauce scraping and tea-bag saving seems miserly and therefore ridiculous. Americans go to lengths of achieving "convenience," in packaging cheese for example, that strike the Dutch as crazy, imprudent, highly un-*zuinig*. Let's see: how about *pre-cutting* the cheese so that you don't have to bother cutting your own chunks, then packaging them together with the crackers, so you don't even have to reach over to the cracker box? "The American," my brother John McCloskey notes, "sees no sacred cause in cutting his own cheese—he'd rather subcontract the effort."[4] To follow Dutch habits of cheese paring would be considered, as the Americans say, "cheap." In the 1930s Chicagoans would joke about Goldblatt's, a low-end department store then on State Street, that when birds flew over it they cried, "Cheap, cheap, cheap." The joke would puzzle the Dutch, and certainly not because of some defect in their grasp of the English language. *Goedkoop*, cheap, is literally a "good buy," and is an act of sacred goodness in being Dutch.

The children's books by Annie M. G. Schmidt that helped define bourgeois life in the Netherlands during and after the 1950s had as protagonists the little boy Jip (pronounced "Yip") and the little girl Janneke ("YAN-uh-ku"), about four years old. In one episode Jip and Janneke are looking enviously out the window at the birds, who can fly away at will, even to Africa. Janneke asks Mother, "Shall we also leave in the winter? To the South? To Africa? And then in the spring come back again?"

> "I would find that wonderful," says Mother. "But the birds have wings. They can fly. And we can't."
> "We can too fly," says Jip. "With an airplane."
> "That costs a lot of money," says Mother. "And we don't have that."
> Jip and Janneke gaze a long time at the birds. Who can go away so far. With their own wings. A great bargain [*heel goedkoop*].
> And they are jealous.[5]

Heel goedkoop. The remark in such circumstances is impossible in America.

An economist might object that children's books, such as David C. McClelland used long ago in a similar way, do not settle the issue of cultural differences.[6] But such attitudes pervade Dutch culture, high and low. Americans believe, as Huey Long said, "Every man a king." Kings are not supposed to bargain over olive oil or save tiny dollops of spaghetti sauce or think of birds as having cheap airfares to their advantage. Those would be absurd, ignoble things for a king to do or think.

Dutch people believe, on the contrary, We're all in this together. Standing out in an aristocratic way is discouraged, even by the tiny group of literal aristocrats. To engage in non-*zuinig* consumption is the act of a nouveau riche; good Lord, even a Walloon. It would be absurd, presumptuous to imagine one could be a "king" and take on the "egotistical" trappings of royalty. We Dutch are bourgeois, huddled in little cities fighting the Spanish king for eight decades, eating rats during sieges, at length in the 1940s harrying the German occupiers, collectively, and are not ashamed to show it.

An American CEO feels on the contrary that he *should* in honor to his noble rank buy an expensive lunch. He leaves a big tip for the same reason. Tipping in fact is an easy-to-observe outcome of a sacred decision, like going to church. Some nations that tip in restaurants are the United States (with the highest percentage of the bill internationally: 16.7 percent by survey), Canada, the UK, Mexico, Egypt. Some that don't tip much or at all are the Netherlands, Denmark, Sweden, Finland, Estonia, Japan, Australia, and New Zealand.[7] France and Italy occupy a nonsacred middle ground of *service compris*.

Hmm. A pattern of church-or-temple-going associated with high tipping, yes? Perhaps not. John McCloskey suggests again that "eating out at a restaurant is regarded more as a form of entertainment in the U.S., calling for an extravagant ritual of generosity. In other countries, eating at a restaurant is just one of the communal daily rounds, with more shared value between waiter and diner and therefore less need for extra compensation." He notes further that "in American restaurants that have the lowest entertainment value and the most bare, utilitarian purpose—fast food—there is no tipping. And no community."[8] One is reminded of the culinary advice on coming to a small American town: "If you find a restaurant called 'Mom's,' keep looking. But if the only other restaurant in town is called 'Eats' . . . go back to Mom's."

All serious researchers on tipping agree that one cannot devise an explanation of tipping on the basis of simple, first-order prudence.[9] Either you honor your Australian values of egalitarianism by sitting in the front seat with the cab driver and not giving him a tip; or you show your American desire to be liked, yet show also your comfortableness with power differentials, by tipping generously in the United States. No simply prudent purpose is served, unless you think the anonymous cab driver in New York whom you stiff may take out a gun and shoot you.

Robert Frank argues persuasively that "the decision to tip in a distant city is about the kinds of character traits one wishes to cultivate."[10] He then goes to some lengths—some of it persuasive—to tell a story of *P*-motivated decisions to become a certain character. Frank, like me, is an economist, sworn to find *P* Only every chance he gets. That, and the secret handshake. He is trying to reduce *S* to a sort of elevated *P*. But as I've already noted about his line of argument, I think he would agree that many if not all variations in S-behavior are best explained as just S, not as stalking horses for various sorts of hidden Prudence.

The economist could reply that bargaining over a little olive oil and scraping a little spaghetti sauce and even tipping at restaurants are minor matters. Eric Jones calls it the assumption of "cultural nullity." He observes that the noneconomist's recitation of instances of irrational attachment to *zuinigheid* "is followed by a heroic leap to the assumption that because certain classes of social behavior visibly differ from place to place, they must be significant, even dominant, influences on how people behave with respect to larger matters."[11] In larger matters, the economist would say—Jones himself reserves judgment—such people are governed by P Only. Max U suffices. Jones quotes as an extreme example the views of an admirable economist, the late Julian Simon, on fertility: "Culture and values do not have independent lives . . . [but] serve as intermediate variables between economic conditions and fertility."[12] So Mr. Economist.

I think not—though of course the question is scientific and cannot be settled at last by dueling anecdotes. Yet consider. The Dutch have a style of doing their business that entails great amounts of committee time, known as *overleg, overleg*, "consultation, consultation."[13] As an American in Holland I am often requested to make an appointment to consult about what will be consulted about when we actually meet to consult. It is maddeningly inefficient. The big van Dalen Dutch-English dictionary gives the example "de politici wilden de hele dag overleggen," "the politicians wanted to spend the whole day consulting." Yeah. As Theo van Gogh was being murdered on the streets of Amsterdam by Mohammed Bouyeri in 2004 he is reported to have said to his attacker, "Sure we can talk about this."

The Dutch film of 1962, *De Overval* ("The Silent Raid") has a long, long scene in which the local leaders of the Resistance in Leeuwarden in 1944 meet in a houseboat and then another long, long scene in a church at a higher level of the organization to *overleg, overleg* endlessly about breaking into a German prison to free their colleagues. The scenes are of a length quite impossible in an American adventure film. In *Von Ryan's Express* (1965) the very complicated plans about a similar matter, involving hundreds of men, are portrayed as being formed with practically no discussion.

Coming from a quarterback-who-calls-the-plays culture of getting things done, an American imagines that 5 percent of Dutch national income—maybe 10 percent—is tossed away annually in *overleg, overleg,* fueled by endless little cups of *koffie,* a consultation having no productive function but to satisfy everyone that all views have been heard. The Dutch seem always to be saying: listen to the other side.

Often as not, the *overleg,* or the listening, is phony. The fix is in, decided by the *politici* out in the walking-corridors of the Parliament building, *de wandelgangen,* man to man. Elaborate rule books are devised by the regent class to keep the mere residents in line. The rule books, the regents intone, are to be followed absolutely without exception. The commonest response one gets on application to a bureaucrat or a shop-keeper in the Netherlands is "That can't be done." But the rule book is then cast away in an instant, with no discussion, when some side deal emerges. After all, the Dutch have been for six centuries masterful deal makers. The Netherlanders didn't get that way by passing up *goedkopen* when they come along.

The hypocrisy doesn't make the American any more patient with the sacred custom of the Dutch. Come on, guys, she thinks without being so rude as to say so. Quit the phony "consultation," the endless fixed meetings, to which one must arrive exactly on time, wasting entire afternoons in what seems to an American a pointless ceremony. The Dutch proverb "Overleg is halve werk" fits in the same cultural place as "Plan ahead" or "A stitch in time saves nine." But its literal meaning is suggestive to the irritated American. Sometimes in the Netherlands the sacred consultation does seem "half the work."

That is to look at the matter from the individual's point of view. In her brilliantly wide-ranging and readable survey of the limits of *P*-Only social thinking, Irene van Staveren (1999, 2001) looks at it from the eighth floor, so to speak. In the manner common to the other young scholars such as Wil-fred Dolfsma and Olav Velthuis inspired by Klamer of Erasmus, she distinguishes three spheres: the government, whose virtue is justice; the market, whose virtue is prudence or freedom; and the home, whose virtue is love. The Greek words are *polis, agora,* and *oikos.* The talk of "spheres," by the way, is especially natural in Dutch thought. It goes back to the conservative the-ologian Abraham Kuyper in the late nineteenth century and to the long political tradition in the Netherlands of so-called pillars (*zuilen*) of au-tonomous communities, Dutch Reform, Catholic, socialist, Jewish, and now Muslim.

The key to van Staveren's thinking is this amazing table laying out the three spheres and their modes of ethical values, feelings, reasoning, and action. She criticizes an early version of my argument for mixing up the columns, and in particular including in a bourgeois column "the virtue of 'affection' that Hume found to be furthered outside the market, . . . the virtue of 'trust' that Mill, Polanyi, and Hirschman have located in caring

The Van Staveren Table: The Three Topoi of Ethics

	DOMAIN OF:	FREEDOM	JUSTICE	CARE
	for which the Greek *topos* is:	*agora*	*polis*	*oikos*
	or the French:	*Liberté*	*Egalité*	*Fraternité*
Ethical capabilities ↓	DIMENSIONS			
	Value of the:	individual	public	relationship
	Core value A:	self-esteem	respect	trust
	Core value B:	dignity	fairness	sympathy
Commitment	Core value C:	self-fulfillment	realization of rights	sustain relationships
	Virtue:	**prudence**	**propriety, justice**	**benevolence, love**
	Accumulated:	freedoms	entitlements	social capital
	Feeling:	pride	righteousness	**affection**
Emotion	Motive:	autonomy	solidarity	responsibility
	Others perceived as:	anonymous	equal/unequal	**different**
	Rewards:	extrinsic	collective	intrinsic
	Epistemology:	teleological, or consequences	deontological, or duties	eschatological, or meaningful purposes
Deliberation	Signals:	prices	votes	symbols
	Evaluation:	free choice	legitimacy	responsiveness
	expression, means:	exit	voice	loyalty
	Interaction:	independent	dependent	interdependent
	Relation to others:	competing	rule following	sharing
Interaction	Social mechanism:	exchange	distributive rules	**gift**
	Place of allocation:	market	state	care economy

Source: Slightly modified from van Staveren, *Caring for Economics*, 1999, p. 46.

relationships in the home, in the community, or among consumers of employees but not in a market transaction, . . . the virtue of 'respect' that Mill and Perkins Gilman found to be supported outside the market, . . . and the virtue of 'responsibility' that Hayek and Friedman recognized as belonging outside the market but at the same time as a precondition for market transactions to happen."[14] I agree that I was unclear about just how such virtues arise in market societies. I probably still am. Van Staveren and I also agree that such values are necessary for markets to work, and that a society without a polis or an *oikos*, a domain of justice or of care, will be deficient in them, nightmarish. A virtue such as trust "is a value that markets need."

But we disagree about whether markets can "generate" trust, or whether trust can only be "furthered and nurtured *outside* the market in what I have called the care economy."[15] Van Staveren thinks of the market here as operating overwhelmingly "through calculation, interest, and exchange." Admittedly, such a mechanical thing could not "generate" trust. Without some love or solidarity, like a starter in sourdough bread, no one would trust anybody. Nancy Folbre says, and I agree, that "the invisible hand of [anonymous, mechanical] markets depends on the invisible heart of care. Markets cannot function effectively outside the framework of families and communities built on values of love, obligation, and reciprocity."[16] The philosopher Lester Hunt makes a similar point, based on a similar dichotomy: the power of commerce over the formation of character "is checked by that of other sectors, including especially the radically contrasting institution of the gift."[17]

Granted. But are *P*-Only calculation, interest, and exchange what markets overwhelmingly consist of? I think not. I think, and believe van Staveren and Folbre and Hunt would agree, that actual markets are often infused with *S* values. Consider the last moderately complicated purchase you made, for that remodeled kitchen, say, or a new car. Where exactly each quantum of trust originates is a deeper question of social psychology than any of us economists or philosophers is equipped to handle. But even markets have trust, fairness, symbols built into them. And, I would say, "generated" in them. The columns do mix.

In the end the School of Klamer would acknowledge so. Their purpose is precisely to overturn the *P*-Only orthodoxy of "mainstream," that is, especially, American, conservative economics. Thus the Dutch learning.

THE MYTH OF MODERN RATIONALITY

But likewise in conservative America. *S* is bigger there than the official *P*-Only theories would allow. The economy is embedded in society, and psychology—or rather "sychology," to preserve the *S* as against the *P*. The tough-guy American style of making decisions about the Big Dig in Boston or about the Second Iraq War is a sacred thing, a matter of unexamined *S* shrouded in cost-benefit ceremonies claiming *P*. Often enough it's a matter of the masculine pride of the quarterback in charge. It is an enactment of the simplicities of the American "redemptive self," as Dan McAdams puts it, Jimmy Stewart filibustering the Senate in *Mr. Smith Goes to Washington*, or George W. Bush in his maturity accepting Jesus as his personal savior. Why else would the Bostonians decide to bury a highway? Why else would the second Bush administration lie about the reasons for the Second Iraq War?

A woman friend of mine, once a specialist in billion-dollar bank loans, told me that the merger of Bank One of Chicago in 2004 with Morgan Chase of New York was in good part an ego trip for the male CEOs involved—that, and a prudent plan to pick up the gains left on the street by the irrationalities of Illinois banking law. Another woman friend, a big-time accountant in New York, told me that [male] egos as much as loopholes in the American tax code determine the way offshore business schemes have developed. John Maynard Keynes called the ego trips "animal spirits"— Peter Dougherty offers the phrase "hormonal capitalism."[1] Keynes and Dougherty do not mean that all investment is random. They mean merely that the systematic part of the economist's explanation, the part that depends on close calculations of interest rates and on rational expectations about expected returns, is only a part. It's a P in an equation in which S figures, too.

The claimed P-Only rationality of modern life, celebrated and criticized and worried over by Max Weber, has been exaggerated. Weber thought that decisions were really, now, in 1905, made by calculation, that bureaucracy was really in 1905 depersonalized, that corporations were really in 1905 run along military lines, in an iron cage of rationality. A century after Weber—many social scientists assume—bureaucratic and corporate decision making must be all the more rational and P-dominated, yes? No. Someone who thinks that a business corporation is run like an army at war has never been in a corporation in business—or for that matter in an army at war.

The myth of modern rationality starts early. D'Alembert's *Encyclopédie* of 1751, Bentham's *Introduction to the Principles of Morals and Legislation* of 1789, and Comte's *Système de politique positive* of 1851 are characteristic expressions. Ernest Renan, professor of Hebrew at the Collège de France from 1862 on, and most famous for his claim that Jesus was a good fellow if a trifle primitive and oriental, declared that "we must make a marked distinction between *societies like our own, where everything takes place in the full light of reflection,* and simple and credulous communities," such as those that Jesus preached in.[2] After the events of the twentieth century in Europe, which exhibited anything but the full light of reflection, one stands amazed by such brisk rationalism.

The Danish professor of planning Bent Flyvbjerg and his colleagues have studied the rational estimation of cost of 258 big transportation projects worldwide 1927–1998, averaging $350 million each in final cost. Road projects at their completion date saw cost overruns of 20 percent (in constant 1995 prices), bridges and tunnels 34 percent, and railways 45 percent.[3] The Big Dig, in 1982–2004, at $14,600 million, came in at 500 percent of its original estimate—all right, only 200 or 300 percent allowing for inflation and new features.

This is not of course evidence that the politicians and engineers involved were irrational, personally speaking. It is merely evidence that collective decisions with other people's money are not governed by the same *goedkoop* calculations as are personal expenditures. That and what economists call the "winner's curse" in a bidding war: in a world of bridge-building in which no one quite knows what the correct bid is, the company with the misfortune this time to guess low wins the bidding, and is regularly therefore stuck with cost overruns.

And we all know how far from being governed entirely by rational prudence even our personal expenditures are, with our own hard-earned money. Even without the winner's curse in bidding for a house or an antique—that is, even with fixed and known prices—we buy things that in the end do not prove to have been worth it. Only if we knew exactly what personal valuation to put on that new fur coat would we avoid what could be called the consumer's curse. Since, contrary to the simplest *P*-Only models of economic behavior, we do not know, we make mistakes. Look at automotive expenditures, to take a big and importantly *S*-driven part of consumption. No one who buys a new car, incurring the thousands of dollars of depreciation from the ten seconds it takes to drive the new car off the dealer's lot, is making his decision under the full light of reflection. Or look at your closet, jammed with consuming mistakes.

Flyvbjerg remarks in an editorial piece in *Engineering News-Record* that "the entire structure of incentives is geared towards underestimating costs and overestimating benefits. When a project goes forward a lot of people profit."[4] When I myself in the 1960s worked as a transportation economist, we would laugh at the so-called cost/benefit studies provided by major engineering firms to justify projects in developing countries. The benefits were double- and treble-counted, big elements of the costs ignored, dubious "social benefits" added in, until the government or the World Bank was satisfied. Forget about the winner's curse; this was the winner's con. But the entry of economists into the business has not much improved the situation, even in countries accustomed to transparency and ethical uprightness.

It is well known in Denmark itself, for example, that the Great Belt connecting the Copenhagen island to the mainland, completed in 1998 at a cost of $4.3 billion, was irrational. A tunnel alone would have been cheaper, since the distance was great. But the politicians wanted a beautiful bridge, too, and *they* were not paying for it, so they got it. The payoff period for the loans is said even in official publications to be as long as forty years—in a world in which commercial projects pay back in under ten. Yet the bridge is glorious. Symbolic of Denmark's connection to Europe. *S*-valuable—if not valuable enough to be justified by *P*.

It is not merely public projects, I repeat, that bear traces of *S* "irrationality." Whenever you watch a decision in business big or small you will note how important the egos and biases and hatreds and loves of the decision makers are. Watch a negotiation for a simple house sale and you will see that it depends on dignities and feelings, roles and pretenses, a give-and-take of politeness, veiling of threats, excusing of hardheadedness because, after all, this is business we are doing. It depends, that is, on the "faculty of speech" that Adam Smith thought foundational for the economy, though his followers have ignored it. It depends on the invisible tongue as much as on the invisible hand.[5]

That does not mean that Prudence goes out the window. The sociologist Bruce Carruthers found that in the early eighteenth century the buying and selling of mere stock certificates, which conferred the right to vote for the governors of the East India Company, was strongly affected by Whig-Tory affiliations. Politically active Tories traded mostly with fellow Tories, even though the Whigs were known to offer better deals.[6] The great Swedish economist and historian Eli Heckscher paused in his book of 1931 about seventeenth- and eighteenth-century mercantilism to reflect on the mix of P and S that rules: "People are actuated, to a greater extent than one tends to admit, by their more or less conscious . . . notions of what is right and natural. This does not contradict the view of their being governed by 'self-interest' . . . for they partly interpret their own interests in the light of this conception. . . . They often feel hampered in asserting their interests in such a direction as they themselves consider harmful to the general good."[7]

During the Great Depression American private investment did not recover until Dr. New Deal gave way to Dr. Win-the-War. Part of this was prudence. Unlike Dr. Win-the-War, Dr. New Deal talked terrifyingly of socialism to the economic royalists. A royalist would have been imprudent to invest heavily in a coal mine or auto factory, as Robert Higgs has noted, if the feds were likely to expropriate it next year.[8] But part was the royalists' S-ish animal spirits, too, arrayed viciously against That Man in the White House. A Peter Arno cartoon from the Depression shows a group of idiotically grinning swells in evening dress on the street inviting some others looking out of French windows to "Come along. We're going down to the TransLux and hiss Roosevelt."

It is often a scientific mistake, that is, to rely on P Only, and to reject S. Or, I say as an economist, vice versa. The economist asks the sociologist how much prudent profit was sacrificed by indulging one's political tastes. Since the economist Gary Becker first raised it, the quantitative question has been important in discussions of discrimination by race or gender. But turnabout is fair play. How much does *P* matter by itself? For some cases, admittedly, *P* is overwhelmingly important. If you are trying to explain covered interest arbitrage in the foreign exchanges, or the seizing of a profit of $400 million in the portfolio of Chase Manhattan, I advise you to forget about *S*, pretty much. Love and faith are not going to explain covered interest arbitrage or gigantic banking opportunities. Prudence will. On the other hand, if you are trying to explain voting or ethics or marriage or church attendance, you will fall into what Michael Polanyi in a similar connection once called "voluntary imbecility" if you simply ignore *S* and its interactions with *P*.

In 1952 a woman who wanted a divorce was wrong-footed from the start, though entitled to alimony if she could catch him in a hotel with his mistress. No longer. *S* has changed, and the change has had financial implications. It's not merely that some curve has shifted, as the economists want to put it. No-fault divorce interacted very strangely with the market, and ended up hurting a good many women. Or maybe not so strangely, a feminist might say.

Most economics, and most anthropology/sociology, is persuasion about the quantitative mixture of prudence and solidarity, the Profane and the Sacred, that matters for any particular case, and about how exactly they interact. The right-wing evolutionists of the 1970s, especially E. O. Wilson, were enthusiastically received by economists like Becker. The left-wing evolutionists, especially S. J. Gould and Richard Lewontin, were enthusiastically received by the Union of Radical Political Economists. The debate was at the political level a matter of *P* vs. *S*. (At the scientific level it is perhaps better described as *P* vs. *P* + ε, the [large] error term ε reflecting nonprudent evolutions of spandrels and five fingers merely stumbled into. But we're talking crude intellectual politics here.) The noneconomists see the world as *S*, largely. The economists want the world to be *P* Only. The world isn't buying.

The current debate between evolutionary psychologists such as Steven Pinker of MIT/Harvard or Ralph Messenger of David Lodge's fictional University of Gloucester and a group of sophisticated doubters such as Noam Chomsky and Jerry Fodor raises the issue again. Are we nice to each other because of some hidden, and scientifically undocumented, long-run prudence of evolution which hardwires particular moral precepts? Or are we nice because we subscribe to the Sacred ethical texts of our culture written on a practically blank slate?

As H. Allen Orr observes, Pinker (a *P* man) defends evolutionary psychology, which reinvents Schopenhauer, when it leads to ethically unhelpful theories—for example, "Men rape to spread their seed"—by huffing that after all we still have Sacred morals to oppose such barbarities. Presumably Pinker would give the same answer to complaints about the homophobic theories put forward by some of his very good friends. *S* rescues us, Pinker suggests, from the nastiness of pure *P*. Pinker's program will therefore not, he seems to promise, degenerate into a revival of Paragraph 175, eugenics, and the forced sterilization of the inferior types.

You bet. And "Pinker barely notices," writes Orr, "that the morality that's always there to save the day . . . is itself a legacy of the despised Blank Slate" of Lockean liberalism. Darwinian *P* "may well have endowed us with a crude morality, but this can't explain why kings but not women once had rights, but now women but not kings do."[9] Or as Richard Rorty asks about Pinker's ruminations, "How will this ability [to 'explain' behavior in evolutionary terms] help us figure out what sort of behavior to encourage?"[10] Rorty argues that we get our notions of good behavior from philosophers and, especially, novelists, and that the attempt by Pinker and others to substitute science for values—by treating "platitudes as gee-whiz scientific discoveries," he notes—is a category mistake. What is true about the fact-value split is that What Is cannot simply be taken as being just the same thing as What Should Be. We can't naturalize ethics *that* much.

The moral slate seems in fact to be practically empty of particular precepts. To buttress his theory that we are mostly *not* antisocial precisely because we are hardwired to be nice, Pinker is fond of instancing adult sociopaths, who supposedly are missing some wiring. It may be so. Yet one wonders if Pinker has ever known a two-year-old, or for that matter a fifteen-year-old; or if he has noted the variation country-to-country in niceness. Every human is born in sin, and must seek redemption. It would seem that the superstructure of ethical or aesthetic or social behavior is not determined in much detail by genes. As the biologist Peter Medawar, discussing an earlier outbreak of the nature/nurture controversy, expressed it, "Human beings owe their biological supremacy to a form of inheritance quite unlike that of other animals: exogenetic or exosomatic heredity," namely, culture.[11]

Ethics is like language, whose deep grammar may be hardwired but whose glorious detail is in its software applications. Or often ethics is not softwared at all, Jane Austen and George Orwell would insist, but a matter of individual human choice, the way in language we make up new words by choice—thus "coasties," as a Midwestern sneer about Californians and New Yorkers.

Of course, the answer to the nature/nurture/choice debate depends on what you mean by "detail." If you want to explain the difference between the music of humans and the music of dolphins, genes are a good place to look—though pack by pack the dolphins, by the way, seem to have musical, or maybe linguistic, cultures, too.[12] A female elephant raised close to a highway developed a growl that sounded like the trucks, which she apparently took to be her herd.[13] But if you want to explain the difference between Mozart and rap music, then culture, tradition, irony, choice, politics, the creativity of that exogenetic or exosomatic heredity are better places to look. As Louis Menand observed of Pinker's claims, "Music appreciation . . . seems to be wired in at about the level of 'Hot Cross Buns.' But people learn to enjoy Wagner. They even learn to sing Wagner. One suspects that enjoying Wagner, singing Wagner, anything to do with Wagner, is in gross excess of the requirements of natural selection."[14]

The evolutionary sociologist Jonathan Turner has argued that what did evolve biologically was a hardwired propensity for morality, with not much of its specific content. He speculates that the move to the savannah by early hominids required more connection within the group than was necessary in the more secluded environs of the trees. "Selection worked to give [the new] hominids the ability to use emotions [such as love of solidarity or fear of social sanctions] to build flexible systems of moral codes," adjustable to groups wandering the savannah in search of grubs and game.

It may be. Millions of years of selection back in the trees for "autonomy, weak tie-formation, and fluid social relations" among our proto-great-ape ancestors had to be offset, Turner believes, and in a hurry. A proto-great-ape venturing into the savannah who went on doing his own thing in lofty disdain of morality would get eaten by proto-lions. The new "neurological capacity to construct moral codes," with intensifiers such as ritual and language and labile emotions to go along with them, did the trick, economically.[15]

It's not all good news, this flexible ability to construct moral codes. As the economist Paul Seabright notes, "Like chimpanzees, though with more deadly refinement, human beings are distinguished by their ability to harness the virtues of altruism and solidarity, and the skills of rational reflection, to the end of making brutal and efficient warfare."[16] Thus the First

Crusade was inspired by theories of just war, as nowadays the anticrusade of Muslim martyrs is inspired by parallel theories. But anyway Turner's story seems rather more plausible than Pinker's, and by the way reads less like a politically pointed just-so story helpful to the radical wing of the Republican Party.

Still, one tires of the boyish enthusiasm in philosophy, psychology, economics, sociology, and the fourth estate for neoevolutionary and game-theoretic arguments. The boys do not realize that the Folk Theorem spoils the game. Perhaps the limitless number of solutions implied by the theorem accounts for the limitless parade of pseudo explanations. Recall the learned game theorists: "The prediction that individuals might do anything from a large set of feasible strategies is neither useful nor precise."[17]

It would be nice to see some actual evidence. The evidence from brain science is that so far we know practically nothing about the connection between brains and minds. This doesn't leave much room for confident statements similar to those about the effects of island size on animal size or of sunshine on human melatonin. The mind-brain connections we know about are too loose to help much in explaining ethics. As Jerry Fodor says, "Unlike our minds [and our postures and hair distributions, say], our brains are, by any gross measure, very like those of apes. So it looks as though relatively small alterations of brain structure must have produced very large behavioral discontinuities in the transition from the ancestral apes to us. If that's right, then you don't have to assume that cognitive complexity is shaped by the gradual action of Darwinian selection on pre-human behavioral phenotypes."[18] Fodor is vexed at people like Pinker who claim credit on some future, twenty-third-century brain science today. He counsels humility: "I'd settle for the merest glimpse of what is going on."

Economists, I have noted, want to explain everything—simply everything—from medieval open fields to the productivity of British steelmaking before 1914, with the simplest possible, boy's-own version of P Only. Without being explicit enough, though, some economists, and some of the best, do acknowledge S variables. Theodore Schultz argued in *Transforming Traditional Agriculture* (1964; Nobel 1979) that peasants in poor countries were prudent. He was arguing that it was a mistake to explain their behavior anthropology-style as "behavior equals some constant plus the effect of the sacred, plus an error term for human variability," $B = \alpha + \gamma S + \varepsilon$, with the S variable alone. Schultz said, Even these "traditional" peasants care about

P, too. Add it to the equation. But Schultz did not ignore the *S* variables. The education of women, he argued forcefully, was crucial in making Prudence work, and the education would depend on overcoming sacred patriarchal objections to literate women. He got the evidence.

Many economists go through a *Bildung* of this sort, starting in graduate school as *P*-Only guys—the guys more than the gals, since most of the gals had this figured out sometime before age eight—and coming by age fifty or so to realize that, after all, people are in fact motivated by more than Prudence. I did, for one. And Robert Fogel (born 1926; Nobel 1993) started in his youth, like me, as a *P*-Only Marxist, then became, like me, a *P*-Only economist, and finally discovered, like me, the force of religion in economic behavior. Even Gary Becker (born 1930; Nobel 1992) shows signs of such a development, in seeing that bourgeois virtues are not a betrayal of the science of economics.

GOD'S DEAL

Seest thou a man diligent in his business? He shall stand before kings.
   —Proverbs 22:29

A man may know the remedy,
But if he has not money, what's the use?
He is like one sitting without a goad
On the head of a musk elephant.
   —Vidyākara, "Subhāṣitaratnakoṣa"

The Christian gospels attack wealth, surprisingly harshly by the standards of the rest of the world's religious canon. It is not surprising therefore that in the nineteenth century a bourgeois but Christian Europe invented the idea of socialism. Marx and Engels wrote fiercely about it in 1848: "Nothing is easier than to give Christian asceticism a Socialist tinge. Has not Christianity declaimed against private property . . . ? Christian Socialism is but the holy water with which the priest consecrates the heart-burnings of the aristocrat."[1] The cofounder of the Catholic Worker movement, the French peasant and priest Peter Maurin, used to wander the streets of America in the early twentieth century declaring, "The world would be better off / If people tried to become better. / And people would become better / If they stopped trying to be better off."[2] Do good by doing poorly.

In 1919 Paul Tillich, then a thirty-three-year-year-old Protestant pastor in Germany, wrote with his friend Carl Richard Wegener "Answer to an Inquiry of the Protestant Consistory of Brandenburg" (1919): "The spirit of Christian love accuses a social order which consciously and in principle is built upon economic and political egoism, and it demands a new order in which the feeling of community is the foundation of the social structure. It accuses the deliberate egoism of an economy . . . in which each is the enemy of the other, because his advantage is conditioned by the disadvantage or ruin of the other, and it demands an economy of solidarity of all, and of joy in work rather than in profit."[3] The economy in this view is a zero-sum game. As the economist and theologian Robert Nelson puts it, "If the private pursuit of self-interest was long seen in Christianity as a sign of the continuing presence of sin in the world—a reminder of the fallen condition of humanity since the transgression of Adam and Eve in the garden—a blessing for a market economy has appeared to many people as the religious equivalent of approving of sin."[4]

I said that self-denial against the alleged egoism of a life in markets is a surprisingly Western idea. We Europeans have been accustomed since the first, Romantic Orientalists to thinking of the Orient, not our own Occident, as the place of self-denial—and paradoxically also as a place of wild excess. We Westerners mix notions of the Buddha with tales of *The Arabian Nights*.

We are mistaken. In *A Passage to England* (1959) the Indian professor of English Nirad C. Chaudhuri noted the contrast between the Lord's Prayer requesting merely our daily bread and the Hindu prayer to Durga, the Mother Goddess, "Give me wealth, long life, sons, and all things desirable."[5] One prays as a Hindu to Ganesha the elephant-headed god to overcome obstacles at the outset of any project: "Bow the head and offer obeisance before the son of Gauri . . . [to obtain] longevity, desired powers, and prosperity." The Vedic hymns are filled with passages like the following in a hymn to Agni the god of fire: "I pray to Agni . . . who . . . brings most treasure. . . . Through Agni one may win wealth, and growth from day to day, glorious and most abounding in heroic sons."[6]

A popular goddess in Hindu households, especially popular with women, is Lakshmi, goddess of all wealth, one of whose four arms is portrayed as pouring out gold coins. Contrast Jesus driving the money-changers from the temple, and his hard deal in Matthew 19:21: "If thou wilt be perfect, go and sell that thou hast, and give to the poor, and thou shalt have treasure in heaven: and come and follow me."

True, the Four Noble Truths of Buddhism recommend that the only solution to life's sorrow is the ending of desire. But consider the "Admonition to Singāla," consisting of a few hundred lines in the canon, described as "the longest single passage . . . devoted to lay morality." In the midst of it Buddha is represented as bursting into poetry in praise of friendship. The reward?

> The wise and moral man
>> Shines like a fire on the hilltop,
> Making money like a bee,
>> Who does not hurt the flower.
> Such a man makes his pile
>> As an anthill, gradually.
> The man grown wealthy thus
>> Can help his family
> And firmly binds his friends
>> To himself. He should divide
> His money in four parts;
>> On one part he should live,
> With two expand his trade,
>> And the fourth he should save
> Against a rainy day.[7]

As the editor remarks, the verses "effectively give the lie to the picture, still popular in some circles, of ancient India as a land of 'plain living and high thinking.' The last three verses are evidently a product of a society quite as acquisitive as that of present-day Europe or America."[8] More so, actually, if one is to take literally the recommended savings rate of 75 percent—with no allowance for charity, which bothered the Buddhist commentators on the text.

Thus too in Zoroastrianism a prayer of blessing (Afrinagan Dahman) reads, "I profess myself . . . a follower of Zarathushtra [*sic*]. . . . May these blessings of the Asha-sanctified come into this house, namely, rewards, compensation, and hospitality; and may there now come to this community Asha, possessions, prosperity, good fortune, and easeful life."[9] Zoroastrianism recommends charity to the poor. But it does not condemn fortunes honestly made and devoutly spent, which perhaps has something to do with the unusual prosperity of the tiny group of Zoroastrian Parsis in Pakistan and northwest India and England.

So with other axial faiths. A superficial reading of Confucius finds an emphasis on love and temperance, justice and courage. Not economic prudence. *The Analects* are a celebration of the bureaucratic gentleman, not the market's "small man," which is the sneering Confucian term. Yet the occasional snobbish remarks on wealth-seeking in Confucius do not have the edge and frequency of Jesus' terrifying warnings, such as that the rich man squeezes into heaven as a camel through a needle's eye.

Like these oriental texts, the writings of the Hebrew Bible, known to Christians as the Wisdom Books, and in particular the book of Proverbs, argue that rich men can be good even in their acquisition of riches. The first impulse is to suppose that riches signify the Lord's blessing, and riches await those who are faithful. So frequently in the Psalms: "Trust in the Lord, and do good; / so you will dwell in the land, and enjoy security. / Take delight in the Lord, / and he will give you the desire of your heart" (37:3–4). The promise, a theologically primitive solution to the problem of evil, is reward in this life. One can imagine the terror with which an unsuccessful Calvinist businessman must have read a passage such as "Those blessed by the Lord shall possess the land / but those cursed by him shall be cut off" (Pss. 37:22). The sixteenth-century businessman of Geneva or Edinburgh would naturally have redoubled his efforts to succeed here below at his calling.

About God's faithful servant Job, greatest of all the men of the East, rich in seven thousand sheep and three thousand camels, Satan taunts the Lord: "Thou hast blessed the work of his hands, and his substance is increased in the land. But put forth thine hand now, and touch all that he hath, and he will curse thee to thy face" (Job 1:10–11). As an experiment, therefore, Satan is permitted by God to take all Job's wealth, then his health. Yet the formerly rich and healthy man in the end keeps faith, after two score chapters of debate with his friends about what the suffering of a righteous man might mean.

The reward? "So the Lord blessed the later end of Job more than his beginning: for he had fourteen thousand sheep, and six thousand camels," a doubling (Job 42:12). The neat ending of the folk tale framing the theologically more sophisticated discussion in the middle parts is impossible in later Christianity, or in later Talmudic Judaism. "Lay not up for yourself treasures on earth," says one of the Jewish radicals on the eve of Talmudism, "Seek ye first the kingdom of God, . . . and all these things shall be added unto you"—but in heaven, where neither moth nor rust doth corrupt.

It is not surprising that Jewish herders and traders viewed herding and trading as ethically all right. "Despite certain Talmudic sayings to the contrary," Meir Tamari argues, "no anti-commercial tradition existed in Judaism." Rabbenu Bachya in the thirteenth century declared that "active participation of man in the creation of his own wealth is a sign of spiritual greatness. In this respect we are, as it were, imitators of God."[10] Nor is it surprising that the religion sprung from a brilliant trader of Mecca "protects and endorses the personal right to own what one may freely gain, through legitimate means, such as gifts and the fruits of one's hand or intellect. It is a sacred right."[11] What is surprising is that a Christendom that generalized the bourgeois life and invented modern capitalism was by contrast with these so hostile early and late to commerce, profit, trade, gain.

On the other hand Jesus counsels, too, *prudence* for the ages. As the nineteenth-century liberal Episcopal Bishop of Massachusetts, William Lawrence, noted in 1901, "While every word that can be quoted against the rich is . . . true . . . the parables of our Lord on the stewardship of wealth, His association with the wealthy, strike another note."[12] The very substance of the Christian deal is steeped in a sort of economics, Christ's sacrifice leading to "redemption." The Vulgate's *redemptio* translates Greek [*apo*]*lutrosis*, for example, Romans 3:24 or 1 Corinthians 1:30, connoting the paying in money of ransom or other obligations. Thus Christ in the *Agnus Dei* is *redemptor,* "the redeemer."

God's grace, the free gift unrequited, is no such vulgar deal. In its vulgar form the deal is, according to Joe Hill, "You will eat, bye and bye / In that glorious land in the sky. / Work and pray, live on hay: / You'll get pie in the sky when you die." Frank Knight depended always on a gospel-based statement of the faith—though his Campbellite upbringing emphasized Acts and Paul's Letters. He noted that Christianity is "very much a religion of reward and punishment. . . . [The Christian] is explicitly promised a hundred-fold repayment . . . (Matt. 19:29–30; Mark 10:29–30; Luke 22:29–30)."[13]

Indeed all "Godly" religions, as the sociologist Rodney Stark calls them, are based on such a deal. Mere spirits of the rocks and fields are to be propitiated, perhaps, or at least avoided, by whistling 'round the graveyard. But "because Gods are conscious beings, they are potential exchange partners because all beings are assumed to want something for which they might be induced to give something." Zeus wants the ascending smells from the burning entrails of a sacrificial bull. Jehovah wants his people to keep their side of the covenant made with Abraham and Moses, namely, to worship him, a jealous God. Stark's surprising explanation for mission and monotheism in Godly religions follows from the exchange, in contrast to mere trick-by-trick magic. "In pursuit of [large] other-worldly rewards humans will accept an *extended exchange relationship* with Gods," and "only Gods of great scope offer rewards so valuable as to justify a demand for an *exclusive* exchange relationship."[14]

The very forms of the attacks by Jesus and his followers on worldly wealth use prudential metaphors: "Lay up for yourselves treasures in heaven." They use the rhetoric of the profane to recommend the sacred. The rewards may be heavenly, but they are rewards nonetheless. It is a common rhetorical device. Epictetus in *The Enchiridion* criticizes envy of power as foolish, because the power is "paid for" by attendance on the mighty.[15] One should no more envy the power thus paid for, he says, than someone who buys a head of lettuce. The one who does not buy the lettuce at least keeps his money, and is therefore no worse off than he who buys it. An economist would quibble that Epictetus is ignoring what is known as "surplus," the gain from trade; or the "rent," as economists call profit, that comes from being first in attendance at the mighty's door. Still, Epictetus's rhetoric is close to that of Jesus in the parable of "render unto Caesar" (Matt. 22:21; Mark 12:17; Luke 20:25). The rhetoric uses commercial notions of ownership and trade and power to undermine the glorification of ownership and trade and power.

You can persuade yourself of Jesus' prudent rhetoric by examining Throckmorton's *Gospel Parallels*. The book gives all versions of each episode in the first three of the four gospels, according to Matthew, Mark, and Luke. Therefore each episode of the teachings can be coded without double counting into four categories. The episode is either

Prudent, that is, recommending worldly self-interest, though always of course in aid of the otherworldly, for example, "You are the salt of the earth; but if salt has lost its taste, . . . it is no longer good for anything" (Matt. 5:13; Luke 14:34; Throckmorton uses the New Revised Standard translation of 1989) or "Neither is new wine put into old wineskins; otherwise the skins burst" (Matt. 9:17; Mark 2:22).

Or it is **Imprudent**, recommending the opposite of self-interest, a holy foolishness hostile to the world's reasons, for example, "Follow me, and I will make you fish for people. Immediately they left their nets and followed him" (Matt. 4:19; Mark 1:17) or "We have nothing here but five loaves and two fishes" (Matt. 14:17; Mark 6:38; Luke 9:13).

Or it is **Mixed**, using the rhetoric of gain, but modestly, such as "Give us this day our daily bread" (Matt. 6:11; Luke 11:3); or using the rhetoric of nongain, but with an emphasis on the reward in heaven, such as "Whenever you give alms, do not sound a trumpet before you.... Your Father who sees in secret will reward you" (Matt. 6:2, 4).

Or it is **Neither**, having no reference either positive or negative to matters of prudence. Thus "At sundown . . . he cured many who were sick with various diseases" (Matt. 8:16; Mark 1:32, 34; Luke 4:40) or "At that time Herod the ruler heard reports . . . and said, 'This is John the Baptist . . . raised from the dead'" (Matt. 14:1–2; Mark 6:14; Luke 9:7).

The result is a nonoverlapping count beginning with the first preachings in Galilee, excluding the infancy narratives and the Passion and the post-crucifixion appearances. In a fallen world the classification cannot be perfect. But there is no doubt, I would claim, that Jesus uses an appeal to prudence more than occasionally, and something like two to one in favor of it rather than against it.

Jesus' prudent advice in the Mark 12:17 version to render unto Caesar is the one of the merely ten sentences in the gospels that the "Jesus Seminar," a group of liberal and quantitative biblical scholars, regards as certainly original. The seminar treats "Thomas," a collection of sayings discovered in 1945 in a Coptic manuscript, as a fifth gospel. Of the other nine supposedly

Classification of Jesus' Teachings Enumerated by Episodes in Matthew, Mark, and Luke

For example, the parables of the

Recommending Prudence	38	Faithful and Wise Slave; House Divided; Fig Tree with No Fruit; the Unjust Manager
Criticizing Prudence	18	Birds Neither Sow Nor Reap; Turn the Cheek; Good Samaritan; Mary Chose the Better Part
Mixed	15	God and Mammon; Sit in the Lowest Place; Rich Young Man; Widow's Gift
Neither	104	Jesus Denounces Scribes and Pharisees; Question about Fasting
Total	175	

Source: Throckmorton's *Gospel Parallels*,1992, p. 180.
Note: When a parallel passage occurs earlier in Throckmorton and has already been coded, it is omitted: that is, it is not counted twice. Thus the Parable of the mustard seed in its Luke 13 version (episode 164, p. 129, of Throckmorton) was already classified in its Matthew and Mark versions (p. 78), and is not recounted (it recommends prudence, by the way). That is why the total is 175, as against Throckmorton's numbering of 221 in the teaching sections. I have a sense that my "Neither" category is rather undercounted. What matters, though, are the first three rows.

original sayings of Jesus in the five gospels, five commend love: turn the other cheek, give to the poor, blessed are the poor/hungry/sad, love your enemy, the good Samaritan. But the four others, among them "render unto Caesar," commend prudence, at least in their use of the metaphors of economic life: God's rule as leaven (Luke 13:20–21, Matt. 13:33), the shrewd manager (Luke 16:1–8), the workers in the vineyard (Matt. 20:1–15), the mustard seed, which only in the spare version of Thomas 20:2–4 does the seminar regard as fully original.

John Dominic Crossan, the former chairman of the Jesus Seminar, offered in 1991 a "reconstructed inventory" of "all the words placed on his lips that actually go back to the historical Jesus."[16] One can catalogue them by those in favor of worldly prudence ("No man can serve two masters"), those advocating holy foolishness ("Carry no purse, no bag, no sandals"), and those indifferent on the matter ("Human beings will be forgiven all their sins"). The result is rather similar to the experiment here with *Gospel Parallels*: thirty-eight for prudence, nineteen against (and therefore again about two to one in favor), and forty-seven indifferent.

The seminar proposed a "final general rule of evidence" in the search for the historical Jesus: "Beware of finding a Jesus entirely congenial to you" (Crossan, p. 5). It is not the case that only original remarks by Jesus constitute Christianity. After all, I remind my fellow believers, the Holy Spirit speaks through Moses and the prophets, too, and in latter days through all the saints, and through our holy, catholic, and apostolic church, and indeed through the inner light of men and women at the meeting. Nor is it obvious that the Jesus Seminar has for sure identified the authentic remarks. The seminar is not universally admired by sophisticated biblical scholars, and is detested by literalists. Nor does Jesus' prudential rhetoric imply that he would have thrilled to the modern bourgeoisie.

The point is merely to counter the assumption especially congenial in the West since 1848 that Jesus was bitterly hostile to the propensity to truck and barter. No, he was not. Even the Sermon on the Mount, the most socialist of Christian texts, is saturated with a rhetoric of reward. "Blessed are the poor in spirit, *for theirs is the kingdom of heaven* . . . Blessed are the meek, *for they shall inherit the earth*" (Matt. 5:3, 5). "The kingdom of heaven," said Jesus in a characteristic simile, "is like a merchant in search of fine pearls; on finding one pearl of great value, he went and sold all that he had and bought it" (Matt. 13:45–46).

I am not making the Jesus-as-salesman argument, the pocket-sized God comforting to Babbitt, with which the priest consecrates the heart-burnings of the bourgeois. Nor am I arguing as does Bruce Wilkinson in his astonishingly popular *The Prayer of Jabez: Breaking Through to the Blessed Life* (2000). He claims that First Chronicles 4:10—"Oh, that you would bless me indeed, *and enlarge my territory*"—reveals that "your Father longs to give you so much more than you have ever thought to ask."[17] More yachts and BMWs, he means.

I am noting merely that Jesus the carpenter lived in a thoroughly market-oriented economy and did not ask all the fishermen to drop their nets and become fishers of people. He accepted that honest money changers were necessary to change denarii into ritually acceptable shekels. He offered salvation in the marketplace, not only at the high altar of the temple. He dined with tax gatherers, not only with the Pharisees and the hypocrites of sad countenance.

God is nothing less than perfect Love. Nor is he to be absorbed into an earthbound and utilitarian prudence. But love, I have noted, includes a proper *self*-love. There is nothing wrong with that. As Bernard Williams observed, in God's deal there is no scarcity, and therefore no competition, and therefore "no effective way of aiming at salvation *at the expense of others*."[18] That Christianity need not itself be inconsistent with capitalism shines in the lives of the saints who lived by trade, such as the tinker John Bunyan, or in William Penn's commercial yet godly plans for his woods in the New World, or indeed in the commercial carpentry of our Lord and Savior. Christianity was in its first centuries an urban religion, appealing to high and low in a market economy. It offered a deal that pointed to a non-market realm, but used metaphors from here below.

Jesus is not entirely congenial either to a socialist or to a capitalist. Nor for that matter to many a Christian.

NECESSARY EXCESS?

The world is too much with us; late and soon,
Getting and spending, we lay waste our powers.
      —Wordsworth

The clerisy thinks that capitalist spending is just awful. In 1985 Daniel Horowitz argued that the American clerisy had been since the 1920s in the grip of a "modern moralism" about spending. The traditional moralism of the nineteenth century looked with alarm from the middle class down onto the workers and immigrants drinking beer and obeying Irish priests and in other ways showing their "loss of virtue." Traditional moralists like the U.S. Commissioner of Labor, Carroll D. Wright, "had no basic reservations about the justice and efficacy of the economic system—their questions had to do with the values of workers and immigrants, not the value of capitalism."

The modern moralist, post-1920, in the style of Veblen and Mencken and Sinclair Lewis, looks down instead from the clerisy onto the middle class. Therefore "at the heart of most versions of modern moralism is a critique, sometimes radical and always adversarial, of the economy."[1] Horowitz is polite to his fellow members of the clerisy—Veblen, Stuart Chase, the Lynds, Galbraith, Riesman, Marcuse, Lasch, and Daniel Bell—and does not say that their concerns were simply mistaken. He does observe that "denouncing other people for their profligacy and lack of Culture is a way of reaffirming one's own commitment."[2]

The clerisy doesn't like the spending patterns of hoi polloi. It has been saying since Veblen that the many are in the grips of a tiny group of advertisers. So the spending on Coke and gas grills and automobiles is the result of hidden persuasion or, to use a favorite word of the clerisy, "manipulation." The peculiarly American attribution of gigantic power to thirty-second television spots is puzzling to an economist. If advertising had the powers attributed to it by the clerisy, then unlimited fortunes could be had for the writing. Yet advertising is less than 2 percent of national product, much of it uncontroversially informative—such as shop signs and entries in the Yellow Pages or ads in trade magazines aimed at highly sophisticated buyers. When Vance Packard published his attack on advertising, *The Hidden Persuaders* (1957), he thought he would lose his friends on Madison Avenue. But they were delighted. An adman friend came up and said, "Vance, before your book I was having a devil of a time convincing my clients that advertising worked. Now they think it's magic."

The American clerisy's hostility to advertising is puzzling to a rhetorician. Why would a country adoring of free speech in its higher intellectual circles have such a distaste for commercial free speech? Perhaps the distaste is merely a branch of that great river of antirhetoric rhetoric in the West since Bacon. But anyway if hoi polloi were as rhetorically stupid as most of the clerisy seems to believe, then as I say any reasonably clever ad writer could "manipulate" them with ease. But it ain't so. The TV generation can see through advertising directed at children by age eight, and by age eighteen it bases its humor—see *Saturday Night Live*—on parodies of attempted manipulation.

So mass consumption is supposed to be motiveless, gormless, stupid. And anyway there's too damned much of it. "Why do they buy so much stuff? The dolts. The common consumer does not own a single classical music recording. It is ages, if ever, that she has read a nonfiction book on the bourgeois virtues. She thinks the Three Tenors are classy. Her house is jammed with tasteless rubbish." One is reminded of the disdain c. 1910 on the part of modernist litterateurs like D. H. Lawrence and Virginia Woolf for the nasty little commuters of London. An air of immorality hangs about Waterloo Station and the super mall.

The amount of American *stuff* nowadays is to be sure formidable. A standard photographic ploy is to get a family in Topeka, Kansas, and one in Lagos, Nigeria, to dump the entire contents of their houses out on the front sidewalk, and then pose for the camera *en famille* and *en stuff*. The contrast is remarkable. Americans certainly do have a lot of clothing and gadgets and lawn mowing equipment. Of course, they have twenty times the average productivity and income of Nigerians. And yet the clerisy wants us to feel guilty about unworn dresses in the closet and unused kitchen gadgets in the bottom drawer. In a world of scarcity, they cry, why are we so profligate in spending? On this matter the clerisy flagellates even itself.

Yet we make ourselves with consumption, as anthropologists have observed. Mary Douglas and Baron Isherwood put it so: "Goods that minister to physical needs—food and drink—are no less carriers of meaning than ballet or poetry. Let us put an end to the widespread and misleading distinction between goods that sustain life and health and others that service the mind and heart—spiritual goods."[3] The classic demonstration is Douglas's article on the symbolic structure of working-class meals in England, but in a sense all of anthropology is in this business.[4] Goods wander across the border of the sacred and the profane—the anthropologist Richard Chalfen, for example, shows how home snapshots and movies do.[5] Or as the anthropologist Marshall Sahlins puts it in the new preface to his classic of 1972, *Stone Age Economics*, "economic activity . . . [is] the expression, in a material register, of the values and relations of a particular form of life."[6]

In her survey of Catholic and radical thinking on consumption Christine Firer Hinze worries that in such market makings of selves we might lose our virtues, especially our temperance.[7] She recalls Monsignor John A. Ryan's books of economics in the early twentieth century calculating the costs of dignity as against superfluity. Hinze and I agree that it is possible to make oneself badly—she and I are Aristotelians and Aquinians, with an idea of the virtuous life, not utilitarians refusing to judge consumption. "Structures of sin" are possible in the sociology of consumption. She and I would urge "a virtue approach to consumer culture," and to much else.[8] But what evidence, really, is there that "the market can neither generate nor guarantee respect for . . . moral foundations"?[9] Doubtless not without ethical effort, yes. But "cannot"?

Americans do have a great deal. They have a great deal, I said, because they produce a great deal. Contrary to your grandmother's dictum—"Eat your spinach: think of the starving children in China"—consuming less in rich America would add nothing to the goods available in China. Not a grain of rice. Countries are rich or poor, have a great deal to consume or very little, mainly because they work well or badly, not because some outsider is adding to or stealing from a God-given endowment. To think otherwise is to suppose that goods come literally and directly from God, like manna. They do not. We humans make them.

So having a lot is not immoral. It is the good luck to be born in America. By all means let us spread the good luck around. The luck consisting of reasonably honest courts and reasonably secure property rights and reasonably nonextractive governments and reasonably effective educational systems, and a reasonably long time for the reasonably good ideas to do their work. Growth has little to do with foreign aid or foreign investment or foreign trade. It is mainly domestic.

The Japanese have a similar problem of stuff. Steve Bailey tells how he furnished his house in Osaka when he was teaching there by collecting *gomi*, "oversized household junk," that the Japanese would leave on the street for collection every month. I mean full furnishings: "refrigerators, gas rings, stand-up mirror, color television, VCR, chairs, bookshelf, corner couch, and a beautiful cherrywood table."[10] The shameless foreigners, the *gaijin*, competed with low-status Japanese junk men in raiding the *gomi* piles. The reason this happens in Japan, Bailey explains, is the small size of the houses and the *S* variable taboo on getting or giving second-hand furniture.

The reason it happens in the United States is that same winner's curse I mentioned earlier, in the form of a consumer's curse. Our American houses are filled with our mistaken consumption, items that turned out not to be as delightful as we thought they were going to be. As David Klemm puts it, following Heidegger, "We understand things in their *potentiality* to be."[11] You men, think of your gadgets; women, your clothing. The full houses are not because we are stupid or sinful. They are because, not being omniscient, we make mistakes from time to time about the delight-generating potential of a $250 electrostatic dust remover from the Sharper Image. (Look at *that* trade name for its manipulative power, by the way). So we often buy things that turn out to be not worth the price. When we mistake in the other direction we do not buy, and wait for the dust removers to come down in price. The occasions of optimism mount up, and the stuff piles up in the garage, since there is no point in throwing away the stuff if you have the room—and Americans have the room. Being rich in electrostatic dust removers and the like is not sinful. It does not unjustly take from the poor. It is not always a sign of intemperance. It is merely a sign of capitalism's very great and productive prudence.

Yet everyone thinks that the great consumption at least "keeps the economy going." Even the clerical critic of spending will acknowledge, knowingly, that "the economy" somehow benefits. The theologian Ellen Charry, to give one example among many that could be quoted, believes that advertising keeps the economy growing.[12] Noneconomists imagine that God has so poorly designed the world that a lack of thrift tending to foolhardiness and avarice is, unhappily, necessary to keep the wheels of commerce turning, "creating jobs" or "keeping the money circulating." They imagine that people must buy, buy, buy or else capitalism will collapse and we all will be impoverished. They believe that advertising is necessary for it, though unhappily it corrupts us. They believe that capitalism must be greedy to keep on working.

The argument is the alleged paradox of thrift. Thriftiness, a good thing in Christianity and most certainly in Buddhism and the rest, seems able paradoxically to impoverish us. We will do poorly by doing good. And if we do well, we are probably damned by the sins of greed and gluttony necessary to profit in a nasty world. Choose, ye sinners: God or Mammon. Dorothy Sayers, who was more than a writer of mysteries, though not an economist, complained in 1942 as a Christian about "the appalling squirrel-cage . . . in which we have been madly turning for the last three centuries . . . a society in which consumption has to be artificially stimulated in order to keep production going."[13]

To tell the truth, many economists in the era of the Great Depression had reverted to this noneconomist's way of thinking. The theory was called "stagnationism." It was a balloon theory of capitalism, that people must keep puff-puffing or the balloon would collapse. It's one version of the old claim that expenditure on luxuries at least employs workpeople. Thus Alexander Pope, in a poem of 1731 subtitled "Of the Use of Riches": "Yet hence the poor are clothed, the hungry fed; / Health to himself, and to his infants bread / The labourer bears: what his [the rich man's] hard heart denies, / His charitable vanity supplies.[14] "Providence is justified in giving wealth to be squandered in this manner," Pope writes in the poem's prose Argument, "since it is dispersed to the poor and laborious part of mankind."

Since the 1940s we bourgeois economists have recovered our senses.[15] The balloon theory of the Depression era has popped, and with it the paradox that sin is necessary to "keep production going," the paradox of thrift that vanity can in the end be charitable. It survives in Marxian critiques of the Adorno-Horkheimer type, but is no longer believed by economists of the center or right. The false paradox reflects a grimly Christian, even

Protestant, conviction that we must give up the kingdom of heaven to achieve prosperity on earth. The popping of the balloon allows us to see the sacred and the profane as connected and sometimes even complementary. We can do good by doing well, a modern Christian economist would say, and can do well by doing good.

Nothing would befall the market economy in the long run if we tempered our desires to a thrifty style of life, one beat-up Volvo and a little house with a vegetable garden and a moderate amount of tofu and jug wine from the Co-op. The balloon theory sounds plausible if you focus on an irrelevant mental experiment, namely, that tomorrow, suddenly, without warning, we would all begin to follow Jesus strictly in what we buy. Such a conversion would doubtless be a shock to sales of Hummers and designer dresses at $15,000 a copy. But, the economist observes, people in a Christian economy would at length find other employment, or choose more leisure. That's the relevant mental experiment, the long run.

In the new, luxury-less economy it would still be a fine thing to have lightbulbs and paved roads and other fruits of enterprise. More of these would still be better than less. "In equilibrium"—a phrase with resonance in bourgeois economics similar to "God willing" in Abrahamic religions—the economy would encourage specialization to satisfy human desires in much the same way it does now. People would buy Bibles in koine Greek and spirit-enhancing trips to Yosemite instead of buying Harlequin romances in English and package tours to Disney World. But they would still value high-speed presses for the books and airplanes for the trips, getting more books and more trips for the cost.

The clerisy admits that luxury consumption at least keeps the poor employed. But this too is mistaken.

Smith uses the phrase "the invisible hand" only two times in his published writings. One of the times, unfortunately, he uses it to defend such trickle-down. In *The Theory of Moral Sentiments* (1759) he notes that an eighteenth-century Bill Gates (as it were) cannot after all eat much more than his chauffeur can, speaking of sheer volume and nutrients. Nor can he wear right now more than one pair of Italian designer trousers, speaking of mere leg-covering ability. Nor can he live in more than one enormous room at a time, speaking of gross roofage and wallage. The real Gates as it happens lives in a surprisingly modest home. His palace outside Seattle is merely an architectural folly for parties, he says. But even if he were a spendthrift, he couldn't possibly spend *and use* anything but a tiny portion of what he earns.

The founder of the first dot.com company, the editor and humorist Brad Templeton, reckons that in 2004 Gates earned $300 a second. It was then not worth Gates's while, Templeton calculates, to bend down to pick up a $1,000 bill. For the banner year of 1998, in which he earned $45 billion, it was a $10,000 bill.[16] Millionaires, and especially billionaires, have limits on how much they can use incomes so very much higher than ours for correspondingly unequal consumption—of, say, trousers, put on one leg at a time. So economic growth, however unequally shared as income, is more egalitarian in its distribution of consumption. As the American economist John Bates Clark predicted in 1901, "The typical laborer will increase his wages from one dollar a day to two, from two to four and from four to eight. Such gains will mean infinitely more to him than any possible increase of capital can mean to the rich. . . . This very change will bring with it a continual approach to equality of genuine comfort."[17]

But Smith wants to argue against Rousseau's notion that property brings inequality in its train. He therefore claims cheerily that the rich "are led by an *invisible hand* to make nearly the same distribution of the necessaries of life, which would have been made, had the earth been divided into equal portions among all its inhabitants."[18] The argument is Pope's trickle-down—"Yet hence the poor are clothed, the hungry fed."

Smith is forgetting that if, say, a Saddam Hussein took 50 percent of Iraqi national produce and put it into arms and palaces, the stuff was in consequence not available for ordinary Iraqis to consume as food or fuel or shelter. Iraq was impoverished, and so the necessaries of life were available in nothing like the distribution which would have been made under real equality. The percentage distribution, to be sure, was roughly the same—at any rate, one man, one pair of trousers at any one time—but the absolute amount was reduced by the needless luxury. Saddam Hussein may not have consumed palaces he never visited. But neither did anyone else. Socially speaking, the resources were thrown away. What a rich woman cannot consume, such as the diamond bauble that sits unworn in the back of her jewelry box, is simply wasted, socially speaking. She gets no pleasure from it, except perhaps the happy memory of its purchase. Pope himself gave the correct analysis a few lines later: " 'Tis use alone that sanctifies expense, / And splendor borrows all her rays from sense."

A noneconomist is inclined to reply that after all the diamond bauble and the palaces and the $300 meals at Charlie Trotter's for Bill Gates "put people to work," such as construction workers or diamond cutters or Michelin-two-star cooks. But that's not so. Smith does not make such a mistake, the supposition that the social problem is to find tasks for people to do who otherwise would be idle.

Noneconomists think that economics is about "keeping the money circulating." And so they are impressed by the claim by the owner of the local sports franchises that using tax dollars to build a new stadium will "generate" local sales and "create" new jobs. To a noneconomist the vocabulary of generating and creating jobs out of unthrifty behavior sounds tough and prudential and quantitative. It is not. It is mistaken. No economist of sense would use such locutions, and indeed you can depend on it that an alleged economist on TV is a phony if she talks of "creating jobs." The reply Smith and the other real economists would give to the noneconomist is that the diamond workers would not be idle if "thrown out" of work in the bauble factory. They would in the long run find alternative employment, such as in growing oats for oatmeal or making thatched roofs for peasant houses. We are mostly pressed for time, not duties.

Smith does at the same place, though, make a third, related argument, also in part mistaken, that the sheer act of imagining the pleasure of wealth deceives us into labor. Admittedly the hope that our latest purchase will bring true happiness is a common imagining, by guys in Brookstone and by gals in the kitchen-equipment store. Smith notes that "what pleases these lovers of toys is not so much the utility, as the aptness of the machines which are fitted to promote it. All their pockets are stuffed with little conveniences."[19] We are in fact often deceived into laboring to get such "trinkets of frivolous utility." But the mistake is to think, as Smith says he does, that the deception is desirable: "And it is well that nature imposes upon us in this manner. It is this deception which rouses and keeps in continual motion the industry of mankind."[20] Smith is articulating the paradox of thrift in a jazzed-up version.

Such lack of thrift does indeed prompt us "to invent and improve all the sciences and arts" relevant to the particular item of luxury we lust for. What is correct about the argument is David Hume's "taking delight in praise" and Frank Knight's "final interest," that is, the stimulus of a sacred vanity. The S variables, even dubious ones, do prompt us to invent and improve and to turn "rude forests of nature into agreeable and fertile plains"—an unmarked quotation, Smith's editors note, from Rousseau's "les vastes forêts se changèrent en des champagnes riantes," though in Rousseau with a very different continuation than a Smithian optimism: "which had to be watered with men's sweat, and in which slavery and misery were soon to germinate and grow with the crops."[21]

But as sheer industry, nothing is gained. It's the balloon theory again, the confusion of "continual motion" with desirable motion, directed just *this* way. It is not in itself good to be set to work raising the Great Wall of China, inventing and improving the science and art of great-wall making, when you could be getting on with your life, improving the science and art of making houses and automobiles, universities and museums.

Smith's mistake is what is known among older economists as the "Tang" fallacy, which is not about the Chinese dynasty but about the powdered orange juice of that name, which was asserted in its advertising to be a spin-off of the American space program. The fallacy is to think that we would have missed out on priceless innovations such as Tang if we had left the money in the hands of ordinary people instead of throwing it away on moon shots. "Job creation" through this or that project—the Big Dig in Boston burying a highway, the tunnel under many kilometers of "The Heart of Holland" burying a railway—is not the optimal working of a market economy, but more like its opposite. After all, notably poor economies commonly have plenty of jobs, opening doors or pulling rickshaws. Unemployment was not the problem faced by the slaves in the silver mines of Attica or the quarries of Syracuse. Our leaders, taking delight in praise, buying their power and prestige with our money, building in Japan for example splendid bridges to nowhere, "create jobs" that shouldn't have been.

The Dutch English rhymester Bernard Mandeville articulated the mistaken supposition in 1705: "Vast numbers thronged the fruitful hive; / Yet those vast numbers made them thrive. / Millions endeavoring to supply / Each other's lust and vanity. . . . / Thus every part was full of vice, / Yet the whole mass a paradise." Mandeville's claim is that vice, vanity, folly, greed, and gluttony are the springs of economic growth. The force of sin creates, unintendedly, a rich and vital society.

Mandeville's insight into unintended consequences was important. But his economics was false, though ever since then it has been a comfort to the trickle-down, I've-got-mine school of capitalist ethics. He was answered immediately and correctly by one George Blewhitt (or Bluett), the author of a pamphlet against the 1723 edition of Mandeville. Mandeville had argued that universal honesty would put locksmiths out of work and therefore would damage prosperity. Better for the hive to be dishonest. Blewhitt replied, "The change [to an honest way of life] must necessarily be supposed to be *gradual*; and then it will appear still plainer that there would arise a succession of new trades . . . in proportion as the trades in providing against roguery grew useless and wore off."[22]

Adam Smith loathed Mandeville's embrace of vice. "Such is the system of Dr. Mandeville," wrote Smith in 1759 with palpable irritation, "which once made so much noise in the world, and which, though, perhaps, it never gave occasion to more vice than would have been without it, at least taught [this] vice, which arose from other causes, to appear with more effrontery, and to avow the corruption of its motives with a profligate audaciousness which had never been heard of before."[23] Smith did not say, ever, that greed is good. The men in the Adam Smith ties need to do a little reading of *The Nature and Causes of the Wealth of Nations* and especially of *The Theory of Moral Sentiments* on the train to Westport. The Christian and other opponents of the sin of avarice need to stop conceding the point to the men of Westport. There is no paradox of thrift, not in a properly Christian world. Nor even in the world we lamentably inhabit.

If true, this should be good news for ethical people. We don't need to accept avaricious production or vulgar consumerism or unloving work-obsession on account of some wider social prudence they are supposed to serve, allegedly keeping us employed. "Keeping us employed." Have you ever in your private, homely activities, doing the laundry or planting the garden, seen your main problem as finding jobs at which to be employed? Isn't the main problem the opposite one, a scarcity of hours in which to bake the bread or fix the car or play with the kids or nurture friendships or sing praises unto the Lord thy God? If you agree, then you grasp the great economic principle that, as Adam Smith put it, to repeat, "What is prudence in the conduct of every private family can scarce be folly in that of a great kingdom." And you will grasp why it is not economic prudence to "keep us all at work" by spending on luxuries and working, working, working.

GOOD WORK

Benjamin Hunnicutt argues in his books on the work obsession of Americans, giving substance to Herbert Marcuse's claims, that long hours—which Hunnicutt thinks have not much fallen since the 1930s—are connected to our great Need-Love for commodities, the "New Economic Gospel of Consumption," new in the 1920s. "The job," Hunnicutt writes, "resembles a secular religion, promising personal identity, salvation, purpose and direction, community, and a way for those who believe truly and simply in 'hard work' to make sense out of the confusion of life."[1]

Even in work-mad America and Japan, Hunnicutt is mistaken about the hours worked, because people now start work later in life and add on many years of retirement at the end, which the life chances in the good old days did not permit.[2] But he's right about the making of the job into an idol. It's a specifically bourgeois sin, because only the bourgeoisie thinks of work as a calling.

But it is also, balanced and in moderation, a bourgeois virtue. *Laborare est orare*, to work is to pray, said the Benedictine monks of Monte Cassino in the sixth century, showing in the very phrase a break with the classical world's contempt for manual labor. In the fourteenth and fifteenth centuries in the Greek Orthodox world "painting became a holy and highly respected mode of fulfilling the requirement of manual labor prescribed for all monks."[3] Max Weber claimed that Tibetan and Christian monks represent "the first human being who lives rationally, who works methodically and by rational means toward a goal," namely a religious goal.[4]

Whether or not that is so, the social theorists in thirteenth-century Europe, and specifically the learned Franciscan and Dominican friars at the new urban universities, transferred the attitude to cities. "The ideals of Christian society as formulated in earlier centuries," explains Lester K. Little, "had come to include high regard for creative work, and so the problem of the legitimacy of the merchant's activities generally, as well as of the profit he made, turned largely on the question of whether what he did could properly be considered creative work."[5] "God's work was, of course, creation," writes Jacques Le Goff on the matter. "Any profession, therefore, which did not create was bad or inferior."[6] Little and Le Goff explain how the rise of urban scholasticism in the twelfth and thirteenth centuries changed this, from at least a Christian point of view. The Church became for a while, Le Goff notes, "an early protector of merchants."[7] From an aristocratic point of view, of course, nothing changed: until the dominance of the bourgeoisie, any nonmilitary work, manual or intellectual, continued to be dishonorable.

Now we work. In an ideal world would capitalist work be necessary? I believe so, contrary to a widespread belief among the clerisy that good work and capitalist work are inconsistent with each other. People following Jesus, true, would as I said make the good, plain pottery that an economy of moderation would demand and spend a lot more time with their kids. They would not pursue the illusory immortality of work. But the plain pottery— and therefore more time with the kids, since getting the fancier Wedgwood china would require more hours of work—would still be produced most efficiently, I have claimed, in a market-oriented, free-trade, private property, enterprising, and energetic economy, as in fact it was in the Lower Galilee of Jesus' time.

Choosing the system of natural liberty over the alternatives would make us richer, not poorer, in sacred things. In a competitive economy of enterprise Josiah Wedgwood invented thin-walled cups and teapots for the commoners, which formerly he had exported to the tsarina and her court. The commoners used them in turn to invent high tea for the rich and the sacred cuppa for the poor.

Imagine everyone was an active, believing, even holy and ascetic Christian. What then would be the ideal economy to house such unusual people?

One way to imagine it is to look at the actual economic history of religious communities, from early Christians in the cities of the Roman Empire to the present-day Amish of Kalona, Iowa. Such data are not free of confounding influences, because the historical communities floated in a sea of markets. But it is worth noting, for example, that medieval Cistercian monks and nuns were the venture capitalists of their age, famous in farm management. The earliest forward contracts on grain in medieval Europe were made by them.

The Calvinists of Holland and Switzerland and Britain in the seventeenth century were skilled businesspeople, as of course Max Weber emphasized a century ago. The early Anabaptists cut themselves off from the political world, refusing to bear arms, for example, and were regularly burned at the stake on that account. But they usually did not cut themselves off from the economic world, at any rate those Anabaptists who did not go all the way to boastful communism. The Old Believers in Russia, highly orthodox and in other ways "conservative," constituted the core of the tiny commercial middle class of that sad land during the eighteenth and nineteenth centuries.[8]

English Quakers, besides doing the Lord's work in resisting war and abolishing slavery and espousing the equality of all men and women, made fortunes still resonant: Cadbury, the English chocolate makers; Rowntree, and Fry, the same; Barclay, private banker of London; Lloyd, the same; and Lloyd of the coffeehouse, then of insurance on ships, then of insurance on anything you wish. The American Shakers were briefly brilliant at designing and manufacturing furniture, and inventing and selling to the market for example, the clothespin and the American-style broom. They certainly were Christians. The Church of Jesus Christ of Latter Day Saints made the Great Basin bloom, but not by adopting socialism. And the modern Amishman in Pennsylvania or Indiana is no slouch at striking a bargain for a plow horse. It is not true, as Paul Tillich maintained in 1933, that "any serious Christian must be a socialist."

Anthony Waterman has shown, in fact, that many serious Anglicans in the early nineteenth century approved of capitalism, and on no flimsy grounds. Classical political economy in the writings of the Reverend Malthus, Archdeacon Paley, Bishop Copleston, Archbishop Sumner of Canterbury, Archbishop Whately of Dublin, and the Professor of Divinity at Edinburgh, Thomas Chalmers, was "the mainstream of Anglo-Scottish social theory in the early 19th century," while the philosophical radicalism of the atheistic school of Bentham was viewed at the time as a "backwater."[9]

One can ask whether the examples of holy profit makers show at least that Christianity fits smoothly with capitalism. No, not necessarily, because it could be a case of giving the Devil his due. In a sea of sin the Christian may properly sell Shaker brooms to the unbelievers at a profit for the church, as Jews and Muslims were permitted to take interest on loans to Christians but not among themselves.

One might think that if everyone were Shakers there would be no buying or selling at all. "No buying and selling" is the vision of utopian socialism, or more properly of the anarchism that is supposed to follow the end of private property and the withering away of the state. It is the anarchism of, say, Prince Kropotkin which thrilled me, age fourteen, down at the local Carnegie Library.

Such economic utopianism of Europe in the mid- to late nineteenth century was paid for with interest by the grandchildren in the twentieth century. It looked a good deal like a secular version of the evangelical Christianity, or the oddly parallel Hasidic Judaism, of the mid-eighteenth and early nineteenth centuries in Europe and America. Dorothy Day (1897–1980), another founder of the Catholic Worker movement in the United States, managed a "House of Hospitality," one of thirty or so, and the newspaper *The Catholic Worker* (1931–present) in order "to realize in the individual and society the expressed and implied teachings of Christ." Robert Ellsberg writes that "the value of such a venture is not properly assessed in terms of profits and losses. Objectively speaking, *The Catholic Worker* has aspired to a kind of 'holy folly.' . . . Dorothy displayed a willful indifference to conventional business sense."[10]

But in truth there seems to be no reason why buying and selling and a business sense would vanish in a perfect Christian community. A business sense has not vanished among the Amish. In one utopian, "intentional" community after another the market has burst in, as into the Amana Colonies in Eastern Iowa in 1932, who at one time, quite unlike the capitalist Amish down the road, took even their meals in common; or more recently into the hippie communes of the 1960s.[11]

Even strictly isolated communities would have exchanges, in effect if not in money terms. Brother Jonathon would be the smithy, Sister Helena the baker. Self-sufficiency is an imprudent way to live, and only misanthropes—like survivalists in Idaho or Thoreau in Concord—take it very seriously. And Thoreau got his books and nails for his separative self near Walden Pond by scrounging from people in town.

One might as well get the advantages of specialization and trade, a book or a horseshoe provided for a nail or a loaf, if "only" to have more time to pray, to write, to think, to travel a good deal in Concord. If the community is small, admittedly, there is nothing to be gained by having formal markets. A family, for example, works better with love than with prudence, the mother as a loving and just central planner rather than as auctioneer. A loving family—the adjective "loving" is crucial—presents us with a valid case of economic central planning. The other valid case is the corporation, "islands of conscious power in this [market] ocean of unconscious cooperation like lumps of butter coagulating in a pail of buttermilk," as one economist put it. A smothering socialism retains its attraction, despite its unhappy history, from the analogy with a family, a cozy little family, say, of 292,287,454 Americans, or with a corporation of 292,287 employees. As Tillich and Wegener said, "Socialism demands an economy of solidarity of all, and of joy in work rather than in profit." But when a community gets big and specialized there are often better ways than a loving solidarity to organize for the sacred things we want.

The economist Frank Knight, in an anticlerical fury, mistook the Christian morality of charity for a call to common ownership, the extreme of loving solidarity, and attacked it as unworkable. (It is said that the only time the University of Chicago has actually refunded money to a student was to a Jesuit who took Knight's course on "the history of economic thought" and discovered that it was in fact a sustained and not especially well-informed attack on the Catholic church.) Knight wrote a book with T. W. Merriam in 1945 called *The Economic Order and Religion* which mysteriously asserts that Christian love destroys "the material and social basis of life," and is "fantastically impossible," and is "incompatible with the requirements of everyday life," and entails an "ideal . . . [which is] not merely opposed to civilization and progress but is an impossible one." Under Christian love "continuing social life is patently impossible" and "a high civilization could hardly be maintained long, . . . to say nothing of progress."[12]

It develops that Knight and Merriam are arguing that social life in a large group *with thoroughgoing ownership in common* is impossible. That is what they believe Christian love entails.[13] Their source is always the gospels, never the elaborate compromises with economic reality of other Christian writers, such as Paul or Aquinas or Luther, or the thirty-eighth article of the Anglicans: "The riches and goods of Christians are not common, as touching the right, title, and possession of the same, as certain Anabaptists do falsely boast."

But, yes: social life without private property *is* impossible, at any rate in large groups. So said Pope Leo XIII in 1891 in *Rerum Novarum*, reechoed by Pius XI in 1931, John XXIII in 1961 and 1963, by Paul VI in 1967 and 1971, and by John Paul II in 1981 and 1991.[14] These men were not nineteenth-century liberals—especially, as Michael Novak explains, not in the harsh, Continental sense, the "old liberals" of Jan Gresshof's satiric poem of the 1930s.[15] They celebrated private property—when used with regard to soul and community. They were nothing like the Sermon-on-the-Mount socialists whom Knight and Merriam attack.

Thus Leo: "Private possessions are clearly in accord with nature" (15), following his hero, Aquinas.[16] "The law of nature, . . . by the practice of all ages, has consecrated private possession as something best adapted to man's nature and to peaceful and tranquil living together" (17). "The fundamental principle of Socialism which would make all possessions public property is to be utterly rejected because it injures the very ones whom it seeks to help" (23). "The right of private property must be regarded as sacred" (65). "If incentives to ingenuity and skill in individual persons were to be abolished, the very fountains of wealth would necessarily dry up; and the equality conjured up by the Socialist imagination would, in reality, be nothing but uniform wretchedness and meanness for one and all, without distinction" (22).

Nick Hornby's comic novel *How to Be Good* (2001) shows the difficulties of "to each according to his need, regardless of his property acquired by effort." A generosity that works just fine within a family works very poorly within a large group of adult strangers. The husband of the narrator goes mad and starts giving away his and his wife's money and his children's superfluous toys. He and his guru are going to write a book:

> "'How to Be Good,' we're going to call it. It's about how we should all live our lives. You know, suggestions. Like taking in the homeless, and giving away your money, and what to do about things like property ownership and, I don't know, the Third World and so on."
> "So" [replies his annoyed wife, a hard-working GP in the National Health Service] "this book's aimed at high-ranking employees of the IMF?"[17]

It's the Sermon on the Mount, on the basis of which many people have concluded that Jesus was of course a socialist. "The love-gospel," write Knight and Merriam, "condemning all self-assertion as sin . . . would destroy all values."[18] Knight and Merriam are correct if they mean, as they appear to, that love without other and balancing virtues is a sin. Knight's understanding of

Christianity appears to have derived from his childhood experience in a frontier Protestant sect, the Campbellites (evolved now into the Church of Christ and the Disciples of Christ), and theirs is what he took to be the core teaching of Christianity: "No creed but the Bible. No ethic but love."

But love without prudence, justice, temperance, and the rest is not Christian orthodoxy—for example, the orthodoxy of Aquinas or of Leo XIII. Leo in fact was a close student of Aquinas, and in 1889 elevated him to dogma within the church. And, yes, such a single-virtue ethic would *not* be ethical in a fallen world. Economists would call the actual orthodoxy a "second-best" argument, as against the first best of "if any man will sue thee at the law, and take away thy coat, let him have thy cloak also." Given that people are imperfect, the Christian, or indeed any economist, would say, we need to make allowances, and hire lawyers. Otherwise everyone will live by stealing each other's coats, with a resulting failure to produce coats in the first place, and a descent into poverty for everyone but the chief.

St. Paul himself said so, in his earliest extant letter (1 Thess. 3:8–11): "Neither did we eat any man's bread for naught, but wrought with labor and travail night and day, that we might not be chargeable to any of you . . . to make ourselves an example unto you to follow us. . . . We commanded you that if any would not work, neither should he eat. For we hear that there are some . . . among you disorderly, working not at all." Or to put it more positively, as Michael Novak does, "One must think clearly about what actually does work—in a sinful world—to achieve the liberation of peoples and persons."[19] "In the right of property," wrote the blessed Pope John XXIII in 1961, "the exercise of liberty finds both a safeguard and a stimulus."[20] Frank Knight couldn't have put it better.

Erasmus began all editions of his *Adages* from 1508 onward with "Between friends all things are common," remarking that "if only it were so fixed in men's minds as it is frequent on everybody's lips, most of the evils of our lives would promptly be removed. . . . Nothing was ever said by a pagan philosopher which comes closer to the mind of Christ" as the proposed socialism of goods in Plato's *Republic*.[21] Such is the first best. But Erasmus notes, sadly, "how Christians dislike this common ownership of Plato's, how in fact they cast stones at it." Many of his 4,150 proverbs collected from classical and Christian sources recommend attention to prudence and work, if not quite with the insistence of, say, proverbs he might have collected in his native Dutch. We are not friends, but strangers, and even in the Society of Friends property was not held in common. Knight and Merriam are not really undermining Christian orthodoxy and Christian ethics. They are misunderestimating them.

Charity is not socialism. Generosity is not a system at all. It is of a person, then two, then a few. God arranges such encounters, a Christian might say. But humans want them, too, the gift-economy of grace above material concerns. To make them into a system, *How to Be Good*, is to cancel their virtue. The heroine and narrator of Hornby's novel sees the orthodox point. One owes love to a family first. Property, with the virtue of justice, protects the beloved family. If any would not work, neither should he eat. Work, depending on temperance and prudence, is desirable to create and to acquire the property. So is prudent stewardship in managing it, though the lilies of the field toil not. For large societies of actual humans, she realizes, if not for lilies and families, the right prescription is bourgeois virtue. True, she cannot quite get rid of the notion that "maybe the desire for nice evenings with people I know and love is essentially bourgeois, reprehensible—depraved, even."[22] Such is the agony of the left liberal.

WAGE SLAVERY

On the side of production the capitalist system provides a field in which ordinary people can exercise their abilities harmlessly. Indeed, helpfully. Business can be, as Max Weber and Michael Novak put it, a "calling," a *Beruf*, a "vocation." "A career in business," writes Novak, "is not only a morally serious vocation but a morally noble one. Those who are called to it have reason to take pride in it and rejoice in it."[1] But of course that is not what the clerisy thinks. Quite the contrary: "If you actually made money yourself, . . . maybe starting from nothing, you are given the subtle impression . . . such a career is rather sweaty, vulgar, and morally suspect."[2]

When I initiated a course in business history at the business school at the University of Chicago in 1979, I started it with Mesopotamia, having the kids read business letters from 2000 BC collected at the Oriental Institute, because I wanted them to know that they were embarking on an ancient and honorable profession, not, as the clerisy believes, a dirty modern aberration. As Novak says, to think of business as a calling—he and I have God in mind here—"would help tie [the young businesspeople] more profoundly to traditions going far back into the past."[3]

Making and selling steel or hamburgers is not the most prestigious field among intellectuals. Writing long books is. Or among artists, installing artworks or making movies is. But running a fruit stall with energy and intelligence shares in the exhilaration of creativity.[4] Don't laugh. By doing so you exhibit a nasty snobbishness, you misled member of the Western clerisy. And you exhibit an undemocratic ignorance of the world's work to boot. Shame on you. Maimonides left no doubt that the clerisy's pretension is a mistake. "One who makes his mind up to study Torah and not to work but to live on charity profanes the name of God, brings the Torah into contempt, extinguishes the light of religion, brings evil upon himself, and deprives himself of the life hereafter."[5]

The psychologist Mihaly Csikszentmihalyi [CHICK-sent-me-high] calls the feeling of creativity "flow," those "flashes of intense living," "when a person's skills are fully involved in overcoming a challenge that is just about manageable." "It is the full involvement of flow, rather than happiness, that makes for excellence in life."[6] By "happiness" here he means mere consumption, "happiness" according to the grossest sort of utilitarianism or Epicureanism, not his Aristotle-derived ideal of the exercise of vital powers. As Martha Nussbaum notes, "Most Greeks would understand *eudaimonia* to be something essentially active, of which praiseworthy activities are not just productive means, but actual constituent parts."[7]

Even the management of possessions provided by the work of others gives an opportunity for flow, as in the housewife's artful arrangement of her furniture or the collector's absorbed passion for his goods, heedless of capital gain. The curatorial art is aristocratic, as may be seen in our Bernard Berensons and Kenneth Clarks (Clark studied as a young man with Berenson, and ended life a baron), but capitalism permits the bourgeoisie to participate. And Berenson at least was a very busy and canny and, some say, unscrupulous businessman, as many an aristocrat has been in fact.

But it is work that is the main opportunity for a flowful life. Csikszentmihalyi tells of Joe, who worked in the cacophony of a railcar factory, and

> who had trained himself to understand and to fix every piece of equipment in the factory. He loved to take on machinery that didn't work, figure out what was wrong with it, and set it right again. . . . The hundred or so welders who worked at the same plant respected Joe, even though they couldn't quite make him out . . . . Many claimed that without Joe the factory might just as well close. . . . I have met many CEOs of major corporations . . . and several dozen Nobel Prize-winners—eminent people who in many ways led excellent lives, but none that was better than Joe's.[8]

In other words it is not merely through the piling up of goods that the market system succeeds. It is through the jobs themselves. Respect for work, I have noted, has been historically rare. Until the quickening of commerce in bourgeois societies, in fact, work except for praying and fighting was despised. It was the rare Stoic philosopher who viewed physical labor as anything but dishonoring. The historically antiwork attitude may have been what prevented classical Mediterranean civilization or medieval Chinese society from industrializing. The Afrikaners of 1910 had no experience of work and no respect for it, which determined their policies toward hard-working Xhosa peasants and hard-working Jewish immigrants. Nowadays it is a problem for many poor societies. Women and slaves work. Real men smoke.

Englishmen in the seventeenth century, for example, had no conception of dignity beyond what the sociologists call "ascription," that is, rank. The result is that seventeenth-century science used gentlemanly status as a warrant for believability. William Petty (1623–1687), one of the founders of the English Royal Society, spoke of a gentleman as someone who had "such estate, real and personal, as whereby he is able to subsist without the practice of any mercenary employments."[9] Only a gentleman could have honor, which was only gradually coming to mean our "honesty."

A gentleman was precisely someone without an occupation. The contemporary French phrase was *l'honnête homme*, the "honorable" man being one who did not work. The early twentieth-century irony about this convention is to call a bum a "gentleman of the road," as earlier a highwayman was a "gentleman of the highway." Such a man is very willing to brawl, but not to be seen to *work* even at that. Thus the Prince Hal of *Henry IV* drinks and whores away the days and nights with Falstaff through parts 1 and 2, and we are indulgently amused. We look for virtue in this romanticizing of idleness, on the circular argument that an idle man is a sort of gentleman and therefore must be virtuous. Prince Hal explains, and Shakespeare in his proto-bourgeois way was recommending, that princes need this common touch.

Down to the nineteenth century, with fading echoes even now, the phrase "a gentleman of business" was considered an absurdity, a flat contradiction. The economist David Ricardo wrote in 1817 that a remission of rent to farmers from their landlords "would only enable some farmers to live like gentlemen."[10] He feared that having an income without work would corrupt active men of business: "gentlemen" were nonworkers. Dickens reasoned similarly. He portrayed gentlemen without occupations as parasites.[11] Yet his heroes, all of them crypto-gentlemen, achieve success not by working but by inheriting. He had a conservative's nostalgia for a simpler time when the rich were charitable and the poor unspoilt and income came down on a gentleman like a gentle rain.

The piling up of goods, even from the nasty, guilt-inducing goad we name "profit," has had the direct effect of giving billions of ordinary people the scope with which to pursue something other than subsistence. But the point here is that on the other side of subsistence, so to speak, the market has provided the billions with meaning in their lives, the opportunity for hope and faith, through that very participation in the making of things for the market. Only an undemocratic snob, you might say, if you were inclined to speak frankly about antibourgeois and antieconomic prejudices since 1848, denies dignity to anything but what priests or aristocrats do. As Knight put it, "We are impelled to look for ends in the economic process itself, and to give thoughtful consideration to the possibilities of participation in economic activity as a sphere of self-expression and creative achievement."[12]

Work in capitalism is not always alienating. Tzvetan Todorov quotes the protagonist of *Forever Flowing*, the posthumously published novel of Vasily Grossman (1905–1964), whom he says was the sole example of a successful Stalinist writer who converted wholly to anti-Communism ("The slave in him died, and a free man arose"): "I used to think freedom was freedom of speech, freedom of the press, freedom of conscience. Here is what it amounts to: you have to have the right to sow what you wish to, to make shoes or coats, to bake into bread the flour ground from the grain you have sown, and to sell it or not sell it as you wish; for the lathe-operator, the steel-worker, and the artist it's a matter of being able to live as you wish and work as you wish and not as they order you."[13]

If you are sure this is wrong, that under capitalism workers are slaves, as I tell you they are under socialism—"Under capitalism, man exploits man; under socialism, it's the other way around"—consider where you got the idea. If from your own actual experience at your life's employment, or even from a blue- or pink-collar summer job, or a few months as a journalist getting nickeled and dimed in minimum wage jobs, you have at least the scientific spirit. You, I, and Barbara Ehrenreich can sit down and think through the balance of the evidence together. But if by any chance you got it unsullied from Marx, or from the numerous people influenced by Marx, I ask you to consider that Marx, like many of us aristocratic priests, had never worked at anything but philosophy and journalism, never picked up a shovel for pay, never so much as set foot in a factory or farm. Marx—Engels was different—had not troubled to look at manual work, much less try it out for himself. He preferred his angry theorizing in the Reading Room of the British Museum.

Studs Terkel in *Working* says that the job "is a search, too, for daily meaning as well as daily bread, for astonishment rather than torpor; in short, for
a sort of life rather than a Monday through Friday sort of dying."[14] It struck
Marisa Bowe while editing a follow-on to Terkel that "very few of those we
talked to"—and the interviewers seem to have talked to American workers
pretty much at random—"hate their jobs, and even among the ones who
do, almost none said 'not working' was their ultimate goal."[15]

> You need not see what someone is doing
> To know it is his vocation,
>
> you have only to watch his eyes:
> a cook mixing his sauce, a surgeon
>
> making a primary incision,
> a clerk completing a bill of lading
>
> wear the same rapt expression,
> forgetting themselves in a function.[16]

It's flow. A Cincinnati sewer worker interviewed on National Public
Radio on August 29, 2002, joked that at first he viewed his job as a way of
claiming credit with hippie girls that he was an "environmental" worker. But
of course that's what he is. And he grew, he declared, to love his work, just
love it, crawling around sewer mains. True, he earns $60,000 a year for his
trouble, as the sand hogs digging tunnels for New York's water supply earn
$150,000 a year. But that condition of a laboring vocation nowadays is made
possible by the goods-piling-up machinery of capitalism.

A traveler from the (ideal, gentle) Communist planet in Ursula Le Guin's
The Dispossessed is startled by the prosperity of the "sturdy, self-respecting-
looking people" in the (ideal, but not-so-gentle) capitalist planet: "It puzzled him. He had assumed that if you removed a human being's natural
incentive to work—his initiative, his creative energy—and replaced it with
external motivation . . . he would become a lazy and careless worker. But no
careless workers kept those lovely farmlands, or made the superb cars and
comfortable trains. The lure of *profit* . . . was evidently a much more effective replacement of the natural initiative than he had been led to believe."[17]

Le Guin overlooks, though, the better case for capitalism, which is not
that profit deftly replaces the instinct of workmanship. On the contrary,
profit and the capitalism dependent on profit nourish it. Marx, Thorstein

Veblen, Karl Polanyi, and others have been mistaken on the point. Good, well-paid workers are not alienated or careless. Watch a team of trash men working the public barrels from a truck along a Chicago street, working fast and accurately, skimming the empty plastic barrels back to their places, tipping them back into the cast-iron holders, riding easily on the lip of the shoot, stormy, husky, brawling. I do not condescend. I've worked trash trucks in my day, and know the feeling.

Chaplin's 1936 movie *Modern Times* or the opening scenes of Sillitoe's angry-young-man novel *The Loneliness of the Long Distance Runner* (1959; movie 1962) say that many factory jobs are monotonous. Granted. I have not worked in a factory. But the monotony is of course pretty common in nonindustrial society, too. Planting rice is never fun. The idiocy of rural life is not always better for the soul than the idiocy of urban life. I *have* worked as a farm laborer. Ironically, only since Romanticism and the rise of prosperous, healthy cities—London stopped killing more people than it bred only at the end of the eighteenth century—have Europeans looked fondly back on their village roots.

For centuries, in every country worldwide, poor people have moved from the village to the city, freely if not joyously, even when the cities were killers. Witness the several hundreds of millions of Chinese peasants who moved since the 1990s to the cities of eastern China, the largest such migration in history. Living in a factory dorm room in the city of Changshu north of Shanghai and working seventy-seven hours a week for eleven months a year making IV drips for Western hospitals to bring home $500 in net pay, if she is very careful, seemed in 2004 better to the nineteen-year-old young woman Bai Lin than staying in her home village of Two Dragons.[18]

If you as a well-off Western city-dweller and office worker think that outdoor work must be so much nicer than being cooped up, it's a good bet you have never worked for more than a day or two in the out-of-doors, never made hay in Wiltshire or made roads in Massachusetts, not to speak of planting rice in Two Dragons. There's a reason that most people, when given the choice, prefer to work under roofs and inside heated and air-conditioned offices and in the busy cities.

A commercial society provides on a unique scale opportunities for fully flowful jobs—which would not describe Bai Lin's eleven-hour days cutting rubber sheets, but does describe her older brother Bai Li Peng's job as a foreman in a factory near Hong Kong. The skilled craftsperson of olden times was much admired by late Romantics such as Morris and Ruskin. But sculpting masons and master builders were a tiny fraction of the medieval workforce, and in their own day were not admired. No one who had to work with his hands, including a painter or sculptor, was admired. Most medievals were closer to the Monty Python vision of the groveling peasant than to the pre-Raphaelite vision of the noble saint of labor, admitting that both are fictions.

Think of the clerkly professions in this way—being a college professor, for example. There are very roughly a million of them today in the United States, about one out of every 150 workers, more people employed now in postsecondary education than the cumulative total in all the centuries everywhere before, say, 1945. The great-great grandparents of the average college teacher worked with their hands, often at jobs providing less scope for flow. Like everyone else's, since that's what a nonmodern economy had on offer, my own ancestors were dirt farmers and lumberjacks and housewives—though my mother's mother took pride in her housewifery, in an age of home canning and home sewing and home making of the sort Cheryl Mendelson celebrates in *Home Comforts: The Art and Science of Keeping House* (1999); and I expect that some others of my ancestors and yours wielded a spade or spindle joyfully by God's grace.

But nonclerkly jobs in a market society provide more scope, too. The uncommon but by no means unheard-of Chicago bus driver who works joyfully at welcoming his passengers and works conscientiously at arriving at each stop exactly on time, navigating the snowy streets of the South Side con brio, is living a flowful life on the job. The textbook salesman who pushes the envelope (he would say), venturing into new academic buildings to confront new curmudgeons in English or accounting, armed only with his open and sunny personality and a giant catalogue he has memorized of Macmillan books, is testing the limits of his skill.

Of course you can refuse to live flowfully, even in a rich, Western society. The tram drivers of Rotterdam are known for leaving just as the university student running to make the tram gets close to the door. They speed up to ram harder when the track is blocked by a careless auto driver. They get satisfaction no doubt in paying back the middle class. One wonders if they wouldn't do better to join it, and make their trams into little sites of bourgeois virtues.

Many college professors treat their fascinating jobs as though they were routine, and become, as Adam Smith said of the effects of repetitive work,

"as stupid and as ignorant as it is possible for a human creature to become."
As they stroll between their few hours of classes a week they lament the
appalling stress of their lives, and form trade unions in a fantasy of proletarian status. True, the college administration encourages the fantasy, by itself
playing the role of the corporate suits, conspiring against common sense, stuff-
ing their executive suites with auto-busy assistant and associate and vice-thises
and thats. But anyway such college professors are refusing flow. Immanuel
Kant lectured every morning, all morning, including Saturdays, easily twice the
average contact hours of a modern college professor, and was uncomplaining
about it. As the son of a saddler he knew hard physical work. Yet in his spare
time he managed to write—slowly, admittedly, by the frenetic standards of
modern academic life—a few books revolutionizing Western philosophy.

"When the job presents clear goals," Csikszentmihalyi writes, "unambiguous feedback, a sense of control, challenges that match the worker's
skills, and few distractions, the feelings it provides are not that different
from what one experiences in a sport or an artistic performance."[19] Or in
reckless driving or in street fighting—the news from flow is not all good.

The pay matters. It is a thrill unique to a market society to find that people are willing to pay for one's product, to surrender their hard-earned
money, as we put it. Remember your first paycheck and the feeling it gave of
adulthood, of pulling your own weight. Remember when you last sold for a
professional's price something you produced. In his play and novella *Home
Truths* David Lodge imagines a conversation in a cottage in Sussex between
two old friends, one a man who writes TV plays and will in a few hours take
a flight from Gatwick to Hollywood, the other a woman comfortably well
off in retirement who makes pottery:

> He picked up a pottery vase. "This is nice. Did you make it?"
> "Yes."
> "Very nice . . . Is it for sale?"
> "Not to you, Sam. If you like it, have it as a present."
> "No way. Would a hundred be fair?"
> "Far too much."
> "I'll give you seventy-five." He took out his chequebook.
> "That's very generous. I *am* selling the odd piece now, actually. It's very
> satisfying."[20]

It's satisfying especially to a married woman accustomed to giving care for
no pay, whose independence in a commercial society depends on a pay
packet. As Peggy Seeger sang,

I really wish that I could be a lady—
I could do all the lovely things a lady's s'posed to do.
I wouldn't even mind if they would pay me,
And I could be a person too.

. . . . But now that times are harder and my Jimmy's got the sack
I went down to Vicker's, they were glad to have me back.
I'm a third-class citizen, my wages tell me that,
But I'm a first-class engineer.[21]

Work in a capitalist society can fulfill the Greek ideal of happiness, reiterated to the boys at English private schools in the nineteenth century as "the exercise of vital powers along lines of excellence in a life affording them scope." One can be an excellent mother in bringing up Connor and Lily to a full adult life, or an excellent carpenter making a staircase with winding treads and housed stringers, or an excellent clerk completing an intricate bill of lading, or an excellent repairer of railcar-making machinery.[22] At least one can in a modern capitalist society.

46

THE RICH

Mr. Strahan put Johnson in mind of a remark which he had made to him; "There are few ways in which a man can be more innocently employed than in getting money." "The more one thinks of this, (said Strahan,) the juster it will appear."
—Johnson, Boswell's *Life*

There are geniuses in trade, as well as in war. . . . Nature seems to authorize trade, as soon as you see the natural merchant, who appears not so much as a private agent, as her factor and Minister of Commerce. His natural probity combines with his insight into the fabric of society to put him above tricks. . . . The habit of his mind is a reference to standards of natural equity and public advantage; and he inspires respect, and the wish to deal with him, both for the quiet spirit of honor which attends him, and for the intellectual pastime which the spectacle of so much ability affords.
—Emerson, 1844

Of course the very rich are always with us. In the railcar factory Happy Joe had a boss, who grew rich as we say "on Joe's back." Any discussion about the ethics of the market tends to devolve rapidly into a discussion of winners and losers, where losers are taken to be the workers. It's part of the zero-sum game that most noneconomists imagine is how the economy works.

Be warned, though, that the metaphor of profit and managerial incomes being "on the back of" the worker is just that, a metaphor, more or less apt, whose aptness remains to be determined. It's not simply reality, as many noneconomists suppose. If you speak of the rich as parasites on real workers, you are depending on a dichotomy of capital and labor devised before 1848, when workers were unspeakably poor, when human capital was rare, when local monopolies prevailed, when land was an important input, before capitalism had grown up. The labor theory of value, I report from economics, is simply mistaken, as almost everyone agrees who has studied the question.[1]

But what *about* those darn capitalists and their grotesquely high incomes? Do I believe in good capitalists? My answer is like the old joke, "Do I believe in infant baptism? Goodness, I've *seen* it!" Do I believe in good capitalists? Goodness, I've *seen* them, for example, Lionel Rothschild, Andrew Carnegie, J. P. Morgan, and John D. Rockefeller. The first, third, and fourth, by the way, were pious followers of an Abrahamic religion, as Jew, Episcopalian, and Baptist. And Carnegie was raised among such people.

We have been told since the muckraking journalists of the early 1900s, or in another rich tradition the anti-Semites then and later, that these were just terrible men. I mean, how else did they get so rich? If you are inclined to think this way, I suggest gently that you may have bought into a theory that the only way to get rich is by stealing. Zero-sum: your gain is my loss. Tillich and Wegener again: each person in a capitalist society "is the enemy of the other, because his advantage is conditioned by the disadvantage or ruin of the other." Or Comte-Sponville: "Western prosperity depends, directly or indirectly, on Third World poverty, which the West in some cases merely takes advantage of and in others actually causes."

In the playroom that's true. Jip gets more toys—short of a subsidy from Mother—only by violence against Janneke. But such a theory is mistaken in a market economy, in which food and toys and other goods and services are made afresh daily, not merely reallocated from a God-given stock. And it is the more mistaken the more quickly the goods-making skills of the economy are growing. Free-market economies are positive sum.

Economies grow slowly—or not at all—when stealing or taxing become simpler ways to wealth than working and selling. The stealing and taxes discourage production, and so the outcome is worse even than zero-sum. Such negative-sum alternatives to exchange have historically been the norm, which is one reason that sustained economic growth happened only once. According to Tacitus, the ancient German man thought it "tame and spiritless to accumulate slowly by the sweat of his brow what can be gotten quickly by the loss of a little blood."[2] In a society dominated by aristocrats, whether of the sword or the pen, manual work had little prestige. Along the Heroin Road from Afghanistan through Turkey to the streets of London, easy money gotten quickly by the loss of a little blood corrupts the young.

Why finish high school, why acquire skills on a building site, when you can earn a workingman's yearly income in a week of bold smuggling?

"Real wealth" in the economist's way of thinking is not a pile of finished stuff merely to be allocated, as in the children's playroom. Nor does wealth consist of those tokens of ownership such as money in your pocket or stocks in your pension plan or profits from your drug deal. Wealth is the real ability in arm or brain or machine to produce more stuff, the "real" backing for the tokens. The recovery of Europe from the Second World War did not depend, as popular fable has it, on the U.S. of A. and the Marshall Plan, gracious though the gesture of the plan was. The plan was the equivalent of about one year of private European investment: very welcome, but not the whole story. Recovery depended chiefly on European arms and brains, their real wealth. That the bricks had been toppled by bombs was only a temporary setback.[3]

The real wealth behind your pension is the ability in arm or brain or machine of employed labor or capital, that is, your kids' generation paying with their abilities in production your Medicare bills. Who owns the stream of disposable income from the real wealth is a separate matter. If the government has plausibly promised to tax your kids to pay for your health care, you in a sense own that stream of income. But anyway the real wealth of the nation as a whole—you and the kids together—is the productive power of the economy, not the promises on tongue or paper.

Private property and unfettered exchange—in a phrase, modern capitalism —is not the kingdom of heaven, Lord knows. But for allocating scarce goods and especially for making more of them, well . . . it is the worst system, except for all those others that have been tried from time to time. And its ethical effect, I have been arguing, is by no means entirely bad. James Boyd White declares that "the market economy . . . is really a system of dominance and acquisition. . . . [It shows] the acquisitive values and calculating behavior of the economic sphere."[4] No, it is not, except in the minds of hardnosed if deluded theorists on the right from Machiavelli to Richard Posner. For one thing, the market is embedded socially and ethically. For another, no other system has been more free from dominance, acquisition, and calculating behavior. A dollar is a dollar, and a poor man has as much claim to its value as a rich man. No dominance there, and less than in a society of aristocratic status or Socialist Party membership. Anyway, name the society that has ever actually existed that has not been dominated by acquisitiveness and calculating behavior. And note the wide scope in modern bourgeois society for people like Jim White and me to preach against such nasty people.

A market is better than Jip's violence in the playroom. It is better than the drug dealer's gun or the aristocrat's sword. It is better than beauty contests depending on race, class, gender, culture, region, politics. Capitalism routinely transcends such categories. It works better for the average person, as we saw 1917–1989, than so-called central planning backed by a Cheka or a KGB. A nonmarket method of allocation gives the goods to the wrong people, usually. People who belong to the Party, say. And especially it doesn't encourage the production of more toys or food or onionskin Greek editions of the New Testament in the first place. Property and trade do so, tempting producers into working to get your attention and your offers. If Brave Sir Botany appropriates the barley crop of the peasants, the peasants have less incentive to use their arms and brains to grow more. If Sir Botany must tempt the peasants with offers of educational services or consultation on interior decorating in order to get the barley, then both he and the peasants are better off compared with the pretrade situation. If he just grabs it, only he is better off, and they worse off.

Unlike stealing or taxing or highhandedly appropriating, that is, exchange is a positive-, not a zero- or negative-, sum game. If I buy low and sell high, I am doing both of the people with whom I deal a favor. That's three favors done—to the seller, to the buyer, and to me in the middle, and no one hurt, except by envy's sting. The seller and buyer didn't have to enter the deal, and by their willingness they show they are made better off.

One can say it more strongly. *Only* such deals are just. As Robert Nozick puts it, "No one has a right to something whose realization requires certain uses of things and activities that other people have rights and entitlements to."[5] I do not have the right to use your house, even when you are on vacation. I do not have the right to make you work for me, unless we have entered a deal to that effect. I do not have the right to be equal to you in beauty, education, income, health. The envious, jealous, spiteful, or begrudging person will want to bring in the state and its monopoly of violence to achieve such rights for himself. The charitable and sympathetic person will want to achieve the right to use your house or education or food on behalf of the poor. It is a good impulse, to help the poor. But it sets up the state as a Brave Sir Botany. State compulsion is not the voluntary cooperation that capitalism and our wealth is built on. The envious or poor man, Nozick says, "must put together, with the cooperation of others, a feasible package."[6] He must deal, not steal.

In *The Invisible Heart* (2001) Russell Roberts imagines a high-school teacher of economics, Sam Gordon, trying to convert a high-school teacher of English, Laura Silver, over coffee at the local Starbucks. It is significant, by the way, that in the same year that Roberts published a book called *The Invisible Heart*, viewed from the libertarian right, Nancy Folbre published a book with the same title, viewed from the *marxisant* left, in mutual unawareness. They were making related points, Folbre that the society *should* have a heart, Roberts that the market *does*. As Roberts's Sam Gordon put it, "I'm not saying that the gentle and caring people of the world are found at the top of the modern corporation. But the scum of the earth can't make it to the top either," which is surely true, and truer of the business world than of many others.

Politicians, police, soldiers, bureaucrats, even ministers of religion and professors of political science can be scum of the earth and get away with it for decades. J. Edgar Hoover comes to mind, or Pinochet and his friends, or the pedophile priests protected by the Roman hierarchy. You can provide your own examples. Laura replies to Sam with a superior smile, expressing the conventional calumny, "I doubt goodness counts for much of anything in the boardroom or in the marketplace." "But it does" Sam urges—Sam is so earnest. Says he: "Meaning what you say, keeping your word, and serving others without resentment are probably more valuable in the business world than elsewhere."

To suppose that the world of profit always kills caring is the mistake that Nancy Folbre makes in her own book. She criticizes Adam Smith—whom she admires on the whole as much as I do—for ignoring "the possibility that the expansion of an economy based on self-interest might weaken moral sentiments."[7] Oh, I dunno. A lawyer friend of mine says that the worst liars and cheats he has encountered are not property developers or city planners, the capitalists or the haughty clerisy, but . . . church people, the literal clerics, officially devoted to humble, caring behavior toward us all. He says that they regard themselves as exempt from merely commercial promise-keeping. After all, they are on God's mission, not Mammon's. So nonprofit organizations are commonly filled with *Dilbert*-like bad actors. It is not profit that makes people bad; often enough it is the lack of it.

Sam continues: "Take a look at the best-selling business books. They aren't about manipulating the customer or exploiting employees," though they *are* about rhetoric—roughly a third, I reckon. "Rhetoric" is not the same thing as dishonest persuasion. On the contrary, business rhetoric is finding the available means of mainly honest persuasion in the one-quarter of national income earned from sweet talk.[8] The sweet talkers include managers above all, but also teachers, social workers, salespeople, politicians, lawyers, bankers, bureaucrats, teachers, journalists. Such people spend much of their working lives changing other peoples' minds, without compulsion.

It is cooperation, not competition or compulsion, that Adam Smith admired. There are realms of compulsion even in a free and liberal society, such as the violent side of police work, though the police will tell you correctly that most of their work is persuasive. A slave society, such as Russia 1917–1989, needs overseers with chains and knouts, not sweet talk. But that's not what most modern, capitalist life entails.

Therefore the business books, Sam claims, are "often about integrity. Leadership. Motivation. Many of them apply religious principles to business," such as Gary Moore's *Faithful Finances 101* (2003). Laura is not to be persuaded: "I find that hard to believe." Oh, Laura: have a look sometime at the business section of the bookstore, and see for yourself. "But to be honest, I have a confession to make," Laura remarks sarcastically. "I'm glad you're sitting down—this will shock you. I don't read many business books." Fun*ny*. *Brilliant* wit.

Laura is proud to be living off a business civilization and yet to remain ignorant of how it actually works. Thus the clerisy of Europe since 1848. Sam is patient: "But that means you're probably getting your perspective on business from a Dickens novel [*Great Expectations*, say] or Hollywood [*Wall Street*] or a television show [*Dallas*]." He returns to his original theme: "Monsters don't often succeed in business. The sweeter competition offering good service and low prices is a better bet [thus `sweet talk']. There's an invisible heart at the core of the marketplace, serving the customer and doing it joyously." A trifle twee, you will reply, if you are of Laura's camp. But consider that you may be mistaken.

Sam: Can I get you a refill?
Laura: Thanks. Decaf this time. If the choice is available.
Sam: Of course, *madame.* (*He stands up and nods politely in mock servitude.*)
Capitalism at your service.

Now if the market deal is a cheat, then of course the victim is not benefited. But it's mainly outsiders to the business world, not insiders, who think that a lot of money is to be made by cheating. P. T. Barnum, John Mueller points out, did not say, ever, that a "sucker is born every minute." Nothing like it. On the contrary, Mueller explains, Barnum and the Ringling Brothers rescued the circus industry from extinction by offering the customers a novelty—*honest*, inexpensive entertainment. They patrolled their grounds with detectives, for example, instead of encouraging pickpockets to strip the rubes. They hired interesting acts instead of hiring "Monday men" to rob the customers' houses when they were at the circus. Mueller quotes George Ade on the nineteenth-century circus kings: they "found the business in the hands of vagabonds and put it into the hands of gentlemen."[9] Well . . . "gentlemen" by an American and nineteenth-century and bourgeois definition. Profit is seldom a con game. Not in a bourgeois society.

True, if I buy low and sell high I get the profit. At any rate I get it until more buyers-low turn up and spoil my game, turning the former profit into a gain to consumers from our competition in a proliferation of Home Depots and Costcos and T.J. Maxxes, or of Microsofts and Yahoos and Googles. But I earn the profit because of a scarce virtue I have, my "alertness," as the economist and rabbi Israel Kirzner puts it.[10] One could also call it " judgment" (*gnomē*), as Aristotle did, and ally it with *phronēsis*, practical wisdom. It is a virtue which is good for *me*, to be sure. But it is also good for other people.

We want to encourage such alertness/judgment/*phronēsis*/enterprise, for the same reason we want to encourage Thomas Edisons and Albert Einsteins. I alertly *notice* what for its best use should be moved from one person to another, that is, moved to its highest-valued use. Profit comes from noticing that people might want to buy the works of the reformed graffiti sprayer Keith Haring. It doesn't come from routine deals—simply because "routine" means "the competitors have entered," and supernormal profits are no longer to be gained. Barnum noticed that people wanted what was described as a "Sunday-school" approach to circuses, and so he provided it, moving resources from pickpocketing to high wire acts. What's the beef?

The beef was well expressed on the eve of the new bourgeois ideology by Louis Thomassin, a French theologian of the late seventeenth century, "a plain man of stupendous erudition," who among other tasks in his posthumous multivolume *Traités historiques et dogmatiques* of 1697 attacked profit making.[11] He criticizes, in a figure of argument going back to Aristotle, "those who accumulate possessions *without end and without measure.*"[12] The Greek word is *apeiros,* without limit. It finds echo in modern characterizations of capitalism from the left, the myth of *Kapitalismus* I mentioned earlier—an allegedly new propensity to accumulate for accumulation's sake without limit. The Greek *to apeiron,* the unlimited (greed), is the very meaning of "capitalism" in Marx and others, such as R. H. Tawney, among Marx's followers.

Thomassin instances "those who hoard huge quantities of wheat in order to sell at what to them is the opportune moment." They foolishly think "they are doing nothing . . . against divine law, because, as they imagine, they do no harm." By contrast, wrote Thomassin, "if no one acquired . . . more than he needed for his maintenance [that is, did not hoard wheat] . . . there would be no destitute in the world at all." In other words, as Father Maurin said, "people would become better / if they stopped trying to be better off." Plato and Aristotle, incidentally, were not especially interested in the causes of such destitution, since that, until the eighteenth century, was a concern to slaves, not aristocrats.

The Thomassin-Maurin argument is especially Christian, arising from a monkish vision of poverty as a result of greed in a world of postlapsarian limits. It finds expression in the late nineteenth-century writings of the Protestant social-gospel movement and in the parallel doubts about free-market capitalism among progressive and conservative Roman Catholics. "Christianity is pre-eminently the religion of slaves," and the slaves favor redistributing the loot. But there is a different, liberal Christian tradition of the urban friars, such as Aquinas. "Albert the Great and [his student, St.] Thomas," writes Lester K. Little, "brought about the emancipation of Christian merchants." They were not commending unlimited greed, but a purposeful buying low and selling high. "The honest merchant, for all these writers, was a man deserving of the profit he made, for they considered it as payment for his labor (*quasi stipendium laboris*)."[13] Profit paid for alertness.

A modern economist, with the Scholastic theologians, notes that buying wheat at a low price to sell at a high price is helpful to those who sell at the low price and to those who buy at the high price. Thomassin, who after all lived in an increasingly commercial age, realized this was true. The arbitrage would "benefit those who would otherwise fall into great necessity," that is, those who would have no wheat in a famine at all if the capitalist granary had not stored it "in huge quantities."

Nonetheless he cannot let go of the notion that it is "this urge to acquire more and more which brings so many poor people to penury." The notion, though mistaken, has as I say become fixed Catholic doctrine by now, expressed in numerous papal encyclicals and bishops' letters. It is part of the leftist dogma that "Western prosperity depends, directly or indirectly, on Third World poverty, which the West in some cases merely takes advantage of and in others actually causes." The pursuit of wealth is claimed to make people poor.

To which economics replies: no, it makes the poor less poor. If you understand "wealth" correctly you understand that to "pursue" it is to build roads or to make more shoes or to notice that wheat wasted in a year of abundance can be moved to a year of dearth, benefiting all. The wheat is allocated better across time as a result of the speculator's enterprise. And the pursuit of profit, I repeat, produces *more* wheat in the first place. The larger riches for the businessman, his "quasi rent" earned before competitors learn from his alertness, results in more, not less, wealth for his customers and employees.

The supposedly *apeiros,* unlimited, profit that makes the system produce so much more is in fact surprisingly small. Most people who have not looked into the matter greatly overestimate how much profit is earned under capitalism. Profit margins in American department stores are approximately 3 or 4 percent of sales. Wal-Mart, which is a tough bargainer with manufacturers for the benefit of the American consumer, has earned a mere 4 percent on sales for decades. Profit margins in American grocery stores are approximately. . . . but wait, let's see if you really do understand American capitalism. Go ahead, take a guess right now at the profit margin on groceries, the cents per dollar of your expenditure at the store going to the owners of the store. What d'you think? No peeking. Ten cents on the dollar? Twenty percent? Thirty?

A different concept, all profit as a share of all incomes in the United States, is about 14 percent. Social accounting can show that such a figure would imply a much lower one at the industry-by-industry level, at which the margin is on all costs, including services and materials purchased from other companies, not just on labor and machinery and buildings and land used directly, "value added," as the economists put it. The profit would be perhaps a high single digit of percentage on your next purchase of clothing or auto repair. The 14 percent of national income is composed of those evil corporate profits after taxes of 5.4 percent plus 8.6 percent from proprietors' income—for example, farms, ma-and-pa stores, your mechanic, your hair-dresser, the 19 million sole proprietorships in the United States, one for every eight workers. Whoever earns it, anyway, national product goes up from making deals, and deals are alertly noticed because of the profit—and punished by the loss: every year 10 percent of firms die. That's one way that capitalism works.

On the 1 to 2 percent profit margin of American grocery stores.

GOOD BARONS

Only a temperate prudence, not an intemperate greed, I say, is required to keep an economy running well. The Wall Street investment advisor Gary Moore argues in *Faithful Finances 101* (2003) that a focus on the spiritual purposes of our lives even when we manage portfolios makes sense. He reports that "I . . . invested my son's education fund in South Shore Bank of Chicago, an inner-city bank that uses investors' money to rehabilitate affordable housing for the poor, and found myself sleeping better knowing I had played a role in defusing racial tensions."[1] Aimless greed, he argues, is a temporary, bubble-stage of speculation. "Some of my friends laughed at my 5 percent as they bought Internet stocks." After the bubble burst, Moore laughed, with God.

In my economics courses I illustrate the argument by dropping a twenty-dollar bill on the floor for all to see. "The scientific power of economics is well illustrated here," I declare, following an argument I first heard from S. N. S. Cheung of the University of Hong Kong. "What would the laws of mere *physics* say about what will happen to the bill if I leave the room?" The students get the joke. The serious scientific point is that the modest amount of prudence to pick up a twenty-dollar bill lying on the floor is enough to keep an economy working just fine.

The degree of "rationality" required is small. No elaborate calculations. You see your opportunity, and you take it. Highly irrational people, bad at calculations of cost and benefit—as we actually are, even in a bourgeois society trained in such calculations and honoring them—would arrive at about the same allocation of any given bundle of goods as would soulless human computers rushing about calculating what economists are pleased to call "marginal utility." Early in the resistance to a new and precisely mathematical expression of a Benthamite Max U, Thorstein Veblen, I have noted, attacked the notion that people were "lightning calculators." But such precision is not necessary to get the more important results of economics, and Veblen's criticism falls flat. This could be proven easily with our massive computing capacity nowadays. If you were to simulate a toy economy of 1,000 consumers and producers, you would find that even approximate maximizing would put the economy very near to where it would be with super rationality.

Interpreting a broad, contextual, rhetorical prudence as the same thing as a narrow, rationalist, first-order predicate logic of "rationality" has always been a mistake. Plato committed it. Modern economists commit it with gusto. Their allies in sociobiology and evolutionary psychology delight in it. In a review of a book by one of the present-day committers of the mistake, Steven Pinker, the philosopher Jerry Fodor notes that "as far as anyone knows, relevance, strength, simplicity, centrality and the like are properties, not of single sentences, but of whole belief systems; and there's no reason at all to suppose that such global properties of belief systems are syntactic. In my view, the cognitive science that we've got so far has hardly begun to face this issue."[2] Relevance, strength, simplicity, and so forth are therefore not reducible to a Turing machine. That is, they are not the formal inferences of the rational theory of mind, such as that "all bachelors are men; John is a bachelor; therefore [triumphantly concluded, in case we hadn't already noticed it] John is a man." The same could be said of metaphor, irony, narrative, jokes. They are local properties of whole belief systems, not of single sentences.

Allocation of goods to the use of the highest value is one result of profit. The other is invention, which in a larger view is just another form of alertness in buying (ideas) low and selling high. The American economy in the late nineteenth century was a deal-making, inventive place, with secure private property and reasonably honest courts in which deals could be repaired when things went wrong, and a society that accorded work very high prestige. National product per head therefore went up smartly 1870–1900, slower than it did in the 1990s, for example, but very respectably for the time. If you look into the way Carnegie and Rockefeller actually got their fortunes, it turns out that it was mainly by making steel and transporting oil cheaper than their competitors did. They did not get it by hurting consumers with monopolies. Nor did they get it by hurting workers by paying less than other people did.

Yes, I understand. You are indignant that I should make such an assertion. I realize that it feels like an attack on your core beliefs, your faith. Everyone knows that the robber barons were, well, robbers.

But consider that you may be mistaken. Consider it possible that our image of the barons of the so-called Gilded Age has less to do with the facts of monopoly and with permanent ethico-political values and more to do with, for instance, the careers of cartoonists and other journalists when cheap paper and steam presses and full color printing were being perfected.[3] Consider that it might possibly be that indignation about new methods of finance reflected less an alleged evil of "stock watering" and more the ancient hostility toward middlemen, soon to be given official state sanction in American Populism and European anti-Semitism. Consider that the muckrakers and other Progressives were disproportionately the children of Protestant clergymen reacting to its new prosperity as the clerisy did, with guilt, and with envy of the businessmen among parishioners even more prosperous. Consider that historical accounts of the visible hand of corporate capitalism in the United States 1865–1914 may have less to do with actual robbery by the trusts and more to do with back-projections of later socialism triumphant.

Steel rails sold for about $100 a hundredweight around 1870 and about $25 a hundredweight around 1900. Crude petroleum sold for about $3.50 a barrel around 1870 and about 90 cents a barrel around 1900. Some robbery. As Michael Novak put the point, "Carnegie's staggering wealth . . . owed nothing to an 'original distribution.'" Andrew started poor. "Neither had he robbed banks or otherwise gained his fortune immorally or illegally. He invented whole new ways of making iron, and later steel, and above all wholly new ways of organizing and administering a business."[4]

In 1870 the average American produced and consumed $2,460 worth of goods and services in 1990 prices, roughly what the average Latin American produced and consumed in 1950.[5] By 1900, with Carnegie's fortune already made and Rockefeller's almost made, the figure was $4,100. That's a rise of $1,640 in thirty years, or 66 percent. In the thirty years after 1950, to give a scale, Latin America did better, about 100 percent. But still, a 2/3 increase per capita in thirty years is not chopped liver. In America 1870–1900, to put it another way, the entire flow of goods and services—the average multiplied by the number of people—increased by $214,000 millions. Theft reallocates things; it does not increase them by millions. Some robbery.

Now: Carnegie's $300 millions when he sold out to J. P. Morgan and his consortium in 1901 made him the richest man in the world, a Croesus, a very Bill Gates. But it was only one-and-a-half one thousandths of the rise in production he helped deliver. To put it another way, this richest man in the capitalist world possessed about $1 out of every $20,800 of American human and physical capital, taking annual personal income as a return of 5 percent on human or physical capital. Some Croesus.

Carnegie himself is said to have made the same point in another way. A socialist came to his office and argued to him that the wealthy should redistribute their wealth to the poor of the earth. Carnegie asked an assistant to go get him a rough estimate of his current wealth and of the population of the earth. The assistant returned shortly with the figures, and according to the anecdote Carnegie performed a calculation, then turned to the assistant and said, "Give this gentleman sixteen cents. That's his share of the wealth."[6]

And then Carnegie gave every dime of his wealth away, in accord with his gospel of wealth. Another businesslike Scot, Adam Smith, by the way, also gave away his considerable fortune, though, unlike Carnegie, he did not sound a trumpet before him when he did his alms.[7] Carnegie viewed the rich as many did in the first age of Darwin as men who had by that very fact of richness proven themselves the best stewards of the world's wealth. But he viewed himself, by a doctrine parallel to the Jewish one of *tzedakah*, as the good steward only for life and only if he spent his wealth in good works. "The man who dies thus rich dies disgraced. Such, in my opinion, is the true gospel concerning wealth, obedience to which is destined some day to solve the problem of the rich and the poor."[8]

It did not solve the problem, and could not. The proud foundations have a tiny share of the nation's wealth to redistribute to college professors and community organizers. The problem is really solved by the education of the workers and the entrepreneurship of the bosses, many of the bosses being, like Carnegie himself, former workers. That is, it is solved by the accumulation of real capital, not by the reallocation of sixteen cents worth of paper wealth.

But Carnegie carried through on his gospel, and did not die rich. He gave to Carnegie Hall in New York, the Peace Palace at the Hague, the Carnegie

Endowment for International Peace, and to that library in Wakefield, Massachusetts, where I first read the anticapitalist classics. "Has Andhrew Carnaygie given ye a libry yet?" asked Mr. Dooley. "Not that I know iv," said Mr. Hennessy. "He will," said Mr. Dooley. "Ye'll not escape him."[9] Notice that you have not heard of a Carnegie line of millionaires. It vanished with the millions. So of course did the British Rothschild give some of his fortune away, though less proportionately than did Carnegie. You *have* heard of a Rothschild line.

You've also heard of Carnegie-Mellon University. The other half is from Andrew Mellon, another of those wretched robber barons, who gave his art collection and the first building for the National Gallery in Washington, and part of the rest of his fortune to the Mellon Foundation, for the betterment of college professors. Collis Huntington of Central and Southern Pacific fame gave millions to Tuskegee and Hampton Institutes and his art collection to the Metropolitan Museum. His nephew and heir, the interurban king Henry Huntington, gave his rare book collections to the Huntington Library, delighting again generations of college professors.

J. P. Morgan gave freely to the Metropolitan and other causes during his life and in his will. In the words of Jean Strouse, a recent biographer, "He was essentially in business importing financial capital to fuel the growing American economy [for example, he financed Edison's light] and in his off-hours he was also importing cultural capital, basically stocking America's libraries and museums with the great treasures of the past."[10] Carnegie's henchman Henry Frick—whose last message to his former boss was "Tell Mr. Carnegie I'll see him in hell, where we both are going"—gave away the Frick Collection in New York and most of the rest of his $50 million fortune.

Old John D. Rockefeller gave gobs and gobs of money away, as a devout Baptist who raised his son and by proxy his five grandsons to a gospel of public service. He gave away $500 million, many billions in present dollars. But it was not every dime he had. He needed to keep some to distribute to children for the newsreel cameras, advised to do this by his PR man. And unlike Carnegie, he did give large sums to those grandsons, and to a granddaughter in whom the gospel of wealth did not shine.

George Soros, who was in 2002 worth $6 billion, plans to give it all away by 2010. The Gates Foundation gives away about as much as Soros's entire fortune every year. In 2004 Gates gave away to his foundation all the

$3 billion he collected from Microsoft's first-time paying of dividends. This is the virtue of the liberal man, in Aquinas's words: "By reason of his not being a lover of money, it follows that a man readily makes use of it, whether for himself, or for the good of others, or for God's glory."[11]

You'll want to reply, if you remain in thrall to the anticapitalist opinions of the Progressives, "Yeah, but they stole it in the first place." No, dear, they did not. Please try to listen more carefully. "The genius and labors of the so-called robber barons," writes Michael Novak, "transformed social possibilities . . . and set the lives of millions on an upward path"—including Novak's Slovak American ancestors working in Carnegie's and Morgan's steel mills.[12]

Admittedly, they corrupted politics. But when have the rich not done that? Yon Cassius hath a lean and hungry look. As the barons said in extenuation, weren't the politicians themselves at fault? We're just playing the game. Mark Twain remarked in 1897, in "Pudd'nhead Wilson's New Calendar," that it could "probably be shown by facts and figures that there is no distinctly native American criminal class except Congress."[13] As Collis Huntington wrote in 1877, "If you have to pay money [to a politician] to have the right thing done, it is only just and fair to do it. . . . If a [politician] has the power to do great evil and won't do right unless he is bribed to do it, I think . . . it is a man's duty to go up and bribe."[14] Honest graft.

Seriously, now, these men were not saints of love or justice in their work. But they were not pirates, either. Their Pinkertons broke up labor unions, true. And people like Marshall Field and George Pullman in Chicago conspired to sic the police on law-abiding anarchists. Yet many other business leaders in Chicago in the Gilded Age, such as Montgomery Ward, looked forward even in the 1880s to a capitalism-enriched world in which workers like you and me would have to be *enticed* to come to work, paid $60,000 to work in Cincinnati's sewers, for example. Even Pullman looked forward to such a future, at least when he was allowed to boss people around in his lovely little town for the workers south of Chicago and resist the unionization of his Pullman porters.

Carnegie, who before the Homestead Strike had spent a good deal of wind preaching cooperation between labor and capital, was in fact appalled by the outcome—though he had left the dirty business to Frick, and hid out on his estate in Scotland. He told Frick to break the unions, corresponding with Pittsburgh daily by telegraph, approving the steps taken. Later he never would admit that he had had a hand in Homestead.

These are serious ethical failures, and good reasons to think less of Huntington and Pullman and Carnegie. Novak says of the robber barons that "they sinned gravely" and of Carnegie that "he certainly was a moral coward."[15] But such sins, failures, cowardices are not peculiar to capitalism. They are human and political, and can be found everywhere in any era. The specifically economic actions of the robber barons were not robbery, not at all. That businesspeople buy low and sell high in a particularly alert and advantageous way does not make them bad, unless any trading is bad, unless when you yourself shop prudently you are bad, unless any tall poppy needs to be cut down, unless we wish to run our ethical lives on the sin of envy.

The clerisy is sure of its ground, but hasn't much considered that it may be mistaken. The late Robert Heilbroner's *The Worldly Philosophers* (1953 and six later editions) enticed me among many others to major in economics. Though we long disagreed about Marxism, I honor Bob, who in his last years decided that capitalism was the best of those systems that have been tried from time to time. But in his 1953 chapter on his hero Veblen he gives a "head-spinning example" of why the robber barons were bad that does not stand up very well to scrutiny.[16] William Rockefeller—John D.'s younger brother—and Henry Rogers bought Anaconda Copper in 1899 for $39 million, which they did not have in their bank accounts. They quickly covered the $39 million check by getting a loan from a banker friend, and then sold the company to the stock market for $75 million, and paid back the banker. Result? A $36 million profit in a trice without risking a dime of their own money.

Bad? Not so obviously as Heilbroner thinks. The Anaconda deal outraged the muckrakers, and Heilbroner joins in the general condemnation. "This free-for-all involved staggering dishonesty," he claims. Where exactly the dishonesty lies is not so clear. It appears that the deal came to be notorious as an instance of bad barons chiefly because Samuel Untermyer, a lawyer for Rockefeller and Rogers at the time of the deal who felt he had not himself received enough out of it, became counsel to a House committee in 1912–1913 investigating the money trust.[17]

What exactly is the beef? Rockefeller and Rogers had noticed that Anaconda was undervalued—that its old owners were willing to sell it for less than the stock market, they reckoned, would value it at. There is no evidence put forward in the tale that Rockefeller and Rogers *fooled* the stock market. The new company did not fall in value when they cleared out, and in fact they did not clear out entirely, as Heilbroner to the contrary implies. They sold only half the stock, and would therefore have had no interest in allowing its market value to fall. It didn't. The company was now correctly valued, the barons getting their profit from alertness.

They bought it without having the money in the bank, and persuaded the seller to wait to cash the check. So what? There is nothing unusual about this, in capitalism or out. True, Rockefeller and Rogers were condemned at the time by the financial community. But it's hard to see anything but envy as a basis for the condemnation: "Why didn't *we* think of that?" On the seller's side it was an open-eyed deal. The seller was extending credit to Rockefeller and Rogers, credit which they deserved to have. They had shown themselves to be smart cookies, and anyway had Standard Oil to back them. If the seller thought that Anaconda was worth only $39 million, there's no reason why he shouldn't accommodate the buyers by holding the check uncashed for a while, if he knew them to be reliable chaps, as he did. Indeed they quickly showed they were both smart and reliable, by covering the check and then by promptly repaying the bank loan that had covered it.

The Anaconda deal was routine, the same you enter when you buy any business—say, a house on speculation—and finance the purchase with a loan. If you have been correct in your assessment that the market will value the business more than you paid for it, then you can cash in your capital gain right away by reselling the business and paying off the loan. Rockefeller and Rogers were correct, and did cash in. That's not bad. That's good. Companies should be correctly valued, or else their real assets will be poorly employed. In the matter of Anaconda, William Rockefeller and Henry Rogers were good barons, not robbers.

The American experience with capitalist fortunes has been odd, intertwined with the peculiarly devout American attitude toward God. Fully 96 percent of Americans profess a belief in God, exceeded in this only by Nigeria, Brazil, South Africa, Ireland, Poland, and Northern Ireland.[18] It was well said in the 1980s that the two most religious countries in the world were the Islamic Republic of Iran and . . . the United States of America. Or alternatively that

India is the most religious country and Sweden the least, and the United States is . . . an India whose clerisy is Swedish.

In France or Britain a fortune starts a dynasty, as the Rothschilds show. In America—and especially generously in America and Japan—rich people endow colleges, finance hospitals, support the opera. It's a civic impulse, often tied to a religious impulse, as in the many hundreds of private colleges. Rockefeller's University of Chicago was a Baptist institution. So was Denison University in Ohio. The new university in Chicago got money from that devout Baptist, John D. Rockefeller, though not as much as one might think. He gave to Chicago, instead of adding to his earlier and generous gifts to Denison, in part because the administration at Denison didn't take his advice seriously. Big mistake. If they had taken his advice, the great private research university of the Midwest would be in Granville, Ohio, not in Chicago, Illinois.

Wesleyan University is not so called idly. Harvard, of course, was Congregational, for training up a literate ministry, "First flower of their wilderness / Star of their night." And so on across the country, to Pepperdine in far Malibu (Church of Christ). A French millionaire assumes correctly, au contraire, that *l'Etat* will provide. He is more interested in buying that chateau in the Loire valley or that vineyard outside Bordeaux, playing at aristocracy, like Carnegie on his Scottish estate, than "giving back to the community," as American millionaires are always putting it. To repeat, though, they didn't *take* it in the first place. They made deals. Rich people in America have more often than elsewhere showed a townsperson's public spirit, bourgeois virtues.

Any society, religious or not, has a sacred sphere and a profane, as I have said, *S* and *P*, a sphere in which love and justice determine largely who gets what as against a sphere in which prudence and courage largely do so. But "largely" is not "exclusively." Life in a market is not exclusively a matter of the profane. Buyers and sellers show their sacred qualities, too. The economy is, as the sociologists like to put it, "embedded," which is to say that the economy is not a sphere of Prudence Only independent of other ethical considerations. Or as we Episcopalians say, "Almighty God, whose Son Jesus Christ in his earthly life shared our toil and hallowed our labor; Be present with your people when they work."[19] And when they exchange and get rich, since alert trade is work.

THE ANXIETIES OF BOURGEOIS VIRTUES

I am recommending what might be thought of, philosophically speaking, as a libertarian version of Aristotelianism. Or perhaps, theologically speaking, a capitalist version of Pelagianism. Or an anti-Tillichian theological humanism with a dose of economics.

The always-present alternative to Kant and Bentham was Hobbes and Locke, that is to say, contractarianism, the third way in modern European ethical philosophy. But after Smith died, his simple and obvious system of natural liberty to make a contract was unmoored from the virtue ethics he espoused early and late. This was an ethical catastrophe. The theory of bourgeois virtues, almost complete in Smith, was abandoned by later exponents of contractarianism.

The result has been a long line of contractarian theorists trying to solve the Hobbes Problem—namely, "Can a group of asocial monsters, who have never been children and have never loved anything, never had faith or hope or justice or temperance, be shown on a blackboard to create out of rational self-interest a civil society?" The problem can be shown rigorously to be insoluble, at least under Prudence-Only axioms of strict self-interest. But this has not stopped academic men from trying to solve it again and again and again, 1651 to the present. They want to found society on contract without ethics—morals by agreement, ethics within the limits of reason. I am recommending that we go back to Smith, and do both: both agreement and morals, both reason and ethics. The case can be put in a little table. It has been shown mathematically and experimentally, I claim, that the first, Hobbesian column is in fact unsustainable without its last row, that is,

Three Ethical / Political Philosophies
Hobbesian, Smithian, Socialist

SOCIAL THEORY	Hobbesian	Smithian	Utopian socialist
THEOLOGY	Augustinian	Pelagian, Aquinian	Liberation
CHARACTER	Max U	Embedded bourgeois	Hopeful cleric
LITERARY VICTORIAN	Mr. Moneybags in *Das Kapital* (1867)	Lapham in *The Rise of Silas Lapham* (1885)	Julian West in *Looking Backward* (1887)
VIRTUES	P Only	P plus Temperance, Courage, Justice, Love, Faith, Hope	L & J & H Only
SUSTAINING EQUILIBRIUM	Can't cheat and survive	Wouldn't think of cheating	Sweetened nature of humankind under socialism
LAST HOPE	Other virtues supplied ad hoc	Not demoralized by the P-only theories of the clerisy	No Lenins or Maos or Shining Paths come to power

unless virtues come down from the stage scenery miraculously. The life of
man is solitary and poor unless miraculously the Max U's cooperate—as in
fact experimental subjects do cooperate, because they *have* been children
and *have* loved someone and are not monsters of P Only. They cooperate,
that is, for reasons inconsistent with the assumption of P Only.

The P-Only science of economics has no place for what Smith called "the
faculty of speech." Yet it is well known in experimental economics that
"simply allowing individuals to talk with one another [love, faith, justice] is
a sufficient change in the decision environment to make a substantial difference in behavior. . . . Individuals who start as strangers with no normative relationship to one another [in the style of P Only] may soon begin to
discuss a problem . . . and eventually acquire a sense of community [love,
faith] and moral responsibility [justice]."[1]

But in truth that last, saving, ethical row is necessary for *any* of the three
columns to work. Even my beloved second column, which is the way
capitalism actually operates, pretty much, can be undermined by Max U
ideologies. I stress that such ideologies are seen not only on the right, politically speaking. The hard left, too, with Marx, sees capitalism as a field for

Mr. Moneybags and "endless accumulation" for its own sake, whatever that might mean. The hard left's heaven, likewise, a communist society without private property, depends on Jesus rather than Satan being a member of the Politburo. In actually existing socialism Satan has had a more successful political career than Jesus.

The philosopher Edward Feser has usefully outlined three grounds for what he calls "principled libertarianism." The three Enlightenment philosophies show up once again. The libertarianism of Smith's "simple and obvious system of natural liberty" can be justified on utilitarian grounds, as maximizing national income. Or it can be justified, as Feser himself and Robert Nozick do, on natural rights and Kantian grounds: "the only system compatible with respect for individuals' natural rights to life, liberty, and property is a libertarian one."[2] Or it can be justified on contractarian grounds, as John Rawls does, being what one would choose at the Creation.

By Feser's definitions I am not in fact a "principled" libertarian—which is not to say that I am unprincipled in the nonphilosophical way of talking, but that I am pragmatic in the philosophical way of talking. That's fine with me. Such libertarians, Feser puts it, "tend to appeal to empirical considerations, eschewing philosophical analysis in favor of economic arguments and historical and sociological studies comparing the results of free-market policies with those of government intervention."[3] That's right, as I have tried to do here. As a mere economist and historian I am incapable of the fantasies that the people of principle are so gifted at. I keep being brought up short by the world as it is, at least as I can discern it through a glass darkly.

But if I had to be principled I would reach back before the French Enlightenment, or back into the Scottish Enlightenment, and offer a fourth justification for the free society, namely, that it leads to and depends on flourishing human lives of virtue. My so-called principle shares some features with the "postmodernist bourgeois liberalism" of Richard Rorty, or the "agonistic liberalism" of Isaiah Berlin, or the "dystopic liberalism" of Judith Shklar, or the rhetorical pluralism of Stuart Hampshire, or the "biblical realism" of Reinhold Niebuhr and Michael Novak, or the "cooperation to mutual benefit" plus "light" of Robert Nozick, or the feminist virtue ethics of Annette Baier or Carol Gilligan.[4]

Such impure mixes have not been popular in the West after Kant and Bentham and Locke. But they are not therefore merely confused. One does not, for example, have to be an antimarket communitarian to be an

Aristotelian, or a socialist to be a Christian. Hursthouse quotes Daniel Stat-
man as asserting that communitarianism "might turn out to be the political
aspect of virtue ethics."[5] I hope you are persuaded by now that this aspect is
not the only one that can be discerned. Bourgeois virtue is as plausible a
political entailment of virtue ethics as is the Green Party.

Nor to be a libertarian does one have to be a egoist. The right wing, I have
said, has too often embraced the analysis of its enemies that capitalism
works only through a sociopathic egoism, à la Hobbes, with left and right
therefore agreeing on the amoral character of markets. Quentin Skinner
worried that "contemporary liberalism, especially in its so-called libertarian
form, is in danger of sweeping the public bare of any concepts save those of
self-interest and individual rights." I admit there is such a danger, in the
form of a vulgar version of neoliberalism advocated at the country club and
in some classrooms and in some Cabinet rooms.

But as Skinner in turn admits, there is a path between MacIntyre's communitarianism and Ayn Rand's individualism. I would characterize the way
as a positive duty to be a good bourgeois—many exemplars of which you
and I know personally. As Skinner puts it, "Unless we place our duties before
our rights, we must expect to find our rights themselves undermined."[6]
Placing duties ahead of rights comes naturally to a burgher of Delft or to a
citizen of Rapid City.

A bourgeois version of the virtues deriving ultimately from Aristotle +
Augustine = Aquinas is also called liberalism. The bourgeois moment is
Smith, whom I have claimed as something like a secular Aquinian—though
note that Aquinas and his generation were busy in the mid-thirteenth century proving that "an honest, modest, charitable merchant was indeed able
to lead a good, Christian life."[7] I have noted that Robert Nelson argued in
detail in his first book on "economic theology" that "American economics
follows . . . closely in the Roman tradition, associated with ideas of natural
law as revealed through exercise of faculties of human reason, given a leading theological exposition by Thomas Aquinas."[8] The darker "Protestant"
tradition in economics, "seeing a sinful . . . world . . . where the powers of
human reasoning have been fatally weakened by the . . . corruption
of human nature," he detects in the line of Plato, Augustine, Luther, and
Marx.

Some liberal theorists would deny their heritage in virtue ethics, claiming that liberalism, for example, is at heart simply radical democratic

thought—which itself, though, comes from the Augustinian part of the equation.[9] Other liberals claim, with Lockeans (if not with Locke), and quite contrary to the first group, that the trading of rights under contract will suffice: no need to get entangled in the ethical tradition of the West. Thus David Strauss asserts that "importing a full Aristotelian vocabulary is not only unnecessary but incompatible with liberal premises."[10] He is correct if "full" means such things as having a free male Greek aristocrat's attitude toward institutions such as slavery, or placing at the head of all of them a virtue such as "great-souledness." But Strauss doesn't really show that the two virtues he identifies as necessary for liberalism—toleration of the views of others and a flexibility in life plans—"have nothing particularly Aristotelian" about them. He admits, for example, that flexibility in life is "a kind of moral courage, a willingness to face one's life without having its most important contours already determined."[11] And toleration can be viewed—and was in the debates over it in Holland in the 1620s, for example—as a species of humility, which is in turn composed, noted Aquinas, of temperance and justice, which were pagan, not only Christian, virtues.

The bourgeois vices reflect commonly the anxieties of the middleman, as in the many bourgeois characters of Molière straining for respectability. *Le bourgeois gentilhomme* is a joke in its very title, I have noted, since in French as in English in 1670 such a phrase was an absurdity, meaning "the burgher m'lord."[12]

Yet consider the bourgeois virtues contrasted with the earlier alternatives. The aristocratic virtues elevate an I. The Christian/peasant virtues elevate a Thou. The priestly virtues elevate an It. The bourgeois virtues speak instead of We, negotiating between I and Thou with reference to It, as civilized people must. Abram is renamed Abraham, the father of a multitude, when he enters into a covenant with the Lord, literally a property deal. Later Abraham bargains like a rug merchant to stay the Lord's hand over the city of Sodom: "Wilt thou also destroy the righteous with the wicked? Peradventure there may be fifty righteous within the city. . . . Peradventure there shall lack five of the fifty righteous: wilt thou destroy all the city for lack of five?" And so by mathematical induction to a mere ten. God at that juncture stays his hand. From the beginning Abraham shows the bourgeois virtues. A peasant prostrates himself before the gods; an aristocrat curses them; a priest organizes their worship. The bourgeois argues with his God and makes a little deal. I can get it for you wholesale.

The project here is to revive such an beneficent ideology of deal making for the middle class—or rather the project is to make it respectable again among the clerisy, since it does not need to be "revived" in capitalist practice. Vibrant ideologies of the aristocrat and the peasant still persist, I have argued, doing some good and a lot of evil. We need to revive a serious ethical conversation about middle-class life, the life of towns, the forum and agora. We need to get beyond the project of damning a man of business because he is neither an exalted aristocrat nor an unassuming peasant-proletarian. The conservative program of handing things over to a class of pseudoaristocrats trained at Andover and Yale or the radical program of handing things over to a proletariat-friendly party of bourgeois-born young men has not worked out very well. We need an ethical bourgeoisie.

The point is that merely heroic courage or merely Christian love, at any rate in their vulgar forms, are not usefully complete accounts of the virtues appropriate to a commercial society. The two vocabularies are heard in the camp and in the common. Achilles struts the camp in his Hephaestian armor, exercising his noble wrath. Jesus stands barefoot on the mount, preaching to the very least of the commoners. Camp and common.

And yet we live now in the town, we bourgeois, or are moving to the town and townly occupations as fast as we can manage. "Everyone nowadays," said Adam Smith as early as 1776, "becomes in some measure a merchant."[13] The prediction that the proletariat would become the universal class has proven to be mistaken. The nineteenth-century idea that the middleman stood for capital against labor looks wrong today, when the financial side of capital is an anonymous fund from London and Tokyo, much of it pension funds owned by employees, and when over half the productive real capital stock in rich countries is in fact human capital, the skills of the machinist in Cedar Rapids or the lawyer in Cape Town.[14]

The historian Jürgen Kocka has written of the failure of embourgeoisement of the working class in nineteenth-century Germany: "Lack of independence, market-dependent, the manual character of labor, small income, cramped living conditions, and the need for all members of the family to contribute to the family income—these were the factors which stood in the way of a real [embourgeoisement] of the workers in the nineteenth century."[15] That's right: and when the proletariat gets financial independence, college education, word-work, large income, the large suburban house, and late entry into the workforce, it becomes . . . bourgeois. It happened first in

America. The proletariat, an urban and secular version of the rural and religious peasantry, has been able when lucky to send its children to Notre Dame and thence to careers in plastics. The clerisy may lament, churchmen wail, bohemians jeer. Yet the universal class into which the other classes are slowly melting is the detested bourgeoisie.

Half of employment in rich countries is white collar, steadily rising. Thirty percent of the workforce qualifies in Richard Florida's opinion for the "Creative Class," as against 10 percent in 1900, the talkers and designers and managers. There are about 140 million employees in the United States now, but 19 million sole proprietorships and 2.5 million partnerships. Count them up in the telephone book; you will be amazed. Each proprietorship represents by definition 1.0 and each partnership at least 2.0 and each small corporation perhaps 2.0 or 3.0 little capitalists. Including small corporations, that's a total of perhaps 25 million small businesspeople, out of 215 million people age 20 or older.

Jobs for peasants, proletarians, and aristocrats are shrinking. Even soldiers are bourgeois. The production of things has become and will continue to become cheaper relative to most services. A piece of cotton cloth that sold for 70 or 80 shillings in the 1780s sold in the 1850s for 5 shillings.[16] The cheapening first led spinning out of the home, then weaving, men's clothing, women's clothing, baking, brewing, canning, and finally most other cooking. It then led peasants off the land: three-quarters of American workers in 1800 worked on farms; 40 percent in 1900; 8 percent in 1960; 2.5 percent in 1990. The 2.5 percent produced a lot more than the three-quarters had. Yet a barber or a professor was not much more productive in 1990 than in 1800. It still takes fifteen minutes with a pair of scissors to do short back and sides; it still takes fifty minutes with a piece of chalk to convey the notion of comparative advantage to undergraduates. But the farmer has become more productive by a factor of thirty-six. We cannot eat thirty-six times more food—I have tried: it doesn't work—and so the farmer's share in employment has fallen toward nil.

The making of things in factories will go the same way as the preparing of food in kitchens and the growing of crops on farms. Calculators that sold for four hundred dollars in 1970 sold for four dollars in 1990, and four cents now. Actually, by Moore's Law, the cost of the sheer calculating power of the machines—adding, multiplying, and carrying—fell in the ratio of $100 at the beginning to now a tiny fraction of a cent. The joke is that if

Maseratis had fallen in price 1970 to 2000 the way calculation did, they would by 2000 have sold for twenty-three cents per car. The proletarian labor required to make a radio, a windowpane, or a car is disappearing toward nil. Workers on the line in manufacturing peaked at about a fifth of the labor force after World War II in the United States and have since been disappearing, at first slowly and now quickly. What is left is bussing tables on the one side and bourgeois occupations on the other. In fifty years a maker of things on an assembly line in the United States will be as rare as a farmer.

That's not because the "jobs go overseas," as noneconomists think. Even if they stay at home, fewer and fewer people push the buttons. And that's a good thing, not bad, whether accomplished through foreign trade or through automation, or both, because it is another way of saying that we can get more per person. There is no such thing in the moderately long run as technological or foreign-trade unemployment. If on the contrary what you read in the newspaper about "losing jobs" were good economics, then practically no one would still be employed. There are no jobs nowadays for tens of thousands of canal-boat teamsters c. 1850 or tens of thousands of blacksmiths c. 1900. Understand: I advocate ample provision for those hurt by change. But I advocate, too, change. If the Internet replaces professorial lectures I will retire gracefully, on a pension income earned from the great productivity of the American economy.

The change is making proletarian occupations fewer and the enlarged bourgeoisie richer. The Creative Class edges ever upward in size, to the *benefit* of the remaining poor. Engels wrote to Marx ("Dear Moor") in October 1858 that "the English proletariat is actually becoming more and more bourgeois, so that the ultimate aim of this most bourgeois of nations would appear to be the possession, *alongside* the bourgeois, of a bourgeois aristocracy and the bourgeois proletariat."[17]

In 1933 a German writer declared that "the Bourgeois epoch is coming to an end. . . . Today it does not look as if the youth were of a mind to enter into [the inheritance of bourgeois life]. They have no feeling for the *Bürgertum*'s particular virtues, its particular mix of commitment and humane moderation. The mixture has been a distinguishing feature of liberalism, which is much maligned today."[18] So it has frequently been said. And yet—admitting the seriousness of the challenge to bourgeois virtues mounted in the 1930s and 1940s—from the 1950s to the present the bourgeoisie and its values and its liberalism has spread. The Good Germans of our era, for example, have precisely that mixture of commitment and humane moderation.

Nonetheless it is still routine to idealize a pagan or a Christian story of the virtues and then to sound a lament that in these latter days, alas, no one achieves the ideal. We live in a vulgar age of iron, or of plastic, it is said, not pagan gold or Christian silver. In the ethical accounting of artists and intellectuals since 1848 the townsfolk are perhaps useful, even necessary; but virtuous? The aristocracy and peasantry-proletariat, it is reported by the clerisy, join in disdain for the merchant, who has neither the martial honor of a knight nor the solidarity of a serf. The bourgeois virtues have been reduced to the single vice of greed.

Michael Novak reports on the Roman Catholic nostalgia for an imagined precapitalism of guilds and peasants, workers and beloved lords, warmly greeting each other on Sunday after mass. Catholic social thinkers, he writes,

> fail to envisage the hundreds of millions of the world's Catholics who work in small businesses of their own. They ignore the barbers and beauticians, the tobacco shop owners, the storekeepers, the electrical contractors, the plumbing and heating firms, the bakery owners, the butchers, the restaurateurs, the publishers of ethnic newspapers, the rug merchants, the cabinetmakers, the owners of jewelry stores, the managers of fast-food restaurants, the ice-cream vendors, the auto mechanics, the proprietors of hardware stores and appliance shops, the tailors, the makers of ecclesiastical candles, the lacemakers.[19]

He continues his encomium on small business in terms that Montaigne or Montesquieu could have used: "Commerce requires attention to small losses and small gains; teaches care, discipline, frugality, clear accounting, providential forethought, and respect for regular reckonings; instructs in courtesy; softens the barbaric instincts and demands attention to manners; teaches fidelity to contracts, honesty in fair dealings, and concern for one's moral reputation."[20] Novak has the petite bourgeoisie in mind. But I would extend his encomium to the grande as well, with a rather different set of virtues. Neither class is perfect, because we live in an imperfect world. But both are pretty good, as John Mueller would put it—within the limits of original sin, as Novak and I would. And, Novak observes, "these qualities are, of course, ridiculed by artists and aristocrats, the passionate and the wild at heart."

Thomas Mann was surely, as Amos Oz calls him, "the lover, mocker, elegist and immortalizer of the bourgeois age."[21] In his first successful novel,

Buddenbrooks (1901), which mocks and elegizes his own North German merchant ancestors, the fortune hunter Bendix Grünlich ("greenish") flatters Frau Consul for the hand of Antonie. Frau Consul's family is Duchamps, "of the field," expressing a nostalgia for the pastoral aristocracy; compare Jack London's sarcasm about "Van Weyden." "This would be a better world if there were more families like them in it," declares the ingratiating Mr. Greenish. "They have religion, benevolence, and genuine piety; in short, they are my ideal of the true Christian spirit. And in them it is united to a rare degree with a brilliant cosmopolitanism, an elegance, an aristocratic bearing."[22] It would be a better world, in other words, with Christian aristocrats and no third estate. Later he "communicated the [false] fact that his father had been a clergyman, a Christian, and at the same time a highly cosmopolitan gentleman" (p. 79), claiming Christian-peasant and pagan-aristocratic virtues in combination.

The combination of peasant and aristocratic virtues cannot be genuine in a bourgeois. And so it proves in Grünlich.

Christian rhetoric in *Buddenbrooks* is used as a mere instrument of ambition or pride, as when Johann diverts his daughter Antonie from her infatuation with an unsuitable young man, one in fact embodying the liberal ideals of 1848: "It is my Christian conviction, my dear daughter, that one must have regard for the feelings of others," namely, Father Johann's. The passionate Christianity of the bourgeoisie in the early nineteenth century, Mann implies, was a transient novelty, at least by the standard of religious sobriety in Germany after the Thirty Years' War: "The deceased Consul's [Johann's father] fanatical love of God and of the Savior had been an emotion foreign to his forebears, who never cherished other than the normal, every-day sentiments proper to good citizens." Johann has drifted away from enthusiastic religion, the bourgeois or even proletarian correlate of the Sentimental Revolution among the gentry and aristocracy, and uses the memory of it merely as a rhetorical trick.

Aristocratic rhetoric as well, Mann implies, is false in the bourgeoisie, and dangerous. Gerda, born Arnoldsen in Amsterdam, mother of future Buddenbrooks, is "an artist, an individual, a puzzling, fascinating creature," thinks bourgeois Tom, who marries her. Peter Gay notes that Mann never allows himself inside her head. She is seen ominously as "aristocratic"— though as a Dutch woman this is something of an absurdity at the outset.[23] She reinforces the bohemian strain in the family, evinced by Tom's brother, called significantly Christian, who ends in a madhouse, and in Tom's only son and heir, called Hanno, who is like his "aristocratic" mother music-obsessed, and who dies at fifteen, ending the hopes for the firm.[24]

In 1944 Sartre claimed with some justice that "most members of the middle class and most Christians are not authentic." The word "authenticity" is a master term in Sartre, taken from Heidegger, meaning that *les bourgeois* without authenticity "refuse to live up to their middle-class or Christian condition fully and that they always conceal certain parts of themselves from themselves."[25] As Ruth Benedict observed at about the same troubled time, "Men who have accepted a system of values by which to live cannot without courting inefficiency and chaos keep for long a fenced-off portion of their lives where they think and behave according to a contrary set of values."[26]

I quoted Aristotle's sneering remark that the bourgeoisie have lives "ignoble and inimical to goodness/excellence." Aristotle's reasoning is that the polis required "men who are absolutely just, and not men who are merely just in relation to some particular standard," that is, their own particular bottom line, which is no justice at all.[27] In this he is correct. Adam Smith argued on similar grounds that landlords, not merchants, were the best representatives of the whole community. Prudence Only is not an ideal constitution. But Smith, unlike Aristotle, knew and loved actual bourgeois people. And so he knew, as the Western clerisy hostile to the bourgeoisie does not, that a good society can be founded on actually existing bourgeois virtues. Forgetting Smith in a commercial society has orphaned the virtues. It is the ethical tragedy of the modern West.

What then are the bourgeois virtues? You ask me to preach. I'll preach to thee.

The leading bourgeois virtue is the Prudence to buy low and sell high. I admit it. There. But it is also the prudence to trade rather than to invade, to calculate the consequences, to pursue the good with competence—Herbert Hoover, for example, energetically rescuing many Europeans from starvation after 1918.

Another bourgeois virtue is the Temperance to save and accumulate, of course. But it is also the temperance to educate oneself in business and in life, to listen to the customer humbly, to resist the temptations to cheat, to ask quietly whether there might be a compromise here—Eleanor Roosevelt negotiating the United Nations Declaration of Human Rights in 1948.

A third is the Justice to insist on private property honestly acquired. But it is also the justice to pay willingly for good work, to honor labor, to break down privilege, to value people for what they can do rather than for who they are, to view success without envy, making capitalism work since 1776.

A fourth is the Courage to venture on new ways of business. But it is also the courage to overcome the fear of change, to bear defeat unto bankruptcy, to be courteous to new ideas, to wake up next morning and face fresh work with cheer, resisting the despairing pessimism of the clerisy 1848 to the present. And so the bourgeoisie can have Prudence, Temperance, Justice, and Courage, the pagan four. Or the Scottish three—Prudence, Temperance, and Justice, the artificial virtues—plus enterprise, that is, Courage with another dose of Temperance.

Beyond the pagan virtues is the Love to take care of one's own, yes. But it is also a bourgeois love to care for employees and partners and colleagues and customers and fellow citizens, to wish well of humankind, to seek God, finding human and transcendent connection in the marketplace in 2006, and in a Scottish benevolence c. 1759.

Another is the Faith to honor one's community of business. But it is also the faith to build monuments to the glorious past, to sustain traditions of commerce, of learning, of religion, finding identity in Amsterdam and Chicago and Osaka.

Another is the Hope to imagine a better machine. But it is also the hope to see the future as something other than stagnation or eternal recurrence, to infuse the day's work with a purpose, seeing one's labor as a glorious calling, 1533 to the present. So the bourgeoisie can have Faith, Hope, and Love, these three, the theological virtues.

That is, the bourgeois virtues are merely the seven virtues exercised in a commercial society. They are not hypothetical. For centuries in Venice and Holland and then in England and Scotland and British North America, then in Belgium, Northern France, the Rhineland, Sydney, Cleveland, Los Angeles, Bombay, Shanghai, and in a widening array of places elsewhere, against hardy traditions of aristocratic and peasant virtues, we have practiced them. We have fallen repeatedly, of course, into bourgeois vices. Sin is original. But we live in a commercial society, most of us, and capitalism is not automatically vicious or sinful. Rather the contrary.

"Bourgeois virtues" is no contradiction. It is the way we live now, mainly, at work, on our good days, and the way we should, Mondays through Fridays.

THE UNFINISHED CASE FOR THE

BOURGEOIS VIRTUES

When I began to write this work, I divided it into three parts, supposing that one volume
would contain a full discussion of the arguments which seemed to me to arise naturally from
a few simple principles; but fresh illustrations occurring as I advanced, I now present only
the first part to the public.
   —Mary Wollstonecraft, *A Vindication of the Rights of Woman*, 1792

I must desire the reader not to take any assertion alone by itself, but to consider the whole of
what is said upon it: because this is necessary . . . to see the very meaning of the assertion.
   —Bishop Butler, *Fifteen Sermons*, 1725

The Bourgeois Virtues, vol. 2, *Bourgeois Towns: How a Capitalist Ethic Grew in the Dutch and English Lands, 1600–1800*

HOW IN THE SEVENTEENTH AND EIGHTEENTH CENTURIES THE
VIRTUES FARED IN NORTHWESTERN EUROPE, AND WITH WHAT
CONSEQUENCES FOR THE NINETEENTH CENTURY

14   The Bourgeois Revolutions and a Certain Freedom
     And capitalism made people free, for one thing by spreading owner-
     ship, as Jefferson and others argued (but this is the lesser reason, for
     capitalism can also corrupt, as in Jefferson's ownership of slaves,
     for example, or as in the selfishness of manufacturers for their own
     interests, as Smith noted). The greater reason is the substitution of
     contract for status, and the spread of radical egalitarianism of a
     Protestant sort.

The Bourgeois Virtues, vol. 3, *The Treason of the Clerisy:
How Capitalism Was Demoralized in the Age of Romance*
THE TRAGIC TURN AFTER 1848 AGAINST THE BOURGEOISIE BY THE
ARTISTS AND INTELLECTUALS OF EUROPE AND ITS OFFSHOOTS

1   Bentham and the Modern Chaos of Precise Ideas
     But the modern project of making an ethic for a commercial society
     started to fall apart around 1800. One part into which it fell was Ben-
     thamism, that is, the elevation of Prudence Only to a philosophical
     principle.

2   I Choose Never to Stoop: Romanticism
     The opposite of Benthamism was Romanticism, the idea beloved in
     Germany that Love and Courage Alone sufficed.

3   Why Romance?
     Romanticism was a reaction to a fading faith in God, not a reaction to
     capitalism.

4 & 5   Evangelicalism and Economics
     Love of God and love of gain danced for a while together in the early
     nineteenth century, in a revived but tough-minded evangelicalism, in
     England and the United States, for example.

6   The Angel in the House
     But Prudence and Courage vs. the rest of the virtues became gender-
     ized, through a separation of spheres.

7 & 8   The Great Conversion
     Which is perhaps one reason why in the mid-nineteenth century so
     many of the male artists and intellectuals of Europe and its offshoots
     turned against capitalism, as a vulgar Prudence unworthy of a secular-
     ized Faith and Hope. A *trahison des clercs* ensued, a century and a half
     of the "intellectual organization of political hatreds."

The Bourgeois Virtues, vol. 4, *Defending the Defensible: The Case for an Ethical Capitalism*

WHAT IS ALLEGED TO BE WRONG WITH BOURGEOIS SOCIETY, AND WHY
THE ALLEGATIONS ARE MOSTLY FALSE

Part 1 THE CHARGES

14 Restarting Adam Smith

The way forward is to go back to the blessed Adam Smith, or at any rate to his project, shared with figures like Montesquieu or Thomas Paine, of a commercial yet virtuous society. And humanistic economics.

15 New Stories, New Arts

And the arts—novels, movies, songs, painting—are where we do most of our ethical thinking, at least if we are secular, and even (I would argue) if we are not. It is in art that the bourgeois virtues must be renewed. But the economics should become unified with the art.

NOTES

PREFACE

   1. Dougherty, *Who's Afraid of Adam Smith?*, 2002, p. xi.

APOLOGY

   1. Appiah, *Ethics of Identity*, 2005, p. xi.

   2. Mueller, *Capitalism, Democracy*, 1999, p. 17.

   3. Mueller, *Capitalism, Democracy*, 1999, p. 7.

   4. Weber, *Protestant Ethic*, 1904–1905, p. 69.

   5. Macfarlane, *Riddle of the Modern*, 2000, p. 271.

   6. Mueller disagrees: *Capitalism, Democracy*, 1999, p. 83ff.

   7. Marshall's *Principles*, 1890 (1920), bk. 1, chap. 1, in paragraph 1, p. 1.

   8. Novak, *Business as a Calling*, 1996, p. 7.

   9. Jones, *Christian Socialist Revival*, 1968, pp. 85–86, n.2.

   10. Comte-Sponville, *On the Virtues*, 1996, p. 89. The fount of such views in France was Merleau-Ponty. Compare Aron, *Memoirs*, 1983, p. 216: when Merleau-Ponty writes in 1947 "as though it were an obvious truth, that 'the moral and material civilization of England presupposes the exploitation of colonies,' he flippantly resolves a still open question."

   11. White, *Justice as Translation*, 1990 , p. 71.

   12. Gray, *False Dawn*, 1998, p. 36.

   13. Nozick, *Anarchy, State*, 1974, p. x.

   14. Najita, *Visions of Virtue in Tokugawa*, 1987, for example, p. 71ff.

   15. Macaulay, "Southey's Colloquies," 1830, p. 184–187.

   16. Marx and Engels, *Communist Manifesto*, 1848, p. 64.

   17. Graña, *Bohemian versus Bourgeois*, 1964, p. xii.

   18. You may examine it in forty-nine languages at http://home.planet.nl/~elder180/ internationale/).

   19. Etymological wisdom not otherwise attributed is from the *Oxford English Dictionary*, from which is taken the quotation by Emerson here ("clerisy").

20. So it is given in Baudelaire, "Further Notes," 1857, p. 97; but an editor of Poe 1849 (Poe died that same year) at http://www.eapoe.org/works/misc/fiftysc.htm believes "old" may have been meant to be "odd." The peskiness of editors. But that Baudelaire believed it "old" is itself significant.

21. Shaw, *Introduction to Hard Times*, 1912, pp. 334–335. Compare Holmes to Pollock, Dec. 29, 1915: "The first half of the 19th century was unhygienic but jovial. We now have improved hygiene and all manner of intelligent isms but don't seem to get a good time out of it" (Holmes, *Holmes-Pollock*, vol. 1, p. 229).

22. Butler, *Fifteen Sermons*, 1725, preface, p. 349. I have modernized spelling and punctuation here and elsewhere, to avoid distancing the authors. Stephen Greenblatt praises the Oxford edition's (1986) modernizing of Shakespeare's spelling for avoiding "a certain cozy, Olde-English quaintness" (Greenblatt, General Introduction to *The Norton Shakespeare*, 1997, p. 73). The distance of the olde ffolke should depend on their thoughts, not their spelling conventions. For the same reason I have changed British spellings to American, "honour" to "honor" and the like. Sometimes I cannot resist retaining "-eth" in sixteenth-century quotations. It's so cozy and quaint.

23. Smith, *Moral Sentiments*, 1749 (1790) 7.2.4.12, p. 312.

24. Oz, "The Discreet Charms of Zionism," 1977, in *Under This Blazing Light*, 1979, p. 108.

25. Marx, *Capital*, 1867, chap. 31, last page (p. 834 of Modern Library ed.).

26. Schumpeter, *Capitalism, Socialism*, 1942, part 2, "Can Capitalism Survive?" para. 3, p. 61 of Harper Torchbook ed.

27. Weber 1904–1905, p. 17; in his *General Economic History* (1923 [trans. Frank Knight 1927], p. 355) he writes, "The notion that our rationalistic and capitalistic age is characterized by a stronger economic interest than other periods is childish."

28. Mokyr, *Gifts*, 2002, chap. 7, "Institutions, Knowledge, and Economic Growth."

29. Weber, *Protestant Ethic*, 1904–1905 (1958), p. 52. But it did not have the *modern* spirit of holy accumulation and rationality, he adds.

30. Goody, *East in the West*, 1996, p. 237.

31. Sartre, *Anti-Semite*, 1944, p. 57.

32. Lasch, *The Culture of Narcissism*, 1979, p. 18.

33. http://www.freedomhouse.org/research/freeworld/2004/charts2004.pdf.

34. See the book of amazing economic facts by the economic historian Angus Maddison, *World Economy*, 2001, summarizing the work over the past decades by our colleagues in economic history.

35. Wells, *Journey of Man*, 2002, p. 151, implies a rise from some few thousands out of Africa to 10 million by 8500 BC, to the full 1,000 million in 1800. On these time scales the past two centuries are surely the *fastest* rise.

36. Maddison, *World Economy*, 2001, p. 28, table 1–2: "world" and "Average Group A" and "Africa."

37. The terse entries were discovered by the historian Laurel Thatcher Ulrich, were transcribed by a husband-wife team in ten years of evening labor, and were dramatized in a film of 1997 by Laurie Kahn-Leavitt and Richard Rogers. Ulrich wrote a book about the life in 1990.

38. Kahn-Leavitt and others (1997), transcript of the video, spelling and punctuation modernized. http://www.dohistory.org/diary/1785/01/17850101_txt.html.

39. John Donnelly, *Boston Globe*, "Over Half World's Homes Have Running Water, WHO Report Finds. But Progress Stalls on Sanitation Goal." August 26, 2004.

40. Maddison, *World Economy*, 2001, p. 30, table 1-5a; Riley, *Rising Life Expectancy: A Global History*, 2001, reckons it at 30 years in 1800 and 67 years now; compare Oeppen and Vaupel, "Broken Limits," 2002. The notion that AIDS is itself somehow connected to capitalism, as you will sometimes hear, is strange. Why would capitalists kill their workers and customers?

41. In Sweden and England/Wales, in which the statistics are good (Human Mortality Data Base at http://www.demog.berkeley.edu, Dec. 2003), life tables back to the mid-nineteenth century imply additional years of life expected at ages 15–19 of 43 years (England/Wales for men and women born 1841–1849) rising to 62.5 years for people born 1990–1999; and 46.4 years (Sweden, 1861–1899) to 64.1. The rise is about a factor of 1.5, not the 2 used here, but the rise has surely been larger in places like China and South Asia.

42. I'm assuming that everyone in the population has survived to adulthood, which is of course contrary to fact. Allowing for the fact would result in an even higher ratio of increase than 6 to 1, because the assumption is less true in 1800 than in 2000.

43. Scherer, *Quarter Notes*, 2003, pp. 31–33.

44. Mueller, *Capitalism, Democracy*, 1999, pp. 198–199, 201, 252; Sen, *Development as Freedom*, 2000, pp. 149–151.

45. Schumpeter, *Capitalism Socialism*, 1942, part 2, chap. 5, p. 67.

46. Stiglitz, *Globalization*, 2002, pp. 248–249. Note Stiglitz's quantitative estimate, relative to a world population of 6 billion.

47. Calomiris, *Globalist Manifesto*, 2002, p. 69.

48. Muller, *Mind and Market*, 2002, p. 17.

49. Arguments such as that "the poor are fitted for such a life"; "poverty frees one from concern for earthly things." Fleischacker, *Distributive Justice*, 2004, pp. 9–10.

50. Coleridge in Jackson, ed., p. 13.

51. Fogel, *Escape from Hunger*, 2004, p. 74.

52. McCracken, *Plenitude*, 1997, p. 23.

53. Jones, *Culture and the Price of Information*, forthcoming, Princeton University Press.

54. Vargas Llosa, "Culture of Liberty," 2001.

55. Here's some good news. In the manner of interest rates the growth gathered force, and so the factor of increase in adult materially supplied years was much less in 1913, at the second peak of bourgeois self-confidence, than it is by now, at the third peak—the first was in 1832, when all this got going in earnest. In 1913 it was, as an economist had characterized it a little before, merely the "rude first steps in material civilization." To get from 1 to a factor of 2, 4, 8, . . . 102 takes 6.5 doublings. Try it on your calculator. The low estimate of adult materially supplied years, therefore, would take, in a total of 200 years, about 30.8 years for each doubling. Each doubling takes the same amount of time. By the Rule of 72 (that something growing at 1 percent per year doubles in 72 years) the required growth per year is an apparently moderate $(72/30.8) \times 1\% = 2\%$ per year. But the rate is only apparently "moderate," since a doubling on a doubling on a doubling every century or so yields in two centuries an immoderate amount of change, that factor of 102. Check

it out, I say: you will be amazed. You can see without calculation the reasonableness of the immoderate force of interest. Something growing at a mere 1 percent gets to be *of course* at least 72 percent larger in 72 years: that much you can see without any mysterious Rule, since of course 72 times 1 percent is 72 percent. The rest of the doubling (to 100 percent = a doubling in 72 years, that is) comes from the compounding. And if something doubles during 72 years growing at 1 percent per year, it will of course double in half that time if it grows twice as fast, 2 percent per year. The encouragements to art or science or liberation feeding on themselves in a nonlinear way were therefore in 1913 less strong—at this 2 percent rate of growth per year 1800 to 1913 rising to merely 13.3 or so on the scale from 1 to 100. Then in the politics-disturbed spurts of the twentieth century it went the rest of the way to 100 percent of the change, 100 percent of that factor of 102, or from the other point of view 100 percent of that factor of 255.

56. Nozick, *Anarchy, State,* 1974, pp. 328–329.

57. Sen, *Development as Freedom,* 2000, pp. 6, 112.

58. Sen, *Development as Freedom,* 2000, pp. 115, 201.

59. National Public Radio in Chicago, around 11:00 a.m., October 3, 2005.

60. Quoted in Sen, *Development as Freedom,* 2000, p. 114.

61. Granovetter, "Economic Action," 1985. Novak, *Catholic Social Thought,* 1984 (1989), p. 24.

62. Sacks, *Dignity of Difference,* 2002, pp. 32, 16, 22, 14.

63. Wollstonecraft, *Rights of Women,* 1792, p. 149.

64. Tocqueville, *Democracy in America,* 1840 [1954], vol. 2, p. 131.

65. Hunt, *Character and Culture,* 1997, p. 211.

66. For example, Marx and Engels, *Communist Manifesto,* 1848, p. 66, "Pauperism develops more rapidly than population and wealth."

67. Marx and Engels, *Communist Manifesto,* 1848, p. 69, "Private property . . . for the few is solely due to its non-existence in the hands of those nine-tenths."

68. Marx and Engels, *Communist Manifesto,* 1848, p. 70, "Culture . . . is, for the enormous majority, a mere training to act as a machine."

69. Schweiker, *Theological Ethics,* 2004, p. xiii.

70. See again Najita, *Visions of Virtue in Togugawa,* 1987, for example, p. 5.

71. In 1973 David Friedman reckoned the figure was at most about 5 percent (*The Machinery of Freedom,* pp. xiv, xv, quoted in Nozick, *Anarchy, State,* 1974, p. 177n.)

72. As Johan Van Overtveldt points out to me.

73. Margo, "Labor Force," 2000, p. 213, table 5.3; McCloskey, "Industrial Revolution," 1981, p. 127.

74. Rousseau, *Origin of Inequality,* 1755, p. 60.

75. Schmidtz 1994, quoted in Feser, *On Nozick,* 2004, p. 84.

76. Compare Lindert, *Fertility and Scarcity,* 1978. Some Georgist friends tell me that I am wrong, and that you can get the share of all rents up to 10 percent if you include income from things like the (God-given and unaugmentable) electronic spectrum. But as I say, they would agree that a determinism of "resources" as noneconomists understand the word is unjustified. And some of my Austrian economics friends retort that *taxing* such resources would result in distortions of the economy. All agree with the main present point, however: that human capital has become much larger.

77. Thus again Peter Lindert, this time "Voice and Growth," 2003.

78. Smith, *Wealth*, 1776, p. 267. Spelling modernized.

79. Smith, *Wealth*, 1776, 4.7.c, p. 613. Italics supplied.

80. Todorov, *Hope and Memory*, 2000, pp. 45, 47.

81. Smith, *Wealth*, 1776, 4.1, p. 446.

82. Macfarlane, *Riddle of the Modern*, 2000, p. 275.

83. McNeill, *Human Condition*, 1980, p. 68; compare Charles Tilly, *Coercion, Capital*, 1990. McNeill elsewhere (*Venice*, 1974, p. 127) observes that as nation-state coalesced "Venetians (and other Italians) fond it harder to secure favorable treatment by threatening to take their business elsewhere to another jurisdiction."

84. Macfarlane, *Riddle of the Modern*, 2000, p. 262, quoting Gellner's *Conditions of Liberty, Civil Society and Its Rivals* (1995).

85. Daly, *Autocracy Under Siege* 1998; and *Watchful State*, 2004.

86. Higgs, *Crisis and Leviathan*, 1987; and *Against Leviathan*, 2004.

87. Constant, "Liberty of the Ancients," 1819, pp. 311, 316.

88. Fairbank et al., *East Asia*, 1989, p. 409.

89. Henshall, *History of Japan*, 2004, p. 55.

90. Nakane, Introduction, to *Tokugawa Japan*, 1990, p. 8.

91. Heckscher, *Mercantilism*, 1931, vol. 1, p. 173.

92. Heckscher, *Mercantilism*, 1931, vol. 1, p. 173.

93. Fairbank et al., *East Asia*, 1989, pp. 234, 486.

94. Baechler, *Evolution of Capitalism*, 1971, p. 113.

95. Macfarlane, *Riddle of the Modern*, 2000, pp. 274–275.

96. Mokyr, *Gifts of Athena*, 2002, p. 278.

97. NcNeill, *Human Condition*, 1980, p. 63.

98. Parker, *Military Revolution*, 2nd ed., 1996, pp. 140, 143.

99. Mokyr, *Gifts*, 2002, p. 297.

100. Mokyr, *Gifts*, 2002, p. 278. On pp. 279–282 he examines the bad side of fragmentation.

101. Friedman, "Life of a Laureate," 1985, in Breit and Hirsch, *Lives of the Laureates*, 2004, p. 72.

102. Higgs, "Where Figures Fail," 1983.

103. Folbre, *Invisible Heart*, 2001, p. 226; and pp. 227, 148, 133, and throughout.

104. Gertrude Himmelfarb, *Idea of Poverty*, 1984, p. 46, quoted in Fleischacker 2004b, *Short History*, p. 64.

105. Fleischacker, *Short History*, 2004b, p. 2 and throughout.

106. Feser, *On Nozick*, 2004, pp. 52–53.

107. See, for example, Mark White's criticism of social economics on this ground, White, "Kantian Dignity," 2003.

108. Cox and Alm, *Myths of Rich and Poor*, 1999, p. 73.

109. Gottschalk and Danziger, "Family Income Mobility," 1997, p. 36, table 3.

110. Long and Ferrie, "Tale of Two Labor Markets," 2005, tables 1 and 2. Rates in the United States were similar in the third quarter of the nineteenth century, and much lower at the time in Britain (p. 22).

111. Rousseau, *Political Economy,* 1755 (1987), p. 133, and quoted with enthusiasm in Fleischacker, *Short History,* 2004, p. 60.

112. Sen, *Development as Freedom,* 2000, p. 1; compare pp. 43, 152, 178ff, 182ff.

113. Sen, *Development as Freedom,* 2000, p. 43.

114. Guest, *Shackled Continent,* 2004, p. 214.

115. Ellis, *Founding Brothers,* 2000, p. 4. Ellis perhaps gets carried away in his praise for the United States as "the oldest enduring republic in world history" (p. 5). One could instance Rome 509 BC–27 BC.

116. Ridley, *Origins of Virtue,* 1996, p. 263.

117. Ridley, *Origins of Virtue,* 1996, p. 263. Compare Kropotkin, *Mutual Aid,* 1902, with a very similar vision.

118. Selznick, *Moral Commonwealth,* 1992, p. 534.

119. Coase, "Lighthouse," 1974.

120. Selznick, *Moral Commonwealth,* 1992, pp. 511, 517.

121. Sen, *Development as Freedom,* 2000, p. 40.

122. Slivinski, "Corporate Welfare," 2001. I admit that stock ownership is widespread. But the point is, you can't make people better off by taxing them to give subsidies to themselves.

123. Rush Limbaugh, TV show (10/5/95, quoted at http://www.fair.org/extra/0311/limbaugh-drugs.html).

124. Constant, "Liberty of the Ancients," 1819, p. 327.

125. Calomiris, *Globalist Manifesto,* 2002, pp. 68–69. And, for some other of my claims, my colleagues writing in McCloskey, ed. *Second Thoughts,* 1993.

APPEAL

1. *Hoi autoi tois autois tōn autōn ta auta,* Richard Lanham tells me.

2. Winters, *The Displaced of Capital,* 2004, "The Displaced of Capital," p. 12.

3. Bellow, *It All Adds Up,* 1994, p. 308.

CHAPTER 1: THE VERY WORD "VIRTUE"

1. Geertz, *Works and Lives,* 1988, p. 107.

2. Benedict, *Chrysanthemum,* 1946, p. 13.

3. MacIntyre, *After Virtue,* 1981, p. 178.

4. As cancer cures and cleft-palate operations and the coloring of hair, for example, are unnatural, contrary to God's evident will for the person in question. An obsession with unnatural sex defaces the work of the otherwise insightful natural-law theorist J. Budziszewski.

5. The father/mother rhetoric is the burden of Lakoff, *Moral Politics,* 1996.

6. Holmes, "Address," 1895, p. 265.

7. Quoted in Vinen, *History in Fragments,* 2000, p. 148.

8. Lakoff, *Moral Politics,* 1996.

9. Aristotle, *Nic. Ethics,* c. 330 BC, 4.7.1.1127a.

10. Murdoch, "On 'God' and 'Good,' " 1969, pp. 57, 58. "Ordinary language": Murdoch was an Oxford philosopher as well as a novelist.

CHAPTER 2: THE VERY WORD "BOURGEOIS"

1. Huddie "Leadbelly" Ledbetter, "Bourgeois Blues," 1937 (copyright 1959 Folkways Music Publisher).

2. Mencken, "Types of Men," 1922.

3. Quoted in Johnston, *Radical Middle Class*, 2003, p. 5, which contains a good analysis of the phenomenon of the antibourgeois bourgeoisie.

4. Hartz, *Liberal Tradition*, 1955, following Tocqueville.

5. Murphy, "American Presidents," 2004.

6. On Switzerland, see Kocka, "The European Pattern," 1988 (1993), p. 26.

7. Hobsbawm, "English Middle Class," 1988 (1993), pp. 134, 138, 145.

8. Davidoff and Hall, *Family Fortunes*, 1987, p. 264.

9. Graña, *Bohemian versus Bourgeois*, 1964, p. 17.

10. Florida, *Creative Class*, 2002, p. 332.

11. Reprinted and translated in Horst, *Low Sky*, 1996, p. 142. The poem was called "Liefdesverklaring," or "Love-Declaration."

12. In such matters the Dutch were perhaps a little more democratic even before the war than, say, the English or the French. Accompanying the representatives of the *Bildungsbürgertum* on their evening stroll in Gresshof's poem was a representative from the petite bourgeoisie, "en 't klerkje dat vandaag wat vroeger klaar is," "and a little clerk who today is finished a bit early."

13. Johnston, *Radical Middle Class*, 2003, p. 28.

14. See Johnston's review of the critics of the Lasswell-Lipset-Mayer theory of petit bourgeois reaction, chap. 6 of *Radical Middle Class*.

15. Johnston, *Radical Middle Class*, 2003, p. 13.

16. Greenblatt, *Will in the World*, 2004, p. 76.

17. Remember: unattributed word-lore is from *The Oxford English Dictionary*.

18. Quoted in Greenblatt, *Will in the World*, 2004, p. 77.

19. Gilman, *Women and Economics*, 1898, p. 157.

20. Thompson, *Virtuous Marketplace*, 2000, p. 174.

21. Quoted in Johnston, *Radical Middle Class*, 2003, p. 264.

22. Jefferson to John Jay, August 23, 1785, http://wikisource.org/wiki/Letter_to_John_Jay_-_August_23,_1785.

CHAPTER 3: ON NOT BEING SPOOKED BY THE WORD "BOURGEOIS"

1. Huizinga, "Spirit of the Netherlands," 1935 (1968), p. 111.

2. *On the Social Contract*, bk. I, chap. 6, end, and footnote, in *Basic Political Writings*. Mansfield points this out in Mansfield, "Liberty and Virtue," 2003, p. 9. Rousseau says in footnote 4 that "quand Bodin a voulu parler de nos citoyens et bourgeois, il a fait une lourde bévue en prenant les uns pour les autres" ("When [Jean] Bodin wanted to speak of our citizens and bourgeois, he committed a terrible blunder in taking the one for the other"). http://un2sg4.unige.ch/athena/rousseau/jjr_cont.html#4.

3. Schama, *Embarrassment*, 1987, p. 568.

4. Schama, *Embarrassment*, 1987, p. 567.

5. Schama, *Embarrassment*, 1987, p. 11.

6. Schama, *Embarrassment*, 1987, p. 420.

7. Schama, *Embarrassment*, 1987, p. 420.

8. Schama, *Embarrassment*, 1987, p. 609.

9. Parks, "Cosimos," 2002, p. 76.

10. Parks, "Cosimos," 2002, p. 75.

11. Schama, *Embarrassment*, 1987, p. 49.

12. Schama, *Embarrassment*, 1987, p. 399.

13. Schama, *Embarrassment*, 1987, p. 388.

14. Felltham, *A Brief Character of the Low Countries*, 1652, quoted in Gross, *The New Oxford Book of English Prose*, 2000, pp. 95–96.

15. Schama, *Embarrassment*, 1987, p. 47.

16. Ross, "American Exceptionalism," 1995, p. 22.

17. De Vries, *European Urbanization*, 1984, pp. 270–277, cited in Maddison, *World Economy*, 2001, p. 54. Compare, however, the northern Italians of bourgeois character in Milan, Venice, Florence, Genoa, Pisa, Siena, and the like. In 1600 only Paris and London were in the club of over-100,000-population with Naples, Venice, Milan, Rome, and Palermo.

18. Israel, *Dutch Republic*, 1995, pp. 115, 328; Maddison, *World Economy*, 2001, p. 54.

19. De Vries, *European Urbanization*, 1984, pp. 30, 36, 39, and 46, quoted in Maddison, *World Economy*, 2001, p. 248.

20. "Vivent les Gueux," Israel, *Dutch Republic*, 1995, p. 148.

CHAPTER 4: THE FIRST VIRTUE: LOVE PROFANE AND SACRED

1. For example, by Budziszewski, "Escape from Nihilism," n. d.

2. Murdoch, "Sovereignty of Good," 1967, p. 103.

3. Tompkins, "Me and My Shadow," 1987 (2001), p. 2143.

4. Willey, *English Moralists*, 1964, pp. 107–108.

5. *Essais de morale* (1671), in Clark, ed., *Commerce, Culture*, 2003, pp. 57, 59.

6. Morgan quoted in Held, *Feminist Morality*, 1993, pp. 48–49.

7. Hornby, *How to Be Good*, 2001, p. 200; Munro, "Nettles" in Munro, *Hateship*, 2003.

8. Lewis, *Four Loves*, 1960, p. 142.

9. Casey, *Pagan Virtue*, 1990, p. 163.

10. Aquinas, *Summa contra gentiles*, c. 1259–1264, bk. 3, pt. 3, chap. 124, "That Marriage ought to be between one Man and one Woman."

11. Plato had applied it of course to both heterosexual and homosexual unions. The Wife of Bath had at church door husbands five, but recent scholarship has found that *homosexual* unions were routinely honored in the Middle Ages and Renaissance at the same place (Boswell, *Same Sex Unions*, 1994, pp. 191, 264, 267, 280–281).

12. Macfarlane, *Riddle of the Modern*, pp. 176, 183, 189.

13. Macfarlane, *Riddle of the Modern*, pp. 199, 175 (quoting Steele), 336 (quoting Thompson), 343.

14. Duffy, "Cradle Will Rock," 2002, p. 61.

15. Quoted in Duffy, "Cradle Will Rock," 2002, p. 62.

16. Saller, "Family Values in Ancient Rome," 2001, at http://fathom.lib.uchicago.edu/1/777777121908/.

17. Bradstreet, *Works*, 1678, pp. 232, 234.

18. Bradstreet, *Works*, 1678, p. 225.

19. Quoted in Cole, *Simone Weil*, 2001, p. 116.

20. MacIntyre, *After Virtue*, 1981, p. 172.

21. Lewis, "On Ethics" c. 1941–1942, pp. 68, 76.

22. Plato, *Republic*, c. 360 BC, 4, Stephanus, 442b–d, pp. 1073–1074.

23. Johnson, *Practical Philosophy*, 2002.

24. Aquinas, as understood by Schockenhoff, "Virtue of Charity," 2002, p. 248.

25. The English word "care," by the way, is Germanic, as in Old English *caru, cearu*, "sorrow," from Indo-European **gar-*, "to cry out," whence via Latin *garrīre* > "garrulous." The Latin cousin is *cūra*. "Care" is not, as you would think, from the Latin *cārus* (whence "charity," "caress," cherish"), which is instead from IE **kā*, "to desire," whence also English "whore," Sanskrit *kamasutra*. *Amor* seems to originate in *amma* = "mama," in babbling.

26. Hartman, *Unmediated Vision*, 1954, p. 4, italics supplied.

27. Klemm, "Material Grace," 2004, p. 235.

28. Hartman, *Unmediated Vision*, 1954, pp. 4–5.

29. As A. N. Wilson observes in *God's Funeral*, 1999, p. 45.

30. Milton, *Paradise Lost*, 1667, 8.588–594.

31. Greeley, *The Catholic Imagination*, 2000, p. 7; and chap. 2, "Sacred Desire." Annette Baier argues that Kant, Descartes, and the rest see humans as despicable and love for them as impossible (Baier, "Ethics," 1994, pp. 36, 38).

CHAPTER 5: LOVE AND THE TRANSCENDENT

1. Lewis, *Four Loves*, 1960, pp. 135–136.

2. Klemm, "Material Grace," 2004, p. 226.

3. Klemm, "Material Grace," 2004, p. 233.

4. Klemm, "Material Grace," 2004, p. 226.

5. Lewis, *Four Loves*, 1960, p. 32.

6. Schweiker, *Theological Ethics*, 2004, pp. xii, 201.

7. Schweiker, *Theological Ethics*, 2004, p. xv.

8. Weil, *Gravity and Grace*, 1942 (1949), pp. 164–165, 166, 168–169.

9. Erasmus, *Adages*, 1500–1533, selected by William Barker (2001), 2.69, p. 40.

10. Schweiker, *Theological Ethics*, 2004, p. xvi.

11. Bellah, *Imagining Japan*, 2003, pp. 20, 13.

12. From his sermons, quoted in Allison, *The Rise of Moralism*, 1966, p. 4, punctuation modernized.

13. Allison, *The Rise of Moralism*, 1966, pp. 7, 24. Allison (who, incidentally, was the Episcopal bishop of South Carolina) shows the slide in late sixteenth-century Anglicanism toward the Catholic view of works, thence to deism and then to atheism, the view that Christ was a Good Man only: "the imputation of *our* righteousness, not the imputation of Christ's righteousness, became that by which we are justified" (p. 204).

14. Wood, *Broken Estate,* 1999.

15. Murdoch, "Sovereignty of Good," 1967, p. 100.

16. Nussbaum, *Fragility of Goodness,* 1986, p. 361.

17. William Alfred found this on a Vermont tombstone, and made it the motto of his play *Agamemnon.*

18. Augustine, *Confessions,* AD 398, 4.10.

19. Nussbaum, *Fragility of Goodness,* 1986, p. 420.

20. Matt. 22:37–40 and a dozen or so other places in the New Testament (for example, Matt. 7:12, reexposited in Paul's Letter to the Romans 13:8); Tractate Shabbos 31a; and Lev. 19:18.

21. Tillich, *Courage to Be,* 1952, pp. 9, 101.

22. Weil, *Waiting for God,* 1950, p. 195.

23. Tillich, *Courage to Be,* 1952, p. 120.

24. Halwani, *Virtuous Liaisons,* 2003, pp. 19, 27, 73ff.

25. Smith, *Moral Sentiments,* 1759, 1790, pt. 3, chap. 3, para. 4, p. 136. Compare Rousseau *Political Economy,* 1755, p. 121.

26. Smith, *Wealth,* 1776, 3.3.5, p. 137. I wish he hadn't said "reason," which makes the passage sound Kantian.

27. Lewis, *Screwtape Letters,* 1943, p. 37.

28. Murdoch, *Metaphysics,* 1992, p. 17.

29. Tronto, *Moral Boundaries,* 1993, p. 161; compare p. 135, "the dangers faced by the vulnerable at the hands of their caregivers."

30. Tronto, *Moral Boundaries,* 1993, p. 167.

CHAPTER 6: SWEET LOVE VS. INTEREST

1. Lewis, *Screwtape Letters,* 1943, p. 86.

2. Hobbes, *Leviathan,* 1651, vol. 1, chap. 6, p. 24.

3. Aquinas, *Disputed Questions on Virtue* (section *On Hope*), c. 1269–1272, quoted in Cessario, "Hope," 2002, p. 237. See the similar analysis in *Summa theologiae,* c. 1270, Ia, IIae, q. 26, art. 4, objection 3, "On the contrary." By the way, the great *Summa* is sometimes referred to as *Theologica* and sometimes *Theologiae.* The professionals, for example, those in Pope, ed., *Ethics of Aquinas,* seem these days to prefer *Theologiae.*

4. Klemm, "Material Grace," 2004, p. 224.

5. Stocker, "Schizophrenia of Modern Ethical Theories," 1976, pp. 68–69, 71.

6. Becker and Tomes, "Equilibrium Theory," 1979, p. 1161.

7. Folbre, *Invisible Heart,* 2001, p. 112.

8. Becker, "Theory of Marriage," 1974 (1976), pp. 236, 237. A "preference function" is economic jargon for tastes.

9. Whitehead, *Modes of Thought,* 1938 (1968), p.23.

10. Hampshire, Postscript, 1982, to Hampshire, *Thought and Action,* 1959, p. 274.

11. Held, *Feminist Morality,* 1993, p. 8.

12. Yuengert, *Boundaries,* 2004, p. 12.

13. MacIntyre, *After Virtue,* 1981, pp. 185.

14. Abbing, *Why Are Artists So Poor?* 2002.

15. Sen, *Ethics and Economics*, 1987, p. 41.

16. Schmidtz, "Reasons for Altruism," 1993, pp. 164–165. My italics on "concern" and "respect."

17. Tronto, *Moral Boundaries*, 1993, pp. 127–137.

18. Pinker, *How the Mind Works*, 1997, quoted in Fodor, "Trouble with Psychological Darwinism," 1998.

19. Fodor, "Trouble with Psychological Darwinism," 1998.

20. Nozick, *Invariances*, 2001, p. 300.

21. Frankfurt, *Reasons of Love*, 2004, pp. 79–80, italics supplied.

22. Nozick, *Anarchy, State*, 1974, p. 168.

23. Veblen, "Why Is Economics Not an Evolutionary Science?" 1898.

24. Sugden, "Thinking as a Team," 1993.

25. Lewis, *Four Loves*, 1960, p. 168.

26. Lewis, *Four Loves*, 1960, pp. 191, 180, 168, 163.

27. Wilbur, "A Wedding Toast," in *Poems*, 1971 (1988), p. 61.

CHAPTER 7: BOURGEOIS ECONOMISTS AGAINST LOVE

1. Yeats, *Estrangement*, 1909, entry 51, p. 334.

2. Whitehead, *Modes of Thought*, 1938, p. 31.

3. Sen, *Ethics and Economics*, 1987, p 2.

4. Smith, *Wealth*, 1776, 4.2.12, p. 183.

5. Baier, "Ethics," 1994, p. 10.

6. Field, *Altruistically Inclined?* 2003, p. 300.

7. Field, *Altruistically Inclined?* 2003, p. 313.

8. Friedman, "Social Responsibility of Business," 1970.

9. Friedman, "Social Responsibility of Business," 1970, p 33, emphasis added, as Daniel G. Arce M. does when quoting this passage ("Conspicuous by Its Absence," 2004, p. 263).

10. Quoted in Arce M., "Conspicuous by Its Absence," 2004, p. 265.

11. Daviss, "Profits from Principle," 1999 (2003), pp. 203, 209.

12. Donaldson, "Adding Corporate Ethics," 2000 (2003), p. 100.

13. Najita, *Visions of Virtue in Togugawa*, 1987, p. 91.

14. Smith, *Wealth*, 1776, 1.2, pp. 28–30.

15. Totman, *Early Modern Japan*, 1993, pp. 181, 359.

16. Najita, *Visions of Virtue in Togugawa*, 1987, pp. 88–89.

17. Nakai Chikuzan, around 1760, quoted in Totman, *Early Modern Japan*, 1993, p. 359.

18. Solomon, *Ethics and Excellence*, 1992, p. 21 and throughout.

19. Murray, *Stoic Philosophy*, 1915, p. 30.

20. Epictetus, *The Book of Epictetus*, c. AD 130, Fragments, p. 286.

21. Aristotle, *Rhetoric*, c. 350 BC, 1367a, p. 81.

22. Hooker, *Laws*, 1593, 1.10.2, p. 189.

23. Koehn, "Virtue Ethics," 2005, p. 536.

24. Lewis, *Screwtape Letters*, 1943, p. ix.

25. Schmidtz, "Reasons for Altruism," 1993, p. 170.

26. Nozick, *Anarchy, State,* 1974, pp. 42–44. William James posed a similar question in *Pragmatism,* 1907.

27. Nozick, *Examined Life,* 1989, p. 102.

28. Roberts, *Invisible Heart,* 2001, p. 138.

29. Koehn, "Virtue Ethics," 2005, p. 535.

30. Sen, *Ethics and Economics,* 1987, p. 43, and p. 55: "Self-interested behavior can scarcely suffice when agency is important on its own."

31. As Nozick asks, "For ethics, might the content of the attribute of having a soul simply be that the being strives, or is capable of striving, to give meaning to its life?" (Nozick, *Anarchy, State,* 1974, p. 50).

32. Held, *Feminist Morality,* 1993, p. 8.

33. Compare White, "Kantian Critique," 2005, MS p. 6. The example is Kantian.

CHAPTER 8: LOVE AND THE BOURGEOISIE

1. Ostrom, Gardner, and Walker, *Rules, Games,* 1994, p. 322.

2. A guide to the devastation is Hargreaves-Heap and Varoufakis, *Game Theory,* 2004, for example, on defection in finite games (for instance, Nash backward induction), p. 122 and the pages leading up to it, as well as p. 203 (quoting Roger Myerson); on the Folk Theorem, pp. 202, 206, 208, and 247: "A new type of Folk Theorem . . . ends all hope that evolutionary [game] theory will be indeterminacy's death knell." The Folk Theorem is a mathematical hell.

3. Field, "Review of North," 2005.

4. Searle, *Speech Acts,* 1969; and Fish, *Is There a Text?* 1980.

5. V. Smith, Letter to Frans B. M. de Waal, April 9, 2005.

6. Macaulay, "Non-Contractual Relations," 1963, p. 196.

7. Macaulay, "Non-Contractual Relations," 1963, p. 197.

8. Macaulay, "Non-Contractual Relations," 1963, p. 195.

9. Macaulay, "Non-Contractual Relations," 1963, p. 198.

10. Macaulay, "Non-Contractual Relations," 1963, p. 199.

11. McClay, "The Strange Career of *The Lonely Crowd,*" 1993, p. 432. The Bender book he is admiring is *Community and Social Change in America* (1978).

12. Uzzi, "Embeddedness," 1999.

13. Novak, *Business as a Calling,* 1996, pp. 8, 10, and chap. 3.

14. Kamin, "Monuments to Mediocrity," 2003, p. 6.

15. Frank, "Motives," 2005, p. 370.

16. Frankfurt, *Reasons of Love,* 2004, p. 90.

17. Schaefer, *Shane,* 1949, p. 97.

18. Lewis, *Four Loves,* 1960, pp. 98–99. I am told that Antoine de Saint-Exupéry somewhere says much the same.

19. Frey, *Not Just For the Money,* 1997; Frey and Stutzer, *Happiness & Economics,* 2002.

20. Murdoch, " 'God' and 'Good,' " 1969, p. 53.

21. Aristotle, *Nic. Ethics,* c. 330 BC, 8.3.6 (1156b).

22. Stocker, "Schizophrenia," 1976, p. 72.

23. Quoted in Sen, "Rational Fools," 1977, p. 326.

24. Sen, "Rational Fools," 1977, p. 326.

25. Sen, "Rational Fools," 1977, p. 328.

26. Sen, "Rational Fools," 1977, p. 329.

27. Sen, "Rational Fools," 1977, p. 336.

28. Quoted in Ridley, *Origins of Virtue*, 1996, p. 263, pp. 260–261.

29. Solomon, *Ethics and Excellence*, 1992, p. 104.

30. Freeman, "Not Your Father's (or Mum's) Union," 2003.

31. Snyder, "Winter Work," 1995 (1997), p. 74.

32. Roback Morse's summary of her *Love and Economics*, 2001, at http://www.hooverdigest.org/013/morse.html.

CHAPTER 9: SOLIDARITY REGAINED

1. Selznick, *Moral Commonwealth*, 1992, pp. 6, 8.

2. Hanawalt, *Crime and Conflict*, 1979, pp. 271–272.

3. Raftis, *Tenure and Mobility*, 1964, chaps. 6–8.

4. Wrigley and Schofield, *Population History*, 1981.

5. Coontz, *The Way We Never Were*, 1992.

6. Dennison and Carus, "Invention of the Russian Rural Commune," 2003. For the attachment to the figment, see Engels's first footnote to the 1888 English translation of *The Communist Manifesto*, in which Haxthausen's notions about the *mir* are praised.

7. Samuel Popkin, *The Rational Peasant*, 1979.

8. Folbre, *Invisible Heart*, 2001, p. 20.

9. Bellah et al., *Habits*, 1985, p. 284.

10. Bellah et al., *Habits*, 1985, p. xlii.

11. Bellah et al., *Habits*, 1985, p. 291.

12. Bellah et al., *Habits*, 1985, p. 286.

13. Folbre, *Invisible Heart*, 2001, p. 32.

14. See Muller, *Mind and Market*, 2002, pp. 263, 280.

15. Bellah et al., *Habits*, 1985, p. xvii.

16. Freeman, "Not Your Mother's Union," 2003.

17. Berlin, letter to Norman Birnbaum, quoted in Ignatieff, *Isaiah Berlin*, 1998, p. 251. Compare Nozick, *Anarchy, State*, 1974, p. 297: "That it is impossible simultaneously and continually to realize all social and ethical goods is a regrettable fact about the human condition, worth investigating and lamenting." But a fact.

18. Mussolini and Gentile, "Doctrine of Fascism," 1932, para. 10.

19. Florida, *Creative Class*, 2002, chap. 15.

20. Butler, *Fifteen Sermons*, 1725, sermon 1, p. 367, italics supplied.

21. Florida, *Creative Class*, 2002, p. 277.

22. Sennett, *Corrosion of Character*, 1998, p. 24.

23. Sennett, *Corrosion of Character*, 1988, p. 23.

24. Butler, *Fifteen Sermons*, 1725, preface, p. 343.

25. Smith, *Wealth*, 1776, 2.3.31, p. 343; and Lukács quoted in Lendvai, *Hungarians*, 1999, p. 491.

26. See, for example, Ignatieff, *Isaiah Berlin*, 1998, pp. 245, 247, 248.

27. Muller, *Mind and Market*, 2002, p. 280.

28. Bellah et al., *Habits*, 1985, p. 292.

29. Bellah et al., *Habits*, 1985, p. 290.

30. Bellah et al., *Habits*, 1985, p. 7.

31. Innes, *Labor in a New Land*, 1983.

32. Mansfield, "Liberty and Virtue," 2003, p. 9n. Mansfield is uncertain whether Shklar was praising the bourgeoisie or dissing "virtue." It seems unlikely that one who spoke so often of the republican virtues intended the latter.

33. Bellah et al., *Habits*, p. 286.

CHAPTER 10: FAITH AS IDENTITY

1. Aquinas, *Disputed Questions*, 1269–1272, "Virtues in General," art. 12, p. 89.

2. Aquinas, *Lauda, Sion, salvatorem*, verse 6, at http://www.ewtn.com/library/PRAYER/LAUDA.TXT.

3. Budziszewski, "Religion and Civic Culture," 1992, p. 51.

4. Davis and Hersh, *Descartes' Dream*, 1986, for example, p. 232.

5. "Faith," in *Oxford Dictionary of the Christian Church*, pp. 491–492.

6. Barr, *Physics and Faith*, 2003, p. 266.

7. Merton, *New Seeds of Contemplation*, 1962, pp. 127, 135–136.

8. Quoted in Kirsch, "Get Happy," 2004, p. 97.

9. Lewis, *Mere Christianity*, 1943–1945, pp. 123–126.

10. Appiah, *Ethics of Identity*, 2005, p. 137.

11. J. Q. Wilson, *Moral Sense*, 1993, pp. 99–117.

12. J. Q. Wilson, *Moral Sense*, 1993, p. xiii.

13. Cicero, *De amicitia*, 44 BC, 5.20.

14. Aristotle, *Nich. Ethics*, c. 330 BC, 1156a20, Broadie and Rowe trans.

15. Bellah et al., *Habits*, 1985.

16. Ingram and Roberts, "Friendship among Competitors," 2000, p. 417.

17. Ingram and Roberts, "Friendship among Competitors," 2000, p. 420; compare Mueller, *Capitalism Democracy*, 1999, p. 39.

18. Ingram and Roberts, "Friendship among Competitors," 2000, p. 418.

19. Pahl, *Friendship*, 2000, pp. 53–54.

20. Quoted in Pahl, *Friendship*, 2000, p. 30.

21. Greenblatt, *Will in the World*, 2004, chap. 3.

22. Quoted in Pahl, *Friendship*, 2000, p. 53.

23. Branca, ed., *Merchant Writers*, 1986, pp. 48, 68. Compare Cicero's similar advice in *De amicitia*, 44 BC, for example, 17.63 and 19.67; and before him Hesiod, *Works and Days*, c. 700 BC, lines 371–372: "Even with your brother smile—and get a witness; for trust and mistrust alike ruin men."

24. Branca, *Merchant Writers*, 1986, pp. 48, 73.

25. Cicero, *De amicitia* 9.32, 12.46, 14.52.

26. Evensky, "Ethics and the Invisible Hand," 1993; and "Adam Smith's Lost Legacy," 2001.

27. Arce M., "Conspicuous by Its Absence," 2004, p. 263.

28. Pahl, *Friendship,* 2000, p. 55.

29. Seabright, *Company of Strangers,* 2004, p. 8.

30. Shakespeare, *Hen. V,* 2.2.3 ff.

CHAPTER 11: HOPE AND ITS BANISHMENT

1. Cessario, "The Theological Virtue of Hope," 2002, p. 234.

2. Shields, *Dressing Up,* 2000, pp. 46, 50, 53.

3. Wilbur, "On the Marginal Way," 1969, in *New and Collected Poems,* 1988, p. 122.

4. Aristotle, *Nich. Ethics,* c. 330 BC, 1123a35 ff.

5. Cessario, "The Theological Virtue of Hope," 2002, p. 238.

6. Aquinas, *Summa Theologiae,* c. 1270, IIa, IIae, q. 161, art. 4. The citation is in the usual form. It means the second [*secunda*] half of the second [*secundae*] Part—note the Latin case endings, -*a* and -*ae*. Aquinas organized his inquiry around questions ("q.") and broke down his dialectic answers into a few or a half dozen articles (art.). I generally use the New Advent Web site for the translation, but occasionally use my own translation, too.

7. I am indebted to Marijke Prins for these ideas.

8. Harvey, *Condition of Postmodernity,* 1990.

9. Berman, *All That Is Solid,* 1982, p. 15.

10. Item 2359006705, category 15897.

11. Schweiker, *Theological Ethics,* 2004, p. x.

12. An amazing reproduction of the actual French text of the 1740 Amsterdam edition is available at http://www.lib.uchicago.edu/efts/ARTFL/projects/dicos/BAYLE/search.fulltext.form.html.

13. Pocock, "Cambridge Paradigms," 1983, p. 241.

14. Arnold, "The Study of Poetry," 1880, pp. 320–321.

15. Arnold, "The Study of Poetry," 1880, p. 301.

16. A. N. Wilson, *God's Funeral,* 1999, p. 25.

17. Keynes, "Marshall," 1924, p. 134.

18. Schumpeter, *History,* 1954, p. 772 n 2.

19. A. N. Wilson, *God's Funeral,* 1999, p. 125. Compare Novak, *Catholic Social Thought,* 1984, p. 64.

20. A. N. Wilson, *God's Funeral,* 1999, p. 9.

21. Schumpeter, *History,* 1954, p. 772 n 2.

CHAPTER 12: AGAINST THE SACRED

1. Hursthouse, *Virtue Ethics,* 1999, index. I am counting multiple pages at their total: thus "benevolence, Humean, 99–102" counts as four pages.

2. Hursthouse, *Virtue Ethics,* 1999, pp. 232–233; compare 218: "But what could this fifth end be?"

3. Comte-Sponville, *On the Virtues,* 1996, p. 92.

4. Comte-Sponville, *On the Virtues,* 1996, pp. 17, 19.

5. Comte-Sponville, *On the Virtues,* 1996, p. 21.

6. Comte-Sponville, *On the Virtues,* 1996, p. 25.

7. Comte-Sponville, *On the Virtues*, 1996, p. 28.

8. A. N. Wilson, *God's Funeral*, 1999, p. 59.

9. Comte-Sponville, *On the Virtues*, 1996, p. 53, italics supplied.

10. Quoted from Groopman, *Anatomy of Hope*, 2003, in *Publishers Weekly*, itself quoted at http://www.amazon.com/exec/obidos/tg/detail/-/0375506381/002–8162323–5258406?v=glance.

11. Comte-Sponville, *On the Virtues*, 1996, p. 26.

12. Comte-Sponville, *On the Virtues*, 1996, p. 295n20.

13. Comte-Sponville, *On the Virtues*, 1996, p. 288.

14. Russell, "A Free Man's Worship," 1903 (1957), p. 106.

15. Comte-Sponville, *On the Virtues*, 1996, p. 295n20.

16. Hampshire, Postscript, 1982, to Hampshire, *Thought and Action*, 1959, p. 283.

17. Aristotle, *History of Animals*, c. 350 BC, 8.1.

18. Muir, "The Animals," at http:www.poemhunter.com/p/m/poem.asp?poet=6684 &poem=28779.

19. Lodge, *Thinks . . .* , 2001, p. 318.

20. A. N. Wilson, *God's Funeral*, 1999, p. 59.

21. Mazzini in Gangulee, ed., *Selected Writings*, 1830–1872, pp. 106, 103.

22. Mazzini in Gangulee, ed., *Selected Writings*, 1830–1872, p. 105.

23. Totman, *Early Modern Japan*, 1993, pp. 349, 361–364, 369–370, 378.

24. *Classic Peanuts*, *Chicago Tribune*, March 24, 2005.

25. Johnson, *Birth of the Modern*, 1991, pp. 600–601.

26. Heinich, *Glory of Van Gogh*, 1991 (1996), p. 148.

27. Donald Miller, *City of the Century*, 1996, pp. 387–391, 422.

CHAPTER 13: VAN GOGH AND THE TRANSCENDENT PROFANE

1. Van Gogh, "Letter to Aurier," early Feb. 1890, pp. 195–197 in Stein, *Van Gogh*, 1986.

2. Bellow, *Humboldt's Gift*, quoted in Kirsch, "Get Happy," 2004, p. 91.

3. Read, *Meaning of Art*, 1931 (1969), p. 202.

4. Pascoe and Catling, *Eyewitness*, 1995.

5. Van Baar and Kok, *De Millenium*, 1999, pp. 32–33. Nietzsche's syphilis, by the way, appears to be still another mad artist/scientist myth. He seems to have had in fact a slow-developing brain tumor.

6. Kirsch, "Get Happy," 2004, p. 92.

7. Johanna van Gogh, quoted in van Gogh (1883–1890), *Letters*, p. 509.

8. Van Gogh, ed. Leeuw, *Letters*, 1883–1890, p. 509, xix.

9. Van Gogh, ed. Leeuw, *Letters*, 1883–1890, p. 365.

10. Van Gogh, ed. Leeuw, *Letters*, 1883–1890, p. 365.

11. John McCloskey has helped me with these ideas, as with many others.

12. Van Gogh, ed. Leeuw, *Letters*, 1996, pp. x, xi.

13. Van Gogh, ed. Leeuw, *Letters*, 1996, p. 326–327.

14. Van Gogh, ed. Leeuw, *Letters*, 1996, p. 395.

15. Leighton, ed. *100 Masterpieces*, 2002, plate 75, "Wheatfields with Crows," text by Willem-stein.

16. Stein, ed., *Van Gogh*, 1986, pp. 246, 257–258; compare de Meester's article of March 1891, p. 261ff in Stein, ed.

17. Stein, ed., *Van Gogh*, 1986, p. 107, italics his.

18. Stein, ed., *Van Gogh*, 1986, p. 374.

19. About September 29, 1888, (van Gogh, *Verzamelde Brieven*, 1883–1890, no. 543, p. 321), quoted in Druick and Zegers, *Van Gogh and Gauguin*, 2001, p. 138, underlining in French original.

20. Van Gogh, *Verzamelde Brieven*, 1883–1890, no. 531, quoted in Druick and Zegers, *Van Gogh and Gauguin*, 2001, p. 138.

21. Letter, 28 May 1888, quoted in Druick and Zegers, *Van Gogh and Gauguin*, 2001, p. 108. Contrast by the way Aurier's praise for "the isolate."

22. Van Gogh, 1883–1890, *Letters*, pp. 342–343.

23. Van Baar and Kok, *De Millenium*, 1999, p. 32.

24. Todorov, *Hope and Memory*, 2000, p. 32.

25. Ignatieff, *Needs of Strangers*, 1984, p. 21.

CHAPTER 14: HUMILITY AND TRUTH

1. Aquinas, *Summa Theologiae*, c. 1270, IIa, IIae, q. 161, art. 3, "I answer that . . . ," quoted in Pope, "Overview," in Pope, "Overview," 2002, p. 45.

2. Cor. 2:12, quoted by Aquinas, and himself quoted in Pope, "Overview," 2002, p. 45.

3. Quoted in Brinton, *Friends*, 1964, p. 36.

4. Day, in Day, *Selected Writings*, 1983, p. 124.

5. Sacks, *Dignity of Difference*, 2002, pp. 64–65.

6. Rorty, "Experiments in Philosophic Genre," 1983, p. 562.

7. IIa, IIae, q. 161, art. 1, quoted in Houser in Pope, ed., *Ethics of Aquinas*, 2002, p. 311.

8. Sweeney in Pope, ed., *Ethics of Aquinas*, 2002, p. 163.

9. Milton, *Paradise Lost*, 1667, 5.656–666.

10. Fish, *How Milton Works*, 2001.

11. Pope, "Overview," in Pope, ed., *Ethics of Aquinas*, 2002, p. 45; Comte-Sponville cannot get this, or any other Christian virtue, right: *On the Virtues*, 1996, pp. 140–148.

12. Charry, "Happiness," 2004, p. 24.

13. Charry, "Happiness," 2004, p. 25.

14. Weil, *Gravity and Grace*, 1942, p. 40, in a chapter entitled "Self-Effacement."

15. Merton, *Thoughts*, 1956, p. 55.

16. Saiving, "Human Situation," 1960, p. 109.

17. Mill, *Subjection of Women*, 1869, chap. 2, p. 41.

18. Dickens, *David Copperfield*, 1850, chap. 39.

19. Franklin, *Autobiography*, 1771–1784, p. 159.

20. Murdoch, "Sovereignty of Good," 1967, p. 95.

21. Richard Palmer, quoted in Pool, "Strange Bedfellows," 1989, p. 700. Compare Cicero, *De divinatione*, 2.13.30, "physicus, quo genere nihil adrogantius." Palmer, and Cicero, did not perhaps know any professor of surgery.

22. Murdoch, "Sovereignty of Good," 1967, p. 103.

23. White, *Justice as Translation*, 1989, p. 42. Our mutual acquaintance Richard Posner does not know how to read this way. See my review of White's book, a book by Stanley Fish, and a book by Posner: McCloskey, "Essential Rhetoric of Law," 1991.

24. Lavoie, ed., Introduction to *Economics and Hermeneutics*, 1992.

25. Smith, *Wealth*, 1776, 1.2, para. 2, p. 25.

26. Fleischacker, "Economics and the Ordinary Person," 2004.

27. Eliade, *Sacred and Profane*, 1957, p. 23.

28. Budziszewski, 'Religion and Civic Culture," 1992, p. 52.

29. Mencken, "Theodore Dreiser," 1916, p. 49.

30. Mencken, "Theodore Dreiser," 1916, p. 51.

31. Murdoch, " 'God' and 'Good,' " 1969, p. 50.

32. Mencken, "On Being an American," 1922, p. 19 and throughout. Compare Mark Twain in *Following the Equator* (1897), motto to chap. 28, quoted from *Pudd'nhead Wilson's New Calendar, Century Magazine*: "Let us be thankful for the fools. But for them the rest of us could not succeed."

33. Koehn, "Virtue Ethics," 2005, p. 535.

34. Holmes, "Address," 1895, p. 266.

35. Quoted in Alschuler, *Law without Values*, 2000, p. 43.

36. Kant, *Critique of Practical Reason*, 1788, Conclusion.

CHAPTER 15: ECONOMIC THEOLOGY

1. Sen, *Ethics and Economics*, 1987, p. 50.

2. These are the titles of three of his other books, of 1977, 1983, and 2000.

3. Nelson, *Economics as Religion*, 2001, p. 267.

4. Nelson, *Reaching for Heaven on Earth*, 1991.

5. http://www.perc.org/aboutperc/index.php.

6. Hirschman, *Exit, Voice, and Loyalty*, 1970.

CHAPTER 16: THE GOOD OF COURAGE

1. *Oxford Latin Dictionary*, 1982, "uirtus," "uir," "mulier."

2. For example, Tacitus, *Germania*, 18, *Ne se mulier extra* virtutem . . . *putet*; 19, 30 (*virtutem numerare*: count on bravery); *pudicitia*, p. 19. Compare Plutarch, "Gaius Marius," para. 19, on the women of the Ambrones, apparently also *Germani*, "armed with swords and axes," enduring battle "to the end with unbroken spirits."

3. Milton, *Paradise Lost*, 1667, 5.772, as reported by Raphael. By no accident the same phrase is used by God earlier in the book in promising the Messiah (5.601).

4. Personal discussion, October 2003.

5. Strauss, *Thoughts on Machiavelli*, 1958 p. 47.

6. Mansfield, *Machiavelli's Virtue*, 1966, pp. 31, 36; and last quotation, p. 42, italics supplied.

7. Mansfield and Tarcov, Introduction, 1996, to Machiavelli, *Discourses on Livy*, p. xxi.

8. Davidoff and Hall, *Family Fortunes*, 1987, p. 229.

9. Holmes, "Address," 1895, p. 265.

10. Smith, *Lectures on Jurisprudence*, 1766, sec. 300, p. 527.

11. Lattimore, trans. *The Iliad of Homer*, 1951, bk. 1, 225–226, 149.

12. Weil, "The *Iliad*," 1940, p. 163.

13. Herbert, *Still Life with a Bridle*, 1991, pp. 114–115.

14. Homer, *Odyssey*, Fitzgerald, trans., p. 239.

15. White, *Heracles' Bow*, 1984, chap. 1; *Philoctetes*, c. 409 BC, line 111, where Odysseus says, "When one does something for gain, one need not blush."

16. *Njal's Saga*, c. 1275, sec. 19, p. 73.

17. Macaulay, "Horatius," 1842, stanzas 36–50, 57.

18. T. Livius, *Ab urbe condita*, 2.10.9, "undique." By the way, archaeological evidence suggests that despite Horatius's heroics the Etruscans did in fact reconquer Rome.

19. Hanson, *Western Way of War*, 1989, p. 5.

20. Hanson, "Land Warfare in Thucydides," 1996, pp. 606–607. And see Hanson, *Western Way of War*, 1989, chap. 4.

21. Keeley, *War Before Civilization*, 1996, pp. 34, 189.

22. McNeill, *Pursuit of Power*, 1982, p. 128.

23. U.S. labor force in Protective Services (table 629, minus firefighters, brave but not aggressive) and in the Armed Forces (table 542), mostly men, from U.S. Bureau of the Census, *Statistical Abstract of the United States: 1992* (Government Printing Office, 1992).

24. Nederlands Instituut, "Srebrenica: A Safe Area," 2002, pp. 5, 6.

25. Nederlands Instituut, "Srebrenica: A Safe Area," 2002, p. 3.

26. Nederlands Instituut, "Srebrenica: A Safe Area," 2002, p. 4.

27. Nederlands Instituut, "Srebrenica: A Safe Area," 2002, p. 6.

28. Nederlands Instituut, "Srebrenica: A Safe Area," 2002, p. 6.

29. Nederlands Instituut, "Srebrenica: A Safe Area," 2002, p. 4.

30. Quoted in Emerson, "Napoleon," 1850, p. 345.

31. Jullien, *Treatise of Efficacy*, 1996.

32. Sun Tzu, *The Art of War*, Giles translation (1910), chap. 4, at http://www.chinapage.com/sunzi-e.html.

33. Jullien, *Treatise on Efficacy*, 1996, p. 197.

CHAPTER 17: ANACHRONISTIC COURAGE IN THE BOURGEOISIE

1. Quoted in Everitt, *Cicero*, 2001, p. 46. The translation is that of Fagles, *The Iliad*, 1990, 6.247 (p. 202), whose "my boy" is not literally in the Greek (6.208), but does seem to capture the tone of the passage.

2. Hanson, *Western Way of War*, 1989, p. 41.

3. Page, *Chronicles of Vikings*, 1995, p. 25.

4. Byock, *Viking Age*, 2001, pp. 149–158.

5. Langford, *Polite and Commercial People*, 1992, p. 34.

6. Cannadine, *Decline and Fall*, 1990, appendix B, p. 711; and discussion pp. 206–222.

7. Hollingsworth, "A Demographic Study of the British Ducal Families," 1957, table 3.

8. Mill, *Subjection of Women*, 1869, p. 43.

9. Reddy, *Navigation of Feeling*, 2001.

10. McNeill, *Pursuit of Power,* 1982, pp. 104–105.

11. Austen, *Persuasion,* 1818, pp. 73, 74.

12. Keegan, *The Face of Battle,* 1976 (1978), pp. 190, 322, italics supplied.

13. Tompkins, *West of Everything,* 1992, pp. 145, 146.

14. Bill Brown, *Reading the West,* 1997, p. 269.

15. Schaefer, "Interview," in Schaefer, *Shane,* 1984, ed. J. C. Work, p. 278.

16. Dykstra, *Cattle Towns,* 1968, pp. 146, 148, 143.

17. Lacy and Ashe, *The Arthurian Handbook,* 1997, pp. 3–4.

18. Fadiman, Introduction, to Van Tilburg Clark, *The Ox-Bow Incident* (1941), 1942, p. vii.

19. Quoted in Brown, "Reading the West," 1997, p. 2.

20. Wheeler, *Deadwood Dick,* 1877, pp. 357–358.

21. McPherson, "Confederate Guerrilla," 2003, p. 21.

22. Shakespeare, *Rich. II,* 4.1.128, 134–135.

23. Brown, "Reading the West," 1997, pp. 35, 38, 40.

CHAPTER 18: TACITURN COURAGE AGAINST THE "FEMININE"

1. Tompkins, *West of Everything,* 1992.

2. Tompkins, *West of Everything,* 1992.

3. Homer, *Iliad,* Lombardo trans., 1997, pp. 506–513.

4. Rose, *Gender and Heroism,* 2002, p. xii.

5. Milton, *Paradise Regained,* 1671, 4.1–7.

6. Tompkins, *West of Everything,* 1992, p. 51, 52. Countryman and von Heussen-Countryman, *Shane,* 1999, pp. 15, 17.

7. Schaefer, *Shane,* 1949, pp. 72–73, 82.

8. Richard Fried, "Operation Polecat," 2002; and "Voting Against the Hammer and Sickle," 2003.

9. Lomax, *Cowboy Songs,* 1910.

10. French, *Cowboy Metaphysics,* 1997, p. 32.

11. Tompkins, "Me and My Shadow," 1987 (2001), p. 2141.

12. Mozart, *The Magic Flute,* 1791, act 2, scenes 2 and 19.

13. Pierpont, "Tough Guy," 2002, p. 68.

14. Hurston, *Their Eyes,* 1937, pp. 85, 74.

15. Tompkins, *West of Everything,* 1992, p. 44.

16. Brands, *TR: The Last Romantic,* 1997.

17. Cannadine, *Aspects,* 1994, p. 157.

18. Holmes numbers are given in Alschuler, *Law without Values,* 2000, p. 39.

19. Williams, "Transitional," *The Tempers,* 1913, at http://www.english.uiuc.edu/maps/poets/s_z/williams/additionalpoems.htm.

20. Rotella, "Synonymous with Kept," 2001, p. 242, with elisions.

21. Mann, *Death in Venice,* 1912, p. 72.

22. Brands, *TR,* 1997, pp. 32, xi–xii, 797–799, 802, 812; Dalton, *Theodore Roosevelt,* 2002, p. 504; Cannadine, *Aspects,* 1994, p. 157.

23. Tompkins, *West of Everything,* 1992, p. 33.

CHAPTER 19: BOURGEOIS VS. QUEER

1. D'Emilio and Freedman, *Intimate Matters*, 1997, p. v.

2. Aquinas, *Summa contra gentiles*, c. 1259–1264, bk. 3, pt. 3, chap. 122.

3. Boswell, *Christianity*, 1980, chap. 10, and esp. chap. 11, pp. 318–330 on Aquinas.

4. Gunther, *La construction*, 1995.

5. Vinen, *History in Fragments*, 2000, pp. 116–118, 114.

6. Schama, *Embarrassment*, 1987, p. 601. The next quotation is from p. 605.

7. Quinn, *Same-Sex Dynamics*, 1996, p. 367.

8. Vinen, *History in Fragments*, 2000, p. 154.

9. Chauncey, *Gay New York*, 1994, p. 353.

10. Sinfield, *Wilde Century*, 1994, pp. 3, 140.

11. Vyvyan Holland, *Son of Oscar Wilde* (1954), quoted in Sinfield, *The Wilde Century*, 1994, p. 126.

12. D'Emilio and Freedman, *Sexual Matters*, 1997, pp. 124, 129.

13. Vinen, *History in Fragments*, 2000, p. 117.

14. Hodges, *Alan Turing*, 1983, pp. 458, 462, 471.

15. London, *Sea Wolf*, 1904, pp. 3, 7, 9, 12, 14, 17, 20, 280; "I did it," p. 274. "My man," p. 280.

16. Hammett, *Maltese Falcon*, 1929, chaps. 4 and 5 (pp. 46–47, 49–50, 53).

17. Dickey, see p. 539n12 below.

18. Pierpont, "Tough Guy," 2002, p. 70.

19. Brown, "Reading the West," p. 38.

20. Vol. 1, no. 1, chap. 18, "Stanford's Dime Novel and Story Paper Collection," http://www-sul.stanford.edu/depts/dp/pennies/home.html.

21. Quinn, *Same-Sex Dynamics*, 1996, p. 35, quoting Stuart Henry, *Conquering Our Great American Plains*, 1930: Hickok "seemed effeminate," "feminine," "sissy," pp. 271, 275–276, 288.

22. Hemingway, *Sun Also Rises*, 1926, p. 28.

23. Willingham, "Sun Hasn't Set," 2002, p. 42; and Wagner-Martin, "The Romance of Desire," 2002, p. 54.

24. Mailer, *Naked and the Dead*, 1948, p. 340.

25. Willingham, "Sun Hasn't Set," 2002, throughout.

CHAPTER 20: BALANCING COURAGE

1. Lewis, *Babbitt*, 1922, chap. 3.

2. Thurber, "Secret Life," 1939, first paragraphs.

3. Knight, "Ethics of Competition," 1923, p. 39; compare p. 59.

4. Jackson, *Business Ethics*, 1996, p. 80.

5. Knight, "Ethics of Competition," 1923, p. 39, his italics.

6. Schumpeter, *Theory*, 1912, pp. 93–94.

7. Schumpeter, *Capitalism, Socialism*, 1942, chap. 11, pp. 127–128.

8. Dawidoff, *Fly Swatter*, pp. 12, 13, 15, 42, 91, 313–320, 336.

9. Lewis, *Screwtape Letters*, 1942, p. 31.

10. As Byock observes, *Viking Age*, 2001, p. 229.

11. Foot, "Virtues and Vices," 1978, pp. 2–3.

12. Johnson, *Journey*, 1775, p. 99, punctuation modernized.

13. Pincoffs, *Quandaries*, 1986, p. 78.

14. Hursthouse, *Virtue Ethics*, 1999, pp. 198–202.

15. Knight, "Ethics and the Economic," 1922, p. 30.

16. MacIntyre, *After Virtue*, 1981, p. 183. Elshtain, *Women and War*, 1987, pp. 52–56.

17. Berlin, "The Originality of Machiavelli," 1953, pp. 72, 76.

18. Plato, *Republic*, c. 360 BC, 4, Stephanus 442c–d, p. 1074.

19. Aristotle, *Politics*, c. 330 BC, 7.1.11, p. 281.

20. MacIntyre, *After Virtue*, 1981, p. 181.

21. Prindle, *Politics and Economics*, 2003, pp. 98, 70.

22. Aristotle, *Politics*, c. 330 BC, 7.1.4 (1323a), p. 280.

23. David Cannadine, *Aspects of Aristocracy*, 1994, p. 159; Vinen, *History in Fragments*, 2000, p. 159.

24. Foot, "Virtues and Vices," 1978, p. 18.

25. Dickens, *Dombey and Son*, 1848, p. 54.

26. Wolf, "Moral Saints," 1982, p. 81.

CHAPTER 21

1. Gadamer, *Truth and Method*, 1965, p. xxxviii.

2. Aristotle, *Nic. Ethics*, c. 330 BC, 1.6.15 (1097a).

3. Pufendorf, *On the Duty of Man*, 1673, bk. 1, chap. 5, "On duty to oneself," p. 46.

4. Williams, "Virtue," 1995, p. 707.

5. Coontz, *Way We Never Were*, 1992, p. 60.

6. Foot, *Natural Goodness*, 2001, p. 17.

7. Charry, "Happiness," 2004, p. 21.

8. Kant, *Grounding*, 1785.

9. Plato, *Definitions*, c. 350 BC, Stephanus 411d, p. 1679.

10. Aquinas, *Summa Theologiae*, c. 1270, Ia, IIae, q. 61, art. 3 and 4 (Aquinas, *Treatise on the Virtues*, c. 1270, pp. 112–113).

11. Aquinas, *Summa Theologiae*, c. 1270, Ia, IIae, q. 58, art. 4 (Aquinas, *Treatise on the Virtues*, p. 86). Also Ia, IIae, q. 65, art. 2 (Aquinas, *Treatise on the Virtues*, p. 143).

12. Aquinas, *Disputed Questions*, 1269–1273, "The Cardinal Virtues," art. 1, p. 109.

13. Yuengert, *Boundaries*, 2004, p. 13.

14. Hariman, Preface, 2003, p. viii.

15. Rorty, "Contemplation in Aristotle's *Ethics*," 1980, p. 380.

16. Aquinas, *Treatise on the Virtues*, c. 1270, q. 61, art. 3, 4.

17. Aristotle, *Nic. Ethics*, c. 330 BC, 6.5.

18. MacIntyre, *After Virtue*, 1981, pp. 178, 207–208.

19. Wolf, "Moral Saints," 1982, p. 80, line 7, "improving the welfare of others or of society as a whole," among many other places, four times on p. 80, for example; on p. 81; p. 85, middle; taken back on p. 93, top, but then, "This approach seems unlikely to succeed."

20. Butler, *Fifteen Sermons*, 1725, sermon 1, p. 371.

21. Shaftesbury, *Characteristics*, 1713 (1732), vol. 2, pp. 13–14. The evolutionary cast of the book is notable. For example, again, vol. 2, p. 18, "If the affection be . . . [an] advantage to the society . . . this must necessarily constitute what we call equity and right."

22. Stocker, "Schizophrenia," 1976, p. 72.

23. Quoted in Hariman, "Radical Sociality," 1999, p. 10.

24. Orwell, "Reflections on Gandhi," 1949, p. 1353.

25. I am indebted to Robin Rapp for this example.

26. I am indebted to Eduard Bonet for this *punt.*

27. Hughes, *Barcelona*, 1992, p. 26.

28. Cervantes, *Don Quixote*, 1604/1614, pt. 2, chap. 11, p. 534; pt. 1, chap. 13, p. 96; Sancho: pt. 1, chap. 10, p. 81; pt. 2, chap. 11, p. 533. Compare George Borrow in 1843 (*The Bible in Spain*, Preface): "You may draw the last cuarto from a Spaniard [or at any rate a Castilian], provided you will concede to him the title of cavalier, and rich man, for the old leaven still works as powerfully as in the time of the first Philip."

29. For example, Andreau, *Banking and Business in the Roman World*, 1987, p. 13: "Although it was fashionable to deplore moneylending for interest, the Greek and Latin elite members—in these periods at least—appear to have been at great pains to conceal their investments."

30. Aristotle, *Nic. Ethics*, c. 330 BC, 5.5 passim; compare 5.2.13.

31. Carney, *The Shape of the Past*, 1975, p. 197, quoted in Crossan, *Historical Jesus*, 1991, p. 55.

32. Plato, *Republic*, c. 360 BC, 4, Stephanus 550E.

33. Aristotle, *Politics*, c. 330 BC, end of 1258a, p. 28.

34. Aristotle, *Politics*, c. 330 BC, 1338b, p. 301.

35. Cicero, *On Duties*, 44 BC, 1.150–151.

36. Aristotle, *Nic. Ethics*, quoted in R. E. Houser, "The Virtue of Courage," 2002, p. 305.

CHAPTER 22: THE MONOMANIA OF IMMANUEL KANT

1. Aristotle, *Nic. Ethics*, c. 330 BC, 1.6.16 (1097a).

2. Kant, *Grounding*, 1785, p. 56–57.

3. Kant, *Grounding*, 1785, p. 57.

4. See Lisska, *Aquinas's Theory*, 1996, pp. 57, 73.

5. Hume, *Human Understanding*, 1748, last page, his italics.

6. Compare Putnam, *Realism*, 1990, p. 115; and discussion in McCloskey, *Knowledge and Persuasion*, 1994, p. 277 and p. 95ff.

7. Richard Rumbold, speech on the gallows, Edinburgh, 1685, from *The World's Famous Orations: Great Britain: I (710–1777)*, 1906. In full at http://www.bartleby.com/268/3/15.html.

8. Frederick II, *Anti-Machiavel*, 1740, chap. 1.

9. Macaulay, "Frederic the Great," 1842, p. 188.

10. Kuehn, *Kant*, 2001, p. 272.

11. Pluhar, Translator's Introduction, 1987, p. xxxi, note 8.

12. Kuehn, *Kant*, 2001, p. 281; compare pp. 27, 43.

13. Quoted in Kuehn, *Kant,* 2001, p. 43.

14. I am such an incompetent scholar of Kant and of Boswell that on finding this on the Internet I believed for a day or so that it was genuine.

15. Kuehn, *Kant,* 2001, p. 157.

16. Kuehn, *Kant,* 2001, p. 241.

17. Kuehn, *Kant,* 2001, p. 163.

18. Kuehn, *Kant,* 2001, p. 155.

19. Kuehn, *Kant,* 2001, p. 155.

20. Kuehn, *Kant,* 2001, p. 156.

21. Williams, *Ethics,* 1985, pp. 197, 127.

22. Rumbold's speech on the gallows: http://www.bartleby.com/268/3/15.html.

CHAPTER 23: THE STORIED CHARACTER OF VIRTUE

1. Hursthouse, "Virtue Theory and Abortion," 1991, p. 224, and her comparison of virtue theory with Kantian and utilitarian theories at pp. 217–219.

2. Nussbaum, *Fragility of Goodness,* 1986, p. 14.

3. Hursthouse, *Virtue Ethics,* 1999, pp. 18, 59. Notice that Hursthouse uses "moral" and "ethical" as synonyms.

4. Mill, "The Mind and Character of Jeremy Bentham," 1838, p. 317.

5. Hariman, "Theory without Modernity," 2003, p. 7.

6. Lanham, *Electronic Word,* 1993, pp. 79ff.

7. McCloskey, *If You're So Smart,* 1990.

8. A point made by the economist Gary Walton in *Beyond Winning,* 1991.

9. Williams and Underwood, *Science of Hitting,* 1986 (1970), p. 7.

10. Brodkey, "Writing," 1994.

11. Shaftesbury, *Characteristics,* 1713 (1732), vol. 2, p. 99.

12. Compare McDowell, "Virtue and Reason," 1979, pp. 144–147.

13. Hursthouse, *Virtue Ethics,* 1999, p. 35.

14. Hursthouse, *Virtue Ethics,* 1999, pp. 60, 39ff, 57–58.

15. Upchurch, *Convicted in the Womb,* 1996, pp. 81–84.

16. Kant, *Grounding,* 1785, p. 398.

17. Murdoch, "Sovereignty of Good," 1967, p. 80.

18. Murdoch, "Sovereignty of Good," 1967, p. 80.

CHAPTER 24: EVIL AS IMBALANCE, INNER AND OUTER

1. Williams, *Moral Luck,* 1981, p. x.

2. Hursthouse, *Virtue Ethics,* 1999, p. 22.

3. MacIntyre, *Whose Justice,* 1988, p. 175, italics supplied.

4. MacIntyre, *After Virtue,* 1981, p. 206.

5. Wolfe, *Moral Freedom,* 2001, pp. 21, 23ff.

6. Murdoch, "Sovereignty of Good," 1967, p. 95.

7. Midgley, *Wickedness,* 1984, p. 147. Shakespeare, *Othello,* 1.1.154 (in the Oxford edition given in Greenblatt, ed., *The Norton Shakespeare*).

8. Coleridge, *Omniana* (1812), quoted at http://www.clicknotes.com/othello/motiveless. html.

9. Fish, *How Milton Works*, 2001, throughout, for example, pp. 47, 57, 92.

10. Lewis, "Satan," 1942, p. 200.

11. Lewis, *Screwtape Letters*, 1943, p. xi.

12. Milton, *Paradise Lost*, 1667, 4.108–110; 1.262–263. London's use of Milton: James Dickey, Introduction to his edition of *The Call of the Wild, White Fang, and Other Stories* (1961), quoted in Jack London, *The Sea Wolf*, ed. Gary Kinder, (New York: Modern Library, 2000), p. 293.

13. Ryan, "Human Nature," 1987, p. 218.

14. Sartre, *Anti-Semite*, 1944, pp. 46–47.

15. http://us.imdb.com/title/tt0025913/

16. Doris, *Lack of Character*, 2002, p. 54.

17. Doris, *Lack of Character*, 2002, pp. 39–51 and throughout.

18. Quoted in Elshtain, "Addams, Jane," 1995, p. 14.

19. Butler, *Fifteen Sermons*, 1725, preface, p. 352.

20. Midgley, *Wickedness*, 1984, p. 14.

21. Foot, *Natural Goodness*, 2001, pp. 16, 116.

22. Aquinas, *Summa contra gentiles*, c. 1259–1264, bk. 3, pt. 3.

23. Midgley, *Wickedness*, 1984, p. 14.

24. Aquinas, *Disputed Questions*, 1269–1272, "The Cardinal Virtues," art. 1, p. 106.

25. Aristotle, *Nic. Ethics*, c. 330 BC, 7.1.4 (1155b).

26. Justinian, *Institutes*, AD 533, p. 1, "Iustitia est constans et perpetua voluntas ius suum cuique tribunes."

27. Aristotle, *Nic. Ethics*, c. 330 BC, 5.6.8 (1134b).

28. Sacks, 2002, *Dignity of Difference*, p. 92.

29. Fleischacker, *Short History*, 2004b, p. 2 and throughout.

30. Fleischacker, *Short History*, 2004b; and "Economics and the Ordinary," 2004c.

31. Cannadine, *Class in Britain*, 1998, p. 167.

CHAPTER 25: THE PAGAN-ETHICAL BOURGEOIS

1. For the following: Kraaij, *Royal Palace*, 1997, pp. 10, 12, 14, 23, 42–47; Huisken, *Royal Palace*, 1996, pp. 22–23; Goossens, *Treasure Wrought*, 1996, pp. 16–17, 22, 28.

2. Geyl, *Netherlands*, 1936, p. 540.

3. Rosand, *Myths of Venice*, 2001, p. 97.

4. Hoxby, *Mammon's Music*, 2002, p. 107.

5. Eddy de Jongh, who started the business of reading moral messages in paintings like a text, has some second thoughts in Jongh, "Some Notes on Interpretation," 1991. In the same volume Eric Sluijter mounts a brilliant assault on the didactic hypothesis.

6. Fuchs, *Dutch Painting*, 1978.

7. Temple, *Observations*, 1673, 4, p. 92; "not" and "hopes": *sic.*

8. Temple, *Observations*, 1673, 4, p. 84.

9. Huizinga, "Dutch Civilization," 1941, p. 20; Israel, *Dutch Republic*, 1995, p. 222.

10. Huizinga, "Spirit of the Netherlands," 1935, p. 31.

11. Quoted in Houser, "Virtue of Courage," 2002, p. 306.

12. Cicero, *On Duties*, 44 BC, 1.61.

13. Justinian, *Institutes*, 533 BC, p. 1, sec. 1.1.

14. Complete, scannable texts are given at http://www-tech.mit.edu/Shakespeare/.

15. Shaftesbury, *Characteristics*, 1713, vol. 4, p. 4. Compare p. 8: "honest or moral character."

16. For example, Shakespeare, *Othello*, 1.3.283, 293, 382; and 2.1.198; 2.3.6, 125, 160, 230, 249, 309–315; 3.1.20–21, 38; 3.2.5; 3.3.105–107, 123, 130, 134, 158, 229, 247, 262, 380–389, 417, 438; 5.1.32; 5.2.79, 155, 161 (*Norton Shakespeare*).

17. Casey, *Pagan Virtue*, 1990, p. 83.

18. Ruskin, *Stones of Venice*, 1851–1853, vol. 2, chap. 8, "The Ducal Palace," para. 64, p. 328.

19. Bellah, *Imagining Japan*, 2003, p. 42.

20. Aron, *Memoirs*, 1983, p. 330.

21. Santoni, *Bad Faith, Good Faith*, 1995, pp. xvi–xvii.

22. Quoted in Todorov, *Hope and Memory*, 2000, p. 35.

23. Santoni, *Bad Faith, Good Faith*, 1995, p. 187.

24. Shklar, "Montesquieu," 1990, p. 268.

CHAPTER 26: THE SYSTEM OF THE VIRTUES

1. Aquinas, *Summa Theologiae*, c. 1270, Iae, Ia, q. 96, art. 3; and q. 54, art. 2, to which he refers, quoted in Lisska, *Aquinas's Theory*, 1996, p. 285, is the source of the motto by Aquinas.

2. See the discussion of this in Rudi Keller, *On Language Change*, 1990, for example, p. 46.

3. Smith, *Moral Sentiments*, 1790, p. 237.

4. Smith, *Moral Sentiments*, 1790, pp. 237–238. Compare pp. 268–269, 271. He has a confusing discussion on p. 189 (an older section) in which he analyses prudence as temperance plus wisdom, *sophia*. But in the passage I quote he is adhering to Aquinian divisions.

5. MacIntyre, *Dependent Rational Animals*, 1999, p. 5; compare pp. 155–156.

6. Charry, "Happiness," 2004, p. 28.

7. Schweiker, *Theological Ethics*, 2004.

8. Frankfurt, *Reasons of Love*, 2004, p. 7.

9. Frankfurt, *Reasons of Love*, 2004, p. 8.

10. Frankfurt, *Reasons of Love*, 2004, p. 11.

11. Frankfurt, *Reasons of Love*, 2004, p. 28.

12. Foot, *Natural Goodness*, 2001, p. 14.

13. The phrase from Frankfurt, *Reasons of Love*, 2004, is from p. 29.

14. Knight, "Ethics and the Economic," 1922, in Knight, *Ethics of Competition*, 1935, p. 22.

15. Ignatieff, *Needs of Strangers*, 1984, pp. 17, 15.

16. Held, *Feminist Morality*, 1993, p. 62.

17. Baier, *Moral Prejudices*, 1994, pp. 53, 62–63.

18. Tillich, *Courage to Be*, 1952, pp. 86–96.

19. Nelson, *Feminism, Objectivity*, 1996, pp. 10–19, 28–34, 45.

20. Nelson, *Feminism, Objectivity*, 1996, p. 136.

21. Hursthouse, *Virtue Ethics*, 1999, p. 41.

22. Hursthouse, *Virtue Ethics*, 1999, p. 155.

CHAPTER 27: A PHILOSOPHICAL PSYCHOLOGY?

1. Danielson, personal conversation, January 2005. At the University of British Columbia Danielson runs an amazing inquiry into what people actually think about the virtues.

2. Peterson and Seligman, *Character Strengths and Virtues*, 2004, p. 13.

3. Peterson and Seligman, *Character Strengths and Virtues*, 2004, p. 30.

4. Aquinas, *Summa theologiae*, c. 1270, Ia, IIae, q. 57, art. 1 (Aquinas, *Treatise on the Virtues*).

5. Haslam in Peterson and Seligman, *Character Strengths and Virtues*, 2004, p. 480; Cicero, *On Duties*, 1.27.93.

6. Aquinas, *Summa Theologiae*, c. 1270, Ia, IIae, q. 61, art. 3 and 4 (Aquinas, *Treatise on the Virtues*, pp. 112–113).

7. Aquinas, *Summa Theologiae*, c. 1270, Ia, IIae, q. 58, art. 4 (Aquinas, *Treatise on the Virtues*, p. 86). Also Ia, IIae, q. 65, art. 2 (Aquinas, *Treatise on the Virtues*, p. 143).

8. As do Jonsen and Toulmin, *Casuistry*, 1988, pp. 58–74.

9. Cited in Novak, *Business as a Calling*, 1996, p. 2.

10. Quoted in Peterson and Seligman, *Character Strengths and Virtues*, 2004, p. 39.

11. Peterson and Seligman, *Character Strengths and Virtues*, 2004, p. 39. The other two of his dimensions are analytic and creative intelligence. Sternberg, by the way, suffered from test anxiety as a child and has become an eloquent spokesman against one-dimensional theories of intelligence.

12. Sarah Broadie accepts her coeditor Christopher Rowe's translation of "wisdom" unmodified as the word for *phronesis*. But she makes clear that it is practical, not theoretical, as the Philosopher himself said (Broadie, "Philosophical Introduction," 2002, p. 46).

13. Haslam, "Prudence," in Peterson and Seligman, *Character Strengths and Virtues*, 2004, p. 482.

14. Haslam, "Prudence," in Peterson and Seligman, *Character Strengths and Virtues*, 2004, p. 480, italics supplied.

15. Doris, *Lack of Character*, 2002, p. 114.

16. Doris, *Lack of Character*, 2002, p. 105.

17. Doris, *Lack of Character*, 2002, p. 169. This is the last page—a short book, in which nonetheless Doris makes use of fully 750 items of bibliography, ranging from thorough use of Lifton on the Nazis to Conrad on Lord Jim.

CHAPTER 28: ETHICAL STRIVING

1. Rachels, *Elements*, 1999, p. 19.

2. White, "A Kantian Critique," 2005, p. 15.

3. Baier, "Ethics," 1994, p. 6.

4. The passage is noted and the identification with Smith asserted by a German translator in 1926 of *The Theory of Moral Sentiments*, Walther Eckstein, quoted in Raphael and Macfie, eds., Introduction to *Theory* (ed. of 1976), p. 31.

5. Berkowitz, Introduction, to *Virtue and the Making of Modern Liberalism*, 1999, at http://www.pupress.princeton.edu/chapters/i6565.html.

6. Frankfurt, *Reasons of Love*, 2004, pp. 26, 28.

7. Putnam, *Realism with a Human Face*, 1990; later works. McCloskey, *Knowledge and Persuasion*, 1994, chaps. 17 and 19, esp. p. 277.

8. If you think that, say, a National Academy of Science ensures that the science under its sponsorship is true and ethical, google "Lynn Conway," and find out from her how the National Academy under Bush has followed a program of unscientific homo- and transphobia.

9. Sayre, *Rosalind Franklin*, 1975, pp. 18–23, 191–194.

10. Sykes, *Seven Daughters*, 2001, pp. 152, 165.

11. McInerny, Preface to Aquinas, *Disputed Questions*, 1999, p. xv.

12. DePaul and Zagzebski, eds., *Intellectual Virtue*, 2003. No one in the volume seems to know that Putnam is now a supporter of this position.

13. Anscombe, "Modern Moral Philosophy," 1958, p. 34.

14. Rorty, "Science as Solidarity," 1987, p. 42.

15. Rorty, "Ethics without Principles," 1994 (1999), pp. 82–83.

16. Hampshire, Postscript, 1982, to Hampshire, *Thought and Action*, 1959, p. 289.

17. Charry, *Renewing of Your Minds*, 1997, p. 236.

18. Charry, *Renewing of Your Minds*, 1997, p. 232.

19. Charry, *Renewing of Your Minds*, 1997, p. viii.

20. Sayre, *Rosalind Franklin*, 1975, p. 195.

21. Coase, "Lives of the Laureates," 1994, p. 190.

22. Buchanan, "Lives of the Laureates," 1987, p. 139.

23. Hariman, "Theory without Modernity," 2003, p. 7.

24. *Book of Knowledge*, vol. 14, p. 4445. One of the pleasures for a child reading the books was their system of continuous pagination, producing heroically large sums to read up to, such as 4445.

25. Compare Hursthouse, *Virtue Ethics*, 1999, p. 142n: "In the modern, English-speaking world, it is easy to forget that many children used to be brought up on stories in which the heroes (and sometimes heroines) constantly spoke of what was noble."

26. Green, "The Bookie of Virtue," 2003.

27. Miller, *Death*, 1949, p. 41.

28. Miller, *Death*, 1949, p. 28.

29. Miller, *Death*, 1949, pp. 64–65.

30. Miller, *Death*, 1949, pp. 29–30.

31. Miller, *Death*, 1949, pp. 50–51.

32. Van Staveren, *Caring for Economics*, 1999, p. 170; and see her book from this, *Values of Economics*, 2001.

33. Hariman, *Prudence*, 2003, p. 13.

34. Van Staveren, *Caring for Economics*, 1999, p. 171.

CHAPTER 29: ETHICAL REALISM

1. Keegan, *Face of Battle*, 1976 (1978), chap. 1.

2. James, *Pragmatism*, 1907, p. 262.

3. Rorty, *Consequences*, 1982, p. xiv.

4. James, *Pragmatism*, 1907, p. 259.

5. McCloskey, *Rhetoric of Economics*, 1985, pp. 45–46.

6. Booth, *Modern Dogma*, 1974.

7. Putnam, *Realism*, 1990, pp. vii, 115.

8. Toulmin, *Human Understanding*, 1972, p. vii.

9. Harré, *Varieties of Realism*, 1986, p. 90.

10. Blaug, *Methodology of Economics*, 1980, p. 131.

11. Hausman and McPherson, *Economic Analysis and Moral Philosophy*, 1996, p. 212.

12. Hausman and McPherson, *Economic Analysis and Moral Philosophy*, 1996, p. 212.

13. Lewis, *Mere Christianity*, 1952, p. 35.

14. Murdoch, *Metaphysics*, 1992, p. 26.

15. Hampshire, Postscript, 1982, to Hampshire, *Thought and Action*, 1959, p. 274.

16. Kant, *Practical Reason*, 1788, 6, problem 2, "Remark."

CHAPTER 30: AGAINST REDUCTION

1. Mill, "The Mind and Character of Jeremy Bentham," 1838, p. 318, italics his.

2. I am indebted to Eli Berman of the University of California at San Diego for a discussion of these matters.

3. Frank, *What Price the Moral High Ground?* 2004, p. 26.

4. Sen, *Ethics and Economics*, 1987, p. 13.

5. Hammett, *Maltese Falcon*, 1929, p. 215.

6. Frank, *Passions within Reason*, 1988, p. xi.

7. Frankfurt, *Reasons of Love*, 2004, p. 42.

8. Peterson and Seligman, eds., *Character Strengths and Virtues*, 2004, p. 19.

9. Tocqueville, *Democracy in America*, 1840, vol. 2, p. 130.

10. Nozick, *Invariances*, 2001, p. 244. The next two quotations are from pp. 246 and 256.

11. Nozick, *Invariances*, 2001, p. 248.

12. Nozick, *Invariances*, 2001, p. 280. *The Examined Life*, 1989, pp. 212–215.

13. Nozick, *Philosophical Explanations*, 1981, chap. 5, pp. 499–570. Notably, the last book (2001) has the same structure as the 1981 one: epistemology, metaphysics (especially free will), and ethics.

14. Nozick, *The Examined Life*, 1989, pp. 214–215.

15. Nozick, *Philosophical Explanations*, 1981, pp. 515ff.

16. Nozick, *Invariances*, 2001, p. 288.

17. This is the model pioneered by Lawrence Iannoccone in the 1970s, explained in Iannoccone, "Introduction to the Economics of Religion," 1998.

18. Cox, *Imperial Fault Lines*, 2002, and personal correspondence.

19. White 2004, "Weakness of Will," surveys the contributions, pp. 4–6.

20. Strachey, *Eminent Victorians* 1918, p. 84.

CHAPTER 31: CHARACTER(S)

1. Smith, *Moral Sentiments*, 1790, pp. 294, 137; and part 1, "Of the Propriety of Action," to which merit (part 2), duty (3), utility (4), and custom (5) are subordinated.

2. Hariman, "Theory without Modernity," 2003, p. 8.

3. Gray, *Isaiah Berlin*, 1996, p. 44, italics omitted.

4. Lomasky, *Persons, Rights*, 1987; Nozick, *Anarchy, State*, 1974, p. 245.

5. Hampshire, 1989, p. 108, quoted in Gray, *Isaiah Berlin*, 1996, p. 54.

6. Lewis, *The Four Loves*, 1960, p. 116.

7. Novak, *Business as a Calling*.

CHAPTER 32: ANTIMONISM AGAIN

1. Hampshire, "Justice is Strife," 1991.

2. Arendt, *Human Condition*, 1958, p. 17.

3. Collins, *Artificial Experts*, 1990.

4. Hursthouse, *Virtue Ethics*, 1999, p. 54.

5. Jonsen and Toulmin, *Casuistry*, 1988, p. 286.

6. Jonsen and Toulmin, *Casuistry*, 1988, p. 289.

7. Fordyce, *Element of Moral Philosophy*, 1754, pp. 98–99.

8. Thomas Kennedy, Introduction (2003) to Fordyce, *Element of Moral Philosophy*, 1754, p. x.

9. MacIntyre, *After Virtue*, 1981, p. 180.

10. Aristotle, *Nic. Ethics*, c. 330 BC, 3.3.10 (1112b), and the long discussion at 3.2 (of choice) and 3.3 (of deliberation).

11. McDowell, "Virtue and Reason," 1979, p. 162.

12. Fodor, "The Trouble with Psychological Darwinism," 1998.

13. Berlin, *Crooked Timber*, 1998, pp. 11–12.

14. Gray, *Isaiah Berlin*, 1996, p. 25. In a review of Gray's book in *Reason* magazine, Chandran Kukathas, "What's the Big Idea?" 1996, plausibly disputes that Berlin was quite such a hedgehog.

15. Nozick, *Anarchy, State*, 1974, p. 310.

16. Gray, *Isaiah Berlin*, 1996, pp. 45–46.

17. Berlin, *Against the Current*, 1979, p. 74.

18. Sen, *Development as Freedom*, 2000, pp. 1242–1245.

19. Leopardi, *Pensieri*, 1845, p. 29.

20. See, for example, Robert Shalhope, "American Revolution," 1995, p. 24.

21. Hodges, *Alan Turing*, 1983, p. 154, quoting from *Wittgenstein's Lectures on the Foundations of Mathematics*, Cambridge, 1939.

22. Compare David Schmidtz's "ethical dualism" in Schmidtz, *Rational Choice*, 1995.

23. Stock 1992 , quoted in Johnston, *Radical Middle Class*, 2003, p. 11.

CHAPTER 33: WHY NOT ONE VIRTUE?

1. Aquinas, *Disputed Questions*, 1269–1272, "The Cardinal Virtues," art. 1, p. 112.

2. Cates, "Virtue of Temperance," 2002, p. 330.

3. Aquinas, *Summa Theologiae*, c. 1270, IIa, IIae, q. 151, art. 1 (Aquinas, *Treatise on the Virtues*).

4. Aquinas, *Summa Theologiae*, c. 1270, IIa, IIae, q. 117, art. 5 (Aquinas, *Treatise on the Virtues*).

5. Deursen, "Dutch Republic," 1999, p. 171.

6. As Philippa Foot wrote in 1978, "*Summa Theologica* is one of the best sources we have for moral philosophy, and moreover . . . St. Thomas' ethical writings are as useful to the atheist as to the . . . Christian believer" ("Virtues and Vices," p. 2).

7. Murdoch, "Sovereignty of Good," 1967, p. 98.

8. Murdoch, "Sovereignty of Good," 1967, p. 99.

9. Murdoch, "Sovereignty of Good," 1967, p. 98.

10. Dreiser, *American Tragedy*, 1925, pp. 65–66.

11. McInerny, Preface to Aquinas, *Disputed Questions*, 1999, p. xi.

12. Murdoch, "Sovereignty of Good," 1967, p. 95.

13. Budziszewski, *The Resurrection of Nature*, 1986, p. 156.

14. Smith, *Theory*, 1790, p. 20. See Solomon, "Sympathy for Adam Smith," 2004, p. 6.

15. Smith, *Theory*, 1790, p. 113.

16. Chap. 13, sec. 4, of Hobbes, *Elements of Law*, 1640.

CHAPTER 34: DROPPING THE VIRTUES, 1532–1958

1. Quoted by West, ed., in Bacon, *Essays*, 1625, p. xiii.

2. Ginzburg, "Diventare Machiavelli," n.d.

3. Aquinas, *Summa Theologiae*, c. 1270, Ia, IIae, q. 57, art. 4, "Response" (Aquinas, *Treatise on the Virtues*, p. 73); compare art. 3, "Response" (Aquinas, *Treatise on the Virtues*, p. 71). Compare McInerny, Preface to Aquinas, *Disputed Questions*, 1999, p. xiii.

4. Hobbes, *Leviathan*, 1651, vol. 1, chap. 6.

5. Hobbes, *Leviathan*, 1651, vol. 1, chap. 4.

6. Hariman, "Theory without Modernity," 2003, p. 7, and especially note 28 on p. 29.

7. Jonsen and Toulmin, *Casuistry*, 1988, p. 19.

8. Jonsen and Toulmin, *Casuistry*, 1988, p. 8.

9. Little, *Religious Poverty*, 1978, p. 174.

10. Jonsen and Toulmin, *Casuistry*, 1988, p. 88.

11. Lanham, *Motives of Eloquence*, 1976, pp. 150–153.

12. I am indebted to my colleague Walter Benn Michaels for this point.

13. Woolf, "Jane Austen," 1925, p. 142.

14. Iser, "Interaction between Text and Reader," 1980, pp. 110–111.

15. Butler, *Jane Austen and the War of Ideas*, 1975, p. 271, quoted in Casey 1990, p. 164.

16. Casey, *Pagan Virtue*, 1990, p. 160.

17. Austen, *Selected Letters*, Chapman, ed., 1955, pp. 172–175 (Nov. 18, 1814).

18. Robert Conquest, "George Orwell," 1969, quoted in Hitchens, *Orwell's Victory*, 2002, p. 1.

19. Orwell, "Charles Dickens," 1940, p. 185.

20. Orwell, "As I Please," p. 707.

21. Orwell, "Review," 1944, p. 550.

22. Orwell, "Charles Dickens," 1940, p. 150.

23. Frye, "Dickens and the Comedy of Humors," 1968, p. 232.

24. Marx and Engels, *Communist Manifesto*, 1848, p. 76.

25. Hitchens, *Orwell's Victory*, 2002, pp. 30–31.

26. Orwell, "Charles Dickens," 1940, pp. 150–151.

27. Quoted in Hitchens, *Orwell's Victory*, 2002, p. 10.

CHAPTER 35: OTHER LISTS

1. Katherine Dahlsgaard was in charge of "lessons of history" in the project; Peterson and Seligman, *Character Strengths and Virtues*, 2004, p. 33.

2. Peterson and Seligman, *Character Strengths and Virtues*, 2004, chap. 3, pp. 53–85.

3. Weil, *The Need for Roots*, 1943 (1949), p, 10ff.

4. Gray, *Simone Weil*, 2001, pp. 43–44.

5. Reproduced in Godin, *Rules of Life*, 1996, pp. 50–51. Godin gives fifty-eight codes in full, from "Alcoholics Anonymous: The Twelve Steps" to "The Young Man's Training for an Effective Life." Compare *Peanuts*. Lucy: "Life is a mystery, Charlie Brown. . . . Do you have an answer?" Charlie: "Be kind, Don't smoke, Be prompt, Smile a lot, Eat sensibly, Avoid cavities, and Mark your ballot carefully. . . . Avoid too much sun, Send overseas packages early, Love all creatures above and below, Insure your belongings, and Try to keep the ball low." Lucy: "Hold real still because I'm going to hit you a very sharp blow on the nose" (*Classic Peanuts*, reproduced in the *Chicago Tribune*, March 23, 2005).

6. Jankélévitch's book on the philosophy of music was translated in 2003 and his *Forgiveness* in 2005.

7. DePaul and Zagzebski, eds., *Intellectual Virtue*, 2003, pp. 281–289.

CHAPTER 36: EASTERN AND OTHER WAYS

1. Murdoch, " 'God' and 'Good,' " 1969, p. 58.

2. Ivanhoe, *Confucian Moral*, 2000, pp. ix. I am retailing here chaps. 1 and especially 2 of his book.

3. Hursthouse, *Virtue Ethics*, 1999, p. 14.

4. The bibliography in Hursthouse, *Virtue Ethics*, 1999, is Oxbridge-centered. No Eastern philosopher figures are mentioned, and among past ethicists only Aristotle and Kant (Aquinas, for example, is mentioned once, but is not cited and does not appear to have influenced Hursthouse's thinking).

5. White, *Justice as Translation*, 1989, p. 65.

6. Lau's introduction to Confucius, *The Analects*, c. 497, p. 24.

7. Confucius, *Analects*, 10.8, p. 103. For a similarly relaxed attitude toward the pleasures of this world, compare Jesus at the wedding feast turning water into wine, to keep the party going.

8. Confucius, *Analects*, 9.31, p. 100.

9. *Dīgha Nikāya*, 3.180ff, reprinted in Embree, ed., *Sources*, 1988, p. 121.

10. *Vimalakirti Sutra*, AD 406, pp. 33–34.

11. Benedict, *Chrysanthemum*, 1946, p. 116. The vocabulary of "circles" is not peculiar to Benedict. Compare Iwao Taka, "Business Ethics in Japan," 1997.

12. Benedict, *Chrysanthemum*, 1946, p. 195.

13. Benedict, *Chrysanthemum*, 1946, p. 196.

14. Bellah, *Imagining Japan*, 2003, pp. 46–47.

15. Benedict, *Chrysanthemum*, 1946, p. 197.

16. Peterson and Seligman, *Character Strengths and Virtues*, 2004, p. 50.

17. Reddy, *Navigation of Feeling*, 2001, for example, p. 20.

18. Rorty, "Postmodernist Bourgeois Liberalism," 1985, p. 214.

19. Rorty, "Postmodernist Bourgeois Liberalism," 1985, p. 215. Rorty was here classifying "prudence" as amoral selfishness. I would not, and it matters for my disagreements with Rorty about *economics* (we agree about most other things) that I would not.

CHAPTER 37: NEEDING VIRTUES

1. Knight, "Ethics of Competition," 1923, p. 62.

2. Polanyi, *Logic of Liberty*, 1951, p. 106.

3. From chap. 7, proposition 3 of the Internet text of Hobbes's early *Elements of Law*, which Richard Tuck ("Hobbes," 1987, through whom the quotation was found) notes "contains the essentials of all his later political thought" (p. 210). www.knuten.liu.se/~bjoch509/works/hobbes/elements.txt.

4. Holmes, letter to Lady Pollock, Sept. 6, 1902, *Holmes-Pollock Letters*, 1941, vol. 1, p. 105.

5. Holmes, *Address . . . at the Dedication of the Northwestern University Law School Building*, quoted in Alschuler, *Law without Values*, 2000, p. 24.

6. Holmes, *Holmes-Laski Letters*, Dec. 3, 1917, quoted in Luban, "Justice Holmes," 1992, p. 244.

7. Holmes, *Holmes-Pollock Letters*, 1941, vol. 2, p. 36 (Feb. 1, 1920).

8. Holmes, "Natural Law" (1918), quoted in Alschuler, *Law without Values*, 2000, p. 192.

9. Masson, *Final Analysis*, 1990, pp. 39–40.

10. Booth, *Modern Dogma*, 1974, p. 13.

11. Booth, *Modern Dogma*, 1974, p. xi and chap. 2.

12. Santayana, *Persons and Places*, 1943–1953, p. 441.

13. Orwell, "Dickens," 1940, p. 184.

14. Blaug, *Methodology of Economics*, 1980, pp. 132–133.

15. Robbins, *Nature and Significance*, 1932, p. 134. Sen says that such a view was "quite unfashionable then" (Sen, *Ethics and Economics*, 1987). Not, I think, among the reigning fashionistas of 1932.

16. Russell, *Education and the Social Order*, quoted in James F. Perry, "The Dream Hypothesis, Transitions, and the Very Idea of Humanity," at http://www.bu.edu/wcp/Papers/Teac/TeacPerr.htm.

17. MacIntyre, *After Virtue*, 1981, p. 11, his italics.

18. Hobbes, *Leviathan*, 1651, vol. 1, chap. 15, p. 82; and vol. 1, chap. 6, p. 24.

19. Thucydides, *Peloponnesian War*, c. 404 BC, 5.89–111.

20. Rachels, *Elements*, 1999, p. 79.

21. Hariman, *Political Style*, 1995, pp. 29, 33.

22. Hariman, "Theory without Modernity," 2003, p. 27, note 15, quoting his own 1995 *Political Style*.

23. Maus, "Introduction to *Richard II*," 1997, p. 948.

24. Yuengert, *Boundaries*, 2004, p. 120.

25. Williams, *Morality*, 1972, p. 6; compare Murdoch, " 'God' and 'Good,' " 1969, p. 49.

26. Budziszewski, "The Real Issue: Escape from Nihilism," http://www.leaderu.com/real/ri9801/budziszewski.html. He is referring to Nietzsche's *Ecce Homo*: "Whoever knows how to breathe the air of my writings knows that it is an air of heights, a strong air. One must be made for it, otherwise there is no small danger to become chilled by it. The ice is near, the solitude is immense."

27. Quoted on p. 86 in MacFarquhar, "Bench Burner," 2001.

28. Luban, "Justice Holmes," 1992, p. 252.

29. Alschuler, *Law without Values*, 2000, p. 6.

30. Holmes, "Address," 1895, p. 265.

31. Trotsky, *The Defence of Terrorism* (*Terrorizm i Kommunizm*, 1920) quoted in Kolakowski, *Main Currents of Marxism*, vol. 2. p. 510. Compare Callicles in the *Gorgias* 483d: "Nature itself reveals that it's a just thing for the better man and more capable man to have a greater share" (trans. D. J. Zeyl).

32. Holmes, *Holmes-Pollock Letters*, 1941, vol. 2, p. 14 (May 26, 1919).

33. Holmes, *Holmes-Pollock Letters*, 1941, vol. 1, p. 75 (July 20, 1897).

34. Lombardo, "Eugenic Sterilization Laws," n.d.

35. Isacsson, "Sweden: Sterilization Policy," 1997.

36. White, "Kantian Critique," 2005, MS pp. 8-9.

37. Posner, *The Economics of Justice* (1983), quoted in White, "Kantian Critique," 2005, MS p. 12.

38. Holmes, "Address," 1895, p. 264.

39. Holmes, *Holmes-Laski Letters*, vol. 1, pp. 761-762, quoted in Alschuler, *Law without Values*, 2000, p. 6.

40. Ignatieff, *Needs of Strangers*, 1984, p. 30.

CHAPTER 38: *P & S* AND THE CAPITALIST LIFE

1. Eliade, *Sacred and Profane*, 1957, p. 14.

2. Stark, *One True God*, 2001, p.20.

3. See again Bellah, *Imagining Japan*, 2003, p. 13.

4. Benedict, *Chrysanthemum*, 1946, pp. 142-143, 121, 113, 115.

5. Fodor, "Trouble with Psychological Darwinism," 1998.

6. Sen, *Ethics and Economics*, 1987, p. 71.

7. McClay, "Strange Career of *The Lonely Crowd*," 1993, p. 397.

8. Mill, *Principles*, 1871, "Preliminary Remarks," p. 2.

9. MacIntyre, *After Virtue*, 1981, p. 187.

10. Hoffman and Spitzer, "Entitlements," 1985. Hoffman and Spitzer, with, for example, Forsythe, Horowitz, Savin, and Sefton, "Fairness," 1994, try to find a "rational," that is, a pure prudence, explanation for moral sentiments. The point is that they fail, as, for example, Eckel and Grossman, "Altruism," 1996, demonstrate.

11. Knight, "Economic Theory and Nationalism," 1934, pp. 306-307.

12. White, *Justice as Translation*, 1989, p. 70.

13. Nye, "Thinking about the State," 1997, pp. 132-133.

14. Heilbroner, *The Worldly Philosophers*, 1953, p. 201. Compare p. 156, "an owner-entrepreneur engaged in an endless race," and so forth.

15. Weber, *Protestant Ethic*, 1904–1905, p. 53.

16. Weber, *Protestant Ethic*, 1904–1905, p. 51, italics supplied.

17. Tronto, *Moral Boundaries*, 1993, p. 29.

18. Macfarlane, *Culture of Capitalism*, 1987, p. 226.

19. Smith, *Theory*, 1790, p. 173.

20. Jones, *Increasing Returns*, 1933, should be better known among economists. A student of Marshall, he anticipated the mathematics of the "residual." He died young, and his work was forgotten except by economic historians.

21. Dworkin, "Is Wealth a Value?" 1980. Posner conceded the point, but characteristically did not let his concession change his theory or his practice of law.

22. Aristotle, *Nich. Eth.* 1.5.8 (Rackham trans.), italics supplied.

23. Frank, *Passions within Reason*, 1988, p. 211.

24. Frank, *Passions within Reason*, 1988, p. 196ff. Bob: believe me on this one.

25. Frank, *Passions within Reason*, 1988, p. 256.

26. Frank, *Passions within Reason*, 1988, p. 258.

CHAPTER 39: SACRED REASONS

1. Velthuis, "The Instrumental," 1996,

2. Schjeldahl, "Dealership," 2004, p. 41.

3. Velthuis, "The Instrumental," 1996, [82].

4. Velthuis, "The Instrumental," 1996, [90].

5. Velthuis, "The Instrumental," 1996, [96].

6. Schjeldahl, "Dealership," 2004, p. 41.

7. Arjo Klamer, personal conversation.

8. http://www.doctorswithoutborders-usa.org/donate/, read on January 4, 2005.

9. Quoted in Pahl, *Friendship*, 2000, p. 62; compare Gray, *Isaiah Berlin*, 1996, p. 63: "We do not charge a consultation fee for listening to our friends' troubles and, if we did, that would signify the death of friendship as a practice among us."

10. Sen, *Ethics and Economics*, 1987, p. 19.

11. Greenblatt, *Will in the World*, 2004, p. 112.

12. Mill, "Essay V," 1874, para. 39.

13. Hume, *Principle of Morals*, app. II, pp. 301–302.

14. Butler, *Fifteen Sermons*, 1725, preface, p. 351.

15. Cicero, *De amicitia*, 21.80; p. 189 of Falconer trans.

16. Schmidtz, "Reasons for Altruism," 1993, p. 168.

17. Frankfurt, *Reasons of Love*, 2004, pp. 16, 22.

18. Damasio, *Descartes' Error*, 1994.

19. Frijda 1994 and Bower 1992 quoted in Reddy, *Navigation of Feeling*, 2001, pp. 23–24.

20. Schmidtz, "Reasons for Altruism," 1993, p. 167.

21. Emerson, "Napoleon," 1850, pp. 341, 351–352.

22. Johnson, *Napoleon*, 2002, p. 9.

CHAPTER 40: NOT BY *P* ALONE

1. Novak, *Business as a Calling*, 1996, p. 4.

2. Ulrich, *Martha Ballard*, 1990, p. 203.

3. If you wish for some reason to say it the way the Dutch do, say the vowel *ui* high in your mouth, like the *ou* in *out* the way Ontarians say it; and say the *g* the way Scots say the *ch* in *loch*: "zou-nich."

4. Personal correspondence, February 2005.

5. Schmidt, *Jip and Janneke 3*, 1956–1958, p. 95, italics mine.

6. McClelland, *Achievement Society*, 1961.

7. Lynn and Lynn, "National Values and Tipping," 2004, table 1, pp. 15–17 of the manuscript version. It is not entirely clear how to interpret blanks in the table. I think they mean "no tipping beyond compulsory additions to the bill" (as, for example, in Italy; I am puzzled by the 15 percent for France). Japan is not in the table: I am using travel handbooks, as Lynn and Lynn did in compiling their data.

8. Personal correspondence, February 2005.

9. At present Michael Lynn, a psychologist at the Cornell University School of Hotel Administration, and Ofer Azar, an economist at Northwestern University, seem to be the most prominent students of the matter.

10. Frank, *Passions within Reason*, 1988, p. 18. By "simply prudent" I mean "non-rule utilitarianism," the rule utilitarianism that Frank is invoking.

11. Jones, *Culture*, forthcoming, chap. 1.

12. Jones, *Culture*, forthcoming, chap. 1.

13. If you want to pronounce *overleg* as Dutch, make that last *g* into a *ch* as in Scots *loch* or German *ich*.

14. Van Staveren, *Caring for Economics*, 1999, p. 83.

15. Van Staveren, *Caring for Economics*, 1999, p. 88. A little surprisingly, she is summarizing and agreeing with Oliver Williamson here. What is surprising is that a Samuelsonian economist would be making such a point. But he is.

16. Folbre, *Invisible Heart*, 2001, p. vii.

17. Hunt, *Character and Culture*, 1997, p. 211.

CHAPTER 41: THE MYTH OF MODERN RATIONALITY

1. Dougherty, *Who's Afraid of Adam Smith?*, 2002, p. 83.

2. Quoted in Wood, *Broken Estate*, 1999, p. 262.

3. Flyvbjerg et al., "Cost Overruns," 2003. I thank Jens Jorgensen for telling me about Flyvbjerg's work.

4. Flyvbjerg, "Megaprojects," 2004, p. 87. But he needs to consider the Winner's Curse.

5. For the phrase the "invisible tongue" I thank a friend of Chuck Middleton.

6. Carruthers, "Trading," 1996.

7. Heckscher, *Mercantilism*, 1931, vol. 2, p. 137.

8. Higgs, "Regime Uncertainty," 1997.

9. Orr, "Darwinian Storytelling," 2003, p. 18.

10. Rorty, "Philosophy Envy," 2004, p. 21.

11. Medawar, *New York Review of Books*, Feb. 3, 1977, quoted in Hearnshaw, *Cyril Burt*, 1979, p. 317.

12. MacIntyre, *Dependent Rational Animals*, 1999, chap. 3, "The Intelligence of Dolphins."

13. Poole et al., "Animal Behavior," 2005.

14. Menand, "What Comes Naturally," 2002.

15. Turner, *Origins of Human Emotions*, 2000, pp. 52–59; compare Richerson and Boyd, *Not by Genes Alone*, 2004.

16. Seabright, *Company of Strangers*, 2004, p. 7.

17. Ostrom, Gardner, and Walker, *Rules, Games*, 1994, p. 322.

18. Fodor, "Trouble with Psychological Darwinism," 1998.

CHAPTER 42

1. Marx and Engels, *Communist Manifesto* 1848, p. 77.

2. Ellsberg, Introduction to Day, *Selected Writings*, 1983, p. xxv.

3. Tillich and Wegener, "Answer," 1919.

4. Nelson, *Economics as Religion*, 2001, p. 331.

5. Chaudhuri, *Passage to England*, 1959, p. 178; compare his chap. 5, "Money and the Englishman."

6. Knott, *Hinduism*, 1998, p. 15. Compare another translation in Embree, ed. *Sources of Indian Tradition*, 1988, vol. 1, p. 9. Sanskrit's cousinhood to Latin shows in *Agni: ignus*, hearth.

7. *Dīgha Nikāya*, 3.180ff., reprinted in Embree, ed., *Sources of Indian Tradition*, 1988, vol. 1, p. 120.

8. A. L. Basham, in Embree, ed., *Sources of Indian Tradition*, 1988, vol. 1, p. 151.

9. http://www.avesta.org/avesta.html, at Afrinagan Dahman.

10. Quoted in Sacks, *Dignity of Difference*, 2002, p. 87.

11. Both of these are mottoes to chap. 2 in Novak, *Business as a Calling*, 1996, p. 41.

12. Lawrence, 1901, p. 69.

13. Knight and Merriam, *Economic Order and Religion*, 1945, p. 36; the agreement of verse numbers is spooky but, especially for Matthew and Mark, literally so.

14. Stark, *One True God*, 2001, pp. 15, 19, 22, his italics.

15. Epictetus, *Book of Epictetus*, c. AD 130, p. xxv.

16. Crossan, *Historical Jesus*, 1991, p. xiii.

17. Wilkinson, *Prayer of Jabez*, 2000, p. 4, italics supplied.

18. Williams, *Morality*, 1972, p. 70.

CHAPTER 43: NECESSARY EXCESS?

1. Horowitz, *Morality of Spending*, 1985, pp. 166–167.

2. Horowitz, *Morality of Spending*, 1985, p. 168.

3. Douglas and Isherwood, 1979, quoted in van Staveren, *Caring for Economics*, 1999, p. 92.

4. Douglas, "Deciphering a Meal," 1972.

5. Chalfen, *Snapshot*, 1987.

6. Sahlins, *Stone Age Economics*, 1972, preface to 2003 ed., p. ix.

7. Hinze, "What is Enough?" 2004, esp. p. 179.

8. Hinze, "What is Enough?" 2004, p. 177.

9. Hinze, "What is Enough?" 2004, p. 179 again.

10. Bailey, "Of *Gomi* and *Gaijin*," 1999, p. 147.

11. Klemm, "Material Grace," 2004, p. 232.

12. Charry, "Happiness," 2004, p. 30.

13. Sayer, 1942, in Heath, ed., p. 432.

14. Pope, "Epistle to Burlington," 1732, lines 169–172.

15. Robert Fogel gives some interesting evidence on the rise and fall of stagnationism in Fogel, "Reconsidering Expectations," 2005.

16. http://www.templetons.com/brad/billg.html.

17. Clark, "Society of the Future," 1901.

18. Smith, *Theory*, 1790, p. 184ff. The suggestion that Smith is here contradicting Rousseau is H. B. Acton's, reported by the editors in note 6 on pp. 183–184.

19. Smith, *Theory*, 1790, p. 180.

20. Smith, *Theory*, 1790, p. 183. MacIntyre, *Dependent Rational Animals*, 1999, p. 2, criticizes Smith on similar grounds.

21. Rousseau, *Origin of Inequality*, 1755, pt. 2, p. 65.

22. Blewhitt in Clark, ed., *Commerce, Culture*, 2003, p. 228.

23. Smith, *Theory*, 1790, p. 313.

CHAPTER 44: GOOD WORK

1. Hunnicutt, *Kellogg's Six-Hour Day*, 1996, p. 12.

2. Fogel, *Escape from Hunger*, 2004, pp. 70–71.

3. McNeill, *Venice*, 1974, p. 100.

4. Weber, *General Economic History*, 1923, p. 365.

5. Little, *Religious Poverty*, 1978, p. 178, citing Le Goff, "Licit and Illicit Trades in the Medieval West," 1963 (trans. 1980).

6. Le Goff, "Licit and Illicit Trades," 1963, p. 61.

7. Le Goff, "Licit and Illicit Trades," 1963, p. 70.

8. Gerschenkron, *Europe in the Russian Mirror*, 1970, esp. chaps. 1 and 2.

9. Waterman, *Revolution, Economics, and Religion*, 1991, p. 14.

10. Ellsberg, "Introduction" to Day, *Selected Writings*, 1983, p. xvi.

11. Cosgel, "Religious Culture," 1993, on the Amish, and his work with others on the Shakers, for example, Murray and Cosgel, "Between God and Market," 1999.

12. Knight and Merriam, *Economic Order and Religion*, 1945, pp. 29, 30, 31, 46.

13. See, for example, Knight and Merriam, *Economic Order and Religion*, 1945, p. 48.

14. These are Pius: *Quadragesimo Anno*; John: *Mater et Magistra* and *Pacem in Terris*; Paul: *Populorum Progressio* and *Octogesima Adveniens*; and John Paul: *Laborem Exercens* and *Centesimus Annus*. Michael Novak is my guide here: *Catholic Social Thought*, 1984, chaps. 6–8.

15. Novak, *Catholic Social Thought*, 1984.

16. Leo XIII, 1891, *Rerum Novarum*, paragraph numbers given. See Aquinas *Summa Theologiae*, c. 1270, IIa, IIae, q. 66, quoted and discussed in Fleischacker, *A Short History*, 2004, p. 35 and note 40.

17. Hornby, *How to Be Good*, 2001, p. 210.

18. Knight and Merriam, *Economic Order and Religion*, 1945, p. 50.

19. Novak, *Catholic Social Thought*, 1984, p. xvi.

20. From the encyclical *Mater et Magistra*, 1961, quoted in Novak, *Catholic Social Thought*, 1984, p. xxii.

21. Erasmus, *Adages*, 1500–1533, 1508 onward, 1.1.1, p. 29 of Barker, ed.

22. Hornby, *How to Be Good*, 2001, p. 218.

CHAPTER 45: WAGE SLAVERY

1. Novak, *Business as a Calling*, 1996, p. 13.

2. Novak, *Business as a Calling*, 1996, p. 5.

3. Novak, *Business as a Calling*, 1996, p. 37.

4. Thus James Norwood Corbett, pp. 250–254, in Bowe, Bowe, and Streeter, *Gig*, 2000.

5. Maimonides, *Mishnah Torah*, c. 1200, quoted in Sacks, *Dignity of Difference*, 2000, p. 95.

6. Csikszentmihalyi, *Finding Flow*, 1997, pp. 31, 30, 32.

7. Nussbaum, *Fragility of Goodness*, 1986, p. 6, note 2. *Eudaimonia* is translated as "happiness," but means literally "the property of having a good guardian spirit."

8. Csikszentmihalyi, *Finding Flow*, 1997, pp. 2–3.

9. Shapin, *History of Truth*, 1994, p. 50.

10. Ricardo, *Principles of Political Economy*, 1817, p. 98.

11. Frye, "Dickens," 1968, p. 230.

12. Knight, "Ethics of Competition," 1923, p. 51.

13. Todorov, *Hope and Memory*, 2000, pp. 69–70, p. 48.

14. Terkel, *Working*.

15. Bowe, Bowe, and Streeter, *Gig*, 2000, p. xiii.

16. Auden, "Horae Canonicae," 1949–1954, sec. 3, Sext, 1, p. 477. When he wasn't being a poet, though, Auden had conventional leftish attitudes about alienation.

17. Le Guin, *Dispossessed*, 1974, p. 66, italics hers.

18. Lev, "The Great Migration of China," 2004, Dec. 27.

19. P. 38; compare Knight, "Ethics of Competition," 1923, p. 54: i.

20. Lodge, *Home Truths*, 1999, pp. 26–27.

21. Seeger, "I'm Gonna be an Engineer" (1971) © 1976, 1979 by Stormking Music, Inc. All rights reserved.

22. Schuttner, *Basic Stairbuilding*, 1998, p. 67ff.

CHAPTER 46: THE RICH

1. Nozick, *Anarchy, State*, 1974, pp. 156–162, is an accessible demolition.

2. Tacitus, *Germania*, AD 98, 14, p. 114.

3. Gordon and Walton, "A Theory of Regenerative Growth," 1982.

4. White, *Justice as Translation*, 1989, p. 74.

5. Nozick, *Anarchy, State*, 1974, p. 238.

6. Nozick, *Anarchy, State*, 1974, p. 238.

7. Folbre, *Invisible Heart*, 2001, p. xiii.

8. McCloskey and Klamer, "One Quarter," 1995.

9. Mueller, *Capitalism, Democracy,* 1999, pp. 24–25.

10. Kirzner, *Competition,* 1973, pp. 35, 65.

11. Quoted by Muller, *Mind and Market,* 2002, p. 3.

12. Aristotle, *Politics,* c. 430 BC, 1257b35.

13. Little, *Religious Poverty,* 1978, p. 178.

CHAPTER 47: GOOD BARONS

1. Moore, *Faithful Finances,* 2003, p. 50.

2. Fodor, "Trouble with Psychological Darwinism," 1998.

3. John, "Rich Man's Mail," 2004. John tells me that the current thinking is that the term "robber barons" came from German immigrant journalists like Carl Schurz, who were thinking of the Rhine River tolls.

4. Novak, *Business as a Calling,* 1996, p. 59.

5. Maddison, *Monitoring,* 1995, p. 196; Maddison has made some slight adjustments to these figures in Maddison, *World Economy,* 2001.

6. "Is said" and "according to the anecdote" because it is attested as far as I know only in Edmund Fuller, *2500 Anecdotes for All Occasions* (N.Y.: Crown, 1943) in Fadiman and Bernard, *Bartlett's Book of Anecdotes,* 1985, 2000.

7. Muller, *Mind and Market,* 2002, p. 54.

8. Carnegie, "Wealth," 1889, p. 64.

9. Dunne, *Mr. Dooley,* 1906, p. 112.

10. Strouse to Wall Street Books, at http://www.cyberhaven.com/WallStreetBooks/morgan.html.

11. Aquinas, *Summa Theologiae,* c. 1270, IIa, IIae, q. 117, art. 6.

12. Novak, *Business as a Calling,* 1996, p. 76.

13. "Pudd'nhead Wilson's New Calendar," in *Following the Equator* (1897). Compare Nozick, *Anarchy, State,* 1974, p. 14: "Is there really anyone who, searching for a group of wise and sensitive persons to regulate him for his own good, would choose that group of people who constitute the membership of both houses of Congress?"

14. DeLong, "Robber Barons," 1998.

15. Novak, *Business as a Calling,* 1996, pp. 61–62.

16. Heilbroner, *Worldly Philosophers,* 1953, pp. 216–217.

17. Delong, "The Robber Barons," 1998. I do not mean to say that Untermyer, who was over his long career a prominent trustbuster and community figure, was motivated entirely by spite; only partly.

18. Inglehart et al., *Human Values,* 1998, table 166, from 31,000 responses to 1990–1993 surveys; though the median is surprisingly high: Iceland 85, Britain 78.

19. *Book of Common Prayer,* 1979, p. 259.

CHAPTER 48: THE ANXIETIES OF BOURGEOIS VIRTUES

1. Ostrom, Gardner, and Walker, *Rules, Games,* 1994, p. 320.

2. Feser, *On Nozick,* 2004, p. 14.

3. Feser, *On Nozick,* 2004, p. 13.

4. Shklar herself called her vision "bare-bones liberalism." See Benhabib, "Judith Shklar's Dystopic Liberalism," 1994.

5. Hursthouse, *Virtue Ethics,* 1999, p. 6.

6. Skinner, "Republican Ideal," 1990, p. 309.

7. Little, *Religious Poverty,* 1978, p. 179.

8. As summarized in the second book, Nelson, *Reaching for Heaven,* 2001, p. xxi.

9. McCloskey, *American Conservativism,* 1951, pp. 5–7.

10. Strauss, "Liberal Virtues," 1992, p. 197.

11. Strauss, "Liberal Virtues," 1992, pp. 201, 199.

12. See Molière, *Le bourgeois gentilhomme,* 2.5, for example: "If you walk about dressed like a burgher [*habillé en bourgeois*]," M. Jourdain notes, "no one will say to you, 'M'lord' [*Mon gentilhomme*]." The tailor's assistants, encouraged by his tips, go on to call him "my [feudal] master" [*monseigneur*] and then even "excellency" [*votre grandeur*]. The buying of honor was already common in France.

13. Smith, *Wealth,* 1776, p. 37.

14. You can see the truth of this in the facts of the share of labor, including entrepreneurial labor, in national income, which was about 33 percent in 1800 in a place like England and is now about 90 percent. That is, the return to physical capital and especially land has fallen as a share of national income. It has been replaced by the 57 percent (90 minus 33) going to new skills over and above raw labor.

15. Kocka, "European Pattern," 1988, p. 35, note 18. The German word is *Verbürgerlichung.*

16. McCloskey, "Industrial Revolution," 1981, p. 110.

17. *Marx-Engels Collected Works,* vol. 40, p. 343, given at http://www.marxists.org/archive/marx/works/1858/letters/58_10_07.htm. "Most bourgeois of nations": Engels had not lived in the United States.

18. Rudolf Smend, quoted in Kocka, "European Pattern," 1988, p. 36, note 26.

19. Novak, *Catholic Social Thought,* 1984, p. 179.

20. Novak, *Catholic Social Thought,* 1984, p. 179.

21. Oz, *Under This Blazing Light,* 1979, p. 45.

22. Mann, *Buddenbrooks,* 1901, p. 74.

23. Gay, *Savage Reprisals,* 2002, p. 130.

24. Mann, *Buddenbrooks,* 1901, pp. 113, 202–203, 66, 227.

25. Sartre, *Anti-Semite,* 1944, p. 90.

26. Benedict, *Chrysanthemum,* 1946, p. 12.

27. Aristotle, *Politics,* c. 330 BC, 1328b, p. 301.

WORKS CITED

Abbing, Hans. 2002. *Why Are Artists So Poor? The Exceptional Economy of the Arts*. Amsterdam: Amsterdam University Press.

Adams, Jeremy. 2000. *Thomas Aquinas: Angelic Doctor*. Chantilly, Va.: Teaching Company.

Allison, C. FitzSimons. *The Rise of Moralism: The Proclamation of the Gospel from Hooker to Baxter*. New York: Seabury.

Alschuler, Albert W. 2000. *Law without Values: The Life, Work, and Legacy of Justice Holmes*. Chicago: University of Chicago Press.

Andreau, Jean. 1987. *Banking and Business in the Roman World*. Trans. Janet Lloyd. Cambridge: Cambridge University Press, 1999.

Anscombe, G. Elizabeth M. 1958. "Modern Moral Philosophy." *Philosophy* 33: 1–19. Pp. 26–44 in Crisp and Slote, eds., *Virtue Ethics*.

Appiah, Kwame Anthony. 2005. *The Ethics of Identity*. Princeton: Princeton University Press.

Aquinas, St. Thomas, c. 1259–1264. *Summa contra Gentiles*. An Annotated Translation (With some Abridgement) by Joseph Rickaby, S. J. London: Burns and Oates, 1905. Reprinted at Jacques Maritain CenterWeb site, http://www.nd.edu/Departments/Maritain/etext/gc.htm.

Aquinas, St. Thomas. c. 1269–1273. *Disputed Questions on Virtue* [*Quaestio disputata de vertibus in commune* and *Quaestio . . . cardinalibus*]. Trans. and preface by Ralph McInerny. South Bend, Ind.: St. Augustine's Press, 1999.

Aquinas, St. Thomas. c. 1270. *Summa Theologica* [*Theologiae*], entire, in English. Trans. Fathers of the English Dominican Province. 2nd ed., 1920. New Advent website: http://www.newadvent.org/summa/315100.htm.

Aquinas, St. Thomas. c. 1270. *Treatise on the Virtues* [*Summa Theologiae*, First Half of the Second Part, questions 49–67], Trans. and ed. John A. Oesterle. Notre Dame, Ind.: University of Notre Dame Press, 1984.

Arce M., Daniel G. 2004. "Conspicuous by Its Absence: Ethics and Managerial Economics." *Journal of Business Ethics* 54: 261–277.

Arendt, Hannah. 1958. *The Human Condition.* Chicago: University of Chicago Press.

Aristotle. c. 350 BC. *The History of Animals.* Trans. D'Arcy Wentworth Thompson, 1910. Available at http://classics. mit.edu/Aristotle/history_anim.html.

Aristotle. c. 330 BC. *Nicomachean Ethics.* Trans. H. Rackham. Cambridge, Mass.: Harvard University Press, 1934.

Aristotle. c. 330 BC. *Politics.* Trans. Earnest Barker. Oxford: Oxford University Press, 1968 (orig. 1946).

Aristotle. c. 350 BC. *Rhetoric.* Trans. George A. Kennedy. Oxford: Oxford University Press, 1991.

Arnold, Matthew. 1880. "The Study of Poetry." Pp. 299–331 in Lionel Trilling, ed. *The Portable Matthew Arnold.* New York: Viking, 1949.

Aron, Raymond. 1983. *Memoirs.* Trans. George Holoch, abridged edition. New York: Holmes and Meier, 1990.

Auden, W. H. 1940. "New Year Letter (January 1)." Pp. 159–193 in E. Mendelson, ed., *W. H. Auden: Collected Poems.* New York: Random House, 1976.

Auden, W. H. 1949–1954. "Horae Canonicae." Pp. 475–486 in E. Mendelson, ed., *W. H. Auden: Collected Poems.* New York: Random House, 1976.

Augustine, St. AD 398. *Confessions.* Trans. F. J. Sheed. New York: Sheed and Ward.

Austen, Jane. 1818. *Persuasion.* Oxford: Oxford World Classics, 1930. London: Hamlyn, 1987.

Baar, Dirk-Jan van, and Auke Kok. 1999. *De Millenium Top-40.* No place [Netherlands, Belgium]: HP-De Tijd.

Bacon, Francis. 1625. *Essays.* 3rd ed. A. S. West, ed. Cambridge: Cambridge University Press, 1899.

Baechler, Jean. 1971. *Les origines du capitalisme* (The origins of capitalism). Paris: Gallimard. Oxford: Basil Blackwell, 1975.

Baier, Annette C. 1985. "What Do Women Want with a Moral Theory?" *Nous* 19:53–63. Reprinted as pp. 1–17 in her *Moral Prejudices,* 1994 and as pp. 263–277 in Crisp and Slote, eds., *Virtue Ethics.*

Baier, Annette C. 1994. "Ethics in Many Different Voices." From her *Moral Prejudices: Essays on Ethics.* Cambridge, Mass.: Harvard University Press, 1994. Reprinted as pp. 247–268 in Jane Adamson, R. Freadman, and David Parker, eds. *Renegotiating Ethics in Literature, Philosophy, and Theory.* Cambridge: Cambridge University Press, 1998.

Bailey, Steve. 1999. "Of *Gomi* and *Gaijin.*" Pp. 147–149 in D. W. George and Amy G. Carlson, eds. *Japan: True Stories of Life on the Road.* San Francisco: Travelers' Tales.

Barr, Stephen. 2003. *Modern Physics and Modern Faith.* Notre Dame, Ind.: University of Notre Dame Press.

Baudelaire, Charles. 1857. "Further Notes on Edgar Poe." Pp. 93–110 in J. Mayne, ed. and trans. *The Painter of Modern Life and Other Essays: Charles Baudelaire.* 2nd ed. 1995 (orig. 1964). London: Phaidon.

Beck, Lewis White. 1979. *Mr. Boswell Dines with Professor Kant: Being a part of James Boswell's Journal, until now unknown, found in the Castle of Balmeanach on the Isle of Muck in the Inner Hebrides.* Edinburgh: Tragara Press. Bristol: Thoemmes Press, 1995. Also at http://www. thoemmes.com/bos_kant.htm.

Becker, Gary S. 1974. "A Theory of Marriage." *Journal of Political Economy* July/August.

Reprinted as pp. 205–250 in Becker, *The Economic Approach to Human Behavior*. Chicago: University of Chicago Press, 1976.

Becker, Gary, and Nigel Tomes. 1979. "An Equilibrium Theory of the Distribution of Income and Intergenerational Mobility." *Journal of Political Economy* 87: 1153–1189.

Bell, Daniel. 1976. *The Cultural Contradictions of Capitalism*. New York: Basic Books.

Bellah, Robert. 2003. *Imagining Japan: The Japanese Tradition and Its Modern Interpretation*. Berkeley: University of California Press.

Bellah, Robert N., Richard Madsen, William M. Sullivan, Ann Swidler, and Steven M. Tipton. 1985. *Habits of the Heart: Individualism and Commitment in American Life*. Updated edition. Berkeley: University of California Press, 1996.

Bellow, Saul. 1994. *It All Adds Up: From the Dim Past to an Uncertain Future*. New York: Penguin.

Benedict, Ruth. 1946. *The Chrysanthemum and the Sword: Patterns of Japanese Culture*. Boston: Houghton Mifflin, 1989.

Benhabib, Selya. 1994. "Judith Shklar's Dystopic Liberalism." *Social Research* 61 (Summer): 477–488.

Bennett, William J., ed. 1993. *The Book of Virtues: A Treasury of Great Moral Stories*. New York: Simon and Schuster.

Bentham, Jeremy. 1789. *A Fragment on Government, with an Introduction to the Principles of Morals and Legislation*. W. Harrison, ed. Oxford: Basil Blackwell, 1948.

Berlin, Isaiah. 1953. "The Originality of Machiavelli." Pp. 25–79 in *Against the Current*. First delivered to the British section of the Political Studies Association, 1953. First published in M. P. Gilmore, ed., *Studies in Machiavelli*, 1972.

Berlin, Isaiah. 1965. *The Roots of Romanticism: The Mellon Lectures*. Henry Hardy, ed. Princeton: Princeton University Press, 1999.

Berlin, Isaiah. 1975. "The Apotheosis of the Romantic Will." Pp. 207–237 in Berlin, *The Crooked Timber of Humanity*. Henry Hardy, ed. London: John Murray, 1990. Fontana, 1991. First published in Italian.

Berlin, Isaiah. 1979. *Against the Current: Essays in the History of Ideas*. H. Hardy, ed. Oxford: Clarendon Press, 1981.

Berlin, Isaiah. 1981. *Personal Impressions*. H. Hardy, ed. New York: Viking Penguin.

Berlin, Isaiah. 1996 (delivered 1960). "The Romantic Revolution: A Crisis in the History of Modern Thought." Pp. 168–193 in *The Sense of Reality*.

Berlin, Isaiah. 1996 (delivered 1961). "Rabindranath Tagore and the Consciousness of Nationality." Pp. 249–266 in Berlin, *The Sense of Reality*.

Berlin, Isaiah. 1996 (delivered 1972). "Kant as an Unfamiliar Source of Nationalism." Pp. 232–248 in Berlin, *The Sense of Reality*.

Berlin, Isaiah. 1996. *The Sense of Reality: Studies in Ideas and their History*, H. Hardy, ed. New York: Farrar, Straus, and Giroux, 1997.

Berlin, Isaiah. 1998. *The Crooked Timber of Humanity: Chapters in the History of Ideas*. H. Hardy, ed. Princeton: Princeton University Press.

Berman, Marshall. 1982. *All That Is Solid Melts into Air: The Experience of Modernity*. New York: Penguin.

Blaug, Marc. 1980. *The Methodology of Economics: Or, How Economists Explain*. Cambridge: Cambridge University Press.

Bock, Gisela, Quentin Skinner, and Maurizio Viroli, eds. 1990. *Machiavelli and Republicanism*. Cambridge: Cambridge University Press.

Bonkovsky, H. L., E. E. Cable, J. W. Cable, S. E. Donohue, E. C. White, Y. Greene, et al. 1992. "Porphyrogenic properties of the terpenes camphor, pinene, and thujone (with a note on historic implications for absinthe and the illness of Vincent van Gogh)." *Biochemical Pharmacology* 43: 2359–2368.

Book of Common Prayer. 1979. Episcopal Church. New York: Church Hymnal Corporation.

Book of Knowledge: The Children's Encyclopaedia. 1911. New York: Grolier Society; London: Education Book Co.

Booth, Wayne C. 1974. *Modern Dogma and the Rhetoric of Assent*. Chicago: University of Chicago Press.

Boswell, James. 1791. *The Life of Samuel Johnson, LL. D*. Everyman's Library, in two vols. Vol. 1. London: Dent, 1949.

Boswell, John. 1980. *Christianity, Social Tolerance, and Homosexuality*. Chicago: University of Chicago Press.

Boswell, John. 1994. *Same Sex Unions in Pre-Modern Europe*. New York: Villard.

Bourdieu, Pierre. 1984. *Distinction: A Social Critique of the Judgment of Taste*. Trans. from the French ed. of 1979. Cambridge, Mass.: Harvard University Press. With added preface.

Bowe, John, Marisa Bowe, and Sabin Streeter, eds. 2000. *Gig: Americans Talk about Their Jobs*. New York: Crown (New York: Random House, 2001).

Bradstreet, Anne. 1650, 1678. *The Works of Anne Bradstreet*. Jeannine Hensley, ed. Cambridge, Mass.: Harvard University Press, 1967.

Branca, Vittore. 1986. *Merchant Writers of the Italian Renaissance*. Trans. Murtha Baca. New York: Marsilio, 1999.

Brands, H. W. 1997. *TR: The Last Romantic*. New York: Basic Books.

Breit, William, and Barry T. Hirsch, eds. 2004. *Lives of the Laureates: Eighteen Nobel Economists*. 4th ed. Cambridge: MIT Press.

Brinton, Howard H. 1964. *Friends for 300 Years*. Wallingford, Pa.: Pendle Hill Publications, 2002.

Broadie, Sarah. 2002. "Philosophical Introduction." Pp. 9–91 in Broadie and Christopher Rowe (trans.), eds., *Aristotle: Nicomachean Ethics*. Oxford: Oxford University Press.

Brodkey, Linda. 1994. "Writing on the Bias." *College English* 56 (Oct): 527–547.

Broer, Lawrence R., and Gloria Holland, eds. 2002. *Hemingway and Women: Female Critics and the Female Voice*. Tuscaloosa: University of Alabama Press.

Brown, Bill. 1997. "Reading the West: Cultural and Historical Background." Pp. 1–40 in Brown, *Reading the West*.

Brown, Bill. 1997. *Reading the West: An Anthology of Dime Westerns*. Bedford Cultural edition. Boston: Bedford Books.

Buchanan, James. 1987. "Lives of the Laureates: Buchanan." Pp. 137–151 in Breit and Hirsch, eds., *Lives*.

Budziszewski, J. 1986. *The Resurrection of Nature: Political Theory and the Human Character*. Ithaca: Cornell University Press.

Budziszewski, J. 1992. "Religion and Civic Culture." Pp. 49–68 in Chapman and Galston, eds., *Virtue*.

Budziszewski, J. 2003. "The Real Issue: Escape from Nihilism." Christian Leadership Ministries, http://www. leaderu.com/real/ri9801/budziszewski.html.

Butler, Joseph, Bishop. 1725. *Fifteen Sermons*. Pp. 335–528 in *The Analogy of Religion and Fifteen Sermons*. 1736. London: The Religious Tract Society.

Byock, Jesse. 2001. *Viking Age Iceland*. London: Penguin.

Calomiris, Charles. 2002. *A Globalist Manifesto for Public Policy*. London: Institute of Economic Affairs.

Cannadine, David. 1990. *The Decline and Fall of the British Aristocracy*. New Haven: Yale University Press.

Cannadine, David. 1994. *Aspects of Aristocracy*. London: Penguin ed., 1995.

Cannadine, David. 1998. *Class in Britain*. New Haven: Yale University Press. (Penguin 2000).

Carnegie, Andrew. 1889. "Wealth." *North American Review* 148 (June): 653–664. Text at http://alpha.furman.edu/~benson/docs/carnegie.htm.

Carruthers, Bruce G. 1996. "Trading on the London Stock Market." Chap. 7 in Carruthers, *City of Capital: Politics and Markets in the English Financial Revolution*. Princeton: Princeton University Press. Reprinted as pp. 457–481 in Frank Dobbin, ed., *The New Economic Sociology: A Reader*. Princeton: Princeton University Press, 2004.

Casey, John. 1990. *Pagan Virtue: An Essay in Ethics*. Cambridge: Cambridge University Press.

Cates, Diana Fritz. 2002. "The Virtue of Temperance." Pp. 321–339 in Pope, ed., *The Ethics of Aquinas*.

Cervantes, Miguel. 1604/1614. *The Adventures of Don Quixote*. Trans. J. M. Cohen. Harmondsworth: Penguin, 1950.

Cessario, Romanus. 2002. "The Theological Virtue of Hope." Pp. 232–243 in Pope, ed., *The Ethics of Aquinas*.

Chalfen, Richard. 1987. *Snapshot: Versions of a Life*. Bowling Green, Ohio: Bowling Green University Press.

Chapman, John W., and William A. Galston, eds. 1992. *Virtue: Nomos XXXIV*. New York: New York University Press.

Chapman, R. W., ed. 1925. *The Works of Jane Austen*. 6 vols. London: Oxford University Press, 1954. Standard scholarly edition. All cites to this.

Charry, Ellen T. 1997. *By the Renewing of Your Minds: The Pastoral Function of Christian Doctrine*. New York: Oxford University Press.

Charry, Ellen T. 2004. "On Happiness." *Anglican Theological Review*. 86 (Winter): 19–33.

Chase, Alston. 1986. *Playing God in Yellowstone: The Destruction of America's First National Park*. Boston: Atlantic Monthly Press.

Chaudhuri, Nirad C. 1959. *A Passage to England*. London: Oxford University Press.

Chauncey, George. 1994. *Gay New York: Gender, Urban Culture, and the Making of the Gay Male World, 1890–1940*. New York: Basic Books.

Cicero, Marcus Tullius. 44 BC. *De amicitia* [Concerning Friendship]. Trans. W. A. Falconer. Loeb edition. Cambridge, Mass.: Harvard University Press, 1938.

Cicero, Marcus Tullius. 44 BC. *De officiis* [On Duties]. Trans. W. Miller. Loeb edition. Cambridge, Mass.: Harvard University Press, 1913.

Clark, Henry C., ed. 2003. *Commerce, Culture, and Liberty: Readings on Capitalism before Adam Smith.* Indianapolis: Liberty Fund.

Clark, John Bates. 1901. "The Society of the Future." *Independent* 53 (July 18): 1649–1651. Reprinted as pp. 77–80 in Gail Kennedy, ed., *Democracy and the Gospel of Wealth.* Boston: Heath, 1949.

Coase, Ronald H. 1974. "The Lighthouse in Economics." *Journal of Law and Economics* 17 (2) (October): 357–376.

Coase, Ronald. 1994. "Lives of the Laureates: Coase." Pp. 189–206 in Breit and Hirsch, eds., *Lives.*

Cole, Robert. 2001. *Simone Weil: A Modern Pilgrimage.* Woodstock, Vt.: Skylight Paths.

Coleridge, Samuel Taylor. 2003. *A Book I Value: Selected Marginalia.* Ed. H. J. Jackson. Princeton: Princeton University Press.

Collins, Harry. 1990. *Artificial Experts: Social Knowledge and Intelligent Machines.* Cambridge, Mass.: MIT Press.

Comte-Sponville, André. 1996. *A Small Treatise on the Great Virtues.* Trans. Catherine Temerson. New York: Henry Holt, Metropolitan/Owl Books, 2001.

Confucius. c. 497. *The Analects.* Trans. with an introduction by D. C. Lau. London: Penguin, 1979.

Constant, Benjamin. 1814. *The Spirit of Conquest and Usurpation.* Trans. and ed. Biancamaria Fontana. Pp. 45–167 in *Benjamin Constant: Political Writings.* Cambridge Texts in the History of Political Thought. Cambridge: Cambridge University Press, 1988.

Constant, Benjamin. 1819. "The Liberty of the Ancients Compared with That of the Moderns." Pp. 309–328 in *Benjamin Constant: Political Writings.* Cambridge Texts in the History of Political Thought. Cambridge: Cambridge University Press, 1988.

Coontz, Stephanie. 1992. *The Way We Never Were: American Families and the Nostalgia Trap.* New York: Basic Books. Paperback ed. 2000.

Cosgel, Metin M. 1993. "Religious Culture and Economic Performance: Agricultural Productivity of the Amish, 1850–80." *Journal of Economic History* 53 (June): 319–331.

Countryman, E., and E. von Heussen-Countryman. 1999. *Shane.* London: British Film Institute.

Cox, Jeffrey. 2002. *Imperial Fault Lines: Christianity and Colonial Power in India, 1818–1940.* Stanford: Stanford University Press.

Cox, W. Michael, and Richard Alm. 1999. *Myths of Rich and Poor: Why We're Better Off Than We Think.* New York: Basic.

Crisp, Roger, and Michael Slote, eds. 1997. *Virtue Ethics.* Cambridge: Cambridge University Press.

Cross, F. L., ed. 1957. *The Oxford Dictionary of the Christian Church.* London: Oxford University Press.

Crossan, John Dominic. 1991. *The Historical Jesus: The Life of a Mediterranean Jewish Peasant.* New York: HarperCollins.

Csikszentmihalyi, Mihaly. 1997. *Finding Flow: The Psychology of Engagement with Everyday Life.* New York: Basic Books.

D'Emilio, John, and Estelle B. Freedman. 1997. *Intimate Matters: A History of Sexuality in America.* 2nd ed. Chicago: University of Chicago Press.

Dalton, Kathleen. 2002. *Theodore Roosevelt: A Strenuous Life.* New York: Knopf.

Daly, Jonathan W. 1998. *Autocracy Under Siege: Security Police and Opposition in Russia, 1866–1905.* DeKalb: Northern Illinois University Press.

Daly, Jonathan W. 2004. *The Watchful State: Security Police and Opposition in Russia, 1906–1917.* DeKalb: Northern Illinois University Press.

Damasio, Antonio. 1994. *Descartes' Error: Emotion, Reason, and the Human Brain.* New York: Grosset/Putnam.

Davidoff, Leonore, and Catherine Hall. 1987. *Family Fortunes: Men and Women of the English Middle Class, 1780–1850.* Chicago: University of Chicago Press.

Davis, Philip J., and Reuben Hersh. 1986. *Descartes' Dream: The World According to Mathematics.* New York: Harcourt Brace Jovanovich.

Daviss, Bennett. 1999. "Profits from Principle: Corporations Are Finding That Social Responsibility Pays Off." *Futurist,* March, pp. 28–32. Reprinted as pp. 203–209 in John E. Richardson, ed., *Business Ethics,* 15th ed. Guildford, Conn.: McGraw Hill/Dushkin, 2004.

Dawidoff, Nicholas. 2002. *The Fly Swatter: How My Grandfather Made His Way in the World.* New York: Pantheon.

Day, Dorothy. 1983. *Selected Writings.* R. Ellsberg, ed. Maryknoll, N.Y.: Orbis ed.

De Vries, Jan. 1984. *European Urbanization, 1500–1800.* London: Methuen.

DeLong, J. Bradford. 1998. "The Robber Barons." University of California at Berkeley, and NBER. http://econ161.berkeley.edu/Econ_Articles/carnegie/DeLong_Moscow_paper2.html.

Dennison, Tracy K., and A. W. Carus. 2003. "The Invention of the Russian Rural Commune: Haxthausen and the Evidence." *Historical Journal* 46 (3): 561–582.

DePaul, Michael, and Linda Zagzebski, eds. 2003. *Intellectual Virtue: Perspectives from Ethics and Epistemology.* Oxford: Oxford University Press.

Deursen, A. Th. van. 1999. "The Dutch Republic." Pp. 143–218 in J. C. H. Blom and E. Lamberts, eds. *History of the Low Countries.* New York: Berghahn Books.

Dickens, Charles. 1848. *Dombey and Son.* London: Penguin, 1970, 1985.

Dickens, Charles. 1854. *Hard Times.* Norton Critical Edition. G. Ford and S. Monod, eds., 2nd ed. New York: W. W. Norton, 1990.

Donaldson, Thomas. 2000. "Adding Corporate Ethics to the Bottom Line." *Financial Times,* Nov 13. Reprinted as pp. 98–101 in J. E. Richardson, ed., *Business Ethics,* 15th ed. Guildford, Conn.: McGraw-Hill/Dushkin, 2003.

Donnelly, John. 2004. "Over Half World's Homes Have Running Water, WHO Report Finds. But Progress Stalls on Sanitation Goal." *Boston Globe,* August 26.

Doris, John M. 2002. *Lack of Character: Personality and Moral Behavior.* Cambridge: Cambridge University Press.

Dougherty, Peter J. 2002. *Who's Afraid of Adam Smith? How the Market Got Its Soul.* New York: Wiley.

Douglas, Mary. 1972. "Deciphering a Meal." Pp. 249–275 in Douglas, *Implicit Meanings.* London: Routledge and Kegan Paul, 1979.

Dreiser, Theodore. 1925. *An American Tragedy.* New York: Penguin Putnam, Library of America, 2003.

Druik, Douglas W., and Peter Kort Zegers. 2001. *Van Gogh and Gauguin: The Studio of the South.* New York: Thames and Hudson.

Duffy, Eamon. 2002. "The Cradle Will Rock." Reviews of three books on Medieval childhood. *New York Review of Books,* December 19, pp. 61–63.

Dunne, Peter Finley. 1906. *Dissertations by Mr. Dooley.* New York: Harper & Bros.

Dworkin, Ronald. 1980. "Is Wealth a Value?" *Journal of Legal Issues* 9: 191–226.

Dwyer, June. 1989. *Jane Austen.* New York: Continuum.

Dykstra, Robert R. 1968. *The Cattle Towns.* New York: Knopf.

Easterlin, Richard A. 1999. "How Beneficent Is the Market? A Look at the Modern History of Mortality." *European Review of Economic History* 3.

Eckel, Catherine C., and Philip J. Grossman. 1996. "Altruism in Anonymous Dictator Games." *Games and Economic Behavior* 16: 181–191. Reprinted at http://www.econ.vt.edu/people/profiles/EckelGrossmanAltruism.pdf.

Eliade, Mircea. 1957. *The Sacred and the Profane: The Nature of Religion.* Trans. from the French by W. R. Trask. New York: Knopf. New York: Harcourt, Brace & World, 1959.

Ellis, Joseph J. 2000. *Founding Brothers: The Revolutionary Generation.* New York: Vintage/Random House.

Ellsberg, Robert. 1983. Introduction. Pp. xv–xli in Dorothy Day, *Selected Writings.*

Elshtain, Jean Bethke. 1987. *Women and War.* New York: Basic Books.

Elshtain, Jean Bethke. 1995. "Adams, Jane." Pp. 14–16 in Fox and Kloppenberg, eds., *Companion.*

Embree, Ainslee, ed. 1988. *Sources of Indian Tradition.* Vol. 1, *From the Beginning to 1800.* 2nd ed. New York: Columbia University Press. *Digha Nikaya,* 3.180ff, pp. 120, 123.

Emerson, Ralph Waldo. 1850. "Napoleon; Or, the Man of the World." Pp. 337–359 in Emerson, *Selected Essays.* L. Ziff, ed. New York: Viking Penguin, 1982.

Epictetus. c. AD 130. *The Book of Epictetus, Being the Enchiridion, together with Chapters from the Discourses and Selections from the Fragments of Epictetus.* T. W. Rolleston, ed.; trans. Elizabeth Carter. London: George G. Harrap & Co., n.d.

Erasmus, Desiderius, of Rotterdam. 1500–1533. *The Adages of Erasmus.* Selected by William Barker. Toronto: University of Toronto Press, 2001.

Evensky, Jerry. 1993. "Retrospectives: Ethics and the Invisible Hand." *Journal of Economic Perspectives* 7 (2): 197–205.

Evensky, Jerry. 2001. "Adam Smith's Lost Legacy." *Southern Economic Journal* 6 (3): 497–517.

Everitt, Anthony. 2003. *Cicero: The Life and Times of Rome's Greatest Politician.* New York: Random House.

Fadiman, Clifton. 1942. Introduction to Readers Club ed. of Walter van Tilburg Clark, *The Ox-Bow Incident,* pp. vii–xi. New York: Readers Club.

Fairbank, John K., Edwin O. Reischauer, and Albert M. Craig. 1989. *East Asia: Tradition and Transformation.* Boston: Houghton Mifflin.

Feser, Edward. 2004. *On Nozick.* Belmont, Calif.: Wadsworth.

Field, Alexander. 2003. *Altruistically Inclined? The Behavioral Sciences, Evolutionary Theory, and the Origins of Reciprocity.* Ann Arbor: University of Michigan Press.

Field, Alexander. 2005. Review of Douglass North, *Understanding the Process of Economic Change*. eh.net-review@eh.net. February 15.

Fish, Stanley. 1980. *Is There a Text in This Class? The Authority of Interpretive Communities*. Cambridge, Mass.: Harvard University Press.

Fish, Stanley. 2001. *How Milton Works*. Cambridge, Mass.: Harvard University Press.

Fleischacker, Samuel. 1999. *A Third Concept of Liberty: Judgment and Freedom in Kant and Adam Smith*. Princeton: Princeton University Press.

Fleischacker, Samuel. 2004. "Economics and the Ordinary Person: Re-reading Adam Smith." Library of Economics and Liberty, October 4. At http://www.econlib.org/library/Columns/y2004/FleischackerSmith.html.

Fleischacker, Samuel. 2004. *On Adam Smith's* Wealth of Nations: *A Philosophical Companion*. Princeton: Princeton University Press.

Fleischacker, Samuel. 2004. *A Short History of Distributive Justice*. Cambridge, Mass.: Harvard University Press.

Florida, Richard. 2002. *The Rise of the Creative Class: And How It's Transforming Work, Leisure, Community, and Everyday Life*. New York: Basic Books.

Flyvbjerg, Bent. 2004. "Megaprojects: Misrepresentation Drives Projects." *Engineering News Record*. January 5, p. 87 only. Copy in http://www.plan.aau.dk/~flyvbjerg/pub.htm

Flyvbjerg, Bent, Mette K. Skamris Holm, Søren L. Buhl. 2003. "How Common and How Large Are Cost Overruns in Transport Infrastructure Projects?" *Transport Reviews* 23 (1): 71–88. Copy in http://www.plan.aau.dk/~flyvbjerg/pub.htm.

Fodor, Jerry. 1998. "The Trouble with Psychological Darwinism" Review of *How the Mind Works*, by Steven Pinker; and *Evolution in Mind*, by Henry Plotkin. London *Review of Books* 20 (2). Reprinted at http://humanities.uchicago.edu/faculty/goldsmith/CogSciCourse/Fodor.htm and at http://www.homestead.com/flowstate/files/fodor.html.

Fogel, Robert W. 1999. *The Fourth Great Awakening and the Future of Egalitarianism*. Chicago: University of Chicago Press.

Fogel, Robert W. 2004. *The Escape from Hunger and Premature Death, 1700–2100*. Cambridge, Mass.: Cambridge University Press.

Fogel, Robert W. 2005. "Reconsidering Expectations of Economic Growth after World War II from the Perspective of 2004." National Bureau of Economic Research. Working paper no. W11125.

Folbre, Nancy. 2001. *The Invisible Heart: Economics and Family Values*. New York: The New Press.

Foot, Philippa. 1978. "Virtues and Vices." Pp. 1–18 in Foot, *Virtues and Vices*.

Foot, Philippa. 1978. *Virtues and Vices and Other Essays in Moral Philosophy*. Berkeley: University of California Press.

Foot, Philippa. 2001. *Natural Goodness*. Oxford: Clarendon Press.

Fordyce, David. 1754. *The Element of Moral Philosophy*. Thomas D. Kennedy, ed. Indianapolis: Liberty Fund, 2003.

Forsythe, Robert, Joel L. Horowitz, N. Eugene Savin, and M. Sefton. 1994. "Fairness in Simple Bargaining Experiments." *Games and Economic Behavior* 6: 347–369.

Fox, Richard Wightman, and James T. Kloppenberg, eds. 1995. *A Companion to American Thought*. Oxford: Blackwell.

Frank, Robert. 1988. *Passions within Reason: The Strategic Role of the Emotions.* New York: W. W. Norton.

Frank, Robert. 1999. *Luxury Fever.* New York: Free Press.

Frank, Robert. 2004. *What Price the Moral High Ground? Ethical Dilemmas in Competitive Environments.* Princeton: Princeton University Press.

Frank, Robert. 2005. "Motives and Self-interest." Pp. 369f in *The Blackwell Encyclopedia of Management.,* 2nd ed., vol. 2, *Business Ethics.* Patricia Werhane and R. E. Freeman, eds. Oxford: Blackwell.

Frankfurt, Harry. 2004. *The Reasons of Love.* Princeton: Princeton University Press.

Franklin, Benjamin. 1771–1774. *The Autobiography of Benjamin Franklin.* L. W. Larabee, R. L. Ketcham, H. C. Boatfield, and H. M. Fineman, eds. New Haven: Yale University Press, 1964.

Frederick II, known as the Great. 1740. *Anti-Machiavel.* Trans. at http://www.geocities.com/danielmacryan/antimac.html.

Freeman, Richard. 2003. "Not Your Father's (or Mum's) Union." Speech to the 32nd Conference of Economists, Canberra, Australia, 29 September–1 October.

French, Peter A. 1997. *Cowboy Metaphysics: Ethics and Death in Westerns.* Lanham, Md.: Rowman & Littlefield.

Frey, Bruno S. 1997. *Not Just For the Money: An Economic Theory of Personal Motivation.* Cheltenham: Edward Elgar.

Frey, Bruno S., and Alois Stutzer. 2002. *Happiness & Economics.* Princeton: Princeton University Press.

Fried, Richard. 1990. *Nightmare in Red: The McCarthy Era in Perspective.* New York: Oxford University Press.

Fried, Richard. 2002. "'Operation Polecat': Tom Dewey and the Origins of the McCarthy Era." Talk to the Department of History, University of Illinois at Chicago, Dec. 4.

Fried, Richard. 2003. "Voting Against the Hammer and Sickle: Communism as an Issue in American Politics." Pp. 99–127 in W. H. Chafe, ed., *The Achievement of American Liberalism: The New Deal and Its Legacies.* New York: Columbia University Press.

Friedman, Milton. 1970. "The Social Responsibility of Business Is to Increase Its Profits." *New York Times Sunday Magazine* (Sept. 13).

Friedman, Milton. 1985. "Lives of the Laureates: Friedman." Pp. 65–77 in Breit and Hirsch, eds., *Lives.*

Frye, Northrop. 1968. "Dickens and the Comedy of Humors." Reprinted as pp. 218–240 in Frye, *The Stubborn Structure: Essays on Criticism and Society.* Ithaca: Cornell University Press, 1970.

Fuchs, R. H. 1978. *Dutch Painting.* London: Thames and Hudson.

Fukuyama, Francis. 1999. *The Great Disruption.* New York: Touchstone (Simon and Schuster).

Funk, Robert W., Roy W. Hoover, and the Jesus Seminar. 1993. *The Five Gospels: The Search for the Authentic Words of Jesus.* San Francisco: HarperCollins; paperback ed., 1997.

Gadamer, Hans-Georg. 1965. *Truth and Method.* 2nd ed. Trans. Joel Weinsheimer and Donald G. Marshall. New York: Crossroad, 1989.

Gay, Peter. 2002. *Savage Reprisals: Bleak House, Madame Bovary, Buddenbrooks.* New York: Norton.

Geertz, Clifford. 1988. *Works and Lives.* Stanford: Stanford University Press.

George, David. 2004. *Preference Pollution: How Markets Create the Desires We Dislike.* Ann Arbor: University of Michigan Press.

Gerschenkron, Alexander. 1970. *Europe in the Russian Mirror: Four Lectures in Economic History.* Cambridge: Cambridge University Press.

Geyl, Pieter. 1936. *The Netherlands in the Seventeenth Century, 1609–1648.* London: Phoenix Press, 2001.

Gilman, Charlotte Perkins. 1898. *Women and Economics.* New York: Harper, 1966.

Ginzburg, Carlo. N.d. "Diventare Machiavelli: Una nuova lettera dei *Ghiribizzi al Soderni.*" Paper, Department of History, University of California, Los Angeles.

Godin, Seth. 1996. *The Official Rules of Life.* New York: Simon and Schuster.

Goody, Jack. 1996. *The East in the West.* Cambridge: Cambridge University Press.

Goossens, Eymert-Jan. 1996. *Treasure Wrought by Chisel and Brush: The Amsterdam Town Hall in the Golden Age.* Zwolle: Waanders/Royal Palace Amsterdam.

Gopnik, Adam. 2001. "The First Comedian: Molière's Middle-Class Manner." *New Yorker,* June 11, pp. 82–88.

Gordon, Donald F., and Gary M. Walton. 1982. "A Theory of Regenerative Growth and the Experience of Post–World War II West Germany." Pp. 169–190 in R. Ransom, R. Sutch, and G. Walton, eds., *Explorations in the New Economic History: Essays in Honor of Douglass C. North.* New York: Academic Press.

Gottschalk, Peter, and Sheldon Danziger. 1997. "Family Income Mobility: How Much Is There and Has It Changed?" Boston College, MS at http://fmwww.bc.edu/EC-P/WP398.pdf.

Grampp, William D. 1973. "Classical Economics and Its Moral Critics." *History of Political Economy* 5.

Graña, César. 1964. *Bohemian versus Bourgeois: French Society and the French Man of Letters in the Nineteenth Century.* New York: Basic.

Granovetter, Mark. 1985. "Economic Action and Social Structure: The Problem of Embeddedness." *American Journal of Sociology* 91 (November): 481–510. Reprinted as pp. 51–74 in Granovetter and Swedberg, eds., *The Sociology of Economic Life.*

Granovetter, Mark, and Richard Swedberg, eds. 2001. *The Sociology of Economic Life.* Boulder: Westview.

Gray, Francine Du Plessix. 2001. *Simone Weil.* New York: Viking Penguin.

Gray, John. 1996. *Isaiah Berlin.* Princeton: Princeton University Press.

Gray, John. 1997. *Endgames: Questions in Late Modern Political Thought.* Malden, Mass.: Polity Press, 1997.

Gray, John. 1998. *False Dawn: The Delusions of Global Capitalism.* New York: New Press.

Greeley, Andrew. 2000. *The Catholic Imagination.* Berkeley: University of California Press.

Green, Joshua. 2003. "The Bookie of Virtue." *Washington Monthly,* June. http://www.washingtonmonthly.com/features/2003/0306.green.html.

Greenblatt, Stephen J. 1997. Introduction. Pp. 1–76 in Greenblatt, ed., *Norton Shakespeare.*

Greenblatt, Stephen J., ed. 1997. *The Norton Shakespeare, Based on the Oxford Edition.* New York: W. W. Norton.

Greenblatt, Stephen J. 2004. *Will in the World: How Shakespeare Became Shakespeare.* New York: W. W. Norton,

Greenspan, Alan. 1999. Commencement Address at Harvard University, June. Reproduced in the *Harvard Magazine*, July-August 1999, pp. 68–69.

Gross, John. 2000. *The New Oxford Book of English Prose.* Oxford: Oxford University Press.

Guest, Robert. 2004. *The Shackled Continent: Africa's Past, Present, and Future.* Basingstoke, UK: Macmillan.

Gunther, Scott E. 1995. *La construction de l'identité homosexuelle dans les lois aux Etats-Unis et en France.* Mémoire de DEA. Paris: Ecole Normale Supérieure & Ecole des Hautes Etudes en Sciences Sociales. http://homepages.nyu.edu/~seg9045/cv.htm.

Hagen, Everett E. 1962. *On the Theory of Social Change: How Economic Growth Began.* Homewood, Ill.: Dorsey Press.

Halwani, Raja. 2003. *Virtuous Liaisons: Care, Love, Sex, and Virtue Ethics.* Chicago: Open Court.

Hammett, Dashiell. 1929. *The Maltese Falcon.* New York: Knopf, Vintage ed. of 1984, with notes by James Dickey.

Hampshire, Stuart. 1959. *Thought and Action.* New ed. Notre Dame: Notre Dame University Press, 1982.

Hampshire, Stuart. 1991. "Justice Is Strife." Presidential Address to the 65th Annual Pacific Division Meeting of the American Philosophical Association, San Francisco, March 29. Excerpted in http://caae.phil.cmu.edu/Cavalier/Forum/meta/background/Hampshire.html.

Hanawalt, Barbara. 1979. *Crime and Conflict in English Communities, 1300–1348.* Cambridge, Mass.: Harvard University Press.

Hanson, Victor Davis. 1989. *The Western Way of War: Infantry Battle in Classical Greece.* New York: Knopf.

Hanson, Victor Davis. 1996. "Land Warfare in Thucydides." Appendix F, pp. 603–607 in *The Landmark Thucydides*, ed. Robert B. Strassler, trans. R. Crawley. New York: Free Press.

Hargreaves-Heap, Shaun, and Yanis Varoufakis. 2004. *Game Theory: A Critical Text.* 2nd ed. London: Routledge.

Hariman, Robert. 1995. *Political Style: The Artistry of Power.* Chicago: University of Chicago Press.

Hariman, Robert. 1999. "Radical Sociality and Christian Detachment in Erasmus' *Praise of Folly*." *World Order* 31: 9–23.

Hariman, Robert. 2003. Preface. Pp. vii–ix in Hariman, ed. *Prudence.*

Hariman, Robert. 2003. "Theory without Modernity." Pp. 1–32 in Hariman, ed. *Prudence.*

Hariman, Robert, ed. 2003. *Prudence: Classical Virtue, Postmodern Practice.* University Park: Pennsylvania State University Press.

Harré, Rom. 1986. *Varieties of Realism: A Rationale for the Natural Sciences.* Oxford: Basil Blackwell.

Hartman, Geoffrey. 1954. *The Unmediated Vision: An Interpretation of Wordsworth, Hopkins, Rilke, and Valéry.* New Haven: Yale University Press.

Hartz, Louis. 1955. *The Liberal Tradition in America: An Interpretation of American Political Thought since the Revolution.* New York: Harcourt Brace.

Harvey, David. 1990. *The Condition of Postmodernity: An Enquiry into the Origins of Cultural Change.* Cambridge, Mass.: Blackwell.

Haslam, Nick. 2004. "Prudence." Pp. 477–497 in Peterson and Seligman, *Character Strengths and Virtues*.

Hausman, Daniel M., and Michael S. McPherson. 1996. *Economic Analysis and Moral Philosophy*. Cambridge: Cambridge University Press.

Hearnshaw, L. S. 1979. *Cyril Burt: Psychologist*. Ithaca: Cornell University Press.

Heckscher, Eli. F. 1931. *Mercantilism*. Trans. Mendel Shapiro. London: Allen and Unwin, 1934.

Heilbroner, Robert. 1953. *The Worldly Philosophers: The Lives, Times, and Ideas of the Great Economic Thinkers*. 7th ed. New York: Simon and Schuster, 1999.

Heinich, Nathalie. 1991. *The Glory of Van Gogh: An Anthology of Admiration*. Trans. from the French by Paul Leduc Browne. Princeton: Princeton University Press, 1996.

Held, Virginia. 1993. *Feminist Morality: Transforming Culture, Society, and Politics*. Chicago: University of Chicago Press.

Hemingway, Ernest. 1986. *The Garden of Eden*. Assembled by Thomas Jenks. New York: Scribner.

Hemingway, Ernest. 1926. *The Sun Also Rises*. New York: Scribner. Reprinted Simon and Schuster, n.d.

Henshall, Kenneth. 2004. *A History of Japan: From Stone Age to Superpower*. 2nd ed. Basingstoke: Palgrace Macmillan.

Herbert, Zbigniew. 1991. *Still Life with a Bridle: Essays and Apocryphas*. Trans. J. and Bogdana Carpenter. Hopewell, N.J.: Echo.

Herlihy, David. "The Economy of Traditional Europe." *Journal of Economic History* 31 (1) (1971): 153–164.

Hesiod. c. 700 BC. *Works and Days*. In H. G. Evelyn-White, trans., *Hesiod: The Homeric Hymns and Homerica*. Loeb Library. Cambridge, Mass.: Harvard University Press.

Higgs, Robert. 1983. "Where Figures Fail: Measuring the Growth of Big Government." *The Freeman* 33 (3) (March 1983). At http://www.libertyhaven.com/politicsandcurrentevents/governmentreformitsrealrole/figuresfail.html.

Higgs, Robert. 1987. *Crisis and Leviathan: Critical Episodes in the Growth of American Government*. New York: Oxford University Press.

Higgs, Robert. 1997. "Regime Uncertainty: Why the Great Depression Lasted So Long and Why Prosperity Resumed after the War." *Independent Review* 1: 561–590.

Higgs, Robert. 2004. *Against Leviathan: Government Power and a Free Society*. Oakland: The Independent Institute.

Himmelfarb, Gertrude. 1977. "Social History and the Moral Imagination." Pp. 28–58 in Quentin Anderson, ed. *Art, Politics and Will—Essays in Honor of Lionel Trilling*. New York: Basic. Reprinted as pp. 248–270 in Neale 1983.

Himmelfarb, Gertrude. 1984. *The Idea of Poverty*. New York: Knopf.

Hinze, Christine Firer. 2004. "What Is Enough? Catholic Social Thought, Consumption, and Material Sufficiency." Pp. 162–188 in Schweiker and Mathewes, eds., *Having*.

Hirschman, Albert O. 1970. *Exit, Voice and Loyalty: Responses to Decline in Firms, Organizations, and States*. Cambridge, Mass.: Harvard University Press.

Hirschman, Albert O. 1977. *The Passions and the Interests: Political Arguments for Capitalism before Its Triumph*. Princeton: Princeton University Press.

Hirschman, Albert O. 1981. *Essays in Trespassing: Economics to Politics and Beyond*. Cambridge: Cambridge University Press.

Hitchens, Christopher. 2002. *Orwell's Victory*. London: Penguin (Allen Lane).

Hobbes, Thomas. 1640. *The Elements of Law Natural and Politic*. Internet edition: www.knuten.liu.se/~bjoch509/works /hobbes/elements.txt.

Hobbes, Thomas. 1651. *Leviathan*. Everyman edition. London: J. M. Dent: E. P. Dutton, 1914.

Hobsbawm, Eric. 1988. "The Example of the." Pp. 127–150 in Kocka and Mitchell, eds., *Bourgeois Society*.

Hodges, Andrew. 1983. *Alan Turing: The Enigma*. New York: Simon and Schuster.

Hoffer, Eric. 1979. *Before the Sabbath*. New York: Harper and Row.

Hoffman, Elizabeth, and Matthew Spitzer. 1985. "Entitlements, Rights, and Fairness: An Experimental Examination of Subjects' Concepts of Distributive Justice." *Journal of Legal Studies* 14: 259–298.

Hollander, Anne. 1999. *Feeding the Eye*. New York: Farrar, Straus and Giroux.

Hollingsworth, T. H. 1957. "A Demographic Study of the British Ducal Families." *Population Studies* 11 (1): 4–26.

Holmes, Oliver Wendell, Jr. 1895. From "An Address Delivered on Memorial Day, May 30." Pp. 263–270 in Joseph T. Cox, ed., *The Written Wars: American Prose through the Civil War*. North Haven, Conn.: Archon.

Holmes, Oliver Wendell, Jr., and Sir Frederick Pollock. 1941. *Holmes-Pollock Letters*. M. D. Howe, ed. Cambridge, Mass.: Harvard University Press.

Homer. c. 700 BC. *The Iliad*. Trans. Stanley Lombardo. Intro. Sheila Murnaghan. Indianapolis: Hackett Publishing, 1997.

Homer. c. 700 BC. *The Iliad*. Trans. Robert Fagles. New York: Viking Penguin, 1990.

Hont, Istvan, and Michael Ignatieff. 1983. *Wealth and Virtue: The Shaping of Political Economy in the Scottish Enlightenment*. Cambridge: Cambridge University Press.

Hooker, Richard. 1593. *On the Laws of Ecclesiastical Polity*. Vol. 1 (Books 1–4). London: Dent (Everyman, 1907).

Hornby, Nick. 2001. *How to Be Good*. New York: Penguin Putnam.

Horowitz, Daniel. 1985. *The Morality of Spending: Attitudes toward the Consumer Society in America, 1875–1940*. Baltimore: Johns Hopkins University Press.

Horst, Han van der. 1996. *The Low Sky: Understanding the Dutch*. Schiedam: Scriptum.

Houser, R. E. 2002. "The Virtue of Courage." Pp. 304–320 in Pope, ed., *The Ethics of Aquinas*.

Hoxby, Blair. 2002. *Mammon's Music: Literature and Economics in the Age of Milton*. New Haven: Yale University Press.

Hugh of St. Victor. c. AD 1125. *The Didascalicon of Hugh of St. Victor: A Medieval Guide to the Arts*. Trans. Jerome Taylor. New York: Columbia University Press, 1961.

Hughes, Robert. 1992. *Barcelona*. New York: Knopf.

Huisken, Jacobine E. 1996. *'s Kongins Paleis op den Dam* [*The royal palace on the dam in a historical view.*] Abcoude, Netherlands: Uniepers.

Huizinga, Johan H. 1935. "The Spirit of the Netherlands." Pp. 105–137 in Huizinga, *Dutch Civilization in the Seventeenth Century and Other Essays*, Pieter Geyl and F. W. N. Hugenholtz, eds.; A. J. Pomerans, trans. London: Collins, 1968.

Huizinga, Johan H. 1941. "Dutch Civilization in the Seventeenth Century." Pp. 9–104 in Huizinga, *Dutch Civilization in the Seventeenth Century and Other Essays*, Pieter Geyl and F. W. N. Hugenholtz, eds.; A. J. Pomerans, trans. London: Collins, 1968.

Hume, David. 1741–1742. *Essays, Moral, Political, and Literary*. Rev. ed. Eugene F. Miller, ed. Indianapolis: Liberty Fund.

Hume, David. 1748. *An Inquiry Concerning Human Understanding and Concerning the Principles of Morals*. Ed. L. A. Selby-Bigge. 3rd ed., revised by P. H. Nidditch. Oxford: Clarendon Press, 1975.

Hume, David. 1751. *Enquiry Concerning the Principles of Morals*. Oxford: Oxford University Press, 1902.

Hunnicutt, Benjamin Kline. 1988. *Work without End: Abandoning Shorter Hours for the Right to Work*. Philadelphia: Temple University Press.

Hunnicutt, Benjamin Kline. 1996. *Kellogg's Six-Hour Day*. Philadelphia: Temple University Press.

Hunt, Lester H. 1997. *Character and Culture*. Lanham, Md.: Rowman & Littlefield.

Hursthouse, Rosalind. 1991. "Virtue Theory and Abortion." *Philosophy and Public Affairs* 20: 223–246. Reprinted as pp. 217–238 in Crisp and Slote, eds., *Virtue Ethics*.

Hursthouse, Rosalind. 1999. *On Virtue Ethics*. Oxford: Oxford University Press.

Hurston, Nora Zeale. 1937. *Their Eyes Were Watching God*. New York: Harper-Collins, 1990.

Iannoccone, Lawrence R. 1998. "Introduction to the Economics of Religion." *Journal of Economic Literature* 36: 1465–1494.

Ignatieff, Michael. 1984. *The Needs of Strangers*. New York: Viking Penguin Books. Picador ed., 2001.

Ignatieff, Michael. 1998. *Isaiah Berlin: A Life*. New York: Henry Holt (Metropolitan).

Ingalls, D. H. H., ed. c. 1100 AD. *An Anthology of Sanskrit Court Poetry*. Cambridge, Mass.: Harvard University Press, 1965.

Inglehart, Ronald, Miguel Basanez, and Alejandro Moreno. 1998. *Human Values and Beliefs: A Cross-Cultural Sourcebook*. Ann Arbor: University of Michigan Press.

Ingram, Paul, and Peter W. Roberts. 2000. "Friendship among Competitors in the Sydney Hotel Industry." *American Journal of Sociology* 16 (Sept): 387–423.

Innes, Stephen. 1983. *Labor in a New Land: Economy and Society in Seventeenth-Century Springfield*. Princeton: Princeton University Press.

Inoue, Kyoko. 1991. *MacArthur's Japanese Constitution: A Linguistic and Cultural Study of Its Making*. Chicago: University of Chicago Press.

Inoue, Kyoko. 2001. *Individual Dignity in Modern Japanese Thought: The Evolution of the Concept of Jinkaku in Moral and Educational Discourse*. Ann Arbor: Center for Japanese Studies, University of Michigan Press.

Inoue, Kyoko. 2002. "Individual Dignity and Human Rights: Why the Two Are Not Necessarily Linked in Japanese Democratic Thought." MS, Department of English, University of Illinois at Chicago.

Isacsson, Birgitta. 1997. "Sweden: Sterilization Policy Sparks Debate." *Militant* 61 (33) (September 28). Reproduced at http://www.themilitant.com/1997/6133/6133_18.html.

Iser, Wolfgang. 1980. "The Interaction between Text and Reader." Pp. 106–119 in S. R. Suleiman and I. Crosman, eds., *The Reader in the Text*. Princeton: Princeton University Press.

Israel, Jonathan. 1995. *The Dutch Republic: Its Greatness, Rise, and Fall, 1477–1806*. Oxford: Clarendon Press.

Ivanhoe, Philip J. 2000. *Confucian Moral Self Cultivation.* Indianapolis: Hackett.

Jackson, Jennifer. 1996. *An Introduction to Business Ethics.* Oxford: Blackwell.

James, William. 1907. *Pragmatism: A New Name for Some Old Ways of Thinking.* Reprinted, with pagination of the 1907 edition. New York: Longmans, Green, 1949.

Jankélévitch, Vladimir. 1967. *Forgiveness.* Trans. Andrew Kelley. Chicago: University of Chicago Press, 2005.

Jankélévitch, Vladimir. 2003. *Music and the Ineffable.* Trans. Carolyn Abbate. Princeton: Princeton University Press.

John, Richard. 2004. "Rich Man's Mail: Western Union's Gilded Age." Paper, Department of History, University of Illinois at Chicago. A chapter in his forthcoming book, tentatively entitled *Making Connections: The Advent of American Telecommunications.*

John, Richard. Forthcoming. *Making Connections: The Advent of American Telecommunications.* Cambridge, Mass.: Harvard University Press.

Johnson, Luke Timothy. 2002. *Practical Philosophy: The Greco-Roman Moralists.* Chantilly, Va.: The Teaching Company.

Johnson, Mark. 1993. *Moral Imagination: Implication of Cognitive Science for Ethics.* Chicago: University of Chicago Press.

Johnson, Paul. 1988. *The Intellectuals.* New York: Harper and Row, 1990.

Johnson, Paul. 1991. *The Birth of the Modern: World Society 1815–1830.* New York: HarperCollins.

Johnson, Paul. 2002. *Napoleon.* New York: Lipper/Viking/Penguin.

Johnson, Samuel, and James Boswell. 1775, 1785. *A Journey to the Western Isles & The Journal of a Tour to the Hebrides.* Harmondsworth: Penguin, 1984.

Johnston, Robert D. 2003. *The Radical Middle Class: Populist Democracy and the Question of Capitalism in Progressive Era Portland, Oregon.* Princeton: Princeton University Press.

Jones, Eric L. 1987. *The European Miracle: Environments, Economics, and Geopolitics in the History of Europe and Asia.* Cambridge: Cambridge University Press.

Jones, Eric L. 2000. *Growth Recurring: Economic Change in World History.* Princeton: Princeton University Press.

Jones, Eric L. Forthcoming. *Culture and the Price of Information.* Princeton: Princeton University Press.

Jones, G. T. 1933. *Increasing Returns.* Cambridge: Cambridge University Press.

Jones, Peter d'A. 1968. The *Christian Socialist Revival, 1877–1914.* Princeton: Princeton University Press.

Jongh, Eddy de. 1991. "Some Notes on Interpretation." Pp. 119–136 in David Freedberg and Jan de Vries, eds. *Art in History, History in Art.* Santa Monica, Calif.: Getty Center for the History of Art and the Humanities, University of Chicago Press.

Jonsen, Albert R., and Stephen Toulmin. 1988. *The Abuse of Casuistry: A History of Moral Reasoning.* Berkeley: University of California Press.

Jullien, François. 1996. *A Treatise on Efficacy: Between Western and Chinese Thinking.* Trans. Janet Lloyd. Honolulu: University of Hawaii Press, 2004.

Justinian [by Tribonian and Dorotheus]. AD 533. *Institutes.* Trans. P. Birks and G. McLeod. With the Latin text of P. Krueger. Ithaca: Cornell University Press, 1987.

Kahn-Leavitt, Laurie, Richard P. Rogers, and Laurel Thatcher Ulrich. 1997. Transcript of *A Midwife's Tale*. Blueberry Hill Productions, PBS Home Video, at http://www.pbs.org/wgbh/amex/midwife/index.html.

Kamin, Blair. 2003. "Monuments to Mediocrity." *Chicago Tribune*, August 10, sec. 7, pp. 1, 6, 7.

Kant, Immanuel. 1785. *Grounding for the Metaphysics of Morals*. Trans. James Ellington. Indianapolis: Hackett, 1993.

Kant, Immanuel. 1788. *The Critique of Practical Reason*. Trans. Thomas Kingsmill Abbott, editions 1889–1913. Reprinted at http://eserver.org/philosophy/kant/critique-of-practical-reaso.txt.

Keegan, John. 1976. *The Face of Battle: A Study of Agincourt, Waterloo, and the Somme*. New York: Viking. Penguin ed. 1978.

Keeley, Lawrence H. 1996. *War Before Civilization: The Myth of the Peaceful Savage*. Oxford: Oxford University Press.

Keller, Rudi. 1990. *On Language Change: The Invisible Hand in Language*. London: Taylor and Francis, 1994.

Keynes, John Maynard. 1924. "Alfred Marshall." Pp. 125–217 in Keynes, *Essays in Biography*. New York: Horizon Press, 1951. Reprinted New York: W. W. Norton, 1963.

Kirsch, Adam. 2004. "Get Happy." *New Yorker*, Nov 22.

Kirzner, Israel. 1973. *Competition and Entrepreneurship*. Chicago: University of Chicago Press.

Klemm, David. 2004. "Material Grace: The Paradox of Property and Possession." Pp. 222–245 in Schweiker and Mathewes, eds. *Having*.

Knight, Frank H. 1922. "Ethics and the Economic Interpretation." *Quarterly Journal of Economics* 36 (3) (May): 454–481. Reprinted as pp. 11–32 in Knight, *The Ethics of Competition*, 1935.

Knight, Frank H. 1923. "The Ethics of Competition." *Quarterly Journal of Economics*. Reprinted as pp. 33–67 in Knight, *The Ethics of Competition*, 1935.

Knight, Frank H. 1934. "Economic Theory and Nationalism." Pp. 268–351 in Knight, *The Ethics of Competition*, 1935.

Knight, Frank H. 1935. *The Ethics of Competition*. With a new introduction by Richard Boyd. New Brunswick, N.J.: Transaction Publishers, 1997.

Knight, Frank H., and T. W. Merriam. 1945. *The Economic Order and Religion*. New York: Harper and Bros.

Kocka, Jürgen. 1988. "The European Pattern and the German Case." Pp. 3–39 in Kocka and Mitchell, eds., *Bourgeois Society*.

Kocka, Jürgen, and Allan Mitchell, eds. 1988. *Bourgeois Society in Nineteenth-Century Europe*. Translated from the German edition. Oxford: Berg, 1993.

Koehn, Daryl. 2005. "Virtue Ethics." Pp. 535–538 in *The Blackwell Encyclopedia of Management*, 2nd ed., vol. 2, *Business Ethics*. Patricia Werhane and R. E. Freeman, eds. Oxford: Blackwell.

Kolakowski, Leszek. 1978. *Main Currents of Marxism*. Vol. 2, *The Golden Age*. Oxford: Oxford University Press.

Kors, Allan. 1998. *The Birth of the Modern Mind: An Intellectual History of the 17th and 18th Centuries*. Chantilly, Va.: Teaching Company.

Kraaij, Harry J. 1997. *The Royal Palace in Amsterdam: A Brief History of the Building and Its Uses*. Amsterdam: Stichting Koninklijk Paleis te Amsterdam.

Kropotkin, P. A., Prince. 1901. "Modern Science and Anarchism." Trans. 1903. Reprinted as pp. 57–93 in E. Capouya and K. Tompkins, eds., *The Essential Kropotkin*. New York: Liveright, 1975.

Kropotkin, P. A., Prince. 1902. *Mutual Aid: A Factor of Evolution*. New York: New York University Press, 1972.

Kuehn, Manfred. 2001. *Kant: A Biography*. Cambridge: Cambridge University Press.

Kukathas, Chandran. 1996. "What's the Big Idea?" *Reason* (November)

Lacy, Norris J., and Geoffrey Ashe. 1997. *The Arthurian Handbook*. 2nd ed. New York: Garland.

Lakoff, George. 1996. *Moral Politics: How Liberals and Conservatives Think*. Chicago: University of Chicago Press. 2nd ed., 2002.

Langford, Paul. 1992. *A Polite and Commercial People: England 1727–1783*. Oxford: Oxford University Press.

Lanham, Richard. 1976. *Motives of Eloquence: Literary Rhetoric in the Renaissance*. New Haven: Yale University Press.

Lanham, Richard A. 1993. *The Electronic Word: Democracy, Technology, and the Arts*. Chicago: University of Chicago Press.

Lasch, Christopher. 1979. *The Culture of Narcissism: American Life in an Age of Diminishing Expectations*. New York: Norton (Warner Book paper).

Lavoie, Don C. 1990. Introduction. Pp. 1–18 in Lavoie, ed. *Economics and Hermeneutics*.

Lavoie, Don, ed. 1991. *Economics and Hermeneutics*. London: Routledge.

Lawrence, D. H. 1936. "Morality and the Novel." From *Phoenix I*. Reprinted as pp. 127–131 in David Lodge, ed., *20th Century Literary Criticism: A Reader*. London: Longman, 1972.

Le Goff, Jacques. 1963. "Licit and Illicit Trades in the Medieval West." Trans. A. Goldhammer. Pp. 58–70 in Le Goff, *Time, Work, and Culture in the Middle Ages*. Chicago: University of Chicago Press, 1980.

Le Guin, Ursula K. 1969. *The Left Hand of Darkness*. New York: Ace Books.

Le Guin, Ursula K. 1974. *The Dispossessed*. New York: Harper and Row, Avon Book edition.

Ledbetter, Huddie "Leadbelly." 1937. "The Bourgeois Blues." P. 77 in J. A. Lomax and A. Lomax, eds., *Leadbelly: A Collection of World-Famous Songs*. New York: Folkways Music Publishers, 1959.

Leighton, John, ed. 2002. *100 Masterpieces of the Van Gogh Museum*. Text by Denise Willemstein. Amsterdam: Van Gogh Museum Enterprises.

Lendvai, Paul. 1999. *The Hungarians: A Thousand Years of Victory in Defeat*. Trans. from the German by Ann Major. Princeton: Princeton University Press, 2003.

Leo XIII. 1891. *Rerum Novarum (On the Condition of the Working Classes)*. Encyclical Letter issued on May 15. English translation at Archdiocese of St. Paul and Minneapolis, Office for Social Justice, at http://www.osjspm.org/cst/rn.htm.

Leopardi, Giacomo. 1845. *Pensieri: A Bilingual Edition*. Trans. W. S. Di Piero. New York: Oxford University Press, 1984.

Lev, Michael A. 2004. "The Great Migration of China." *Chicago Tribune*, Dec. 27, 28, 29.

Lewis, C. S. c. 1941–1942. "On Ethics." First published in *Christian Reflections*, W. Hooper, ed. London: Bles, 1967. New York: Harper Collins, 1981.

Lewis, C. S. 1942. "Satan." From his *A Preface to "Paradise Lost."* Reprinted as pp. 196–204 in Arthur E. Barjer, ed. *Milton: Modern Essays in Criticism*. New York: Oxford University Press, 1965.

Lewis, C. S. 1943. *The Screwtape Letters, and Screwtape Proposes a Toast*. London: Macmillan, 1961.

Lewis, C. S. 1943–1945. *Mere Christianity*. London: Macmillan, 1952. Touchstone Book, 1996.

Lewis, C. S. 1960. *The Four Loves*. New York: Harcourt, Brace.

Lewis, Sinclair. 1922. *Babbitt*. New York: Harcourt Brace Jovanovich.

Lindert, Peter H. 1978. *Fertility and Scarcity in America*. Princeton: Princeton University Press.

Lindert, Peter H. 2003. "Voice and Growth: Was Churchill Right?" *Journal of Economic History* 63 (June): 315–350.

Lisska, Anthony. 1996. *Aquinas's Theory of Natural Law: An Analytic Reconstruction*. Oxford: Oxford University Press.

Little, Lester K. 1978. *Religious Poverty and the Profit Economy in Medieval Europe*. Ithaca: Cornell University Press.

Lodge, David. 1988. *Nice Work*. Harmondsworth: Penguin, 1990.

Lodge, David. 1999. *Home Truths: A Novella*. London: Penguin, 2000.

Lodge, David. 2001. *Thinks . . .* London: Penguin.

Loftus, L. S., and W. N. Arnold. 1991. "Vincent van Gogh's Illness: Acute Intermittent Porphyria?" *British Medical Journal* 303: 1589–1591.

Lomasky, Loren. 1987. *Persons, Rights, and the Moral Community*. Oxford: Oxford University Press.

Lomax, John A. 1910. *Cowboys Songs and Other Frontier Ballads*. New York: Sturgis & Walton.

Lombardo, Paul. N.d. "Eugenic Sterilization Laws." MS, University of Virginia Medical School. At http://www.eugenicsarchive.org/html/eugenics/essay8text.html.

London, Jack. 1904. *The Sea Wolf*. New York: Modern Library ed., 2000.

Long, Jason, and Joseph Ferrie. 2005. "A Tale of Two Labor Markets: Intergenerational Occupational Mobility in Britain and the U.S. since 1850." Working paper 11253. Cambridge: National Bureau of Economic Research.

Luban, David. 1992. "Justice Holmes and Judicial Virtue." Pp. 235–264 in Chapman and Galston, eds., *Virtue*.

Lynn, Michael, and Ann Lynn. 2004. "National Values and Tipping Customs: A Replication and Extension." *Journal of Hospitality and Tourist Research* 28: 356–364, in MS at http://www.people.cornell.edu/pages/wml3/working_papers.htm.

Macaulay, Stewart. 1963. "Non-Contractual Relations in Business: A Preliminary Study." *American Sociological Review* 28: 55–67. Reprinted as pp. 191–205 in Granovetter and Swedberg, 2001.

Macaulay, T. B. 1830. "Southey's Colloquies on Society." *Edinburgh Review,* Jan. Reprinted in *Critical, Historical, and Miscellaneous Essays by Lord Macaulay*. Boston, 1860 (1881 ed.), vol. 2, pp. 132–187.

Macaulay, T. B. 1837. "Lord Bacon." *Edinburgh Review,* July. Reprinted in *Essays*, vol. 3, pp. 336–495.

Macaulay, T. B. 1842. "Frederic the Great." *Edinburgh Review,* April. Reprinted in *Essays*, vol. 5, pp. 148–247.

Macaulay, T. B. 1842. "Horatius at the Bridge." From *Lays of Ancient Rome*. Pp. 807–824 in G. M. Young, ed. *Macaulay*. Cambridge, Mass.: Harvard University Press, 1952 [1967].

Macfarlane, Alan. 1987. *The Culture of Capitalism*. Oxford: Basil Blackwell.

Macfarlane, Alan. 2000. *The Riddle of the Modern World: Of Liberty, Wealth, and Equality*. Basingstoke, Hampshire: Palgrave.

MacFarquhar, Larissa. 2001. "The Bench Burner." *New Yorker,* Dec. 10, pp. 78–89.

MacIntyre, Alasdair. 1981. *After Virtue: A Study in Moral Theory.* Notre Dame: University of Notre Dame Press.

MacIntyre, Alasdair. 1988. *Whose Justice? Whose Rationality?* London: Duckworth.

MacIntyre, Alasdair. 1999. *Dependent Rational Animals: Why Human Beings Need the Virtues.* Chicago, Ill.: Open Court.

Maddison, Angus. 1995. *Monitoring the World Economy, 1820–1992.* Paris: Organization for Economic Cooperation and Development.

Maddison, Angus. 2001. *The World Economy: A Millennial Perspective.* Paris: Organization for Economic Cooperation and Development.

Mailer, Norman. 1948. *The Naked and the Dead.* New York: Random House (Modern Library ed.).

Mailer, Norman. 1997. *The Gospel According to the Son.* New York: Random House, Abacus Book.

Mailer, Norman. 2002. "Birds and Lions: Writing from the Inside Out." *New Yorker,* Dec. 23 and 30, pp. 76–84.

Malthus, T. R. 1798. *An Essay on the Principle of Population.* Reprinted in Wrigley and Souden 1986.

Mann, Thomas. 1901. *Buddenbrooks.* Trans. H. T. Lowe-Porter. New York: Vintage, 1952.

Mann, Thomas. 1912. *Death in Venice.* Trans. (1930) H. T. Lowe-Porter. In Mann, *Death in Venice and Seven Other Stories.* New York: Vintage Books, n.d.

Mansfield, Harvey C. 1966. *Machiavelli's Virtue.* Chicago: University of Chicago Press.

Mansfield, Harvey C. 2003. "Liberty and Virtue in the American Founding." Pp. 3–28 in Peter Berkowitz, ed. *Never a Matter of Indifference: Sustaining Virtue in a Free Republic.* Stanford, Calif.: Hoover Institution Press. Reprinted at http://www-hoover.stanford.edu/publications/books/fulltext/virtue/3.pdf.

Mansfield, Harvey C., and Nathan Tarcov, trans. and eds. 1996. Introduction. Machiavelli, *Discourses on Livy.* Chicago: University of Chicago Press.

Margo, Robert. 2000. "The Labor Force in the Nineteenth Century." Pp. 207–243 in S. L. Engerman and R. E. Gallman, eds., *The Cambridge Economic History of the United States,* vol. 2, *The Long Nineteenth Century.* Cambridge: Cambridge University Press.

Margolis, Howard. 1982. *Selfishness, Altruism, and Rationality.* Cambridge, Mass.: Harvard University Press.

Marshall, Alfred. 1890. *Principles of Economics.* 8th ed. London: Macmillan, 1920.

Marx, Karl. 1867. *Capital: A Critique of Political Economy.* Trans. E. Undermann from the 4th German ed., F. Engels ed. Chicago: Charles H. Kerr & Co., 1906. New York: Modern Library (Random House), n.d.

Marx, Karl, and Friedrich Engels. 1848. *The Communist Manifesto.* Trans., with additional notes and introduction, F. L. Bender, 1888. Norton Critical Edition. New York: W. W. Norton, 1988.

Masson, Jeffrey Moussaieff. 1990. *Final Analysis: The Making and Unmaking of a Psychoanalyst.* New York: Simon and Schuster, Pocket Books.

Maus, Katharine Eisaman. 1997. "Introduction to *Richard II.*" Pp. 943–951 in S. Greenblatt et al., eds. *The Norton Shakespeare.* New York: W. W. Norton.

Mazzini, Giuseppe. 1830–1872. *Selected Writings.* N. Gangulee, ed. London: Lindsay Drummond, 1945.

McClay, Wilfred. 1993. "The Strange Career of *The Lonely Crowd;* or, The Antinomies of Autonomy." Pp. 397–440 in T. L. Haskell and R. F. Teichgraeber III, eds., *The Culture of the Market: Historical Essays.* Cambridge: Cambridge University Press.

McClelland, David C. 1961. *The Achievement Society.* Princeton: Van Nostrand.

McCloskey, Deirdre N. 1981. "The Industrial Revolution, 1780–1860: A Survey." Chap. 6 in Floud and McCloskey eds., *The Economic History of Britain, 1700–Present,* vol. 1, pp. 103–127. Cambridge: Cambridge University Press.

McCloskey, Deirdre N. 1985. *The Applied Theory of Price,* 2nd ed. New York: Macmillan.

McCloskey, Deirdre. 1985. *The Rhetoric of Economics.* Madison: University of Wisconsin Press.

McCloskey, Deirdre N. 1990. *If You're So Smart: The Narrative of Economic Expertise.* Chicago: University of Chicago Press.

McCloskey, Deirdre N. 1991. "The Essential Rhetoric of Law, Literature, and Liberty." Review of Posner's *Law as Literature,* Fish's *Doing What Comes Naturally,* and White's *Justice as Translation. Critical Review* 5 (1) (Spring): 203–223.

McCloskey, Deirdre N. 1994. "Bourgeois Virtue." *American Scholar* 63 (2, Spring): 177–191.

McCloskey, Deirdre N. 1994. *Knowledge and Persuasion in Economics.* Cambridge: Cambridge University Press.

McCloskey, Deirdre N., ed. 1993. *Second Thoughts: Myths and Morals of U.S. Economic History.* New York: Oxford University Press.

McCloskey, Deirdre N., and Arjo Klamer. 1995. "One Quarter of GDP Is Persuasion." *American Economic Review* 85 (May): 191–195.

McCloskey, Helen S. 2003. *The Strain of Roots: A Collection of Poems.* Lunenburg, Vt.: Stinehour Press.

McCloskey, Robert G. 1951. *American Conservatism in the Age of Enterprise: A Study of William Graham Sumner, Stephen J. Field, and Andrew Carnegie.* Cambridge, Mass.: Harvard University Press.

McCracken, Grant. 1997. *Plenitude.* Toronto: Periph.: Fluide.

McDowell, John. 1979. "Virtue and Reason." *Monist* 62: 331–350. Reprinted as pp. 141–162 in Crisp and Slote, eds., *Virtue Ethics.*

McInerny,, Ralph. 1999. Preface to his edition of Aquinas, *Disputed Questions on Virtue.* South Bend, IN: St. Augustine Press.

McNeill, William H. 1974. *Venice: The Hinge of Europe, 1081–1797.* Chicago: University of Chicago Press.

McNeill, William H. 1980. *The Human Condition: An Ecological and Historical View.* Princeton: Princeton University Press.

McNeill, William H. 1982. *The Pursuit of Power: Technology, Armed Force, and Society since A.D. 1000.* Chicago: University of Chicago Press.

McPherson, James M. 2003. "A Confederate Guerrilla." Review of T. J. Stiles, *Jesse James. New York Review of Books,* Feb. 27, pp. 21–22.

Menand, Louis. 2002. "What Comes Naturally: Does Evolution Explain Who We Are?" Review of S. Pinker, *The Blank Slate. New Yorker,* Nov 25. Posted at http://www.newyorker.com/critics/books/?021125crbo_books.

Mencken, H. L. 1916. "Theodore Dreiser." From *A Book of Prefaces.* Reprinted as pp. 35–56 in A. Cooke, ed., *The Vintage Mencken.* New York: Vintage, 1956.

Mencken, H. L. 1919. "Professor Veblen." In *Prejudices,* 1st ser. Reprinted as pp. 200–210 in H. Cairns, ed., H. L. Mencken, *The American Scene: A Reader.* New York: Knopf, 1965.

Mencken, H. L. 1922. "Beethoven." *Baltimore Sun* and *American Mercury.* Reprinted in *Prejudices,* 5th ser., 1926, and as pp. 424–428 in H. L. Mencken, *The American Scene: A Reader,* H. Cairns, ed. New York: Knopf, 1965.

Mencken, H. L. 1922. "On Being an American." In *Prejudices*, 3rd ser. Reprinted as pp. 6–38 in Mencken, *The American Scene: A Reader*. H. Cairns, ed. New York: Knopf, 1965.

Mencken, H. L. 1922. *Prejudices*. 3rd ser. New York: Knopf.

Mencken, H. L. 1922. "Types of Men." In *Prejudices*, 3rd ser. New York: Knopf.

Merton, Thomas. 1956. *Thoughts in Solitude*. New York: Farrar, Straus and Giroux.

Merton, Thomas. 1962. *New Seeds of Contemplation*. New York: New Directions, 1972.

Midgley, Mary. 1984. *Wickedness: A Philosophical Essay*. London: Routledge.

Mill, John Stuart. 1838. "The Mind and Character of Jeremy Bentham." *Westminster Review*. Excerpted pp. 316–318 in Dickens, *Hard Times*, Norton Critical Edition.

Mill, John Stuart. 1869. *On the Subjection of Women*. Sue Mansfield, ed. Croft Classics. Arlington Heights, Ill.: Harlan Davidson, 1980.

Mill, John Stuart. 1871. *Principles of Political Economy, with Some of Their Applications to Social Philosophy*. London: Longmans, Green, 1909.

Mill, John Stuart. 1874 [1844]. "Essay V." In his *Essays on Some Unsettled Issues in Political Economy*. 2nd ed. London.

Miller, Arthur. 1949. *Death of a Salesman*. In Gerald Weales, ed., *Death of a Salesman: Text and Criticism*. New York: Viking Press, 1967.

Miller, Arthur. 1957. Introduction to *Collected Plays*. Reprinted pp. 155–171 in Gerald Weales, ed., *Death of a Salesman: Text and Criticism*. New York: Viking Press, 1967.

Miller, Arthur. 1959, "Morality and Modern Drama: Interview with Phillip Gelb." *Educational Theatre Journal*, Oct. Reprinted as pp. 172–186 in Gerald Weales, ed., *Death of a Salesman: Text and Criticism*. New York: Viking Press, 1967.

Miller, Donald L. 1996. *City of the Century: The Epic of Chicago and the Making of America*. New York: Simon and Schuster. Trade paperback, 2003.

Milton, John. 1667. *Paradise Lost*. Alastair Fowler, ed. 2nd ed. London: Longman, 1998.

Milton, John. 1671. *Paradise Regained*. Pp. 407–462 in Milton, *The Complete Poems*. John Leonard, ed. London: Penguin, 1998.

Mokyr, Joel. 2002. *The Gifts of Athena: Historical Origins of the Knowledge Economy*. Princeton: Princeton University Press.

Molière, J. B. P. 1670. *Le bourgeois gentilhomme*. Trans. A. R. Waller as *The Citizen Turn'd Gentleman*, vol. 7. Edinburgh: John Grant, 1926.

Moore, Gary. 2003. *Faithful Finances 101*. West Conshohocken, Pa.: Templeton Foundation Press.

Morse, Jennifer Roback. 2001. *Love and Economics: Why the Laissez Faire Family Doesn't Work*. Dallas: Spence.

Mueller, John. 1999. *Capitalism, Democracy, and Ralph's Pretty Good Grocery*. Princeton: Princeton University Press.

Muller, Jerry. 2002. *The Mind and the Market: Capitalism in Modern European Thought*. New York: Knopf.

Munro, Alice. 2003. *Hateship, Friendship, Courtship, Loveship, Marriage: Stories*. New York: Vintage.

Murdoch, Iris. 1967. "The Sovereignty of Good over Other Concepts." Leslie Stephen Lecture. Pp. 77–104 in Murdoch, *The Sovereignty of Good*. London: Routledge, 1970, 1985.

Murdoch, Iris. 1969. "On 'God' and 'Good.'" From *The Anatomy of Knowledge*, republished as pp. 46–76 in Murdoch, *The Sovereignty of Good*. London: Routledge, 1970, 1985.

Murdoch, Iris. 1992. *Metaphysics as a Guide to Morals.* Based on the 1982 Gifford Lecture. University of Edinburgh. London: Penguin.

Murphy, Sean. 2004. "American Presidents with Irish Ancestors." Bray, Co. Wicklow, Ireland: Centre for Irish Genealogical and Historical Studies. http://homepage.eircom.net/ ~seanjmurphy/dir/pres.htm.

Murray, Gilbert. 1915. *The Stoic Philosophy.* London: Allen and Unwin.

Murray, John E., and Metin M. Cosgel. 1999. "Between God and Market: Influences of Economy and Spirit on Shaker Communal Dairying, 1830–1875." *Social Science History* 23 (Spring): 41–65.

Mussolini, Benito, and Giovanni Gentile. 1932. "La dottrina del fascismo" [The doctrine of Fascism]. *Enciclopedia Italiana,* trans. at http://www.worldfuturefund.org/wffmaster/ Reading/Germany/mussolini.htm.

Najita, Tetsuo. 1987. *Visions of Virtue in Togugawa Japan: The Kaitokudo Merchant Academy of Osaka.* Honolulu: University of Hawai'i Press.

Nakane, Chie. 1990. Introduction. Pp. 3–9 in Nakane and S. Oishi, eds. *Tokugawa Japan: The Social and Economic Antecedents of Modern Japan.* Tokyo: University of Tokyo Press.

Nederlands Instituut voor Oorlogsdocumentatie. April 10, 2002. "Srebrenica: A Safe Area." "Presentation Speech." At http://www. srebrenica.nl/en/a_index.htm.

Nelson, Julie A. 1996. *Feminism, Objectivity, and Economics.* London: Routledge.

Nelson, Robert H. 1991. *Reaching for Heaven on Earth: The Theological Meaning of Economics.* Lanham, Md.: Rowman & Littlefield.

Nelson, Robert H. 2001. *Economics as Religion: From Samuelson to Chicago and Beyond.* University Park: Pennsylvania State University Press.

Njàl's Saga. c. AD 1275. Trans. with an introduction by Magnus Magnusson and Hermann Pálsson. London: Penguin, 1960.

Noddings, Nel. 1984. *Caring: A Feminine Approach to Ethics and Moral Education.* Berkeley: University of California Press.

Novak, Michael. 1984. *Catholic Social Thought and Liberal Institutions: Freedom with Justice.* 2nd ed. New Brunswick: Transaction, 1989.

Novak, Michael. 1996. *Business as a Calling: Work and the Examined Life.* New York: Free Press.

Nozick, Robert. 1974. *Anarchy, State, and Utopia.* New York: Basic Books.

Nozick, Robert. 1981. *Philosophical Explanations.* Cambridge, Mass.: Harvard University Press.

Nozick, Robert. 1989. *The Examined Life: Philosophical Meditations.* New York: Simon and Schuster.

Nozick, Robert. 2001. *Invariances: The Structure of the Objective World.* Cambridge, Mass.: Harvard University Press.

Nussbaum, Martha. 1986. *The Fragility of Goodness: Luck and Ethics in Greek Tragedy and Philosophy.* Cambridge: Cambridge University Press.

Nye, John V. C. 1997. "Thinking about the State: Property Rights, Trade, and Changing Contractual Arrangements in a World with Coercion." Pp. 121–142 in John Drobak and John Nye, eds. *The Frontiers of the New Institutional Economics.* New York: Academic Press.

Oeppen, Jim, and James W. Vaupel. 2002. "Broken Limits to Life Expectancy." *Science* 296 (May): 1028–1029.

Orr, H. Allen. 2003. "Darwinian Storytelling." Review of Steven Pinker, *The Blank Slate. New York Review of Books* Feb. 27, pp. 17–18.

Orwell, George. 1940. "Charles Dickens." Pp. 135–185 in Orwell, *Essays*, 2002.

Orwell, George. 1944. "As I Please 37." *Tribune*, August 11. Pp. 705–708 in Orwell, *Essays*.

Orwell, George. 1944. Review of *The Edge of the Abyss* by Alfred Noyes. *Observer*, February 27. Pp. 549–552 in Orwell, *Essays*.

Orwell, George. 1949. "Reflections on Gandhi." *Partisan Review*, Jan. Pp. 1349–1357 in Orwell, *Essays*, 2002.

Orwell, George. 2002. *Essays*. John Carey, ed. Everyman Library. New York: Knopf.

Ostrom, Elinor, Roy Gardner, and James Walker. 1994. *Rules, Games, and Common-Pool Resources*. Ann Arbor: University of Michigan Press.

Oz, Amos. 1979. *Under This Blazing Light*. Trans. Nicolas de Lange. Cambridge: Cambridge University Press, 1995.

Page, R. I. 1995. *Chronicles of the Vikings: Records, Memorials, and Myths*. London: British Museum Press.

Pahl, Ray. 2000. *On Friendship*. Cambridge: Polity.

Parker, Geoffrey. 1996. *The Military Revolution.: Military Innovation and the Rise of the West, 1500–1800*. 2nd ed. Cambridge: Cambridge University Press.

Parks, Tim. 2002. "The Cosimos." Review of Kent, *Cosimo de' Medici;* and of Luchinat and others, *The Medici. New York Review of Books*, December 19, pp. 75–77.

Pascoe, Robin, and Christopher Catling. 1995. *Eyewitness Travel Guide to Amsterdam*. London: Dorling Kindersley.

Peterson, Christopher, and Martin E. P. Seligman. 2004. *Character Strengths and Virtues: A Handbook and Classification*. Oxford: Oxford University Press.

Pierpont, Claudia Roth. 2002. "Tough Guy: The Mystery of Dashiell Hammett." *New Yorker*, Feb. 11, 66–81.

Pincoffs, Edmund. 1986. *Quandaries and Virtues: Against Reductivism in Ethics*. Lawrence: University of Kansas Press.

Pinker, Steven. 1997. *How the Mind Works*. New York: Norton.

Plato. c. 360 BC. *The Republic*. Trans. G. M. A. Grube; rev. ed. C. D. C. Reeve. Pp. 971–1223 in J. M. Cooper, ed., *Plato: Complete Works*. Indianapolis: Hackett, 1997.

Plato. c. 350 BC. *Definitions*. Trans. D. S. Hutchinson. Pp. 1677–1686 in J. M. Cooper, ed., *Plato: Complete Works*. Indianapolis/Cambridge: Hackett, 1997.

Pluhar, Werner S. 1987. Translator's Introduction. Pp. xxiii–cix in Immanuel Kant, *Critique of Judgment*, 1790, trans. Pluhar. Indianapolis: Hackett.

Pocock, J. G. A. 1983. "Cambridge Paradigms and Scottish Philosophers." Pp. 235–252 in Hont and Ignatieff.

Poe, Edgar Allan. 1849. "Fifty Suggestions." *Graham's Magazine*, May, pp. 317–319.

Polanyi, Michael. 1951. *The Logic of Liberty*. Chicago: University of Chicago Press.

Pool, Robert. 1989. "Strange Bedfellows." *Science* 245 (18 Aug.): 700–703.

Poole, Joyce H., P. L. Tyack, Angela S. Stoeger-Horwathm, and Stephanie Watwood. 2005. "Animal Behavior: Elephants Are Capable of Vocal Learning." *Nature* 434 (24 March): 455–456.

Pope, Alexander. 1731. "Epistle IV to Richard Boyle, Earl of Burlington." Pp. 314–321 in *Pope: Poetical Works*, H. Davis, ed. Oxford: Oxford University Press, 1966.

Pope, Stephen J. 2002. "Overview of the Ethics of St. Thomas Aquinas." Pp. 30–53 in Pope, ed., *The Ethics of Aquinas.*

Pope, Stephen J., ed. 2002. *The Ethics of Aquinas.* Washington, D.C.: Georgetown University Press.

Popkin, Samuel L. 1979. *The Rational Peasant: The Political Economy of Rural Society in Vietnam.* Berkeley: University of California Press.

Posner, Richard. 1992. *Economic Analysis of Law.* 4th ed. Boston: Little, Brown.

Prindle, David. 2003. *The Search for Democratic Capitalism: Politics and Economics in American Thought.* MS, Department of Government, University of Texas at Austin. Forthcoming 2006, Johns Hopkins University Press.

Pufendorf, Samuel. 1673. *On the Duty of Man and Citizen.* James Tilly, ed.; trans. Michael Silverthorne. Cambridge: Cambridge University Press, 1991.

Putnam, Hilary. 1990. *Realism with a Human Face.* J. Conant, ed. Cambridge, Mass.: Harvard University Press.

Putnam, Hilary. 2002. *The Collapse of the Fact/Value Dichotomy, and Other Essays.* Cambridge, Mass.: Harvard University Press.

Quinn, D. Michael. 1996. *Same-Sex Dynamics among Nineteenth-Century Americans: A Mormon Example.* Urbana: University of Illinois Press.

Rachels, James. 1999. *The Elements of Moral Philosophy.* 3rd ed. New York: McGraw-Hill.

Raftis, J. Ambrose. 1964. *Tenure and Mobility: Studies in the Social History of the Medieval English Village.* Toronto: Pontifical Institute of Medieval Studies.

Read, Herbert. 1931. *The Meaning of Art.* New edition. New York: Praeger, 1969.

Reddy, William. 2001. *The Navigation of Feeling: A Framework for the History of Emotions.* Cambridge: Cambridge University Press.

Reich, Robert. 1991. *The Work of Nations: Preparing Ourselves for 21st Century Capitalism.* New York: Knopf.

Reich, Robert. 2003. *I'll Be Short: Essentials for a Decent Working Society.* Boston: Beacon.

Ricardo, David. 1817. *Principles of Political Economy and Taxation.* R. M. Hartwell, ed. Harmondsworth: Penguin, 1971.

Richerson, Peter J., and Robert Boyd. 2004. *Not by Genes Alone: How Culture Transformed Human Evolution.* Chicago: University of Chicago Press.

Ridley, Matt. 1996. *The Origins of Virtue: Human Instincts and the Evolution of Cooperation.* New York: Penguin.

Riley, James. 2001. *Rising Life Expectancy: A Global History.* Cambridge: Cambridge University Press.

Robbins, Lionel. 1932. *The Nature and Significance of Economic Science.* London: Macmillan.

Roberts, Russell. 2001. *The Invisible Heart: An Economic Romance.* Cambridge: MIT Press.

Roget, Peter Mark. 1962. *Roget's International Thesaurus.* 3rd ed. New York: Crowell.

Rorty, Amélie Oksenberg. 1980. "The Place of Contemplation in Aristotle's *Nicomachean Ethics.*" Pp. 377–394 in Rorty, ed., *Essays on Aristotle's Ethics.* Los Angeles: University of California Press.

Rorty, Amélie Oksenberg. 1983. "Experiments in Philosophic Genre: Descartes' Meditations." *Critical Inquiry* 9 (March): 545–565.

Rorty, Richard. 1987. "Science as Solidarity." Pp. 38–52 in John Nelson, Allan Megill, and Deirdre McCloskey, eds., *The Rhetoric of the Human Science: Language and Argument in Scholarship and Public Affairs*. Madison: University of Wisconsin Press.

Rorty, Richard. 2004. "Philosophy Envy." *Daedalus* (Fall): 18–24. Reprinted at http://www.amacad.org/publications/fall2004/rorty.pdf.

Rorty, Richard. 1979. *Philosophy and the Mirror of Nature*. Princeton: Princeton University Press.

Rorty, Richard. 1982. *Consequences of Pragmatism (Essays: 1972–1980)*. Minneapolis: University of Minnesota Press.

Rorty, Richard. 1985. "Postmodernist Bourgeois Liberalism." Pp. 214–221 in Robert Hollinger, ed. *Hermeneutics and Praxis*. Notre Dame, Ind.: University of Notre Dame Press.

Rorty, Richard. 1994. "Ethics without Principles." Reprinted in *Philosophy and Social Hope*. London: Penguin, 1999. Available at http://www.philosophy.uncc.edu/mleldrid/cmt/EWOP.html.

Rosand, David. 2001. *Myths of Venice: The Figuration of a State*. Chapel Hill: University of North Carolina Press.

Rose, Mary Beth. 2002. *Gender and Heroism in Early Modern English Literature*. Chicago: University of Chicago Press.

Ross, Dorothy. 1995. "American Exceptionalism." Pp. 22–23 in Fox and Kloppenberg, eds., *Companion*.

Rotella, Guy. 2001. "Synonymous with Kept: Frost and Economics." Pp. 241–260 in Robert Faggen, ed., *The Cambridge Companion to Robert Frost*. Cambridge: Cambridge University Press.

Rousseau, Jean-Jacques. 1755. *Discourse on the Origin of Inequality*. Pp. 25–109 in D. A. Cress, trans. and ed., *Jean-Jacques Rousseau: Basic Political Writings*. Indianapolis: Hackett, 1987

Rousseau, Jean-Jacques. 1755. *Discourse on Political Economy*. Pp. 111–138 in D. A. Cress, trans. and ed., *Jean-Jacques Rousseau: Basic Political Writings*. Indianapolis: Hackett, 1987.

Ruskin, John. 1851–1853. *The Stones of Venice*. New York: Peter Fenelon Collier, 1900.

Russell, Bertrand. 1903. "A Free Man's Worship." *Independent Review*. Reprinted in *Why I Am Not a Christian and Other Essays on Religion and Related Subject*. New York: Simon and Schuster, 1957.

Ryan, Alan. 1987. "Human Nature." in Janet Coleman, William Connolly, Alan Ryan, eds., *The Blackwell Encyclopedia of Political Thought*. London: Blackwell Reference.

Sacks, Jonathan. 2002. *The Dignity of Difference: How to Avoid the Clash of Civilizations*. London: Continuum.

Sahlins, Marshall. 1972. *Stone Age Economics*. New ed. London: Routledge, 2003.

Saiving, Valerie. 1960. "The Human Situation: A Feminine View." *Journal of Religion* 40 (April): 100–112.

Sali-I-Martin, X. 2002. "The Disturbing 'Rise' of Global Income Inequality." National Bureau of Economic Research, working paper no. 8904.

Santayana, George. 1943–1953. *Persons and Places*. Vol. 1 of *The Works of George Santayana*. Cambridge, Mass.: MIT Press, 1986.

Santoni, Ronald E. 1995. *Bad Faith, Good Faith, and Authenticity in Sartre's Early Philosophy.* Philadelphia: Temple University Press.

Sartre, Jean-Paul. 1944. *Anti-Semite and Jew: An Exploration of the Etiology of Hate.* Trans. G. L. Becker, 1948, with a new preface by Michael Walzer. New York: Schocken, 1995.

Sayre, Anne. 1975. *Rosalind Franklin and DNA.* New York: Norton.

Schaefer, Jack. 1949. *Shane.* Boston: Houghton Mifflin. *The Critical Edition.* J. C. Work, ed. Lincoln: University of Nebraska Press, 1984.

Schama, Simon. 1987. *The Embarrassment of Riches: An Interpretation of Dutch Culture in the Golden Age.* Berkeley: University of California Press.

Scherer, F. M. 2003. *Quarter Notes and Bank Notes: The Economics of Music Composition in the Eighteenth and Nineteenth Centuries.* Princeton: Princeton University Press.

Schjeldahl, Peter. 2004. "Dealership: How Marian Goodman Quietly Changed the Contemporary-Art Market." *New Yorker*, Feb. 2: 36–41.

Schmidt, Annie M. G. 1954–1956. *Jip en Janneke 2.* Amsterdam and Antwerp: Querido, 1964, 1984.

Schmidt, Annie M. G. 1956–1958. *Jip and Janneke 3.* Amsterdam: Querido, 1964.

Schmidtz, David. 1993. "Reasons for Altruism." Pp. 52–68 in Ellen Frankel Paul, Fred D. Miller, and Jeffrey Paul, eds., *Altruism.* Cambridge: Cambridge University Press. Reprinted as pp. 164–175 in Aafke E. Komter, ed. *The Gift: An Interdisciplinary Perspective.* Amsterdam: University of Amsterdam Press, 1996.

Schmidtz, David. 1995. *Rational Choice and Moral Agency.* Princeton: Princeton University Press.

Schockenhoff, Eberhard. 2002. "The Theological Virtue of Charity." Pp. 244–258 in Pope, ed., *The Ethics of Aquinas..*

Schumpeter, Joseph A. 1912. *The Theory of Economic Development.* Trans. R. Opie. Cambridge, Mass.: Harvard University Press, 1934.

Schumpeter, Joseph A. 1942. *Capitalism, Socialism and Democracy.* 3rd. ed. New York: Harper and Row, 1950. Harper Torchbook ed. 1962.

Schumpeter, Joseph A. 1954. *History of Economic Analysis.* Elizabeth B. Schumpeter, ed. New York: Oxford University Press.

Schuttner, Scott. 1998. *Basic Stairbuilding.* Newtown, Conn.: Taunton Press.

Schweiker, William. 2004. *Theological Ethics and Global Dynamics in the Time of Many Worlds.* Oxford: Blackwell.

Schweiker, William, and Charles Mathewes, eds. 2004. *Having: Property and Possession in Religious and Social Life.* Grand Rapids. Mich.: Eerdmans.

Seabright, Paul. 2004. *The Company of Strangers: A Natural History of Economic Life.* Princeton: Princeton University Press.

Searle, John. 1969. *Speech Acts: An Essay in the Philosophy of Language.* Cambridge: Cambridge University Press.

Selznick, Philip. 1992. *The Moral Commonwealth: Social Theory and the Promise of Community.* Berkeley: University of California Press.

Sen, Amartya. 1977. "Rational Fools: A Critique of the Behavioral Foundations of Economic Theory." *Philosophy and Public Affairs* 6 (4): 317–344.

Sen, Amartya. 1987. *On Ethics and Economics.* Oxford: Blackwell.

Sen, Amartya. 2000. *Development as Freedom.* New York: Knopf.

Seneca, Lucius Annaeus. Before 65 BC. *De Tranquillitate Animi.* [On the tranquility of the mind.] Trans. William Bell Langsdorf (1900), revised and edited by Michael S. Russo. Sophia Project. http://www.molloy.edu/academic/philosophy/sophia/Seneca/tranquility.htm.

Sennett, Richard. 1998. *The Corrosion of Character: The Personal Consequences of Work in the New Capitalism.* New York: Norton.

Shaftesbury, Anthony Ashley Cooper, 3rd Earl of. 1713. *Characteristics of Men, Manners, Opinions, Times.* 6th edition, 1732, introduced by D. Den Uyl. Indianapolis: Liberty Fund, 2001.

Shalhope, Robert. 1995. "American Revolution." Pp. 23–26 in Fox and Kloppenberg, eds., *Companion.*

Shapin, Steven. 1994. *A History of Truth: Civility and Science in Seventeenth-century England.* Chicago: University of Chicago Press.

Shaw, George Bernard. 1912. *Introduction to Hard Times* (London: Waverly), portion reprinted as pp. 333–340 in G. Ford and S. Monod, eds. *Charles Dickens, Hard Times.* Norton Critical Edition, 2nd ed. New York: W. W. Norton, 1990.

Shields, Carol. 2000. *Dressing Up for the Carnival.* London: Fourth Estate.

Shklar, Judith. 1990. "Montesquieu and the New Republicanism." Pp. 265–279 in Gisela Bock et al., eds., *Machiavelli and Republicanism.*

Silver, Allan. 1990. "Friendship in Commercial Society: Eighteenth Century Social Theory and Modern Sociology." *American Journal of Sociology* 95: 1474–1504.

Sinfield, Alan. 1994. *The Wilde Century: Effeminacy, Oscar Wilde, and the Queer Movement.* New York: Columbia University Press.

Skinner, Quentin. 1990. "The Republican Ideal of Political Liberty." Pp. 293–309 in Gisela Bock et al., eds., *Machiavelli and Republicanism.*

Slivinski, Stephen. 2001. "The Corporate Welfare Budget Bigger Than Ever." Cato Policy Analysis no. 415, October 10. http://www.cato.org/pubs/pas/pa-415es.html.

Sluijter, Eric J. 1991. "Didactic and Disguised Meanings." Pp. 175–207 in David Freedberg and Jan de Vries, eds. *Art in History, History in Art.* Santa Monica, Calif.: Getty Center for the History of Art and the Humanities, University of Chicago Press.

Smith, Adam. 1759, 1790. *The Theory of Moral Sentiments.* Glasgow edition. D. D. Raphael and A. L. Macfie, eds. Indianapolis: Liberty Classics, 1976, 1982.

Smith, Adam. 1762–1763, 1766. *Lectures on Jurisprudence.* R. L. Meek, D. D. Raphael, P. G. Stein, eds. Glasgow edition. Oxford: Oxford University Press, 1978, 1982.

Smith, Adam. 1776. *An Inquiry into the Nature and Causes of the Wealth of Nations.* Glasgow edition. Campbell, Skinner, and Todd, eds. 2 vols. Indianapolis: Liberty Classics, 1976, 1981.

Smith, Adam. 1977. *Correspondence of Adam Smith.* E. C. Mossner and I. S. Ross, eds. Glasgow edition. Oxford: Oxford University Press.

Smith, Adam. 1980. *Essays on Philosophical Subjects.* W. P. D. Wightman and J. J. Bryce, eds. Glasgow edition. Oxford: Oxford University Press.

Smith, Vernon. 2005. Letter to Frans B. M. de Waal. April 9. Submitted to *Scientific American.*

Snyder, Don J. 1995. "Winter Work." *Harper's* Magazine (November). Reprinted as pp. 67–89 in Kathryn Rhett, ed. *Survival Stories: Memoirs of Crisis.* New York: Anchor, 1997.

Solomon, Robert. 1992. *Ethics and Excellence: Cooperation and Integrity in Business.* New York: Oxford University Press.

Solomon, Robert. 2004. "Sympathy for Adam Smith: Some Contemporary Philosophical and Psychological Considerations." Paper, University of Texas at Austin.

Sophocles. c. 409 BC. *Philoctetes*. Trans. D. Grene. Chicago: University of Chicago Press, 1957.

Stark, Rodney. 2001. *One True God: Historical Consequences of Monotheism*. Princeton: Princeton University Press.

Staveren, Irene van. 1999. *Caring for Economics: An Aristotelian Perspective*. Proefschrift [Ph.D. diss.], Erasmus Universiteit Rotterdam. Delft: Eburon Academische Uitverij.

Staveren, Irene van. 2001. *The Values of Economics: An Aristotelian Perspective*. London: Routledge.

Stein, Susan Alyson, ed. 1986. *Van Gogh: A Retrospective*. No place: Beaux Arts editions.

Stiglitz, Joseph. 2002. *Globalization and Its Discontents*. London: Penguin.

Stocker, Michael. 1976. "The Schizophrenia of Modern Ethical Theories." *Journal of Philosophy* 73: 453–466. Reprinted as pp. 66–78 in Crisp and Slote, eds., *Virtue Ethics*.

Strachey, Lytton. 1918. *Eminent Victorians*. Illustrated edition. London: Albion Press, 1988.

Strauss, David A. 1992. "The Liberal Virtues." Pp. 197–203 in Chapman and Galston, eds., *Virtue*.

Strauss, Leo. 1958. *Thoughts on Machiavelli*. Chicago: University of Chicago Press.

Sugden, Robert. 1993. "Thinking as a Team: Towards an Explanation of Non-Selfish Behavior." *Social Philosophy and Policy* 10: 69–89.

Sweeney, Eileen. 2002. "Vice and Sin." Pp. 151–168 in Pope, ed., *The Ethics of Aquinas*.

Sykes, Bryan. 2001. *The Seven Daughters of Eve*. New York: Norton.

Tacitus, Cornelius. AD 98. *Germania*. D. R. Stuart, ed. New York: Macmillan, 1916.

Tacitus, Cornelius. AD 98 *The Agricola and the Germania*. Trans. H. Mattingly, S. A. Handford. Harmondsworth: Penguin, 1948, 1970.

Taka, Iwao. 1997. "Business Ethics in Japan." Pp. 80–86 in *The Blackwell Encyclopedia of Management*, 2nd ed. , vol. 2, *Business Ethics*. Patricia Werhane and R. E. Freeman, eds. Oxford: Blackwell.

Temple, Sir William. 1673. *Observations upon the United Provinces of the Netherlands*. G. Clark, ed. Oxford: Oxford University Press, 1972.

Thompson, Victoria E. 2000. *The Virtuous Marketplace: Women and Men, Money and Politics in Paris, 1830–1870*. Baltimore: Johns Hopkins University Press.

Throckmorton, Burton H. 1992. *Gospel Parallels: A Comparison of the Synoptic Gospels*. Nashville: Thomas Nelson.

Thucydides. c. 404 BC. *Peloponnesian War*. Trans. R. Crawley. In Robert B. Strassler, ed., *The Landmark Thucydides*. New York: Free Press, 1996.

Thurber, James. 1939. "The Secret Life of Walter Mitty." *New Yorker*, March 18.

Tillich, Paul. 1933. *Die sozialistische Entscheidung*. Potsdam: Protte, 1933. Trans. as *The Socialist Decision*, trans. Franklin Sherman. New York: Harper & Row, 1977.

Tillich, Paul. 1952. *The Courage to Be*. New Haven: Yale University Press. 2nd ed. Introduction by P. J. Gomes, 2000.

Tillich, Paul, and Carl Richard Wegener. 1919. "Answer to an Inquiry of the Protestant Consistory of Brandenburg."

Tilly, Charles. 1990. *Coercion, Capital, and European States, AD 990–1900*. Oxford: Blackwell.

Tocqueville, Alexis de. 1840. *Democracy in America*. Vol. 2. Trans. Phillips Bradley. New York: Knopf, 1945 (Vintage edition 1954).

Todorov, Tzvetan. 2000. *Hope and Memory: Lessons from the Twentieth Century.* David Bellos, trans. Princeton: Princeton University Press, 2003.

Tompkins, Jane. 1987. "Me and My Shadow." *New Literary History* 19. Reprinted as pp. 2129–2143 in *The Norton Anthology of Theory and Criticism,* ed. Vincent B. Leitch. New York: W. W. Norton, 2001.

Tompkins, Jane. 1992. *West of Everything: The Inner Life of Westerns.* New York: Oxford University Press.

Totman, Conrad. 1993. *Early Modern Japan.* Berkeley: University of California Press.

Toulmin, Stephen. 1972. *Human Understanding: The Collective Use and Evolution of Concepts.* Princeton: Princeton University Press.

Tronto, Joan C. 1993. *Moral Boundaries: A Political Argument for an Ethics of Care.* New York: Routledge.

Tuck, Richard. 1987. "Hobbes." Pp. 210–213 in J. Coleman, W. Connolly, and A. Ryan, eds., *The Blackwell Encyclopedia of Political Thought.* Oxford: Basil Blackwell.

Turner, Jonathan H. 2000. *On the Origins of Human Emotions.* Princeton: Princeton University Press.

Ulrich, Laurel Thatcher. 1990. *A Midwife's Tale: The Life of Martha Ballard, Based on Her Diary, 1785–1812.* New York: Vintage/Random House.

U.S. Bureau of the Census. 1992. *Statistical Abstract of the United States, 1981–82.* 103rd ed. Washington, D.C.: Government Printing Office.

Upchurch, Carl. 1996. *Convicted in the Womb: One Man's Journey from Prison to Peacemaker.* New York: Bantam, paperback, 1997.

Uzzi, Brian. 1999. "Embeddedness in the Making of Capital." *American Journal of Sociology* 64: 481–505.

van Gogh, Vincent. 1883–1890. *The Letters of Vincent van Gogh.* Ronald de Leeuw, ed.; trans. A. Pomerans. London: Penguin, 1996, 1997.

van Gogh, Vincent. 1883–1890. *Verzamelde Brieven van* [Collected letters from] *Vincent van Gogh.* 1953. Derde deel [3rd vol.] (1883–1890). Amsterdam: Wereldbibliotheek.

Vargas Llosa, Mario. 2001. "The Culture of Liberty." *Foreign Policy* (Jan-Feb). Internet version at http://www.globalpolicy.org/globaliz/cultural/llosa.htm.

Veblen, Thorstein. 1898. "Why Is Economics Not an Evolutionary Science?" *Quarterly Journal of Economics* 12: 373–397. Available on line at http://cepa.newschool.edu/het/profiles/veblen.htm.

Velthuis, Olav. 1996. "The Instrumental and the Intrinsic." Paper, Kunst-en Cultuurwetenschappen, Erasmus University of Rotterdam.

Velthuis, Olav. 2005. *Talking Prices: Meanings of Prices on the Market for Contemporary Art.* Princeton: Princeton University Press.

Vimalakirti Sutra. AD 406. Trans. Burton Watson. New York: Columbia University Press, 1997.

Vinen, Richard. 2000. *A History in Fragments: Europe in the Twentieth Century.* Boston: Little, Brown.

Voltaire. 1733, 1734. *Philosophical Letters.* E. Dilworth, ed. and trans. 1956. New York: Modern Library ed. 1992.

Wagner-Martin, Linda. 2002. "The Romance of Desire in Hemingway's Fiction." Pp. 54–69 in Broer and Holland, eds., *Hemingway and Women.*

Walton, Gary. 1991. *Beyond Winning: The Timeless Wisdom of Great Philosopher Coaches.* Champaign, Ill.: Human Kinetics Publishers.

Waterman, A. M. C. 1991. *Revolution, Economics, and Religion: Christian Political Economy, 1798–1833.* Cambridge: Cambridge University Press.

Weber, Max. 1904–1905. *The Protestant Ethic and the Spirit of Capitalism.* Trans. T. Parsons, 1930, from the 1920 German edition. New York: Scribner's, 1958.

Weber, Max. 1923. *General Economic History* [*Wirtschaftsgeschichte*]. Trans. Frank Knight (Greenberg, 1927). New Brunswick, N.J.: Transaction Books, 1981.

Weil, Simone. 1940. "The *Iliad*, or, The Poem of Force." Trans. Mary McCarthy. *Politics* (Nov. 1945). Reprinted as pp. 162–195 in *Simone Weil: An Anthology*, ed. Siân Miles. London: Weidenfeld and Nicolson, 1986.

Weil, Simone. 1947. *Gravity and Grace.* [*La pesanteur et la grâce*]. Trans. Emma Crawford and Marion von der Ruhr. London: Routledge & Kegan Paul, 1952 (London: Routledge Classics 2002).

Weil, Simone. 1943. *The Need for Roots: Prelude to a Declaration of Duties towards Mankind* [*L'enracinement*, 1949]. Trans. Arthur Wills, with a preface by T. S. Eliot. London: Routledge & Kegan Paul, 1952. London: Routledge Classics, 2002.

Weil, Simone. *Waiting for God.* 1950. [*L'attende de Dieu.*] Trans. Emma Crauford. New York: G. P. Putnam, 1951 (Harper Colophon 1973).

Weinstein, Arnold. 1997. *Classics of American Literature.* Chantilly, Va.: Teaching Company.

Weinstein, Arnold. 1998. *20th-Century American Fiction.* Chantilly, Va.: Teaching Company.

Wells, Spencer. 2002. *The Journey of Man: A Genetic Odyssey.* Princeton: Princeton University Press.

Wheeler, Edward L. 1877. *Deadwood Dick, The Prince of the Road; or, The Black Rider of the Black Hills.* Pp. 173–358 in Brown, *Reading the West.*

White, James Boyd. 1984. *Heracles' Bow: Essays on the Rhetoric and Poetics of the Law.* Madison: University of Wisconsin Press.

White, James Boyd. 1990. *Justice as Translation: An Essay in Cultural and Legal Criticism.* Chicago: University of Chicago Press.

White, Mark D. 2003. "Kantian Dignity and Social Economics." *Forum for Social Economics* 32 (Spring): 1–11.

White, Mark D. 2004. "Multiple Utilities and Weakness of Will: A Kantian Analysis." MS, Department of Political Science, Economics and Philosophy, College of Staten Island. Forthcoming, *Review of Social Economy.*

White, Mark D. 2005. "A Kantian Critique of Neoclassical Law and Economics." MS, Department of Political Science, Economics, and Philosophy, College of Staten Island. Forthcoming, *Review of Political Economy.*

Whitehead, Alfred North. 1938. *Modes of Thought.* New York: Macmillan (ed. of 1968, Free Press).

Wilbur, Richard. 1988. *New and Collected Poems.* New York: Harcourt Brace.

Wilkinson, Bruce. 2000. *The Prayer of Jabez: Breaking Through to the Blessed Life.* Sister, Ore.: Multnomah.

Willey, Basil. 1964. *English Moralists.* London: Chatto & Windus.

Williams, Bernard. 1972. *Morality: An Introduction to Ethics.* Cambridge: Cambridge University Press. Canto ed., 1993.

Williams, Bernard. 1981. *Moral Luck: Philosophical Papers 1973–1980*. Cambridge: Cambridge University Press.

Williams, Bernard. 1985. *Ethics and the Limits of Philosophy*. Cambridge: Harvard University Press.

Williams, H. H. 1910–1911. "Ethics" (in part). *The Encyclopaedia Britannica*. London: Encyclopaedia Britannica.

Williams, Joan. 1995. "Virtue." Pp. 706–709 in Fox and Kloppenberg, eds., *Companion*.

Williams, Ted, and John Underwood. 1970. *The Science of Hitting*. Revised and updated edition. New York: Simon and Schuster, 1986.

Willingham, Kathy G. 2002. "The Sun Hasn't Set Yet: Brett Ashley and the Hero Code Debate." Pp. 34–53 in Broer and Holland, eds., *Hemingway and Women*.

Wilson, A. N. 1999. *God's Funeral: A Biography of Faith and Doubt in Western Civilization*. New York: Ballantine.

Wilson, James Q. 1993. *The Moral Sense*. New York: Free Press.

Winters, Anne. 2004. *The Displaced of Capital*. Chicago: University of Chicago Press.

Wolf, Susan. 1982. "Moral Saints." *Journal of Philosophy* 79: 419–439. Reprinted as pp. 79–98 in Crisp and Slote, eds., *Virtue Ethics*.

Wolfe, Alan. 2001. *Moral Freedom: The Search for Virtue in a World of Choice*. New York: Norton.

Wollstonecraft, Mary. 1792. *A Vindication of the Rights of Woman*. Norton Critical Edition, Carol E. Poston, ed. New York: Norton, 1975.

Wood, James. 1999. *The Broken Estate: Essays on Literature and Belief*. New York: Random House.

Woolf, Virginia. 1925. "Jane Austen." In *The Common Reader*, 1st ser. New York, Harcourt Brace Jovanovich, 1953.

Wrigley, E. A., and Roger Schofield. 1981. *The Population History of England, 1540–1871*. Cambridge: Cambridge University Press.

Yeats, William Butler. 1909. *Estrangement: Extracts from a Diary Kept in 1909*. Reprinted in *The Autobiography of William Butler Yeats*. London: Macmillan, 1965.

Yuengert, Andrew. 2004. *The Boundaries of Technique: Ordering Positive and Normative Concerns in Economic Research*. Lanham, Md.: Lexington Books.

INDEX

1848: and ethics of bourgeoisie, 505; Graña
on paradox, 8–9; paradox of, 8–9, 73;
pessimism about capitalism since:
described, 2, 7, 9–10, 11, 7–58, 74, 349, 511;
vs. success of capitalism since, 9, 12, 478;
summarized, 31–32; and theories of
bourgeois motivation, 146; and turn
against hope and faith, 167, 173, 384;
vol. 3 treats, 56, 511–512; and work, 472
1960s: admired, 11, 240; detested by neoconservatives, 11, 329; socialist, 11
Abbing, Hans: on why artists are poor,
524n14 (chap. 6)
acedia, despair: 101, 160, 250; Aquinas on,
186; of clerisy since 1848, 508; glorified by
Russell, 171; Holmes and, 401; Read on
van Gogh's, 177
Achilles: charted, 300, 304; Elshtain on, 246;
imperfect in pagan virtues, 200, 203–204,
249, 502
Addams, Jane: art and elevating poor, 175;
tragic ethical conflict, 285, 360
adult years of goods-supplied life: defined,
20; implications for culture in rise since
1800, 20
advertising: American clerisy's suspicion of,
452; and paradox of thrift, 455; value of,
59, 513
Africa: access to drinking water in, 18; benefits
from modern economic growth, 16; educational expenditures in, 46; German
colonialism in, 287; governments predatory in, 52; origin of language in, 16, 21, 173

agape. See love
agency. *See* Sen
Akerlof, George: preferences for preferences,
344; sacred in, 415; on scientific failure of
Max U, 135, 415
Albert, St., the Great: pagan virtues, 294
alertness, 191, 489, 494–496
Alfred, William: on love and mortality,
524n17
Allison, C. Fitzsimmons: quoting Hooker's
sermons, 523n13
Alm, Richard: on mobility in United States,
44
Alschuler, Albert: count of Holmes's letters,
534n18 (chap. 18); Holmes's "aftershave
virtues," 401; quoting young Holmes,
532n35
altruistic hedonism: prudence-only love, 115;
relation to Max U, 106, 114
Ambrose, St.: pagan virtues "cardinal," 96
American Gothic: painting, temperance, 250
American Tragedy: ethical choice, 366
amiability: in Austen, 375, 377; in Roget's,
362–363
Amish: and business, 191, 464
Anderson, Terry, 197
Andreau, Jean: on money lending and class
among ancients, 537n29
Anscombe, Elizabeth: naming virtues, 324;
on revival of virtue ethics, 91
antibourgeois bourgeois: Ehrenreich, 69;
Johnston, 521n3; John McCloskey, 530n11
(chap. 13); and van Gogh myth, 179